INDUSTRIAL ORGANIZATION
and
MANAGEMENT

INDUSTRIAL ORGANIZATION and MANAGEMENT

SIXTH EDITION

James L. Riggs
Professor and Head
Department of Industrial and General Engineering
Oregon State University

Lawrence L. Bethel
Late President, Fashion Institute of Technology

Franklin S. Atwater
Industrial Executive

George H. E. Smith
Late Lawyer and Economist

Harvey A. Stackman, Jr.
Research Economist
University of South Carolina

McGRAW-HILL BOOK COMPANY
New York St. Louis San Francisco Auckland Bogotá Düsseldorf
Johannesburg London Madrid Mexico Montreal New Delhi
Panama Paris São Paulo Singapore Sydney Tokyo Toronto

INDUSTRIAL ORGANIZATION AND MANAGEMENT

1 2 3 4 5 6 7 8 9 0 FGRFGR 7 8 3 2 1 0 9

This book was set in Baskerville by Cobb/Dunlop Publisher Services
Incorporated. The editor was Julienne V. Brown; the designer was Elliot
Epstein; the production supervisor was Donna Piligra.
Fairfield Graphics was printer and binder.

Library of Congress Cataloguing in Publication Data

Main entry under title:

Industrial organization and management.

    Fifth ed., 1971 entered under Bethel, Lawrence L.
    Bibliography: p.
    Includes index.
    1. Industrial organization. 2. Industrial manage-
ment. I. Riggs, James L. II. Bethel, Lawrence L.
Industrial organization and management. III. Title.
HD31.B43   1979   658   78–17148
ISBN   0–07–052854–3

CONTENTS

PREFACE

Publication of the sixth edition of Industrial Organization and Management marks the text's 34th anniversary in print. Over the years it has tutored hundreds of thousands of students in the United States and it has been translated for use by students in other nations. The six editions have recorded the tremendous changes in industrial practices and technology which have occurred since World War II, while stressing the continued reliance on sound principles of management required to accomodate those changes. The original objectives of the text remain intact: "to present an overview of the operations of an industrial organization, the interrelationship of functions, and the fundamental principles of management which lead toward effective coordination and control."

The intent of the new edition is to survey the overall workings of industrial systems while highlighting the individual skills needed to make an enterprise work better. Implementation of this intent led to extensive revisions. Presentations in some areas are more succinct to allow greater coverage of recent developments. Added attention is devoted to managerial practices and techniques of general applicability. Interactions among consumers, government, and industry are explored to help anticipate industrial challenges of the 1980s.

The most prominent new feature is the addition of "Perspectives." Over a hundred short digests and discussions of special topics drawn from recent literature are spotted throughout the text. Some offer controversial opinions or expand on the conventional interpretation of operating policies. Others focus on current concerns critical to the long-term health of industry, such as

- coping with the paperwork explosion

- expectations for improving the quality of working life

- corporate ethics and white-collar crime

- the push for productivity

- effects of the consumer movement

- elimination of discrimination

- environmental protection and industrial growth

- conservation of resources, especially energy

- safety and social obligations of industry

In response to suggestions from users of the previous edition, subjects of less importance or those with which the reader is likely already familiar have been shortened. The result is a more compact renditian that overviews the total production/distribution system, yet provides detailed operational considerations and procedures in the more immediately useful topics. The flow of subjects, following the introduction, progresses from *management structures* to *resource planning* to *production operations* to *personnel relationships* to *organizational control.* This chain links 20 chapters that successively develop the input-output sequences of industrial operations. Individual chapters start with a key-subject digest and end with student exercises, including review questions and cases for discussion.

As apparent from the foregoing, the theme for the book is still that created by Professors Bethel, Atwater, Smith, and Stackman. Credit for excerpts included in the Perspectives are owed to many authors and their publishers, primarily *Fortune, Harvard Business Review,* and *Industrial Engineering.* The resulting synthesis of time-honored subjects with recent advances and current concerns about future developments provides a challenging tour of the industrial scene.

May the journey be rewarding.

James L. Riggs

1

INTRODUCTION: AMERICAN INDUSTRY

From its very beginning over 200 years ago, the United States has been engaged in a continuous social, technological, and scientific revolution. It has moved from water power to steam to electric to nuclear power; from handicraft to mechanical to automated to robotic mass production; through mineral, chemical, metallurgical, electronic, and miniaturization innovations; and the effects have spread over the world and into outer space. Despite the technological gains of other industrial nations, especially the U.S.S.R. and Japan, the United States still stands foremost in the volume of production, in the general application of science and technology to production, and in the wide distribution of goods and services among its people. How and why has this come about? What factors and influences shaped the American economy? How is the economy organized and controlled? How is American industry managed?

1 INTRODUCTION: AMERICAN INDUSTRY

1-1 MAJOR STAGES OF U.S. ECONOMIC GROWTH

In 1976 the United States of America celebrated its 200th anniversary. From its birth to now the country has passed through periods of hardship and prosperity, war and peace, insecurity and confidence, but with maturity came the powerful industrial muscle needed to support its stature as a world leader. Its development can be divided into six stages that span the period from the early colonial settlements of the seventeenth century to current times.

1-1.1 Colonial Industries

The earliest manufactures revolved wholly around the problem of subsistence in a raw unsettled country. Food and other agricultural production, lumbering, shipbuilding, and ship fitting heavily occupied the early colonists. But beside the woodsman's ax, the gun and trap of the fur gatherer, the farmer's plow, the fishing smack, and the whaler were the household and village shops of simple craftsmen who toiled to turn out the stern necessities and rarer luxuries demanded by a pioneer people.

1-1.2 Exploitation of Natural Resources

The second stage extended approximately from 1800 to 1860. It centered largely about the manufacture of goods to meet the demands of a fast growing population cut off by protective legislation from imports from abroad and the exploitation of natural resources opened up by settlers moving westward.

   The first definitely protective tariff encouraging home manufactures was enacted in 1816, and in the same year the Second National Bank was set up for the further development of American sources of capital and credit. By the Constitution, free trade between the states held the way open for a brisk commerce as the different sections of the country were settled. Although agriculture predominated in the economy of the nation and furnished increasing exports to Europe, Americans turned with feverish energy to the development of all other natural resources with which the country abounded. Household industries and village shops continued to be the prevailing methods of conducting industrial operations but, as the period drew to a close, factory production rose in importance.

1-1.3 The Factory System

The major characteristic of the third stage of development is the expansion of the factory system until, by 1890, industry exceeded agriculture as the dominant economic activity of the nation. The factory system brought the several processes of manufacture under one roof, centralized and increased the use of power, introduced specialized tools and machines, and hired workers for fixed wages and hours. Individual proprietors and partnerships owned the greater part of these enterprises, and capital came partly from the slow process of accumulation and partly from sources abroad. The exploitation of natural resources continued unabated all through this period, but of great significance was the shift in important industries away from dependence upon agricultural raw materials and over to the minerals and metals, particularly coal, iron, and steel. The growth of industry during this period was especially marked by technological developments: the great increase in inventions of products and processes, the wider use of steam engines as prime movers, the application of mechanical science to industrial processes, greater specialization in tools, machines, and labor, and the rapid expansion of the principle of interchangeable parts introduced successfully in America by Eli Whitney as early as 1798.

Natural increases in the population, augmented by waves of immigrants, furnished expanding markets and provided a growing labor force. Invested capital grew enormously, and more and more of it was being generated by the rapidly increasing economic activity within the country, while reliance upon foreign capital was reduced. In accumulating capital and making it available to producers, a change took place in the method of organizing enterprises. The incorporated company rose in importance compared to the simpler forms of individual and partnership enterprises. This development opened up larger possibilities for the further expansion of the principle of the factory system—the integration of industrial processes and the combination of enterprises.

1-1.4 The Spread of Scientific and Technological Innovations

The fourth stage constitutes an industrial revolution peculiarly American. What took place between 1890 and 1930 was much more than the further growth of the factory system; it was a complete transformation of the whole field of industrial production. By the introduction of new sources of power —notably the electric dynamo and the gasoline engine—power was specialized and brought to the work instead of the work having to be taken to the power, as was largely the case with steam. A whole series of new inventions came into wide everyday use, of which the telephone, automobile, motion-picture visual and sound apparatus, radio, airplane, and automatic machine tools are the most conspicuous end products. They revolutionized communication and transportation, amounting to a conquest of time and space hitherto undreamed.

The World War from 1914 to 1918 intensified the entire development. But the war also left a trail of maladjustments, particularly a decline in agricultural income, lack of balance between production and consumption,

3

and a speculative rise in securities, which by 1929 combined with an accumulation of other factors to cause the greatest depression the nation ever experienced.

Great change took place in production processes. By the science of time and motion studies; by the scientific arrangement of materials, machines, and processes; by the standardization of products; and by the redesign of factory buildings, the crude benchwork of the factory system was converted into the flexible assembly line of continuous mass production. Skill, precision, great power, multiple operations, and automatic controls were built into machines. The crude products of iron and steel were refined by the use of alloys, making metals lighter, more durable, and adaptable to wider uses. New chemical processes and products emerged from the laboratories that were rapidly being established in industry after industry.

Production was integrated and concentrated, bringing together under single management the many processes of manufacture from the raw materials to the finished products. This was obviously accompanied by greater combinations in the field of business organization. By almost every yardstick other than number of establishments, the corporation exceeded individual proprietorships and partnerships as the prevailing form of business organization. But more than that, the corporation itself, in many fields of industry, was merely a subsidiary unit in larger corporate structures such as the trust and holding company. Through outright merger and by other methods of business combination, many complementary and associated corporations were brought under one management. The largest companies in the most flourishing period of the simple factory system were dwarfed by the great industrial empires built up in the first quarter of the present century.

1-1.5 The Socioeconomic Revolution

A fifth stage, extending from the Great Depression of 1929 through the Korean conflict of 1950, marked a significant change in American economic development. During the depression years, when economic conditions failed to reach a new equilibrium capable of achieving recovery and full employment, the Federal government intervened in the economy on an unprecedented scale. No field of American life was untouched. The Federal government intervened in agriculture, industry, finance, state and local affairs, and for the health, welfare, and security of the people. It put the force of government behind the union organization of labor and took an active part in labor-management relations. Billions of dollars were spent on successive programs of "relief, recovery, and reform."

While the Federal government aimed at economic recovery and reemployment, its major accomplishment was to establish social-welfare measures so far-reaching as to amount to a socioeconomic revolution. With all its outpouring of money and its wide extension of government operations, the "New Deal"[1] found no permanent solution for unemployment. Approximately 14 million persons were out of work in 1933, and after 7 years of extraordinary effort to solve the problem some nine million remained unemployed. Affairs were in this unsatisfactory state when war broke out in Europe in September, 1939. Entrance into the war against Germany, Italy, and Japan finally threw the United States into the high gear of production based on a war economy.

The production system in the war economy which finally emerged had the following characteristics: (1) outright abandonment of the production of civilian goods in many lines, especially the metals, and the subordination of all other civilian production to military preferences; (2) government-controlled production through a program of designated end-use products, supported by priorities and allocations of raw materials; (3) manpower allocation between civilian and military requirements by the Selective Service Administration, United States employment services, and through some indirect "freezing" of civilian workers in certain industries and areas; (4) price control and rationing of consumer goods; and (5) government supervisory direction and control over all associated elements of the economy in the interests of war. The goal sought was to organize the entire industrial system into one gigantic machine geared to maximum war production with the absolute minimum of civilian supply and maintenance.

Conditions in the postwar world gave little opportunity for peacetime economic relations. After a brief and incomplete attempt to convert from war to peace, the United States became involved in a "cold war" of defensive resistance to a militant communism spearheaded by Soviet Russia. From time to time this conflict flared up into hostile situations in Europe and Asia. It involved the United States and members of the United Nations in armed operations in Korea in 1950.

1-1.6 International Expansion and Domestic Consolidation

Many of the trends which started prior to 1950 have continued since then, often at an accelerated pace. A significant portion of the national budget was allocated to military expenditures for the cold war of the 1950s; these expenditures increased during the next decade for the hot war in Viet Nam and were still large in the 1970s. At the same time, foreign aid sent huge quantities of food, building, and military supplies to many countries. Occasionally the ebb and flow of exports resulting from shifting diplomatic relationships or national objectives caused domestic industrial disruptions. For example, the cutback in the space exploration program caused massive layoffs in the aerospace industry, and the grain sales to Russia

---

[1]The political slogan of the Franklin D. Roosevelt campaign in 1932 and successive years. For a detailed description of the times, see Charles A. Beard and George H. E. Smith, "The Future Comes: A Study of the New Deal" (1934), and "The Old Deal and the New" (1940), New York: The Macmillan Company.

in 1974 affected both food consumers and producers throughout the United States.

Economic conditions were generally healthy in the sixties and seventies, although depression tendencies appeared in 1960–1961, 1969–1970, and 1973–1974. The last recession period was particularly frustrating to economic planners in the government because prices rose or continued at high levels while employment dropped. Contrary to previous experience, lower demand by consumers during the business slowdown did not drag prices down commensurately, and government actions aimed at increasing business activity to relieve unemployment fueled more inflation. High rates of inflation throughout the world linger on to worry managers and influence their financial decisions.

Social obligations of American industry were affected in the 1960s and 1970s by legislation and changing public expectations. Some of the more significant influences are listed below.

1. Safety and health standards were established and enforced by new government agencies. So widespread were the regulations that nearly all segments of industry were affected.

2. Laws designed to protect the environment caused major expenditures by corporations and municipalities to limit or to correct pollution of water, air, and land.

3. Groups with ecological concerns successfully aroused public opinion to oppose both government and industrial activities. Products such as the supersonic transport were terminated in the development stage, and ecological safeguards were inserted in projects such as the Alaska pipe line.

4. Class-action law suits and consumer advocates forced more attention on the quality of products, their repair, and how they were advertised.

5. Efforts to eliminate discrimination due to sex, color, creed, age, and physical or mental disability resulted in modifications to personnel practices and facilities.

6. Workers' expectations for more satisfying jobs, in conjunction with legislative actions, frequently effected more pleasant work places and innovative management practices.

The growing awareness of resource limitations is having an ever greater effect on industrial operations and planning. Potential energy shortages stirred the most concern in the United States. Anticipated increases in fuel costs have spurred manufacturers to invest in fuel-saving facilities, distributors to reorganize supply channels, and nearly all organizations to initiate energy conservation programs. Automobile makers were directed by Congress to build cars that would travel more miles per gallon of gasoline. Industrial responses to resource shortages, such as the substitution of plentiful for scarce materials and extensive recycling or recovery of waste materials, will be critical management considerations for the rest of this century.

American companies operate all over the world. The movement of investment abroad began after World War II and was accelerated by military, economic, and technical aid programs devised to assist the war-devastated or developing nations. Expansion continued in order to exploit natural resources, to utilize low-cost labor, and to develop new markets available in foreign countries. In most cases, both the United States and the host countries benefited: the United States gained access to raw materials and profited from lower costs for imported products sold domestically, and the host countries were enriched by the access to new technology, jobs created by plant construction and operation, and currency earned from exports.

A result of international trading has been the growth of *multinational* companies. Such companies are typified by branches in many countries in which research, development, and manufacturing are conducted, and where the managers and stockholders represent several nationalities. The origin of multinationals can be traced to the great trading companies of the 18th century, but their present state of integrated, globe-encompassing activities has been fostered by a favorable political climate and the development of rapid worldwide communications.

Perspective 1A   THE SHRINKING WORLD

In effect, technology has decreased the size of the world by increasing the speed of transportation and message transmission. The result has been more travel and trade between distant nations. Now major sporting events anywhere may become global television spectacles, and fads speed around the world almost as quickly as they start. The following statistics spotlight causes and effects of our shrinking globe:

	1950	1975–1976
A Trip to Europe (Washington, D.C. to London)	17 hours	3½ hours
Pieces of mail sent abroad from the United States	417 million	933 million
Telephone calls to and from the United States	900,000	50.5 million
Americans visiting overseas	651,000	7.7 million
Foreigners coming to the United States, excluding Canadian and Mexican visitors	288,000	4.4 million
Exports by free-world nations	$56 billion	$875 billion
Foreign direct investment in the United States	$3.4 billion	$26.7 billion
United States direct investment abroad	$11.8 billion	$133.2 billion

SOURCE: U.S. News and World Report, July 18, 1977.

COMMENT   The quick and relatively convenient flow of money, products, styles, and information between nations has impacted American industry in many ways. Competition, both at home and abroad, is an obvious result, but more subtle economic and managerial concerns are also significant: trends originating abroad that affect consumers and workers, knowledge made available by the exchange of students and consultants, irregular fluctuations of monetary values, coordination of activities made difficult by cultural differences, and many more.

1-2 BASIC ECONOMIC PROCESSES

Stripped of all detail, four major processes cover the material activities of people in any economic system: the primary raw-material industries, manufacturing, distribution, and the service industries (see Fig. 1–1).

First, there is the process that provides the raw materials needed in modern economy: the minerals and fuels; the grains and other vegetable and animal food products; wool, cotton, flax, and other fibers; lumber; stone, sand, and clay; leather, hides, and skin; and like commodities. This is the work of enterprises engaged in agriculture, mining, lumber-

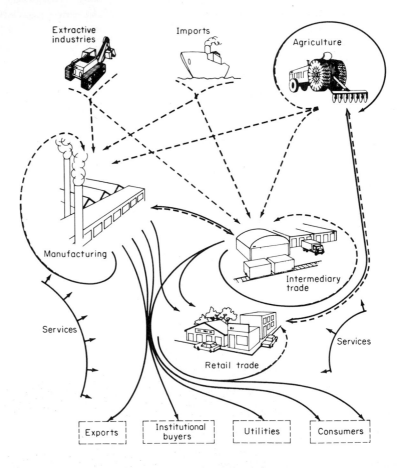

Figure 1-1 The economic process in the United States. General flow of production and distribution. Services are provided for all processes and trade.

ing, hunting, and fishing—often called the extractive, or "primary industries."

Second, there is the process by which these raw materials are manufactured or converted into different forms, i.e., the manufacturing process carried on chiefly in factory enterprises. The products turned out here fall into two general classes: semimanufactures, which are partly fabricated goods passing from producer to producer for further processing, and finished goods to be sold to the ultimate consumer. Thousands of enterprises carry on the manufacturing process.

The third is the distributive process by which raw materials and manufactured goods are passed from producer to producer and from producers to consumers. Here are found the commercial and trading enterprises. They facilitate the passage of goods from the crude raw materials through the many stages of processing and manufacture to the ultimate consumers. In the main, their operations consist of buying and selling as middlemen, storing, sorting, grading, packaging, and moving goods about to places where they are most needed.

The fourth element—the furnishing of services in the economy—has rapidly grown to prominence in recent years. While many are thus engaged in producing and handling tangible goods, there are others who render an infinite variety of services at every point in the economic system: domestic services; financial and professional services to individuals and to business enterprises; mechanical services in factories and in the community; general public services such as transportation, communication, the furnishing of heat, light, and power, and similar services commonly classed as public utilities; and government services. Although the performance of services is not a process like agriculture and manufacturing, it is one of the four broad fields into which an economic system is divided.

Here, then, is the essence of economic life: people making goods and performing services while in turn they use the products and benefit by the services of others. The need for organizing economic life springs from the fact that man's wants are unlimited, but the means of satisfying those wants are scarce. The material basis of daily living is thus a cooperative cycle of making and using goods and services. All four fields of economic activity are mutually dependent parts of the larger whole, the national economy. And because the nation is not a self-sufficient economic unit, it carries this cooperative cycle beyond its borders by taking part with other nations in the international exchange of goods and services.

Perspective 1B PRODUCTION GOES UP, BUT SO DO PRICES

The total output of American factories, mines, and utilities, as shown by the solid line in the chart, has gone up quite steadily since the depths of the depression in the 1930s. However, consumer prices have also risen, as indicated by the dashed line, and in recent years the rate of increase has been a cause of alarm.

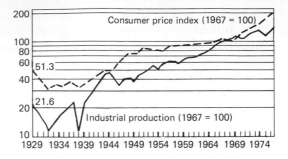

COMMENT   Industrial production is a pivotal factor in the economic health of the nation. It provides employment and income. In 1977 employment was at an all-time high, but unemployment was over 7 per cent, a level considered to be too high. Average income has increased by about 130 per cent (corrected for inflation) since the thirties to nearly $6,000 per person after taxes, but there are still too many people with incomes below the poverty level. Inflation affects both the public and the producers in their decisions about what to buy, when to buy, how much to buy, and why certain items should be bought rather than others.

1-3   INDUSTRIAL ENTERPRISE

Having glanced briefly at the economic system as a whole, we pass now to the important but narrower field with which this book is concerned. Of the four great processes which together form the framework of the economic system, we are primarily concerned with the field of the manufacturing industries, or "industrial enterprise," as it is commonly called. What is industrial enterprise? *Guided by management, an industrial enterprise combines land, labor, and capital in variable proportions to make a producing unit turning out tangible goods.*[2]

The essence of industrial production is the transformation by factory methods of raw materials into things wanted by society. Industries are divided into broad classes according to the nature of the industry, the use made of the product, and the amount of service obtained from the product before it is consumed or becomes unfit for further use. Thus, industries which manufacture materials, tools, machines, and equipment for use in the operations of other factories are *producer-goods industries.* Those which turn out products intended for direct use of the people in daily living are *consum-*

---

[2]The term "land" covers not only "standing room," i.e., physical location of industrial plant, but also natural resources (natural raw materials), character of the soil, rainfall, temperature, the earth's waters, and other features associated with land. "Labor" includes brainwork, manual work, and all the characteristics of individuals engaged in personal services. "Capital" refers chiefly to buildings, tools, machines, equipment, and materials, produced by man and used in further production. In common use, capital often lumps together land, money, buildings, equipment, and materials as being the total investment in an industrial enterprise.

er-goods industries. Each is further classified as *durable-goods, nondurable-goods,* and *semidurable-goods* industries. A durable item, like a dynamo, an automobile, or a watch, provides service over a long period of time. Nondurable goods, like industrial catalysts or fuel, are used up in one or a few operations. The semidurable goods fall in between. The type of goods produced is especially important to management. It strongly influences, as we shall see in many chapters of this book, the organization, finances, business policies, labor supply, production methods, marketing channels, and general prosperity of the industrial enterprise.

Within the field of industrial enterprise we see hundreds of thousands of producing units at work. These units vary in form of ownership and in the way they are organized for operation. A knowledge of this basic industrial structure is essential to successful management of an enterprise because it largely determines the conditions of production.

1-3.1 Division of Labor and Specialization

The entire field of industrial activity, like the economic system as a whole, is pervaded by the principle of division of labor and its refinement, specialization. In its simplest form, division of labor means dividing up the work on the principle that different people and different places are best fitted for different things depending on influences stemming from geography, natural conditions, personal aptitudes, and skills. Specialization is a refinement of this principle and is carried furthest in the manufacturing industries. Land is put to special uses; labor to minutely specialized tasks; buildings, tools, and machines to particular operations. Within the single establishment there is specialization in organization and function, subdivision of activities by departments and sections, and further specialization by process and by operation until a single machine, tool, or worker performs a minute task exclusively. The latest development—automation—integrates several such specialized tasks or operations into single units (such as multiple-operation machines) and groups machines and processes together in a line or sequence automatically controlled by mechanical and electronic devices.

Specialization yields enormous benefits in greater quantities of goods in less time and with less effort, wider varieties, better quality, less waste, more efficient employment of land, labor, and capital, and generally rising standards of living. Specialization has its disadvantages, too. It depends upon the extent of the market and upon the smooth flow of goods between markets (trade). But chiefly it creates a dependence not only within the economic system and among industries, but among all departments, sections, processes, and operations within a single enterprise, which makes the enterprise (and often the entire economy, as in depressions) vulnerable to miscalculations and disruptions.

These facts have significance in the field of industrial management. Upon management and those who share in the responsibility for industrial operations falls the burden of discovering the extent to which specialization can be carried with good rather than bad effects. Within the single enterprise, it means that management continuously must study and make decisions necessary to achieve sound organization and financing; proper selection and use of people, materials, tools, and machines; smooth labor relations; skillful coordination of all parts of the enterprise; frequent checks and constant control over performance; and careful appraisal of end results. In the wider sphere of the national economy, it means also that there must be closer coordination among enterprises, between industry and industry, and among all industries and other elements of the economy for the good of the country as a whole.

1-3.2 Types of Ownership

Ownership is a legal term. Most commonly it means the legal title to a thing, the right of possession, control, and disposal. Applied to an industrial enterprise it means title to and possession of the assets of the enterprise, the power to determine the policies of operation, and the right to receive and dispose of the proceeds. When an enterprise is so organized that individuals exercise and enjoy these rights in their own interest, the ownership is said to be *private*. If they attach to political bodies, i.e., to municipal, state, or Federal government, or to any agencies created by them, the ownership is *public*. In a very few cases, the business unit may have some private and some public elements of ownership (e.g., government-owned ships managed by private operators) and thus may be said to be *mixed* business units. A government-owned plant operated by a private contractor is another example.

Just as the economic system as a whole is a mixed one, the ownership of enterprises within it is also mixed. Private persons and partnerships own and operate a great many enterprises. Individuals and families own many small and medium-size enterprises under corporate forms. Larger enterprises, which are relatively few in number but produce the largest amount of goods and services, are owned by corporate stockholders who entrust operations to hired managers. Industrial enterprises today, even when completely private in ownership, distribute the end results of their operations to managers (salaries, bonuses, pensions, stock options), to labor (wages, pensions, fringe benefits), to financial institutions (interest), to governments (taxes), to local community projects (charitable and other contributions), to educational institutions (gifts), and to stockholders, who are the real owners (dividends).

Perspective 1C   WHO OWNS AMERICAN INDUSTRY?

A major shift appears to be underway in the ownership of American companies. More of U.S. industry is coming to be owned by banks, pension funds, and other large financial institutions, while individual investors own less. The table reveals that recent slides in stockholdings by individuals and mutual funds are being compensated for by rising holdings by institutions.

Investor Groups	1970 Stockholdings* (billion $)	(percentage of total)	1977 Stockholdings* (billion $)	(percentage of total)
Individuals	582.1	66.9	508.6	53.2
Bank trust funds	84.2	9.7	103.2	10.8
Private pension funds	61.4	7.0	109.7	11.5
Mutual funds	51.3	5.9	48.9	5.1
Insurance companies	27.0	3.1	51.6	5.4
Foreign investors	26.9	3.1	61.4	6.4
Foundations	20.0	2.3	27.1	2.8
College educational endowments	7.6	0.9	10.4	1.1
State and local retirement funds	7.3	0.8	30.1	3.2
Mutual savings banks	2.5	0.3	4.4	0.5
Total	870.3	100.0	955.4	100.0

*Investment-company shares held by other institutional groups are counted twice, by amounts of $4 billion in 1970 and by $10 billion in 1977.
SOURCE: U.S. Securities and Exchange Commission.

COMMENT More people than ever before have a stake in the stock market, but fewer individuals buy and sell for themselves. From a high of 31 million stockholders in 1970, the number fell to less than 25 million by 1977. This drop is even more noticeable when the 1977 percentage of ownership, 53.2 per cent, is compared with the 70 per cent owned by individuals in 1960.

Concentration of buying power in institutions has made the exercise of that power more demanding. The purchase or sale of large blocks of stock in a company may drive prices sharply up or down, owing to the limited supply of floating shares. This feature has encouraged institutions to search for investment opportunities in smaller companies that have good records.

1-3.3 Forms of Ownership

Whenever an enterprise is started, the promoters or prospective managers must first make the policy decisions necessary to establish the legal form. Privately owned industrial enterprises take four basic forms: individual proprietorship, partnership, corporation, and cooperative (including mutual) organization. A manufacturing enterprise may be organized in any one of these forms, but usually one form is more desirable than others for the particular enterprise.

The choice of form depends upon a careful consideration of a number of factors, including the following: who the promoters are and what ideas they hold toward the several forms of organization; the nature and size of the business to be started; the capital required and the means of procuring it; the length of time the enterprise is expected to operate; technical conditions affecting the enterprise; type of products to be manufactured; method and volume of production; kind of markets to be supplied and methods of marketing; competitive conditions in the chosen industry; methods of sharing the benefits and obligations of the enterprise; and the influence that all laws and government regulations exert upon private enterprise.

1-3.4   Individual Proprietorships and Partnerships

Enterprises which are small, require little capital, and lend themselves readily to control by one or a few persons take the form of the individual proprietorship or the partnership. The small machine shop, woodworking plant, printing establishment, canning factory, and thousands of similar enterprises exist in these forms of ownership. The individual or partnership promotes the enterprise; gets together the necessary land, buildings, machinery, and labor; and conducts the actual manufacturing and marketing operations. Such enterprises have the advantage of easy formation, simple control by the persons involved, direct association with operations, flexibility in making quick decisions and seizing opportunities, and some tax advantages. But more and more, especially in manufacturing, the trend is toward the corporate form. This is to overcome the disadvantages often attached to individual ownership and partnerships (e.g., insufficient capital, limited managerial talent, unlimited personal liability, effect upon the enterprise of the death of individual owners, etc.) and to gain the broader advantages of corporate organization.

1-3.5   Cooperative Organizations

A cooperative association has some elements of a large partnership and also many features of the corporation, although it is distinct from both. The principal theory of the true cooperative association is the elimination of profit, the idea being to provide goods and services to members at cost. In most states a special section of law deals with the formation of cooperative associations. When so formed, the cooperative society functions very much like a corporation, with elected officers, a board of directors, and periodic shareholders' meetings. Members pay fees or buy shares in the association, and profits are periodically redistributed to members. To prevent concentration of control in a few members, each member has only one vote, and the purchase of shares may be limited. The two chief forms of cooperative enterprises are *consumer cooperatives,* in retail trade and services, and *producer cooperatives,* organized for group buying and selling such items as dairy products, grain, fruits, and livestock and for buying producers' supplies.

1-3.6   Corporations

Corporations dominate the manufacturing field in the United States. The corporation is a legally created business unit with a simple basic structure. It is composed of any number of stock- or shareholders who are the real owners of the company, a board of directors elected by the membership to fix policies, and a group of top-ranking officers chosen by the directors to manage the company's operations.

A corporation is usually formed by a small group of persons who may put up the money, land, buildings, equipment, patents, and other assets to get the company started. They decide upon the name, location, character of the business, and capitalization. This and other pertinent information is embodied in an application for a charter. After compliance with appropriate state and Federal laws, a certificate is granted (as provided in state laws) which approves the corporate charter and authorizes the company to complete its organization and commence business.

ORGANIZATIONAL ADVANTAGES OF THE CORPORATION The corporation has great advantages in meeting the ownership, financing, and operational problems of modern industrial enterprise. By the sale of thousands of shares to many large and small investors who have only limited liability, the corporation can get together capital in considerable amounts, and the company remains stable as owners come and go. By means of its large capital the corporation is ideally suited to large-scale manufacture. It permits extended specialization in management, plant and equipment, factory organization, labor, and marketing. Although like all other forms of economic organization the corporation is subject to corrupt use, inefficiency, and stagnation, nevertheless it is not likely to continue for long in those conditions because it is subject to searching criticism from investors, labor, government, competitors, and the public. On balance, taking good and bad in the history of business units, no finer instrument exists with which to meet the complex problems of modern enterprise.

1-3.7   Corporate Combinations

The ingenuity which produced the simple corporation as a business unit did not stop with that achievement. Many of the conditions which led to the development of the corporation suggested a further step—the combining of two or more corporations under one management, such as *informal associations, voting trusts, mergers,* and *holding companies.*

For reasons of public policy, informal associations and trusts are no longer used today. They ran afoul of antitrust laws. Legitimate corporate combinations usually take the form of the merger and the holding company. In the merger, one corporation acquires the assets of one or more other corporations and either merges them in its existing organization or forms a new corporation. The common procedure in forming the holding company is for the promoters to negotiate with a number of enterprises and agree upon a purchase price for each. A holding company is then formed and capitalized for enough to acquire control of all the enterprises by cash or by an exchange of securities. The identity of the original enterprises is retained, but they become subsidiaries of the parent holding company. A more recent development is for two or more established corporations to set up a separate corporation for joint participation in some special project.

From the standpoint of operating complexity the corporate combination is important and interesting. Many types of combinations are found in American industry today. *Horizontal combinations* bring together a number of plants engaged in the same or similar activities in one industrial field, such as a chain of bread-baking companies. *Vertical combinations* join together plants performing successive functions in the chain of processes from raw material to finished product. A company logging its own forest area, operating sawmills, running a planing and woodworking shop for dressed and fabricated wood products, and perhaps including a furniture manufactory is an example.

A third group of combinations is based upon *divergent functions* such as those involved in joint products, by-products, and like processes. In the *joint-product* group, the manufacture of any one of the different products might be discontinued without affecting the others produced, as, for example, when butter and cheese are produced from milk. Combinations in the *by-product* group depend upon the main product, as in the meat industry where the animal is turned into fresh meat, glue and gelatin, grease, soap, animal shortening, sausage casings, fertilizer, and other products, in different establishments. Where *like* processes are employed, many industrial combinations turn out varied products. Printing and publishing combinations, for example, employ like processes to turn out newspapers and periodicals in one industry group and book, music, and job printing in another industry group.

A fourth group consists of combinations on *convergent functions.* The plants in a combination of this kind may start out with different products but, somewhere in the course of operations from raw materials to market, the different products are combined into a single product or meet in a common market. Combinations of this type may deal with *complementary products,* as when one plant of a combination makes cigars and another makes boxes, the two being combined in the single box of cigars sold to the trade. Some combinations employing convergent functions include plants dealing with *auxiliary products.* The auxiliary product is needed in the manufacture of the final product but does not add to the physical material of the finished goods. A company making ice cream may also control another plant making ice to use in its operations. In some combinations the different products or processes do not converge at any stage of the manufacture but meet in a common market. Thus, a manufacturer of electric refrigerators may set up another plant to produce electric ranges because the two products reach the same market.

In the current merger movement, combinations are being formed to bring together all kinds of *unrelated functions and products* (often called lateral or conglomerate diversification). Some of the traditional reasons for these combinations, such as technological relationship, complementary lines of business and industry, and coordinated operations, lie behind this movement, as well as more recent policies of corporate management to even out the business cycle, spread the risk, and give security to the enterprise. But also, there is a tendency for the management of some corporations to buy and sell companies as if they were "commodities," regardless of any particular line or lines of business, or to build business combinations as if they were financial holding companies.

The reasons for combinations are innumerable. One main reason is to increase profits through the economies of large-scale enterprise. Combination brings purchasing advantages, manufacturing economies, easier and more adequate financing, selling advantages, and administrative efficiency and economies. Technology and research often lead to combinations to exploit the results. The desire to control raw materials and semimanufactured products going into a finished article may lead to combinations of plants for that purpose. The desire to eliminate competition is another cause. Idle plants and resources often induce a firm to enter different industrial fields. A company is often forced into the manufacture of many different products by the need for a full line, by changes in demand, by new methods of marketing, by consumer financing conditions, by requests of large buyers. Waste materials and salvage may result in a new plant. The linking together of corporations producing diverse products is also an attempt to use diversity to attain economic stability, or to acquire experienced and specialized management personnel. Sometimes the purpose is to secure tax advantages. The reasons are practically endless. Each combination must be examined by itself if one wants to understand the reasons and conditions that influenced its formation. While certain basic patterns of combination appear such as those described above, many other mergers occur by chance or have no rational basis for their creation unless it be, giving a new twist to the old adage, to say that many different eggs in one basket provides a new sense of security.

1-3.8   Public Ownership

Public welfare and necessity are the chief reasons for the establishment on three levels of government—Federal, state, and local—of public-owned enterprises. These are mainly of the public-utility or public-service type and when established are operated very much like private enterprises. The range of government enterprises has been widening in recent years under the drive toward socialization, but except for prison industries and certain national-defense operations, governments have remained aloof from the field of general manufacturing. The two chief forms of public enterprises are the *public corporation*, organized and chartered like private corporations, and the *nonincorporated public enterprise*, operated by a regular department of government or by a special agency created for the purpose. Some of these public enterprises are operated in something like a partnership between the Federal government and state and local bodies in special and multipurpose undertakings as in certain public-utility and other enterprises; others are quasi-partnership relationships with private enterprise as in the field of atomic energy and certain national defense plants. These mixed business relationships have been in process of evolution for more than a generation and have raised considerable controversy in public policy, but the trend continues and may ultimately result in new forms of coordinated public and private enterprises.

1-4 CONTROLS IN A MIXED ECONOMY

The American economy today is a mixed economy—partly *private* enterprise, partly *public* enterprise, and partly *mixed* units in which private entrepreneurs, governments, labor organizations, and institutional bodies join in various undertakings. It is highly important for management in the future to appreciate how such a mixed economy is controlled.

Control, in the sense here used, means the power to determine how the resources of the nation are to be allocated for various purposes, what goods and services shall be produced and who shall produce them, how and among whom the wealth and income shall be distributed and in what proportions. Some controls come from the nature of our institutions, customs, laws, and processes. For example, our system of economy, featuring individual initiative, private ownership, and operation of the means of production, is a controlling force. Competition among producers, among buyers, among sellers, and between buyers and sellers is another controlling force. These traditional controls tended to make the economy self-regulating to a considerable degree. In addition to these institutional controls, government and organized labor now exert controlling forces in the economy. The combined effect of all these forces keeps the economy working—providing jobs, goods, and services which advance the general welfare of all our people. Let us examine these controlling forces a little more closely.

1-4.1 The System as a Controlling Force

Historically, freedom to engage in whatever enterprise appeared promising and to shift from job to job as opportunity arose was ensured to the individual by natural conditions and by the form and practice of government in America. Incentives to produce goods and render services came largely from the desires of men for subsistence and improvement of their own welfare. An undeveloped, rich country afforded raw materials and opportunities in abundance. The law protected the right of contract and private ownership and the right to enjoy rewards (including profits) derived from them. A nationwide communication and free-market network and a uniform monetary system facilitated the exchange of goods and services. The owners (and later the hired managers) determined the internal policies and operations of the particular enterprise and a good part of the general conditions of production as well. Freedom to work and produce, competition, and the price system were relied upon to regulate activity and to ensure balance and equity. The consumer, within certain limitations, exercising his free choice to buy or not to buy, to shift favor from seller to seller and from one product to another, was a powerful factor in the control of enterprise. With government maintaining order and enforcing a few "general rules of the game," these were the main lines of control which prevailed in America from colonial days until the turn of the twentieth century.

Controlling modern industrial enterprise is a complex process. Many of the controlling forces inherent in a private-enterprise system continue to function in today's American economy, but they are hedged about by numerous qualifications and restrictions developed in the course of changing times. Subject to those changes individuals may still enter and leave enterprises as they choose, contract freely, and own and dispose of property. Business undertakings are more costly and troublesome to start and operate, but opportunity is not foreclosed. Within a framework of a variety of limitations, management still makes the decisions on the kind and location of the plant it will operate, the kind and quantity of product it will produce, the organization and working conditions of the enterprise, how it will market the product, and how it will distribute the proceeds. Consumers also exercise free choice to buy or not to buy and to shift favor from seller to seller and from one product to another. Competition contains elements of monopoly, of price and other rigidities, and of striving for quality superiority, but it is scarcely less intense than it was before the turn of the century. Perhaps the most significant development in modern times is the expansion of the public sector of the economy (government) and the growth in numbers and power of organized labor to the point where both government and labor, along with management, now share in the control of industrial enterprise.

1-4.2 Government as a Controlling Force

As part of its function to maintain law and order, government had from time to time intervened to alleviate some of the harsher effects of this relatively free and highly individualistic economic system. Beginning with the Interstate Commerce Commission Act of 1887, such intervention by the Federal government broadened into many fields of regulation under the interstate-commerce clause of the Constitution. Among the many reasons accounting for the increased participation of the Federal government in economic life were the large growth and urbanization of the population, growth in size and power of business organizations, nationwide expansion of industry and commerce, enlargement of the scope of wars in which the nation became involved, the spread of education, public concern with natural resources, and the inability of the separate states to deal with the resulting effects. The growth of science and technology and the need to undertake activities of greater scope and cost than could be undertaken either by the states or by private enterprise were also contributing factors. Finally, as the private-enterprise system found it more and more difficult to deal with economic crises of increasing severity which accompanied industrialization of the country, the Federal government began to participate actively in all phases of the economic system. This was most apparent during the sustained economic depression of 1929–1939 when the Federal government undertook far-reaching economic and social operations.

Government as an active element sharing in the control of economic operations shows itself in eight ways: (1) by regulations affecting almost every field of activity, every enterprise, and every process of economic life; (2) by deliberate manipulation of the banking and monetary system; (3) by provision of an elaborate array of government services; (4) by considerable participation as promotor, financier, and operator of large-scale public enterprises; (5) by commodity controls, purchases, and other stabilization operations; (6) by the employment of taxation and other fiscal devices to transfer wealth and income from the more to the less fortunate groups in the population through loans, grants, subsidies, benefits, and social-welfare services; (7) by the control, almost exclusive in some cases, of economic relations between the United States and the rest of the world; and (8) by the political action of executive departments of government allying themselves with special-interest groups to expand government powers and activities.

In addition to the obvious effects of government taxing and spending, government exerts other influences on the nation's economic system. These include influences stemming from the size and management of the public debt and effects on interest rates, savings, and investments from government borrowing, lending, and refinancing operations. The Federal government in particular influences all parts of the economy through policies and operations of the Treasury in cooperation with the Federal Reserve System in the field of money and credit. While their operations fall short of managed money and credit, they exert a powerful regulatory force on both, which affects every activity in the nation.

Perspective 1D   ECONOMIC BENEFIT VERSUS ENVIRONMENTAL HAZARD

Two chemists from the University of California, Irvine, suggested in 1974 that molecules of fluorocarbons from more than 1½ billion aerosol cans sold annually may be rising into the stratosphere. There these gas molecules could break down the earth's ozone shield that prevents the sun's most harmful ultraviolet radiation from reaching the earth. If more of this radiation gets through, some scientists fear it would increase cataracts and human skin cancer, and might even cause genetic damage to plant and animal life.

Environmentalists took the challenge and called for a ban on the use of fluorocarbon gases. Industry spokesmen reacted by pointing out that estimates of the danger varied widely and that a complete ban on the gases would seriously affect refrigeration and foamed-plastic industries as well as spray-can makers. The production, packaging, and marketing of fluorocarbons was estimated as an $8 billion U.S. industry involving nearly a million workers.

The stage was thus set for a classic confrontation between economic benefit and environmental peril. The government was judge and jury through its legislative bodies and regulatory agencies. Both sides presented witnesses. A recess was called in 1976 to allow an investigation by a special government-appointed task force. It reported back that "there seems to be legitimate concern" about the effects of hydrocarbons on ozone, but more evidence is needed to make a final verdict.

COMMENT   The ozone controversy typifies how special-interest groups can influence the legislative and regulatory process, and thereby affect the economic welfare of many people not intimately concerned with a specific issue. It is also a poignant example of the difficulties an industrial society has in weighing economic advantages against environmental hazards. Banning the gases would cause economic dislocations, but if they are not banned, irreparable damage could conceivably be inflicted on the whole human race.

1-4.3   Organized Labor as a Controlling Force

During the same period in which the Federal government emerged as a participant in the control of the economic system, organized labor grew to exert a similar power. Many of the same conditions which led to government intervention in economic life also furthered the growth of labor organizations. It is an interesting coincidence that the Federal regulation of private economic activities in 1887 began almost at the same time that the formation of the American Federation of Labor signaled the beginning of the modern labor movement.

The power of organized labor to exert controlling forces on the economy can be readily understood when its methods of operations are stated. These are: (1) labor's traditional economic power to affect industry through wage, hour, working-conditions, and benefits contracts in collective bargaining and through a variety of strikes, slowdowns, boycotts, and other work stoppages—some capable of permanently damaging private enterprises and crippling the national economy; (2) the persuasive effect of mass organizations upon industrial policies, standards, and operations; and (3) labor's political power through alliance with political parties, influence on voting habits of an organized minority, and pressures on law-making bodies at all levels of government.

Other developments in organized labor indicate that it will continue to be heard in economic affairs. It has an assured income from the checkoff system for collecting dues. It has large welfare and pension funds to invest and administer. Union leaders exercise strong control over the internal affairs of unions and union workers. Alliances between unions for common ends have become more frequent and more effective. The result is that even though organized labor covers only a portion of the nation's total working force, it exerts considerable influence on the decisions affecting specific industries as well as on the economic system as a whole. Conversely, there is now placed upon organized labor a new and grave responsibility for the operation of industry which until recent times rarely rested upon the worker or upon management.

Perspective 1E LIFETIME SECURITY FOR INDUSTRIAL WORKERS

Job tenure is traditionally associated with professors. Some labor unions would like to see the tenure system extended to their members. They cite the security currently afforded to educators, government employees, and Japanese industrial workers as prototypes. The intent of a lifetime security arrangement is to insulate employment from the ups and downs of business cycles.

To some extent income security is already included in many union contracts. Those workers covered by such contracts can collect supplemental unemployment benefits (S.U.B.) on top of regular unemployment compensation if they are laid off work. However, S.U.B. now lasts a year at most, and companies are not obliged to keep paying when reserves run low. An ideal lifetime security plan would guarantee full pay indefinitely, regardless of fluctuations in the national economy or local business downturns.

Employers are concerned about the adverse consequences of tenure proposals. Increased costs would entail higher prices. There would be less mobility in the labor force and a greater incentive to replace people with machines. A probable reaction to a tenured work force would be to rely more on subcontractors and temporary workers during periods of strong demand, instead of hiring additional permanent employees.

COMMENT The famous Japanese lifetime-employment system allows more management discretion in assigning workers to jobs than is permitted by American labor unions. In addition to greater labor-management cooperation in the Japanese mold, wage bargaining would have to recognize the value of eliminating the risk of joblessness. Then there is the chance that too much success in bargaining for top wages plus guaranteed employment could come back to haunt the negotiators in the form of business and work lost to nonunion competitors.

1-5 INDUSTRIAL MANAGEMENT

The driving force behind every industrial organization is its management team. Different teams operate in different ways. There are no universal truths of management to define the one best way, just concepts that explain why some operations were managed successfully in the past and guidelines to suggest what can be done to increase chances of success in the future.

Some companies have reputations for conservatism based on years of steady, if not spectacular, growth. Others have go-go reputations built on rapid expansion and spurts of impressive earnings. Their reputations are manifestations of divergent management philosophies, and the success with which those philosophies have been converted to practice.

1-5.1 Managers

A manager may sit behind a broad desk in a tall, deep-cushioned chair. Large windows expose a panoramic view. At the touch of a finger he can talk with people anywhere in the company or with worldwide business associates. Few see his activities, but many feel the effects of his decisions.

Another manager sits behind a drawing board on a tall, stiff stool. The board is also his desk, and it is cluttered. When he wants to speak to associates, he yells because his office is a nook in the modest shop he runs. His contacts include equipment salesmen, bill collectors, and customers. His decisions depend more on quick judgments than careful planning, but their effects are important to those near him.

These two managers are far apart on the scale of prestige, yet they have much in common. Their mission is to plan, coordinate, control, and accomplish. Though each has his own traits of personal dedication and ambition, their achievements can probably be traced to their success in managing people. Similarly, people at every tier of corporate hierarchy exercise essentially the same management principles to lead other people toward the accomplishment of organizational objectives.

Managerial competence is a function of a manager's character, knowledge, and experience. These three ingredients interact to mold a particular style of management. Styles may be altered or fashioned by education gained from formal training and work seasoning. An advantage of studying management techniques is the opportunity it allows to explore and develop managerial skills without suffering the consequences of trial and error learning.

Perspective 1F   IS MANAGEMENT AN ART OR A SCIENCE?

The argument that management is a science rests on the concept that there are basic principles of management which are appropriate for any type of business. The rebuttal that management is an art recognizes that people-to-people contacts are involved and that various aspects of managerial expertise are too subtle to capture by rules of conduct or by optimization formulas. The two arguments are blended nicely by Stafford Beer:

. . . To say that there can be a science of management is not to deny that management is an art. The man with the genius for designing buildings is not less of an artist because he is a competent architect. It is a very good thing for us all that he is. . . . The science of a subject is always about its very nature; it is not about virtuosity.*

*source: *Management Science—The Business Use of Operations Research,* Garden City, N.Y.: Doubleday & Company, Inc., 1968.

COMMENT   It may well be that some aspects of management are so personal—social behavior, sensitivity, creativity, and ability to react flexibly and rationally to changing situations—that managerial skills defy systematic development. However, the abundance of mail-order, custom-seminar, and college courses in salesmanship, leadership, and general management suggest otherwise. Just a few centuries ago sciences such as chemistry were believed too special to be passed along by mass education. Now even the mysteries of management can be examined conveniently in the classroom rather than by an exhaustive apprenticeship.

1-5.2 Management Science

The history of the human race implies mankind has practiced management for thousands of years, though written records on the subject date back only a couple of centuries. Earliest accounts are rather sketchy as they are more biographical records of managerial exploits than explanations of how to manage. Around the turn of this century management writings became more definitive. In the last three decades the literature has grown from a trickle to a flood. Much of the recent advance has emphasized the quantitative aspects under the banner of *management science.*

Two developments supported the growth of management science as a distinguished discipline: operations research and computers. The former evolved from task-force approaches taken to solve large, complex problems during World War II. Operations research teams were composed of natural scientists, mathematicians, and engineers whose common language was mathematics. After the war similar methods of analysis were applied to industrial problems. During this same period, computers were being developed that could accommodate the tremendous number of mathematical manipulations required to utilize the quantitative models of operations. These fortuitous events provided the foundations from which management science applications have extended to most areas of industry.

Perspective 1G MANAGEMENT MODELS

A model is a representation of reality. In management science, a model includes selected relevant factors of an actual system and is designed to explain certain aspects of that system. The model generally simplifies reality but closely approximates the more important elements under investigation.

Some models are intended to describe ongoing operations, known as descriptive models, and others to characterize how things ought to be arranged to accomplish a particular objective, called normative models. They can take three-dimensional, graphical, or symbolic forms. The use of symbols or numbers is the most abstract version and the one most common in management science. For instance, a graphical model of cost relationships frequently found in industrial operations is shown on page 25. The number of units that minimize total cost is indicated by the lowest point on the total cost curve. The same cost relationships could be described by a mathematical model:

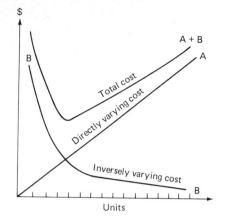

Total cost $= Ax + B/x$
where x = design variable (number of units)
        A = cost per unit (constant cost for all units)
        B = unit cost (constant cost for total number of units)

Then the number of units that minimize the total cost could be determined mathematically as $x = \sqrt{B/A}$ (see Chapt. 11).

COMMENT   Scientists have been developing models of physical systems for a long time. $E = mc^2$ is Einstein's famous, familiar, but seldom fully understood expression of a governing physical phenomenon. $P = R - C$ (profit equals revenue minus cost) is a businessman's formula. Rather crude expressions of basic cost relationships have been around the business world for many years, but extensive use of sophisticated models by American industry is quite recent. Acceptance of more elaborate modeling is retarded by lack of understanding, even some distrust, of how models can assist in management decision making. But the complex web of factors in which many of today's operating decisions are tangled makes the use of management models more of a necessity than a fancy assist.

1-6 STUDYING AMERICAN INDUSTRY

American industry is a very broad subject. The previous pages provided a brief glimpse of its character. All the subjects so far encountered will be enlarged upon in subsequent chapters where more detailed discussions are provided of operational components and the way they mesh to meet the needs of consumers. As shown in Figure 1-2, the rest of this book is divided into five major sections portrayed as links in the chain connecting *input* (raw materials, land, labor, etc.) to *output* (finished products, services, etc.).

• Chapters within the *Management* section examine the responsibilities of managers and the tools available to assist them.

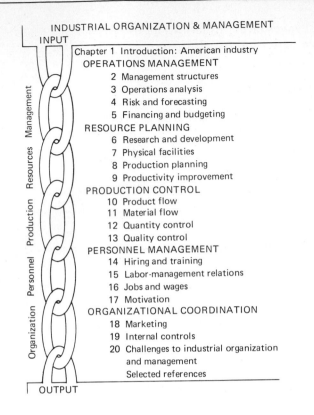

Figure 1-2 Flow of text material for the study of organization and management in American industry.

- The *Resource* section looks at ways to utilize inputs most effectively.

- In the *Production* section attention is focused on the processes and controls needed to transform raw materials into finished products.

- The *Personnel* section recognizes that people are the most critical factor in industrial organization and management, and the most challenging.

- Coordination is the theme of the *Organization* section in which chapters discuss how the output of the industrial system reaches consumers and what developments can be expected in the future.

It would take an enormous book to completely examine all the factors and issues affecting American industry, if indeed such an exhaustive tome could ever be compiled. And it would be out of date as soon as it was written. Conditions change continually: new products and technology, revised regulations, shifts in demands and supplies, rising expectations of workers and consumers, and so on. Yet there are basic relationships and functions that must be understood before the consequences of change can be appreciated. It is the intent of this book to provide a survey of these basics that reveals the challenges facing American industry and the opportunities available to promote better industrial organization and management.

1-7 REVIEW QUESTIONS

1. What are the six stages of growth of the American economy? Discuss the significance of each stage.

2. What part does manufacturing play in an economic system?

3. What are the advantages and disadvantages of specialization?

4. List the different types of manufacturing industries, and provide an example of a typical product from each.

5. What are the major distinctions between a corporate form of organization and a partnership?

6. Comment on the following statement: In manufacturing the tendency is toward more and larger corporations.

7. Utilize an example to distinguish between horizontal combination and vertical combination.

8. Distinguish between the three controlling forces of the national economy by commenting on the sources and constituents of each.

9. If there are indeed no "universal truths" of management upon which to base content, how can the subject legitimately be taught by educational institutions? How does the concept of *management science* fit the subject?

1-8 TOPICS FOR DISCUSSION

1. Consult one or more standard economic texts, and then explain how the following concepts exert controlling and regulating influences on the economic system:

   a. Individual initiative
   b. Private ownership of the means of production
   c. Competition among producers
   d. Competition among buyers
   e. Competition among sellers
   f. Bargaining between buyers and sellers
   g. Consumers' freedom of choice

2. Since governments and organized labor now participate substantially in the control and operation of the economy, what significant changes do you see in our system of economy, which in the past has been characterized by individual initiative and enterprise?

3. American industrial history discloses a persistent tendency toward combinations and mergers of industrial operations and business units. What economic, social, and political implications does this trend have? What are the possible effects on private enterprise? (In your discussion give special emphasis to such subjects as control of enterprise, prices, competition, invention, patents, employment, and profits.)

4. Take a position and argue *for* or *against* the proposition: "The trend in the last 25 years in the United States, as among other industrial countries of the world, is toward the socialization of industrial enterprise with consequent reduction of opportunity for private enterprise."

5. Study the diagram on the economic process in the United States (Fig. 1-1). Describe:

   a. All the relationships you can discover between (1) the raw material and extractive industries and the manufacturing industries; (2) the manufacturing industries and intermediary trade; (3) the intermediary trade and retail trade.
   b. What relationships can you discover between imports and exports in the diagram?
   c. Under the processes entitled (1) primary industries, (2) manufacturing, and (3) distributive industries, list as many "service" industries as you can find connected with each economic process. (The purpose of question 5 is to acquire a more thorough understanding of the interrelationships and coordination of the American economic system.)

6. Fears have been expressed that the concentration of ownership of U.S. companies by relatively few institutions, as discussed in Perspective 1C, might tempt the institutions to exert control over the companies in which they own a significant share. What factors tend to limit this potential influence?

7. Discuss both sides of an environmental–industry controversy similar to the ozone issue in Perspective 1D.

8. The chart in Perspective 1G could represent a repair problem, when units of time are given on the horizontal scale. Then line *A* would designate the cost of an idle facility (renting equipment, extra cost owed to buying parts not produced because production equipment was being repaired, etc.) and line *B* would show the cost of making repairs (decreasing repair time disproportionately increases the cost due to overtime payments, hiring extra help, more supervisory help required, etc.). Thus the point on the time scale directly below the bottom point of the total cost curve (*A* + *B*) would mark the most economical repair time.

   Describe another industrial operation that could be represented by the lines in the chart. Discuss factors that set the shape of each line and how the minimum point on the total cost curve indicates the best solution to the problem.

9. Case 1A: *The Smell of Money*
   On a bright Sunday afternoon Al Notz sat in his office with the shades drawn, contemplating what he should say at tomorrow's annual meeting of the company's stockholders. The facts and figures he had to deliver were discouraging. Revenue was up and operating costs had not increased proportionately, but major capital expenditures had been made to meet new clean-air standards. The end result was that the usual dividend on stock had to be halved.
   Besides the angry stockholders expected to be present at the meeting, Al had heard rumors that a contingent of environmentalists from a nearby university would picket the meeting. They wanted still more controls, both to further reduce the odor from the paper-making process of the plant and to eliminate untreated wastes being discharged into Cedar Creek. As manager of the plant, Al knew that the State Environmental Quality Department had approved a schedule for gradually controlling the remaining air and water contamination. The authorities recognized how expensive more controls would be and took that into consideration in stretching out modifications, but the plant location alongside a busy highway made it a natural target for groups seeking to protect the environment.
   The paper company was started 22 years ago. The original owners later made it a public corporation in order to finance a major expansion that allowed the use of a new process for converting wood chips into Kraft paper. The odor from the process had always been pretty strong, but the community used to be more tolerant, calling it the smell of money. Also, most of the stock

had been sold locally, and the stockholders had come to expect substantial dividends from their holdings.

Al was worried that the stockholders and environmentalists would clash. In addition, he felt obliged to report that next year's dividends would also suffer from plant modifications required to meet higher safety standards in compliance with OSHA (Occupational Safety and Health Act) regulations. What depressed him most was the provable fact that the company was more productive than ever before, but the bottom line on the profit and loss statement did not reflect this achievement.

Questions

1. What approach would you recommend for Al to take at tomorrow's meeting—stress productivity gains and blame the government for higher costs, emphasize the benefits to the community from new pollution controls stressing that these activities are responsibilities of ownership, etc.?

2. Put yourself in the role of a stockholder. Should Al be blamed for "giving in" too easily or too quickly to demands for environmental improvements and be directed to spend more effort in the future protecting dividends instead of the environment? What would be your feelings toward the picketers?

2

MANAGEMENT AND ORGANIZATION STRUCTURE

We have viewed the industrial enterprise, in the preceding chapter, in terms of its historical development, its major changes, and its place in the total economy as it exists today. Attention is now directed to its management and organization structure. Industrial organization is a means by which human resources, physical assets, money, and time are coordinated into efficient production of products and services. What are the major functions that constitute the operation of an enterprise, and by what means can it be organized to bring these varied functions into coordination? What are the fundamental principles of organization and management that must permeate its operations? How should an enterprise be structured to foster better management?

2 MANAGEMENT AND ORGANIZATION STRUCTURE

2-1 EFFECTS OF INTERNAL ORGANIZATION ON MANAGEMENT

An industrial enterprise may possess the most modern plant and equipment, a highly skilled and experienced labor and sales force, ample financial resources, and an adequate source of raw materials, yet be a failure in its purpose of making a profit. There may be many reasons and circumstances responsible for this failure, but the most frequent reason is *poor management.*

It is the intent of a manufacturing enterprise, through the efforts of people and machines, to transform materials or parts into products of greater usefulness to others who will purchase these products. An extractive industry, on the other hand, will provide material for other producers and consumers. Some enterprises may be engaged primarily in the distribution of products to users. Others may be engaged in the servicing of products already in use. Others produce and distribute energy; still others supply means of transportation for products, materials, and people. Fundamentally, all these enterprises are selling the time of their workers, machines, plant, patents, and money. The extent to which they make efficient use of the time of these assets will largely determine the extent of profit—the primary goal of those who have invested effort and capital in the enterprise. *Organization* is a plan for bringing these assets into the position of greatest effectiveness, or *productivity.* The plan consists of the grouping of operations (people and machines) to achieve the advantages of specialization, the designation of those who are to *supervise* each of these groups of operations, and those who are to *serve* these operations.

In the small enterprise the organizational structure may be very simple. The owner frequently is the manager. He may have daily contact with all the people of the company. He is the one who establishes policies, assigns the jobs to be done, and follows up on the jobs for the purpose of direction and coordination.

As the enterprise grows larger, the problems of organization for grouping, supervising, and serving operations become more complex. Today we find many companies that may be divided into more than 100 divisions scattered throughout the nation and foreign countries, some employing many thousands in one division. Each division is a huge industrial enterprise within itself, yet all divisions must be brought into coordination with established policies. There must be coordination among those who procure the orders, those who process and supply the material, those who produce the different parts that comprise the finished product, those who assemble these parts, those who get the product off the shipping platform and on the way to the customer, and those who serve and maintain personnel, plant, and equipment. When this coordination does not exist, we find orders delayed beyond the promised date of delivery, idle personnel, idle machines, shortages of some materials and excess of other materials, grumbling and dissatisfaction on the part of personnel, ulcers on the part of the president, and, ultimately, financial difficulties on the part of the company.

A common fault of management is its failure to adapt its organization structure, policies, and procedures to the growth in size and complexity of the enterprise. This is particularly true where an owner-manager has been highly successful with his little company "three doors down from the corner." He naturally fears to change his way of doing things as his company grows larger lest he lose the one ingredient that has made him successful; furthermore, he is not at all sure *which* ingredient that may be.

We can better understand the complexities that face us in the management of an industrial enterprise if we review briefly at this point the separate major functions required in today's industrial economy.

2-2 MAJOR FUNCTIONS OF THE INDUSTRIAL ENTERPRISE

In an industrial enterprise the functions may be divided broadly into two groups: (1) the policy group and (2) the administrative group. The *policy* group, although responsible for the establishment of policies for all segments of the enterprise, has direct operating responsiblity for relations with stockholders, external investments, public relations exclusive of customer and vendor relations, and legal relations both internal and external.

The *administrative* group includes all other functions, primarily internal in nature, which operate under broad instructions or policies established by the top management or policy group. These functions include:

1. Product development

2. Purchasing

3. Industrial relations

4. Manufacturing

5. Marketing

6. Internal finance and office services

Before we go further into organization structures for the coordination of these functions in the administrative group, it will be helpful to consider briefly the general scope of each. One or more subsequent chapters will be devoted to the details of each of these functions.

2-2.1 Product Development

In some companies product development plays a vital role. For example, in the automobile industry, which is highly competitive, research and design are of special significance. Furthermore, the nature of the product of the automobile industry, in comparison with cutlery or paper, requires more research and experimentation. In the latter industries, research is essential, but because the products do not have moving parts and mechanical gadgets, the problems of design are simpler and more limited.

2-2.2 Purchasing

This function encompasses all activities connected with the procurement from outside vendors of materials, parts, supplies, equipment, and tooling. It usually includes:

1. Procurement

2. Materials investigation

3. Subcontracting

Here again practice will vary in the scope of function. Often *receiving* and perhaps *storage* and *internal transportation* may be included in the purchasing function.

2-2.3 Industrial Relations

The industrial-relations function has had especially significant growth during recent years, both in scope and in recognition. The American labor movement and a growing social consciousness have been strong contributing factors.

Industrial relations consists primarily of six parts:

1. Employment

2. Training and communications

3. Health and safety

4. Employee services and benefits

5. Labor relations

6. Wage and salary administration

2-2.4 Manufacturing

The manufacturing function includes the operations directly concerned with the making of the product, including the processing of materials. It also includes various services to these *productive* operations.[1] The following, however, are typical of these manufacturing services:

[1]Although accounting practice differs, the term "productive operations" or "productive labor" in industrial manufacturing generally refers to operations of labor that change the form, size, or physical or chemical characteristics of the product or of its components.

1. Industrial engineering, including production planning and standards and methods

2. Plant service, including shipping, receiving, storage, and internal transportation

3. Plant engineering, including mechanical engineering, electrical engineering, tools, power, and maintenance

2-2.5 Marketing

The distribution of the product is usually considered to be of two parts, *sales* and *promotion.* A third part, *service,* is essential when the company manufactures a product for which service by the company is required. For example, a machinery manufacturer might need to supply service for his product after installation in the customer's plant, while a manufacturer of paper boxes would not.

Promotion is considered a highly specialized activity requiring personnel qualified for the handling of all types of advertising and customer relations. There is, of course, a considerable amount of effective promotion work performed by the salespersons in the field. Promotion, therefore, cannot be segregated entirely from the selling function.

2-2.6 Internal Finance and Office Services

Internal finance and office services actually are two functions or groups of functions but are frequently grouped into one for convenience of organization. Often the individual responsible for the supervision of internal finance is fully qualified by background and training to supervise the office services. Then, too, the office services, such as stenography, duplicating, filing, mailing, and control of records and reports, are so closely related to finance that a natural grouping results. However, it should be recognized that these office services extend throughout the organization and are not limited to the "business office." In fact, the nature of the business may cause the major portion of office-service time to be directed toward operations outside the business office—manufacturing, sales, industrial relations, and other functions. This often leads to the decentralization of office services so that each major function of the organization has its own services.

Perspective 2A   ORGANIZATION MUTATION

Peter Drucker, the well-known author and management consultant, warns that traditional structures are no longer adequate for today's complex organizations:

The classical organization structures of the 1920s and 1930s, which still serve as textbook examples, stood for decades without needing more than an occasional touching up. American Telephone & Telegraph, General Motors, Du Pont, Unilever, and Sears Roebuck maintained their organizational concepts, structures, and basic components through several management generations and major changes in the size and scope of the business. Today, however, a company no sooner finishes a major job of reorganizing itself than it starts all over again.*

Drucker suggests that there are five basic organization structures. Two are in the classical mold:

1. *Functional structures.* Each management unit is associated with a particular function, such as manufacturing, engineering, purchasing, and sales departments within one company.
2. *Product division.* Functional subunits are grouped according to the product produced in the company, such as the manufacturing, engineering, and sales groups operating within a single division of a large company to produce a certain type of product.

The other three structures are modern variations:

3. *Team organization.* Groups comprising several functional skills are organized to perform specific assignments.
4. *Simulated product divisions.* Related subunits are artificially treated as separate profit and loss centers, like real product divisions, although they are actually segments of a common, larger process.
5. *Systems structure.* A combination of designs 3 and 4 as utilized in large government bodies and transnational companies.

*SOURCE: "New Templates for Today's Organization," *Harvard Business Review,* January-February, 1974.

COMMENT   There apparently is no ideal organization design to emulate. A management structure is a means of attaining the objectives and goals of an institution, and therefore must be responsive to respective needs and changes in those needs. As Drucker concludes, " 'Perfect organization' is like 'perfect health': the test is the ills it does not have and therefore does not have to cure."

2-3   MANAGEMENT STRUCTURE

The primary purpose of a management structure is to facilitate the coordination and control over the activities of the company. There are many factors to consider in determining the design for a given company. No two companies are identical. Each company must be studied in terms of its purposes, its size, and the nature of the product manufactured or provided. There are, however, a few basic principles that can be used for guidance in considering the management needs of any company. These will be discussed in the remainder of this chapter.

2-3.1   Lines of Responsibility and Authority

It is easily recognized that in any sizable organization there must be delegation of responsibility. In the first place, it is a physical impossibility for any one person to control effectively all the work of a large organization through personal contact with it. Managers must rely on other individuals to be responsible for designated phases of the work. Second, no one person possesses the skills essential to guide personally the highly specialized activities in a modern industry. Instead, an expert on finance assumes responsibility for the financial activities of the enterprise. An industrial engineer analyzes the manufacturing processes of the company and develops the most efficient methods for manufacturing a product of maximum quality at minimum cost. And so, throughout the organization, top management must segregate these highly specialized activities and obtain individuals with the necessary knowledge and skill to be responsible for them.

This principle of delegation of authority extends all the way through the company from the president and general manager to the heads of divisions, the supervisors, the straw bosses, and the workers at the bench. Lines of responsibility must be fixed. Everyone in a company should know to whom they are responsible. Lines of responsibility that are "fringy" or indistinct lead to grumbling and misunderstanding throughout the personnel of the organization. One supervisor will order the work performed in one way and another will order the worker to stop operations and proceed in a different way. The result is dissatisfaction on the part of workers and supervisors and loss in the efficiency of operations.

Consider also the position of the supervisor who cannot be sure of the bounds of his responsibility. He lives in fear of the possibility that he is either "meddling with someone else's business" or neglecting a responsibility of which he is unaware. Lines of responsibility work two ways: from the executive to the supervisor and to the workers that come under his jurisdiction and, conversely, from the worker to those who are in authority over him. These lines must be kept clear at all times in order to facilitate the ready flow of communication and control.

2-3.2 The Meaning of Responsibility and Authority

A famous professor of administration is credited with a definition of "hell" as *responsibility without authority.* Many people, by their actions, seem constantly to seek authority but evade responsibility. The latter we refer to as "buck-passing." Authority and responsibility must go together. We are much more willing to agree to the necessity of authority in doing a job than to accept the resulting responsibilities once we are aware of the full implications of these responsibilities.

If you as an individual were given the complete authority for the selection of production processes and equipment, would you also be willing to assume the complete responsibility? These elements not only require extensive research but also in the end require selective experience for the exercise of judgment in making final choices. These are elements which play an important role in determining the relative competitive position of the manufacturer. The enterprise must continually exploit all its resources for the improvement of processes and equipment lest it be knocked out of the market by a more efficient competitor. Would you be willing to assume this responsibility alone?

If you were given authority to act in disciplinary cases including suspension or discharge, would you be willing to assume complete responsibility for the avoidance of strikes and consequent shutdowns tht might result from an unintentional error in your actions?

If your answer to these questions is in the affirmative, your employer should very quickly put you in isolated quarters where you can cause no serious destruction to life or property. No one is infallible. We are all capable of errors. You as an individual might be willing to risk the possibility of such errors, but the stockholders, the board of directors, the president, your management superiors, and the employees cannot afford to place that much confidence in you.

These reasons are the source of the principle which says that *authority can never be completely delegated—it can only be shared.* The president is still held responsible for quality of product and for the causes of strikes. Then why does he delegate any of the authority and responsibility? He does so because he must *share* if he expects to obtain the necessary counsel of specialists in production, cost, labor relations, and the many other varied activities of the company. Such counsel, given by persons who do not share in the responsibility, would be of questionable value.

Yet even with the aid of responsible specialists there is always the element of risk in decisions. The true scientist will be the first to admit the possibility of error in his findings and recommendations. Who is to assume the risk? Who is to make the decision? Probably the best answer is that decisions should result from the *pooling of judgment* of those who share in the responsibility and authority in the situation in question.

In the selection of processes and equipment, basic policies governing the procedures to be used in the selection are established and approved by top management. However, even these policies are the outgrowth of recommendations coming from specialized staff personnel and approved by the production foremen, the production-control manager, the cost-control manager, the superintendent, and the maintenance superintendent.

Perspective 2B   STEEPED, ROUNDED, AND SQUASHED ORGANIZATION PATTERNS

The vast majority of organizations can be represented by a triangular shape in which higher levels of the structure are inhabited by successively fewer people. The degree of steepness of the triangle is both the cause and the result of the way management operates. Three versions of a triangular organization with associated character implications are shown on page 39.

COMMENT   Because all organizational triangles narrow as they get taller, responsibilities at the top tiers tend to be similar, regardless of the type of industry or government body represented by the triangle. Job characteristics that vary inversely with the number of job holders include

1. *Planning horizons*   Top level managers plan operations months or years in advance, while bottom level workers have short range, if any, options to consider.

ORGANIZATION PATTERN

IMPLICATION OF
ORGANIZATION PATTERN

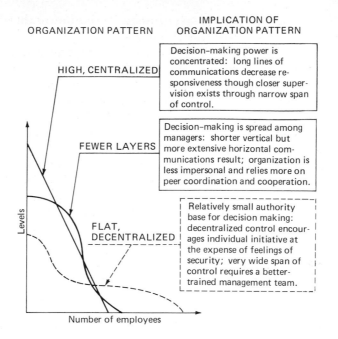

HIGH, CENTRALIZED

Decision–making power is
concentrated: long lines of
communications decrease re-
sponsiveness though closer supervision exists through narrow span
of control.

FEWER LAYERS

Decision–making is spread among
managers: shorter vertical but
more extensive horizontal communications result; organization is
less impersonal and relies more on
peer coordination and cooperation.

FLAT,
DECENTRALIZED

Relatively small authority
base for decision making:
decentralized control encourages individual initiative at
the expense of feelings of
security; very wide span of
control requires a better-
trained management team.

Levels

Number of employees

2. *Freedom of action*   Many companies set expenditure limits for each level of management; for instance, a department manager could be allowed to make a single expenditure of $2,000 without seeking the boss' approval, and that boss, in turn, could authorize $10,000 expenditures without prior approval.

3. *Variety of work*   Work assignments become less repetitive at progressively higher levels of the organization.

4. *More pay for more responsibility*   Activity coordination automatically includes the more significant events from all lower levels; this accumulated accountability is a source of take-home duties and frayed nerves popularly associated with managers of managers.

2-3.3   Trends Toward Decentralization of Authority and Responsibility

Mention has been made earlier of the trend toward the merger of companies into large multiplant corporations. One of the difficulties accompanying these mergers has been the extended line of communication and action. The headquarters office may be located in New York City with plants scattered throughout the United States and even beyond. The products of the plants may be greatly diversified—textiles, motion-picture production, airplane-engine parts, food, chemicals, transportation. To what extent should this corporation attempt centralized purchasing—the pooling of all purchasing through one central office? To what extent shall it attempt to enforce a single standard of safety practices? Should it attempt nationwide labor bargaining? Should it attempt corporation-wide personnel policies and practices? The same question may be asked regarding all the major staff functions.

We have considered earlier in this chapter the importance of sharing responsibility and authority, and the value of pooled judgment in making decisions on policies and practices. This becomes practically impossible in the large multiplant organization with centralized-staff departments. The staff person from headquarters is almost a stranger to the distant plant. Each plant will have problems peculiarly its own. It will have special material problems. It will have labor problems peculiar to its own locality. Differences in production operations will result in differences in production problems. A staff department must live with those differences to be able to understand them.

Companies have attempted to solve this problem by locating staff representatives permanently in designated plants but requiring that they will be responsible directly to the central-staff offices. This only half-solved the problem. The central office had a better-informed spokesman, but two major phases of the problem remained unsolved: (1) delay in communication and action; and (2) split authority within the plant since the plant manager did not have direct authority over the staff representatives. This led to friction, "buck-passing," and lack of cooperation. It was exceedingly difficult, if not impossible, for the staff representative to become a part of the plant "team."

This situation has led in recent years to the *decentralization* of staff functions in large multiplant organizations, even in companies with little diversification in products. By this plan each plant or separate operating unit has its own staff departments responsible to plant organization. The central-headquarters offices may still retain staff departments and serve in general as resource centers. The plant executive, however, is responsible for all operations within his plant. With this responsibility goes the authority for the acceptance or rejection of suggested changes. Certain functions in some companies may be excepted, e.g., labor bargaining. The trend, however, seems to be toward decentralization wherever possible.

2-3.4 Available Personnel

The organization of a company is dependent not only upon the type and arrangement of work in the company but also upon the special abilities and skills of personnel to perform the work. This is especially true in the establishment of leaders, supervisors, and foremen. Two factors are here especially significant: (1) the need for close supervision as judged by the skill of the workers and the difficulty of the operations; and (2) the availability of experienced and trustworthy personnel capable of acting in supervisory capacities. Operations of a routine, unskilled nature might require little supervision. In this case a large number of operators could be grouped together under one supervisor or foreman. On the other hand, during a period of rapid expansion when large numbers of new personnel are being brought into the plant, it is usually advisable to decrease the number of operators per supervisor in order that each worker may receive more attention and help in becoming familiar with the work.

One of the greatest difficulties encountered by industry is the ever-present shortage of people capable of leadership and supervision of others. This may be due primarily to lack of incentive in the supervisory positions, inadequate or ineffective recruitment of those possessing potential leadership ability, and insufficient training of present and potential supervisory personnel. These factors will be discussed more fully in the industrial-relations section of this book. It will suffice here merely to state that the shortage usually exists, except possibly in times of serious unemployment.

Scarcity of capable supervisory personnel has its effect on the organization of the company in that the company must often group the work according to the abilities of the leaders who are available rather than attempt to fit the leaders into preconceived work groupings. An especially capable leader and administrator may have more and more assignments added to his or her responsibilities while the less capable may have functions taken away or at least remain status quo. Two short illustrations will perhaps explain how this influence operates in actual practice.

The first illustration is of a company that found it necessary to set up two superintendents of production, rather than expand the duties of one, merely because of the inadequacies and inflexibility of the individual involved. This was an old New England manufacturer of consumer products, who early in World War II was offered a contract for the production of machine-gun parts. Although the same basic equipment was involved, the production on the new contract required new setups and much closer tolerances in contrast with the principal product of the company. This meant close supervision of operations, new quality-control procedures, and careful scheduling. The production superintendent had been with the company for 30 years. Because of his experience he was highly valuable to the company in spite of his strong resistance to new methods of production. It was considered inadvisable to depend on him to organize the new production unit or to give him jurisdiction over it. Instead, a younger man with wide experience both in and out of the company was appointed to the position of war production coordinator. He reported directly to the executive vice-president and had authority over all operations on war products. If, in contrast, the production superintendent had possessed the desired flexibility and initiative, the logical organization in a company of this size would have called for the appointment of an assistant to aid him in the organization and operation of the new unit.

The second illustration is in direct contrast to the first. This case shows how a chief stock clerk, because of his unusual leadership abilities, had more and more responsibilities added to his position—far beyond what would be expected of a position carrying the title of stock clerk. This case is told by a consultant who had been called upon to assist in picking a man to fill the vacated position of the chief stock clerk, who was being promoted to assistant to the president. The consultant found that, in addition to the usual responsibilities of controlling inventories, the position also carried jurisdiction over production control, cost control, purchasing, shipping, receiving, materials handling, and personnel. The former holder of the position was a man of distinctly superior administrative ability. In recognition of his ability, the company over a period of many years had added difficult problem areas to his assignment but did not change his title. Obviously, the consultant recommended that in attempting a replacement there should be some reorganization of these functions. Actually, the company hired two men as a result of the reorganization—a chief stock clerk and an assistant works manager.

Perspective 2C   HOW MANY PEOPLE SHOULD A LEADER LEAD?

The number of subordinates who report directly to a superior establishes his or her "span of control." As the number of subordinates increases arithmetically, the number of potential interactions increases geometrically. For example, one supervisor and a single subordinate interact only with each other, 1:1. A span of control of two has six interactions: the supervisor with each subordinate singularly (2), with either subordinate acting as the leader for the pair (2), and the subordinates with each other as initiated by either one (2). These two relationship patterns as well as a span of three are depicted in the diagrams below where the supervisor is represented by *S* and the subordinates by numbers.

Single-headed arrows show one-to-one relationships, multiple-headed arrows show sequences, and dashed arrows indicate contacts between subordinates sponsored by

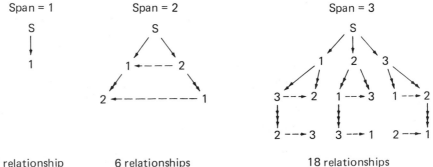

Span = 1	Span = 2	Span = 3
1 relationship	6 relationships	18 relationships

one or the other. For instance, the chain S→1↠3 indicates a contact with subordinate 1 who represents the pair of 1 and 3, while S→1↠3↠↠2 indicates the supervisor has a relationship with 1 who represents the trio of 1, 2, and 3. A span of control of 10 has 5210 potential relationships.

A survey by Ernest Dade in 1967 of 100 large companies revealed that the span of control of chief executives ranged from 1 to 24, with a median of 8 or 9. About two-thirds of the spans were between 5 and 11.*

*SOURCE: *Organization*, New York: American Management Association, 1967.

COMMENT Counting the interactions among a crew and its leader is a striking way to highlight the difficulties of leadership. If it is believed that each potential relationship is important to success, then the size should be limited. It is likely, however, that only a few of the potential transactions occur in any given day, limiting the monitoring duties of the superior. What span of control is appropriate depends on the nature of the work, the competence of the personnel, and the environment. Top management spans, as those described in the survey of chief executives, are normally smaller than spans lower in the hierarchy.

2-3.5   Lines of Coordination and Facilitation

Many executives object to the charting of lines of authority and responsibility for, they say, an organization does not work that way. Here a distinction can be made between authority and facilitation or persuasion. By authority, people in parallel positions are responsible not to one another but to superior executives. Actually, however, the majority of problems affecting these two people may have been solved by mutual agreement before ever reaching the superior officers. This is merely a recognition of the fact that courteous, informal discussion by individuals nearest a problem may simplify the solution and avoid extraneous influences such as misunderstanding and distrust.

Of course, free interplay of discussion between individuals of different departments can develop into a serious weakness in organization. First, it can result in a needless waste of time if a supervisor can call an employment interviewer and discuss in detail the routine requirements of a job to be filled or if he can call a follow-up clerk in the purchasing department and ask for special consideration on an order of material. Such abuse would also serve to destroy lines of coordination and control. Executives who are supposed to be in positions where they can view problems in better perspective and with recognition for the welfare of the department or the enterprise are "by-passed" and made ineffective.

For these reasons lines of facilitation are recognized for their value but are carefully confined to points where they are actually needed.

2-4 TYPES OF ORGANIZATIONS

It has been stated that details of organizational structure may differ in terms of the peculiar needs of a given industrial enterprise. There are, however, four principal organization types with varying degrees of complexity appropriate to the enterprise in terms of size and type of product. These types are: (1) line or military; (2) line and staff; (3) functional (pure); and (4) line and functional staff.

2-4.1 Line Organization

Line organization is the simplest form of structure. It is the framework on which a more complex organization may be built as needs arise. It assumes a direct straight-line responsibility and control from the general manager to the superintendent, to foremen, and to the workers (see Fig. 2-1).

Line organization has frequently been referred to as military organization. It acquired this name through the fact that there are direct single lines of authority and responsibility between an officer and his subordinates. However, any similarity that might have existed previously between this form of organization and the organization of the military services is now outmoded. Branches of the military service now have special divisions with horizontal as well as vertical lines of authority and responsibility.

2-4.2 Line and Staff Organization

Industrial leaders have recognized, as their companies grew from simple to complex organizations, that a small number of executives could not personally assume direct responsibility for all functions such as research, planning, distribution, public relations, industrial relations, and the many other varied

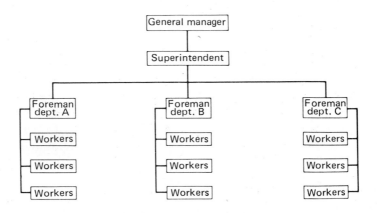

Figure 2-1 Line organization.

gabytes) usable

act

1

activities. Therefore, one of the first moves toward reorganization as a company grew in size and complexity was to appoint assistants to executives. Specific advisory responsibilities were delegated to these assistants. Executives and general foremen retained supervisory authority and control over the activities of the personnel of their particular departments. They were the coordinating force that worked toward the preservation of harmony and good personnel relations between the workers and the special executive assistants. These assistants frequently carried the title of process engineer, design engineer, industrial engineer, or budget officer, as shown in Figure 2-2. As the activities of these assistants increased, other personnel were added to assist in the activities. Eventually, the work centering around a special assistant was organized into a department which was known as a *staff* department, supplementing the *line* organization of the enterprise.

2-4.3   Functional Organization (Pure)

The development of staff departments led quite naturally to attempts toward complete reorganization on a functional basis. This removed the staff specialist from his "assisting" capacity and gave him authority and responsibility for supervision and administration of the function, replacing the operating foreman. The movement was led by Frederick W. Taylor, a pioneer in what was known as scientific management.

This functional organization proved to be a failure because each worker had a multiplicity of bosses, i.e., one for production preparation and scheduling, one for inspection, one for maintenance, etc. Such a system is a direct violation of one of the principles of organization.

Although no longer in use, this type of organization is mentioned here historically because the idea occurs frequently in the minds of students of management that it should be possible to combine the work of the specialist

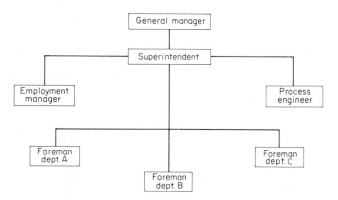

Figure 2-2   Simple line and staff organization.

and the foreman. Furthermore, this is intended as a warning to the staff specialist who may trap himself into feeling that he is in complete charge of his function and is resentful of the right of any operating foreman to challenge him.

2-4.4 Line and Functional Staff Organization

The functionalized organization of foremen as advocated by Taylor led to the establishment of functional staff departments whereby many of the advantages of both the line and staff organization and the functional type of organization could be retained. This has come to be known as line and functional staff organization. Through this type of organization, functional staff departments were given responsibility and authority, within company policy established in consultation with the line organization, over specialized activities such as inspection, time study, employment, purchasing, internal transportation, and shipping. Note that these are service functions performed by specialized personnel apart from the line operators who are responsible to their line supervisors.

Under this type of organization, however, the staff department directs its function in the production units up to the point where disagreement occurs, e.g., interpretation of quality standards used in the rejection of finished work. The disagreement is then taken to the administrative heads of the production and the staff units involved, and ultimately may be carried to higher management (see Fig. 2-3).

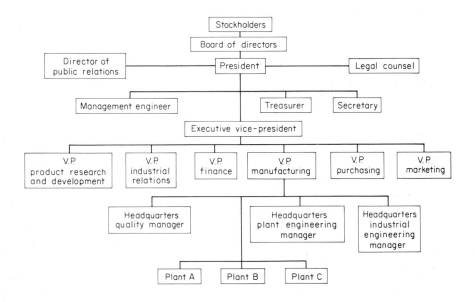

Figure 2-3 Organization chart of the management group of a large multiplant organization that illustrates line and functional staff relationships.

Perspective 2D READING BETWEEN THE LINES OF AN ORGANIZATION CHART

Most organizations publish a chart that theoretically purports its managerial structure. Boxes, labeled with work functions or titles, are arranged to show superior-subordinate relationships; they imply the flow of delegated responsibility and attendant accountability. But many relationships are tenuous, and actual positions of authority may be reversed or simply not revealed.

Harold Stieglitz commented on the potential for misinterpretation:

To some people, inclusion on the organization chart is, in itself, a status symbol. The physical location on the chart—linear distance from the chief executive—is viewed as a measure of importance. And there's the rub. Given the limitations of a piece of paper, not everyone can be charted equidistant from the chief executive. Reassurances like 'size and position of boxes do not reflect importance or status' are seldom reassuring enough. The incumbent charted in a particular spot may realize the truth of this statement; but he may fear that the 'other fellows may not,' or vice versa. . . . Most people still rely on the pay envelope as a more accurate reflection of relative importance. And the organization chart just isn't designed to reflect the pay structure of the company.*

*source: "What's Not on the Organization Chart," *The Conference Board Record,* September, 1964.

COMMENT It should not surprise anyone that actual degrees of responsibility and authority do not coincide with those charted. A table of organization may be outdated before it is published because activities of an organization can change rapidly. Similarly, people change positions, and the influence of successive position holders may differ vastly due to personal characteristics. Insiders know where to go to get something done, even if it means traveling through the white spaces of the organization chart.

Despite its limitations, a conventional organization chart is still valuable. At a minimum it displays the skeletal structure which imparts to both insiders and outsiders the formal channels of communication and authority. But only the naive believe that it exposes the complete picture of the organization.

2-5 COMMITTEES

In order to facilitate a cooperative relationship within a large industrial enterprise, many companies now add a network of committees to the line and staff organization. Committees are formed for the performance of special duties. These committees may be either permanent, sometimes referred to as standing committees, or they may be organized to serve a temporary function only.

2-5.1 The Need for Committees

The test of administrators is their ability to get others to work with them toward a common goal. They should be free to devote attention to special problems as they arise and to new developments for the general improvement of operations. However, if they attempt to dictate quickly the solution of a problem or the structure of a new project, they find that they alone must follow it through to completion. Their subordinates and colleagues are far behind in their thinking. There is no enthusiasm for the plan. Probably the most common faults of administrators are their impatience and reluctance to share the process of planning with those who must work with them in developing and operating the project—those who must translate plans into action.

The importance of enthusiastic, cooperative effort can best be explained through studying the probabilities of a given situation. For example, let us consider the organization of a training program. The director of industrial relations, of the dictatorial variety, would probably call the supervisors together and announce that the company is to have a training program. He would set forth the details of the program as he had planned them. He would make it perfectly clear that the plans were to be followed and were not to be questioned. Under these circumstances the supervisors and all executives through the company would have a natural tendency to resist the development of the program (1) because of their dislike for the methods of the director and (2) because some of their own pet ideas have not been included. The result of such a situation would undoubtedly be an accumulation of hindrance to the program such as enforced overtime for trainees, unwillingness to transfer trainees from one department to another, and unwillingness on the part of supervisors to take an active part in training on the job.

Nor can an administrator be a person who sits idly by and expects others to provide all the ideas and the work required for their development. An idea must be nurtured. It must be given support through the personal assistance of the administrator and other personnel of the organization who can contribute to its development. A suggestion should seldom be quickly answered "yes" or "no." If the answer is "yes" and the individual is told to go ahead, there will almost inevitably be floundering, disagreement, and delay. Usually the idea is only in an embryo stage. It lacks clarity of definition. Its full pattern has not been thought through. If the answer is quickly "no," the one making the suggestion feels that he or she has not been given adequate consideration and is discouraged from making other suggestions in the future. Instead, he or she should patiently be assisted in arriving at his or her own decision that the suggestion lacks sufficient merit to receive adoption. Frequently this can be attained only through permitting the individual to attempt an elaboration of plans with the help and criticism of associates.

A committee is a tool for the development of ideas and recommendations of policy and procedure. It is a means whereby ideas can be pooled and offered for criticism. It is a powerful mechanism for tactful administrators who realize the importance of getting their people to work together in the solution of their own problems.

2-5.2 Basic Principles of Committee Organization

Committees, like other phases of organization, should be varied in terms of the needs of a given enterprise. However, there are at least four basic principles to be considered:

1. The organization of a committee should grow out of a need that is recognized by representatives of the departments and the personnel affected.

2. The personnel of a committee should be representative of the function and the personnel concerned and should represent variations in opinion among personnel.

3. Duties, authority, and responsibility must be clearly defined even if, owing to circumstances, they must be subject to change.

4. The organization and operation of a committee should be a cooperative development.

2-5.3 Weaknesses of Committees

The principal weaknesses of committee operation are that it (1) is slow, (2) wastes time, and (3) tends to hang on after its usefulness is over. Slow action and wasted time are characteristics of the democratic process wherever applied, but such weaknesses are a small price to pay for the values of pooled judgment, eventual understanding, and agreement. As for the dissolution of inactive committees, this can be overcome by clarifying their purposes and fixing a definite time for their termination. Moreover, recognizing that action by committees is slow, there are times when emergencies call for executive action. The wise executive does not fear or shirk these emergency decisions; at the same time he knows that they are temporary expedients and explains his action to the committees.

Policies growing out of this pooling of judgment and approved by top management should include statements of principles governing the procedures to be followed and the group to be consulted when the situation warrants. This does not mean that every time a piece of equipment is bought a committee must be called together for approval of the purchase. Instead, the individuals directly charged with the responsibility are given prescribed areas of responsibility in which to act. In the purchase of miscellaneous supplies, a department may requisition through purchasing within the limits of its budget without further authorization. However, major replacements or additions might be placed by policy in another category requiring consultation with a larger number of affected parties. The extent of agreement or disagreement within a group also may determine how many people in the ladder of responsibility and authority must be included.

There may be instances when the president or chief executive officer is in disagreement with the majority judgment of the group. In such cases there are two alternatives:

1. To exercise the right of final authority and reverse the majority recommendation. In such case full responsibility is assumed and those in opposition are released from responsiblity for the possible error of the decision.

2. To carry the issue to higher authority for recommendation.

Utilization of these alternatives should be necessary only on rare occasion. Frequent use will lead to a "one-person company." If such reversals prove to be necessary on frequent occasions, the company is not receiving the quality of specialized counsel which it is seeking and deserves. Therefore, ultimately, the company should call for changes in personnel.

Perspective 2E   THE GRAPEVINE CIRCUIT

Only the very rare organization lacks a grapevine—a casual but penetrating communications network. Some critics call it a rumor mill or gossip line. Nearly everyone has occasion to marvel at its speed. Almost no one acclaims its accuracy. The way a message can pass into the grapevine, whirl through the circuit, and emerge almost

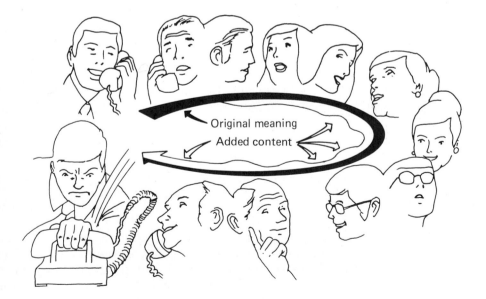

unrecognizable due to the distortions and embellishments accumulated along the way is depicted below.

COMMENT   Just as each enterprise has its own formal organization pattern, it also has its own grapevine pattern. Membership in the grapevine network varies with time and the topic being transmitted. However, some groups and individuals are more stable members than others. These active transmitters usually enjoy a reputation for having "hot news" or a "pipeline to the top." A manager who is aware of the more energetic newsmongers knows where to seek or plant reports. But there is no assurance of the results. The spontaneous nature of a grapevine reduces reliability. Sometimes only the good part of the news is passed along to protect the listener's feelings, or only the bad part is told to satisfy some motive of the teller. Always there is the chance for misinterpretation owing to the choice of words used in the transmission.

2-6   REVIEW QUESTIONS

1. What is the purpose of an organization?

2. Why is it possible that a good organization with a relatively poor product can sometimes drive a good product backed by a poor organization out of the marketplace?

3. Comment on the statement that authority and responsibility must go together.

4. What distinguishes a line from a staff function?

5. To what extent does the line-and-staff organization overcome the disadvantages of a simple line organization?

6. Why are management committees often ridiculed?

7. If you were chairman of a committee, what precautions could you take to give your committee a better chance to operate efficiently?

2-7   TOPICS FOR DISCUSSION

1. Executives of industry contend that the most common deterrent to effective expansion of an enterprise is the scarcity of capable management personnel. Can you account for the probable causes of this condition?

2. One of the most frequent ills of organization is the lack of clarity in the separation of functions and in the establishment of lines of authority and responsibility. Referring to the functions described in this chapter, including the subdivision of major functions, indicate where these separations might be most apt to become fringy or overlap.

3. Some people contend that an organization never should be changed to fit a given individual in it. Others claim that such change may be advisable. Comment on this difference in opinion.

4. By what criteria may a company claim "the right to exist and make a profit"?

5. For each of the five organization patterns listed in Perspective 2A, name a company that exhibits that pattern and describe the structure.

6. List and discuss examples of wage-payment plans in which individuals that are apparently lower in rank than those holding higher positions in the organization structure actually receive much higher earnings.

7. Discuss the advantages and disadvantages of having fewer subordinates reporting to a single supervisor.

8. Case 2A: *An Organizational Box*

Rectangular, matrix, product, or project management, whichever it is called, is a relatively new pattern of organization. Some say it was conceived by the Procter and Gamble Company in the 1930s, and others credit General Electric with a later introduction. Only in the last decade, however, has it received very much attention. Most of that attention was created by its application to weapons production.

Developments in weaponry of almost science-fiction design are characterized by huge expenditures, highly advanced technology, complex coordination problems, and an urgency for completion. A special form of organization emerged to cope with these large-scale, diverse factors. The pattern that evolved was a two-dimensional matrix, one dimension being the different weapons under development and the other the regular functional line-staff components. As displayed in Figure 2-4, the rows of the matrix represent independent products or projects (weapon-systems code names) and the columns are the support units for the projects (line departments).

Civilian counterparts to weapon programs are based on well-identified production or service projects such as a dam, section of a highway, educational unit, etc.

The project manager is theoretically the boss of the bosses. He exerts authority across traditional department lines. Though he does not have exclusive "command" over functional line managers, he has final say for any reasonable alternative within the realm of his project. He spends much of his time coordinating detachments from the regular line departments to accomplish project missions. Since the project manager is accountable for all conditions affecting completion of his project, he exercises complete budgetary control. Power of the purse confirms and consolidates his sweeping authority.

Questions

1. Compare the matrix organization pattern with the traditional line structure and comment on the most glaring departure from conventional supervisory principles.

9. Case 2B: *Who Is Responsible?*

People in positions of responsibility are frequently tempted to "pass the buck" on emotional or sensitive issues. In this era of active social concern and consumerism, it is sometimes difficult

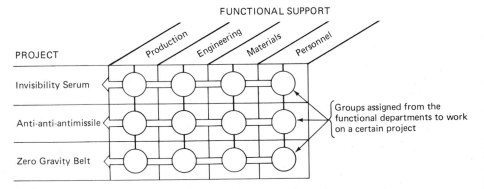

Figure 2-4 Format of a matrix organization.

to say who is really responsible for certain events, yet companies and regulatory agencies are obliged to trace actions to their source in order to avoid similar circumstances in the future. In considering the following incidents, decide who you feel is responsible, state your reasons, and discuss the question of restitution.

   a. Rejected products are placed in a special stall for reprocessing after being declared faulty by inspection. A rejected batch of dye is accidently included in a shipment to a woolen mill where some cloth is ruined by the poor quality. Who is responsible—inspectors, shift foreman, delivery personnel, or the plant manager?

   b. A feature story in a newspaper is inaccurate and offensive to a large segment of readers. Who is responsible—the writer, news editor, editor in chief, or publisher?

   c. A new drug successfully passes numerous acceptability and safety tests administered by the developers and government agencies. After it has been sold for 2 years, a new investigation links it with cancer. Who is responsible—the researchers who developed the drug, the company that produced the drug, government agencies that initially approved its sale, or doctors who prescribed it?

10. Case 2C: *The International Oil Consortium*

   The International Oil Consortium possesses extensive domestic and foreign operations. In the past it has been a highly centralized organization in its United States operations.

   Recently the company has taken some steps toward decentralization of its United States operations through organization by regional divisions. In this reorganization, functional staff departments are established in each regional division. Staff counterparts are maintained in the home office in New York for research and development but are intended to be advisory only and not in control of divisional staffs. Figure 2-5 shows a chart of one regional division.

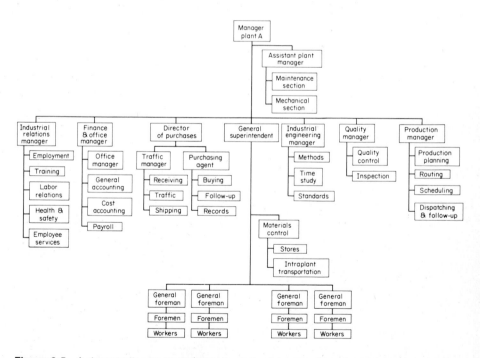

Figure 2-5 A decentralized organization chart showing one plant of a multiplant company. Each of the staff departments is responsible directly to the plant manager but receives assistance from its counterpart in headquarters offices.

Questions

1. Thinking only in terms of the principles of internal organization, comment on this division organization as shown in Figure 2-5 and its probable effectiveness as a means toward the promotion and coordination of the activities of the division.

2. Can you suggest how this organization might be improved?

11. Case 2D: *The B and G Manufacturing Company*

The B and G Manufacturing Company is a metalworking plant under the direction of a plant manager who is known as a strict disciplinarian. One day a foreman noticed Jim White, one of the workers, at the time clock punching out two cards—his own and the card of Pete Boynton, a fellow worker. Since it was the rule of the company that each person must punch out his or her own card, the foreman asked Jim to accompany him to the personnel director. The personnel director interpreted the incident as a direct violation of a rule and gave immediate notice of discharge to both workers.

The two workers came to see the personnel director on the following day. Pete claimed innocence on the ground that he had not asked that his card be punched and did not know at the time that it was being punched. He had been offered a ride by a friend who had already punched out and who could not wait for him to go through the punch-out procedure. Pete was worried about his wife, who was ill at home and was anxious to reach home as quickly as possible. He planned to take his card to the foreman the next morning for reinstatement, a provision sometimes exercised in such cases.

These circumstances were verified by Jim. He claimed that he had punched Pete's card the same time he punched his own, not being conscious of any wrongdoing.

The personnel director was inclined to believe the story of the two men but did not feel he could reverse the action taken. He recognized that these men were good workers and had good records prior to this incident. Nevertheless, they had violated a rule for which the penalty was immediate discharge. He also reminded them that it was the policy of the company to enforce the rules without exception.

A few days later the personnel director, the plant manager, and the sales manager sat together at lunch. The sales manager reported that he was faced with the necessity of notifying one of their best customers that his order must be delayed because of the inability of one department to conform to schedule. The department in question was the one from which the two workers had been discharged. Not only had it been impossible to replace these men to date, but disgruntlement over the incident had led to significant decline in the cooperation of other workers.

The personnel director and the sales manager took the position that the discharge of these two valuable men could have been avoided if there had been provision for considering the circumstances of the case. They pointed out that the incident was costly to the company in the possible loss of a customer, in the dissatisfaction within the employee group, and in the time and money that would be involved in recruiting and training replacements.

The plant manager could not agree with this point of view. "We must have rules if we are to have efficiency; and the rules are no good unless we enforce them. Furthermore, if we start considering all these variations in circumstances, we will find ourselves loaded down with everybody thinking he is an exception." He admitted that the grievances were frequent but countered with the point that they could be of little consequence if the contract agreed to by the union was followed to the *letter*.

Questions

1. Place yourself in the position of the personnel director in this situation. Which of the following courses of action would you have chosen in consideration of the information which he had available at the time of the decision?

a. Would you have discharged both men?

b. Would you have discharged Jim White only?

c. Would you have discharged Pete Boynton only?

d. Would you have discharged neither of them?

Justify your choice of decision.

2. What policy and procedure changes would you recommend for the handling of future cases of this type?

OPERATIONS ANALYSIS

Knowledge is power. Management's knowledge of the operations of the enterprise, of its weakness and vulnerability, and of its strengths and opportunities is essential to successful leadership. Then leaders must know what managerial techniques and supporting facilities are available to make best use of their knowledge of operations. By what means can management be assured that the necessary stream of appropriate information will be kept flowing at a speed sufficient to form the basis for both short- and long-range action? What are the basic sources of information? What technical aids are available to process this information? How can managers benefit from the quantitative approaches to problem solving, associated with management science and operations research, to assist their decision making? These are the challenges of operations analysis.

3 OPERATIONS ANALYSIS

3-1 THE ROLE OF MANAGEMENT

We observed in the last chapter how organizations are structured to promote better management. We also recognized that it is the performance of
the people who fill the positions, not the organizational design, that determines the success of the enterprise. These managers can draw upon a
variety of information-processing and decision-making tools to help them
meet their responsibilities. In this chapter we shall examine several of these
tools.

Electronic assistance is a rapidly expanding, yet still controversial, influence on managerial activities. When the potential of computers was first
recognized, fears were expressed that middle management levels would
become obsolete; the computer with its unfailing memory and tremendous
calculating speed would digest data from the factory floor and prepare
reports according to programmed decision rules for delivery directly to top
management. Such fears of managerial centralization have been largely
unrealized. Instead, instant access to operational information has tended to
support greater decentralization, and computer capabilities have opened
new vistas for machine-assisted decision making at all management levels.

But the increasing capacity and rapacity of automated record keeping has
inspired symbolic cries such as, "I'm human! Don't fold, spindle or mutilate
me." Such rhetoric is a continuing reminder that the human resource is still
the most critical operating factor.

3-1.1 Coordination

To be effective, human activities have to be coordinated. Efficient coordination requires much more than an organization framework. Figure 3–1
presents a sequence of building blocks that have to be erected to support
the organization's operations.

At the top of the foundation is *coordination*. This is the attribute that
integrates all the elements of an organization into an operating unity. Experience has shown that high productivity in a business is dependent upon the
interest and willing *cooperation* of both managers and workers, the second
listing in the sequence. Where machines may have a standard of efficiency
and be set to run at a given speed, human beings, whether managers or
workers, cannot be so easily regulated to a predetermined point of productivity. Human beings, preferably, should be led by goals which they accept
as justifiable, worthy, and fair to all concerned. This leads us to *human
relations* as the third element in the sequence. It has been proved many times
that the application of good human relations "pays off" through cooperative
coordination and hence greater productivity. For example, a study of the

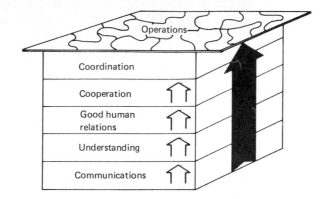

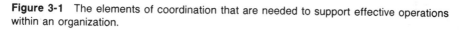

Figure 3-1 The elements of coordination that are needed to support effective operations within an organization.

home office of an insurance company revealed that the major differences in high- and low-producing groups in this company were in large part related to supervisory practices and attitudes. The supervisors with the higher producing sections in general were following a more liberal philosophy of management. They were giving more attention to the problems of motivating workers.

Good human relations, in turn, is dependent upon *understanding*. There must be understanding of the goals which are common to the various members of the organization and to the organization as a whole. There must be understanding of the interrelationship among jobs and the significance of any one job to the total product and to the company.

In order that there may be understanding among people, there must be effective means of *communication* among them. One of the greatest powers of man is his facility in communicating with others. Yet in our technological progress in production, we have taken away many of the conditions favorable to effective communication. If people can talk with one another long enough, the chances are great that they will be able to iron out their differences and discover common goals. This is because they will come to better understanding. It is difficult for us to understand the actions and motives of the person with whom we have not been able to communicate.

3-1.2 Control

Since it is not possible for the executive to keep in touch personally with routine details of the operations of a large company, he must develop *managerial controls*. *Webster's New Collegiate Dictionary* defines the verb *control* as "to check or regulate . . . to keep within limits." Yet managerial control carries a much broader connotation, i.e., to apply not only the check rein but also the whip; not only to regulate but also to stimulate.

To control, the executive must have information revealing those points that require his attention, in accordance with the *exception principle,* to be discussed later in this chapter. These may be activities that require restrictive or corrective action, such as excessive rejections of finished products due to poor quality in production, excessive labor turnover, disproportionate labor costs, or undue equipment failures. On the other hand, appropriate control information may reveal areas of strength in the operations which should be utilized more fully, such as a developing trend of popularity of a particular product or line of products of the company, an increasing backlog of orders that would justify an additional labor shift or the reopening of another production division, and the opening up of a favorable source of material that should be contracted before other competitors monopolize it. These are all points that require management action and will be accomplished only if management is made aware that the conditions exist. But it should be borne in mind that controls only *lead up* to specific management action, revealing the necessity for action and variation from routine.

In general, managerial control operates through:

1. *Management by predetermined policies*   Here management attempts control by laying down the policies which guide the entire enterprise in advance. All parts of the organization must conform to these policies, or a change in management personnel is indicated.

2. *Management by predetermined operations standards*   Here the predetermined standards of operation provide automatic control. Responsible personnel throughout the organization must conform to these standards. If one or more of these people feels that a change in standard is needed, he is obligated to report and substantiate this feeling promptly to appropriate authority. But until such change is approved, the standard is in force.

3. *Management by action on the exception principle*   If steps 1 and 2 are carried out, control is actually being exercised either by management policies or by operations standards. But exceptions in the form of problems will occur. With management freed from routines, appropriate attention can be given to these exceptions, utilizing the real qualities of active management—talent, skill, experience, judgment, etc.

4. *Management by responsible personnel*   Line and staff personnel are supposedly competent people and should be dealing with the functions of the enterprise in a responsible manner. They should be exercising control tools and techniques in each division of the enterprise. If things go wrong, corrections should be made by reference to predetermined policies, by predetermined standards, by dealing with problems on the exception principle, or by replacing line and staff personnel.

Each chapter of this book deals with a different aspect of control tools and techniques; it is the task of top management to see that these controls function.

Perspective 3A ADVICE FROM THE PAST

Frederick W. Taylor was a pioneer in operations analysis. A few of his accomplishments are described in the following section. The paragraphs below relate his concerns about the role of management.

Among the risks of a manufacturing business, by far the greatest is that of bad management; and of the three managing departments, the commercial, the financiering, and the productive, the latter, in most cases, receives the least attention from those that have invested their money in the business, and contains the greatest elements of risk. This risk arises not so much from the evident mismanagement, which plainly discloses itself through occasional strikes and similar troubles, as from the daily more insidious and fatal failure on the part of the superintendents to secure anything even approaching the maximum from their men and machines.

It is not unusual for the manager of a manufacturing business to go most minutely into every detail of the buying and selling and financiering, and arrange every element of these branches in the most systematic manner, and according to principles that have been carefully planned to insure the business against almost any contingency which may arise, while the manufacturing is turned over to a superintendent or foreman, with little or no restrictions as to the principles and methods which he is to pursue, either in the management of his men or the care of the company's plant.

The modern manufacturer, however, seeks not only to secure the best superintendents and workmen, but to surround each department of his manufacture with the most carefully woven network of system and method, which should render the business, for a considerable period, at least, independent of the loss of any one man, and frequently of any combination of men.

Even after fully realizing the importance of adopting the best possible system and methods of management for securing a proper return from employees and as an insurance against strikes and the carelessness and laziness of men, there are difficulties in the problem of selecting methods of management which shall be adequate to the purpose, and yet be free from red tape, and inexpensive.*

*SOURCE: Frederick W. Taylor, *Two Papers on Scientific Management,* London: George Routledge & Sons, 1919.

COMMENT Taylor's advice, written over 60 years ago, is remarkably contemporary.

3-2 MANAGEMENT SCIENCE

As industry itself has widened its horizons from rule-of-thumb and empirical methods to precision and scientific techniques, the character of industrial management also has changed. Specialization has carved out new occupations for the management personnel who direct the constantly enlarging subdivisions of an industrial enterprise. As in every evolving field, there is a tendency to define and crystallize functions and to find some distinctive names for them. This will be obvious from descriptions in this text of functions practiced in modern industrial organization and management. We now refer to a term commonly applied to functions which touch upon many phases of an enterprise—management science.

In substance, management science is applied by a functional staff management member or a consultant (individual practitioner or firm member) who provides an integrated viewpoint to operations analysis based on the application of scientific research methods to business problems. Two disciplines intimately associated with management science are industrial engineering and operations research.

The roots of management science extend to the work of Frederick W. Taylor, the father of scientific management.[1] Taylor is known for his systematic development of management techniques, which he started at the Midvale Steel Company in Philadelphia around 1880. His work began with an effort to develop a piecework system, but he soon found all management actions closely interrelated. Taylor spent the next 30 years perfecting his system in wood-pulp mills, machinery plants, building-construction projects, the Bethlehem Steel Company, and others. He developed what he called his four principles of management: *research, standardization, control,* and *cooperation.* When installed at the Link Belt Engineering Company in 1905, the system included cost accounting, unit time study, inventory control, production control, planning, output scheduling, functional operation, standardized procedures, a mnemonic system of classification, and means for maintaining quality production. All these were developed by the application of inductive research to industrial operations.

Associated with Taylor in those early years were other important pioneers of scientific management—Carl G. Barth, Henry L. Gantt, Sanford E. Thompson, H. King Hathaway, and many others. Barth brought to the work of scientific management the use of research mathematics, which he merged with his extensive knowledge of machine tools. Gantt contributed the recognition of worker psychology, the development of a bonus plan, and the charts used in production scheduling.

Some of these early contributors to scientific management were graduates of engineering schools, but many were practitioners who learned in industry a working knowledge of engineering principles, research methods, and modern management. Engineering thus came to be closely associated with the management of the enterprise. Out of this came the term "industrial engineering," which today is descriptive of the work of functional staffs responsible for such activities as incentive standards, methods analysis, quality control, production control, cost control, and materials handling.

Executives noted the benefits of industrial engineering in connection with production operations and began to call upon the industrial engineer to apply the same scientific approach to problems in organization, sales, finance, office operations, inventory and tool control, and, in fact, all phases of business. This expansion had the effects of: (1) enlarging the scope of techniques, often calling for the addition of specialists who possessed skill

[1]Taylor himself called his system "task management" until the last 5 years of his life. It was given the more popular misnomer by attorney Louis Brandeis (later a justice of the Supreme Court) in 1910 at hearings on railroad-rate increases. In the United States the term "scientific management" still refers to "Taylor system." In England and much of the rest of the world "scientific management" is used to mean merely "modern management."

in the physical or social sciences or in mathematics; and (2) teaching managers to rely increasingly on the systematic approach and to experiment to acquire facts, rather than to use the rule of thumb in decisions.

The systematic approach to the solution of problems in industrial management is nothing more than the application of the scientific method used in scientific research for generations—going back, in fact, to the work of Francis Bacon. It was the foundation of the work of Taylor referred to earlier. Only recently, however, has it been recognized that the same methodology is applicable to a varied assortment of problems encountered in the different segments of an industrial enterprise.

This approach is a methodology which sets forth a sequence of steps to be followed. The exact words describing the steps may vary, but the idea remains the same:

1. Obtain the facts pertaining to the situation. These facts must be verified, sifted, clarified, and amplified to obtain accuracy and meaning.

2. Identify the problem involved in the situation.

3. Enumerate the principles or laws applicable to the problem and select those which appear to predominate.

4. Formulate alternative solutions.

5. Select the solution or combination of solutions most appropriate.

6. Test the solution for possible results.

7. Apply the solution to the specific problem situation.

Obviously, the steps of this approach are elementary to the student of science. They have also been widely practiced in industry in relation to the more tangible scientific phases of operations. But in other areas, such as distribution, advertising, and human relations, there are managers even today who rely on emotionalism, tradition, and rule of thumb for guidance in making decisions. The management scientist seeks to bring orderliness and system to the solution of all major business problems.

Perspective 3B   THE BUSINESS BRANCH OF SCIENCE

Judging from the number of printed words devoted to it in business journals, management science is the "in" subject. A few detractors berate it as simply a collection of solutions looking for a problem, but the freshness of its approach continues to claim new advocates. The still expanding boundaries of the subject make difficult an accurate assessment of its potential. Their broadness is attested to by David Miller and Martin Starr:

Management science is concerned with both short- and long-range planning. At present, it is likely to be far more effective (directly) in short-range circumstances. Nevertheless, it attempts to establish whatever relationships exist between an organization's objectives and its resources. In this way, it cuts across the traditional areas of management. Such crossing of boundaries characterizes management science, which is *problem-oriented.* *

*SOURCE: *Executive Decisions and Operations Research,* 2d ed., Englewood Cliffs, N.J.: Prentice-Hall, Inc., 1969.

COMMENT   The obvious strength of management science is its objective, quantitative treatment of management problems. This treatment is characterized by: (1) a statement of the problem in a mathematical form; (2) reliance on measurable qualities such as costs and revenues; (3) use of computers; and (4) a dedication to rational decision making.

3-3   OPERATIONS RESEARCH

Closely associated with management science is the specialty *operations research,* defined by John F. Magee as:

. . . the organized application of the methods and techniques of science, particularly the physical sciences, to the study of operating problems in business, government, or the military. The objective of this work is to gain an explicit quantitative understanding of the essential elements of an operation and the factors affecting results, in order to give management a sounder basis for decisions.

As the name implies, it is experimental research aimed at solving complex operating problems. It attempts wherever possible to translate facts into quantitative terms so that cause-and-effect relationships may be analyzed through the use of mathematical and other scientific formulas.

During the 10 years just after World War II a great deal of management engineering was performed under the name of operations research. (In England it was known as "operational research.") The influx of physical scientists, many of whom were unacquainted with modern management administration, into war technology and the pressures of total war with new and terrible weapons gave rise to a rediscovery of a kind of pragmatic scientific management. This merged with an increasingly popular acceptance of statistical quality control in America and the practical development of high-speed electronic calculators to give impetus to the operations-research approach.

Subsequent chapters in this book will discuss the techniques used in operations research, indicate specific problem areas which can be explored by this tool, and point out its strengths, weaknesses, and limitations. It is important here only that we be introduced to the term and that as we meet it on later pages we recognize it to be one of the more important tools of both management and industrial engineering in obtaining quantitative answers to the more complex operating problems of the enterprise.

It would be misleading to imply, however, that operations research is the cure-all for otherwise faulty management decisions. There are difficulties to be encountered as with most problem-solving techniques:

1. Operations research aids in supplying factual data to be used in arriving at management decisions. It still remains the responsibility of management to weigh the evidence so supplied in light of the existing management organization, the current financial position of the company, the short-term and long-term goals of the company, and the many established company policies that would be affected such as personnel, customer service, credit, and others. We cannot expect that higher mathematics or an electronic calculator can turn out management decisions—they can only assist.

2. Operations research, in quantifying a problem, translates assumed business facts into numbers (or symbolic logic). It manipulates those abstractions and translates the results back into words to guide operating executives. The quantifying is an aid since it greatly facilitates the handling of complex data and permits experiments with a mathematical model instead of the actual enterprise. At the same time it presents weaknesses in that the ability to judge the accuracy of the assumed facts, and to translate what businessmen say about business into mathematical symbols, is a rare skill possessed by only a few hybrid scientist-executives. This means that the researcher must have a great deal of fundamental knowledge about the business operation, or that there must be a working team that does have the knowledge. It also means that the executive relying on operations research must have a working knowledge of the statistical assumptions underlying the research plus a knowledge of what data were used.

Perspective 3C   THE MOST USED OPERATIONS-RESEARCH TECHNIQUES

Many mathematical techniques have become associated with the practice of operations research. They range in complexity from basic inventory models to exotic programming methods, and in application from general use by a variety of practitioners to rare use for special cases. A survey of 176 firms from the Fortune 500 list of biggest corporations reveals which operations-research techniques the respondents used most often. Ratings for the seven most applied techniques are shown in the table below.

A second part of the survey questioned the breadth of applications. Simulation was found to have by far the most application areas in production. It was followed by linear programming and regression analysis.

Relative Use of Operations Research Techniques

Techniques	Never 1	2	3	4	Very Frequently 5	Mean
Regression analysis	9.5	2.7	17.6	21.6	48.6	3.97
Linear programming	15.4	14.1	21.8	16.7	32.0	3.36
Simulation	11.4	15.7	25.7	24.3	22.9	3.31
Network models	39.1	29.0	15.9	10.1	5.8	2.14
Queuing theory	36.6	39.4	16.9	5.6	1.4	1.96
Dynamic programming	53.6	36.2	7.2	0.0	2.9	1.62
Game theory	59.7	25.4	8.9	6.0	0.0	1.61

(Degree of Use (per cent))

SOURCE: William Ledbetter and James F. Cox, "Are OR Techniques Being Used?" *Industrial Engineering*, February, 1977.

COMMENT   The operations-research techniques listed in the table could appropriately be claimed tools for industrial engineers, business managers, economists, and several other disciplines which conduct quantitative analyses. The significant issue is that these techniques are of relatively recent origin, or have been made more powerful by recent innovations, and their use indicates a growing role for quantitative tools in operations analysis.

3-4   INFORMATION

A great deal of energy is devoted to acquiring, recording, and disseminating information as factually as possible. This effort amounts to a production process in which the product is information. Raw materials are bits of data. They are received and inspected for accuracy. Bits from several sources are assembled. Some are stored as inventory in files or data banks for later use, and others are packaged for shipment as memos or reports. The shipping lines are the communication channels in and among organizations. Whoever has requested the information is the consumer to be satisfied. Like other products, information may be rejected due to inferior raw materials, careless assembly, unattractive packaging, or staleness caused by delays in distribution.

Figure 3–2 provides an indication of the variety of information flows to which a manager is exposed. To avoid being inundated by a data deluge, managers have to be selective in deciding how much time and reliance

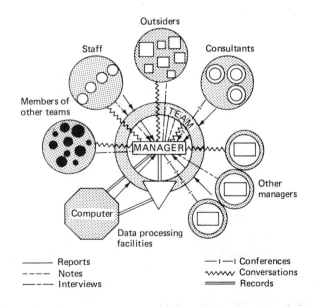

Figure 3-2   A manager taps many sources of information, using several channels. The length of the channels and the filtering effect increase for higher levels of management. Some information passes through the manager's immediate team and other data go directly to her. Her sources of data are both inside and outside her own organization.

should be allocated to each information source. Conversely, it would be damaging to overlook available information that could be useful in controlling operations. In the following sections we shall consider ways to control information flow and ways to obtain information that contributes to operations control.

3-4.1   Technical Controls

Good management works, where possible, toward establishing predetermined decisions and adjustments to be made either by administrative personnel or by automated equipment. Where the problem reaches beyond the limitations of predetermined action, the human being or the machine must refer it to higher management.

Consider, by way of example, the control board in an electric power plant in a large urban area. This large control center, tended by two or three persons, is constructed to make predetermined adjustments for the proper control and distribution of power. Some adjustments are performed automatically by the equipment; some are made by the attendants. The cycle time of generators must be kept constant. As a generator goes off cycle, it shows on the board and automatically is corrected. A generator may burn out, and the control-board equipment will switch to a stand-by generator. The power demand from one section of the city, because of unusual and temporary activity there, may exceed the generating capacity allocated to it. The control equipment will borrow power from another section of the city where it is available.

But let us assume that, because of a series of concurrent power failures and excessive demands, the predetermined adjustments set up in the control equipment have become exhausted, i.e., all alternatives are tried and do not correct the situation. The control board then signals the attendants for help. If the attendants find that their available adjustments are insufficient to correct the problem, they must take emergency action to prevent destruction, and then refer the situation to higher management.

All automation systems make use of *servomechanisms* and *feedback control.* These can be explained easily if you will imagine yourself reaching for a piece of candy from a box of candies. What happens? First, your eyes encourage your brain to send out signals to your arm muscles. There the impulses are amplified and actuate the muscles. When your hand reaches the desired section of the box, your eyes send signals to the brain and thence to the arm muscles to cease working and to the finger muscles to start flexing. A servomechanism—control of motion—is at work. If in the process your hand or fingers have overshot or undershot their mark, your eyes, detecting this fact, tell the brain, which sends necessary corrective information to the proper muscles. Feedback—communication of a result—signals the servomechanism. The analogy to industrial machines is apparent. The feedback principle is not a recent development, having long been used in home thermostats, dial telephones, ship and aircraft steering devices, and picture-stabilizing arrangements in television receivers. It is now being built into many other types of equipment to provide administrative and management personnel with needed information.

3-4.2 Communications

Extensive attention has been given in the past decade to improvement and greater use of communications equipment. This increased emphasis has developed from four primary considerations.

1. *Recognition of the importance of records and reports as management tools for planning, coordinating, and controlling the enterprise.* One of the effects of this recognition has been an increase in the volume of data to be handled and an increase in the emphasis on speed in accumulation and analysis so that it may be available in time for use in the planning and control of current operations.

2. *Reduction of the cost of clerical labor.* As the salaries of office workers increase, either the efficiency of operations must improve or the ultimate cost and consequent price of product or service must increase. Added to the element of increased salaries was the increase in the number of clerical employees required to turn out the increased volume of office work. These two elements caused clerical operations to become one of the prominent costs of the enterprise and therefore deserving of special effort toward simplification and mechanization.

   Much attention has been given to improving the quality of correspondence while attempting to reduce its cost. New methods with tag names such as "word processing" or "electronic secretaries" utilize dictation prerecorded in the form of letter modules. An executive dials the central "dictabank" and records his message using established codes and dictating procedures. Revisions and transcriptions are electronically assisted.

3. *Improvement of customer service.* Competitive marketing conditions of the past decade have emphasized service to customers. Such emphasis demands rapid delivery of product items and in accordance with promised delivery schedule, individual attention to customer complaints, rapid replacement of faulty items, and personal counseling by the salesman or field engineer regarding the use of the product. In order to perform this service without excessive cost, it became necessary to exercise closer planning and control over inventory, production schedules, materials procurement, quality control, and shipping. It also required that salespersons and field engineers be relieved of routine clerical duties where possible in order that more time could be given to service (see Fig. 3–3).

4. *Improvement of working conditions.* This movement toward attempted improvement in working conditions in office operations was a part of a general movement in connection with all operations of the enterprise referred to in earlier chapters. One element of this was the attempted removal of the monotony of routine operations. The advance in the educational level of the population has increased the potential ability of office workers to perform tasks involving human judgment. Although there are many well-educated people who prefer routine positions, many others become frustrated by simple repetitive tasks. Good management

Figure 3-3 The drive-in facilities of the United States National Bank. Both the teller and customer stations are equipped with television cameras and screens. They are connected by an audio system for communications and a pneumatic carrier system for conducting money transactions. This equipment combination allows the convenience of remote service while retaining the security and access to records of a centralized facility.

recognizes that where possible a worker should be used to the extent of his highest ability. The development of office machines to perform repetitive tasks is one means toward the improvement of office working conditions.

Trends toward mechanization and simplification in the communication of information have been more evolutionary than revolutionary. We should think of this whole movement as dating back to the transition from pen and pencil to the typewriter in writing operation. The introduction of stenography and stenotype and dictating and transcribing machines were successive steps in the division of writing operations and the eventual mechanization of them. The adding machine, calculators, and posting machines represented progress in the handling of numbers, adding speed and accuracy to the operations. Progress in filing of records and reports dates from the "pigeonhole" in the roll-top desk, to the vertical file and the visible file, to the use of microfilm and computer memory by which records may be stored in a small space and with improved access.

Perspective 3D ANTIDOTE FOR THE PAPERWORK PLAGUE

It has been estimated that over 25 per cent of the current gross national product is absorbed in the production, processing, and distribution of information. This statistic is vivid evidence of the proverbial information explosion. Its message to managers is to find ways to avoid being wounded by shrapnel from the explosion—bits of information.

Dr. Richard Peterson suggests that managers can benefit from classifying information to determine what is really useful.* He proposes five categories, the first two for use internally by company decision makers and the other three for dissemination to external decision makers such as government agencies, legislators, and consumers.

1. *Decisive information* Data that have a positive value for improving decisions.
2. *Implementation information* Routine data that are needed to increase the efficiency of operations.
3. *Required information* Data generated by a company to meet regulations and to satisfy explicit or implicit commitments.
4. *Restricted information* Confidential data that would be potentially harmful to the organization if they became generally known.
5. *Persuasive information* Filtered information utilized to improve a company's public image or to influence a decision.

*SOURCE: "The Components of Information," *Interfaces,* August, 1977.

COMMENT A U.S. congressional committee calculated that an average of 50 forms is filled out each year for each adult and child in America and that in 1974 alone, some 10 billion pieces of paper passed through the hands of Federal bureaucrats. Industries share the paper plague. One way to slow the flow would be for each paperwork generator to question the significance of the data to be disseminated: Do they really add value? Equivalently, the same questions of significance should help data recipients handle the flow. If a paper does not add value, it should not have been issued; since it was anyway, it does not deserve attention or retention.

3-4.3 Electronic Data Processing

Application of electronics is perhaps the most significant recent development in the area of information. Management decisions and control are dependent upon the accurate accumulation of production and distribution information, the effective analysis of this information, and the availability of the information with sufficient speed and economy to make it of practical use. Management has long recognized that data collected manually are highly susceptible to human error, difficult and expensive to obtain, and generally insufficient for the purpose of making business decisions. One of the first major adaptations of electronics to this need was through the improvement of machine-accounting equipment that would tabulate, sort, and print information for the billing of accounts receivable; aid in the construction and analysis of payroll; assist in the accumulation and sorting of data in market research; and perform other similar tasks. This was done through the use of punched cards and electronic sorting and printing equipment. Developments in recent years, however, have produced an array of *electronic-data-processing* (EDP) equipment from which an enterprise can select and adapt according to its specific requirements. This may vary from one to many integrated units and may be connected with component units in branch offices or warehouses throughout the nation.

Simply stated, an EDP system is fed information for processing and instructions as to how it is to be processed. It stores this information by card, by tape, by record, or by "memory" magnetic drum for future use. On demand it will process designated data through a series of logical or arithmetical operations according to instructions and print the results. Obviously, not all systems will perform all operations; they are restricted or expanded according to the needs and the economical requirements.

A few illustrations may help to explain the potentials of these EDP systems. One equipment manufacturer had developed a system under the name of automatic production recording system. Let us assume that the information wanted by management is as follows: for *accounting purposes*— the number of motors produced, the number that passed inspection, the total productive hours, nonproductive periods by reason or code, and the date; for *quality control*—the troubles encountered with motors that fail to pass inspection and the reasons for their rejection; for *production control*— hourly reports on production, rejection, and repair rates and also instantaneous on-demand readings for these items at any desired time between scheduled hourly readings.

Here is how the system might work on this project. Counting switches are placed on the conveyor lines at strategic places, and unit count is fed to counter panels in the central console. By means of a control unit located at the assembly line, an operator introduces the production order number into the system and signals the passing of the last motor of a given order. The system then correlates a read-out code number, shift number, year, month, and date—previously introduced into the system—with the production number, elapsed job time, and unit count from storage. All this information is then fed automatically to the printer and tape perforator to produce the record for accounting purposes.

A portable keyboard is installed at the motor-repair area, where the production number and repair code for each motor are recorded on the printed document and in punched tape simultaneously. These become the reports for quality-control analysis. An electric impulse is fed to a counter for each operation of the portable keyboard, making available a total of motors repaired for the on-demand printed record. An additional counting switch is located between the production line and the motor-repair area to provide a motors-rejected total.

An hourly read-out, initiated by a control clock, correlates code number, time of day, shift number, quantity finished, quantity rejected, and quantity repaired. This report, printed by the automatic typewriter, provides information necessary for control at stations along the production line. A push button permits a read-out of the same data at any time.

Another example is a company that has an automated information system which permits its salespersons throughout the nation to determine immediately the availability of any product and the status of any order. Continuous production and inventory records are available when dealing with a prospective customer. Once an order is placed, the system checks the credit rating of the customer, automatically processes the order according to preset rules, selects the warehouse shipment, and issues instructions on when and how the shipment is to be made. A similar system is used by airlines for making reservations, providing individual customer service, and controlling flights. Figure 3–4 shows equipment used to access data in central files for use at the production site.

Many of the early difficulties encountered in EDP equipment, such as equipment errors, translation of instructions into the equipment, and provisions for exceptions in instructions, have been almost completely eliminated by automatic devices. Furthermore, significant progress continues in the development of lower cost units for small- and medium-sized business and in the increase of speed of operation.

The greatest difficulty, however, is still that of human error, which stands

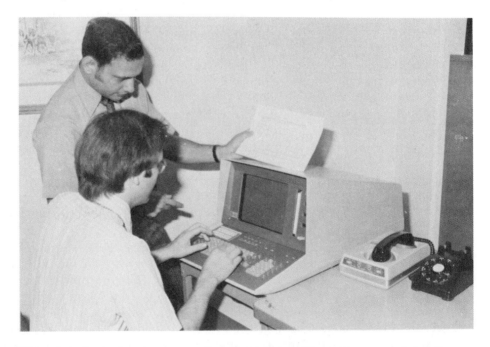

Figure 3-4   Production planners examine shipment data extracted from central data files and converted to graphic form. The CRT terminal and attached hard copy unit allows visual inspection and easy data formatting and manipulation. Data can be transmitted via telephone lines to the corporate data center, or they can be processed locally by the terminal with available software packages. (Courtesy of Proctor and Gamble Company.)

as a constant threat to accuracy. A machine can be only as accurate as the information that is fed to it. The aim is to build more and more of the manual recording and analysis operations into automatic equipment systems and thus increase the efficiency in terms of both accuracy and availability of management information.

Perspective 3E COMPUTERS MAKE MISTAKES TOO

Consumers are getting more and more frustrated with the impersonal machines that have been programmed to deal with them. Businesses are forced to rely increasingly on electronic data processing to handle the records of our data-dependent society, sometimes with disastrous results. The examples below are indicative of the growing disgruntlement.

- A computer system intended to cut waste in the State of Michigan's 32-million-dollar-a-day day-care program went haywire, turning the whole thing into a financial nightmare. Because of a complex of errors, many of the State's 20,000 individuals who provide day-care services were underpaid, overpaid, or not paid at all.
- The Social Security Administration's computer notified a New Jersey man of his death and cut off his monthly benefits.
- A major hotel in Chicago recently ordered a form letter sent out to its past customers, thanking them for their patronage and telling of the hotel's new modernization plan.

  Unfortunately, the printer who mailed out the letters sent them to a different customer's mailing list. The result: Hundreds of Chicago housewives opened letters thanking their husbands for patronizing the hotel. Calls then poured in to the hotel from husbands demanding an explanation for their wives, who were threatening divorce.

  The blame was laid to the printer's computer, but it stemmed from an error by the programmer.*

*SOURCE: "When Computers Goof—Consumers Air Their Frustrations," *U.S. News & World Report,* May 2, 1977.

COMMENT Computers do not err, of course; the programming is at fault, but that does not cool a victim's wrath. So many complaints have accumulated that corporations are setting up special procedures to provide a human interface between the machines and customers. These efforts include toll-free telephone lines, more customer-relations staffs, and even a computer programmed to deal with complaints by issuing individualized replies with trigger copies sent to affected departments. With an estimated 110,-000 computers now in use in the United States, of which 80 per cent are involved in processing personal and financial data, irritation caused by cold communications from unresponsive machines will not be easily relieved.

3-4.4 Personnel

Technical controls for supplying information are extremely important, but they are not enough. Even with these, the chief executive may be the most poorly informed person in the organization unless he establishes necessary rapport with the personnel inside and outside the organization upon whom he must depend. New conditions and circumstances are always developing for which technical controls have not been established and which must therefore come to attention only by personal observation and interpretation. If the executive merely sits back and waits for problems and opportunities to be brought to his attention, he may find that reluctant or unimaginative subordinates have allowed him to drift into insurmountable difficulties. The question then is how much control and what kinds of control shall be exercised over his assistants? This question applies not only to the chief executive but to all levels of administration.

Fundamentally, the answer to this question lies in the proper training and development of assistants. The executive, in molding his team, must give special attention to achieving a careful understanding on the part of each participant regarding: (1) What action must be reported to the superior officer prior to performance? (2) What action may be taken and then reported? (3) What action may be taken and not reported unless questions, difficulties, or unusual circumstances result? It is readily recognized that it is not practical to predetermine precisely the classification into which each activity would be placed. There must be some reliance on the use of judgment on the part of the assistant. His is not a rule-book position. It is the development of judgment that we are seeking in the training of assistants so that they will be able to distinguish between an emergency and a routine action—will know when to consult with others and when to proceed independently. For example, companies usually establish limits on the authority of designated administrative personnel in the amount of expenditure that may be authorized for one item without clearing with the superior officer. However, if an emergency breakdown in equipment occurs in a remote field installation that requires immediate expenditure to avoid costly damages, the assistant in charge would be expected to take corrective action even if the expenditure does exceed the established limit.

The chapter on Hiring and Training will indicate some of the fundamental principles and practices that may be used in the development of administrative personnel. Mention may be made here, however, that much of the development must come through the working association of the assistant and his superior. A new industrial-engineering assistant may be asked to report at the end of each day or each week, "What have I accomplished?" This is a part of his training—training in planning, self-inventory, and in sharing problems and pertinent information with his superior officer. As time establishes confidence between the two persons they then reach an understanding on what kinds of information should be reported—some at regular intervals and others when the occasion demands. This is where the *exception principle,* mentioned earlier in this chapter, comes into use. Each major function of the enterprise will have its established schedule of records. They are instruments of control through which management exercises its directive influence. Records become a part of the *system* throughout which mass details are placed under routines that are acted on by those directly in charge but which at the same time reveal *exceptions* that must be reported to superior officers.

3-4.5 Consultants

Ideally, perhaps, an enterprise of at least medium size should be able to investigate its own problems and construct its own solutions. But with the mounting complexity of business it is often helpful, if not absolutely essential, to seek outside consultation. This consultation may come from a local or national association, such as the chamber of commerce, the various manufacturers' associations, and the American Management Association, or it may come from a private consulting firm or from members of a university faculty. The associations are especially helpful in supplying literature or even special reports on research and experiences in other companies with similar problems. The consulting firms or individuals go a step further and actually make analysis of the problem of the company in question. The consultant brings to the company the breadth of experience gained in many different companies. But even more important, he is often better able to view the problem without bias and vested interest. The outsider may see at once what is obvious except to the individuals who have been living with it. Then, too, business people often call in the outsider merely to confirm what they think they already know. It provides an independent check on their own appraisal and seems to add a bit of authority, soundness, and confidence to the situation, leading to more ready acceptance within the organization.

When consultants are used, they often prefer to work in cooperation with executives and staff and in an advisory capacity only. It is the job of the consultant to analyze and make recommendations. It is the job of management and its organization structure to accept or reject the recommendations. If changes are made as a result of this process, the installation of changes is usually done by the company itself, perhaps with the continuing advice of the consultant.

3-5 MANAGING THE MANAGEMENT INFORMATION SYSTEM

A management information system (MIS) is designed to provide information access and decision-input capabilities to support management decision making at all levels. Most of the data are derived from continuous monitoring of operating units and regular reports from outside sources. This information constitutes a data file for information retrieval that can be tapped by individual managers to assist their particular needs. Periodic information reports, in which the data have been statistically analyzed, are generated for more general dissemination. Finally, the MIS includes decision models, simulation capabilities, and files specially structured to allow the examination of alternative courses of action.

The complexity and power of MIS can be better appreciated by tracing its development. Computers were first utilized for clerical or record-keeping functions. They were very effective in this role. But these systems were built to deal with individual processing requirements, such as personnel and payroll records, and there was seldom any coordination among different files. The next step was to combine these single data files into a *data base,* an integrated file in which transactions are recorded as soon as possible, and once recorded, are available for all applications which may need them. A management information system is the next level of sophistication. It relies on the comprehensive data base and integrated processing, but also includes models that provide informational support for decision making. Consequently, the MIS concept is difficult to initiate, but many organizations feel the potential rewards are worth the effort.

The worth of any management system lies ultimately in its contribution to more effective operations. Three areas stand out as beneficiaries of a well-managed MIS. It should increase the productivity of office labor, and since this is the largest single occupational category in the United States (approximately 22 per cent of the total labor force in 1973 with an associated overhead cost estimated at $350 billion), there is plenty of room for improvement. A second area is in the control of operations for which the value of real-time information to monitor or correct ongoing activities can be indispensible. The third area is the impact of digested information on the decision processes of management. The opportunity to examine the consequences of possible actions by simulation and to observe "optimal solutions" from modeled conditions is a privilege some managers have today that yesteryear managers could not even envision.

Perspective 3F   COMPUTERIZED CROOKS

Computers are modernizing the ancient art of embezzling. Embezzlement, the social disease of corporations, involves the theft of property by someone to whom the property has been entrusted. It is estimated that embezzlers take two to three hundred million dollars a year in the United States. A growing proportion of this theft is accomplished by computerized crooks who have mastered computer technology to siphon funds from corporate accounts by manipulating accounting and record-keeping systems. Examples are cited by Professor Brandt Allen:

By entering fraudulent data into the bank's computer from a remote terminal in his branch office, a chief teller of a major New York savings bank stole a million and a half dollars from hundreds of accounts. When quarterly interest was due, he would simply either redeposit some of the money or indicate that it had been redeposited. The manual auditing and the computer controls failed to show any fraudulent manipulation. The teller was not detected until a police raid on a gambling operation revealed that he was betting up to $30,000 a day on professional sports. Even then the teller had to explain his manipulations to the bank executives for them to fully understand what he had done.

An employee in the data center at the welfare department of a large city entered fraudulent data into the payroll system and stole $2.75 million over a 9-month period. He and several of his friends created a fictitious work force identified by fake social security numbers that were processed weekly through the payroll routine. The computer would automatically print a check for each fake employee, then the conspirators would intercept the checks, endorse them, and cash them. The conspirators were uncovered when a policeman discovered a batch of over a hundred of the fraudulent checks in an overdue rental car he found illegally parked.*

*SOURCE: "Embezzler's Guide to the Computer," *Harvard Business Review,* July–August, 1975.

COMMENT It is an uncomfortable, but not too surprising, reality that thieves as well as honest managers have grasped the advances in computer technology and management science to advance their work. Bank robberies have been planned with the assistance of operations research techniques. The examples above of computerized theft could be just a token indication of computer fraud because all *successful* embezzlement remains undetected.

In addition to direct thefts, there may be a host of minor irregularities stemming from access to personal data in computer files that allows confidential information to be used inappropriately. Public protests have led to regulations designed to control the invasion of privacy from illegal or unethical use of data in computer files. It appears that any technological advance may have its grim side, which provides the impetus for another advance to correct imperfections, which. . . .

3-6 FUTURE OPERATIONS ANALYSES

It has been predicted that within a few years a computer will be the world's chess champion. The significance to industry of this prediction is that computers will likely get even faster, have larger memories, and offer more convenient operating features, but they will still need defined objectives and unambiguous rules to follow in solving problems.

While the introduction of large-scale computer systems has been well publicized, the relatively quiet growth of small-scale systems may have even more profound effects. The capabilities of minicomputers have increased while their prices have declined. This trend, along with the development of more convenient programming methods, has opened the way for small businesses to take advantage of electronic assistance. The use of minicomputers is not limited to payroll and bookkeeping activities. They can be used for real-time computer control over operations such as directing the flow of products and materials through a shop, while simultaneously keeping track of each item in inventory.

New techniques for problem solving are continuously being developed within the realm of management science. Ill-structured problems are succumbing to solution algorithms arising from operations research and industrial engineering. More elaborate simulation techniques provide closer links between the symbolic world of laboratory investigations and the industrial environment of the real world. The increasingly realistic simulations are powerful tools for experiencing the difficulties of operations management without the limitations and consequences of actual performance. These improved solution procedures provide the software needed to gain full advantage of the more powerful computer hardware developments.

Steps are being made to tie together behavioral systems, data-processing systems, production and processing systems, information systems, transportation and inventory systems, record systems, and other systems into a total management system. New pieces of hardware and improved analytical programs cannot alone accomplish the objective; operating managers will have to understand the language, philosophy, and technology before the total system concept can be made workable. And the objective is deserving of the managers' efforts: some form of workable system integration must be developed to cope with the growing complexities of operations management.

3-7 REVIEW QUESTIONS

1. What is the overall objective of management in an industrial enterprise?

2. What does management mean by "action on the exception principle"?

3. What is meant by the term "management science"? What is the scope of its application?

4. What is operations research? How is it used?

5. How does an organization obtain its operational information? What are its two principal sources?

6. What is meant by feedback control? Give an example.

7. Distinguish between an EDP system and a management information system.

3-8 TOPICS FOR DISCUSSION

1. What should be the long-term national effects, economically and sociologically, of improvement in technical managerial controls?

2. How may growth in technical controls change the requirements and qualifications of management officials?

3. How can small business gain advantage from these improvements in technical controls?

4. How may we determine the extent to which we permit administrative personnel to "go their own way" vs. action with permission or consultation? What guiding principles or policies can be established?

5. Briefly describe the content and intent of each of the operations research techniques listed in the table of Perspective 3C. Recognizing that these are the most used operations research tools, what can be said about the nature of the discipline?

6. How can an implemented management information system be expected to yield improvements in the areas of office labor, shop control, and managerial decisions? Compare the MIS approach to traditional methods in discussing the improvements.

7. Case 3A: *Plane Devices, Inc.*
   A mechanical-electrical engineer was the principal owner and founder of this company in Los Angeles. He had a special flair for working with airplane manufacturers, taking their designs of

various small devices and subcontracting component parts, and producing them on a contract basis. He operated a small factory where he inspected and assembled parts purchased outside and tested and shipped the completed assemblies.

Subsequently, in order to meet competition which sprang up, he decided to manufacture his own parts, which represented the greater part of the total value of his products. In order to have a favorable labor market and a climate that was good for his type of manufacturing, he located his new plant in Arizona, several hundred miles from Los Angeles. Not only did he set up the parts manufacturing here, but he moved the testing and assembling operations here as well. The owner, however, remained in Los Angeles, in his executive headquarters, with a small group of sales engineers. This permitted him to maintain the same close contacts with his customers that had made him successful.

A qualified factory manager had been put in charge of the new plant. During the starting-up period, the owner made frequent trips to the plant, keeping in touch first hand with what was going on and providing leadership and motivation to the local management. But as time went on, these trips became less and less frequent as the complexity of his personal activities made his continuing presence in Los Angeles more and more compelling. Accordingly, the time came when full responsibility for the factory operation had been shifted to the manager, with the owner depending completely upon the manager's activities and results.

Soon the owner began to hear from several of his customers that some of his prices were not competitive, some deliveries were seriously late, and quality was not up to the expected high standard. A sense of disquietude began to develop on the part of the owner. His uneasiness reached a point where he procured the services of a consulting management engineer.

On his introductory trip through the plant, the consulting engineer got the impression that a rather slow working tempo prevailed. This led him to review the payroll records. Here he learned that for several months workers' productivity had been slipping. An investigation showed that it was due to delays and slowing down of workers caused by an uneven flow of work. When this was explored more deeply, the cause of the uneven flow proved to be a combination of substandard materials and inadequate machine maintenance. Working backward, the consulting engineer unearthed the root of this difficulty—poor control of materials. Purchased materials were not up to original standards. At first this caused low productivity, which increased labor costs. Then, in order to compensate for this, a drive toward overhead cost reduction ensued, which included a cutback in maintenance personnel. The result served only to lower productivity still more. All this resulted in higher overall cost, lower capacity, and poorer quality, which showed up later in customer complaints.

A meeting of the owner, factory manager, and consulting engineer revealed that deterioration in purchased materials and parts was due to a misguided program on the part of the factory manager to reduce production costs by saving on purchases. The use of substitute materials created other cost increases that overbalanced several times the slight saving on purchases.

Questions

1. What managerial controls should be established to avoid the recurrence of such difficulties?

2. How might these controls be used by the owner to provide leadership and motivation to the factory manager?

8. Case 3B: *The Bell-Miller Appliance Company*

Ed Miller was the principal stockholder and general manager of the Miller Automatic Controls Company. He was a trained electrical engineer and possessed an outstanding flair for inventing and developing product items as well as machinery and equipment for manufacturing. It was his nature to devote most of his time and effort to the drawing board, the toolmakers, and experimental mechanics. A group of assistants had grown up over the years to whom he delegated the commercial activities, i.e., selling, buying, accounting, etc. From years of experience they handled these in a satisfactory manner, coming to Miller with problems outside the routine. He handled the working force of about 300 workers through six foremen who had grown up in the company. Labor cost was controlled through piecework, and the rates were set by the foremen. These rates were reviewed and modified, according to individual circumstances, by Mr. Miller, who had developed a speaking acquaintanceship with most of his workers and an understanding of their operations and their problems. This procedure, in conjunction with the efficient equipment that Mr. Miller had designed, resulted in economical manufacturing costs.

One of Mr. Miller's largest customers was the Bell Appliance Company in the same city. Mr. Bell, the president, was an astute merchandiser, clever businessman, and a well-trained and effective administrator. In spite of the fact that he was successful, he sorely needed improvement in product design and production cost. In his buying contacts with the Miller Automatic Controls Company, it became apparent that Mr. Miller would be the ideal man to bolster these weaknesses in Mr. Bell's company. This was considered priority number one. To obtain Miller, a merger was proposed and eventually consummated with acquiescence to the demand by Mr. Miller that he become vice-president of the combined Bell–Miller Appliance Company in charge of product development and manufacturing. In this capacity he carried both the priority item of redoing the Bell merchandise and machinery and also the supervision of operations in both plants. With Mr. Bell as president, the two factories were continued in their separate locations but headquarters for both were established at the Bell plant, where the working force was about 400 people.

Mr. Bell recognized at once that there needed to be a more scientific way of dealing with piece rates and piecework problems than by individual negotiation with the vice-president. Accordingly, in consultation with Mr. Miller, he decided to install a modern labor-standard and wage-incentive system, and a firm of consulting industrial engineers was engaged for that purpose.

These engineers took over, and during the next 6 months, while standards were being set, they also handled the piecework problems that came up. They spent an additional 2 months switching over to the new incentive system and working with the operators, supervisors, and staff in bringing the production and wages up to proper levels. Since the consulting engineers took over this responsibility, Mr. Miller was able, during the time they were there, to concentrate in large measure on the development of the product and production equipment, and excellent progress was made in this direction.

At the end of this 8-month period, the engineers had finished their installation and the time had come for them to turn back to the management the responsibility for wages and productivity. Since Mr. Miller was vice-president in charge of manufacturing as well as of product development, this responsibility fell on his shoulders.

Not long thereafter, difficulties started in connection with workers' earnings, labor costs, and volume of production. As a result of the incentive system, earnings of the workers had been brought up to a level considerably higher than existed previously. Now, however, with the engineers gone and with no followup from them, earnings started to slip. In working out arrangements in advance with the union to install the incentive system, guarantees were made as to minimum levels of earnings for various job classifications. As time went on, actual hourly earnings on incentive rates fell and broke through these guaranteed minimums in many instances. As a result, both labor costs and volume of production suffered. While this became a matter of great concern to management, even graver was the growing dissatisfaction of the working force with shrinking earnings. The seriousness of the situation forced a switch of emphasis on Mr. Miller's part to these problems and made it necessary to slight the development activity that had gotten off to such a good start. But in spite of the vice-president's new concentration on problems of productivity, the desired improvement in earnings was not achieved. It was not long, therefore, before the union threatened to strike. Action was now imperative, and it was decided to call back the consulting industrial engineers, who had installed the incentive system, to reestablish satisfactory hourly earnings. On this basis the union agreed to hold the threatened strike in abeyance.

When the engineers returned, they investigated the causes of the low productivity and found it was due primarily to idle time. This was time that workers were unable to use productively, either because equipment was not in proper condition or work was not being supplied to the operator as fast as needed. Production checks showed that if such delays were eliminated, workers could readily turn out the proper amount of production to yield anticipated earnings. A report was then made to the management explaining the nature of the delays and what was needed to be done to overcome them. The report established the fact that the delays were due primarily to missing materials, improper work flow, inadequate maintenance, and poor supervision.

Questions

1. Indicate the fundamental problems involved in arriving at a solution to this case.

2. What are the principles applicable to these problems?

3. How would you approach a solution?

RISK AND FORECASTING

In a free economy a business venture may be promoted and launched by anyone, provided the general rules of the game (commercial law) are complied with and certain standards safeguarding health, safety, and morals are observed. But freedom to enter business and to launch new products is no guarantee of success. First there is the need for accurate forecasts of market potential and resource availability. A venture is generally ill conceived when it caters to a declining market or relies on human and material resources which may become unavailable in the future. Assuming the enterprise is well conceived, it is still beset with risks all along the way. The challenging problem before management is how to anticipate and minimize these risks. What methods are available to forecast future business conditions? How may risks concerning the product be avoided? What are the risks of inadequate financing, of faulty accounting? What risks must be minimized in manufacturing operations? Can insurance compensate for all the risks? Unless satisfactory answers to these questions are found and adopted by the enterprise, efficiency will be reduced, costly damage may ensue, profits may be drained away, and business failures will be inevitable.

4 RISK AND FORECASTING

4-1 ANTICIPATING RISK

Risks arise generally from uncertainties in nature, in the economic system, and in human nature. They are often created by improper organization, faulty product development, unsound financing, and bad management. Many risks in industry may be likened to leaks in a water system: unless minimized or eliminated, the leaks will drain off the profits to the point where the enterprise ceases to be a solvent operation. In considering the subject of business risk, let us keep the focus on the industrial enterprise in action and note the risks it must meet in the course of its operations.

The *product* is the all-important center of an industrial enterprise. It is for the sake of the product that the whole organization of management, plant, equipment, materials, and workers exists. The product gives meaning to production. It is the source of profits, one of the chief incentives for which people labor. More product and better quality of product are the chief ends for all we do in the name of efficiency, whether that product is a manufactured good or a service.

When carefully analyzed, many failures attributed to financing, organization, and other causes turn out to be failures in the product. By "failure of product" we mean the larger sense of the problem—failure in the relation of the product to the enterprise producing it, in marketing the product, and in calculating the place that the product fills in the scale of human needs.

The general problem of business risk thus begins with a study of the product, its physical nature, and its commercial possibilities. We shall deal in later chapters with specific problems of product development and engineering; here we are concerned with avoiding risks of product failure. What must management do to know the product, to be sure that there is a satisfactory demand for it, to prepare the company for the undertaking, to find the basis for cost, price, and production schedules, and to guard the enterprise against adverse business conditions? The object of inquiries on these lines is to make reasonably certain that risks to the company from the possibility of product failure are minimized or eliminated.

4-1.1 Is the Product Well Conceived and Useful?

Clues about the utility of a product are revealed by a thorough study. In other words, what do you have to sell? This involves a careful consideration of such factors as physical appearance, structure, functional style and design, component materials, and the detailed uses for which the product or service is intended. This necessarily means close coordination among several departments: research, engineering, production, sales, and finance (see Chap. 2). Is the product to be used directly by people in the process of living (a consumer good) or by other manufacturers in further production (a producer good)? Is it a durable good (of long life when used), nondurable (consumed almost immediately), or semidurable? How is the product identified as to industrial group and commercial class? Do patents and trademarks adequately protect the product? Patent-infringement suits often put a stop to a new enterprise. If patents of others are to be used, are the use and royalty agreements drawn properly? Have the effects of these agreements on production costs and marketing factors been carefully calculated so that sufficient margin exists to meet the pressure of competitors' prices and also to provide a profit substantial enough to warrant continued production? Have government and trade regulations affecting the production and use of the product been checked so as to avoid interference with the business from these sources? Has a tax analysis of the product been made? Have service factors been thoroughly weighed? What guarantees are to be made? How are the responsibility and cost of servicing to be borne and by whom? Will service parts constitute a secondary line of products on which profits may be made? These are only a few of the questions which should be asked about the product for the implications they have on every phase of the company's operations.

4-1.2   Is There a Demand for the Product?

After it is certain that the product is well conceived (although it may not be completely perfected) and that no obstacles stemming from the product itself will hamper its production and sale, the next step is to find out whether there is a satisfactory demand for it. Just because a product is the firm's "baby," there is no automatic assurance that the public will cuddle it, as many firms have discovered to their surprise and disappointment. A market study to avoid this risk is best made in two stages: (1) the *preliminary survey,* to determine potential demand; and (2) the *intensive market study,* which is used as the basis for production plans and sales campaigns. A preliminary survey shows the probable nature, extent, and depth of the market. If properly conducted, it may point up defects in the product and indicate desirable changes which would be costly to make after production is in full swing. It may show that plans for the enterprise are too ambitious and ought to be cut to smaller scale, or it may indicate the reverse, that the original plans are too modest and not scaled to take full advantage of the demand that really exists.

The intensive market study begins where the preliminary survey leaves off and it enlarges the range and degree of coverage. It aims to discover how much of the *potential* demand can be turned into *actual sales.* Such information is highly important for many reasons. It is a guide to price and production schedules, labor and materials commitments, marketing plans and sales terms, credit and collection policies, and financial requirements. This is the time to tighten up on the risks before too much is ventured on too little thought and information.

The material for the market studies must be drawn from many quarters and by various means. An established company has invaluable information within its own organization and experience. This should be systematically collected and put in useful form. But much data will have to come from outside sources: from government agencies and from surveys made by newspapers, magazines, radio networks, advertising agencies, chambers of commerce, universities, and various privately endowed research organizations. Every effort should be made to identify the prospective buyers, to learn their circumstances and characteristics, to chart the conditions under which they are likely to buy, to determine the type of effort necessary to sell to them, to discover if and how they are being serviced by competing firms or with comparable products, and what obstacles the firm will encounter in any attempt to distribute the product in the market outlined. No assumptions or guesswork in an inquiry of this kind can substitute for the patient collection and study of the most detailed information to be found.

4-1.3　How Does the Product Relate to the Enterprise?

From a study of the product and from market studies, it will be wise to reexamine the relation of the product to the enterprise if risks are to be avoided or minimized. Important decisions will hinge upon whether the product is to be launched along with a *new* enterprise, or whether it is a new product of an *established* company. Of like importance is the question whether the company is to be based upon the single product, a line of related products, or several diversified products. In other words, the place that the product is to occupy in the company and the purpose for which the company conceives the product are of considerable importance in forecasting and calculating the risks.

Production factors are of first consideration in relating the product to the enterprise. Are the proposed or existing plant and equipment adequate for efficient production, for contemplated quality and volume? What raw materials are required, what substitutes can be used, how adequate is the supply, and how dependable is the source of materials? Is there anything in the processing, cost conditions, and transportation of the materials to be used from the crude state to the point where needed that will create risks for production and marketing plans? Is the labor supply appropriate and dependable for the manufacture of the particular product? Are proper provisions being made for product development and improvement, for product form, design, packaging, and shipment? Has an analysis of government laws and regulations, trade customs and requirements, labor laws and union agreements affecting plant, equipment, and production been made? Has a graph of projected production been made, taking into account seasonal factors, production for stock, market, and order; allowing for necessary idle time and use of machinery and equipment for other products; and covering similar factors affecting production? Where possible, from a pilot plant, from test runs, and from engineering estimates, has a careful cost analysis been made? Many chapters of this book are devoted to answering these questions. The object of inquiring about them here is to make certain that all risks concerning the manufacture of the product are disclosed and measures taken to safeguard against them.

In like manner the product should be considered in conjunction with other departments of the enterprise. Is the sales organization properly formed for the marketing of the product as a specialty or line of products? Has a careful promotion, advertising, and sales campaign been formulated? Has a careful financing forecast been made? What demands will the manufacture of the particular product make upon financial arrangements?

Perspective 4A POPULATION PROFILES AND PRODUCT PLANNING

A critical factor in anticipating future risks in production is the shifting population profile. It is relatively easy to recognize lineal changes in age groupings and to spot shifts in the geographic distribution of the population, but it is more difficult to estimate their influence on particular products. Changes in the regional and age mix for the next decade from 1977, as estimated by the U.S. Bureau of Census, are shown below.

1. Overall U.S. population up 10 per cent, from 216.8 million to 228.6 million in 1987.
2. Regional increases in the U.S. population:

New England	6.8%
Mid Atlantic	3%
South Atlantic	16.4%
North Central—East	5.4%
South Central—East	9.1%
North Central—West	5.5%
South Central—West	14.5%
Mountain	24%
Pacific	14.6%
Children, under 13	up 11%
Teenagers, 13–20	down 17%
Young adults, 20–34	up 13%
Young middle age, 35–49	up 31%
Older middle age, 50–64	down 1%
Elderly, 65 and older	up 19%

3. Changes in age groups between 1977 and 1987:

Autos	Slower rise in demand
Houses	Substantial increase
Apartments	Moderate growth
Furniture	Increase in demand
Travel	Up sharply
Entertainment	Substantial increase
Appliances	Rising demand
Teenage clothing	Down somewhat

As some age groups grow faster than others, the nation's needs for goods and services also shift. The following effects on key markets are predicted:

Baby food, clothing, toys . . . . Expanding market
Adult clothing . . . . Up substantially
School construction . . . . Sharply cut back
Alcoholic Beverages . . . . Continued increase
Medical services . . . . Up sharply
Adult education . . . . Continued growth
Fuel . . . . Slow increase in demand
Metals . . . . Steady increase, except for autos

COMMENT   Nearly every industry can be affected by population shifts. Some will gain markets and others will lose. But the risks are reasonably predictable. Products for babies and toddlers, which suffered from the low birth rates of the 1970s, will probably pick up in the 1980s. Teenage products—blue jeans, tapes, records, and new high schools—should level off. The demand for houses will likely increase, with the greatest gains in the South and West.

Associated with the changing product mix is a change in the profile of the workforce. The U.S. Labor Department estimates that the nation's workforce will increase by only 15 per cent between 1977 and 1987, compared with an increase of 24 per cent in the previous 10 years. But to reduce unemployment to 5 per cent, 16 million additional jobs must be created. The size and composition of the future workforce can affect the demand for products and services as well as the workers available to produce them. Both are risks for production planning.

4-2   FORECASTING RISK

Business success and survival in modern times demand that management pay increasing attention to general economic conditions. This is true whether a new enterprise is to be established, a new product is to be launched, or whether an established firm wishes to improve its relative position in a competitive market. The uncertainties of economic life create many risks for industrial enterprise; while some are beyond the control of the individual firm, many others may be avoided or cushioned by working with business barometers and forecasts, even when these aids fall short of absolute reliability.

4-2.1   Relationship of the Enterprise to General Economic Conditions

The economic present and future are conditioned by three sets of forces or influences, each of which is made up of many different elements. These are the seasonal influences, the long-time trends, and business cycles. All three are at work, effecting economic change, concurrently. Stated another way, seasonal influences and business cycles are of relatively short duration and occur, so to speak, within the longer time framework of the long-time trends which are also working economic changes. Economic forecasting studies each of these three sets of influences, seeks to discover the way they work and the effects they produce separately and in combination, and then tries to interpret them in terms of future probability as a basis for practical economic action.

Figure 4–1 represents a time-series analysis based on past sales, indicated by circles. The wave-like line connecting the circles shows the rising trend of annual sales, and possibly some effects of a business cycle. These two factors in combination are the basis for the dashed *trend line,* or regression line, which smooths out the variations. A forecast for future sales levels is obtained by extending the trend line beyond the current date. Then the average value for the percentage of annual sales made each month, as shown by the insert to the right, is utilized to anticipate demand during a particular month; the forecasted annual sales figure is multiplied by the charted percentage of sales that have historically occurred for the month in question.

SEASONAL VARIATIONS Seasonal variations stem from the yearly cycle of weather and from the social seasons set up by custom and traditions. Businessmen have already learned much in the way of adapting their operations to these predictable changes. They know substantially what to expect in spring, summer, fall, and winter. They know how to translate Easter, vacation time, Thanksgiving, and Christmas into economic terms. They manufacture for inventory in off seasons, diversify the line of products so as to stabilize production and labor, offset weather by artificial devices, offer special sales inducements to off-season buying, adjust price schedules to take up part of the risk of seasonal business, anticipate the season (as when women's spring hats are introduced in January), develop off-season uses for seasonal products, exploit complementary markets when the season in one closes while the season in the other opens, and stagger vacations—the list of off-setting techniques is endless.

LONG-TERM TRENDS Long-term trends indicate structural changes in the economy occurring in a slow, cumulative way. They come about through

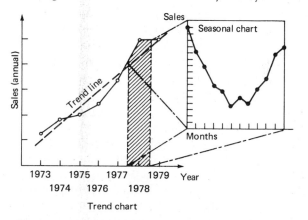

Figure 4-1 Sales data from which a forecast is derived by time-series analysis. Circles on the main chart indicate annual sales. The seasonal distribution of sales within 1 year, denoted by the shaded area, is shown in the insert. (SOURCE: James L. Riggs, *Production Systems: Planning, Analysis and Control* (2nd ed.), New York: John Wiley & Sons, Inc., 1976.)

changes in productive ability, social institutions, and individual habits and usually manifest themselves in industrial growth or decadence. Obviously, this involves many elements such as population trends, technological developments, condition and use of natural resources, long-term stages or types of economic growth, changes in social institutions and customs and in individual habits. Forecasters study these long-term trends. Where possible, they project them into the future and interpret their significance in economic affairs. Some data are sufficiently refined and reliable to be of direct assistance to industrial groups and even to individual enterprises. Many industries have either ignored these long-term trends or have made inadequate adaptation to them. Some examples are rail transportation as affected by automobiles, airplanes, pipelines and trucking lines; the coal industry as affected by oil; the textile industry as affected by imported fabrics; and the phonograph-record industry, which was almost eclipsed by radio before it staged a healthy comeback. Much has been learned from the past, and today there is far greater awareness in industry and business of the need for appraising long-term trends and adapting the enterprise to them.

The individual enterprise can obtain or make up from available studies a list of these long-term trends, arranging them according to the degrees of positive and negative effects they may have on the enterprise. It may then interpret them in terms of adjustments to be made in planning the future of the enterprise, in arranging its capital investment, in determining the type, volume, and nature of its production, in formulating labor and other policies and similar detailed applications. Care will have to be taken that long-term trends serve only as a broad guide which must be brought into relation with seasonal and business-cycle changes. The effort to do this will be valuable even though the reliability of long-term forecasting remains in considerable doubt.

THE BUSINESS CYCLE   In duration, the business cycle covers a time period longer than seasonal fluctuations and much shorter than long-term trends. Stated differently, many seasonal fluctuations take place within a business cycle, and many business cycles occur in the progress of a long-term trend. The business cycle is made up of recurrent fluctuations revolving around a state of balance. These fluctuations make up a pattern according to which business activity experiences an *upswing*, carrying it far above balance to what may be termed "overproduction," and then enters upon a *downswing* extending far below balance to a point we may call "underproduction." These two extremes are popularly called "prosperity" and "depression." A complete cycle is described when business activity moves, let us say, from the peak of prosperity through the downswing to depression and back up again to prosperity; or in similar manner from depression to depression. The length of the cycle varies widely. Although the cycle is recurrent, i.e., occurs again and again, it does not do so in clear, stated periods; and it does not swing from one extreme to the opposite extreme in any consistent pattern.

The Great Depression that began in 1929 was a vivid and unforgettable experience of the havoc worked in every phase of life by cycles of extreme severity. Major depressions of comparable severity occurred in 1815–1821, 1837–1843, and 1873–1878, although the relative degree of severity cannot be satisfactorily established. Between 1878 and 1933, some 15 cycles are traced, 7 considered major and 8 minor, according to the extent of deviation from normal. Since 1933, recessions of varied severity have occurred in 1937–1938, 1949, 1957–1958, 1960–1961, and 1973–1975. Each cycle is unique in that different factors and different combinations of factors distinguish it from others. And, to make things even more difficult for the practical businessman, it is believed that, in addition to these cycles affecting total economic activity, there is also a *specific* cycle for an individual industry or process.

Much greater attention has been given to business cycles since the depression of the 1930s. Government, in particular, has developed a wide array of automatic stabilizers, cushioning effects, and compensating elements. Industry has also moved in many ways which tend to make business crises less likely and less severe. But there is no absolute assurance that business cycles can be smoothed out or depressions avoided. An individual enterprise cannot hope to isolate itself from the business cycle, but by judicious adjustment in accordance with the business "barometers" used by experts to study business cycles, management may go far to protect itself against the worst effects of cyclic changes.

4-2.2 Business Barometers

Since business cycles affect every phase of economic life, forecasters have made minute studies of economic operations and conditions in an effort to find either the causes or the indicators of cyclic behavior. They have studied stock-market activity, industrial production, employment, prices, construction contracts, electric-power output, bank debits, income inventories, trade, and similar features of economic activity. They have divided many of these larger activities into subclassifications for more intensive study as, for example, stock prices, world prices, commodity prices, retail prices, agricultural prices, industrial prices, and such aggregate price behavior as the general price level. By careful search of past conditions, they have succeeded in projecting many of these economic activities over fairly long periods of time to gain the perspective that business-cycle study requires.

Aside from their use in studying economic cycles, these compilations of data may be used by the practical business executive as guides in operating the specific enterprise. As projected in time, the data on any given item, such as industrial production, bank debits, retail prices, or department-store sales, are termed a *series*. Wherever possible the data are converted into *index numbers* which are statistical devices used for convenience in measuring and comparing data. A single series may be used for many purposes; or many series may be combined in one general index (as they usually are) for the purpose of bringing related data together. In order to measure *general business activity,* for example, a compiler will select and combine several different series which he believes are keys or indicators to the course of general business conditions. Many government and private statistical organizations as well as business magazines and the business pages of newspapers provide compilations of this kind. The most comprehensive may be those compiled by the U.S. Department of Commerce.[1]

The managers of any enterprise can examine and select a group of business indicators that measure and compare data having some direct bearing on the particular enterprise. Specifically, the sales manager can find and use indicators of regional business conditions and indexes of producer and consumer goods; of production, shipments, and inventories; of price behavior in many fields of his interest; of trade conditions, wholesale and retail; of income, wage payments, and credit conditions; and of commercial failures and the state of general business prospects. The purchasing agent can watch the trend of purchases, production, inventories, general prices, specific commodity prices, and money and credit conditions. The production manager, personnel manager, treasurer, and other company officials can find special indexes of value to them in their work. With careful selection it is possible to construct a workable barometer for the particular enterprise. While the risks of economic uncertainties may never be overcome, much can be done to plan ahead and cushion their effects on the company's operations.

4-3 METHODS OF FORECASTING

The essence of each forecasting method is the different manner by which past performances are translated into predictions of future performance. Techniques range from subjective opinions to objective numerical calculations. There is no universally preferred technique because the expectations from forecasting vary so widely. Some firms are satisfied with a vague estimate of future demand. For such enterprises, elaborate forecasting computations would not pay for themselves. Where reliable forecasts are necessary, the extra effort and cost involved in making better predictions are expected and accepted.

---

[1]Twelve leading indicators are the average factory work week, the rate of hiring in manufacturing industry, the layoff rate, new orders received by manufacturers of durable goods, the number of new homes on which construction is started, new contracts placed for commercial and industrial construction (measured in floor space), the net change in the number of businesses in operation, the liability of commercial and industrial businesses that have failed, corporate profits after taxes, Standard and Poor's index for industrial, railroad, and utility common-stock prices, the change in business inventories, and prices of industrial raw materials. One or more of these indicators may correlate closely with a company's sales and thereby provide a convenient relationship from which to forecast operating conditions.

4-3.1   Subjective Methods

The majority of industrial enterprises rely on informal forecasting methods. They watch certain economic trends and relate them to short-range operations. The result of a pessimistic view of future business could be a reduction of inventories or a cancellation of specific activities. Conversely, a forecast of increased sales could trigger plans for higher production. Such views evolve from opinions voiced by salespersons, retailers, managers, and other cognizant individuals within the organization. Conflicting opinions are usually resolved by a consensus of key executives.

Predictions by educated guesses, sometimes obtained by the *Delphi method,* have both advantages and weaknesses. On the plus side is the opportunity to use proprietary knowledge gained from experience with the firm's products and competitive position. A wide sample of qualified opinions tends to balance overly enthusiastic estimates against overly pessimistic opinions and to include divergent perspectives. The absence of formal forecasting training and detailed data evaluation keeps the cost low.

4-3.2   Objective Methods

Many forms of statistical analysis have been developed to relate historical data to future occurrences. A *time series analysis* attempts to identify the pattern of trends, business cycles, and seasonal variations. The patterns are expressed mathematically. A line fitted to a plot of past performances (or the quantitative expression of the line) can be extrapolated to show anticipated future performance. In doing so, it is assumed that the factors affecting previous behavior will similarly influence the future (see Figure 4–1).

A slightly different approach is to give unequal weighting to the historical data points. The most recent occurrences are usually weighted to show more importance. In the *moving average method* a forecast for the next period results from averaging a set number of the most recent observations. When the true value for the forecast period is known, it replaces the oldest observation in the span to be averaged for the next forecast. The *exponential smoothing method* develops a new forecast by adjusting the previous prediction according to a selected fraction of the differences between the prediction and what actually occurred. Selection of larger fractions makes the new forecast more sensitive to recent data. The extreme condition (where the fraction is 1.0), sometimes called "persistence forecasting," is to use the latest observation as the forecast for the next period.

Correlation analysis is employed to determine how well an index relates to data of interest to the firm, such as sales. Business barometers as mentioned previously are readily available and inexpensive. A correlation study reveals how much reliance can be put on these indexes to foretell associated futures. For instance, the number of new housing starts is a likely indicator of future demand for prefabricated windows, carpenters, plumbing services, and similar construction-oriented industries. Higher correlations (a correlation coefficient of ±1.0 identifies a perfect match) mean that more faith can be put in the forecasts from the indexes.

Forecasting charts are often used for interpretive purposes and for control. Quantitative data are plotted as points directly on the chart, and the resulting pattern is evaluated with the assistance of statistical limits. Where the data are qualitative, the logical inferences may be set up in a list of favorable and unfavorable factors relating to the product or enterprise. Various degrees of favorability and unfavorability may be determined upon and represented by symbols. Interpretative conclusions can be worked out for each point value and symbol and for various groupings of indicators. A system of periodic ratings of business factors will be necessary because the business picture is constantly changing. For the individual enterprise, these evaluations should always be in terms of that enterprise. In other words, what may be an unfavorable condition in the business cycle as regards the total economy may be a favorable one in terms of the individual enterprise.

When the chart and the evaluation bases are carefully worked out, the points and symbols may be grouped into various patterns indicating different effects on the enterprise and pointing toward several possibilities for corrective action. Patterns may be related to certain key policies, operations, and decisions. Thus, definite patterns may be developed for guidance on overall expansion or retrenchment, investment in plant and equipment, short- and long-term financing; on price and credit policies; on production schedules, inventory policies, labor force, and wage rates; on sales campaigns, and on budget construction. It is this end product of such a chart —these patterns highlighting conditions and indicating actions and decisions required on key policies—that will be of most service to the general management. Much experimentation, testing, and many mistakes will have to be made before a working tool of this kind can be constructed, but it is not beyond the range of possibility. Even if there should be complete failure in the attempt to make a reliable forecast of all business risks, the experience will yield many by-products in the direction of more efficient conduct of the business for those who make the try.

Several forecasting techniques are related in Figure 4–2 to the stages of product development where they are likely to be most useful. The life cycle of a successful product is divided into three stages: (1) development and introduction; (2) rapid growth; and (3) mature or steady-state condition. Each stage places different demands on forecast preparation, and the forecaster typically responds with the method most suitable to produce the data needed to make timely decisions. Some of the more popular methods are listed beneath the activities to which the forecasts are applied.

Perspective 4B   PREDICTION PRACTICES AND PRACTITIONERS

A survey of 127 companies by Steven C. Wheelwright and Darral G. Clarke found that most companies have a substantial commitment to forecasting and they employ a wide range of techniques. The top seven techniques used for forecasting are shown in the table below.

Forecasting Method	Use of the Method by Those Familiar with It	Ongoing Use of the Method by Those Who Have Tried It	Those Unfamiliar with the Method
Jury of executive opinion	82 (%)	89 (%)	6 (%)
Regression analysis	76	91	8
Time-series smoothing	75	84	13
Sales force composite	74	82	10
Index numbers	67	85	33
Econometric models	65	88	12
Customers' expectations	57	78	15

SOURCE: "Corporate Forecasting: Promise and Reality," *Harvard Business Review,* November-December, 1976.

COMMENT In addition to rating the forecasting techniques, the survey by Wheelwright and Clarke also revealed that many companies do not feel they are getting their money's worth from their investment in forecasting. Such beliefs are understandable from the nature of the forecasting function. There is no "best way" to forecast, thus leaving the way open to second guessing; and good forecasting, like good planning for a trip, is seldom remembered, while an inaccurate forecast and a disappointing trip are seldom forgotten. The authors suggest better communications between the preparers and users of forecasts as one way to improve the situation.

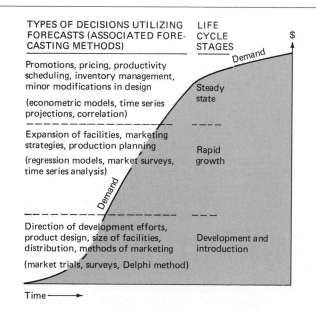

Figure 4-2 Types of management decisions associated with the life cycle of a product and the forecasting methods used to provide data for the decisions. (SOURCE: James L. Riggs, *Production Systems: Planning, Analysis and Control* (2nd ed.), New York: John Wiley & Sons, Inc., 1976.)

4-4 SPECIFIC RISKS IN INDUSTRIAL OPERATIONS

Aside from the general business and forecasting risks involved in launching a new product or maintaining an established line, there are many other risks which the going concern must meet. Most of these are specific and well known, even if their occurrence is unpredictable. Consequently, many methods have been worked out to deal with them. An excellent procedure is to have a small committee prepare a *risk survey* for the enterprise, to be used as a check list and guide for protective measures. Attacking risks at the point of prevention rather than at the point of loss is good business. The following categories indicate some of these risks.

1. *Risks centering around the physical property* Title to the company's real estate and such rights or obligations as ingress and egress roadways, easements, and riparian rights on streams, if defective, may cause considerable inconvenience and expense. These are matters for the company attorney. The plant engineering department may be charged with the task of guarding against hazards to the physical property and to the safety and health of employees on or about the property. Included here are risks from fire; storm damage; unsafe stairs, floors, and passageways; machinery, materials, power transmission, and conveyor systems; defective wiring; boiler explosions; and a whole range of similar dangers which can be very costly. Most of these risks can be eliminated, and all can be minimized.

2. *Risks centering around administration* Building a proper administrative staff whose members can carry on competently if ill health, accident, or death removes key individuals is a wise policy even though insurance may be held on the lives of selected executives. Care in fostering the loyalty and honesty of officials who handle large sums of money is a strong reinforcement of any fidelity insurance that may be carried. Credit losses are best prevented by careful extension of credit. Many financial losses are avoidable by proper accounting methods and budgetary controls which can give the danger signals. Reserves against contingencies cushion the blows of the unexpected and, if not needed, are pleasing additions to net worth. Where possible, plan ahead, diversify the sources of income, and iron out seasonal variations. Avoid the complacency which literally carries the enterprise in a state of frozen assets. The term "frozen assets" is a paradox; most of the assets disappear with the thawing. Weed out the complacent, unprogressive managerial personnel. In short, in the handling of administrative risks, as with all risks, preventive action is preferable to offsetting the losses after they occur.

3. *Risks in connection with the labor force* The health, morale, and safety of the labor force in the course of productive operations are direct responsibilities of management. Many firms insist upon and pay for medical examinations for prospective workers. They encourage group health, hospitalization, accident, and life insurance. An emergency sickroom with an industrial nurse in charge often catches injuries before they become heavy liabilities. Even if workmen's compensation insurance meets part of the problem of industrial accidents, it is better to go to the sources of trouble. Treating the workers as human beings entitled to every consideration commensurate with efficient production is also good insurance

against absenteeism and labor turnover, against damage to materials and equipment through carelessness and indifference, and against labor trouble. In short, adequate personnel administration can go a long way toward preventing risks centering around the worker and his operations.

4. *Risks in connection with materials*   Many risks arise in connection with materials. Proper forecasts, forward buying, or hedging will go far toward eliminating price surprises. Supply deficiencies may be met by changes in inventory policies, by contracting out, by developing captive suppliers, or by a careful survey of alternative sources and substitutes. Simplification of product and standardization of parts often yield amazing reductions in high-cost materials. Proper storage cuts down losses from deterioration.

5. *Risks of technological change*   We live in a day of rapid technological changes in machinery, equipment, materials, and methods of production. These involve the risks of changing costs of production which along with market prices lie at the heart of the profit equation. They also affect the nature, quality, style, durability, and use of the product. Risks such as these are best met by a policy of constant research, no matter how small the company may be. A firm alert to these risks can find invaluable suggestions in industry and trade-association literature which it can adapt to its own purposes at small cost.

This brief survey of specific risks centering around the enterprise as a whole, its administrative and production activities, merely indicates the type and range of risks likely to be encountered in the average industrial enterprise. A company survey will bring out the specialized and detailed risks that each individual enterprise will have to meet. Other chapters of this book develop many of these risks in detail and discuss the different methods of handling them. With the aid of this material a company committee may explore the nature of risk in its own plant. Knowledge of the risk is the first essential toward eliminating or reducing it. After the facts are thoroughly developed, methods to handle the risk may be put into operation. A residue of risk is likely to remain about which nothing, apparently, can be done. Here, a rough estimate of the probability of the event or happening must be weighed against the cost of compensating for losses, probably through insurance. If the chance of loss or injury is reasonably probable, and the approximate amount of loss is likely to be large, insurance should be sought as an offset.

Perspective 4C   TECHNOLOGICAL ASSESSMENT

Most new products are variations of already established products. The risk in deviating slightly from a successfully marketed item is less than introducing a mutation; the producer does not know if the novel product will perform as expected or if its performance will be appreciated by customers. There is also some risk that the mutation will actually be harmful to related sales, the company's reputation, or the general welfare of the consumers.

Technological assessment is a relatively new field of study in which the intent is to examine the consequences of introducing new technology. While such studies cannot possibly anticipate all future impacts of technological innovations, they can collect all the currently known facts about the subject, what is feared and what is welcomed, and what considerations deserve special attention. Sherry R. Arnstein discusses side effects and unintended social changes resulting from a well-known technological innovation:

> For example, if a comprehensive TA (technological assessment) had been done on the birth control pill in the 1950s, it might have alerted health decision makers to the advisability of conducting additional field tests on biological side effects. It might have alerted health planners to the need to expand the nation's delivery system for venereal disease control as well as the need to reduce the size of obstetrical facilities. Moreover, it might have signaled the school officials on the reduced need for classroom construction, the manpower and education officials on the need for fewer teachers, the social security planners on the huge deficit that would result from the change in the income-producing and benefits-receiving populations, the housing officials on the impending change in design demands for dwelling units, and the clerical leaders on the need to be responsive to the socioreligious perturbations triggered by the availability of the device.*

*SOURCE: "Technological Assessment: Opportunities and Obstacles," *IEEE Transactions on Systems, Man, and Cybernetics,* August, 1977.

COMMENT Industrial companies and government agencies are becoming more concerned that some technologies are providing new benefits to selected sectors of society at the expense of other sectors. Urban freeways, power plants, drugs, and energy-intensive products are examples. Efforts to forecast the impacts of emerging technologies use extrapolation of present trends into the future to observe the effects and interpolation from possible futures back to the present to examine the causes. The methods employed include cross-impact analysis, dynamic modeling, opinion surveys, sensitivity analysis, relevance trees, Delphi, and other analysis techniques. Teams drawn from different interest groups and disciplines conduct the studies. This task force approach is costly, but the magnitude of potential damages from ill-conceived technologies permits a large investment for wise counsel.

4-5 INSURANCE

Insurance should be the last resort, not the first, in meeting business risk. Insurance increases the current cost of doing business and thus narrows the profit margin and makes the product more vulnerable to competition. Insurance does not eliminate the risk. It never fairly compensates for all the loss. At first glance, it appears that insurance shifts the risk to others, but this means simply that others are also shifting part of their risks to you. Each enterprise does not escape its share of the total loss to the economy as a whole. If this merely shared the losses equally among all firms, only the economy as a whole would be likely to suffer. But all enterprises do not have the same cost of production. Some operate with very wide profit margins and can easily bear their share of total economic loss. Others are high-cost firms, operating with a very narrow margin between cost and selling price in what may be a highly competitive field. If total economic losses become large enough so that insurance premiums run high, the marginal firm is likely to find itself vulnerable to business failure and bankruptcy. The best policy for all firms is not to shift the risk, if it can be eliminated altogether, and to reduce all risks wherever possible. It is a better policy, for example, to use safety devices to decrease accidents than to rely upon workmen's compensation insurance to pay for injuries.

Where a residue of risk remains without possibility of elimination, insurance is perhaps the best method to cushion the loss if it should occur. The range of insurance has steadily widened over the years and now includes coverage for almost all calculable risks. There is the usual insurance against fire, earthquake, tornado, windstorm, hailstorm, explosion, burglary and theft, riots, and public disturbances. Various grades and types of insurance cover rolling stock, delivery equipment, and other transportation risks. Personal liability insurance and property damage are available to cover almost every injury to persons and property. Surety and fidelity insurance cover cases such as defalcation and embezzlement. Where necessary, the lives of key executives can be insured to protect the firm against losses growing out of heavy dependence upon one person or a group of persons. Insurance may be had against credit losses and to cover fixed charges and overhead during the incapacitation of the plant.

An increasing array of insurance services (even where the service is government supported or partly subsidized and not strictly on the insurance principle) covers contingencies affecting the labor force. Workmen's compensation insurance is firmly established; and group health, hospitalization, and life insurance is already widely acceptable. Unemployment insurance and the social security system give every indication that such services will be enlarged. Extension of these so-called "social services" in the economy undoubtedly will work temporary hardships on many individual firms, but adjustment will come in the long run. Painful as the present adjustments are, they are deemed more desirable than to let the social risks of accidents, ill health, hospitalization costs, unemployment, and old-age dependency continue and accumulate until they burst forth in the often uncontrollable upheavals of revolution and reform. Even in normal conditions, much of what is called government "interference" in business may be traced back to the unwillingness or inability of the private economy to recognize and safeguard against the risks that affect large groups of people.

4-6 REVIEW QUESTIONS

1. Why bother to pose the three questions listed in the chapter pertaining to product acceptance?

2. Clearly distinguish between the two types of product demand surveys.

3. Distinguish among seasonal variations, business cycles, and long-term trends.

4. What is the objective of forecasting, and what benefits can be attained from achieving the objective?

5. What is meant by the terms "series" and "index numbers"?

6. How is a subjective method different from an objective method of forecasting? Of which type are each of the forecasting techniques that are rated in Perspective 4B? What do the ratings indicate about the preference for objective or subjective forecasting methods?

7. How are specific risks different than general business risks? Can these risks be completely eliminated?

8. Insurance should be the last resort, not the first, in meeting business risk. Comment.

4-7 TOPICS FOR DISCUSSION

1. Several risk considerations influenced by population changes were presented in Perspective 4A. What additional implications can be drawn from the data presented? For example, what buying habits and disposable income levels are associated with the different age groups? What industries could benefit from such observations?

2. In the case of the Novelty Game Company (see Topic 6, case 4A, below), develop how you would go about determining whether there is a demand for this product.

3. How can a producer of a final product, depending upon several subassemblies of component parts, guard against the risks in connection with patent infringement, materials, defective workmanship, labor troubles, and changing costs of production due to technological change?

4. List, discuss, and tell how the automatic stabilizers which have been developed by private enterprise and government in the last 25 years make economic recessions less severe.

5. What is the answer to this question: Why bother about risks when we can get insurance to cover any contingency that arises?

6. Case 4A: *The Novelty Game Company*
   You may recall the amazing profit history of Mah Jong, Monopoly, and Scrabble. The word game with lettered tiles, for example, was invented during the depression of the 1930s, but lay dormant for want of an interested manufacturer. Some 15 years later a friend took it over, named it Scrabble, and began production with parts assembled in the living room of his home. In 1948, the first full year of operation, some 2,251 games were sold and the producer lost $450. The game was still losing in 1952, but suddenly in the last quarter of the year sales jumped sharply and the business expanded to an abandoned schoolhouse and then to a converted woodworking shop. By 1953 some 35 employees were turning out 6,000 sets a week. Promotion was largely by word of mouth, but retailers did a little advertising. Finally, with sales booming, an established New York game-manufacturing firm took over. The game became a fabulous success.
   In the 1972 presidential campaign several games dealing with politics came on the market. The hope was to cash in on the interest, excitement, and magnitude of popular participation in the election contest. One game, introduced by a small independent company formed for the purpose, The Novelty Game Company, consisted of a lithographed playing board, six candidate "men" (plastic player tabs), a deck of instruction cards, and a spinner, in an attractive package, which retailed at $3.50. The game was instructive and interesting. The price seemed reasonable. Sales, however, proved very disappointing. The company faced failure. No other single political game arose to repeat the great successes in the game field.

Questions

1. Bearing in mind the history of Scrabble, as well as the idea of a political game in the 1972 campaign, what three factors do you think accounted for the Novelty Game Company's failure?

2. What would you suggest the companies do with their games? Explain.

7. Case 4B: *Million Air Conditioning Corp*

Although the Million Air Conditioning Corp. is not among the top leaders of commercial and home air-conditioning manufacturers, it has successfully developed and patented a home room air conditioner which combines a cooling unit for summer use with an electrical heating element that can be used to heat individual rooms. While not adequate for full winter heating, the heater serves very well on cold days in the spring and fall months of the year. The company has heretofore confined its marketing area to regions (such as the border area between the Northern and Southern states) where the appeal of a combined cooling–heating unit seems to have the greatest response. The result has been to give the company a fairly lucrative regional market free from the price competition of leading brands of air-conditioning manufacturers who specialize in cooling units exclusively. They sell cooling units at a lower price in national markets, but they cannot sell a cooling–heating unit at a lower price than Million offers in the regional market. By confining itself to a regional market, however, Million has always had excess plant capacity relative to volume and has been searching for a new channel for expansion.

Currently, Million is studying three propositions: (1) expanding sales by more extensive advertising and increased dealerships in other regional markets; (2) using its present business as a base for developing and marketing a regular cool air conditioner in competition for national markets; or (3) acquiring by merger the patents, fixtures, dies, and other assets (including a 10-year lease of a small manufacturing plant with 6 years to go) of the Humidaire Company, which lacks enterprising management and financing to make a go of two good products—a portable electric dehumidifier appliance and a small nonelectric humidifier unit sold to furnace manufacturers and to consumers as an accessory. (Assume that the Humidaire Company can be acquired at a reasonable figure through an exchange of Million's common stock; that Million's excess capacity and the leased premises can be fully utilized; and that the carry-forward tax loss is sufficient to increase Million's reserves until the new acquisition reaches a break-even point in increased sales—the actual figures are not essential to discussion of the principles involved.)

Questions

1. Discuss the risks involved in Million Air's three propositions, and which do you conclude is the most promising for Million to undertake?

8. Case 4C: *A Miniature Recorder*

Jo Burban, an electronic engineer, developed a miniature recording device in her home workshop. She conceives the instrument to be useful for dictation, in business and library research, recording conversations, and similar uses. Her finished pilot model is partly an assembly job of standard components available in the open market and partly her own work and improvements. It is her idea to set up her own enterprise to produce and market the instrument.

Questions

1. Outline at least six steps Burban should take *before* commencing the enterprise or seeking finances for it.

2. If you were Burban, how would you go about launching this enterprise?

9. Case 4D: *A Doctor's Light*

Bostwicker developed a fountain-pen light with a swivel head and spot bulb, and patented it. He gave it a catchy name identifying its use directly with doctors. The anodized colored aluminum case is the size and shape of a large cigar, about ¾ inch thick, 5½ to 6 inches long, weighs about 5 ounces, holds batteries in the barrel, and has an outside fountain-pen clip. No careful calculation of production cost has been made, but Bostwicker estimates the light could sell for about $13.50. He seeks equity financing to produce and market the light.

Questions

1. What do you see in these facts to counsel caution before you would invest in an enterprise to produce and market this light?

5

FINANCING AND BUDGETING

Without sufficient financing a business cannot get started, and without adequate budgeting a business, once started, cannot reach its full potential. Money is a universal lubricant which keeps a business enterprise dynamic. The business must have a sound capital structure to support its growth. It also needs a sound profit plan (budget) to guide and control its day-to-day operations. Thus a healthy industrial organization is one which has access to sufficient capital and the capability of controlling its cash flow; both attributes require careful planning. What are the sources of money capital, and how are they tapped? What special characteristics of the company must be considered in financing operations? Why should the time value of money be considered? How much working capital is needed and how can its availability be assured? What alternative types of budgets may be selected to best serve the company's needs. What information is needed to construct a budget? These questions are addressed in this chapter which concentrates on money matters.

5 FINANCING AND BUDGETING

5-1 KINDS OF CAPITAL

In common usage the word "capital" is the single term used to cover the land, buildings, machinery, tools, and materials of a productive enterprise. Technically, whereas land is capital, it is distinguished from the other means of production because they are reproducible and land is not. Rarely does the businessman make this distinction. In the word capital, he lumps together all the elements he will need to start an enterprise, including the land required. He also takes another step in his thinking which results in a different use of the word capital. He thinks of capital most often in money terms. Promoting a new enterprise is very largely a financial operation. Since money and credit are the chief means for acquiring the instruments of production, the word capital has this financial aspect. And this is the way we shall use it here. Applied to industrial financing, capital means the cash money and credit needed to start and to operate an enterprise.[1]

Financial specialization recognizes different classifications of capital, depending on such features as the use that is to be made of it, the time element involved, and the sources and methods of raising it. These forms of capital are best understood when we examine the capital requirements of an ordinary industrial enterprise. In this way, too, the connection will be clear between money capital and productive capital, the tangible instruments of production. If an industrial enterprise is to be started from the ground up, so to speak, it will need land and buildings, machinery, tools, and equipment. Assets of this kind, intended to be used over and over again in production for a long period of time, are commonly called *fixed capital;* and the money and credit required to pay for such assets take the same name. An enterprise also requires funds to cover its operations—to maintain the plant, to purchase materials and supplies, to pay salaries and wages, to cover storage, transportation, and shipping services, for advertising, and to tide over the enterprise during the time lag between the sale of its products and payment for them. These are current operations, and the funds to cover them are commonly called *working capital.*

5-2 SOURCES OF CAPITAL FUNDS

To finance modern industry, large-scale savings are necessary. By large-scale savings we commonly mean money savings arising in a variety of ways

---

[1]The many technical meanings of the word "capital" are best understood when studied in the context in which they are used. In its broadest meaning capital is synonymous with wealth, all useful articles owned by man. Land and its resources are often called *natural capital* to distinguish them from produced or *artificial capital* such as buildings, machinery, tools, materials. In corporate finance, *paid-in capital* means the amount paid for that percentage of the stock which has been sold. In accounting, *capital net value* is the total assets of an enterprise less the debts owed to others (the equity capital). In other words, the meaning of the word capital depends on its technical usage and upon the context.

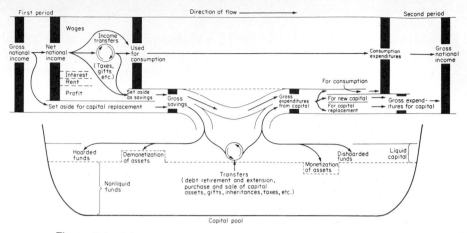

Figure 5-1 Capital pool.

throughout the economy. Individuals, rich and poor, save. The rich save directly, largely because their income exceeds even the large spending they do for themselves and their families. They also save indirectly as when they pay life insurance premiums, purchase annuities, establish funds, etc. From the wealthy to the lower income groups there are gradations in the amount of direct savings like savings bank accounts, building and loan shares, savings bonds; and much of the steady savings is done through such indirect means as life insurance. The very poor cannot save for themselves at all; their income is all used up in living expenses. But the spendings of all individuals from the very poor to the wealthiest contribute indirectly to the stream of savings through the prices paid for goods that work back through the entire economic process, providing business profits and reserves that are invested. It is through this element that a second large group of savings —business savings—take place. Governments make up the third large group of savers. There are about 100,000 government units in the United States —Federal, state, and local. When any one of these units collects more in taxes than is used for operating expenses and uses the balance for public works, the part so used represents government savings.[2] The savings take the form of public works such as highways, river and harbor construction, sewage-disposal and water systems, transportation facilities, public buildings, and the assets in a growing list of government enterprises. In addition, government purchases many billions of dollars' worth of goods and services, a portion of which finds its way into business capital savings for future

[2]Many distinctions in other respects are drawn between government and business savings. The chief one, perhaps, is that business savings are said to be "productive" in the sense that money is spent for goods to be used in further production like factory buildings, machines, and tools; government spendings are declared to be "unproductive" because they go into school buildings, roads, bridges, and other public works, which yield no direct increase in material goods. Although this distinction has been shown repeatedly to be invalid, it still persists in common opinions debating the merits of private enterprise vs. government undertakings. The word "savings" is used here in the economic technical sense and differs somewhat from the lay idea of money deposited by an individual in a bank savings account.

investment. So far as the stream of savings and investments is concerned, government savings perform very much the same function as do business savings. Each takes money from the people's incomes—the one in the form of prices for goods and the other in taxes—and spends part of it for capital goods. All these savings—of individuals, business enterprises, institutions, governments, and others—constitute the capital pool of the national economy (see Fig. 5-1 for a chart showing this flow of funds).

Perspective 5A   INFLATION AND THE COST OF CAPITAL

Capital expenditure for new plants and equipment is an indication of the industrial health of a nation. Investments of capital are needed to create new jobs, raise production efficiency, and improve the quality of the environment and working life. A worldwide shortage of capital was predicted in the mid 1970s. This "capital crunch" failed to materialize, but the rate of return expected from new investments has gone up due to the cost of acquiring capital. An explanation for this condition is given below.

Some businessmen feel that a poor atmosphere for capital spending has become a deeply ingrained characteristic of the mixed economies of the West that rely on the private sector for growth of capital stock, while attempting to satisfy competing claims for rising standards of living through government policies.

The major new product of these mixed economies for the 1970s is, of course, a high rate of inflation and a general expectation that the inflation rate will stay high, at least by the standards of the past, far down the pike. . . .

The negative effect of inflation on capital spending decisions shows up most clearly in its impact on the formulas that companies use to decide on whether to go ahead with new capital investment projects. These formulas almost always involve a threshold rate of return that an investment project must meet if it is to be undertaken. For most companies around the world, that rate is higher now than it was in less inflationary days.*

*SOURCE: "Where is the Capital Spending Boom?", *Business Week,* September 13, 1976.

COMMENT   Inflation decreases the value of investments by reducing the worth of goods they could buy if not spent immediately. Investments are consequently expected to yield returns that both maintain the buying power of invested sums and add to them. Higher inflation rates thus ration capital to those investments that promise the higher returns.

5-3   THE MONEY MARKET

The financial requirements of modern industrial enterprise are so great that a large network is needed to mobilize the money and credit resources needed. The money market does this and is therefore one of the chief reservoirs of capital. What do we mean by the commercial money market? If a definition were attempted, it might read something like this: In its broadest sense, the money market is the total of individuals, firms, institutions, and the process by which money and credit are collected, accumulated, and administered for the financing of economic activities. The market is not a single place, or channel, or institution, but a network of many markets; they are distinguished by the areas they cover, by the different types of loans they make, and by the variety of borrowers they serve.

5-3.1 Long-Term Capital

For long-term capital, industrial borrowers may tap several channels. Large investment banking houses serve large industrial enterprises by undertaking to underwrite and to market stock and bond issues. Insurance companies have lately become an important source for long-term capital funds by taking the security issues of industrial enterprises (particularly utilities) by direct, private placement. Institutional and endowment trust funds may also supply capital by direct placement, but usually they do their investing by purchasing securities distributed by other agencies. In the past, commercial banks dealt mainly in short-term loans, but financial changes in the last 20 years have induced them to seek outlets for their funds in fixed-term investments for as long as 10 to 15 years' maturity. Rarely do wealthy individuals make independent capital loans in competition with these agencies. The sums wanted by the borrowers are too large for any but institutions of great resources and wide connections. But the wealthy do participate in the process indirectly by purchasing stocks and bonds distributed by large corporations and financing agencies.

5-3.2 Intermediate and Short-Term Loans

Whereas intermediate and short-term loans represent different types of financing, both are virtually serviced by the same types of lending agencies. Short-term loans may range from 30 days up to 2 years, and intermediate-term loans to 5 years, depending upon the character and circumstances of the loan. This is the field occupied by the regular commercial banks which in local communities throughout the nation have traditionally served the current credit needs of business enterprises. Some changes have been taking place in this field in recent years. For one thing, the very large industrial companies increasingly tend to finance themselves in matters of intermediate- and short-term credit. On the other hand, the need for bank liquidity, the high lending standards, and the riskiness of small business tend to make commercial banks reluctant to serve the credit needs of small enterprises, unless Federal lending agencies participate with the banks. To a considerable extent also the banks have enlarged their role as a financial service agency in the community in handling the flow of funds. Thus they have increased their activities in making personal, automobile, appliance, and home-improvement loans to individuals and business. Where gaps in financing operations have been left open by the commercial banks, various other lending agencies have become active. These include chattel-mortage companies, miscellaneous finance and investment companies, and commercial factors.

The chattel-mortgage, finance, and investment companies operate in a variety of forms. The rates they charge are likely to be higher, the conditions put upon the borrower more burdensome, and the resultant cost of the loan much higher than regular bank credit. Commercial factors, frequently referred to as the "middlemen of credit," have come to occupy an important place in industrial and business finance. Originally the commercial factor performed merchandising functions for the manufacturer, and in the process realized financial credits which were made available to producers. In time the factor came to deal extensively in financing operations through the purchase of accounts receivable, installment contracts, promissory notes, and other commercial paper based on transactions, inventories, and warehouse stocks. Many of them specialize in aiding struggling enterpreneurs as well as established firms hard pressed for working capital. In most cases they operate in areas where banks are reluctant to enter, and they charge higher rates for accepting the unusual risks. With the aid of a factor a manufacturer can turn orders into cash without waiting weeks and months for a return to be realized. This is an important but costly and sometimes unreliable service to small and medium-sized enterprises whose liquid working capital is often low in proportion to the need to liquidate debts, carry on operations, acquire equipment, or expand.

5-3.3 Trade Credits

Not mentioned as yet, because it is not exactly a lending agency, is the trade credit. This is the mainstay of intermediate and short-term financing, particularly for the small enterprise. It covers not only commodities and supplies, but also machinery, fixtures, equipment, and other items of longer term financing. The small manufacturer simply finds himself partly financed, at least for materials and small equipment, through his regular purchases on credit. A new twist on the trade credit may emerge from the practice by which a large corporation sometimes gives financial aid to some among its cluster of smaller satellite suppliers. In a somewhat similar manner, large buyers such as mail-order houses and department stores sometimes aid those whose production they buy entirely or in substantial part. A new form of financing relationship may grow out of these practices, just as factor financing grew out of merchandising functions originally performed by factors for manufacturers. In boom times and even in times of normal economic activity, trade credits play an important part in short-term financing, but in times of recession, the method tends to fail. At all times, other disadvantages operate to limit its effectiveness as a desirable source of financing.

5-3.4 Credit Instruments

Credit instruments are the legal forms through which loans are made. They differ with the type of loan, the length of time it is to run, the use to which the funds are to be put, and the type of borrower. They differ also by the way in which they affect third parties. Only the more general types of credit instruments can be touched upon here because each case is more or less individual and must be studied specifically.

Long-term credit, if required for equity or fixed capital, usually takes the form of securities—*stocks or bonds* of the borrowing company which ultimately come to be held by individuals, banks, investment trusts, and other investors. Commercial credit for other than fixed capital of permanent nature is usually represented by *promissory notes,* backed by collateral of various kinds, and almost always negotiable. In some cases the collateral takes the form of mortgages against the firm's real estate, machinery, equipment, and other chattels. In other cases the collateral may be securities owned by the firm. Loans may be made, of course, on straight promissory notes, without collateral, but in that case the lender often requires two or more comakers or guarantors.

Short-term credits or commercial loans intended to finance single transactions or a group of transactions that are to be completed in short time are ordinarily evidenced by *promissory notes, drafts, bills of exchange,* or *trade acceptances.* These may or may not be supported by *bills of lading, warehouse receipts,* or *chattel-mortgage contracts* as against materials involved in transactions, and other claims upon property. When *accounts receivable* are accepted as collateral to a loan, or taken over outright by a lending agency, the usual form is to *assign* such accounts to the lender. If the firm markets its products direct to the consumer and takes *installment notes* or *conditional sales contracts,* these may be grouped in series and assigned either outright or as collateral for a circulating capital loan from many lending agencies.

Perspective 5B   VENTURE CAPITAL

The rewards of owning a business lure thousands of people each year to try it. Putting dreams to practice is a severe test of personal confidence and capabilities. The attempt is usually made with an inspiring idea but limited management experience and a dedication to long working hours but limited finances. The risk of failure is large.

A struggling business often needs an infusion of new capital to survive or to "turn the corner" toward success. Private investors may supply the funds through *venture capital*—money to invest in business enterprises in which there is a significant danger of loss as well as a chance for large profits. The venture investor is willing to assume a relatively high degree of risk, providing the prospects are good for high returns on the invested capital. "How high is high?" is answered by Dr. Paul Swadener.

With mortgages at 8½ to 9 per cent, with medium- to high-grade bonds at 8 per cent, with 9 to 12 per cent inflation, with price-to-earnings multiples of 9 to 11, and listed stock yields at 12 to 14 per cent, would 20 to 25 per cent be unreasonably high for undertaking heavy risk?

What does a 25 per cent return convert to in terms of cash? If the investment in the venture is $75,000, a lump sum redemption of the investment at the end of 5 years would be $286,000

$(1.25^5 = 3.8147)$, which is a multiple of nearly 4 to 1. A return of 20 per cent has a 5-year multiple of 2.986 as a lump sum. The venture entrepreneur must be prepared to meet such demands.*

*SOURCE: "Attracting Venture Capital," *Oregon Business Review,* Spring, 1977.

COMMENT Venture investors are normally not interested in being permanently involved with a business firm. They seek high growth potential, and when that potential is attained, they want to sell out at the peak and invest their profits in other promising ventures. They are shrewd judges of venture risk returns, or they would not have the venture capital to invest.

5-4 PLANNING THE FINANCIAL STRUCTURE

Few people will deny that enterprises may still be started on a shoestring and may be developed into large-scale companies. This is less possible in the old-line industries where established firms offer strong competition than it is in the newer industrial fields where demand and supply forces are not fully established. The automotive, airplane, and home-appliance industries are examples of established fields, while plastics, light metals, and electronics are examples of the new fields. The problem of starting a new enterprise is always much more difficult than that of expansion for existing firms. But whether the problem is one of financing a new venture or the expansion of an existing enterprise, modern conditions make financial planning a necessity.

5-4.1 Financing the Noncorporate Enterprise

In the case of the single proprietorship and the partnership, the initial capital comes from the individuals directly interested and possibly through the loans and investments that their friends are willing to make in the business. In addition to cash, these individuals may contribute the actual land, buildings, machinery, and materials needed to make up the productive capital of the business. We shall see later how these enterprises can augment their initial capital with working capital from various sources, but at the start they are largely dependent upon their own resources. Launching a new enterprise through cash and property contributions of individuals personally interested in the venture is one of the oldest forms of business promotion, and it continues to be an important method of financing even today.

5-4.2 Corporate Capitalization

It is the corporate enterprise that is most concerned with the problems of formal capitalization. At the time of incorporation the promoters or prospective managers must make the policy decision as to the total amount at which the enterprise is to be capitalized and what forms the capital structure should take. The chief factors in this decision are the nature and size of the business. From careful analysis of the elements in these factors, analysis of the product, market studies, and a general business forecast of the prospects of the enterprise, it should be possible to make a rough estimate of the fixed capital required. If real estate, buildings, equipment, and other tangible property are contributed by the organizers, the cost or value of such assets will be part of the total. To this sum there will have to be added an amount sufficient to cover necessary promotion, engineering, and developmental expenses. It is essential to have a fund of working capital sufficient in the beginning to carry the firm through the production cycle to the point when substantial and sustained returns from sales may be expected. An estimate of probable earnings may be taken into account in arriving at the total capital figure. In some few cases the capitalization may take account of patents, secret processes, trademarks, and other intangible items, but in the untried enterprise there is little basis for anything other than nominal values on these items. Current legal requirements, state and Federal, will have to be considered because they affect franchise fees, taxation, security sales, and other affairs of the company. Initial capitalization might also be planned with an eye toward future expansion and toward the problem of future marketing of corporate securities, but the danger of over- and undercapitalization should be carefully weighed. The grand total will be the amount of *authorized capital stock* of the enterprise to be used in applying for the corporate charter.

CLASSIFICATION OF STOCK   To complete the basic financial structure, the authorized stock will have to be classified to define the relations of stockholders to the enterprise, to fix the status of the corporation with creditors and the public, and to provide the proper securities and financial base if the company intends to seek funds from the money market.

COMMON STOCK   All the authorized capital stock of a company may be issued in a single classification, *common stock.* No special rights or privileges are attached to common stock. It bears the full risk of the enterprise, its successes and failures. Common-stock holders are in law the real owners of the enterprise, and they are entitled to the net assets of the business. They usually exercise control over the business through the voting power of their stock.

PREFERRED STOCK   Preferred stock is the second of the main classes into which authorized capital stock may be divided. The chief reason for it is to offer inducements to attract investors. The stock may be preferred as to dividends and assets; it may be convertible into common stock on attractive terms; a sinking fund may be set up to guarantee safety of the investment; it may have other rights. On the other hand, it may have limited or no voting power since its other privileges protect it from the risks which common shareholders assume. In each case of preference or limitation, some object is sought which will be of value in the financial administration of the company.

No arbitrary rules can be set for division between common and preferred stock. This is a matter of judgment in each case, in answer to such questions as: How and by whom is the enterprise to be controlled? How much capital will have to be sought from outsiders? To what extent is it wise to burden the company with obligations to pay fixed dividends? What legal and tax considerations are involved? How will the sale of securities be affected by different classes of stock? What financial structure is most assuring to creditors? What is the most desirable basis for the division of earnings and of assets of the company on dissolution? These are a few of the questions entering into the decision when stock is to be set up in classes. After the basic decision is made for classifying stock into common and preferred, similar calculations are made if either stock is further classified, as A and B common or first preferred, second preferred, and other subclasses.

5-4.3 Bond Issues (Company Indebtedness)

When the earnings record is good, assets are substantial, and prospects of expansion favorable, a good method of raising needed capital is to borrow it on bond issues. In essence, bond issues are company promises to repay the loan at stated periods and are backed by a mortgage on part or all of the company's property. They take the form of *bonds, debentures, certificates,* or *notes of issue* based upon a *trust agreement* or *indenture* which contains all the rights and obligations between the company-borrower, the bankers who are to market the issue, the prospective bondholders (represented by the trustee), and the general public (represented by governmental agencies). The essential relationship between the company and the bondholders is that of debtor–creditor. While this means that bondholders have no ownership interest in the company, it also implies that their rights are superior to those of the stockholders until the bonds are retired. A company contemplating a bond issue should make careful studies not only of the varieties of bonds which may be issued, but of the wisdom of floating a bond issue at all. Whereas borrowing for industrial expansion has many advantages, it also carries with it the great risk of loss. Even a temporary failure to pay interest charges or amortization may throw the company into receivership. Money raised through the sale of capital stock is free from this risk.

5-4.4 Working Capital

In the new enterprise, working capital must come largely through the initial financing. After the firm is in operation, other sources will be open to it. Chief of these sources, of course, is the current operations of the enterprise. These operations should be sufficient to produce all the financing required to meet the routine current needs of the enterprise. They may, in addition, yield sufficiently in excess earnings to provide for special reserves and for expansion of the business.

In common usage, *working capital* is the total of current assets consisting of merchandise and materials, cash, accounts receivable, and other liquid assets, less current liabilities. Proper ratios should be sought between current assets and current liabilities and between current assets and capital assets. What these ratios should be depends upon the type of enterprise and other factors; no fixed rule can be applied to all concerns. In general, working capital should be sufficient to meet current liabilities and to enable the company to take immediate advantage of opportunities that present themselves from time to time.

A budget plan is the best device to develop and control the flow of working capital. It sizes up the prospects of the business in advance, proportions the various parts of the enterprise in proper relation, sets the timing of income in relation to expenditures, prepares for contingencies, and keeps a reserve in readiness for unexpected opportunities. A soundly operated enterprise with a realistic budgeting plan will also have far less difficulty when seeking to augment working capital through trade credits and other short-term financing.

5-4.5   Reserves and Expansion

Sound financial administration requires the setting up of reserves for working capital, to liquidate debts, to cover credit losses, against contingencies such as fire, theft, and unexpected liabilities, for depreciation and obsolescence, to offset price fluctuations on inventories, for taxes, to provide for improvements and expansion, and for related purposes. Reserve items may be earmarked cash or property or unidentified as an overall item reflected in the company's balance sheet.

Ordinarily a going concern will accumulate some capital for expansion through operations. Where the competitive price structure allows and in state-regulated enterprises like utilities, the unit price of the product or service may contain a fractional sum to be set aside in the form of reserves for expansion of the business. Closely analogous to financing expansion through a specific part of the price are the common methods of "plowing back the earnings" and depreciation reserves. Taxes, however, have become so burdensome that there is a real problem today in finding the money for growth. In any event, the firm which operates under a complete budget system is in the best position to use these methods to the best advantage.

When greater amounts of capital are needed for expansion, the firm may seek equity capital through sales of stock to employees, customers, sometimes to creditors, and the general public. Stock rights issued to existing shareholders often result in increased equity capital for the company. In recent years sources of expansion funds may be found in community or industrial foundations and investment-development companies, but ordinarily these involve special situations and inducements.

One of the chief methods of expansion, used extensively in the last half century, is to combine two or more enterprises. So far as financing is concerned, combination is a method of raising equity capital and often of strengthening the working capital of the surviving enterprise. It should not be attempted lightly or without a thorough study of the many problems involved. Is the physical property of the concern to be merged in good condition? How long has the company been in business? What advantages or disadvantages will be inherited from its position in the industry and trade? What are its financial history and record of earnings? Are the earnings of the combination likely to exceed those of the separate concerns? Will they justify the full costs of acquisition? Will the combination gain the services of the key persons in charge of the separate concerns and be able to eliminate the incompetents?

These and many other questions must be answered with great care to be certain that the weight of advantage lies with the new company over the former separate concerns. Although a caution sign should always be raised when a successful, going concern considers a merger with another concern in difficulties, business history abounds with just such combinations. Where the company in difficulties has particular weaknesses, such as insufficient working capital, poor management, inadequate sales personnel, or poor distribution network, but possesses a distinctive product, established place in the trade, good physical location and properties, favorable tax features, or other special advantages, merger may be desirable with a successful company able to supply the missing links or to profit by the special advantages. In particular, tax-loss carry forward has come to play a prominent part in many recent mergers. On the other hand, expansion generated by promoters who saw profits in the manipulation of companies rather than in running a sound industrial enterprise has led to great abuses in the past and should be avoided. At all events, the lure of great profits and the dazzle of empire building through expansion should not be permitted to obscure the cold realities of risks which often result when a new concern is fashioned with the patchwork of older companies.

5-4.6 The Special Problem of Small Business

Small enterprise is an important element in the entire economy. Numerically it is the largest sector of the economy, but if measured by employment provided and value of products in the manufacturing field, it is overshadowed by medium- and large-scale enterprises. But these are not the only considerations. Small enterprise provides a source of specialized products and services, a source of supplies and parts for large enterprise, a market for goods and services, a healthy element of competition in the economy, a source of employment for many persons, and a field for individual opportunities and experimentation in business ventures ("seed enterprises") which we associate with dynamic free enterprise.

Because of small size, limited capital and earnings, lack of personnel for specialized management, and intense competition, the small enterprise has difficulty in getting equity capital at the start and in financing itself later through operations. For his initial capital the small enterpriser often has to rely upon his own resources and upon the willingness of friends, relatives, and potential business associates to invest in the business. Until he becomes securely established, the long-term capital market is usually closed to him because his needs are too small and the risk is too great.

Some community banks make short-term loans to small enterprise, but the aid is limited and rarely covers capital expansion. The trade credit is an important mainstay of small-business financing, but it is costly, limited in amount, and not sufficiently reliable. In many cases funds have to be sought from commercial factors, mortgage and finance companies, and personal-loan agencies. For each satisfactory relationship with these sources, there are many other small business concerns which have had painful experiences with this type of financing. Many such loans carry hidden "service" charges, authorize lenders to hold back funds, tie up all available collateral, and allow lenders to interfere in the management of the enterprise. The net effect of all these financing difficulties is to keep the small enterpriser under constant strain and to raise his cost of production so that he is at a competitive disadvantage.

But in many cases the small enterpriser himself is partly at fault for his plight. Small enterprises frequently suffer from bad management, loose accounting practices, too liberal granting of credit to their customers, excessive withdrawals of cash by owners, and premature unwise expansion. These conditions make small enterprises high risks, and lenders who share in those risks seek compensation through high rates and protective devices. In the case of reliable lenders, however, the management aid and supervision they render is a real service to the small business enterprise.

Perspective 5C FINANCIAL LEVERAGE

A measure of the success of a business is its rate of return (RR) or return on investment (ROI)—the percentage of the amount invested in the business (equity) that is earned each year as a return to the owners. A firm which has equity capital of $100,000 and net returns of $10,000 has a rate of return of 10 percent.

The ratio of total debt to total assets is called the *leverage factor*. A firm having assets of $150,000 and a debt of $50,000 has a leverage factor of $50,000/$150,000 = 0.33. One way to increase the rate of return for a successful business is to increase the size of operations by utilizing a greater proportion of borrowed money.

The effects of different leverage factors on the percentage return on equity when earnings vary as a function of economic conditions are portrayed in the table on page 116. Three states of financial leverage are shown for total assets of $1 million with equity proportions of $1 million, $600,000, and $300,000. When all the assets are composed of equity holdings, the after-tax rate of return on investment is equal to half the before-tax rate of return, with the effective income-tax rate at 50 percent. Under

Financial Leverage (In $1,000 Units)	Leverage Factor = 0: Equity = 1000 and Debt = 0			Leverage Factor = 0.4: Equity = 600 and Debt = 400			Leverage Factor = 0.7: Equity = 300 and Debt = 700		
Economic Conditions	Low Sales	Average Sales	High Sales	Low Sales	Average Sales	High Sales	Low Sales	Average Sales	High Sales
RR before taxes and interest	2%	8%	14%	2%	8%	14%	2%	8%	14%
Net earnings before interest and taxes	$20	$80	$140	$20	$80	$140	$20	$80	$140
Interest on debt at i = 8%	0	0	0	$32	$32	$32	$56	$56	$56
Taxable income	$20	$80	$140	–$12	$48	$108	–$36	$24	$84
Taxes at effective tax rate of 50%	$10	$40	$70	0	$24	$54	0	$12	$42
Available for equity returns	$10	$40	$70	–$12	$24	$54	–$36	$12	$42
Percentage return on equity	1%	4%	7%	–2%	4%	9%	–12%	4%	14%

SOURCE: James L. Riggs, *Engineering Economics,* New York: McGraw-Hill Book Co., 1977.

unfavorable conditions causing low sales, the percentage return on equity drops as the leverage factor increases. The trend is reversed when favorable business conditions allow high sales. At average sales, when the before-tax return equals the interest rate for borrowed funds, all three leverage positions result in the same after-tax return on equity investments. In general, whenever favorable business conditions allow a before-tax rate of return greater than the interest rate on debt, the higher the leverage factor, the higher the after-tax percentage return on equity.*

COMMENT   A highly leveraged firm produces very attractive return-on-investment figures during periods of prosperity, yet it can quickly become a target for management criticism or a victim of bankruptcy during a recession. Lenders are often a determinant of the degree of leverage a firm can attain. The credit standing of a borrower is reduced by excessive borrowing, and lenders attempt to protect their loans by limiting the leverage to certain norms. The norms vary among industries with respect to the stability of incomes, and within an industry according to the confidence lenders have in a firm's management; service industries and public utilities typically have very high debt-to-asset ratios (0.6+) and manufacturing has relatively low leverage (0.3 to 0.4). A thriving business can expand faster with the infusion of debt funding, and a sick business may recover more rapidly with the aid of borrowed funds, but a firm weathers brief spells of adversity better when it is less leveraged and not obligated to pay off large debts.

5-5   CAPITAL ALLOCATION

Assuming investment capital is available, there is almost always a choice of ways to invest it. The two most important criteria of worthiness are the risks involved and the pattern of cash flow. An evaluation of risk results from questioning the likelihood of expected returns. Many appropriate questions were posed in the previous chapter. When it is possible to measure probabilities of success for alternative investments, the preferred solution can be obtained quantitatively. In the more common case, where alternatives are risk-rated intuitively, a subjective choice is made between high-return–high-risk and lower-return–lower-risk alternatives.

The time-scaled pattern of receipts and disbursements should always be quantitatively evaluated. The time value of money is synonomous with interest. Interest, or the cost of borrowing capital, has been an accepted aspect of capital management for centuries. In the last 30 years much attention has been given to interest rates as yardsticks of investment quality.

Receiving a dollar today is preferable to receiving it a year from now. Part of the reason is that inflation may detract from the buying power of the delayed dollar, but the more germane consideration is that the dollar received today can be put to work in the interim period. It can earn interest during the year it works before the delayed dollar is received. The amount it earns divided by the amount invested for the year is the interest rate received. This interest rate then becomes a standard by which to measure the attractiveness of the investment.

There are several ways to utilize interest rates in the evaluation of proposed investments—payout period, present worth, equivalent annual cost, capitalized cost, rate of return—but only rate of return will be described here. The rate of return is a percentage figure, equivalent to an interest rate, which indicates the return earned over the life of an investment. It is calculated from the cash-flow stream associated with the investment. The major influence of time is illustrated by Figure 5-2. Three possible cash-flow patterns are shown. All three represent returns over a period of 10 years received from an initial investment of $1,000 made at time 0. Disregarding taxes, the three patterns all have the *same* rate of return. The obvious conclusion to be drawn from studying the cash-flow

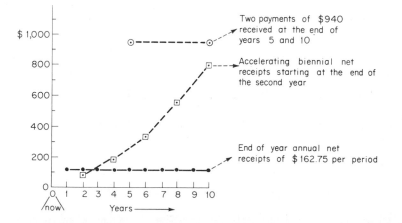

Figure 5-2 Three net cash-flow streams equivalent to a rate of return of 10 per cent on an investment of $1,000 made now and held for 10 years.

streams is that more rapid recovery of investment capital raises the rate of return.

After the rate of return has been computed by discounting the cash flow of each alternative, the final step is to decide which, if any, of the alternative investments should be made. An investment promising a rate of return less than could be earned from investing in conservative bonds would hardly be attractive. Each enterprise has its own minimum acceptable rate of return, larger for high-risk endeavors and lower for conservative operations such as public utilities. Proposals failing to meet the minimum are discarded unless there are very significant intangible benefits involved. The calculated rates of return from several alternatives competing for the same investment funds constitute a preference rating when the alternatives are otherwise equivalent.

5-6   THE BUDGET

It is the long-term responsibility of management to so use investment that it will yield the largest possible profit or return, and it is the function of budgeting to plan that profit picture. Perhaps this planning can be understood better if we first examine the components of profit. Figure 5-3 shows in chart form the basic elements involved in the return on investment. Starting with the upper right-hand corner of the chart we find that working capital is made up of inventories, accounts receivable, and cash. These plus

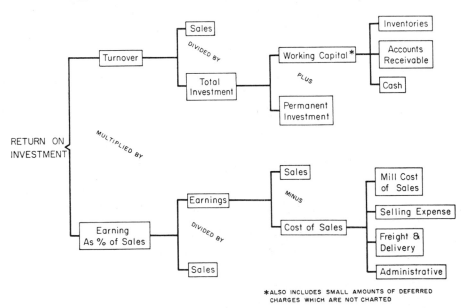

THE Du PONT COMPANY
RELATIONSHIP OF FACTORS AFFECTING RETURN ON INVESTMENT

*ALSO INCLUDES SMALL AMOUNTS OF DEFERRED CHARGES WHICH ARE NOT CHARTED

Figure 5-3   *Note:* Arithmetic calculations progress from right to left. (SOURCE: Alfred M. Watson, *Operations Research and Financial Planning,* New York: American Management Association, Financial Management Series, no. 102.)

the permanent investment in assets such as land, building, and equipment comprise the total investment of the company. We determine how hard this investment is being worked by comparing it with total sales for the designated period of, let us say, one year. If sales were $400,000 and investment $100,000 the turnover of investment for the year would be four or, in other words, it would have been used four times in the year. The more times we are able to use a dollar of investment, the more profit we should receive from it.

The next question, then, is how much did each turnover yield? The lower part of the chart in Figure 5-3 shows the method for calculating earnings in terms of the percentage of the sales dollar. Note that the costs of sales are listed in the lower right-hand corner. These comprise the cost of making the product and getting it to the customers and must be deducted from total income from sales to determine earnings on sales. If we find that earnings on sales is 2½ per cent, then with a turnover of four the return on investment would be 10 per cent.

PLANNING THROUGH THE BUDGET   The task in budgeting is to plan production in accordance with sales estimates and a minimum cost. Recent trends toward decentralization of authority and responsibility, discussed in preceding chapters, are especially applicable in budget planning. Under this system only a relatively small finance staff is maintained at headquarters under the supervision of a controller. He may personally exercise the leadership in budget planning or he may delegate this to a budget director. Each operating division or plant is provided with its own staffs in accounting, industrial engineering, industrial relations, and in some instances product development, where the company is organized on a product basis. The plant or division manager, with the aid of his staffs and material supplied by headquarters, is held responsible for reasonable return on investment, for budgeting, and for the efficient operation of his plant. This is in contrast with some centralized situations, although certainly not all, where the profit budget is prepared in headquarters and the division manager is handed a pattern of operation with predetermined standards against which his operations will be evaluated. In such a situation he feels little concern for profit. Under the decentralized system he is considered an executive in charge of a unit of the investment which is expected to produce its share of the return. Furthermore, it is his responsibility to spread this concern for profit throughout his unit to department heads, supervisors, stenographers, and the people at the bench. The whole philosophy of decentralization tends to make planning for sales, for production, and for the control of costs a cooperative undertaking in the setting of profit goals.

Sales may or may not be decentralized by plants or divisions. If decentralized, sales will operate as a separate staff unit working with the budget director and the plant managers in the establishment of sales goals and production requirements to serve those goals.

In small and medium-sized companies the job of budget planning operates in much the same way that it operates in a division of a larger company except that it may not have the benefit of extensive data gathering and research provided by headquarters of the large company. On the other hand, managers of small companies should have an advantage in promoting an overall operating awareness on the part of the total personnel because of their improved proximity to all operations of the company. This is one of the advantages that large companies are attempting to regain through decentralization.

CONTROL THROUGH THE BUDGET It should be understood that a budget is a means toward an end and is not an end within itself. Budgets are made to be used. They establish goals to which each department and each worker within a department must contribute his designated share in terms of the unified plan. This leads toward precision and confidence. A department head knows what is laid out for his department to accomplish. He knows what is expected of him. He knows when he has done a good job or when and where he is falling behind. Thus, much of the worry of uncertainty is eliminated.

Through recording of actual results against the estimates of the budget, reports are constructed that reveal the points of difficulty and danger—the points which must be analyzed and improved upon. Management operating on the "exception principle" may pick up these points of variation and devote attention to them.

COORDINATION THROUGH THE BUDGET Budgets should be constructive aids to all departments within an organization in achieving their common goals. Unfortunately, however, this purpose is frequently misunderstood. The early emphasis given to budgets as controls of expenditures established in the minds of subordinates the attitude that budgets were negative controls only—devices to limit expenditures. This led to the "padding" of departmental budgets, the idea being for each department to get as large an allotment of expenditures as possible. When all budgets were assembled and reductions were deemed essential, each department felt that it was the subject of discrimination. Thus the budget became a "sore spot" and a factor of disintegration among the personnel.

Budgets, properly constructed and operated, may have a constructive influence on the personnel of an organization. Budgets may serve as a means for bringing about an understanding of the common goals of all who belong to the organization and all who serve it. In this capacity the budget serves as a coordinating and unifying influence.

5-7 TYPES OF BUDGETS

There are two principal types of budgets: the *static,* or fixed, budget and the *variable,* or flexible, budget. The static budget depends upon ability to predict income, sales, or shipments with at least a reasonable degree of accuracy. Using this prediction as a base, fixed sums are allocated for expenditures with a fixed budget of production operations for the period in question. The variable budget recognizes the unreliability of income or sales predictions and makes provisions in advance for variations in production and expenditures in accordance with variations in sales.

1. *The static budget*   Industry inherited the static budget from governmental and institutional organizations. This type of budget served a valuable purpose in the planning and control of certain fixed types of expenditures. The inadequacies of such a budget, however, were soon felt when industry moved into the period of mass production where margins of profit per unit of production were small and planning and control over all operations became more essential. Through study it was found that costs per unit change at different levels of production. The degree of change varies on different products and on different operations involved in the manufacture of the same product.

2. *The variable budget*   The variable budget is constructed in anticipation of variations in sales. It provides in advance for orderly change in the volume of production and in expenditures. This tabulation is based on the recording of costs of previous periods or on the standard costs that have been established through study and experience.

Figure 5-4 is a simplified version of a typical cost curve intended to show the variation in costs as volume increases. Note that three types of cost are illustrated: fixed or stand-by costs representing those items of overhead

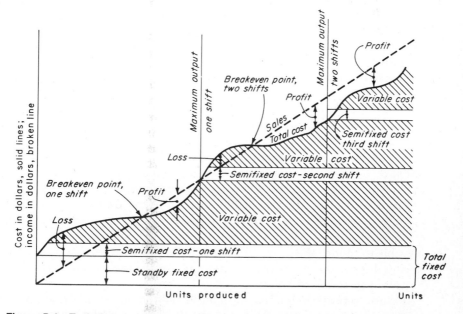

Figure 5-4   Typical cost curve showing how cost varies with the volume of production. Note the effect on the cost elements and on the profit of adding a second and a third shift.

which must be met even though the plant is closed down; semifixed costs; and variable costs. Actually, however, the semifixed costs do not usually follow a straight line but form more of a curve upward as volume increases. For purposes of simplicity and clarity the rise in semifixed costs is indicated at points where the rise is more pronounced, i.e., at points where it becomes necessary to establish additional shifts with the addition of foremen, sweepers, extra maintenance crews, etc. The same effect would be obtained at points where additional buildings have to be opened for increased volume of production. The greatest variation in costs, however, is in those items which are classified as variable costs, such as material and labor. These are the items of greatest concern in budgeting because they are flexible and must be controlled and adjusted as volume increases or decreases.

There are two interpretations of the terms "fixed" and "variable" costs. One interpretation considers a fixed cost as one that is constant in total amount for a given period, while a variable cost increases or decreases in proportion to the volume of production. The second interpretation defines a fixed cost as one that is constant in amount per unit of production but varies in total, while a variable cost changes in amount per unit but remains constant in its total amount for a given period. It will be noted that these two interpretations are directly opposite in their meanings. The classification as described herein assumes the acceptance of the first interpretation. Salaries of major executives, capital taxes, depreciation, etc., remain fixed regardless of the volume of production. These are known as fixed costs. Other items, such as direct labor and direct material, vary almost in proportion to the amount of production and are termed variable costs. Most costs are subject to some variation. Cost of electricity may be considered relatively constant, but even that will vary with extreme changes in volume of production which may require changes in the length of the working day or in the number of working shifts. Therefore, in some enterprises, a third classification of *semifixed* costs is added.

Let us consider for purposes of clarification the application of this classification to a nonindustrial enterprise, an educational institution. Cost items such as library materials, printing, telephone, salaries of the president and deans, and interests on borrowed capital remain constant whether there are 4,000 or 5,000 students registered in a given academic year. These would be considered fixed costs. There are other items, however, that would be reduced with a variation of 1,000 students. One or more residence halls might be closed, thus effecting a saving in light, heat, and janitorial and maid service. A number of class sections might be eliminated, thus making it possible to reduce the instructional staff. Assistant deans might be dismissed during the period of low registration. These are the variable costs that can be varied in terms of volume.

It is not to be expected that variable costs will change in exact proportion to volume of business. Referring to the illustration of the educational institution, if 100 students were added to the school of engineering, instructional costs might remain the same provided the increase was somewhat evenly divided through the four classes. However, if the 100 students were added to the sophomore class alone, it would probably necessitate the increase of instructional expense. The same principle applies to an industrial enterprise. For example, as production volume within a given department or plant increases, there are some variable costs that may decrease per production unit. This may be due to advantages gained through price discounts on increased volume of material purchases or through the decrease of loss resulting from idleness of workers and machines. For this reason variable costs are usually charted to show change in terms of variations in the volume of production.

Holding to the principle of variable budgets, variations in the form of budgeting procedure may be established to meet the peculiar needs of a specific enterprise. In general, we may say that simplicity in budgeting should be held as a primary virtue. Detailed clerical work involved in the preparation and operation of a budget should be held to a minimum. This principle not only leads to the elimination of unnecessary costs in budgeting but in general promotes ease in the interpretation and control of the budget. In a small company where costs are easily identified and controlled or in companies where there is little variation in production volume, a very simple type of budget becomes more practical and appropriate. As an enterprise increases in size and variability, the budget procedure must change to provide the necessary information and control.

Variable budgets are of two principal types. One is the *step budget* which is really a series of budgets set up at different levels of volume of production or sales. These steps are usually established at points in the variation in volume where pronounced changes in costs will occur, such as additional shifts, buildings, and supervisory personnel. The budget for each step recognizes a point of maximum and minimum production. Demands in excess of the maximum or below the minimum require a change in the basic budget or, in other words, the adoption of the budget which has been established for the next step.

The second type of variable budget provides an estimate of the *variable rate of cost* per unit of production or per dollar shipments of sales. Table 5-1 shows a listing of cost classifications. It will be noted that in this case direct material, a variable cost, constitutes 30 cents of the sales dollar.[3] Therefore, if the sales volume is $130,000, the direct material costs would be $39,000. If volume was increased to $150,000, the direct material cost would be increased in direct proportion (150,000 X $0.30 = $45,000). The factory burden cost, however, is divided into two parts, i.e., stand-by, or fixed, cost and variable cost. The fixed cost of $10,000 remaining constant, the variable cost is estimated at 12 cents per sales dollar. Therefore, a sales volume of

[3]See Cost Control in Chap. 19 for a description of types of costs.

Table 5–1   Stand-by and Variable Rate of Costs

Item	Stand-by	Variable Rate per Sales Dollar
Direct material	—	$0.30
Direct labor	—	0.14
Factory burden	$10,000	0.12
Administrative expense	4,000	0.02
Selling expense	9,000	0.04
Total operating cost	$23,000	$0.62

(Sales volume	$130,000)
Direct material—130,000 × $0.30	39,000
Direct labor—130,000 × $0.14	18,200
Factory stand-by burden	10,000
Factory variable burden—130,000 × $0.12	15,600
Administrative stand-by	4,000
Administrative variable—130,000 × $0.02	2,600
Selling expense stand-by	9,000
Selling expense variable—130,000 × $0.04	5,200
Total operating cost	$103,600

$130,000 would result in a factory burden cost of $25,600 (130,000 × $0.12 + $10,000).

Any estimate of the variable *rate* of cost must recognize maximum and minimum volumes. As previously stated, the rate of cost of material may be expected to decrease as volume increases, owing to advantages that may be attained through purchasing in larger lots. Greater labor efficiency, however, may be obtained from the regular force of 1,000 workers than would be realized per unit of production after an additional 500 inexperienced employees had been added to the payroll. Therefore, the variable rate of cost is calculated as an *average* rate between two points of minimum and maximum production.

Perspective 5D   ZERO-BASE BUDGETING

Zero-base budgeting (ZBB) was elevated to prominence when newly elected President Carter prescribed it for the Federal budget. In traditional budgeting the planners start with last year's outlays and decide how much more or less is needed for next year's operations. The ZBB concept requires each budget unit to make a fresh start each year, from a zero outlay level, to decide how much will be needed next year to conduct specifically defined operations. The manager of each unit determines the objectives for that unit's program and alternate ways to meet the objectives. Then budget plans, called decision packages, are developed for two or more spending levels. These packages are submitted to higher level managers who use their broader perspectives to rank the decision packages. The consolidated sets of ranked packages are submitted to the final authorizing group that decides the total expenditure level and allocates funds accordingly to the budget units.

In a memorandum to agency chiefs, President Carter summed up the expected benefits from ZBB: "By working together under a zero-base budgeting system, we can reduce costs and make the Federal government more efficient and effective."*

*SOURCE: "What Zero-base Budgeting Is and How Carter Wants to Use It," *U.S. News & World Report,* April 25, 1977.

COMMENT   Switching to a zero-base budgeting system initially requires a lot of extra work to define and cost-out objectives. However, proponents of ZBB claim it combines planning and budgeting into a single process, causes more cost consciousness, and makes the analysis more comprehensive with greater participation from managers at all levels.

5-8   PREPARING THE BUDGET

Mention was made earlier regarding the function of the budget director, most frequently the controller or assistant controller serving in this capacity. He serves as a coordinator between divisions or departments in budget preparation. Usually the heads of these divisions, together with selected staff representatives, will serve as the budget committee of the company. This committee receives and approves all forecasts, departmental or division budgets, and periodic reports showing comparison of actual and budget. The budget committee may also request special studies of deviations from the budget and consider revisions of budget to meet changed business conditions.

The budget officer must see that all department estimates are prepared with sufficient supporting data to provide an adequate basis for effective consideration by the committee. He has the responsibility for the presentation of these budgets to the committee and for transmitting back to the departments the recommendations of acceptance or revision. The budget officer is also responsible for the organization of a system of regular periodic reports regarding the operations of each department. He may also prepare special reports regarding points of special difficulty and recommended revisions to correct these difficulties.

The preparation of budget estimates within each department should also be a committee proposition. This is in adherence to the same principle of *participation as a means toward cooperation.* Participation in the preparation of a budget serves to familiarize the personnel with the problems involved. With this knowledge of the problems and the feeling of having a part in setting the goals and limitations of the department, the personnel will give more effective cooperation in the operation of the budget. The head of the department may act as chairman of the department committee but, in the case of a large department, he should delegate responsibility for the gathering of details for use by his committee. In other words, he should have an organization within his own department for the preparation of the budget that follows the same general pattern as the budget organization for the enterprise as a whole. He will find that this organization not only will lead to better budget preparation but will prove especially useful in budget control.

5-8.1 Adequate Cost Information

Adequate cost information is a prime essential of budgeting. It constitutes the foundation for the conversion of forecast and business policy into production. Our forecast tells us how much we can sell at a given price level. Our cost information tells us how much it will cost to produce it in the volumes specified. Full realization of cost in advance of budget preparation may cause management to question the advisability of the continuance of certain lines of products, or it may lead to the expansion of a particular line that is able to carry a favorable margin of profit.

Perhaps the most important advantage to be gained through the availability of accurate cost information is that budgeting can be based on facts instead of personal guesswork. The individual who is called upon to provide estimates without facts on which to base these estimates is in the long run facing trouble. Through superior personal judgment he may receive the praise of management when times are good and when production is progressing at a relatively even tempo. If he is wise he will probably allow reasonably safe margins to protect himself from the possible errors of his judgment. This he may be able to do under "normal" conditions. But invariably there will come a time when the "abnormal" occurs—when the "pressure" is put on to decrease the budget of costs in order that the business may continue to operate at a profit. Those are the times when the individual may be forced to eliminate those margins of safety. He promises to operate at less cost yet he does not have a detailed plan approved by management as to just how those costs are to be reduced. The chances are that they will not be reduced and he will be criticized, if not discharged, for poor management of his department. How much better it would be if he could supply facts regarding costs—facts that could be interpreted by any member of the management group. The individual could then relieve himself of reliance on personal judgment alone and present his estimates accompanied by systematically prepared data. Once the estimates are accepted by the budget committee, with full realization of the facts on which they are based, the committee shares the responsibility for the accuracy of those estimates.

5-8.2 The Sales Budget

As previously mentioned, the estimates of future sales set the bounds of limitations for other budgets of the enterprise. There are two principal sources of data for use in the preparation of sales estimates: (1) past performance (sales of previous periods) and (2) market analysis. Both sources are generally used in gaining a composite picture of the relative demand for the different products manufactured and the general changes in business conditions which are pertinent to the future sales of the products of the enterprise.

Salespersons can play a significant role in the preparation of the sales budgets. They are in personal contact with the customer. They are able to obtain firsthand information regarding his wants, his attitude toward future business conditions, his attitude toward the services provided by the enterprise, his attitude toward the program of advertising, etc. If salespersons are trained in the importance of this information and the methods by which it should be produced, the enterprise can develop within its own organization a valuable source of market information. Many companies make the preparation of sales estimates and the introduction of new products to the market a cooperative undertaking which includes participation by vote on the part of each salesperson. A by-product of this procedure is the development of a feeling of responsibility on the part of the salesperson for meeting sales estimates once they are cooperatively established.

5-8.3 Manufacturing Budgets

The number and division of budgets for the manufacturing division of an enterprise will, of course, vary with the size and type of enterprise and the products it manufactures. In general, it may be said that six basic budgets are needed: (1) the production budget which outlines the schedule of product units to be manufactured; (2) the materials budget which specifies the direct material needed to produce the number of units scheduled; (3) the plant and equipment budget that sets forth the requirements of space and machinery; (4) the maintenance budget; (5) the manufacturing expense budget which includes the overhead or burden charges for the period; and (6) the labor budget specifying the productive personnel needed to meet the production schedule.[4]

The production budget is taken directly from the sales estimates, except that it attempts in so far as possible to spread the work evenly over the period. This budget forms the basis for other manufacturing budgets as listed above. With the aid of the materials specifications sheets for each product, the materials budget can be prepared by months for the guidance of the purchasing department. Similarly, the plant and equipment, maintenance, and manufacturing expense budgets must conform to the production

---

[4]Space does not permit the explanation and illustration of the various schedules required in the development of the manufacturing budgets. The purpose here is only to call attention to the nature and scope of budgeting in the manufacturing division. Many excellent references are available for the student of budgeting who wishes to pursue the subject further.

budget for the various departments, not only as to *what* will be needed but also *when.*

The direct labor budget is exceedingly important for reasons previously mentioned and also as a more systematic forecast of the need for recruitment and training. From the production estimates of each department the labor demands can be forecast for each job classification. This forecast is then compared with the roster of present personnel. It may show a probable surplus in one personnel classification and a shortage in another. In such case the company must either discharge from the surplus classification and add to the shortage classification, or plan for the retraining of present personnel for the performance of new jobs. Plans for shifting and retraining become particularly essential when there is a scarcity of labor available for recruitment or when the company is converting to the manufacture of a new product involving new operating skills.

5-8.4 The Financial Budget

The financial budget presents a summary of anticipated receipts and disbursements for the budget period. Its purpose is to plan for the allocation of working capital as represented by the current assets of the enterprise. Data for the financial budget are derived from the budgets as prepared by the various divisions. The financial budget must anticipate the cash receipts by months or at other designated points of the period and make allowance for the raising of additional funds, if needed, to meet current expenses. This means that income from accounts receivable, notes receivable, cash transactions, etc., must be budgeted as accurately as possible. Expenditures may be planned in consideration of two primary factors: (1) the absolute necessities of the budgets of the various divisions, i.e., monthly requirements of materials for production, payroll, etc.; and (2) the limitations of available cash. It is not considered good business to have large amounts of cash lying idle during 10 months of the year in order that funds will be available to meet unusually large expenditures during the other 2 months. Good business policy would suggest that attempts should be made either to spread the added expenses of these two months over a longer period or to borrow additional funds through short-term notes. There are many problems arising out of attempted control of working capital, and there are likewise many possible solutions that may be derived to fit the needs of an individual enterprise. The significant point here is that these problems must be anticipated and avenues selected to meet them. The financial budget is a device intended to serve those objectives.

There are times, of course, when the limitations of capital may make the plans as set forth in the budgets of various divisions prohibitive. This is especially true during periods of rapid expansion when additional plant and equipment must be provided in order to meet the budgeted schedule of production. In such case the financial budget acts as a negative control over other divisions. In most instances, however, the financial budget provides a systematic and positive approach toward the attainment of the coordinated plans of all divisions.

5-9   REVIEW QUESTIONS

1. What is meant by capital? Distinguish between fixed and working capital.

2. Distinguish between short-term, intermediate, and long-term loans. How are these loans financed?

3. What is meant by authorized and capital stock? Distinguish between common and preferred stock.

4. How does the issuing of bonds differ from the issuing of stock?

5. Why is it important for a business to maintain reserves? How does an enterprise achieve its expansion program?

6. Where and how is the rate-of-return method applied? Given equal rates of return and different periods of capital recovery, which alternative is preferable?

7. What is a budget? How does it act as a planning and control mechanism?

8. Distinguish between fixed budget and variable budget. Where is each type used?

9. What are two types of variable budgets? Explain.

10. Why is a sales budget the "key" budget of all budgets? What is the importance of salespersons in the preparation of the sales budget?

5-10   TOPICS FOR DISCUSSION

1. Much is made from time to time of the rise or fall in the number of business failures. What special function, if any, in the national economy is performed by this phenomenon?

2. How and in what ways is saving of vital importance to a free economy? Is saving as essential to a totalitarian economy as it is to a free economy? How do savings affect the cost of capital?

3. Distinguish between internal and external financing of an enterprise.

4. Recognizing that an investor of venture capital is willing to take a risk, expects high returns on any investment, and wants to take his capital out of the business once the period of most rapid growth has passed, what information should an entrepreneur provide to a potential venture investor to convince him to invest?

5. Since budgeting is so broad in scope and involves so many departments of a company, who should be responsible for directing budget preparation and control? Discuss working relationships and specific responsibilities of a budget director.

6. Management seeks constantly to move more items of cost into the *variable* or *semifixed* classifications. Indicate common business costs that you feel must stay in the *fixed* classification.

7. Case 5A: *August Scientific Instruments, Inc.*

ASI, Inc., is a small privately owned company which designs, develops, and produces miniature electromechanical components used by other manufacturers in guidance systems for aircraft and missiles. Practically 100 percent of its products are used in national-defense work. The company is located in a small, nonindustrial, but progressive town whose main center of interest is a Technical Education Institute having a student body and faculty of some 5,000 persons in a total population of about 7,000. The company was started in this town in 1953 in a small shop, with a little capital and seven employees. The company weathered the problems usually faced by new enterprises and grew steadily and soundly, expanding to several vacant store buildings, until in 1958 it enjoyed a capitalization of $300,000 and had some 200 employees, a $67,000 monthly payroll, $115,000 monthly sales, and a backlog of orders exceeding $420,000. By this time, however, the backlog had grown alarmingly, reflecting the company's inability to increase production at a rate to match increased orders. For a while the company sought to meet demands for expansion by bank loans up to 80 percent of accounts receivable, but the urgent need for major expansion persisted. The company was facing a new stage of growth, but the stockholders had exhausted their cash resources; either it had to get outside financial help or freeze the size of the company at an artificially low level.

Analysis of the company's needs indicated that it ought to have (1) a new plant at an estimated cost of $350,000, an amount that exceeded net worth; and (2) long-term financing of about $200,000 to cover additional equipment and machinery and to provide more working capital to finance training of additional personnel. The company considered the possibility of locating in some other city where it had been offered inducements of a new building and tax-free advantages, but it did not want to leave the community where it enjoyed a cooperative arrangement with the scientific educational institution and other advantages. The business community for its part did not wish to lose the company's substantial payroll, a fair portion of which was earned by the students working their way. The local bank was willing to help, but pointed out that the proposed project was more than it could handle. Larger area banks, insurance companies, and other lending sources had been approached but without tangible results. Finally, the Small Business Administration was persuaded to take an interest in the project to see if something could be worked out.

Questions

1. What possible avenues are open to ASI to finance a new plant in its present community? Which seems most likely to succeed and why?

2. Do you see anything in the second phase of ASI's financial problem (that is, the desire to raise $200,000 for new equipment, personnel training, and working capital) to raise the caution signal for management? Why do you think that although ASI offered mortgages as collateral on every free asset the company had, lending institutions might have been reluctant to make this loan?

8. Case 5B: *The Custom and Construction Woodwork Co.*

At one time this company did considerable business in custom and specialty woodwork, but in recent years it has narrowed its operations to handling builder's supplies and lumber. The company feels that it could do a much larger business if it had an increase in its line of credit or more equity capital, but apparently bankers are not rushing in to make loans and investments. They have indicated that the company suffers as much from lack of good management as it does from insufficient financing and have offered the following statements as proof of their views:

Balance Sheet
Dec. 31, 1969

Assets		Liabilities	
Cash	$ 1.896	Notes payable (bank)	$ 14,000
Notes receivable	4,876	Notes receivable, discounted	4,842
Accounts receivable	97,456	Accounts payable	152,240
Inventory	156,822	Accruals	5,440
Total current assets	$261,050	Total current liabilities	$176,522
Land and buildings (at depreciated value)	$ 46,258	Mortgage (real estate)	$ 10,000
Equipment and fixtures (at depreciated values)	11,458	Net worth	133,522
Prepaid	1,278		
Total assets	$320,044	Total liabilities	$320,044

Income Statement

Net sales			$727,116
Cost of goods sold			616,668
Gross profit on sales			$110,448
Operating expenses:			
Wages		$61,378	
Delivery		9,396	
Bad-debt allowance		3,614	
Depreciation allowance		7,200	
Total expenses			$ 81,588
Net profit before other charges			28,860
Other charges:			
Interest		$ 700	
Nonoperating charges		1,000	
Drawings (management accounts)		14,980	
Provisions for taxes		8,656	
Total other charges			$ 25,336
Net profit for period			$ 3,524

Questions

1. Study the statements presented in this case and pick out three weaknesses to illustrate faults in management. Only an elementary knowledge of accounting is necessary to understand this case and write a good answer; the trained accountant could find many other things wrong with this company.

9. Case 5C: *Companies A and B*

Two companies, A and B, are asking for bank loans. You are asked to figure the ratios, explained below, on the accounting data contained in their profit-and-loss statements and their balance sheets. Indicate which is more eligible for a loan and why. This case illustrates how budgeting for turnover, profit, and return on investment affects the total strength of a company.
   Ratios:

$$\text{Current ratio} = \frac{\text{total current assets}}{\text{total current liabilities}} = \text{current credit strength}$$

A 2:1 ratio is generally considered satisfactory. Each dollar of current liabilities is covered by two dollars of current assets.

$$\text{Liquidity ("acid-test") ratio} = \frac{\text{total current assets} - \text{inventory}}{\text{total current liabilities}}$$

These are the "quick" assets (dollar assets or assets readily convertible into dollars) divided by total current liabilities. The "acid-test" ratio is more stringent than the current ratio. A 1:1 is acceptable, i.e., for every dollar of current liabilities, there should be one dollar of current assets with inventory excluded.

Ratios indicating the earning power and financial efficiency of a company:

$$\text{Proprietary ratio} = \frac{\text{total capital}}{\text{total liabilities and capital}}$$

This ratio indicates the dependency of a company upon its creditors for working capital. Considered together with the current ratio over an extended period of time, it provides a trend analysis and shows whether the degree of debt pressure is increasing or decreasing.

$$\text{Rate of earnings on total capital employed} = \frac{\text{net operating profit}}{\text{total liabilities and capital}}$$

This ratio gives the percentage return from business production for every dollar of liabilities and capital employed.

$$\text{Operating ratio} = \frac{\text{cost of goods sold and operating expense}}{\text{net sales}}$$

This shows the percentage of every dollar received from net sales which is needed to meet the cost of production and operation.

Ratios indicating the efficiency of management:

$$\text{Turnover of capital} = \frac{\text{net sales}}{\text{total liabilities and capital}}$$

This ratio undertakes to show what percentage is realized in net sales for every dollar available to management in total liabilities and capital (total assets). It indicates the efficiency of financial management.

$$\text{Number of days' sales in receivables} = \frac{\text{receivables}}{\text{net sales}} \times \left(\begin{array}{l} \text{number of days} \\ \text{covered by profit-} \\ \text{and-loss statement} \end{array} \right)$$

This is the collection ratio. It shows the average length that time accounts are outstanding and is a measure of the efficiency of credit management.

$$\text{Merchandise turnover} = \frac{\text{net sales}}{\text{average inventory}}$$

This is the number of times that inventory is replaced during a given period of time and indicates the degree of efficiency in a company's merchandising.

Ratios important to management in the control of internal operations:

$$\text{Margin percentage} = \frac{\text{gross profit on sales}}{\text{net sales}}$$

For every dollar received from sales, a certain percentage is gross profit. This figure must be large enough to cover all other expenses (not operation expenses alone) if the company is to be profitable. If the quotient in this ratio is subtracted from 100, the percentage of net sales going to cost of goods sold is obtained.

$$\text{Net profit ratio} = \frac{\text{net income (before dividends)}}{\text{net sales}}$$

This ratio shows the percentage of net income for each dollar of net sales.

Profit and Loss Statement for the Year Ended
December 31, 19—,
(thousands of dollars)

	Company A	Company B
Net sales	$22,000	$12,680
Cost of goods sold	10,800	5,500
Gross profit on sales	$11,200	$ 7,180
Operating expenses:		
Maintenance and repairs	$ 600	400
Depreciation	1,520	1,200
Bad-debt expense	360	320
Selling expense	3,700	3,200
Administrative and general	1,260	1,100
Total operating expense	$ 7,440	$ 6,220
Net operating profit	3,760	960
Other income	300	160
Other expense	1,700	800
Net income	$ 2,360	$ 320

Balance Sheet for the Year Ended December 31, 19—,
(thousands of dollars)

	Company A	Company B
Current assets:		
Cash	$ 6,000	$ 3,000
Marketable securities	1,200	1,600
Accounts receivable	1,900	2,540
Inventories	8,000	4,800
Total current assets	$17,100	$11,940
Fixed assets:		
Investments	$ 3,200	$ 4,000
Land, buildings, and equipment (net)	34,600	25,120
Total fixed assets	$37,800	$29,120
Prepaid expenses	1,040	300
Total assets	$55,940	$41,360
Current liabilities:		
Notes payable	$ 700	$ 1,600
Accounts payable	3,200	3,120
Other current liabilities	5,800	4,800
Total current liabilities	$ 9,700	$ 9,520
Fixed liabilities:		
Mortgage payable (due 10 years from date this statement)	$11,160	$18,000
Total liabilities	$20,860	$27,520
Capital:		
Preferred stock—6% cumulative, nonparticipating	$ 8,400	$ 4,000
Common stock	12,000	6,800
Total capital stock	$20,400	$10,800
Surplus:		
Appropriated surplus	$ 4,800	$ 2,160
Unappropriated surplus	9,880	880
Total surplus	$14,680	$ 3,040
Total capital	35,080	13,840
Total liabilities and capital	$55,940	$41,360

6

RESEARCH AND DEVELOPMENT

Over $40 billion per year is currently being invested in research and development. Why? What kinds of research are involved? How are research investigations made? What considerations are uppermost in product development? What management tools are available to aid product development? How is the R&D process organized and operated within the enterprise? These are the fundamental questions to which we turn our attention in the pages that follow.

6 RESEARCH AND DEVELOPMENT

6-1 INDUSTRIAL RESEARCH

In these days of rapidly advancing technology, manufacturing success is most likely to attend those enterprises which persistently and intelligently develop new and better products and new and better ways of making and using old products. While in a few industries the same product sells year after year (e.g., jeweler's rouge, leather, cement), in most industries the product line is constantly changing. Intense competition on processes as well as products makes research and development essential for the very survival of the modern enterprise. Upon R&D hinges the perpetuation of existing jobs and the creation of new opportunities, the maintenance of present sales, and the growth of new markets. Contrariwise, profits fade away where demand is not bolstered by products designed and engineered to the desires of a constantly changing society or made by the most advanced processing techniques developed. Industrial history is replete with examples of enterprises which have fallen by the wayside because they rested upon products and processes which passing technology made obsolete.

An enterprise has the alternative of supplying society with an entirely new service by pioneering a new and original product, or of attempting to compete with another enterprise in supplying society with an existing type of service in the form of a competing product. Where products are competing, they may be similar in design or manufacture, providing patent regulations permit, or one product may depart radically in design and manufacture from the other and merely compete with it in service rendered. Perhaps this can be better explained by an example. Some time ago Polaroid, the first really practical material for polarizing light to be produced commercially, was developed primarily to eliminate the glare from on-coming automobile headlamps without appreciably reducing night vision. As such it attempted to provide an entirely new service. Before long, however, it was found that Polaroid could be used in sun glasses and, when thus used, it went into direct competition with sun glasses fashioned from smoked or colored glass. Thus Polaroid began to render a competing service in the form of a product that was similar in design and manufacture. A third use to which Polaroid was subsequently put was in the field of photoelasticity in instruments for determining stresses and strains. When a piece of transparent plastic is bent or strained and examined under polarized light, bright bands of color appear where stresses are present. The location and number of these color bands give an accurate picture of internal stresses. By this method the design of highly stressed parts such as automotive brake pedals and front-spring control arms can be tested by viewing plastic replicas under polarized light. Where Polaroid is thus used, it competes in service with other stress- and strain-measuring mechanisms, but the application is entirely different as regards design and manufacture.

Naturally when an enterprise attempts the manufacture and sale of a competing product, the service supplied in terms of quality, price, and availability must be comparable or superior to that supplied by a competing enterprise. Otherwise the concern will find little demand for its product. If your mousetrap is not equal to or better than those currently in service, the world is not interested in beating a path to your door.

Once a successful product or range of products is established, the enterprise must then endeavor to keep itself abreast or ahead of the field by the constant improvement of its products. In this rapidly changing world, the demand for products is constantly changing with it. Unlike individuals who inevitably become old and die, industrial enterprises may through the continual development of new products find a sort of "fountain of youth" by which they can retain their youthful vigor and vitality.

Of course, many small enterprises and even some larger ones live on the product designs of their customers. The function of such concerns is to supply materials, parts, and subcontract items for use in the products of other companies. The product-development challenge for these suppliers is to keep abreast or ahead of the parade in developing materials and pioneering physical and chemical advances in their field. Thereby they can increase their usefulness and importance to their customers.

6-1.1 Research Trends

Until shortly after the turn of the century, little thought was given by industry to organized product development. Most new products resulted from the activities of free-lance inventors like Edison, Bell, and Wright. These inventors worked alone or in small independent groups, relied financially upon their own capital or that of friends interested in their projects, and employed cut-and-try methods in their laboratories, which more often than not were located in their kitchens or in nearby barns. Relatively few ever achieved prominence; in fact, many of them were quacks or were ill-advised individuals who squandered their time and money in the search for impossible devices such as the traditional perpetual-motion machine. Very few of those who did contribute worthwhile discoveries ever realized any wealth from them. Free-lance inventors did not concern themselves with yearly and seasonal style changes of products, and in general the progress of products remained static until the same or another free-lance inventor hit upon a new and better basic idea.

In the early 1900s, however, the increasing complexity of manufactured products and processes together with the speeding up of the American way of life through faster transportation and communication facilities left the free-lance inventor unable to cope with the more advanced state of the technical arts. Whereas previously new materials, products, and processes had sprung primarily from practical men and from curious amateurs of an inventive turn of mind working in their own shops, new developments began to come mainly from the organized efforts of trained scientists and engineers engaged cooperatively in specific fields of investigation.[1] Although it is true that lone inventors are still with us, and we hope they always will be, nevertheless their basic inventions usually require the organized effort of a well-equipped research laboratory to test, modify, and extend their ideas before products supplying society with useful services and capable of being manufactured may result. In the past 50-odd years, organized industrial research through the coordination and specialization as well as the intensification of inventive effort has brought about a rate of industrial development previously unequaled. Today organized industrial research stands unchallenged as our greatest medium for achieving better living through new methods and new products.[2]

6-1.2 Public and Private Research Organizations

Industrial research is performed by a number of external agencies as well as by internal organizations of the industrial enterprise. Frequently, companies with excellent research facilities and personnel encounter problems requiring specialized knowledge or equipment best obtained from outside consulting organizations. *Government agencies* today are among the largest conducting research of all kinds (pure, applied, commercial, statistical, social). Practically all Federal government departments are engaged in research and make their findings, except items touching military security, available to industry. In addition, the Federal government finances extensive research carried on in universities and by private research organizations. *Trade associations* frequently sponsor research projects in which the objects sought benefit all members and do not affect their relative competitive positions within the industry. *Special industrial groups* within an industry often carry on research projects of common interest. Small concerns join in establishing a research organization for their common benefit. *Commercial laboratories,* like A. D. Little, Inc., of Cambridge, Mass., and the Battelle Memorial Institute at Columbus, Ohio, specializing in industry-research projects, are frequently employed by manufacturing enterprises for prob-

[1]Even Edison, popularly thought of as a lone-wolf inventor, organized in his Menlo Park laboratory a team of machinists, technicians, and a few scientifically trained people in what might be called a model for today's industrial-research laboratories. There was one difference, however. Edison was always the master, one who used his team to augment his own genius. This is not always the case in today's industrial-research laboratories, where a potential inventive genius may don a white lab coat and become an "organization man" or where he may even be refused employment as "too temperamental" for the team. While today's research laboratory is a fine catalyst for invention, its detractors point out that unless adroitly administered, it can act as a drag on genius.

[2]From 1938 to 1961 the Federal government's annual contribution to R&D rose twentyfold to close to $15 billion, or more than two-thirds of the national outlay. From 1961 to 1967 government-funded R&D increased 5.6 per cent a year and private R&D 7.4 per cent. But from 1967 to 1975 government R&D shrank 3 per cent a year and nongovernment spending rose a modest 1.8 per cent per year.

lems requiring unusual equipment, special technical skill, and a broad approach combining many different fields of knowledge not possessed or readily available in the ordinary enterprise. They are also employed when time and other factors do not permit a company to conduct its own investigation. *Educational institutions* in recent years have entered the commercial research field in response to the closer relationship between pure and applied research, as an incident in their participation in research sponsored by government, and as part of the growing interest of industry in support of education.

An interesting current trend is the development of research parks by industries, laboratories, and research institutions in conjunction with universities, as, for example, "Research Row" on the banks of the Charles River, Cambridge; the development at Princeton, N.J.; the "Research Triangle" in North Carolina; the Detroit-University of Michigan development in automotive and other industrial research; the Southwest Research Institute in San Antonio, Tex.; and the Stanford Research Institute in California. The trend in this direction is likely to grow as basic and applied research draw closer together. Universities can contribute unique facilities and personnel to the fields of industrial research, but industry should recognize the superior obligations of universities to education and should not expect to use the universities in commercial fields.

Perspective 6A A RESEARCH COMMUNITY

A few decades ago, Santa Clara County, California, was a tranquil expanse of apricot, prune, and cherry orchards. Now it's the place where American industry is thrusting out its newest branches and roots. Some 800 pioneering technology companies, along with numerous service and supplier firms, are clustered in the area, forming the densest concentration of innovative industry that exists anywhere in the world.*

How so many research-oriented companies came to be established in one community is fascinating history. The scientific pedigree of the area is traceable to Lee de Forest's development of the vacuum tube. A house in Palo Alto bears a plaque as the "birthplace of electronics"; it was here in 1912 that de Forest was able to amplify the footsteps of a fly to sound like a marching soldier. Late in the 1930s, Frederick Terman of Stanford University encouraged some of his graduate engineering students to start their own companies. Thus William R. Hewlett and David Packard began their spectacularly successful venture. Before long the Varian brothers started a company to perfect their Klystron tube. Once the area acquired enough scientists, companies, and capital to form a critical mass, a chain reaction of new-company formations began—semiconductors, computers, lasers, pollution controls, robot brains, opyoelectronics, etc.

When Terman set out to create a "community of technical scholars," he says, "there wasn't much here and the rest of the world looked awfully big. Now a lot of the rest of the world is here."*

*SOURCE: "California's Great Breeding Ground for Industry," *Fortune,* June, 1974.

COMMENT   The sun-belt climate, closeness to fine educational institutions, availability of venture capital, and a history of technological successes have combined to create a fertile seedbed for R&D advances. Employees of high-technology firms see possibilities for spinoff products and leave to start their own companies. They are encouraged to do so by the evidence of success around them. A study by M.I.T. revealed that one out of five new high-technology companies failed in the first 5 years, whereas four out of five new firms of other types collapsed during the same period.

6-1.3   Time Frame of Research

It should be noted here that product research within an enterprise is a never-ending process with a delayed-action consequence. The success or failure of current research will only become apparent many years hence. As we shall see in the next chapter, there is a long time interval between a product idea and widespread sales. The chemical industry acknowledges that 5 to 7 years are required on the average "from test tube to tank car." Some notable slower-arriving examples: Du Pont spent 12 years in research and development to get nylon into production; Union Carbide put 12 years into developing vinylite.

Tomorrow's profits depend heavily on today's research. Dollars invested now in R&D probably will produce no income for a number of years to come. By pouring money into research, today's industrial managers increase current costs and lower their profits from operations so that in future years their companies—possibly guided by their managerial successors—may reap the fruits.

6-1.4   Scope of Research

Projects involving new technology can be classified into three groups. Definitions of these categories adopted by the National Science Foundation are the following:

1. *Basic research*   Research projects which represent original investigation for the advancement of scientific knowledge and which do not have specific commercial objectives, although they may be in the field of present or potential interest of the reporting company.

2. *Applied research*   Research projects which represent investigation directed to the discovery of new scientific knowledge and which have specific commercial objectives with respect to either products or processes.

3. *Development*   Technical activities concerned with non routine problems which are encountered in translating research findings or other general scientific knowledge into products or processes.

Research, broadly defined, is the systematic search for new knowledge. Charles F. Kettering, who contributed so heavily to industrial research, labeled research as an "organized method of finding out what you are going to do when you can't keep on doing what you are doing now." Table 6-1 shows where the research is done.

6-2 BASIC RESEARCH

Fundamental, or *pure,* research refers to investigation primarily for the sake of knowledge itself. With or without consideration of commercial possibilities, it seeks to find out all there is to know about a particular substance or what happens, and why, when something is done to one or more substances. It deals in the basic sciences. Why is the grass green? What results in the synthesis of long-chain polymers? (Du Pont found out and called it "nylon.") The Bell Telephone Laboratories asked questions in the realm of theoretical physics and predicted the success of the transistor before laboratory experiments were even attempted. The directions in which fundamental investigations are to be pursued frequently are not prescribed in advance, for the avenues of study are determined as the work proceeds and as promising leads are uncovered.

Basic research is aimed at the discovery or explanation of fundamental laws and phenomena of nature, whether physical or organic. Over the last two centuries much of the basic research done has been supported by governments to promote state policies toward health, welfare, and military strength. The dominant support of the U.S. government for basic research is apparent in Table 6-1. The basic-research objectives of industries are to discover relationships or concepts that enable firms to be on the "leading edge" of technology.

Several problems confront supporters of basic research. A declining proportion of R&D funding is allocated to pure research, and that has been concentrated in health and military pursuits. Duplicity of research effort has been criticized, but this may be unavoidable or even advantageous in obtaining results sooner. However, lack of communication between researchers sometimes causes "rediscoveries of the wheel," at a very high cost.

At the interface between basic and applied research, difficulties have been encountered in the *transfer of technology.* In a general sense, transfer of technology pertains to both the transfer of information obtained from basic

Table 6-1 Percentage by Sector of Funds Spent for Three
Classes of Research and Total R&D During 1973

	Percentages of U.S. Research Funds Spent in 1973			
	Basic	Applied	Development	Total
Government	59.7	55.2	60.8	59.4
Industries	17.0	39.4	38.8	36.1
Universities	18.0	3.6	0.1	3.2
Other	5.3	1.8	0.3	1.3

SOURCE: U.S. Department of Commerce.

research to places where it can be adapted for specific applications and to the transfer of results from applied research to other organizations where it can be utilized for related applications. Programs have been initiated at both national and international levels to improve the transfer of technology. In the United States these programs are directed toward making technological innovations which originate from government-supported research, such as the Space Program, available to commercial interests and to transfer technical devices, materials, methods, and information to developing countries.

Perspective 6B   FROM DEATH RAY TO RADAR

The idea of perpetual motion—something for nothing—seems to be a persistent, insidious dream of inventors. It has been around for a long time. Over 2,000 years ago the Chinese searched for an unpowered "everlasting going." Archimedes tried to find it through hydraulics and da Vinci experimented with gravity-powered mechanisms. A perpetual-motion machine was exhibited in New York in 1813. People paid to see little carriers ceaselessly moving up and down inclined planes to drive a wheel which offered free energy. Robert Fulton, of steamboat fame, exposed the hoax by showing that the contraption was connected by a hidden strand of catgut to a handpowered crank in an adjacent room.

Death rays too have been a popular, but unproved, invention. A 1934 experience of the Air Ministry in England with death ray research is described by A. R. Rowe:

For many years the "death ray" had been a hardy annual among optimistic inventors. The usual claim was that by means of a ray emanating from a secret device (known to us in the Air Ministry as a Black Box) the inventor had killed rabbits at short distances, and if only he were given time and money, particularly money, he would produce a bigger and better ray which would destroy any object, such as an aircraft, onto which the ray was directed. Inventors were diffident about discussing the contents of their black boxes and, despite the protection afforded by the patent laws, invariably wanted some of the taxpayers' money before there could be any discussion of their ideas. The Ministry solved the problem by offering £1,000 to any owner of a Black Box who could demonstrate the killing of a sheep at a range of 100 yards, the secret to remain with its owner.

[The mortality rate of sheep was not affected by this offer.*]

*SOURCE: A. R. Rowe, *One Story of Radar*, Cambridge University Press, 1948.

COMMENT   Although the Air Ministry found no death rays, their investigation indirectly led to the development of radar. In answering the question of whether it would be possible to concentrate an electromagnetic beam sufficiently to melt the metal of an airplane, R. A. Watson-Watt said "no," but he indicated that it should be possible to use the concept to locate the position of planes. The first crude but successful demonstration of what eventually evolved into radar was consequently made by Watson-Watt in 1935.

6-3 APPLIED RESEARCH

Applied research, on the other hand, is usually directed at some specific industrial problem. It adapts the basic sciences to materials, products, and other industrial requirements. Frequently, applied research is the specific outgrowth of fundamental research. Once Du Pont had developed nylon, it went to work on applications and uses for the material and, what is more, manufacturing processes whereby nylon could be made commercially into stockings, rope, brush bristles, and numerous other items. Subsidiaries of the Union Carbide and Carbon Corporation have made mass-production industries out of the gases, carbides, batteries, and plastics that are the applied results of some of their pure-research discoveries in carbon and oxygen. Nuclear fission for military destruction is bringing forth, in the field of medicine, useful isotopes which contribute to human preservation.

Applied research in industry embraces (1) marketing; (2) materials; (3) products, and (4) equipment and processes.

6-3.1 Market Research

The chief aims of market research are to test consumer acceptance of products, to develop data for manufacturing schedules and prices, and to provide a source of new ideas for development. Unlike the past, when in small shops custom-made goods were produced through intimate contacts of producer and customer, modern industry is separated from consumers by complicated organization and engages in large-scale production for consumers in the mass whose wants must be explored, developed, and evaluated. The change from intimate producer–consumer contact to wide separation of producers and consumers has been likened to a broken circular chain in which marketing research supplies the missing link (see Fig. 6-1).

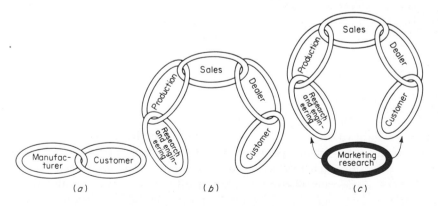

Figure 6-1 The broken chain of modern industry. (a) Relationship which existed between manufacturer and customer under conditions of the one-man shop. (b) In the large modern business institutions, the producer has become separated from the customer, and the intimate relationship no longer exists. (c) Marketing research supplies the missing link to the broken chain and thus rejoins the producer and customer.

6-3.2 Materials Research

Research in materials is linked with product development, since the discovery and improvement of materials frequently lead to new products and lower costs on existing products. Powder metallurgy, for example, now produces finished physical shapes without melting, forging, rolling, extruding, or machining. Hard metals and alloys such as those of tungsten which could not be worked into usable forms by any other method can be put to industrial use in powdered form, as in cemented-carbide cutting tools and in wearing surfaces of inspection gages. By powder metallurgy, softer metals can be formed into small machine parts. Self-lubricating sleeve bearings and ball-bearing retainers, long-wearing oil-pump gears for automobile engines, oil-injector nozzles for diesel engines, fine wire-mesh filter screens, friction faces for brakes and clutches, and self-oiling automobile doorstriker plates are only a few of the many applications resulting from research in powder metallurgy. This type of research and development has played a big part in recent years in making plastics, resins, aluminum and magnesium alloys, synthetic rubber substances, synthetic textile fibers, commercial glass items, and other new materials available in quantity for the manufacture of new products and for improvement in existing products.

6-3.3 Product Research

The importance of product research to the continuing prosperity of the enterprise has already been stressed. It embraces the stimulation of new-product concepts to fill the needs of customers and prospective customers, the process of actually developing new products, and the search for new and original uses for existing products. Allied with these activities are studies to open up new possibilities of by-product utilization. A problem in product research may be approached by directing fundamental research principles toward intensive product application. Or the project may remain from start to finish one of applied product research. A well-rounded research program makes use of both approaches.

6-3.4 Equipment and Process Research

Important to the manufacture of a product is the development of processes that are adequate to produce it in the quantity and quality desired. Frequently a product can be made on a minute scale in a research laboratory, whereas the manufacture of that product on a large scale, utilizing the laboratory process, may be quite impracticable. It is then the function of process research to develop methods of manufacturing it on the scale desired. Similarly, certain standards of quality may be set up for the product which may not be easily adhered to in large-scale production. Here again, research study is required to develop methods of maintaining quality in production manufacture.

Research pertaining to industrial processes is usually directed toward the development of methods of manufacture, tools, and equipment, as well as handling devices that tend to increase productivity. The replacement of human skill and heavy labor by mechanical devices to better the operating efficiency, and the development of methods and mechanisms for increasing the safety of processes are both fertile fields for study.

The decision as to alternative processes is one that is usually vested with the research staff in cooperation with representatives from the industrial- and plant-engineering, production, and cost departments. The part played by the research department in this regard is usually to experiment with available processes, techniques, and equipment and to suggest and try out new ideas. A careful analysis of the relative merits of each process would be made by the research department in cooperation with the other departments concerned to determine which is the best for the product under consideration. Once the basic process has been named, the exact operations and details of the process may be determined by the same cooperative groups.

Where feasible, as in the chemical, military armaments, and other industries, *pilot plants* may be set up to carry on in miniature or in small lots the manufacturing operations involved in full-scale production while the research staff, in cooperation with plant engineers and others, observes and perfects the test runs, equipment, and manufacturing processes. This technique is a relatively simple and inexpensive medium for perfecting processes and operations before large-scale production is undertaken.

Perspective 6C FROM DEATH RAY TO LASER

In 1960 the dazzling flash of the first laser immediately conjured up visions of a "death ray" and also called forth rosy forecasts of all sorts of large-scale commercial applications that were expected to be worth $1 billion a year by 1970. Neither vision has materialized. Though the laser has been finding more and more applications—from eye surgery to burning holes in nipples for baby bottles—there isn't really a laser industry as such. This year, for instance, commercial laser sales are expected to reach only $200 million. And despite a flurry of recent reports touting the laser as a missile melter, that use of the laser appears unlikely, at least from the earth—among other difficulties, it would require war to be waged on cloudless days only, since laser beams don't readily penetrate clouds or fog.*

Although the laser may not be a science-fiction weapon, it still has exciting possibilities for industrial applications. As a component of light-wave technology, a miniature laser beam may be able to transmit voice signals, converted to light, through a glass strand as fine as a human hair to deliver up to 672 simultaneous phone conversations. Another possibility of mind boggling potential is the use of laser beams to synthesize compounds or even to create unknown chemicals. The currently closest commercial application of this laser chemistry is for the separation of isotopes to produce uranium fuels.

*source: Gene Bylinsky, "Laser Alchemy is Just Around the Corner," *Fortune*, September, 1977.

COMMENT Laser applications seem slow in coming, but they have actually arrived in a relatively short time since the basic research state. Some discoveries lie dormant for decades before commercial applications are developed. This time lag and the uncertainty of a payoff are factors that tend to discourage industrial support of research.

6-4 ADMINISTRATION OF INDUSTRIAL RESEARCH

Research conducted within the enterprise may be of two types: (1) that which develops or utilizes the suggestions and ideas that originate with employees or are offered to the company by itinerant inventors; and (2) that which is undertaken entirely within a functionalized research department. Both approaches are vital to the enterprise. If the first alone is used, it is likely to degenerate into a hit-and-miss procedure. Sole reliance on the second may lead to the neglect of the real values which can be found in the experience, interest, and ideas of employees. A coordinated dual approach encourages employees to offer suggestions through the "suggestion box" and other methods; initiates two-way cooperation between the research department and the supervisory force whose responsibility for improvements should be emphasized; brings the research department to the aid of employees and foremen in developing ideas and obtaining patents; and follows a well-publicized policy of equitable remuneration by cash, royalty contracts, and other benefits for all whose suggestions, ideas, and inventions serve the company.

6-4.1 Organization

In small companies it is sufficient to select an appropriate director of research and provide him with such technicians as the company can afford. The organization will be simple, direct, and unitary. Where the department is large, it becomes necessary to organize the research personnel into effective working units. From common experience, organization of the research department may be set up (1) by manufacturing departments or plant units; (2) in terms of specific purposes; and (3) by research techniques.

1. This method meets the need of widely scattered plants and companies having diversified processes and products. Each manufacturing unit has its own research laboratory and personnel devoted mainly to the problems and projects of that unit. They may be loosely integrated through a central research executive. Among the disadvantages are tendencies to neglect collaboration among research units and considerable duplication of personnel, equipment, and effort with a resulting waste of money when projects are conducted along parallel lines.

2. Research in terms of specific purposes refers to division of effort according to products, specific problems, or processes. This eliminates much of the duplication, since each branch of the research department works for the common good of all manufacturing divisions. For example, one research unit may be concerned with the development and control of raw materials, another with new products,

and a third with investigating a source of trouble in some manufacturing operation. Findings of the research department usually go to all manufacturing divisions. One drawback in this method is the tendency of research personnel to confine themselves too closely to the assigned problem, neglecting to follow leads they uncover as by-products of their work.

3. The research department can be organized according to techniques involved. This system is based on a specialization of skills and on the natural divisions of the research sciences. A problem of reclaiming metallic particles from grinding sludge may be one of physics, one of metallurgy, or one of chemistry. Hence it may be turned over successively or simultaneously to the physicists, metallurgists, and chemists, each a specialist group within the research department. Provisions for collaboration, of course, are necessary for complete harmony and effectiveness.

6-4.2 Operating Procedures

Management in each company has the responsibility of studying what its research problems are likely to be and then organizing its research department and procedures along lines which promise maximum effectiveness and a minimum duplication of effort at the lowest cost. Each project must be given a clear-cut path to follow from conception of the idea to launching of the product on the production line. Definite stopping points for review of progress and promise as well as for approval to proceed further should be provided for (see Fig. 6–2 for the biography of a typical research project).

The overall budget of the research department may be based on a percentage of sales, a summation of project-cost estimates, a lump sum subject to periodic review, or the probable financial returns. Each has some drawbacks. If sales are the base, research is likely to become lean in depression years when the need for research is most acute. If the base is the total of project costs, the research department may be too narrowly organized, and there will be little opportunity to exploit new ideas as they develop. In the lump-sum method, the research director has excessive control and responsibility over expenditures, and the research effort may be misdirected. Estimates of financial returns from a specific project comprise the least desirable base, mainly because such forecasts involve too many variables for reliable calculations. To minimize the disadvantages of any one method and at the same time to provide a cross check in controlling expenditures, perhaps the best procedure for budgeting the research department is to use the summation of approved-project-cost estimates for the period as a base and to superimpose upon this base a lump-sum allowance for possible additional worthwhile projects which may be forthcoming during the period.

It is natural to expect that not all research projects will turn out profitably. Some encounter insurmountable difficulties and have to be abandoned. Others prove to be economically unsound. Still others may be shown to have no direct present or future application to the business in which the enterprise is engaged. Obviously it is desirable for unsuccessful projects to be

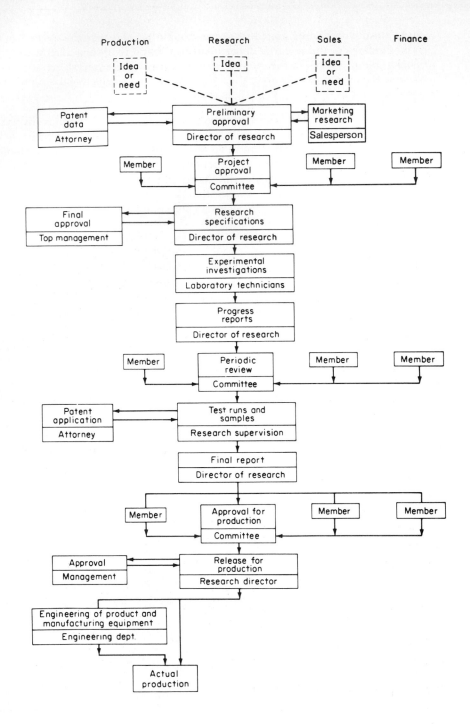

Figure 6-2 The path of a typical research project from its inception to its incorporation into production.

weeded out as early as possible so that additional funds will not be wasted on them. One common method for locating "bad" projects is to make only partial appropriations for each project when it is authorized, so that it must come up for subsequent review and reconsideration when the original allotment has been exhausted. Progress reports not only aid in reviewing projects but also prevent research employees from falling into the undesirable habit of keeping in their heads all information pertaining to their work and findings. These reports enable others to carry on if something happens to the original investigator. They also preserve the experience for future reexamination and to support claims if patent litigation should develop.

6-4.3 Personnel

The industrial research director may be a major executive of the enterprise and devote all or part of his time to the research department, he may be a subexecutive who carries out a policy determined by higher authority, or he may be a college faculty member or a professional research engineer on the staff of some commercial laboratory. He should possess personal research ability, have an orderly mind, and think clearly and instinctively. He should possess one research field in which his talents are recognized, for a director who has won his spurs in research commands the respect of his subordinates.

The research worker, on the other hand, should be a person with a specific area of curiosity together with a facility in that area. His or her talents should be of the type that combines imagination with sound engineering. Facility in any research field is usually best gained by fundamental scientific training of the type offered by the *major scientific schools.* However, as is the case in any other field of endeavor, some good research workers still gain their facility in the *school of experience.*

In stimulating the interest of research personnel, direct wage incentives are often less important than indirect incentives such as special recognition, bonuses for outstanding work, and royalty-sharing policies. Professional or public recognition through publication of achievements, recognition by colleagues, naming of products or processes after the research persons responsible for them, the issuance of patents in the name of the discoverer rather than of the department head—all these are prime incentives to the research worker.

6-5 CREATIVITY

Every researcher and manager welcomes those rare instances when he or she is inspired by an original approach to a question or problem. The person is delighted by the feelings of satisfaction and confidence that accompany a unique solution, but he cannot explain exactly what aroused this creativity. No one can. Creativity embodies both originality and relevance.

Although it is quite easy to spout unique ideas, it is decidedly more difficult to create responses that are relevant to the situation under consideration.

Many studies have been made in recent years to find out what causes and what can promote creative behavior. The mental mechanics of creativity have escaped detection, but several practical observations have been accepted. It appears that creativity is not an inherited talent; we all have it to some degree, and it can be cultivated. There is apparently little or no correlation between high intelligence and greater creativity. Evidence indicates that creative behavior can be encouraged by the right environment and the application of certain techniques.

Brainstorming is the most famous technique for group ideation. It was originated by Alex F. Osborn as a device to increase novelty in advertising. In recent years it has been criticized because it is not the universal solver touted by some proponents, yet it still draws its share of acclaims from practitioners.

Osborn suggests a group size of 5 to 10 people for a brainstorm, although the technique has been used successfully with groups as large as 150. Participants do not have to be experts in the problem area. But they do need to be familiar with the general subject and know the jargon of the trade. It helps to have one or two self-starters in the group to get ideas flowing, and the better the members are at letting themselves go, wildly wrapped up in the discussion, the better the session will be. Fear of looking foolish or fear of being ridiculed will scuttle a session.

The most important person for a successful brainstorm is the leader, but, he or she should not appear important. She should not flout her knowledge or dominate the other members. Instead, after defining the scope of the problem and getting things started, she should limit her activities to keeping the topics in the general problem area and maintaining the informal interplay of ideas. She tries to keep the discussion from degenerating into an inane "bull session" or becoming too formal and restrictive.

Useful guidelines for participants include:

1. Keep the problem as described by the leader clearly in mind.

2. Do not find fault with, or stop to explore in depth, any given idea.

3. Think freely and mention any idea, no matter how wild it is.

4. Maintain a light, humorous, even mock competitive atmosphere.

5. Encourage and support the efforts of other participants.

A productive brainstorming session should produce an idea a minute. All ideas are then recorded. After the session is over, the leader consolidates ideas into natural categories and sends them to the participants for comment. She should not edit the ideas with respect to practicality because an absurd notion could spark a new, significant solution in the second go-around. Eventually the ideas must be graded. The evaluation can be done by having each participant choose a first and second choice in a follow-up meeting in which several groups working on similar problems convene. The leader prepares a final summary with recommended solutions based on previous reviews.

6-6 PRODUCT DEVELOPMENT

From the survey of the broad field of applied research, let us narrow our focus to one of its scenes: product research. Here we should understand the basic considerations that are important to an appraisal of whether or not a specific project of product development is worthwhile. Then, having determined that the product is worthy of continued development, we turn attention to methods of controlling development time and costs.

6-6.1 Consumer Acceptance

Sales depend upon consumer acceptance of the product. Two distinct classes of consumers have to be considered: those who use the product in daily living (the consumer market) and those who use the product in further manufacture (the producer market). Each group of consumers looks for different features in the product, and this indicates the lines of research as well as of marketing.

The ultimate consumer, or general public, usually decides to buy on:

1. Appearance—is the product pleasing and attractive to the eye?

2. Convenience—can it be used readily?

3. Usefulness—does it meet a need or desire?

4. Durability—will it stand up under use?

5. Cost of operation—is it inexpensive to use and keep in good order?

6. Purchase price—how does it compare competitively and in terms of needs met?

7. Diversity of types and sizes from which to choose—does the available variety meet different preferences?

In addition to some of these factors which may be applicable in certain cases, producer consumers look primarily for:

1. Suitability, durability, quality—is the product the best obtainable for use in further production?

2. Stable supply—can it be obtained when required in sustained, desired quantities?

3. Price—can it be bought at a price low enough to keep the *final* cost of the product within the range of competing products in a profitable market?

Frequently ultimate consumers base their decision to buy more on appearance than on the other considerations, and producers endeavoring to cater to that desire stress it in their product designs to the detriment of the other factors. Industrial designers have long been wrestling with the problem of *form design* vs. *functional design,* of appearance vs. utility, for the best design from the standpoint of appearance seldom is the best as regards performance and utility. The automotive industry, for example, in response to demonstrated customer demand, long catered to form design in the evolution of the automobile to the detriment of functional design. Or again, in considering women's stylized shoes, one may be pardoned for wondering if comfort is forgotten in the competition for beauty.

6-6.2 Patent Protection

Before a decision is reached to embark upon an expensive development program, the degree of protection obtainable from patents should be thoroughly explored. A company that is unable thus to protect itself against competition may find that it has lost much of the value of its pioneering efforts. Under the present-day American patent system, a patent may be obtained by any person who has invented or discovered any new and useful process, machine, manufacture, or composition of matter, or any new and useful improvement thereof. In general, invention requires two mental steps: recognition of a need, and a solution that satisfies the need. Moreover, to be inventive and thus subject to patent protection, the idea must not be "obvious" to a person with "ordinary skill in the art." Protection is for a term of 17 years, after which the invention passes into the public domain.

In practice, the patent grant has been used—or misused—by some corporations or corporate combines to perpetuate their control over basic inventions as well as to further monopolies, dictate prices, and regulate production. This perpetuation of control may be accomplished in any of four possible ways. First, there is the simple and usually very reputable practice of obtaining successive improvement patents on a basic invention. Such improvement patents, however, sometimes lose their respectability when they are obtained for the obvious purpose of keeping a basic article on which the patent is about to expire from being thrown on the open market.

The second practice, the so-called "fencing-off device," is that by which the holder of a basic patent surrounds his grant with patents on every conceivable combination of elements, processes, machines, and products, thus heading off competing products developed by different means.

The third use sometimes made of patents is the "fencing-in device." This is just the reverse of the second practice in that a powerful enterprise sometimes is able to secure patents on every possible combination of elements surrounding a basic patent secured by another inventor or company. Thus is the competitor's invention blocked off from further development.

Finally, there is the infringement suit. Nominally, this is purely a legal device for preventing someone from stealing a patented invention. However, it can be used as a controlling device as well. For instance, a competitor desiring to delay or prevent the use of a new discovery may challenge it with or without a clear basis for an independent suit. So costly and long drawn out is such litigation that a financially strong concern may use it as a threat to force into submission a legally right but financially weak competitor.

It is important that the above ramifications of the patent system and their relation to the development program under consideration be carefully studied. Of course, it is sometimes possible for progressive organizations unable to gain patent protection to keep one or more jumps ahead of their competition by improving their products constantly or by introducing new products at frequent intervals. Furthermore, an efficient monopolistic enterprise can often effectively discourage competition simply by manufacturing and marketing its products very cheaply.

6-6.3   Effect on Costs and Profits

Usually before undertaking to develop a particular product, the management of the enterprise must be able to envisage a return on the product that is commensurate with the cost of development. It goes without saying that this requires not only a forecast of the market for the product but also some knowledge of the time, effort, and equipment required in its development. Also important is the estimated cost of manufacturing the product. A product that is developed merely to the point of performing a service is of little practical use unless it can be reproduced commercially. Hence the product design must be carried to a stage where it can be labeled "production design," i.e., a design that can be manufactured in the quantity desired and at a cost in line with the price obtainable for the product.

Sometimes the addition of a new article tends to fill out the line of products; other times the new product competes directly with an existing product and may or may not increase the overall sales and profits of the enterprise.

Many companies, in efforts to broaden their markets, have turned out lower priced "competitive" models of their better products only to have the cheaper model depress the market for the quality goods. In general, the introduction of new products is a good thing, but whether it will be beneficial or detrimental to an established line of products is something to be carefully studied and decided on the merits in each specific case.

A product-development program designed to find ways of utilizing by-products or waste is frequently very worthwhile. A leather-belting company, for example, found markets for waste leather pieces by developing such by-products as shoe soles, dog collars, skate straps, and leather washers. A rubber company developed a pillow market for shredded sponge-rubber waste. A copper smelter learned that rhenium, a metal found in copper ores which formerly went up smelter smokestacks as waste, was better than tungsten for filaments of electronic tubes. Examples such as these have been duplicated thousands of times over. In some cases, profits from products developed from waste may rival those obtained from the main product. Research and imagination are the two chief requisites in turning waste materials into useful products whose value can be many times the cost of development.

Perspective 6D FUTURE TECHNOLOGIES

Basic discoveries made prior to the end of World War II laid the foundations for four outstanding growth industries: jet aircraft, computers, television, and xerography. These four developments are now near their mature stages. At the present time it is difficult to discern any developing technologies that are likely to produce comparable industrial expansion. Five of the more promising R&D areas are listed below.

1. *Solar energy* Improved devices to convert the sun's rays directly into electricity. New types of solar cells used in conjunction with sunlight concentrators could make solar power economically attractive, perhaps within 10 years.
2. *Nuclear power* Thermonuclear fusion controlled to provide safer, cheaper power. The techniques of magnetic confinement, laser fusion, or electron-beam fusion may allow the functioning of a commercial fusion plant within 25 to 35 years.
3. *Geothermal energy* Development of new ways to utilize the earth's heat. By combining advanced technology from chemistry, geology, and hydrology, experiments are underway to directly tap the earth's heat by drilling two holes to the "hot rock" level, then injecting water in one to extract steam from the other.
4. *Transportation* Aircushion or magnetic-suspension vehicles could replace wheel on steel trains. Prototypes are being tested.
5. *Tunnel boring* Earth boring devices using electron beams or nuclear power could make long-distance tube trains feasible.

COMMENT Since so much of the world's attention is focused on energy, research and development activities follow accordingly. But even higher investments in energy research cannot guarantee miracles that will deliver another era of low-cost energy. Foreseeable advances should help us cope with the more acute shortages, but changes in life style—using less energy—will probably be as significant as the effects of future technologies.

6-7 PROGRAM EVALUATION AND REVIEW TECHNIQUE (PERT)

There is a continuing concern among research and development managers about slippages in schedules and overages in cost. The nature of R&D, attempting to do something that has not been done before, postulates uncertainty. Estimates of cost and completion time for original work are admittedly approximate, but the pressure of competitive prices and marketing deadlines has forced greater attention to project control.

Problems of planning and coordinating R&D projects led to the development of the program evaluation and review technique (PERT).[3] PERT is primarily a time management tool, but the planning that goes into the schedule tends also to reduce costs through improved coordination and communication.

The most distinctive feature of a PERT application is the network, a picture of the activities required to complete a project. A sample network is shown in Figure 6–3. Each arrow represents a distinct activity. The circles or nodes denote carefully defined end points and/or beginnings of activities. The sequential arrangement of the arrows corresponds to the project's planned progress. The network thus shows the interrelationships of different parts of the project and which activities are dependent on the successful completion of prerequisite activities.

Figure 6–3 portrays in a skeletal fashion some major steps in developing a new product. The two arrows from the first event indicate that while a preferred preliminary design is being selected, alternative designs will continue to be pursued. The flow of activities from left to right shows successive steps from inception to production. The efforts of different departments, teams, and managers are programmed. Each can observe how related activities depend on their effort.

Once the basic plan is agreed upon, activity duration times must be estimated. In a PERT application, three estimates are given for the duration

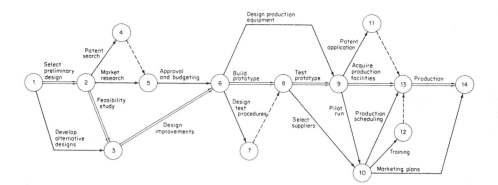

Figure 6-3 A skeletal network for R & D projects. An actual project network would be much more detailed and would include activity durations. The double-lined arrows show a possible critical path for the project. The dashed arrows are called dummies and are used in the network to facilitate different node numbers for all activities. Thus the node numbers at the beginning and end uniquely identify each activity, and they are so described in a computer application of PERT.

[3]PERT is a very close relative of critical path scheduling (CPS). Both are network control techniques first used in 1958. The probabilistic features of PERT make it more suitable for R&D projects, while CPS is more closely associated with construction and industrial scheduling.

of each activity—an optimistic, a pessimistic, and a most likely duration. It is assumed that the actual time to do the activity will fall within the given range with a relative frequency of a prescribed statistical distribution. Under this assumption, a single expected duration is calculated for each activity. Using these single durations, the *critical path* is identified.[4] This path is the chain of activities, stretching the length of the project, that must be completed according to a rigid schedule if the project is to finish when expected. The activities not on the critical path have "float" or slack time which allows leeway in scheduling.

Knowledge of which activities are critical contributes significantly to resource planning and project control. Resources are diverted from noncritical to critical activities whenever there is doubt that planned progress on the critical path can be maintained. Progress is measured frequently by reports from inspectors or evaluating teams. These "updating" reports are used to correct the estimated activity durations and are the bases for resource reassignments. Thus attention is continually redirected to currently lagging activities that will be likely to damage future performance.

The systematic planning required to develop an arrow network and the attention focused by updating reports are probably the most important contributions of a PERT application. However, more refined applications can be made when the stature of the project warrants it. Elaborate cost and resource analysis methods are available. As in the application of all management tools, a decision about which tools to use should be based upon the cost of application compared to the benefits derived.

6-8 REVIEW QUESTIONS

1. What is meant by "research," and why are most companies interested in it?

2. Why is there a trend toward organized research? What are the types of external research organizations?

3. Distinguish between the fundamental and applied research efforts.

4. What factors deserve evaluation before management decides to proceed with a product development program?

5. Of what importance is PERT to management in the development of a product?

6. What is meant by "critical path" and "float"? What is the purpose of updating?

6-9 TOPICS FOR DISCUSSION

1. A typical success story for a small, research-based enterprise reads as follows:
The founder was formerly an engineer in a medium-sized company; he discovered a new principle upon which the company could enlarge its product line. The company declined to

---

[4]Computer programs for PERT and CPS calculations are widely available. The calculations can also be done very easily by hand for networks of a moderate size.

promote the idea, so the engineer left to form his own company for the purpose of developing his new principle. Two years later he successfully tested the first commercial prototype of the product; 2 years thereafter he obtained his first sizable production order and refinanced the enterprise to permit enlarging his facilities to handle this order; and 3 years thereafter he paid his first dividend to stockholders.

What advantages does a new research-based enterprise such as that described above have over an established firm in pioneering a new product? What disadvantages and problems must the new firm overcome in successfully developing, producing, and marketing a new product?

2. Discuss the many ways in which the patent system, despite the grant of a monopoly to a single individual or firm, (a) fosters competition, (b) benefits industry and society in a free-enterprise system, and (c) may become a disservice to the public in some cases when abused.

3. Small-business enterprises rarely have the funds to maintain research departments. How can they assure themselves of the needed research to keep abreast of advancing technology, production techniques, and the science of marketing?

4. Case 6A: *Hyperideation?*

New ideas will hopefully lead to better ways of doing things in regular business activities as well as in formal research programs. One of the reasons brainstorming works for both managers and researchers is explained by the well-known adage that "two heads are better than one." In the case of brainstorming, two or more people exchanging views are likely to generate more ideas because thoughts mentioned by one person tend to spark kindred, but different, thoughts from the listeners. This chain-reaction effect causes "hyperideation."

Try an experiment.

Without talking to anyone else, spend 15 minutes listing all the ideas you can for the proverbial "better mousetrap." Then get two friends together and follow the procedures for a brainstorming session. You act as the recorder to list all the ideas they generate in 15 minutes for new ways to trap mice.

Questions

1. Compare your list of ideas with the list developed from the brainstorming session. Are the lengths of the lists proportional to the number of participants? Comment on the practicality of ideas from both lists.

2. Under what conditions could brainstorming be applied to business situations?

5. Case 6B: *Who's Fooling Who?*

The task of acquiring time estimates for jobs must have started a great while ago; perhaps there was a *P*yramid *ER*ection *T*echnique to help Egyptian schedulers. At any rate they probably had estimating difficulties similar to the ones we now encounter in network scheduling. Ernest O. Codier of General Electric Company gave an address in 1961 to the American Management Association that included the following picturesque tale of modern estimating woes:

There is a traditional man/manager gaming model for time estimating. This game runs approximately as follows: You pick up the phone and with casual and disarming friendliness inquire, "Say, George, just off the top of your head, how long will it take to get out 14 frabastats?" Now George is a very competent fellow and he knows instinctively that it would take 8 weeks to fabricate 14 frabastats provided everything happened the way it *should* happen. But he does not give you this answer immediately because he knows that there will be some normal amount of unforeseen difficulty involved, and he will add a factor to take into account this average uncertainty, say, 2 weeks. Now he has 10 weeks. But George is not misled by the informality of your request; he knows that ultimately in one form or another this is going to show up as a commitment to you, to provide 14 frabastats in a specified time. Furthermore, George knows the nature of the business, and he knows you. He knows that time estimates are traditionally too long, and that somewhere along the line he can expect to get cut back. So at this point he adds the fat, which is his considered opinion as to how severely this time estimate will get cut later on—say 3 weeks. He has now arrived at 13 weeks, and this is the figure *you* get. When this proves to be too long, as it invariably does, since it *is in fact* too long, the time will get cut as George expects. By one or another mechanism you will work the problem backwards and ask for performance 2½ weeks sooner. You have done pretty well as a manager, and have cut out only approximately the amount that George anticipated; he makes routine grumbling noises, because this is proper form, and 10½ weeks becomes his commitment. Now precisely what do you *know* at this point? Not very much. You do *not* know how long the job should take under ideal circumstances, and you have no measure of potential trouble sources which you as George's manager might be able to help him smooth out. Furthermore, if George actually delivers 14 frabastats in 10½ weeks, you are not really sure whether this was an outstanding effort, or whether it was just an average performance. . .

Questions

1. Recognizing that defense tactics such as those employed by George are not atypical, what do you suggest as an alternative?

2. Turning the situation around, put yourself in George's position when he learns that because of an extremely tight contract, he has been scheduled to get out 14 frabastats in 7 weeks without extra assistance. What should he do?

3. Assume further that George protests the rush order given in Question 2, but cannot get the time lengthened because frabastats are vital to the project, and meeting the project's deadline is crucial; so, with much sweat he gets them out in 8 weeks. Should this experience be referenced as the reason for an 8-week estimate for the production of 14 frabastats the next time they are needed? Why?

6. Case 6C: *Government R&D*

Annual expenditures by the Federal government for research and development, primarily in the military field, have recently totaled more than twice the yearly outlay for comparable activity during World War II.

From many voices, pens, and typewriters has come a clamor to eliminate "wasteful duplication," "interservice competition," and "uncoordinated planning" to ensure that the country gets the most from its military R&D dollar. The contention is that while there is no objection to the pursuit of a wide range of *basic* military research projects, once the test tube and the computer probe of technology have been completed, military planners would then step in and determine which new potential weapon system, which one item of military hardware, will best serve the country's objectives and hence should be pursued further. Proponents of this thinking say we need more Manhattan projects, referring to the war-time A-bomb development, and fewer Pershing-Polaris-Minuteman projects, referring to the Army–Navy–Air Force competing ballistic-missile developments of more recent years.

Other people point out that the military cannot afford to put all its eggs in one research basket. This school argues that military R&D already is restricted by too much direction and control, which only serves to slow down the development of promising avenues of offensive and defensive strength.

This question of multiplicity of military research endeavors is of tremendous industrial importance. Not only does it affect the country's security, the well-being of the nation's economy, and the continuity of many R&D projects performed by industry for the government, but also similar questions have been posed concerning competition in private commercial research as among technologists and divisions in a company and among various research organizations.

Questions

1. Should the United States adopt a policy of increased planning and more stringent controls to eliminate duplication and interservice competition related to military R&D projects? Do you take the same stand on competing private research within a company? How do you feel about competition in private research performed by separate companies? Support your positions.

7

PHYSICAL FACILITIES

The successes of R & D efforts take physical form in modifications to existing production facilities or the construction of new ones. The physical facilities of an industrial enterprise consist of the manufacturing and office buildings, the surrounding environment, and the facilities that promote the production of a product or a range of products. This chapter is concerned with the location and design of a plant and its contents to meet production requirements and expectations for comfortable, convenient working conditions.

If a new plant is required, where should it be located? What pollution controls should be considered? In most new and existing buildings, high standards of working conditions today dictate that various facilities be installed for the comfort and effectiveness of employees. What kinds of equipment are involved, and what factors dictate the use of each?

The production equipment of the enterprise is influenced by many factors and in turn affects the plant layout. What criteria can be employed in selecting this equipment to achieve the objectives of the organization? How do product and process requirements influence the plant layout? Why is flexibility in physical facilities necessary?

7 PHYSICAL FACILITIES

7-1 PLANT LOCATION

The decision on locating an industrial plant is frequently one that has a vital effect on the success or failure of the operation of that plant. Hence it should be based upon a careful consideration of all factors pertinent to the business of the particular enterprise. The nature and emphasis of the factors in plant location vary among industries and with changing technical and economic conditions. Some industries have tended to follow their markets in the location of their plants; others, such as the textile industry in Massachusetts, have located around the sources of power; still others, notably Pennsylvania's iron and steel industries, have tended to seek the source of their raw materials. From time to time new or special factors have arisen to outweigh the usual considerations involved in plant location. For example, the current attention given to retaining or improving the quality of the environment has barred some plants from traditional locations. Concern for pollution has made waste disposal a paramount consideration in all plant location studies.

7-1.1 Steps in Selecting the Plant Site

There are three main steps in locating a plant. The first, the *selection of the region* or general area in which the plant is to be located, usually requires consideration of these five factors: (1) proximity to the market; (2) proximity to the necessary materials; (3) availability of transportation facilities; (4) adequacy of public and private services such as power, water, fuel, and gas; and (5) favorable climatic conditions (for most industries, mild winters and comfortable summers).

Once the general area has been determined, the search for a plant site narrows to the second step, the *selection of the particular community.* Which of all the communities in the chosen region can best supply the needs of the individual enterprise? The answer is generally found in (1) a labor supply that is adequate in numbers and in types of skill required; (2) wage scales that are competitive with or lower than those paid by other firms in the same industry; (3) other enterprises in the community which are complementary or supplementary as regards raw materials, products,[1] labor demands, and skills used; (4) a friendly and cooperative attitude toward industry; (5) moderate taxes and the absence of restricting laws and ordinances; and (6)

[1] The pull of raw materials and finished products in plant-size location is well illustrated by the chemical industry. Frequently the finished product of one chemical plant is the raw material of another and a pipeline is the quickest and cheapest method of transportation. At Niagara Falls, N.Y., for example, a number of major chemical plants have settled where they could be interconnected by a maze of pipelines. These range from a few hundred feet to several miles in length and carry from plant to plant such chemicals as acetylene, hydrogen, chlorine, hydrogen chloride, caustic, calcium hypochlorite, and lime slurry.

favorable living conditions and standards which label the community for both key and rank-and-file employees as a good place in which to live. Final decision on the general area, however, occasionally reverts to one of the regional factors in the first step. For example, a town without regular railroad service might be ruled out on that score alone. Electric power rates might tip the scale in favor of a particular community, as might an unlimited supply of water.

The third step is the *selection of the exact plant site* in the favored community. Alternative communities may have to be considered if no available or adequate plant site can be found in the first community selected.

In the search for a site, the principal consideration is land. Is it ample in size, including room for expansion and for the parking of employees' cars? Is the topography right for the type of building desired, and are the soil content and drainage such as to provide the proper foundation?

The second factor in order of importance is very likely to be transportation. Is the potential site as readily accessible to rail, motor, water, or air transportation as may be required? Can employees with and without automobiles conveniently reach the plant?

Then come the miscellaneous factors pertaining to the site's surroundings. Will employees consider it a good place to work? Are there any building and zoning restrictions that would not permit the type of building planned? Is the community fire protection adequate and available to the site? Will the cost of bringing in power and other utilities as well as sewage disposal be prohibitive?

Plant location today is generally a matter of costs tempered by circumstance. Theoretically the most favorable location of a plant is that spot where, in consideration of the business as a whole, the total cost of producing and delivering goods to all customers is the lowest. This total cost includes the cost of all factors listed above which may be pertinent to the enterprise involved as well as any special considerations peculiar to that enterprise. Actually, however, the decision as to plant location is not always based on reason, for more times than management is willing to admit, corporate or financial ties of the enterprise or personal whims of some top executive exercise the balance of power in this regard, and circumstances then takes precedence over cost.

Perspective 7A   CORPORATE MIGRATION

Americans have a well-deserved reputation for mobility—according to the Census Bureau, each year one in five of us moves to a new address. There is nothing new about this: back in the 1850s, Nathaniel Hawthorne observed, "No people on earth have such vagabond habits as ours." American corporations also have a touch of the vagabond in them. In just the last 5 years, for example, 73 of the *Fortune 500,* or almost 15 per cent, have moved their headquarters from one city to another. Several of the 500 have done that more than once during their corporate lifetimes."*

Corporate migration is not a new fad, only the directions have changed. The first wave of relocation, from the 1880s to 1920s, saw a move toward centers of finance and communications—the big cities. The direction reversed during the 1960s as companies left the big cities for the suburbs. The latest wave is toward suburbs or smaller cities in the "sunbelt" of the South and West.

This year 117 of the *Fortune 500* are headquartered in the Sunbelt, compared with just 84 in 1970. (During that same span, 2.5 million Americans moved to the region.) What has happened in recent years is that the development of transportation and communication technology has cut the cords that bound big corporations to the traditional headquarters cities.*

*SOURCE: Herbert E. Meyer, "Why Corporations Are on the Move," *Fortune,* May, 1976.

COMMENT: Besides the calculable factors that point to relocation, such as labor and power costs, accessability to raw materials and markets, support facilities, and taxes, less tangible factors may decide the move. Personal preference of top executives may lead to relocation; more lenient personal taxes, easier commuting, and more desirable living conditions are magnets for migration. Relocation of a corporate headquarters also provides an opportunity to restructure the management and to prune personnel. The fresh start is conducive to shaking things up and may even revitalize operations.

7-1.2 Trends in Plant Location

Five trends in plant location are now discernible. The first is the tendency to locate plants away from the cities, *in the suburbs*[2] or smaller towns. Suburban areas now offer practically all the advantages, facilities, and services supplied by cities and do so with lower assessment values and tax rates. Larger land areas can be obtained at much lower cost in more sparsely settled areas. There is room to spread out the plant, allow for expansion, provide off-street loading and unloading facilities, and furnish adequate parking areas for employees' cars. While travel distance sometimes is greater, travel time usually is less, as city traffic tieups are left behind. The public- and customer-relations value of a modern, functional plant well landscaped in pleasant, roomy surroundings is not to be underestimated.

Second, there is a swing toward planned industrial centers otherwise known as *industrial parks.* These are the industrial equivalent of the community-type residential development, each accommodating a group of manufacturing and distributing plants in a given area. The number of such parks in the country today is estimated to exceed 700, the exact number depend-

[2]There appears to be some indication of a swing back to urban areas. Superhighways radiating to and from most metropolitan areas, major rebuilding and renovation programs to clean up and modernize centers of major cities, and a gradual recognition that many people prefer to live and work in cities, with their diversity of shopping, cultural, entertainment, and professional facilities, all are magnets tending to counteract the suburban trend. Office personnel, in particular, seem to prefer jobs in cities because of the lure of lunch-hour shopping. Certain industries, among them printing, publishing, textiles, and food processors, historically seem to have preferred urban locations.

ing on what constitutes an industrial park.[3] The developer of the center usually provides utilities and other necessary services. He closely controls the site preparation and use of the land in order to achieve an orderly, attractive community of manufacturing concerns. The developer in some instances may even build and finance the plants in the center. In short, it is the cost sharing, construction, and financing advantages provided by these centers which have been largely responsible for their rapid growth in numbers and size in recent years.

A third trend pertains to the *growing competition for industry* among states, municipalities, and community organizations to locate in their midst. This organized competition originally started in the Northeast a number of years ago as communities attempted to fill vacated textile plants. It has since spread to all sections of the country as a method of attracting the dollars and jobs industry brings to the area in which it locates.

Intense competition is found in some Southeastern states where generous concessions are dangled in front of the cost-conscious eyes of industrial managements. As "an expression of welcome," free plant sites sometimes are offered, roads are paved leading to the plant, and water and sewer lines are extended, all at the community's expense. Tax concessions are widespread as new industry is made exempt from all taxes except possibly school levies for a period of years. Other communities will construct the plant building to a company's designs and specifications, assume all taxes and insurance on it, and lease it to the company at absurdly low rates. Apart from such concessions, some companies are attracted to the South and to rural areas in other sections of the country because of their growing economic importance and because wage rates in some nonindustrialized localities are still below rates paid in heavily industrialized areas. Sometimes there is an escapist motive as management uses relocation as a means of dodging featherbedding labor customs and burdensome union agreements generated by employee pressures and management weaknesses of the past.

A word of caution: Confronted with concessions, wage differentials, differences in work effort, and other attractive opportunities if it will but relocate its plant, management has a firm obligation to consider the long-term influence of these factors on the enterprise and on the community itself. Some are at best temporary or apparent advantages. Wage rates soon may be increased by the greater competition for labor's services and by unions moving into the area. Extra training costs, not foreseen, are found necessary to industrialize the labor supply. Other advantages, while more

---

[3]It appears that everyone owning a cow pasture along an express highway or along a railroad track by now has erected a sign proclaiming it to be the site of "a new industrial park." Also, enterprising real-estate men who acquire vacant industrial plants with the intent of subdividing and leasing the space often advertise such property as industrial parks. The minimum qualifications of a bona fide industrial park include adequate land space; a master plan for its development which provides for minimum lot size, land use and setback, architectural requirements, and landscaping; streets ample for truck traffic; available railroad sidings; and water and power in ample supply.

permanent and real, may harm the municipality. The enterprise coming into a community tends to aggravate the community's problems of providing civic facilities and improvements. Unless the enterprise pays its fair share in taxes, it and its employees may be the eventual losers.

Much community industrial planning and much of the industrial migration trend itself is based on sound economic reasoning. Nevertheless, each potential migrant will do well to reflect on which of the rose-colored advantages offered by a new location are real and are sufficiently permanent to justify what of necessity is an expensive and quite irrevocable move.

The fourth trend in plant location is toward *decentralization.* Decentralization, the spreading out of plants of a particular enterprise into new locations, is a trend that began a number of years ago and still continues today but with significantly new motivations. Formerly, industry set up branch plants principally to garner new markets and to provide cheaper and more rapid service to customers.

In recent years, however, a new motive for decentralizing plants has resulted from a recognition of the clumsiness of the gigantic plants so characteristic of the mass-production industries. A large plant is not necessarily more efficient than a smaller plant. On the contrary, a large plant frequently becomes unwieldy, difficult to manage, and a victim of inertia. The management of such a plant is usually so far removed from the operating functions that its decisions become quite impersonal and it tends to lose its perspective of the plant problems. Also the span of administrative control of any one top executive or group of executives is usually such that regardless of the assistance of subordinates, the top management of an extremely large plant is very often unable to comprehend clearly the vastness of the plant under its control. Other factors, such as the difficulty of providing the tremendous supply of personnel necessary, as well as the internal transportation, servicing, and maintenance problems of a large plant, are quite apparent. Not only are several smaller and scattered plants frequently easier to manage than one extremely large plant, but also the production cannot be completely tied up by a fire or other contingencies at any one point.

Basically, decentralization may be accomplished by one of two methods: (1) by the unit or *horizontal method* or (2) by the subsidiary or *vertical method.* Under horizontal decentralization, each branch plant is set up to manufacture a complete product or line of products. Each starts out with raw materials and ends up with the finished article, and the production at each plant is merely *supplementary* to that of the others. Large baking companies buy flour, sugar, shortening, and eggs for their bakeries in various cities throughout the country, and in each one they end up with bread, crackers, and pastry items to be distributed to their local selling outlets.

With the vertical type of decentralization, on the other hand, the basic idea is to remove the manufacture of parts and subassemblies from the main plants to one or more subsidiary plants. The subsidiary or *complementary* plants ship the parts and subassemblies to the main plant, which then performs the assembly operations on the product. Many home-appliance manufacturers have set up a spider web of branch plants to make plastic cases, handles, etc., required on appliances, others to supply electrical parts, and still others to furnish electronic devices. All these items are then assembled into finished appliances at the central plant. A variation of this vertical decentralization is employed by some of the automotive companies, in that the main plant ships parts and subassemblies to its branches scattered about the country, where cars are finally assembled, generally within the market area served.

Pollution control is the fifth trend and is probably the most discussed problem of industry today. The volume of industrial waste is staggering. The four major areas of pollution are water, air, noise, and land.

It was estimated in 1969 that the food, textile, paper and chemical, oil, rubber, metals, machinery, and transportation industries in this country spill a total of 25 trillion gallons of waste water annually. Many rivers and lakes have become so filthy they will not support life, much less provide potable water. Industries that rely on pure water have few choices of location. In addition to the discharge of solids, oil, and chemicals into water, there is the problem of heat dispersion. With the movement toward nuclear plants as a source of electrical power, thermal pollution is receiving more attention because of the huge demands of such plants for cooling water.

Polluted air is present over almost every industrialized community. Much of the blame for the contaminated atmosphere can be directed toward automobile exhaust, but industrial wastes are also big contributors. Factories and electric-power-generating plants emit sulfur oxides and fly ash in the form of carbon, oil, grease, and microscopic pieces of metals or metal oxides. By whatever name, it is serious. Inversion layers of warm air trapping fume-clogged cold air below have caused marked increases in deaths due to respiratory ailments during inversion periods. The obvious warning from increasing concern for air pollution is that old plants will have to install air-purifying equipment, and new plants, even if they contribute minimally to air contamination, will have to locate in areas not subject to inversion cycles.

Noise control within plants has been investigated for many years. Only recently has attention been devoted to industrial noise as an environmental contaminator. The noise level in New York City regularly exceeds 85 decibels, a level some scientists regard as the point above which continuous noise can produce deafness. Less startling, but far more widespread, are the noisy environments that produce stress and lead to more argumentative dispositions at work and at home.

Land spoilage is characterized by unplanned urban sprawls and the sterile ridges of strip mines. Unlike air and water, land has no internal currents to dilute pollutants. Oil and pesticides, once in the ground, stay long after the source of pollution is removed. With land, as with air and water, it is difficult to measure the full effects of exploitation. Chemicals in the land kill vegetation and find their way into humans via pasture lands or gardens. Oxygen-producing vegetation cannot be forever replaced by paving and buildings without some harmful effects. Conservationists point out the value of protecting nature and are more successfully promoting legislation to limit the industrial use of certain natural resources.

The conflicting problems of industrial waste disposal are well exemplified by a comparison of nuclear plants with power-generating plants that utilize oil, gas, or coal. The combustion of fossil fuels contaminates the air. Nuclear plants do not foul the air, but small doses of radioactive material do seep into the cooling water, and the used radioactive fuel must be packaged for burial in caves or dumped at sea. Thus both alternatives contribute to pollution, but still the demand for electrical power increases; the U.S. Bureau of Mines estimates that by the year 2000 energy consumption in the United States could increase from the 1978 rate of about 80 quads per year to 150 (a "quad" represents a quadrillion BTU's which is equivalent to the energy from 175 million barrels of oil or 46 million tons of coal).

7-2 PLANT BUILDINGS

In selecting the plant buildings, a decision must first be made between the *single-story building* and the *multistory building.* Each has its advantages and disadvantages. These must be weighed with respect to the requirements of the particular enterprise. The single-story structure, with its fewer columns and servicing equipment installed in overhead trusses, permits greater flexibility of plant layout. It provides for more uniform illumination, is easier to expand by simply moving a wall, gives greater floor-loading capacity with less vibration, and requires lighter foundations. It permits easier handling and routing of materials and facilitates supervision. The multistory building makes more efficient use of land space and generally results in lower construction costs per square foot of floor space and in lower heating costs. Vertically arranged production areas are possible, which make for more compact layouts and permit the gravity flow of materials.

Allied with the trend toward the location of plants in suburban areas is a trend toward the erection of *single-story buildings* as illustrated in Figure 7-1. Suburban locations frequently offer sufficient land area to accommodate the desired floor space on a single level. Also, the present emphasis on buildings designed around the process, on flexibility in plant layouts, on line production, and on lower materials-handling and routing costs is a strong inducement in favor of the one-story structure. However, for light manufacturing and where gravity flow can be utilized, the multistory building still has it place.

Present thought on building interiors is in the direction of *larger and higher bays.* Column spacings 40 by 60 feet apart are now very popular. Undoubtedly this trend has been influenced by the increased demand for "convertible" plants capable of "vibrating" between the manufacture of military and of nonmilitary goods. There is also widespread use of assembly-line techniques requiring wider and longer bays. Overhead installation of "pack-

Figure 7-1 *Factory* magazine named Omark Industries' Oregon Saw Chain Division plant one of the top 10 in the United States. The 154,500-square-foot plant is attractively landscaped, and original art hangs in the employee lunchroom. The facility uses automatic assembly techniques for saw chain parts and has a computerized inventory control system. (Courtesy of Omark Industries.)

age" servicing equipment (exhaust fans, filters, heaters, and air-conditioning units) has been responsible in part for the increase in plant headroom.

Basements of manufacturing plants are being used increasingly for storage, service tunnels, and employee facilities. Locker rooms, washrooms, and cafeterias are frequently situated there, so that the manufacturing floor is free of such process-interrupting facilities. More window sash and less masonry is to be found in building *walls,* with continuous sash around the building growing in favor. However, some plants for reasons of lower construction and maintenance costs and where the preference is for artificial "controlled" illumination employ solid walls with only a glass "vision strip" to cater to the habitual human desire to see out. Also, because of lower initial and maintenance costs, monitor and saw-tooth *roofs* are giving way to flat roofs. Some plants are using roof ponds or water-spray systems for reflective and evaporative cooling. Plant areas under such roofs are reported to be about 10 degrees cooler in summer.

Office buildings or office areas in industrial buildings range from simple austerity for the office administration which desires minimal, functional facilities to ostentatious luxury for those who, by providing the corporate niceties of life, build a monument to their regime and perhaps divert the office force from the real task at hand. In the midst of these two extremes we find today's typical industrial office about as follows.

It is a simple, brick- and window-walled structure, perhaps two stories high. Movable, "modular," internal office partitions provide layout flexibility over the years, and the module may in some cases surround built-in desks and tables. Acoustical ceilings muffle office-machine clatter and employee chatter, while flexible-tile floors reduce traffic noise and add to the general appearance. Also to be found are air conditioning, flush-mounted fluorescent lights, sun-control drapes or blinds, built-in communication services (e.g., telephone lines, pneumatic tubes, public-address and piped-music systems), and provision for the bane of every office manager's existence, the coffee-break vending machine. Gay colors remove the inherent plainness of the interior. Much attention is paid to the visitor's first-impression focal point, the lobby. It is usually uncluttered and styled for dramatic simplicity, with decorative effects derived from displays or photos of company products and perhaps a painting or two of the company's founding fathers. Cheerful lounges and cafeterias for executive and office personnel are generally provided. In sum, whereas austerity may be false economy and ostentatiousness may fail when tested on the auction block of economic returns, the evolving industrial office is one which supplies pleasant surroundings in which to perform the managerial, professional, and clerical work of the enterprise and does so at moderate cost.

Once a decision is made as to the type of building, its arrangement and position on the plant site must be considered. Drainage, parking, railroad sidings, roadways, location of receiving and shipping docks, zoning restrictions, provision for future expansion, and appearance from adjoining highways and railroad lines are typical of the considerations involved in locating the building on its site. Industrial architects and construction engineers are usually called on to advise in this connection as well as in the design and construction of the building, so vital are these decisions to the future of the enterprise.

Perspective 7B   CLIMBING COSTS FOR PLANT CONSTRUCTION

Many factors have combined in the 1970s to push the cost of plant construction up at an alarming rate. The cost of new electric generating capacity was $107 per kilowatt in 1967 for the American Electric Company; by 1975 the company reported that the cost was $230 a kilowatt and by the 1980s it is expected to reach $550 a kilowatt. DuPont's costs for new plants rose rather consistently from a 2 per cent annual rate up to 9 per cent per year from 1960 to 1973, and then inflated at a 23 per cent rate for 1974.

Factors contributing to construction-cost inflation include construction wages that increased faster than wages in general, higher interest rates for borrowed money, prices of building materials and industrial hardware that increased faster than the broad price index, and the added cost of meeting new antipollution and job-safety standards. These factors hit basic industries the hardest—iron and steel, chemicals, electric utilities, and other capital intensive activities that turn raw resources into materials and energy. And it is in precisely these industries that greater capacity is still needed.

7-3 PLANT SERVICES

The building-equipment items discussed in this section, although not all-inclusive, are those to which industry is today devoting major attention. They point up current trends in management's thinking as regards installations for better process control and manufacturing efficiency as well as for employees' increased comfort and safety. Lest these last named appear to be purely philanthropic benefits, it should be pointed out that they pay dividends in the form of greater productivity and lower accident-compensation costs.

7-3.1 Conditioned Air

Practically all machine tools generate heat. Some are dust, fume, moisture, or smoke producers. Human occupancy of a plant results in lower oxygen content and higher carbon dioxide content. At the same time, human lungs and bodies give off heat and moisture. Odors and bacteria are introduced. Sunlight and artifical lights as well are responsible for an appreciable amount of heat. Winter weather in most sections of the country cools plant interiors. Yet some industrial processes require constant temperatures throughout the year. Others need constant or at least controlled humidity, while still others depend upon the removal of virtually all air-borne dust particles. Thus industrial air conditioning in its broadest sense requires control over temperature, humidity, dust, motion, purity (freshness and bacteria), and odors. Also, there is increased acceptance of comfort conditioning as a factor in maintaining morale and creating good public relations. This trend is found particularly in office and engineering areas, cafeterias, and sales showrooms. However, it is spreading to manufacturing areas as more employees demand more comfortable summertime working conditions and industry finds that increased productivity tends to offset the cost involved.

The control of *temperature* generally involves heating the air in winter and cooling it in summer. However, some plants, in which continuous operations produce considerable heat, require year-round cooling. Heat may be generated from a central heating plant, with the heating medium—usually hot water or steam—piped to heat-radiating devices in the plant areas. "Packaged" or self-contained boilers are becoming popular in the newer plants and are located right in the manufacturing buildings adjacent to the production areas served. For small or remote structures, heating is frequently accomplished by "direct-fired" heaters, each containing a heating element through which air is forced.

Large air-conditioning systems usually pipe the coolant from a centralized compressor plant to local areas where air is run through the coils. For smaller areas, self-contained air conditioners are located directly in the area served. In some sections of the country heat pumps, which both remove and supply heat, are coming into favor for year-round air tempering.

Humidity and *dust* are controlled as part of the temperature conditioning.

Moisture is added to the dry winter air and removed from the moist summer air. Dust is collected by filters and electrostatic air cleaners. *Air motion* and *purity* are encouraged by the proper positioning of incoming air ducts and exhaust outlets to move fresh air throughout the entire area. *Bacteria* and *odors* are removed by means of ozone and germicidal lamps or by passing the air over chemicals.

7-3.2 Illumination

Light and paint are the Siamese twins of illumination. Together they are a team which can banish darkness; one without the other will only half do the job. Good illumination in a plant soon pays for itself in greater productive efficiency, improved morale of employees, fewer accidents, and better housekeeping.

The rapid progress in artificial lighting is attested by the rapid rise in standards of plant illumination. Not many years ago the average industrial illumination achieved by artifical lighting was about 7 footcandles. Today well-lighted work areas receive up to 100 footcandles, and drafting rooms or other areas for very fine work up to 200 footcandles.

Nevertheless, proper intensity for the type of work performed is only one part of good illumination. Even brightness throughout the area without dark shadows is very important, as is elimination of the tunnel or cave effect which was so characteristic of old localized lighting. Furthermore, glare from improperly shielded or poorly placed light sources and reflections from highly reflective walls or shiny surfaces should be minimized. Finally, the light should be "cool," or give off little heat.

Fluorescent lighting properly engineered fills most of these requirements. It is the type of artifical lighting that is most widely used by industry today, having to a great extent replaced incandescent lamps. The advantages of fluorescent lighting are high efficiency, low glare, large area of light source (fewer shadows), little heat, and its availability in colors (daylight, white, green, gold, blue, pink) for different effects and applications. Furthermore, it is more economical in operation, 100 watts of fluorescent lighting being approximately equivalent in footcandle illumination to 300 watts of incandescent lighting.

The other phase of good plant illumination—*color conditioning*—has assumed its present importance only in recent years. The principal objective of color conditioning is "three-dimensional seeing"—the painting of industrial interiors to achieve uniform brightness but with sufficient contrasts so that the work area is more interesting to an employee's eyes than are his surroundings. This means that the walls and the base of the machine must provide uniform seeing conditions without eye-tiring light-dark contrasts. The contrasting colors are then saved for the operating area of the machine upon which the operator should focus his attention.

In actual shop practice, this principle calls for painting ceilings and upper walls light pastel colors, lower walls and machine bases slightly darker but harmonizing colors, and the working areas of machines buff or other contrasting light colors. Color codes further point up obstacles and dangerous objects with yellow or yellow-and-black stripes, fire equipment with red, first-aid equipment with green, etc.

7-3.3   Noise Control

During the past few years industry has displayed an increasing interest in the control of industrial noises. While a reduction or elimination of objectionable noises in a plant lessens the wear and tear on employees' nerves, reduces mental fatigue, and improves morale, such a problem is far from philanthropic. An increase in the amount of work performed, improvement in its quality, and a reduction of costly accidents and of compensation cases involving "industrial deafness" definitely result from the control of noise.

Noise and vibration are partners in crime, and, in fact, noise transmitted to the air directly from the noise-producing equipment may be unimportant compared with that transmitted through vibration of the equipment base to the building structure. Hence the emphasis of much acoustical treatment is on vibration.

The most widely used methods for controlling industrial noise are:

1. Quiet the noise-producing element through proper maintenance and lubrication of the machine, bearings, gears, spindles, etc.

2. Design or redesign machines for quieter operation. The importance of machine-noise factors is now recognized by many machine-tool builders.

3. Isolate the noise source by damping or mounting machines and other equipment on rubber, springs, or felt.

4. Change the plant layout to isolate the noise producers, spread out a noisy battery of machines, or enclose the noise source with sound-resistant partitions.

5. Design or redesign plants for better acoustical properties as by increasing ceiling heights, including noise-confining walls and baffles, or by treating ceilings, walls, and floors acoustically to absorb sound.

7-3.4   Utilities

No treatment of plant installations would be complete unless mention were made of the various plant utilities commonly required in industry today. Three separate *water* systems often are necessary: (1) potable water; (2) water for fire-fighting equipment (usually under higher pressure); and (3) process water for cooling, air conditioning, and toilets (can be drawn from well, lake, or river). *Gas* is also piped through plants to provide process heating. *Steam* is used in power-generating equipment, for process purposes, and sometimes for heating. *Oils,* where used in large quantities, may be stored in underground tanks and pumped to the point of use. This is an efficient way of distributing mixed oils such as machine cutting oils, slushing oils, and solvents, and furthermore it saves trucking, handling, and spillage that otherwise go with the distribution of oils. *Compressed air,* often required as a part of the process and for pneumatic equipment, is supplied by large compressors and piped to the point of use. *Liquid-waste-disposal* systems are increasing in importance today as antipollution regulations are enacted affecting the effluent of plants into rivers and lakes. Similarly, *rubbish* is either burned in an incinerator or compressed in a baler and moved to a dumping area.

Not to be forgotten also is that silent watchman, the *automatic sprinkler system,* which quenches a fire with a water spray before it can gain headway. Frequently an alarm is installed that sounds as soon as water starts to flow through the sprinkler pipes. Allied *fire-fighting equipment* includes portable fire extinguishers and fire engines which, depending upon the type of fire hazard involved, may be filled with a soda-acid solution, foam, powder, gas, carbon tetrachloride, or carbon dioxide. Hydrants, hoses, fog nozzles, fire walls, and fire doors, likewise, should not be overlooked as a part of the plant fire protection.

7-3.5 Employee Services

Included in the category of employee facilities are locker rooms, rest rooms, showers, water coolers, eating facilities, time clocks, plant hospital, and first-aid equipment. Criteria for the design of any of the above installations dictate that they be (1) adequate in capacity for the employee concentration required; (2) readily accessible to the bulk of employees with a minimum of lost production time; (3) easy to keep clean and sanitary; and (4) located and accessible for ease of maintenance. Some recently designed plants locate all employee facilities in the basement or on mezzanines in the center of the production area. Basements also provide the opportunity for subterranean aisles, entrance tunnels, and service passageways without interrupting production. Off-street parking for employees' cars is a requisite in today's plants. Employee recreation areas on company grounds are now commonplace. Fences around the plant or property with properly placed gates help control traffic and trespassers. Also, as a morale booster and for its public-relations effect, more and more companies are landscaping that part of the grounds visible from streets and employee entrances.

7-3.6 Safety Considerations

Although it has not been mentioned explicitly, safety is an implied factor in the selection of particular designs for all the previously mentioned plant qualities. The initial location of the plant may be dictated by the need to protect nearby communities from the effects of a disaster or waste contamination from the plant. The design and construction materials for the plant buildings are often a function of safety considerations for the operating personnel and residents near the plant. Good lighting, noise control,

and employee facilities do contribute to better work performance, and a major share of this contribution is through the reduction of lost-time accidents.

Some specific safety factors are:

1. *High-hazard material* Safe processing and storage of dangerous materials should be part of the basic plant design. Protection should be provided from explosion or the escape of toxic fumes. Facilities for immediate treatment of burns from caustic materials are routinely provided.

2. *Construction* Buildings should be inspected during and after construction to enforce design specifications. After the building is occupied, care must be taken to avoid overloading the upper floors by the installation of heavier than expected equipment.

3. *Utilities* Codes or safety requirements should be rigidly followed in the design of utility systems that are dangerous to personnel if the components are damaged. Steam pipes, high-air-pressure lines, power lines, and other potentially dangerous transmission equipment should be well marked, located outside normal working areas, and guarded.

4. *Passageways* Safe access and egress routes to and within the plant are standard considerations. Sufficient routes should be provided to handle emergencies. Vertical passageways such as elevators and stairs should adhere to basic safety regulations for design and maintenance.

Perspective 7C FACING THE FUTURE WITH FLEXIBILITY

New plants are built to satisfy future demands. Occasionally the demand disappears before a plant is completed. Or a technological breakthrough outdates a process before it gets going. More often demand gradually shifts and technological innovations are eased into existing processes, but even gentle changes can be painful to accommodate without prior planning.

Professors R. J. Craig, J. M. Moore, and W. C. Turner warn,

Facilities planning for the long term require different approaches than those used in short-term planning. Known data extrapolated into the future are satisfactory only for short- or medium-range periods. Long-term plans need to be:

• Approximate (major conceptual aspects only)
• With options (proposing alternative possibilities)
• Open ended (allowing opportunities for change).*

Specific suggestions to increase the flexibility of a plant to cope with future changes include the following:

1. *Building design* Keep the original layout as free as possible from fixed, permanent, or special features—interior walls should be nonload-bearing—and selectively locate fixed installations to reduce conflict with later changes—position a building on its site to allow additions conveniently.

2. *Plant services* Place services (electricity, steam, compressed air, oils, water, etc.) just beneath the floor or below ceilings—use a modular design that allows additional modules or substations to be added without having to replace the entire system.
3. *Equipment* Select material-handling equipment which has general rather than specialized capabilities—avoid permanent tie-downs for production equipment—and use standardized equipment to facilitate changeovers in layout.

*SOURCE: "Planned Production Flexibility," *Industrial Engineering,* October, 1975.

COMMENT The high cost of new construction, as noted in Perspective 7B, is a strong incentive for built-in flexibility. Since the original cost of fixed facilities is usually lower, although the risk of early obsolescence is higher, each flexible feature can and should be economically justified before it is included in the final design.

7-4 PLANT LAYOUT

The ideal procedure for any plant is to build the layout around the productive processes and then design the building around the layout, thus achieving a plant that is completely *functional.* However, this ideal method cannot always be followed. In the case of a going enterprise, some, if not all, buildings may be in existence. Or perhaps the plant site has been selected, and its terrain, size, or shape may not permit the construction of a building to house the utopian layout. Thus plant layout is generally a compromise between the ideal or functional layout and the limitations of plant site and buildings.

Good layouts today are based on the principle of *flow.* Such evidences of steady flow as regular movement of production, absence of bottleneck operations, and minimized backtracking all combine to shorten the manufacturing cycle and reduce the amount of material in process. There is also the matter of flow of people—the arrangement of employee facilities, aisles, plant entrances, and parking areas for uncongested traffic.

7-4.1 Manufacturing Considerations

To obtain an overall view of manufacturing considerations in plant design, production processes can be grouped into three general classifications. Virtually limitless variations of layouts are possible within each class to meet specific manufacturing requirements.

LAYOUT BY PRODUCT FOR SERIALIZED OR PRODUCTION-LINE MANUFACTURE
Here the equipment is laid out according to the sequence of operations so that raw material started at the head of the line is moved progressively to adjacent machines until completion of the item at the other end of the line. By its nature this layout is limited to manufacture of a single part or product or a group of very similar items. It is the type of layout required for all fixed-program automation systems. Advantages over other forms of layout are that it minimizes material handling, reduces the length and time

of the manufacturing cycle, tends to cut inventories of in-process work, saves floor space, makes production control virtually automatic, and facilitates administration over operators, output, and quality. Disadvantages center about its lack of flexibility to meet substantial changes in product design or in production requirements, its maintenance and down-time problems, and its tendency to yield a low utilization of equipment.

Production-line manufacture requires a great deal of planning. The machines, tooling, and auxiliary equipment must all be carefully selected as to both type and capacity to handle the rate of flow desired. Also, a *balanced production line* must be devised by the establishment of the number of operators for optimum line efficiency and an allocation of work elements among the various operators so that each is busy as close to 100 per cent of the time as possible. The *float* or bank of material required ahead of each line must be ascertained, and provision made for its storage in the installation of the line. Sometimes a similar float is necessary between key operations as insurance against stopping the entire line for temporary breakdowns in any one section. At other times, provision of stand-by equipment obviates this need.

Once a line is operating and its "bugs" are ironed out, its operation becomes somewhat routine, being primarily the control of materials, manpower, and quality at each work station so that the line can continue without costly interruptions. With careful planning and control, the efficiency of a layout by product can be really outstanding.

LAYOUT BY OPERATION FOR JOB-LOT MANUFACTURE   Here there is intermittent flow of materials. Thus machines are grouped according to the type of operation they perform. For example, under layout by operation, all lathe turning might be done in one production center or department, grinding in another, plating in a third, assembly in still another, etc. Where a variety of products are produced at irregular intervals, job-lot manufacture obviously is the only type possible. It has the advantage of offering some flexibility to accommodate product variety and demand fluctuations, permits maximum machine utilization, provides for less duplication of tools, jigs, and fixtures, and makes for lower setup and servicing costs. Better control of high-precision or complicated products can be achieved because better specialization of skills is permitted. *Balanced machine loads* are characteristic of this type of manufacture. When some machines become overloaded with work, when certain materials are out of stock, or when absenteeism or machine breakdowns occur, this layout provides the flexibility to minimize the delay.

Of course, in a plant laid out for job-lot manufacture, backtracking is the rule rather than the exception, and substantially higher inventories are necessary. Material must be moved in and out of storerooms, production centers, and inspection stations in batch lots. Delays occur between operations, since any particular batch is not generally moved to the next station until work on the entire lot has been completed at the previous station. Also, since separate production orders are required for each article fabricated, considerable paper work is involved, and the reporting, tracing, and follow-up of material in process are usually laborious and expensive. The handling of material between operations is slow and costly, for work usually must be moved by hand or motorized trucks, and the distance between operations is much greater than where layout by product is involved. For light or small items, this handling problem may be a minor handicap. But for heavy or bulky products, extra handling is one of the serious drawbacks of layout by operation.

LAYOUT BY STATIONARY MATERIAL PRIMARILY FOR MANUFACTURE OF LARGE PARTS AND ASSEMBLIES Here the personnel and equipment are moved to the material, which remains in one place. This type of layout is inherent in shipbuilding and in job welding shops. Advantages include the possibility of assigning one or more skilled workers to a project from start to finish, a maximum flexibility for all sorts of changes in product and process, and the opportunity to take on a number of quite different projects with the same layout. However, because it is based on immobile material, this layout usually presents difficulties in applying proper machine tools and specialized employee skills. The resultant lowering of efficiency tends to limit this layout to large items made singly or in very small lots.

Most layouts incorporate a combination of the foregoing three classes. For example, where layout by product is too inflexible to meet product variety, fluctuations in volume, or irregularity of demand, yet where layout by operation would cause excessive manufacturing costs, a *segmented production line* may be the answer. Here several successive operations on a product are performed by a battery of machines integrated with intermediate handling and feeding devices. Between such batteries are areas for batching and temporary storage of work. Also, operations requiring fixed, extremely heavy, very objectionable, or costly general-purpose equipment (such as that used in heat-treating, plating, forging, or large sheetmetal work) are grouped together in layout by operation. The aim is to retain flexibility for the basic product while capturing the flow and handling advantages of production lines wherever possible. Much of the manufacture of household appliances, farm equipment, and even automobile parts utilizes this segmented approach. Among other combinations is that commonly used by builders of large machinery. Here parts are fabricated in a layout by operation and assembled in a layout by stationary material, the machine base remaining immobile.

7-4.2 Other Considerations

The size of the production center or department is also an important consideration in the making of the layout. Its size is usually dependent more upon the span of administrative control than upon any physical factors involved. A department should not be so large that it is difficult for one person to control. Of course, wherever possible, natural subdivisions should be utilized, as, for example, grouping together people with the same or allied skills, interdependent or related machines, parts, subassemblies, or products.

Service areas should be a part of each production center, or if community service areas are found to be practical, they should be located conveniently to the production personnel and equipment they serve. These include the storage of materials, clerical and supervisory offices, tool and gage cribs, and lavatory, washing, and locker facilities.

Provision should be made in the initial layout for future expansion or a possible rearrangement of machines in the event that the design of the products, methods of manufacture, or production requirements are changed at some subsequent date. To do so may save much grief and costly rearranging of machines should some such changes later take place. Aisles should be adequate not only for the internal transportation of production material and the passage of employees to and from their machines but also for the passage of any of the machines should one or more of them have to be removed from the production center for major repairs. (See Figure 7-2).

However, since floor space in an industrial plant represents money, it is desirable to utilize it to the utmost. Among plants making similar products, the degree of utilization is known as the *relative production density*. A high production density makes for a compact plant, one that is an integrated unit. Furthermore, the plant that can raise its production to a high level thereby prevents the overexpansion of its facilities.

Perspective 7D SPECIAL PURPOSE LAYOUTS

Special design features are incorporated into the overall facility arrangement to satisfy unique requirements or to create a desired environment. Some examples are described below.*

1. *Assembly islands* The physical layout of work stations can assist the implementation of motivational concepts such as job enrichment. Under the assumption that it is more effective to delegate responsibility to groups than to individual workers, the layout should be conducive to group cohesiveness and communication. Two such designs for assembly operations are shown below. The circular table (a) can be stationary for an assembly that is passed by hand from one operation to the next, or it can rotate when workers must abide by a definite cycle time. A conveyor belt for sequential assembly or inspection is U-shaped (b) to make it easier for the group to communicate. Both (a) and (b) encourage eye contact.

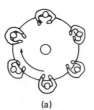

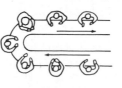

(a)   (b)

Figure 7-2 Models of a plant are used both for new construction and remodeling. The one-sixteenth size model is shown being reviewed to answer such questions as: "Will plant personnel have enough operating and maintenance space after new machines have been installed?" "Does the piping system flow logically?" and "Have all safety and environmental precautions been considered?" (Courtesy of Procter and Gamble Company.)

2. *Markets*   Should the layout for a store be clerk or customer oriented? Exclusive attention to factors that minimize handling costs, may produce an efficient layout that discourages sales. Uniform, uncluttered display cases are convenient to stock and maintain, but they probably fail the retailing objective of maximizing sales per unit of display space. Customer behavioral considerations for market layouts recognize that regular, rectangular layouts provide more display space per unit of floor area, but the space may not be as valuable as angular or freeform layouts that open more merchandise to shoppers' view. Also, aisles should be large enough to accommodate the traffic flow and allow room for lingering, especially in areas of high sales potential such as entrances to department stores and around the perimeter of supermarkets.

3. *Offices*   The "small-group" approach to work structuring is apparent in open designs for offices. Such layouts are characterized by generous spaces between individual workplaces and "think-tank" installations for undisturbed mental work or group discussions. An office layout with half open workplaces and separating walls is shown in the figure below where the numbered areas represent (1) receptionist/waiting area, (2) manager's office, (3) conference room, (4) think tank and discussion room, (5) secretaries, and (6) manager's office.

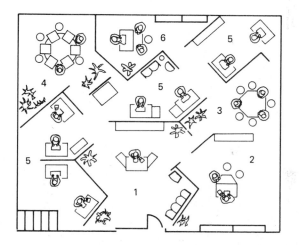

*source: James L. Riggs, *Production Systems: Planning, Analysis, and Control,* 2d ed., New York: John Wiley & Sons, 1976.

7-4.3   Layout Preparation

There are certain tools of plant layout in common use today which are a distinct aid in making or improving the layout of any plant. The first of these is the *process-flow chart,* a graphic map that follows material through its manufacturing cycle and records the sequence of the elements of that cycle as they occur (See Fig. 7-3).

The process-flow chart permits a process to be visualized in such a compact form that possible improvements are usually readily discerned. Repeated static elements of storage, for example, indicate delays in production and perhaps unnecessary transportation of material. The inefficiencies disclosed by such a chart may require the rearranging of work stations or

SUBJECT 182-81630
CHARTED BY E.W.F.
CHART NO. 1 SHEET 1 OF

GENERAL DATA

| SKIDLOAD -100 PIECES |
| 7.2 STOCK TURNOVER - 945 PIECES |
| 9 SKIDS PLUS REQUIRED |
| 582.32 STD HOURS REQUIRED ON PRESENT |

SUMMARY

METHOD	PRES	PROP	SAVE
NO OF OPERATIONS	8	7	1
NO OF OPERATRANSPORTATIONS	13	9	4
NO OF STORAGES	8	6	2
NO OF INSPECTIONS	1	1	0
HOURS STD PER SKID	64702	5515	9.62
DISTANCE TRAVELED	938	625	313
	58332	49635	8597

DATE 1-11-54
DEPT OUTSIDE STORAGE THROUGH MACHINING TO FINISHED GOODS STOREL

PRESENT METHOD

DESCRIPTION OF OPERATION	MEN REQ'D	DIST. MOVED	TIME IN MIN.	EQUIPMENT USED TO MOVE MATERIALS
MOVE SKID FROM OUTSIDE STORAGE TO AIRLOCK	1	150'	.028	GAS FORK TRUCK 4000# CAP
TEMPORARY STORAGE				
MOVE SKID FROM AIRLOCK TO TEMPORARY STORAGE	1	50'	.073	WALKIE TYPE PALLET TRUCK
TEMPORARY STORAGE				
MOVE TO IBM 1	1	35'	.016	WALKIE PALLET TRUCK
ROUGH MACHINE	1		18.000	STD .18/PC
MOVE TO TEMP STORAGE	1	35'	.016	TRANSPORTER
TEMPORARY STORAGE				
MOVE TO IBM 2	1	56'	.018	TRANSPORTER
FINISH MACHINE	1		25.000	STD 25/PC
MOVE TO TEMP. STORAGE	1	56'	.018	TRANSPORTER
TEMPORARY STORAGE				
MOVE TO 6 GRIND	1	20'	.014	TRANSPORTER
GRIND FEET	1		5.000	STD .05/PC
MOVE TO TEMP. STORAGE	1	20'	.014	TRANSPORTER
TEMPORARY STORAGE				
MOVE TO G-23 DRILL	1	68'	.018	TRANSPORTER
DRILL & TAP FOOTHOLES	1		4.200	STD .042/PC
MOVE TO TEMP. STORAGE	1	68'	.018	TRANSPORTER
TEMPORARY STORAGE				
MOVE TO G 15-2 DRILL	1	80'	.019	TRANSPORTER
DRILL & TAP	1		5.000	STD .05/PC PLACE ON CONVEYOR
BENCH	1		6.000	STD .06/PC
INSPECT	1			PARTIAL
STAMP PART NO.	1		.190	STD .0019/PC
PLACE IN SKID	1		.940	STD .0094/PC
MOVE TO TEMP. STORAGE	1	300'	.080	TRANSPORTER
TEMPORARY STORAGE				
MOVE TO PART LOCATION	1	50'	.068	WALKIE TYPE STACKER
PERMANENT STORAGE	TOTAL 938'	64702		TOTALS PER 1 SKID

PROPOSED METHOD #3

DESCRIPTION OF OPERATION	MEN REQ'D	DIST. MOVED	TIME IN MIN.	EQUIPMENT USED TO MOVE MATERIALS
MOVE UNIT LOAD TO TEMPERING	1	100'	.028	GAS FORK TRUCK
TEMPORARY STORAGE				
MOVE TO MILLING MACHINE	1	20'	.022	TRANSPORTER
MILL & PLACE ON CONVEYOR	1		2.500	STD .025/PC
MOVE TO BORING MILL		15'		ROLLER GRAVITY CONVEYOR
TEMPORARY STORAGE				
MACHINE & PLACE ON CONVEY	1		18.00	STD 18/PC
MOVE TO #2 BORING MILL		20'		ROLLER GRAVITY CONVEYOR
TEMPORARY STORAGE				
FINISH MACHINE PUT ON CONV.	1		25.000	STD 25/PC
MOVE TO #1 DRILL		15'		GRAVITY CONVEYOR
TEMPORARY STORAGE				
DRILL & PLACE ON CONVEYOR	1		4.200	STD .042/PC
MOVE TO 2 DRILL		15'		GRAVITY CONVEYOR
TEMPORARY STORAGE				
DRILL & TAP-HANG ON CONV.	1		5.000	STD .05/PC WITH OVERHEAD HOIST
MOVE TO WASH MACHINE		80'		OVERHEAD TROLLEY CONVEYOR
WASH				PROCESS ON CONVEYOR
MOVE TO INSPECTION		80'		OVERHEAD CONVEYOR
INSPECT	1"			PARTIAL (sec) WHILE ON CONVEYOR
MOVE TO STOCK WAREHOUSE		280'		OVERHEAD CONVEYOR
REMOVE FROM CONVEYOR	1	400'		STD .004/PC
PERMANENT STORAGE				
TOTALS / SKID OF 100 PC'S	9	625'	55150	
				7.2 TURNOVER
				945 PCS: 9 SKIDS REQUIRED
				55.15 X 9 SKIDS = 496.35 STD HRS

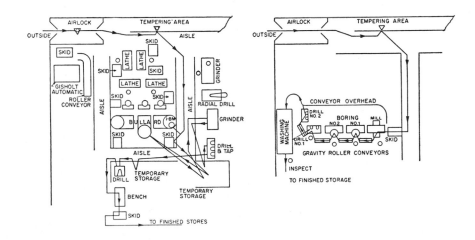

Figure 7-3 Typical process-flow charts and process-flow diagrams. Note how these tools of plant layout reveal inefficiencies in the present layout and point up savings possible under the proposed layout. (Adapted from *Factory.*)

may point the need for better transportation facilities. Analysis may disclose that some operations which add little or nothing to the final value of the product can be eliminated by minor changes in the product design, or that certain tasks previously split into two operations may be combined into a single operation. Similarly, an opportunity may be disclosed by which the sequence of the various elements in the process can be rearranged to eliminate backtracking and unnecessary handling. Once the process has been analyzed through the use of the process-flow chart, any improvements effected can be incorporated into the layout as it is made.

The next layout tool is the familiar *template layout.* It is prepared by cutting out scale templates to denote machines, racks, benches, and other equipment and laying them on a plan drawing that shows building walls, columns, stairs, elevators, and other building limitations affecting layout. A scale of ¼ inch to the foot is generally accepted as standard, although ⅛ inch to the foot is occasionally used where the equipment and the plant are very large. The templates are moved around the drawing to explore various layout possibilities until a layout is obtained that eliminates unnecessary handling, minimizes backtracking of material, makes the most of mechanized handling possibilities, and offers flexibility to meet future changes in production requirements.

An alternative or additional technique makes use of the *scale-model layout.* The models are scaled reproductions of all pieces of equipment laid out on a plan drawing as above. Resembling a child's dollhouse, the model layout aids in determining the amount of space and headroom required by equipment items. While it is a relatively expensive technique, it frequently pays off in laying out new processes. Where neither layout people nor plant supervisors have had much experience with the equipment and the flow of work, these are more readily visualized with models than with templates. Models have also resulted in significant savings in the laying out of refineries and chemical plants. Their complicated problems of piping can be better solved by a visual selection of the best pipe routes on the models. Then the actual piping installation can be made directly from the models, from photos, or from relatively simple drawings prepared from the models.

Steps in making the actual layout are these. First, a *general space layout* or perhaps several alternative layouts are prepared, blocking out possible area allocations, relationship of various activities, and flow of work. Such layouts would draw heavily on information revealed by the process-flow chart or diagram if made, otherwise directly on the knowledge and ideas of operating and engineering personnel. The general space layout finally selected for its merits is then detailed with templates or models. Here again, several specific plans within the confines of the agreed-on general layout may be tried to arrive at one which will most successfully meet the aims and needs of the enterprise (see Fig. 7-4).

After approval of the template or model layout has been obtained from all interested parties, copies of the plan must be made for purposes of installation and permanent record. Sometimes this is accomplished by hav-

Figure 7-4 Views of two scale models. (a) Marketing personnel examining a model of a new service station to evaluate site selection. (b) Engineers discussing construction details of a model of a new processing plant to be constructed. (Courtesy Shell Oil Company.)

ing a draftsman laboriously transfer the layout to a drawing from which prints can be made. At other times the template layout can be photostated. In still other cases the original layout is prepared with translucent plastic or pressure-sensitive tape templates on a plastic grid sheet, all of which can be reproduced photographically.

Better computer programs[4] are being developed to aid plant layout design. The input data to most programs are similar; they include material flow, cost of moving material per unit distance, and space requirements such as the dimensions of buildings, specific building features, and preassigned activity locations. The outputs of all the programs are printed layouts and cost figures. The procedure utilized to produce the output is essentially a computation of the cost of moving the required amount of material through a certain layout pattern. After an initial calculation, exchanges between locations are considered. Each exchange produces a new cost and plant pattern.

Layouts of complex plant designs cannot as yet be done completely by computers, but the speed and systemization afforded by computer-aided design certainly assist rapid layout revisions and the evaluation of standardized patterns. Many different configurations are easily evaluated when the basic data are known. The resulting cost figures highlight areas of significant expense and how the factors influence total cost. However, the planning

[4]Three generally available plant layout planning programs available in the United States include CRAFT (computerized relative allocation of facilities technique), CORELAP (computerized relationship layout planning), and ALDEP (automated layout design program).

details still must be worked out using the previously mentioned layout techniques.

7-5 PRODUCTION EQUIPMENT

The basic manufacturing processes, as we have seen, are determined as part of production planning. The next step is to select each item of productive equipment and its tooling, jigs, fixtures, and gages as best fits the specific product, process, and production requirements. Where production machinery already is available and adaptable to the production plan, it will rather well define the operations to be performed. If the equipment is not on the market, then the operations may be tentatively established and the equipment designed and engineered around them.

7-5.1 Selection

One of the first decisions in the selection of equipment concerns the degree of flexibility or adaptability desired. While product designs are seldom "frozen," some items are subject only to infrequent design changes; others are more unstable, depending upon their relative position on the progress–time curve. The more likely it is that frequent changes in design will occur, the more necessary it becomes to build flexibility into the productive equipment.

Machine tools can be classed as either *general purpose* or *single purpose.* General-purpose machines are the more flexible and constitute the bulk of machine tools in use today. Included in this category are such equipment items as engine and turret lathes, bar machines, universal grinders, welding machines, and induction heaters. Each of these types of machines is designed to perform one or more operations on a variety of sizes and items. A change in product design simply means changing tools, gears, or fixtures, and the same piece of equipment is again ready to start production.

By contrast, special-purpose machines are designed to do one job and that job alone. Such machines generally possess the advantage of performing specific operations more rapidly than do general-purpose machines—an important factor in volume manufacture. However, they are likely to be inflexible, and a change in product design may require scrapping or a complete conversion. Usually the choice between general- and single-purpose equipment is a matter of economics: (1) initial cost which must be charged off during the anticipated useful life of the equipment; (2) direct labor cost; and (3) preparation cost including tooling and setup.

In an attempt to obtain both special-purpose-machine efficiency and general-purpose-machine flexibility, industry is showing increasing interest in *building-block machines.* These are constructed of sectionalized units with standard dimensions for interchangeability of components. Most metal-working machines have six components: a tool that cuts, shears, or presses metal; a tool holder; a powered assembly that moves the holder and its tool into and away from the metal; a carriage which moves the power unit into position; a base which supports the carriage; and a bench, chuck, or other gripping device to hold the metal in place. The useful life of a special-purpose machine built by conventional methods usually ends abruptly once a change in product model or process alters the operation for which it was designed. Not so with a building-block machine. The user may convert it to perform the new job by replacing the tool holder, gripping device, and perhaps some of the other sectionalized units. The remaining sections are reused in the changeover for considerable saving in investment. In some instances the building-block concept makes practical a special-purpose machine where otherwise its inflexibility would dictate use of a less productive general-purpose machine. The increased life expectancy of building-block machines, which permits amortizing their original cost over longer periods of time and slows down their obsolescence rate, makes their purchase more attractive and their future in industry quite promising.

The concept of using general-purpose machines to replace specialized equipment in batch processing has been given the imposing name of "group technology." The use of universal jigs and fixtures reduces the time needed to set up a machine for making changes in a flow of different parts. Maximum use of "universalized" machinery is possible through the organization of parts production into groups on the basis of size, shape, and manufacturing methods. This organization also tends to reduce material handling and inventory costs.

Machine tooling refers to the selection and design of cutting tools, jigs, fixtures, and dies required to perform a specific operation. This field, which is generally called *tool engineering,* has much to do with the operating efficiency of machines. Decision as to whether an air chuck or a mechanical chuck should be used; whether a cemented carbide tool or one made from high-speed steel will perform better; what speeds and feeds produce the most satisfactory results; whether water, oil, or air will serve best as a coolant —these are typical of the problems encountered by the tool engineers.

In the design or selection of any machine, there are two cardinal principles which should be taken into consideration: (1) the machine should be easy to set up, operate, service, and repair; and (2) it should be provided with safety devices to prevent costly difficulties from improper operation. Examples of the latter are electrical heating coils which cut off the power when the equipment has been overloaded and photoelectric interlock devices on furnaces which shut off fuel flow in the event of interruption of the flame. Adequate safety guards should be provided to prevent the operator from being caught in protruding moving parts. Start–stop controls should be placed so that quick stopping is possible. Levers and control movements should be so rigged that their direction coincides with that of the machine part being regulated—otherwise even the best of operators is apt to make a wrong move in an emergency. If possible, the machine should be so designed that the operator may sit comfortably at the machine.

Finally, in making the choice of equipment, there is the question of whether to build or to buy. Many factors bear on such a decision. Where the machine is designed by and purchased from an outside firm, the purchasing company may find itself in the unenviable position of having at least partially financed the development of that equipment and provided the vendor with experience which he can then make available to the company's competitors. Also, an in-plant designed and built item of equipment sometimes more nearly fits that plant's needs than does a similar item of general-purpose design purchased from a machine-tool manufacturer. The ability of the plant to make the equipment, the availability of replacement parts, the knowledge required in that field of design—any of these may govern the decision. Apart from the foregoing considerations there is always the important matter of relative costs.

7-5.2 Capacity

The most accurate and in fact the only scientific method for fixing the number of machines of each type required makes use of anticipated production quantities.

The first information utilized is a forecast of the production required. This forecast usually is based on a breakdown of the sales forecast, and although it may at best be something of a guess on the part of the sales division, nevertheless it is information that is essential to an intelligent appraisal of the production equipment required.

Next a work-schedule policy must be formulated so that the number of hours the equipment is to operate per week can be calculated. The question of the length of the working day together with that of single- or multishift operation is an integral part of the calculation of the available hours of operation. In general, it may be stated that, where floor space and other conditions warrant, single-shift operation for hand jobs and assembly work is preferable because it eliminates the bonus commonly paid to night-shift employees for working less desirable hours. A single-shift schedule is also desirable where the equipment cost is low and hence where the machine-rate charge against the operation performed is correspondingly low. Multishift operation frequently is favored where costly equipment is involved and where 16- or 24-hour-per-day utilization produces a more favorable machine-rate charge against that equipment. Furthermore, in continuous-process industries (as chemical production, papermaking, steel rolling, or brass casting), the 24-hour day is a virtual economic necessity because of the high "warm-up" costs.

Standard production-rate data in the form of minutes per piece or pieces per hour for each product or part to be processed on the equipment involved, together with proper allowances for setup time, maintenance, and repairs, must likewise be considered. These may be obtained from time studies of the equipment and operations performed. If past production records over a period of time are available for that or similar equipment, they may be used as a check against the synthetic data evolved by time studies. Of course, idle-machine allowances or "down time" for setup, maintenance, and repairs will vary considerably among types of machines, nature and precision of the work required, length of the runs permitted, and a host of other conditions. Nevertheless, most enterprises figure that their equipment should be operating between 75 and 80 percent of the theoretical or available hours of operation possible under the work schedule in effect. Failure to measure up to that percentage is usually prima facie evidence that some control is breaking down.

Once the data enumerated above has been assembled, simple mathematical calculations will determine how many machines of each type are necessary for the required product quantities and for the desired work schedule. The primary objective of advance machine planning is the prevention of bottleneck operations. Each type of machine must be capable of absorbing work received from prior operations and of supplying subsequent machines with sufficient material to utilize them to the desired capacity.

7-5.3 Automation

Among the many recent developments in design and application of machine tools, that which has had the greatest impact is expressed by the single word *automation.* Although the term "automatic" has been a part of industry's vocabulary for many years and "automaticity" has contributed much to industry's progress, the word "automation" apparently was first used in the late 1940s. It can best be defined as the addition of handling and control equipment to automatic machines for continuous automatic production through a series of operations without human guidance and control.

In its current state of development, automation in manufacturing takes two forms.[5]

1. *Continuous,* embracing a complete process, fabrication, or assembly. Examples are found in the chemical, oil, baking-mix, steel, automotive, and home-appliance industries wherein continuous, integrated lines and equipment abound.

2. *Segmented,* intermittent automation of sections of a process, fabrication, or assembly with intervals and storage facilities for banks of material among groups of automated equipment. In much of industry's product variety, fluctuations in customer requirements, batch-type or centralized operations (as heat treating, plating, tumbling) in the process, and a host of other limiting conditions plague the would-be continuous "automater" and leave him with segmented automation as the next best thing.

Why is industry devoting so much attention to automation? The answer is to be found in results obtained from successful automated systems. More

---

[5]Among nonmanufacturing forms of automation are office automation and electronic data-processing machines described in Chap. 3. Also in this category are such mechanisms as automatic elevators with electronic timers and detectors, transportation-ticket-selling equipment, and "electronic supervisors" used to schedule various on-and-off operations—all devices which are beyond the scope of this book.

output is obtained from the labor dollar and usually also from the dollar invested in facilities. Quality is more uniform, work is safer, and production scheduling, once the planning of the system has been completed, is virtually automatic. In most instances in-process inventories are substantially reduced because there are few, if any, stopping points in the process.

But automation also has disadvantages. There is considerable investment in facilities, requiring a long period of heavy utilization to recapture the investment. Furthermore, there may be greater manufacturing inflexibility. Product designs must be frozen for long time intervals. In industry where change is rapid or unpredictable, this loss of fluidity may be serious. During a business recession or other times when volume decreases, management cannot lay off an automated line or readily employ it on other work. Finally, the down time of the equipment is apt to be devilishly expensive. There are more mechanical elements to go wrong, and the interdependency of equipment tends to make the system only as reliable as its weakest element. Down time is cumulative. One failure may shut down the entire line. Tool and tool-change costs tend to rise, since all tools are removed simultaneously for inspection and sharpening at regular intervals whether dull or not.

As is true of any major advance in technology, automation has created important economic and social changes. Some of these may be desirable, others undesirable. Industrial mechanization created many dull, routine jobs. Automation appears to be reversing this trend by eliminating those jobs and creating others which require setup ability, maintenance-trade knowledge, engineering, electronics, and mechanics—all fields that are more interesting, more highly skilled, and better paying[6] than the machine-tending, product-assembling jobs introduced by mechanization.

One of the most stirring examples of automation is a plant largely controlled by a computer. Such installations are mostly restricted to continuous or process industries such as oil refineries and chemical or cement plants. Technology is available to wed numerically controlled machines to process-control computers, a combination known as *direct numerical control.* Such a wedding integrates automatic machines into automatic systems—organizations of automatic machines that can function automatically. The problems to overcome in the application of process computers to discrete-item industries are created by the inherent variations characterized by frequent setups and changeovers, interruptible schedules, and uncertainty in demand. The more promising areas of application are for on-line multiproduct production line controls and warehousing. Automation developments in the 1980s should be equivalent to the advances made in the 1970s, with the emphasis changing from the design of individual machines to system controls.

[6]Thus automation may be a partial answer to the problem of how to provide enough interesting industrial jobs for the constantly increasing percentage of people in this country with advanced education. A 1969 report by Professor Eva Mueller of the Wisconsin University's Institute for Social Research concludes, "For the most part, Americans value the equipment they work with, and believe that automation is a good thing for people in their line of work."

Perspective 7E SOFT AUTOMATION WITH ROBOTS

It now seems surpassing innocence that only a few years ago Americans regarded automation as a menace. In 1962, President Kennedy asserted that "the major domestic challenge of the sixties is to maintain full employment at a time when automation is replacing men." . . . unemployment is once again a problem, but few economists blame it on automation, and a number of union leaders are pushing for the acceptance of *more* automation. Even in a year of recovery from a recession, many college students and young blue-collar workers proclaim their intention to shun tedious, unpleasant tasks, no matter what the wages. When asked how these jobs are going to get done, workers and intellectuals alike reply blithely, "Let the machines do them." Gradually, in fact, the willingness to replace men with machines is being transformed from the status of a threat to something like a social necessity.*

"Hard" automation is typified by expensive, fixed-purpose machinery operating for the long-run, high-volume manufacture of many identical items. The automotive industry is a good example of hard automation. "Soft" automation is associated with the computer and its peripheral apparatus. Computers are now used extensively in process industries—oil refineries and chemical industries—to virtually run entire plants, and newer *adaptive control* computers make real-time adjustments to production machines in response to ongoing conditions, such as modifying machine settings to compensate for tool wear that occurs during cutting operations.

The epitome of soft automation is the robot. Limited numbers of machines with human-like versatility are already in use. Though they bear little resemblance to humans, they do possess appendages that vaguely look like human arms and hands. With these appendages they can perform routine and laborious tasks that are distasteful or dangerous to humans.

*SOURCE: Tom Alexander, "The Hard Road to Soft Automation," *Fortune,* July, 1971.

COMMENT Robots have not taken over production duties, as prophesized by some enthusiasts, because they are expensive and lack the sensing ability (primarily vision) to react to irregularities in operating conditions. Experimental robots demonstrate remarkable progress in recognizing their environment, reacting to changing conditions with programmed responses, and even responding to spoken commands. When *artificial intelligence* becomes more reliable and robot components can be purchased off the shelf, the age of "universal automation" will be near. Until then, robots will be candidates mainly for simple but arduous and perilous tasks.

7-6 REVIEW QUESTIONS

1. What are the three steps in selecting the plant site? Explain briefly.

2. Should the raw-material or finished-goods market receive greater consideration in plant location?

3. What are some newer trends in plant location?

4. In designing an industrial building, which factors deserve particular attention? Explain.

5. What is the importance of air conditioning, illumination, noise control, and proper employee facilities in the design of an industrial plant?

6. What safety measures should be included in the design of an industrial plant?

7. What is meant by "special-purpose," "general-purpose," and "building-block" machines?

8. What determines the number of machines required for production?

9. Distinguish between layout by process and layout by product. Where should each be used?

10. Distinguish between two-dimensional and three-dimensional plant layout techniques. What is the difference between a process-flow chart and a process-flow diagram?

11. What is meant by "automation"? What are the two forms of automation?

12. What are the advantages and limitations of automation systems?

7-7 TOPICS FOR DISCUSSION

1. *Factory* magazine reported on replies received from a number of professional industrial-development experts in various sections of the country to questions on industrial site selection. One of the questions was: What are the two most important factors in making site selections? Replies received included the following?

    - Geographic and economic factors; site characteristics
    - Highways; people
    - Transportation (given as most important)
    - Labor; markets
    - Reliable data on proposed sites; community attitude
    - Business climate; good living conditions
    - Markets; people; raw materials

    Why do experts in this field differ so widely on the relative importance of location factors?

2. An important manufacturer of fuel-control systems and accessories for aircraft and missiles occupies a plant originally constructed for processes which did not involve frequent rearrangement of machines and equipment. Aircraft accessory items, however, are continually being phased in or out and require frequent relocation and revamping of facilities and flexibility for rapidly changing processes. What building services and equipment features should now be provided in this plant to supply the desired flexibility?

3. It has been said that in office work, where the rate of production is not standardized and where no minimum requirements must be met consistently, the increase in productivity from air conditioning is more than enough to pay for its cost. What cost and savings factors would you explore in an effort to disprove the accuracy of this statement?

4. A vice-president of the Magazine Publishers Association claims, "There are two things that trigger a sale—exposure and traffic. The checkout counter (in a supermarket) has both. That's where items that are purchased on impulse should be located, and magazines are impulse items."

    Some publishers pay premiums, called retail display allowances, in addition to the normal sales commission to get their magazines displayed at choice spots. In a supermarket the premium position is over the belt where shoppers unload groceries; to the right of the checkout counter is a bad spot because shoppers unloading carts will miss it.

Survey some large grocery or department stores and comment on merchandising techniques related to the position of installations within the store layout.

5. What are the advantages and disadvantages of the following plant-layout techniques, and under what conditions would each be best used:
   a. Drafting on reproducible paper
   b. Two-dimensional templates on cross-ruled paper
   c. Three-dimensional models on cross-ruled paper
   d. Combination of two-dimensional templates and three-dimensional models on cross-ruled paper

6. One observer has defined *man* as a carefully engineered control mechanism weighing about 150 pounds, with five senses, capable of producing circular as well as linear motions, completely self-contained, self-lubricated, and self-powered (except for refueling three times a day). Furthermore, no other control device yet invented is so readily produced by inexperienced labor.

In the light of this definition, evaluate man's future in the "battle" with automation.

7. Case 7A *McGraw-Hill Book Company*

At one time the McGraw-Hill Book Company executive offices, sales headquarters, book warehouse, and distribution center, all were situated in New York City. The rate of growth of the company's book business necessitated increased floor space for this facility, and the heavy congestion of transport in New York led McGraw-Hill management to seek a new site for the book warehouse and distribution center outside the metropolitan area.

McGraw-Hill's major supply sources are located in New York City. Its books for the most part are printed and bound in Pennsylvania, then delivered by truck to the warehouse. At the time the move was under consideration, about seven million copies of various book titles and a smaller stock of motion pictures, text-films, dictation records, and tapes were located in the warehouse. Orders as received at the sales headquarters from schools, colleges, booksellers, and mail-order customers were shipped either by mail or motor freight. As in most large cities, clearance of book shipments through the main post office in New York had become rather slow and difficult because of the steadily mounting work load and lack of modern postal facilities.

In the course of investigating possible relocation sites, McGraw-Hill found 38 acres of rich farmland in Hightstown, N.J. It was determined that approximately 200,000 square feet of floor space would be required, preferably on one floor, except for employee facilities, which could be located on a mezzanine.

Questions

1. What were the most important factors to be considered in relocating McGraw-Hill's warehouse to a new site? List these in the order of their relative importance. In what respects was the Hightstown site favorable under the factors which you have listed?

8. Case 7B *The National Motors Corporation*

A subsidiary of National Motors for a number of years manufactured several models of fractional-horsepower electric motors for household and automotive fans and blowers in facilities that were old and inefficient. The corporation therefore decided that a new plant built around a good layout should be the first step in a program of modernization.

A tract of land 725 by 450 feet was purchased, and the subsidiary's industrial engineering department was given the assignment of preparing a rough space layout to determine size and shape of the proposed building on that site. It was first determined that approximately 120,000 square feet of floor space would be necessary and that the motor assembly line would occupy an area 570 feet long by 50 feet wide, preferably in a straight line.

The industrial engineers explored several possibilities and finally prepared and presented to the corporation management the layout shown in Figure 7-5. The industrial engineers were most enthusiastic over the proposal, claiming that use of the diagonal in the "Siamesed" buildings gives maximum length to the assembly line with minimum building size and lends itself well to supporting operations and services. They also noted that the suggested building shape would permit interesting architectural effects and an impressive central front entrance.

Questions

1. What principles of good layout are found in the plans submitted? What principles appear to have been violated? Suggest any alternatives which you feel would make for a better layout.

9. Case 7C *The N. G. Manufacturing Company*[7]

The N. G. Manufacturing Company makes a precision metal product in a few hundred catalogued sizes ranging in weight from a few ounces to about 50 pounds. The product is used in household appliances, airplanes, automobiles, and many other types of mechanical equipment. The present manufacturing costs and selling prices show that the value of the product varies consistently with its size (e.g., smallest is the least expensive, largest the most costly). All sizes are produced by virtually identical operations on similar equipment with the plant laid out by process.

The N. G. Manufacturing Company management has considered the practicability of automation for its operations. They have concluded that the 12 heaviest selling sizes would warrant automation, that the remaining sizes do not have sufficient volume to permit such a manufacturing-method change. Automated production lines have been engineered and a new, completely separate plant designed and laid out to produce these 12 items. This proposed plant is expected to introduce the following new problems and opportunities:

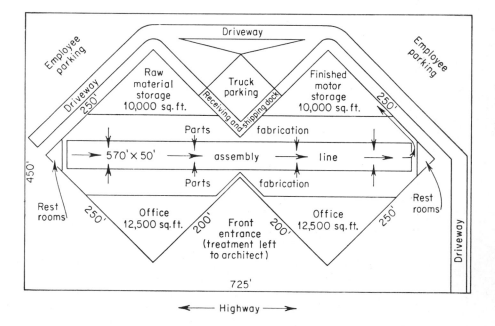

Figure 7-5   Proposed layout for the new National Motors plant.

[7]Company name and facts of the case were altered slightly to hide the identity of the actual company.

1. Cost estimates show that the manufacturing cost of each item produced by automation would be about 75 per cent of its present cost.

2. The sales requirements on the 12 sizes could easily be met in the proposed plant with one-shift operation. If volume justified two shifts, the additional utilization of the high-priced automated equipment required would bring manufacturing costs down even further.

3. Removal of the 12 highest volume sizes from the product mix in the present plant would leave that plant with only the shorter runs. These require more frequent setups and more production-control attention and bring somewhat lower productivity. Thus the unit costs of these remaining items could be expected to rise.

4. The company could substantially reduce prices on the 12 sizes and raise prices on the others slightly to conform to the expected cost pattern. The problem of explaining to customers why they would have to pay considerably more for some items than for other adjacent items in the product line would then arise.

5. A general price reduction might be made throughout the entire line as the way of getting some sales advantages out of the overall manufacturing-cost reduction from automating 12 sizes.

6. The competitive situation on the product is such that competitors would probably soon meet any price reductions made. Thus hope of capturing a substantially increased share of the market is not warranted. However, lower prices on certain automated items might bring in some new uses for the product and swing users from the higher to the lower priced items.

Questions

1. On the basis of the facts presented, advise the company whether or not to go ahead with its automation plans. Give reasons for your advice and explain how the company should act on any problems or opportunities thus introduced.

8

PRODUCTION PLANNING

It may be useful in this study of the industrial enterprise, its organization, and management to stop for a moment and reflect where we are. In previous chapters we were concerned with the external setting, basic organization, and managerial process of the enterprise. We also considered activities in the areas of risk, forecasting, financing, and product research and development.

Now we shall explore the means by which modern industry moves its product concepts toward production realities. How does production planning fit into overall managerial planning? What steps and personnel are involved in preparations for manufacture? How does the nature of the product and its manufacturing processes affect these preparations? What techniques are employed by production planners?

8 PRODUCTION PLANNING

8-1 MANAGERIAL PLANNING

All management is paid to plan—to think, dream, set goals, organize, initiate—then to execute and control. Yet the most common complaint heard today among industrial managers is that they are on such a time-consuming treadmill, simply keeping abreast of the day's events and solving problems —executing and controlling—that they have difficulty finding time to contemplate the future.

The wise manager knows that a proper balance must be maintained in his activities between current and future events. He plans his time around this concept, and along with his administrative duties he sets aside time to contemplate the future. Where, he asks himself, is the enterprise going? What are its goals: immediate, intermediate, long-range? Is it making satisfactory progress against these objectives? Are its organization, financing, products, manufacturing facilities and methods, procedural and control techniques, industrial relations, and marketing all geared to the desired goals? Is the enterprise keeping up with the *accelerated pace of change* in its industrial world as well as in the worlds beyond its own sphere? As we leave our wise manager deep in his contemplation of the future, we note that manufacturing is but one of his several projected worries. Here he pinpoints his concern on ways and means of getting products made. Or, to express it more formally, manufacturing involves processes of changing basic materials by hand or machine into more useful and valuable forms. The activity by which manufacturing ways and means are determined is called production planning.

8-1.1 Scope of Production Planning

Production planning takes a given product or line of products and organizes in advance the work force, materials, machines, and money required for a predetermined output in a given period of time. It starts with a product concept capable of being manufactured, a general idea of the process by which it can be made, and a sales forecast for the discernible future. Sometimes, however, this planning begins simply with a model or mock-up of the desired item. Or occasionally the entire process may have been crystallized in the product development stage by means of a pilot plant.

In the usual sequence of steps, the production-control specialists cooperating with the plant and industrial engineers and the purchasing buyers "explode," or break down, the product into parts and materials. They then determine what is to be made and what purchased. If not already in existence, the physical facilities must next be acquired and organized by the plant and industrial engineers for the level of production desired. These same people also develop and detail the operations and their sequence;

prepare time standards or estimates; determine process quality standards; and plan the tools, jigs, and fixtures as to both type and number necessary for the anticipated production quantities.

Production planning then proceeds with a consideration by the personnel division of the manpower needs. The required skills and number of people are determined from the forecast plus the operation and time data mentioned above. The procurement planning for materials and supplies from external sources, including the setting of time schedules, is performed by the inventory-control and purchasing functions. Still another section, that of cost accounting, estimates the cost of making the product in the forecast quantity.

Coordination of all the planning activities is fundamentally the responsibility of top management. However, in the administration of a going plant with established products and processes, much of the production planning is delegated to the production-control department. That department determines what has to be done to facilitate manufacturing, confers with those who must do it, and follows up to see that it has been done, thus effecting a concerted planning effort from a series of disassociated departments. Of course, this activity of the production-control department sets the stage for its subsequent role in which routines are established that will cause each manufacturing step to be performed in a stipulated manner and at a designated time.

Thus, in summation, it can be said that production planning is a series of related and coordinated activities performed by not one but a number of different departmental groups, each activity being designed to systematize in advance the manufacturing efforts in its area.

8-1.2 Production Planning Objectives

The question, For whom and for what are we planning? is one that should be kept in mind continually by those responsible for planning to operate any industrial enterprise. Why is planning necessary? What are its objectives?

Production planning is aimed at achieving a manufacturing output that will achieve one or more of the following objectives: (1) bring a prescribed level of profit; (2) capture a desired share of the market demand; (3) operate the plant at the predetermined level of efficiency; (4) utilize available plant facilities; and (5) create a specified number of jobs.

In our competitive-enterprise system, the *profit motive* is a predominant factor, for upon it may rest the justification for, and in fact, the very survival of, the enterprise.

Planning provides the necessary information upon which are based manufacturing decisions that to a large extent determine the future profit potential of the enterprise. Whether profits are realized in turn greatly influences the influx of capital, personnel, and customers. No one feels secure about investing in, working for, or doing business with a concern that appears to be skidding downhill.

It is important to understand to what extent the production planners may rely on the sales forecast when translating it into manufacturing requirements. The sales forecast projects product sales over a relatively short period of time: a month, quarter, or year. Even for such short periods, industrial management usually is forced to engage in a guessing game: conjecturing what tack business conditions will take and, more pointedly, what tack the market for a particular product will take. Abundant as are the tools for short-range forecasting, they are far from sharp, and the pet forecasting chart of almost every manager at times is a source of acute embarrassment to him.

Thus, even with the most carefully laid sales plan, the production plan must remain flexible. One common method is through the use of inventories. The amount of material planned to be manufactured differs initially from the sales forecast by the increase or decrease in finished-goods inventory desired for that period. For example, if in anticipation of rising prices, increased sales, or stabilized employment, it is desired to increase finished-goods inventory, the quantity planned to be manufactured will exceed the forecast by the number of units that the inventory is to be increased. Then, if during the period actual sales differ from that forecast, that difference can be absorbed by or "wrung out of" inventory. Other ways of achieving flexibility against changing market demand, as we shall see shortly, are through varying the length of work schedules and through fluctuating employment.

One ideal if not always attainable aim of any plant management is to operate its facilities at their most efficient level of production. This level is seldom the plant's peak capacity, for peak production in any plant involves certain inefficiencies in the use of personnel, equipment, or space, whichever is the limiting factor. At some point below the peak level, then, there is an *optimum plant capacity.* This may be defined as that rate of production which makes the best utilization of work force, equipment, and space combined and which results in the lowest unit cost with respect to all the cost factors involved. In practice, however, the optimum level of production is seldom strictly attainable. It is always interrelated with the other four considerations of production planning herein discussed. It may be subject to certain predetermined decisions such as the number of hours per week the employees wish to work, the number of work shifts the management wishes to employ, or the desire of the owners to expand or contract the plant facilities. At any rate, effective planning procedure takes all such factors into consideration, together with those which determine the operating efficiency, to the end that a rate of production may be achieved with respect to the sales forecast, stock program, or orders that most nearly approximates the optimum plant capacity.

As for the creation of jobs, where in a short period of time a plant successively hires, lays off, and then rehires a fair percentage of its personnel, there is prima facie evidence of poor planning. Pressure of government, unions, and public opinion in recent years has made managements more conscious of their responsibility for keeping people employed. In some states, unemployment-compensation regulations penalize companies with large layoff lists by upping their rates paid for such compensation. Supplemental unemployment-insurance payments made under union contractual agreements also add to costs. These represent a financial stick ready to strike management's posterior if the moral carrot dangling in front of management's nose is not an adequate incentive. Furthermore, seniority-layoff rules in union contracts frequently make layoff and re-hiring procedures complicated and costly to the enterprise. Finally, communities do not look favorably upon companies in their midst wherein there is instability either of work force or of number of hours worked. Thus has production planning assumed a role of increased importance in stabilizing the use of plant facilities, the number of jobs, and the working hours.

This stabilization is achieved by leveling off, as far as is practicable, the normal cyclical and seasonal peaks and valleys in production to the end that equipment and personnel may be kept busy in all seasons and regardless of the trend of the business cycle. Various means are used, such as manufacturing to stock during slack periods in anticipation of future sales, requiring vacations to be taken during such periods, or using idle manufacturing employees for long-term maintenance work. Sometimes, particularly where the slack period is prolonged, certain complementary products can be added to the line of goods made and so selected as to be active during periods when the manufacture of other products would normally be slack. Finally, failing otherwise to keep its employees continually busy, a company can sometimes arrange with other enterprises or agricultural groups to absorb its people temporarily.

In summary, then, to the question "For whom and for what are we planning?" it can be said that we are planning for the owners of the enterprise when we plan to achieve a profit, to operate at the optimum plant capacity, and to utilize the available facilities. We are planning for the employees when we plan to create or maintain jobs. We are planning for the consumers when we plan to meet the market demand. Furthermore, since owners and employees are all consumers, their interest and hence these seemingly divergent objectives of planning are all interrelated. Thus, in effect, we are planning for the productive enterprise in its social setting.

Perspective 8A PLANNING FOR PLANNING

Everyone gives lip service to the value of planning. Students plan vocational careers. Youngsters are urged to develop saving plans and oldsters are supposed to engage in estate planning. Supervisors plan the work to be done by subordinates. Managers plan operations. Resulting schemes range from fanciful to factual. There are occasions for all types of planning; production planning is one of the serious occasions.

Different dimensions of the planning function are listed below.

1. *Planning is a philosophy* Looking ahead is a way of thinking, a concern about the future effects of today's actions. Planning involves a state of mind that recognizes the need for orderliness and the value of direction. Individual planners may sway between optimism and pessimism, but they dare not stray too far from reality.
2. *Planning is integration* Both long- and short-range plans provide a unifying structure to give purpose to the organizational units involved. Broader plans consider the suppliers, customers, and other peripheral contacts of an enterprise. More detailed plans set the framework for coordinated activities within an enterprise. Together they constitute a projection of overall expectations and an explanation for individual contributions.
3. *Planning is a process* Goals and objectives are the most obvious consequence of the planning process. A loose objective of survival or of making a profit is a fuzzy guideline, clearly inadequate for steering an enterprise. A winning plan includes the strategy that defines how much has to be done to achieve the objectives, the sequence of events that satisfies those strategies, and the assignments that lead to the accomplishment of the events.
4. *Planning is a collection of procedures* All companies plan ahead to some extent and apply their own methods in doing so. In a small company, one person may do it all. Larger companies often have standard procedures for formulating and carrying out plans. Forecasting specialists, planning sections that collect and digest data, scheduled meetings at different organizational levels to solicit suggestions and to inform participants, and control measures to check progress contribute to complete planning procedures. Limited procedures are enough for simple plans; more elaborate procedures are necessary for complex plans. Knowing which to apply where is the art of planning.

8-2 MANUFACTURING PROCESSES

Industry today makes use of four basic types of processes: (1) synthetic, (2) analytic, (3) conditioning, and (4) extractive. A *synthetic* process is one that involves the assembly of the component parts of the product. For example, the manufacture of portland cement is a synthetic process involving the mixing of limestone and clay. Automobile assembly lines likewise are typical synthetic processes. An *analytic* process is one that resolves the raw material into its various elements or constituent parts. Such industrial processes as meat packing, which develops a multitude of by-products, and petroleum refining, which converts crude petroleum into gasoline, kerosene, useful oils, etc., are typical analytic processes. A *conditioning* process involves a change in form of physical properties. Most metal-working industries, plastic plants, and leather-tanning shops condition their raw materials to achieve the product. The fourth type of process is *extractive*. It is essentially a process of separation, such as the obtaining of magnesium and bromine from sea water, or metal ore from the earth. Usually, however, manufacturing involves not one but a combination of these productive processes. For example, the manufacture of machine tools involves conditioning processes in the fabrication of the various machine parts, and synthetic processes as far as their assembly into finished products is concerned.

Over the years a multitude of specific processes have been developed for various materials and products. Each has its advantages and limitations in terms of applicability, level of quality, reliability, and economics (overall cost). New processes and adaptations of those already in existence are continually being developed to cope with new products, materials, and desires and to bring higher quality and lower cost. The management of each enterprise must have a thorough knowledge of the manufacturing technology in its field to be able to judge effectively those processes best adapted to its objectives. However, for our purposes here it is desirable simply to note some of the more widely used processes, along with recent trends and emphases. Also, it should be noted that each manufacturing process is made up of a series of operations, each contributing in turn to the progress of the item in its journey from raw material or part to finished product.

8-2.1 Casting

Under the general heading "metal-mold casting" are three specific casting techniques. The so-called *permanent-mold casting* method is similar to sand-casting but makes use of metal or refractory-lined molds and is warranted for volume production at greater precision than is permitted by sand-casting. It is used principally for irregularly shaped articles of moderate size such as automotive engine blocks. *Centrifugal casting* is a similar operation in which the mold is rotated as the metal is poured. The result is a casting which has a dense, clean structure near its outer surface. While centrifugal castings may be of irregular shape, generally they are cylindrical items such as wheels or cylinder barrels. *Die-casting,* which at present is limited to the lower melting alloys of zinc, copper, aluminum, or magnesium, has been defined as "the art of producing accurately dimensioned parts by forcing molten metal under pressure into a steel die." Dimensional tolerances are in the neighborhood of 0.001 inch, very little surface finishing is necessary, and complex and intricate articles ranging in size from the zipper fastener on a lady's handbag to the "massive" radiator grille on her automobile can be produced by this method. Plastic molding is essentially a die-casting technique employing compression and heat on plastic powders. While the cost of the die and the casting machine used for metal items both are high, the operation is incredibly rapid. Consequently die-casting is essentially for volume production.

Investment (or "lost-wax") *casting* starts with wax or plastic replicas which are "invested" into or surrounded by a ceramic material. Upon hardening, the ceramic is fired and the wax or plastic melts away, leaving a ceramic mold into which metal is cast under pressure or centrifugal action. Dimensional accuracy is about 0.001 inch. Certain alloys that are difficult to machine or otherwise form, including those used in the blades and buckets for jet engines, can be cast to shape by this method.

Also on the family tree of casting methods is the technique of powder metallurgy. Metallic powders poured into dies and compressed can then be sintered in a furnace to produce parts of varied strength and porosity to meet specific needs. Small gears, "oilless" bearings, model-train parts, and numerous other items can be produced rapidly and to considerable accuracy (measured in a few thousandths of an inch).

8-2.2   Forming

Forming methods include various forging and extrusion techniques. *Impact-die* or *drop forging* as well as *hot-pressed forging* are performed on heavy forging machines with dies. The metal usually is heated and then pressed or hammered to shape, although smaller articles such as bolts, rivets, and small balls are "cold-headed" at room temperature. Forging dies are fairly costly, making the method one for quantity manufacture. Accuracy in terms of hundredths of an inch is not uncommon. Strength of the metal is improved by forging. Larger items which cannot be machine forged can be *hand forged* on an anvil under a steam-driven hammer. It is essentially a craft operation limited to simple, plain shapes (large crankshafts, steel plates, steel rings) in small quantities.

In *extrusion,* ductile material or material made ductile by heating is caused to flow into dies by the action of a press. In this fashion are produced metal bars and tubes as well as plastic and rubber-base articles. In similar manner, *cold drawing* produces such desired cross sections as hexagons, channels, and ellipses. The blow of a punch press by *impact extrusion* forms ductile metal in a die. Toothpaste tubes are made by this method. New *high-energy forming* techniques are finding increased acceptance, including those involving *hydraulic pressure, air blasts, explosives,* electric-spark discharge in fluid (called *electrohydraulic*), and surges in magnetism (called *electronmagnetic*), all being used on hard-to-form metals and shapes.

8-2.3   Machining

Machining is a term used to embrace the reduction of material to specified shape and dimensions by the action of cutting tools mounted on machinery. Round articles or articles with circular sections, round holes, threads, knurling, etc., can be machined to an accuracy of a few thousandths of an inch on an engine lathe, turret lathe, automatic lathe, hand screw machine, or automatic bar machine depending upon the complexity of the section and the quantity needed. Where only holes or tapped internal surfaces are required, a single- or multiple-spindle drill press may be used. Flat surfaces can be machined on milling machines, shapers, or planers to similar tolerances. Machining techniques are used on a host of materials other than metals, including plastics, rubber, and wood. *Ultrasonic machining* vibrates tiny abrasive particles at ultrasonic frequencies to cut by bombardment gemstones, carbides, and other "unmachinable" materials. Some recent and sophisticated developments in this field include *electric-discharge machining* (known as EDM), where a stream of sparks erodes cavities in electrically conductive materials; *chemical milling,* which employs fluids to etch three-dimensional images in ceramics, glass, and metals; and *electrolytic machining,* a reverse electroplating because the work serves as the anode and the brass or stainless-steel tool as the cathode. Some so-called "superalloys" are best cut by *hot machining* at temperatures of several hundred degrees Fahrenheit or by *subzero machining,* two diametrically opposite techniques of accomplishing the same result: efficient machining with long tool life.

8-2.4 Stamping

Stamping consists of pressing or drawing sheet metal into dies in a press. Intricate shapes, cutout sections, and deep drawings are all possible to tolerances of about 0.001 inch by this method. While it is essentially a process for quantity manufacture, small quantities which do not warrant the high die cost can usually be turned out in an inexpensive "soft" die or by use of a hand-operated shear, bender, and brake. A pressforming method employing heated dies is used to mold slabs of rubber and to bond rubber-to-metal items into various shapes.

8-2.5 Heat Treating

Heat treating of steels and superalloys improves their physical properties to give better fatigue life, ductility, and tensile strength. Heat-treating embraces several processes for changing the physical properties of metals by means of heat. One of these is *hardening,* which, when applied to steel, consists of heating the metal above its critical temperature and quenching suddenly in water or oil or by air blast. *Tempering,* or drawing to give the desired toughness, is accomplished by a subsequent heat-soaking to relieve hardening stresses. *Annealing* is a heat-softening method for parts hardened by heat or cold working. If localized heating is prescribed, it may be done by an *induction heater* wherein heat is generated in any conducting substance by means of a high-frequency magnetic field. Or localized heating can be accomplished by an *acetylene flame* moving along the exterior surface of the part. Both these techniques for local heat treatment are commonly used for case hardening (as gear teeth), for annealing, and for brazing. *Infrared heating* utilizing radiated heat of lamps is a rapid means of preheating, dehydrating, paint drying, or shrink-fitting some articles. Nonmetallic articles may be heated by *radio-frequency power.* It is also useful in pressure-bonding laminated wood, in plywood manufacture, for "compreg" woods, and in the molding of plastics.

8-2.6 Surface Treating

Surface treating includes a variety of processes for chemically or mechanically altering the surface characteristics of any article. *Plating* is an electrolytic process for adding beauty, providing an anticorrosion finish, or enlarging dimensions (of worn or undersized parts) by the addition of chromium, nickel, cadmium, or copper to the surface. *Galvanizing,* a hot-dip process, provides an antirust zinc coating. *Porcelain enameling* gives a hard if somewhat brittle, baked-on, highly protective finish commonly used on kitchenware and on some household appliances. *Metal-blackening,* e.g., gun-metal, embraces electrochemical processes for improving appearance and adding slight antirust protection without increasing the dimensions of the article. *Painting* for appearance and as a preservative makes possible the use of colors. *Plastic coatings* are, however, encroaching into the domain of paints because of their better and more durable finishes. Other surface treatments include surface abrasion by either *tumbling* or *shot blasting* for purposes of cleaning and brightening and *shot-peening,* a means of achieving surface hardness and resistance to fatigue through compressive surface stresses. A youngster in the family of surface treating is the technique of *metal spraying,* in which molten metal is sprayed on parts to build up or alter surfaces.

8-3 MANUFACTURING CONSIDERATIONS

Many production-planning decisions hinge on the variety of products to be manufactured, their volume, and regularity of demand. Running the gamut of manufacturing situations encountered, we find, at one extreme, production of large quantities of a single product in continual process (e.g., automotive parts, light bulbs, and a host of other "mass-production" articles) and, at the other extreme, production of one or perhaps a very few pieces seldom if ever reproduced (e.g., a large electric-power generator, a transoceanic passenger ship). Between these two poles are products made intermittently, ranging from those manufactured at regular intervals to those produced infrequently at unpredictable intervals. To add further variety to the situations encountered, quantities may range from a few pieces to many pieces per lot.

8-3.1 Scheduling

Efficiency dictates that mass-production items be manufactured to master schedules based on depletion of finished-goods inventories, with the machines and equipment integrated by product, i.e., arranged on a production-line basis for *serialized manufacture.* Manufacture of one or a few pieces is based on specific customer order and generally requires that machines be grouped functionally according to type of operation or process performed. It is known as *job-lot manufacture.* Between these two extremes we find many gradations in machine arrangement and manufacturing conditions, which fall into the general category of *semiserialized manufacture.* These are characterized by sporadic production lines or intermittently linked sequential operations interspersed with functionally grouped equipment.

To generalize on planning techniques required to meet this range of manufacturing conditions, it can be noted that for serialized manufacture most of the planning effort goes into a study of best methods and special-purpose equipment, including automatic work-handling and inspection devices, to achieve a *balanced production line* at the desired rate of production. Once the line is established, with its failings and "bugs" ironed out, planning becomes somewhat routine. It is primarily a matter of planning for the control of materials and the control of quality so that the line may operate smoothly without bottlenecks.

Planning for semiserialized manufacture is first a problem of setting up all possible production lines and batteries of related machines and, where this is not practical, grouping machines by process. Second, it is a problem of planning the control of materials and quality. However, semiserialized manufacture, by virtue of the fact that it is not entirely continuous, must facilitate its flow of materials through the use of *balanced schedules.* For this reason subsequent planning is of a more complicated nature than where a fully serialized production line can be employed. Those production lines that can be devised must be sufficiently flexible to manufacture a variety of products or a variety of types and sizes of the same basic product. Hence, to employ all equipment to its optimum capacity, a balanced schedule or relationship usually must be maintained between the sizes and quantities that can be manufactured at any one time on those lines or within the machine groupings. Of course, as we shall discover in Chapter 10, the problem of planning a balanced schedule of production can be eased through the use of matching centers but, nevertheless, the planning of semiserialized manufacture is considerably more complicated than planning where manufacture is serialized.

When we come to the planning of job-lot manufacture, the problems are still more complicated. With the machines grouped by process, the main consideration becomes that of *balanced machine loads.* Scheduling, then, involves careful planning of the work for each machine or battery of machines to ensure that the material in process is spread out evenly among the available equipment and is produced in the desired sequence. Also, since separate production orders are required for each article fabricated, more paper work is involved, material handling and control of quality may become infinitely more difficult, and the reporting and tracing of the progress of material through the plant are invariably more intricate. Here, then, we have some of the prime arguments for the adoption of serialized or at least semiserialized manufacturing methods wherever the volume of production permits, for it can readily be seen that the difficulties and expense of planning may be sharply reduced if such methods can be introduced.

8-3.2 Estimating

Of considerable importance to some plants, particularly those engaged in the job-lot manufacture of products that seldom if ever are reproduced, is the function of *estimating.* As we shall see in Chapter 11, when we consider the problem of quotations through the eyes of the purchasing agent, a customer who wishes to buy a particular product for the first time generally entertains bids from the vendors of such a product before he actually places his order. The quotation must contain among other information the selling price of the article (which requires an estimate of the manufacturing cost) and an estimate of the time required for delivery. These in turn can best be determined through an analysis of the manufacturing techniques required. Thus the estimating of bids is frequently a cooperative function of the production-control, industrial- and plant-engineering, and cost departments.

The sales department, upon receipt of a request for a proposal, refers it to the production-control department which, in the case of new products, variations on standard products, or significant changes in quantity to be manufactured, solicits the aid of engineering and cost. This last-named department makes a cost analysis of the item and prepares a cost estimate, upon the accuracy of which depend not only the opportunity the enterprise has for meeting competition but also the certainty that the expected profit will be realized from the sale.

The cost of producing the first article or batch of a new product is almost invariably higher than that for succeeding articles or batches. In fact, there is a fairly universal pattern where costs of repeat runs of new products are progressively lower, reflecting such factors as increased employee proficiency, methods improvements, engineering changes, and the like. Cost accountants in some industries and in individual companies where there has been considerable new-product development have studied their experience with these products and, finding fairly consistent patterns of cost reduction in the early stages of production of each new product, have plotted these patterns into what are known as *learning curves* for use in future cost prediction. Once the slope of the curve has been established and the initial cost of a new product estimated, the cost department then is able to predict the cost for the five hundredth piece, one thousandth piece, etc. As more research is done on such curves, this fine tool of cost estimating will come into more widespread use (see Perspective 8B).

In the case of products made from standard parts, a price list of such articles or parts can be prepared for use by salespersons in the field. For example, sales engineers for industrial conveyor equipment are supplied with price lists for standard conveyor parts from which the price of most individual installations can be calculated. Also, knock-down wire-grill partitioning used in industrial plants is quoted by sales representatives on a rule-of-thumb price per linear foot.

Of course, products frequently reproduced require virtually no new estimating, for past records furnish actual cost data from which the new bid can be prepared. Also, in some cases when a new product is requested, it may be possible to compare it with some similar product previously manufactured, and the new estimate can be readily projected without a complete analysis.

Perspective 8B   LEARNING CURVES

Learning curves, or cost improvement curves, came to prominence as a cost estimating tool in the aircraft industry during World War II. The basic assumption underlying the curve is that people, individually or as members of a production team, gain proficiency with repetition of the same task or project. Statistical analysis of the learning function indicates that it has a generally predictable pattern. This pattern shows a relatively rapid decrease in direct labor during early repetitions followed by a gradual leveling until little further improvement takes place. Reasons for the reduction in time (cost) per unit are summarized by Professor E. C. Keachie:

"Learning" is a crucial factor but its nature is not just the obvious one of operator learning. A part of the operator learning is physical—rhythmic development of the best motion pattern.

Another part is mental—from simple perception and response to decision making. Beyond this the operator is part of a complex system, even in rather small shops. In addition to the operator's job activity, the system involves him in instructions, standards, scheduling, and varied relationships. His job duties may be changed or he may be moved to a different station or job calling for relearning.

Such changes result from the activities of other persons and the impersonal requirements of the system of production. The designer and his modifications, the planner and his schedule changes, the manager and his decisions, the employees who cause change by their activities and absences are illustrations. Change is the order of the day, and this change includes learning or progress by all hands plus overriding progress of the organization as a whole.

The relationship between the difficulty of the overall task and the ability of the organization to perform it will help to determine the improvement rate. Total learning is evidenced by better coordination, fewer delays in personal and mechanical interactions, stoppages, as well as more production.*

*SOURCE: "Manufacturing Cost Reduction Through the Curve of Natural Productivity Increase," Institute of Business and Economic Research, University of California, Berkeley, 1964.

COMMENT Realization of improved output rates due to learning is important to production planning, but caution must be exercised in determining what learning rate to expect and in anticipating what disruptions to learning might occur in the production process. Deviations from the production plan, late delivery of materials, and similar disruptions can cause "forgetting" which retards, or even reverses, learning effects.

8-4 QUANTITATIVE ANALYSIS

While scientific methods for solving industrial planning and operating problems hark back to the days of Taylor, over the years they have been gradually improved in execution, supplemented in techniques, and expanded in application. Today many of the scientific elements are found grouped under the general heading of *operations research*. Whether all the quantitative methods should be housed under the collective operations-research title or should be associated with their generic origin such as quality or inventory control, is largely an academic question. The more important point is that operations-research has been a rallying discipline for the investigation of ill structured problems throughout the management arena.

Consider a few typical planning problems. A company with seasonal sales wishes to know whether the seasonal demand for its products can be met more cheaply by adding temporary work shift and overtime hours or by a steady year-round work schedule with product stockpiling and increased warehouse costs during the off season. Again, an enterprise with a variety of products, customer requirements ranging from long to short runs, and equipment ranging from high-production long-setup machines to slow-production quick-setup machines, wants to know which product orders to schedule on what machines for lowest cost operation. Also, a company producing a number of products on the same machines seeks the best plant layout of its equipment so as to minimize total material handling for the product mix and volumes anticipated. Still another situation. An oil company is faced with variations in quality of crude oil from different sources and a variety of refining processes, proportions of products (derived chemicals, specialty gasolines, kerosene, diesel oil, and fuel oil), and costs depending on which of its refining plants is employed. In addition, customer demand for each of the above products is continually shifting. What crude oils should be used and to which plants should they be assigned to produce the desired amounts of the various end products at the lowest overall cost?

Such industrial problems as these are beset with related variable factors whose interdependence is not easily visualized or calculated. Until fairly recently, management was faced with making policy decisions on such problems without sound, precise, quantitative information on which to base conclusions. Instead, management had to be content for the most part with historical arithmetic which, like the wails of a "Monday-morning quarterback," told only "how much better off we would be now had we done it differently." Or, confronted with several variable factors, management sometimes arbitrarily fixed one of the variables and then manipulated the others, achieving the best results it could under the self-imposed restrictions.

What is the quantitative approach to such problems? It uses the methods of the researcher—it sometimes involves a team of researchers headed by a management scientist—together with the tools of the mathematician. One member of the team, a specialist in the problem at hand, sets forth the elements that bear on the problem, indicating which are constants, which vary, and how the variables act. From this information, a *model*, usually a mathematical formula or equation, is developed which covers the relationship of the variables. When this is solved for alternative policies, the result is a behavior pattern that can serve as the basis for management's decision. In some instances, the model can be tested for accuracy by inserting data which are known to produce a certain result. Any inaccuracies in the calculated result obtained from the model may indicate that changes are required in the model itself. Several well-respected quantitative techniques are discussed in the following pages.

8-4.1 Linear Programming

One of the mathematical tools used in operations research to solve "optimization" problems is linear programming. With this technique, all the variables are set forth in numerical terms. One is selected; it is optimized; and then the solution is examined in relation to the other variables involved. The numerical information is arrayed in an orderly table called a *matrix*. This is a basic horizontal and vertical columnar work form used in all linear programming problems. While complex problems almost always require large-scale computers, solutions to simpler problems can be arrived at by pencil and desk equipment.

The *transportation method* is an example of a relatively direct manual approach to solving a linear programming problem. Assume there are four plants supplied from three warehouses. The amount required by each plant and the amount available in each warehouse are known. When the shipping costs between plants and warehouses are also known, the problem is directed to deciding the least cost program for transporting supplies.

The compact solution format for these relationships is shown by the transportaton matrix in Figure 8-1. Each column represents a destination or plant. The rows denote the origins or warehouses. The number above the diagonal in each cell in the body of the matrix shows the cost to ship one unit from the origin to the respective destination. The right and lower

Origins	Warehouses $W1$, $W2$, $W3$, shown as triangles
Destinations	Plants $P1$, $P2$, $P3$, $P4$, shown as circles
Supply	20 units at $W1$, 14 units at $W2$, 30 units at $W3$
Demand	16 units at $P1$ and $P2$, 24 units at $P3$, 8 units at $P4$
Costs	Transportation charge per unit shown on arrows

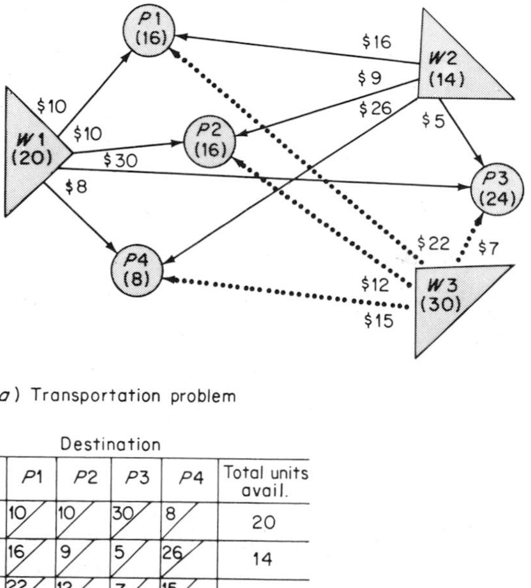

(*a*) Transportation problem

Destination

Origin	$P1$	$P2$	$P3$	$P4$	Total units avail.
$W1$	10	10	30	8	20
$W2$	16	9	5	26	14
$W3$	22	12	7	15	30
Total units req.	16	16	24	8	64 / 64

(*b*) Transportation matrix

Least cost supply pattern	Cost
From $W1$ ship 12 units to $P1$ and 8 units to $P4$:	$184
From $W2$ ship 4 units to $P1$ and 10 units to $P2$:	$154
From $W3$ ship 6 units to $P2$ and 24 units to $P3$:	$240
Total transportation cost:	$578

(*c*) Optimal solution

Figure 8-1 Transportation problem, matrix, and solution.

rims of the matrix define the number of units available at the origins and required at the destinations.

The solution method is essentially a systematic trial and success procedure. A promising feasible solution is developed by following a set of rules. Another set of rules is used to check whether the initial solution is the best possible. If it is not, the check step shows where improvements should be made. The check-revise-check process is continued until no additional improvements are available; the least cost supply routes are then identified. In a large matrix, this sequential process gets tedious, but it is better than seeking a solution without a guiding algorithm. Computer programs are widely available to assist in the more complex linear programming problems.

8-4.2 Queuing Theory

Some operations research problems are solved by "waiting-line," or queuing, theory. This theory can be illustrated by automobiles arriving in random fashion and waiting at a road intersection protected by a traffic light. By varying the timing of the red and green cycles of the light, by permitting or prohibiting "right turn on red," or by changing the number of traffic lanes in each direction, it is possible to alter the "servicing facilities" so as to affect the waiting line of cars. Queuing theory can be used to predict what combination of these changes will maximize the effectiveness of servicing facilities and minimize the waiting line for all concerned. Similarly, in industry production parts arrive and wait at inspection stations, centralized operations, and points of assembly. Receiving and shipping schedules and the routing of transportation vehicles involve waiting-line situations. By use of queuing theory it is possible to balance the cost of letting units wait with that involved in providing increased servicing facilities so as to yield greatest overall effectiveness and efficiency.

As an illustration of a queuing theory application, consider the unloading of supply vans at warehouse docking facilities. When these facilities are inadequate the vans must wait. Conversely, too much unloading capacity means the docking facilities will be idle much of the time. The application of queuing theory seeks a balance between the cost of making the vans wait and the cost of maintaining idle servicing facilities.

This type of problem is easily evaluated by standard queuing formulas when the assumptions upon which the models are based are representative of the physical situation. Some of the more important assumptions for this problem are:

1. Van arrivals follow a Poisson distribution.

2. Arrivals are not affected by the length of the queue.

3. Unloading times follow an exponential distribution.

4. Service at the docks is "first come, first served."

For situations where these assumptions are not valid, the evaluation may not be as straightforward, but it can still be conducted by other methods such as simulation.

We can observe the effect of waiting lines by letting the mean arrival rate be 3 vans per hour and the average service rate be 4 per hour. At first glance it might appear that no vans would ever wait when the service rate exceeds the arrival rate, but the assumption of a Poisson distribution of arrivals means the vans occasionally could arrive in clusters of 3 or 4 and still average just 3 per hour. From formulas based on the given assumptions and using the given data, we can calculate

Average length of the
waiting queue $\qquad = \dfrac{(3)^2}{4 \times (4 - 3)} = 2.25$ vans

Average time a van waits
until unloading is completed $= \dfrac{1}{4 - 3} = 1$ hour

Proportion of the time the
unloading docks are idle $\qquad = 1 - \dfrac{3}{4} = \dfrac{1}{4}$

The effect of different servicing arrangements (such as replacing the single facility with a pair of smaller ones each capable of servicing 2 vans per hour) is evaluated by associating the cost per hour of idle vans with the hourly cost of idle unloading facilities.

8-4.3 Monte Carlo Simulation

An allied technique is known as Monte Carlo simulation, taking its name from the roulette wheel. Useful in problems that defy direct mathematical analysis, it is an empirical approach which relies on the law of probability to simulate actual experience. Random-number tables, computerized random-number generators, or cards bearing numbers in the same proportion as the variables in the problem are used in the simulation exercise, and what is essentially a cut-and-try activity is repeated until the law of probability reveals the optimum solution for the conditions simulated. Waiting-line problems where assumptions for standard formulas are invalid become logical candidates for solution by simulation. Similarly, problems involving the best sequence for scheduling job-lot orders, the amount of safety stock to carry when inventory levels fluctuate unpredictably, and the necessary equipment capacity to meet peak loads can use the Monte Carlo method for solution. Since a large number of trials is necessary to obtain reliable solutions, simulations are almost always computerized.

8-4.4 Critical Path Scheduling

The network-based technique for project planning and coordination, known as critical path scheduling (CPS), was introduced in 1958. Few, if any, management tools have experienced such wide and rapid acceptance as

CPS. One version, program evaluation and review technique (PERT), is tailored to the needs of research and development projects (see Section 6-7). Another version, called the critical path method (CPM), is a standard planning technique for the construction industry. We will group both of these versions and the many other refinements for cost and resource controls under the CPS title.

The most distinguishing feature of a CPS application is the arrow network. As illustrated in Figure 8-2, an arrow network is a picture of the project. Each arrow represents a well-defined activity. The nodes at each end of an activity are the events that distinctly identify when one activity is completed and the next is started. The nodes are numbered to facilitate computer or manual time calculations.

The time to complete each activity is noted below its arrow. These durations are summed across the network to determine how long the project should take. The chain of activities that sets the maximum project duration is known as the critical path. Activities on this path must be carefully controlled if the project is to be completed within the expected time. Activities not on the critical path have leeway or *float* in scheduling. Skillful scheduling of this float with respect to the utilization of personnel, materials, and machines will minimize the project's cost.

A small project such as that shown in Figure 8-2 would hardly be a candidate for a CPS analysis. The value of CPS is most evident for large, one-time projects. When there are 20,000 or 30,000 activities, the systematic CPS routine helps disclose omissions and discover errors of logic. Computer programs are universally available to overcome the huge burden of arithmetic.

After a project passes from the planning to the working stage, CPS techniques also assist in control. The networks, often converted to time-scaled charts, show where extra resources should be applied to keep the project on schedule and, correspondingly, which activities can be delayed without affecting the total project completion time. Potential trouble areas can be anticipated by monitoring progress.

The analysis techniques previously described constitute only a brief survey of some better known routines. Other techniques of applied mathemat-

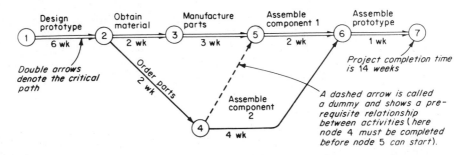

Figure 8-2 Arrow network for a critical path schedule of prototype development.

ics, work sampling, and group decision making are being developed almost daily. Often the solution to a seemingly impossible problem is found in common practice in another industry, laboratory, science, or art. It is not necessary here to know the details or mechanics of all the techniques. Rather, this is the job for the specialist. We are here concerned only with application, with the knowledge that scientific disciplines can be applied to business decision making.

Perspective 8C ANALYSIS OF QUANTITATIVE ANALYSIS METHODS

New methods of quantitative analysis are continually being developed. It is difficult, if not impossible, for people in industry to keep up with what is available and then select which ones are worth mastering. Dr. William T. Morris suggests that the usefulness of quantitative methods can be assessed by examining their stage of maturity.

In making judgments about quantitative methods, it seems helpful to be aware of the almost fad-like nature of their comings and goings. To emphasize the faddish aspect of many of these methods is not to be unnecessarily cynical about them. Many such methods seem to behave as do other types of fads, and this is a very useful observation to have in mind when considering one of the currently popular ones. If one considers the evolution, progress, application, and decline of these methods in relation to the following model, it may be clear that there is a kind of life cycle through which some have already passed, and various stages to which others have just recently progressed.

We might take as an illustrative example, PERT, program evaluation and review technique, a graphical and analytical method of production planning and control. In the first stage there is a reformulation and renaming of some basic ideas. PERT had many direct ancestors including the Gantt chart, for example.

These newly named ideas are then applied to a particular production situation. It is important to build atomic submarines in a hurry, and PERT is applied to help increase the productivity of this program. In the next stage the specific program succeeds and some of the credit, some of the glory, goes to the method. PERT gets some of the credit for the successful ship construction program. At this point, three types of persons enter the picture, stimulated by the publicity which the method has received. The academics enter, generalizing the method, making it more sophisticated, enriching it and publishing articles laying out their results. They are not articles about application, but about the sophistication of the technique itself, a sophistication which may even lead to a whole new body of applied mathematics, where the word "applied" refers only to imagined possibilities. The second group to enter are the consultants who see the favorable publicity as a sound basis for a marketing effort. They begin to market the technique, emphasizing its newness, the "revolutionary" character of the method, and its great universal potential for productivity improvement. The third group consists of people in organizations whose careers are not progressing to their own satisfaction. They decide that it might be possible to build a career on the new method so they become resident advocates and local spokesmen for it. They become leaders and marketers of in-house programs to apply the method, hoping that its success will result also in their own advancement. At this point extensive marketing effort has built up expectations which simply cannot all be realized. A lot of people, however, now have vested interests in the technique, so it is pushed to the point of actual application in a variety of situations. Its implementation produces mixed results, a few successes, but quite a few failures. The technique has been oversold, disappointments are inevitable, reevaluations and "second thoughts" begin to appear in the management literature. The technique generally passes into decline, although it does remain and makes a useful contribution in a few places where it turns out to be appropriate.*

*SOURCE: "Quantitative Methods—A Management Perspective," *Industrial Engineering*, June, 1975.

COMMENT: Most quantitative methods exhibit essentially the same life cycle phases as Dr. Morris describes, some rising to prominence faster and fading at the same rate, others exhibiting more lasting power but still subject to dwindling attention. In appraising the potential use of a technique, the critical indicator is its record of actual accomplishment, how much documented evidence there is of its effectiveness in industrial applications.

8-5   REVIEW QUESTIONS

1. What is meant by "production planning"? What are its objectives?

2. Why is it important to stabilize the use of plant facilities, number of jobs, and working hours?

3. Distinguish among the four types of manufacturing processes given in this chapter.

4. Where is it desirable to have serialized manufacture? Job-lot manufacture?

5. Which type of manufacture requires that cost estimates be prepared for the products? What is meant by "learning curve"?

6. What is the significance of a model in the quantitative approach to production planning?

7. What are the different quantitative techniques described in this chapter? Where can each be used?

8-6   TOPICS FOR DISCUSSION

1. One executive notes that if he had to solve all his everyday problems on the spot, he would not have time to plan ahead. He therefore admits to having a "procrastination drawer" in his desk into which go papers on most of the tough daily problems not of major importance. Periodically, when the drawer becomes full, he goes through it and finds that perhaps 80 per cent of the items which appeared troublesome somehow have straightened themselves out. Occasionally some item bounces back to plague him, but he finds that on the whole his batting average is good. Comment on the merits of this practice.

2. In a profit economy, to what extent is a company justified in sacrificing its optimum profits by:

   a. Cutting prices so that it can capture enough of the available market to become the "General Motors" of its industry?
   b. Refusing customers' orders so as to permit operating the plant at a level deemed "comfortable" by its management?
   c. Employing people to perform on available equipment in the plant work that could be purchased more economically, the motive being to employ a temporary excess of labor in the community?

3. It has been suggested by students of learning curves that the following industries should be able to apply such curves to advantage in connection with their new products: aircraft, electronics, shipbuilding, home appliances, and builders of mass-produced homes. Those in which learning curves would be of little advantage are claimed to be oil refining, chemicals, plastics, most automotive parts, and standard toys. Do you agree with the above contention and why?

4. Case 8A: *The New-Process Manufacturing Co.*

New-Process, a large metalworking company supplying equipment used by most industries in the country, recently acquired the nucleus of an operations-research team. The company management asked division heads to submit to the team problems they faced which they felt might be best solved by operations-research techniques. The following were received:

1. In one manufacturing department of the company a shortage of machine capacity is limiting production. Four different products are involved, and each can be made by two or more alternative methods, depending on which machines are used. There are minimum production requirements per week for each product, but any additional units produced by this department can be sold. What quantity per week of each product and which method for each gives the most profitable use of the available capacity?

2. The company has 12 hand-fed assembly machines performing highly repetitive, short-cycle work. Should these be operated by 12, 6, or 4 operators on a one-machine-, two-machine-, or three-machine-per-operator basis, respectively?

3. Sales of the company are closely related to growth in industrial output of the country. Some expansion of the company's manufacturing capacity now is required. Manufacturing considerations for this expansion dictate three possible sizes of plants, which for simplicity we shall call small, medium, and large. The small plant would bring certain manufacturing economies up to its maximum capacity, beyond which the medium plant would become more economical. It in turn would yield to the economies of the large plant if and when further capacity were necessary. Each of the three plants could be completed within a year's time, and each would probably be obsolete 15 years thereafter. In which size plant should the company invest now?

4. The company's monthly electric-power bill is based on (a) a demand charge computed from the peak amount of power used by the company at any time during the past 12 months, (b) an energy charge calculated from the total amount of power used during the current month, (c) a penalty charge if the power factor is low, and (d) a fuel adjustment charge or credit, depending on the present cost of fuel used by the power company in its power generation. Two alternative rate schedules are available to the company: one providing for a high demand charge and a low energy charge, the other for a low demand charge and a high energy charge. Minor variations between the two schedules also exist in methods of applying power-factor charge and fuel adjustment. Which rate schedule should the company adopt?

5. In a preventive maintenance program for various groups of the company's manufacturing equipment, what is the optimum period of time between inspections to reveal signs of approaching failure?

6. Considering all economic factors involved, what is the most satisfactory number of stockroom clerks in a stockroom of small tools and supplies serving a large number of production employees?

Questions

1. Suggest which, if any, operations-research techniques might be applied to each problem.

2. What common characteristics do you find among the problems you have selected for operations-research solution?

3. What limitations do you see in operations-research problem solving?

5. Case 8B: *Casts, Inc.*

A customer has inquired of Casts, Inc., its prices on 50- and 100-piece lots of a certain casting complete with six drilled holes.

The laying out and drilling of the holes can be done by a skilled mechanic in each casting in 40 minutes. He is paid at the rate of $12.50 per hour, and the shop overhead applied against his time is $12.50 per hour.

A jig could be made costing $1,000 permitting the job to be done on a multiple-spindle drill press in 1.8 minutes per piece including loading and unloading the jig. The machine rate (i.e., overhead) for the multiple-spindle drill press is $7.50 per hour and the operator gets $7.00 per hour.

Questions

1. How would you plan the drilling of this casting in 50-piece lots? In 100-piece lots? What estimated shop costs per piece would you quote the company's sales department in response to the customer's inquiry?

9
PRODUCTIVITY IMPROVEMENT

Productivity gains, as measured by increases in output/input ratios, are necessary for a healthy economy. What are the factors that affect productivity growth? An enterprise must look to constant productivity—to finding ways of bettering the product and making it at lower cost—if it is to keep itself abreast or ahead of competition. The techniques of simplification, diversification, and miniaturization often are employed. How does each fit into the product-improvement audit? For a product to be made economically and perform reliably, it must be carefully engineered. How and when does standardization play a part in product engineering? What can be expected from the disciplines of value engineering and the techniques of reliability engineering? This chapter attempts to throw light on vital concern for productivity improvement.

9 PRODUCTIVITY IMPROVEMENT

9-1 PRODUCTIVITY ADVANCES

Between 1973 and 1975, an unusual economic development occurred. American productivity, which had risen persistently over the past 25 years, stopped growing. For the first time since 1947, the earliest date for quarterly data, the productivity rate in the United States actually declined in six out of seven consecutive quarters. This unfavorable performance reflected the slowdown in economic activity which began at the end of 1973 and resulted in low rates of capacity utilization, rising unemployment, and a reduction in real hourly compensation.

Thoughtful observers of the economic scene were troubled by productivity performance even before the onset of the 1973–1975 recession. Since 1966 the rate at which productivity has fluctuated was well below the postwar average, as is evident in Figure 9-1. Moreover, the average rate of advance in manufacturing productivity in the United States since World War II has been below that of most other industrial nations. Admittedly, the United States started from a much higher level and the level of productivity is still above that of any other nation, but the gap is gradually closing. The lag in productivity growth weakens American industry's ability to compete successfully in world markets.

9-1.1 Meaning of Productivity

Broadly speaking, productivity can be defined as the relationship of the volume of goods and services produced to the physical inputs used in its production. Productivity can therefore be measured in terms of the ratio of output to input of labor, capital, energy, materials, or a combination of these. The most widely used measure relates output to the input of labor time, which includes the time of employees, managers, and the self-employed. Output per hour simply indicates how much labor time is associated with the volume of output. The concept of output per hour does not imply sole or even primary responsibility on the part of the work force for productivity improvement since, in a highly technological society, worker skill and effort are clearly only two of many interrelated sources of improvement.

Productivity growth is influenced by a number of factors—education and skill of the work force, technological innovation, capital and capacity utilization, scale of production, flow of materials, quality of management, state of labor relations, among others. These vary in relative importance, but none may be ignored. Beyond these factors, productivity improvement depends on the efforts of all groups in the economy—business, labor, investors, consumers, and governments at all levels. Cooperation among these groups is fostered by an expanding economy, which provides for maximum employ-

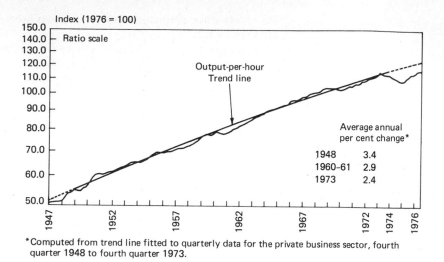

*Computed from trend line fitted to quarterly data for the private business sector, fourth quarter 1948 to fourth quarter 1973.

Figure 9-1 Output-per-hour growth rate in the U.S. private business sector—real gross product per man-hour worked for all persons in the private business sector. SOURCE: Bureau of Labor Statistics, U.S. Department of Labor.

ment and utilization of plants and machines. An expanding economy also creates the basis for efficient rates of operation, increased investment in new plant and equipment, and more job opportunities for those who may be displaced by technological change.

9-1.2 Factors Affecting Productivity Gains

The factors that directly or immediately impinge on productivity fall into three main groups: (1) increase in tangible capital per worker; (2) improvement in the quality of labor; and (3) increase in the efficiency with which capital and labor are put to use in production. Underlying these are the factors which stimulate savings and investment and thereby increase tangible capital, the education and training which improve the quality of labor, and the technological and other advances which raise output per unit of labor and capital.

1. *Tangible capital per worker* Increases in productivity and the higher income thus produced help generate capital formation. The process is mutually reenforcing since capital formation helps increase productivity. Tools, machines, rolling stock, buildings of all sorts, farm and timber lands, roads and dams, stocks of materials, and other goods are often referred to as the "means of production." The more of these items supplied to each worker, the greater the product obtained from an hour of work.

2. *Improvement in the quality of labor* Labor, which is also a form of investment—not in tangible goods, but in human beings, made through education, on-the-job training, and the provision of better health facilities—is a critical factor in the equation of productivity improvement. Quite often such investment by families,

217

government, and employers is not directly related to the production process but rather to improving the quality of human life; but such improvements to "human capital" have positive effects on productivity. The quality of labor may also be affected by changes in the age–sex composition of the labor force. The changes may have a negative or positive effect on productivity growth, depending on whether they produce a better qualified or less qualified labor force, as measured by earning capacity.

3. *More efficient use of capital and labor*   Of the factors that improve the efficiency with which capital and labor are used, the most prominent is technological advance. In its broadest definition, this includes improvements in managerial techniques as well as modifications in tools and equipment. Another influence is the speedier diffusion of technological advances within and between countries as transportation, communication, and education improve.

Higher efficiency may also result from a reduction in the length of the workday or week, better allocation of resources among various economic sectors, and programs that encourage worker cooperation toward productivity improvement goals. Labor-management relations, strikes and lockouts, changes in the business cycle, and even the weather also have impact, although these more directly influence year-to-year changes in productivity rather than long-term trends.

Government economic policy may have an indirect influence on productivity, as the reference to education and diffusion of technology indicates, but it can also have a direct effect. Thus, tax codes which are disincentives to innovation and regulatory activities that are unnecessarily burdensome can impede efforts to increase or maintain efficiency, while positive policies can promote efficiency and greater productivity.

Sources of productivity growth are themselves influenced by even broader forces at work in the economy. These include the incentives that impel people constantly to strive to advance themselves, the motivation to maximize profit, and the wide diffusion of new techniques throughout the economic system. High productivity is the end result of millions of decisions and innovations on the part of millions of people. Productivity cannot be increased simply by government fiat or exhortation. Rather any increase in output per worker-hour depends on the energy, ingenuity, and skill with which all resources of production are managed. Thus productivity improvement is a recurring theme throughout this book because the mechanisms of improvement are so diverse. Sometimes the relationship of industrial activities may seem obscure, as in the following discussions of simplification and diversification, but such considerations do affect the bottom line of industrial efficiency—its productivity.

Perspective 9A PRODUCTIVITY AND RELATIVE PRICES

Virtually all industries have experienced long-term increases in output per worker hour, but the rates of increase have varied greatly. These variations help explain differences in the behavior of industrial prices. As a rule, industries with above-average productivity growth have, either voluntarily or under pressure of competition, shown smaller price increases, as indicated in the chart below.* An extreme example is the hosiery manufacturing industry, where output per worker hour increased at the extraordinary rate of 7 per cent a year between 1960 and 1974 and the industry's selling price declined at the same time, despite a general inflation, at the rate of 1 per cent a year. In contrast, industries with below-average productivity have tended to raise prices more than the general run. An example is footwear, with a growth in output per worker hour of less than 1 per cent a year, and a price increase of nearly 4 per cent a year between 1960 and 1974. Consumers gained from one and paid the cost for the other.

*SOURCE: Bureau of Labor Statistics, U.S. Department of Labor.

COMMENT   While changes in output per hour and price tend to be related, the relationship is not perfect. Output per hour is a major determinant of price, but not the only one. Among the factors that influence the relative prices of an industry's products, in addition to labor productivity, are the prices an industry has to pay for its nonlabor inputs and the efficiency with which materials, fuel, and services purchased from other industries are put to use. For instance, economies in the utilization of coal and petroleum, the prices for which have been surging since 1973, will be important determi-

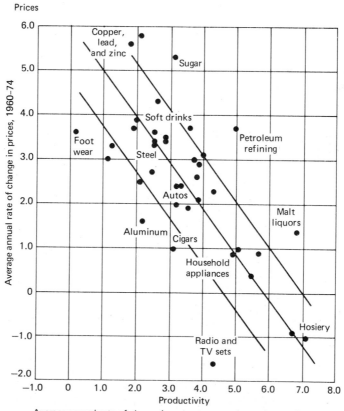

Average annual rate of change in output per employee–hour, 1960–74

nants of the prices charged by the electric power industry. As the prices of energy, materials, and other nonlabor inputs rise relative to general prices and wages, many industries feel pressures to take special measures to reduce waste and scrap in processing and thus increase their materials and energy productivity.

9-2 PRODUCT SIMPLIFICATION AND DIVERSIFICATION

Product simplification means essentially the elimination of extraneous or marginal lines, types, and models of products. It includes a reduction in the range of materials and components used in manufacturing these products and also tends to reduce the complexity of methods and processes of manufacturing. The current trend toward miniaturization is one of the many forms of simplification, as will be discussed below.

Product diversification is the direct opposite of simplification. It involves the addition of lines of products, types, and models. It likewise affects materials, components, and manufacturing methods and processes, but in the direction of increased complexity. There are three basic approaches to product diversification:

First, a company may diversify *horizontally* into new products which, while they do not significantly affect existing products, do utilize the manufacturing, marketing, or financial know-how and facilities of the enterprise. These are known as *complementary products,* produced by like processes or equipment (e.g., printing plants which publish books, magazines, and newspapers and do job printing) or sold in common markets (e.g., refrigerators, ranges, washing machines, and window air conditioners made separately in the home-appliance enterprise but sold through the same distribution facilities). Certain products which are seasonal or for which the demand is not stable are complementary in that they can be so scheduled as to keep manufacturing facilities busy during otherwise slack periods.

The second approach a company may take is to diversify *vertically* by integration into materials, components, or subsequent or satellite products. Here the company's objective is to find greater profit opportunities in "making" rather than "buying"—or "selling." For example, a metalworking-press plant may decide to pickle, roll, and slit its own flat, strip-steel coils rather than *buy* the material from a steel-rolling mill. In the reverse direction, a steel-rolling mill may decide to fabricate its steel and *sell* the subsequent product rather than make the steel alone. Vertical diversification usually calls for know-how, facilities, and marketing techniques different from those previously employed. Satellite products "spin off" from the principal product as in the case of *by-products,* where material from the product can be used in subsidiary items (e.g., meat packing gives rise to glue, gelatin, grease, soap, shortening, fertilizer, and a host of other items) and *auxiliary products,* where one product used in the manufacture of another is offered for sale (e.g., a metalworking company marketing a proprietary machine developed originally for its own processes).

Finally, a company may approach diversification *laterally,* beyond the confines of its own industry and into *unrelated products.* Much of today's diversification into unrelated products takes place through merger with or acquisition of an enterprise in a different industry. Such diversification seldom has economic justification in operating advantages but does "spread the risk" against demand for a particular product falling off and is often the means for exploiting a new "growth" product deemed to have a good profit potential.

Venture into vertical or lateral diversification—or, in reverse, into vertical or lateral simplification—is dependent primarily on the corporate aims and objectives. Only horizontal diversification and simplification affect similar products, and since we are concerned here with the design of products which are related, the following paragraphs will direct our attention only to the horizontal approach.

9-2.1 Factors Affecting Simplification and Diversification

First among these is the nature and use of the product. In the case of a producer of capital goods, fewer types and sizes are necessary than in the case of a producer of consumer goods. Producers buy on performance and economy, while consumers are more influenced by appearance, ornamentation, choice of style, and colors. Hence manufacturers of consumer goods tend more toward diversification than do enterprises making producer goods. Second, highly competitive industries are often compelled to diversify in the effort to attract and hold customers, while less competitive or monopolistic enterprises are freer to concentrate on simplification. A third consideration is the interaction between simplification or diversification and price of the product and sales volume. Simplification may reduce sales appeal but result in such savings that the price can be reduced enough to increase total sales. Conversely, diversification might increase the sales volume more than enough to offset the higher manufacturing costs and prices.

9-2.2 Benefits Derived

The benefits to be derived from simplification are those resulting from the manufacture of fewer products or from products that are less complex to manufacture. In either case, simplification means that fewer types and sizes of raw materials are purchased, smaller and less varied inventories are possible, and large quantities of the remaining materials may be purchased with resultant quantity discounts. It also makes possible the utilization of special-purpose machines or machines tooled up to handle one type of product, as compared with general-purpose or utility machines which may sacrifice productivity for the flexibility required to handle a variety of products. It eases the problems of supervision and of production planning. Simplification may also be extended to individual operations to the end that a greater degree of specialization of work tasks may result. This naturally leads to greater ease in training employees and a greater proficiency of work. Lower manufacturing costs, particularly lower labor costs and lower inventories, mean less money tied up in the enterprise.

The benefits derived from diversification are primarily those resulting from the sale of a broader and, in some cases, more balanced line of products, from more extensive use of some know-how or facility, or from greater overall efficiency and effectiveness. Where sales appeal is important, a variety of competing products tends to meet more exactly each consumer's individual needs and desires. Diversification may reduce the impact on the enterprise caused by a change in demand for a particular product. Sometimes, through the manufacture of a variety of products, it is possible to level off the peaks and valleys of business booms and recessions, making for more steady employment of personnel and equipment.

However, diversification can increase manufacturing and distribution "headaches." Larger and more varied inventories are often necessary, greater investments in manufacturing equipment and tooling may be required, and employees must be taught more skills, sometimes to the point where they are expected to be Jacks-of-all-trades. Supervision under such operating conditions usually must be strengthened, and the difficulties of planning production of diversified manufacture are increased severalfold. Similarly, management problems often are multiplied out of proportion to the number of products added.

In past years, diversification has in many instances been carried to great extremes. Often the practice was as unwise as it was uneconomical. Primarily to outdo competitors, manufacturers of consumer goods each year added fancy, and in some cases useless, gadgets to an ever-widening range of products. Frequently the demand for this ever-increasing variety came not from the customer but from the salespersons who clamored for additional selling points or features in his or her line of products.

A wise management, before deciding on horizontal diversification, asks itself the following questions about each proposed product:

1. Does it fit into the company's aims and objectives?

2. Can use be made of present sales and distribution mechanisms?

3. Can present manufacturing know-how or facilities be utilized?

4. Can resultant financial obligations be met without undue strain on the enterprise?

5. Is competent technical, managerial, and supervisory talent available?

6. Will it increase production and sales volume or level off their peaks and valleys?

7. Will it contribute to profits in proportion to the effort and investment required?

Only if the answer to all or a majority of these questions is in the affirmative, will a wise management favor a policy of diversification of its line of products.

9-3   PRODUCT ENGINEERING

Product design by the research team originally carries the product to the point where it will perform satisfactorily the function intended. Production design by the product-engineering group may then be necessary to develop the product further so that it can be readily reproduced. This group studies the product, its materials and parts, possibly redesigning some parts for simplified manufacture; specifies clearances and tolerances for all components; and determines standards for materials, parts, overall quality, and performance. While these activities may be performed as part of the research organization, in the larger enterprises a separate department is usually set up under a chief product engineer. The duties of the product-engineering department also include preparation of various engineering data, drawings, models, and patterns.

The engineering data commonly developed by the product-engineering function include stress calculations for highly stressed parts together with the redesigning of such parts as may be necessary to achieve the strength characteristics required. Calculations pertaining to performance of the product, its operating speeds, permissible loads, and life characteristics are functions of the product-engineering group, as are the preparation of data and specifications for lubrication, servicing, and replacement of parts.

The engineering department also is responsible for the preparation of engineering drawings. These are usually transparent tracings from which blueprints or whiteprints can be made. Drawings are usually prepared for each part, subassembly, or assembly and serve as the foundation of all instructions issued to the manufacturing units. They show front, side, and "plan" views of the object to be manufactured, together with all necessary dimensions, tolerances, clearances, and specifications. Frequently the establishing of these engineering details, since they vitally affect the manufacturing of the product, is the subject of consultations between the product engineers and the industrial and plant engineers, the latter two groups being concerned with the technical problems arising out of manufacture.

Among the latest trends in product engineering is that toward miniaturization. The term covers more than tendencies to smallness and lightness. It takes several forms: increased performance for the same size and weight, much better performance with a minor increase in size and weight, change in shape and reduction of size and weight without loss of function—all are manifestations of miniaturization. Perhaps its best definition is "More and more for less and less." Like automation, miniaturization is old in practice (e.g., the watch industry) but has taken on new intensity and wider application under the pressure of new demands for compactness, lightness, and higher performance, as in electronics, aircraft, metal products, and other industries.

In some end products, miniaturization is dramatically visible, as, for example, transistor radios, hearing aids, pocket recorders, vest-pocket TV cameras, and briefcase dictating machines. The transistor has helped to reduce the room-size electronic computer to filing-cabinet size. Behind these spectacular end products are the many developments miniaturization is accomplishing in the fields of electronics and mechanics: from miniature bearings, setscrews, and lock nuts to more compact, smaller, and lighter gyroscopes, transformers, motors, machine tools, and even automobiles. It should be noted, however, that while a miniaturized part frequently contributes to a lower cost end product, it can cause substantial increases in the cost of the part itself. Miniaturizing costs come high—both in money and in headaches.

The influence of miniaturization is widely felt in industry. It compels new concepts of manufacturing. In some cases former tolerances become major dimensions and new tolerances are truly microscopic. Performances are now possible which could not have been achieved before. Without miniaturization, missiles would still be in the Fourth-of-July rocket stage and space probes would be reported only in science fiction. Miniaturization challenges industrial designers and demands new skills of manufacturing and maintenance personnel, new equipment for microscopic parts, special gages and weigh-counting scales, and finer lubricants. Some old industries have been able to exploit their former specialties, as in the case of the watch company which set up to manufacture the precision tools it had developed to make its watch parts. Miniaturization has given rise to the so-called "clean rooms" —glassed-in, air-conditioned assembly rooms, with workers gowned like operating surgeons, for products likely to be ruined by minute specks of dust, lint, and chemical traces. The whole trend is contagious and points to new techniques, skills, materials, and approaches to design, manufacture, and performance.

9-4 INDUSTRIAL STANDARDIZATION

A *standard* is essentially a criterion of measurement, quality, performance, or practice, established by custom, consent, or authority and used as a basis for comparison over a period of time. The setting of standards and the coordinating of the industrial factors to comply with these standards and to maintain them during the periods for which they are effective are known as "industrial standardization."

It is rather unfortunate that the terms "simplification" and "standardization" are sometimes loosely used interchangeably. However, it should be noted that simplification, as already defined, refers to lines of products and methods of manufacturing procedure, whereas standardization is concerned principally with a particular product or process. When a manufacturer of electric appliances reduces his line of electric irons from five models to two, he has *simplified* his line of products. When the same manufacturer establishes for each model iron a heating element of a certain wattage and design, a beveled sole plate with tapered toe and made from a casting, a finish of chrome plate of a specified thickness, and also when he stipulates that each iron will bear a 5-year guarantee, he is said to have established *standards* for the product and its manufacturing processes.

Industrial standards may be either *technical* or *operative*. A technical standard is one that involves technical or engineering elements and usually specifies *what* and *how*. An operative standard, on the other hand, deals with the human element and specifies *who, when,* and *why*. Some standards fall naturally into one or the other of these classifications, whereas other standards represent a combination of both types as they involve both technical and human elements. An engineering specification relating to the properties of steel billets, for example, is a technical standard, whereas a set of regulations governing employee-grievance procedure in an industrial plant is an operative standard. A fire-underwriter requirement that suitable exits shall be provided in a public building (technical element) and that these shall be inspected periodically to ensure that they are unlocked and that no obstructions are present (operative element) combines both types of standards.

9-4.1   Range of Industrial Standards

While the range of industrial standards is exceptionally wide, the more common standards deal with products, engineering design, materials, quantity, processes, equipment, safety, and administrative practices.

Product standards establish the ingredients, formulas, physical characteristics, quality, and performance of a particular product or line of products for the purposes of reproduction and sale. These standards are essentially technical descriptions used in advertising, issued in the form of a product catalogue, or set forth on the product package to aid the company's sales representative and the customer in selecting a particular item which meets the latter's needs and desires. In defining product content and capabilities, they are the basis for quality control and may also help eliminate manufacturing errors. Typical of product standards are the nitrogen-phosphorus-potassium content indicated on a bag of commercial fertilizer, the grit, grade, hardness, bond, and maximum-speed specification of an industrial grinding wheel, and the warranty that a child's toy missile will "rise 100 feet in the air." Product standards generally protect and benefit consumers by assuring them of articles that are interchangeable, uniform in quality and performance, and often lower in price.

Some product standards are set on a nationwide basis by the industry concerned, usually through its trade association. Others are laid down by the individual enterprise in lieu of or in conjunction with a brand name for the product. (A can of soup is bought primarily by brand name, but the label indicates the ingredients, the net weight, and the number of servings expected.) Still others are established by government agencies (e.g., certain drugs) or by customer specifications (e.g., a special machine tool). Generally, however, product standards are a set of compromises arising from the desires of customers, the "state of the art" in the product field, the proficiency of the manufacturing processes, and manufacturing costs.

Engineering design standards are concerned directly with the component parts that make up the product. A company making several similar products may standardize on certain sizes of bolts, screws, fittings, etc., which are to be used in the design of its products. Drawings and specifications for these parts are usually catalogued by number, so that a designer or draftsperson confronted with the need for some such part has only to look in the catalogue for the standardized part that best serves his or her purpose. Instead of sketching the part, he or she merely refers to it by number on the drawing. The burden of proof for a request to modify or add to the list of standardized parts rests with the designer.

Design standards play an important part in world trade, with interchangeability one of the principal benefits derived from their universal application. In the past, the United States at times has missed opportunities to join in setting international standards. Today this country finds itself handicapped in competing in the world markets by not meeting international standards on grooved pulleys, V belts, cast-iron pipe, and electrical fittings, to mention only a few. Now industries dealing in foreign trade are in the forefront of those pushing for more international engineering design standards, with participation of the American National Standards Institute in the International Standards Organization.

Material standards are those which concern the composition, form, size, and finish as well as the types of materials used. Any material standards can be readily set forth in a set of specifications listing the required properties of the material desired. For example, a specification for Manila rope might include a notation as to the kind of fiber desired, the diameter, the weight per foot of length, the oil content, as well as the breaking strength. Raw materials are almost always purchased to specifications, but it is equally important that standard specifications also be established for supply items such as tool bits, drills, cutting and lubricating oils, grinding wheels, and belting, as well as for repair parts.

Quantity standards, which will be considered in later chapters dealing with the control of materials, production, and cost, relate to the quantity of the finished product to be completed within a given period, the amount of raw, in-process, and supply materials required, the production rate per person or per machine, the overhead cost per machine-hour, and any number of other similar standards that are in constant use in industry today in the operation of productive facilities.

Process standards include the standardization, first of all, of operating methods and, second, of operational performance or work effort, subjects which will be treated in Chapters 12 and 16 from the point of view of procedures. Considered here primarily from the standpoint of their function, both of these phases of process control are necessary to the efficient operation of the enterprise, the former dealing primarily with the efficiency of the equipment and plant operating practices, and the latter with the efficiency of the employees. In either case, the standards are established from scientific analysis, past experience, or both, to define what should reasonably be expected in the control of processes. Any deviations of the actual results as compared with the standards are carefully scrutinized for opportunities of correction and improvement.

Equipment standards cover the rating, capabilities, installation, and servicing requirements, etc., of processing and materials-handling equipment, tools, jigs, and fixtures. Electrical and dimensional characteristics for machine tools are two areas in which such standards have attracted considerable interest in recent years.

Safety standards are rules, regulations, and practices which assure the safety of employees while on company premises.

Administrative-practice standards are those dealing with clerical and operating procedures, systems, and records in the realm of administering company policy. Examples of such standards are purchasing procedures, inventory routines, production-control methods, personnel records, and accounting systems.

9-4.2 Agencies for the Establishment of Standards

Foremost among the agencies that establish industrial standards is the National Bureau of Standards, a governmental agency which, at the request of private industry or other government bureaus, will test and establish reference or working standards on anything from a baby carriage to a steel I beam. Also included in its activities are the custody and maintenance of the standards of weights and measures, publication of data on the units of measurement, formulation of standards of quality and performance, development of testing apparatus and methods of testing, and research on the properties of metals. It further acts as a clearinghouse through which the producer, distributor, and consumer all can operate to eliminate needless variety of types and sizes—in other words, to simplify product lines. The Food and Drug Administration, agricultural agencies, the Army, the Navy, and other Federal agencies charged with procurement and protection of the public are also active in setting standards. State and local agencies likewise usually establish standards for purchases upon which they solicit bids. Of course, prime contractors set standards for their subcontractors, as do all enterprises in the purchase of their raw materials. These standards not only facilitate the production of vendors by giving them working quality ranges and tolerances but also assure the purchaser of some guarantee of quality, purity, and uniformity.

Also engaged in important work in the field of standardization is the American National Standards Institute (ANSI). This association is composed of a number of trade associations representing industry, various engineering societies, and several government departments. The function of the American National Standards Institute is to coordinate the standardizing activities of committees of its member groups, to approve and publish engineering and industrial standards and safety codes, and to represent American industry in international standardization attempts. Many individual industries, for themselves and in conjunction with related services, engage in standardizing, as, for example, the Underwriters Laboratories (UL) in the electrical field.

Perspective 9B WORLDWIDE STANDARDIZATION

Standards have been around for a long time. The pyramids of Egypt and the water pipes of ancient Rome were constructed of standardized elements. In the year 1502, the Sultan of Turkey established a standard for the manufacture of carpets. In the late 1800s, Austria, England, Germany, and Russia established standardization laboratories. While an Office of Weights and Measures had been set up in the U.S. Coast and Geodetic Survey in 1836, it was 1901 before the National Bureau of Standards was established. The first international body was the International Electrotechnical Commission which was started in 1906. Following World War II, delegates from 25 countries met in London to consider the establishment of a new international organization "whose object shall be to facilitate the international coordination and unification of industrial standards." As a result, the International Organization for Standardization was formed in 1947; by 1976 membership increased to 63 nations.

When considering the motivation for national standardization programs, it is worthwhile to recall the story of the disastrous fire that destroyed Baltimore in 1904. Before the fire had gotten out of control more than a dozen fire engines from surrounding districts were on the scene, but the fire raged on because the hoses of the fire equipment from outside of the town did not fit the gauge of Baltimore's water hydrants. Had the hose sizes of the various fire services been standardized, Baltimore might have been saved.

Numerous cases of inefficiency and wastage still exist throughout the world that could be eliminated by national and international standardization efforts. Introduction of standards in developing countries can be expected to save considerable sums of money and enhance the quality of locally made goods. If a country's standardization program is started relatively early in its industrialization period, say before industrial products represent 20 per cent of the gross national product, it is then relatively simple to develop standards. Markets both at home and abroad will be expanded if products can be turned out in conformity with international standards.*

*SOURCE: Adapted from K. S. Stephens, *Guide to Standardization, Certification, and Quality Control,* Tokyo, Japan: Asian Productivity Organization, 1978.

9-4.3 Introduction of Standards

When to standardize is always a difficult problem in product development. Invention is usually a slow process, starting with faint beginnings, proceeding gradually to development, diffusion, and finally to a state where its social influences are felt. The time span varies but usually covers many years, as the reader may observe in such cases as the automobile, radio and television, and the sound movie. The progress of any new invention can be shown to be a function of time and may be depicted graphically by what is known as a *progress–time curve* (see Fig. 9-2). The life of a new idea is marked by three successive stages: (1) the incipient period; (2) the development period; and (3) the saturation period.

The establishment or introduction of standards at any point on the progress curve results in a temporary fixation of existing conditions. Thus, if standardization is introduced at point *k* on the curve, there is a tendency to stabilize conditions at that level (horizontal line *kk'*). By the time point *k'* is reached, progress has proceeded to point *m*. Thus the line *k'm* represents the magnitude of the "pull" of progress on the existing standardized level which tends to force an upward revision of that level of standards so as to incorporate the improvements made since the standards were established. It is apparent, however, that, as the progress curve levels off at point *e* and the improvements successively come less rapidly and are of a relatively minor nature, any level of standards established thereafter increasingly approximates the curve of progress. Thus there is less pull (magnitude *p'q*) to change the standards during this third period. Hence standards set during this period are valid for a greater length of time.

From the progress–time curve explained above, three basic principles of industrial standardization can be evolved:

1. Standards cannot be effectively established before the third or saturation period in the development of a product. To establish standards at an earlier state makes their almost continual revision necessary to keep pace with progress.

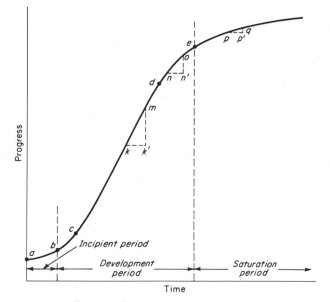

Progress-time curve.

Figure 9-2 Progress–time curve.

2. Standardization "fights" progress by tending to stabilize conditions at an existing level. The upward pull of progress exerted on a standardized level at any point along the progress curve also creates an equal and opposite downward pull operating against the path of progress, with the net results that progress is retarded.

3. Since standards must frequently be revised to keep pace with progress, it is quite necessary that as few basic standards as possible be established so that the program for compliance with, and maintenance of, these standards will be as flexible as possible.

A good example of premature standardization in recent years occurred in the case of television. During the middle 1940s, when this invention was entering its development period, the Federal Communications Commission standardized on 12 television channels and on "black-and-white" video in order that commercial television sets might be manufactured and sold in quantity. This standardization served only to retard subsequent progress in the science of television. Adoption of additional ultrahigh-frequency channels to reduce interference between stations and the introduction of "full-color" video, both fundamental improvements aimed at better television quality, were apparently delayed for many years for fear of their effect on existing equipment, and color television was thrown into confusion by a Commission edict in favor of one transmission and receiving system as against all others. Wide protest and advancing technology finally led the Commission to reconsider, early in 1953, its previous premature action and vacate its ruling. Again, early fixing of standards and prolonged disregard of progress in the case of the Model T resulted in damaging cost to the Ford Motor Company.

Perspective 9C   EXPECTATION FOR METRICATION

The metric system of measurement is *almost* the standard for the world; it is used by over 90 per cent of the world's population.

After nearly 200 years of sporadic debate, the U.S. Congress passed legislation in 1975 to set up a Federal mechanism to help the country shift over to metric measurements. Arguments against the shift warn of huge expenditures required to prepare and meet new standards, develop and purchase new metric production machines, retrain workers, educate consumers, overcome psychological resistance to change, reduce dangers resulting from misuses—as in taking medicines, and avoid adverse trade balances from making U.S. markets more accessible to foreign competition. Conversely, it is argued that a switch to the metric system will make U.S. products more competitive worldwide, provide savings through simplification of measurements—as in eliminating costly errors in production, and actually reduce dangers from mismeasuring, because metric scales are easier to use.

Even without an official commitment and time table for adopting the metric system, the shift is underway. With few exceptions, the language and tools of U.S. science are metric, and many schools now teach the metric system. In 1976 the U.S. Office of Consumer Affairs began using primarily metric units and one of every three automobiles on U.S. roads required metric nuts, bolts, and tools. An increasing variety of consumer goods are measured and identified in metric measures. Metric traffic signs are appearing and weather conditions are often reported in metric measurements.

There will be major costs and difficulties in metrication, even if it is carefully coordinated, but eventually the United States will surely join the rest of the world in using the metric system as the standardized language of measurement.

9-5 RELIABILITY ENGINEERING

The reliability of a product is only as good as its design. Fine manufacturing workmanship and control of quality, while important, can do no more than preserve the reliability engineered into the product—the lasting properties of its materials, components, and assemblies. For some products, reliability is limited primarily by cost considerations: "If we design it stronger or better, we'll price ourselves out of the market." For others, the present state of the art is the determining factor. In space vehicles, for example, no amount of money can buy immediately any desired degrees of performance. Thus the objective of reliability engineering is a product that will perform its intended function in its operating environment for the specified period of time, subject to the limitations of technology and cost.

The initial approach to reliability engineering usually is one of design calculations (physical, chemical, behavioral) which predict inherent capabilities. Engineering-design standards often assist here as proven parts, new parts which have been systematically evaluated, stress data, rating curves, safety factors, and failure rates are available for application to a particular design problem. Once beyond the design stage, empirical part or product testing, often of a destructive nature, is the almost universal proving ground of reliability. Automobiles are given tortuous test-track runs. Jet-engine components are subjected to severe accelerated life tests. Food and drink flavors must pass the palates of professional connoisseurs. All sorts of items from shoes to fabrics to golf balls to mattresses are bent, stretched, pounded, pulled, squeezed, and mauled until they are junk. For some products, instead of laboratory tests simulating actual conditions, controlled consumer tests are made to reveal actual operating results. By these means the manufacturer hopes to learn the strong and weak points of his products and especially what features require improvement. This knowledge is of particular importance to companies which sell "brand-name" products, where one poor model or item can bring harm to the entire branded line.

While much product testing is performed by the manufacturer, some industries, among them the electrical producers, have set up laboratories to prescribe standards of quality, safety, and performance and to publicize their action with a stamp of approval. A number of private, independent testing laboratories, consumer leagues, and laboratories sponsored by household magazines perform similar functions. Government bureaus disseminate consumer bulletins telling how to judge, buy, and conserve many products. Legislation has been passed, and more is urged, regulating the quality of foods and drugs, setting forth uniform standards of size, requiring proper labels, outlawing unfair practices, and enforcing adherence. There is also a developing trend toward self-policing by private enterprise to avoid government intervention to assure maintenance of standards.

Why? Simply because the average private consumer is bewildered by the complexity of many modern products, the wide range of choices, and the conflicting, confusing advertising claims. Furthermore, he is driven to a state of desperation by products which either fail to function upon removal from the packing box or suffer infant mortality or which he is forever buying back from the repair shop. The missile and aircraft industries know only too well the seriousness of an unreliable component. In industry, and in the military, the price paid for inoperative equipment, their maintenance, and necessary spares due to unreliability is stupendous. Some manufacturers include in the purchase price of their products a definite sum to defray the cost of making good on warranties. More may find it necessary to do so if at their present reliability level they are to retain customer goodwill. Also, there is the possibility of damage awards arising out of liability for products which fail or which do not come up to advertised claims. Hence, in recent years, industry as a whole has taken increased interest in planning for and maintaining a higher degree of product performance. Automobile and appliance manufacturers, for example, have extended their guarantee periods, conducted reliability drives among their manufacturing plants, and subjected their parts suppliers to increased reliability scrutiny. Other companies suppress the urge to go into the market place with an untested product, preferring to sacrifice being "first" for evidence that the product is free of "bugs." Still, total reliability as a goal has not been reached. In some industries it is not even in sight. But at least the general direction of travel is right.

9-6 VALUE ENGINEERING

Value engineering (VE) has been defined as an organized effort to attain optimum value in a product, system, or service, by providing the necessary functions at the lowest cost. Some critics say VE is a fancy name given to commonsense operations, and others say it is just a title for cost-reduction techniques already in use. To some extent the criticisms are valid, but the formalized VE approach and the emphatic use of relevant managerial tools deserves more than passing attention.

The VE philosophy or discipline is represented by a national organization with the catchy acronym SAVE (Society of American Value Engineers). Formal value engineering groups are prevalent in private industry and within government departments. The Bureau of Ships in 1954 initiated the first VE program in the Department of Defense. Since 1963 the Department of Defense has officially encouraged VE practices with contract incentives that share with the contractor savings accrued through successful VE programs. "The objective of the value engineering incentive clause is to provide a financial reward to encourage contractors to develop and submit to the government cost-reduction proposals which involve changes in the contract specifications, purchase descriptions, or statement of work."[1]

The philosophy of cost consciousness is no stranger to any successful enterprise. It is the approach of VE to the same goal that makes it distinguishable. A key feature is the stress given to the *function* concept. In the VE approach, functions of a product are described by only two words—a verb and a noun. Both basic and secondary functions are identified. For instance, a tie clip could have the basic function of "position tie" and a secondary function of "provide status." After evaluating the noted functions in terms of use, esteem, and exchange values, the functions of the component parts of the project are described. The purpose of the component descriptions is to identify unnecessary functions built into the product or its components and to forcefully question the way each function is accomplished. The greatest advantage of this routine is gained during the product's design phase, but it is also applicable in keeping the product contemporary with customers' changing preferences.

Functional descriptions are only a small part of a complete engineering package. A team effort is almost a mandatory condition. New VE programs are typically initiated by a training session for a cross section of management levels involved in related work. Small teams seek savings within the company using a systematic approach to problem analysis and emphasizing creativity. The success of training is tied closely to the cooperation and communications engendered.

It is well known that almost any change will have at least some opposition, and the backbone of VE is an insistence on change. Therefore, the VE package must be widely accepted before it can make significant contributions.

Perspective 9D   VALUE OF VALUE ENGINEERING

Cost reduction is a well-trod path that leads to productivity enhancement. Improvements in the design of new products or existing products, which reduce costs while maintaining reliability requirements, raise the output/input ratio of production by decreasing input for the same amount of output. The value engineering approach emphasizes design simplicity and more efficient use of materials. This approach would seem to be self-selling, but it still meets resistance, as recognized by Dr. D. R. Herzog:

In truth, people must be convinced of the savings resulting from an effective value engineering program. There are those who limit their economy measures to such things as turning out lights

---

[1] American Society of Tool and Manufacturing Engineers, "Value Engineering in Manufacturing," Englewood Cliffs, N.J.: Prentice-Hall, Inc., 1967.

and saving pencil stubs, followed by those who are satisfied with insignificant cost reductions of their product. Finally, there are those unimaginative persons who make such statements as:

1. I know it won't work.
2. That's been tried before.
3. We haven't time for detail.
4. We have always made it on a screw machine.
5. It doesn't fit in with our plans.
6. It's been done this way for 20 years, why change?

Evaluation of the functions expected from a product is a basic feature of the VE approach. It is important to realize that the evaluation is concerned with the product itself, not its role in the entire system. Thus a brake is evaluated according to its functional parts that collectively perform at a required level of reliability, not on the potential cost of failure of the whole machine—damage to the vehicle, destruction of other property, and possible loss of life.

For example: a commercial switch rated at 600 volts and 10 amperes originally cost $128. This switch protects $800,000 worth of equipment, but, once again, you don't pay for the consequences of failure, but for essential quality and functioning. Breakdown of the cost into functional areas revealed the following:

1. Electrical	$18
2. Mechanical	12
3. Case and cover	50
4. Labor and overhead	48
5. Total	$128

At first glance, it is obvious that the cost of the case and cover was disproportionately high and that it far exceeded its functional value. Two months of analysis reduced the cost as follows:

1. Electrical	$6
2. Mechanical	10
3. Case and cover	14
4. Labor and overhead	35
5. Total	$65

As seen by the example, this method of dividing the costs into functional areas is valuable in analyzing existing designs as it may indicate where value engineering should start.*

*SOURCE: "Value Engineering for New Product Planning and Development," *Proceedings,* AIIE Annual Conference, 1974.

COMMENT   The three parameters of value engineering are function, reliability, and cost. The intent of a VE program is to identify critical functions with respect to required reliability and then to seek ways to make the product cheaper without "cheapening" its design.

9-7   REVIEW QUESTIONS

1. Define productivity. What are the three primary factors that contribute to productivity gains? Of what value are productivity improvements to society?

2. Define simplification, diversification, and miniaturization. Illustrate each.

3. What are the three means of product diversification? What are the factors affecting the "horizontal" approach?

4. Distinguish between simplification and standardization. What are the two types of standards? Give an example of each.

5. What are the three stages in the life of a given product? When should standardization be introduced? Why?

6. What is the objective of value engineering? At what stage of product development can its principles be applied most advantageously?

7. What are the objectives of reliability engineering and product testing?

9-8 TOPICS FOR DISCUSSION

1. Some observers report a developing trend away from "planned obsolescence" in consumer goods through a deemphasis of annual model changes. Certain of the domestic compact cars, for example, have limited model changes to engineering advances with no basic alterations in styling for several successive years. If this trend continues, what advantages and disadvantages to the consumer can be expected to result?

2. In certain industries companies customarily make but one basic line of products. Examples are steel-rolling mills, dress manufacturers, and producers of antifriction bearings. Such enterprises claim they can achieve adequate diversification in the markets they serve. Do you agree with this claim? Explain your answer.

3. A manufacturing executive has stated: "I fail to see any future in miniaturization of mechanical products. It's O.K. for electronics and for commercial consumer products. Other than these there isn't any need for it." Comment on this statement.

4. National standards are set for many products manufactured by a variety of companies or used in end products manufactured by a variety of companies. Some companies heartily endorse and conform to such standards; others prefer to remain aloof and not adopt them. What are the advantages and disadvantages of each policy?

5. Discuss examples of government actions that have either discouraged or encouraged productivity gains by industry. For instance, new laws that required investments to reduce pollution could have diverted capital that otherwise would have funded productivity-improvement programs, and new laws that established tax credits for investments in new machines could have contributed to productivity gains through the purchases allowed.

6. Answer the following reservations about supporting plans for a productivity-improvement program:
   a. "Why should I cooperate with that new scheme to have us all switch positions on the assembly line every hour so that our jobs will be 'enriched' and we'll all be more 'productive.' All they're trying to do is get us to work faster."
   b. "I don't plan to tell anyone how I can do my job better, even if being more productive is supposed to help everyone. I might get some cash for the suggestion, but then I'd have to live with it forever. Now I can speed up whenever I need to meet the quota quick, and loaf when I want to."

c. "They say that, if we follow all those new methods to improve productivity, we'll put out 20 per cent more units, and the job will be easier too. Maybe my job will be easier, but I figure that before long they'll come back and say one out of every five of us is laid off."

7. Case 9A: *The Continental Can Company*

In 1956 the Continental Can Company, which makes tin cans, plastic bottles, vacuum-type metal closures, and crown caps (bottle caps), acquired the Hazel-Atlas Glass Company, producers of glass containers and screw-type closures.

In 1960 the Antitrust Division of the U.S. Department of Justice instituted a Federal court action against Continental Can, contending that the acquisition was illegal.[2] This action was reported in the *Wall Street Journal,* June 7, 1960, excerpts from which follow:

The Government says it seeks a decision interpreting the Clayton Act, a key antitrust statute, "in a manner which discourages acquisitions between and among close substitute producers."

The government "claims glass containers compete with tin cans and plastic bottles, and that screw-type metal closures are competitors of crown caps and vacuum-type closures.

Continental Can's defense . . . is that "metal, glass, and plastic containers have sufficiently peculiar characteristics and uses to bar commingling them in any line of commerce." The company says that "the same is true of crown caps, screw-type closures, and vacuum closures."

Government and company attorneys clash on their interpretations of what constitutes the valid lines of commerce in this case.

In the eyes of Continental Can's lawyers, there are six distinct lines of commerce: metal cans, glass containers, plastic bottles, crown caps, vacuum-type closures, and screw-type closures. They argue that "the characteristics of containers and the consuming public's reactions to them are such that each of the various end products which are packed in containers tends to move in a preferred container." They add that "the selections of containers are not made at random, and they do not shift from day to day, or from year to year." They cite mayonnaise and fruit preserves in glass jars, corn and paint in tin cans.

The Government divides the market into 10 relevant lines of commerce. But in the first six it bases its division on the activity of the purchaser of the product. It says there are three lines of commerce in which both metal cans and glass bottles compete, consisting of the canning industry, the beer industry, and the soft drink industry. It also says there are three lines of commerce in which plastic, metal, and glass containers compete, including toiletries and cosmetics, medicines and health, and household chemicals.

In addition, it sets up four additional lines of commerce which it classifies as the can industry, the glass container industry, metal closure . . . , and the packaging industry.

Continental Can maintains, however, that the Government in its first six classifications is attempting to "fragment" or "gerrymander the market to coincide with its preconceived theory of the case." It declares that according to the logic of the Government's theory "a can of beer is not the same as a can for soft drinks, but a beer can is the same as a beer bottle; a can for tomato juice is not the same as a can for soft drinks, but a tomato juice can is the same as both a tuna fish can and a mayonnaise jar."

"There is, in the U.S., no more of a business of supplying containers to the "canning industry" or to other specified packers and processors than there is a business of supplying neckties to lawyers," asserts Continental Can.

Questions

1. Omitting all consideration of the legal aspects and in light of the opposing views on lines of commerce in the container industry presented above, analyze Continental Can's acquisition of Hazel-Atlas from the standpoint of diversification. Include discussion of the kinds of diversification you find are involved and competitive advantages and disadvantages derived therefrom.

[2]This suit later was dismissed in the United States District Court.

8. Case 9B: *Wonderful Washing Machine Company*

In 1975 the Wonderful Washing Machine Company experienced a slump in sales of its laundry appliances, contrary to sales trends in the rest of the industry. Investigation revealed that public confidence in the company's line of washers and washer-dryers had been shaken as the result of generally poor experience with the line of models produced and sold during the preceding 3 years. These machines, the investigation revealed, were causing their owners, on the average, six repair calls per year compared with two or three such calls per year for competing makes of machines. These annoying and costly repairs had won for the Wonderful machines the general reputation that they were "lemons."

A survey of service centers and spare-part depots showed that the largest number of failures centered about clutches, filters, and transmissions. The problems with these items varied but were found to include materials, workmanship, and design.

The company decided to offer each owner of one model of washing machine a brand-new, and hopefully more trouble-free, model machine at a cost to the customer of $100. It further offered to exchange a combination model washer-dryer on which severe problems had been encountered with new, individual washer and dryer units delivered, installed, and initially serviced free of charge. On other models the company offered to replace the transmission free of charge. The total cost of this replacement program was estimated to exceed $7,500,000. Yet this expenditure was deemed essential if the company ever wished to regain public confidence in its line of laundry appliances.

Questions

1. Detail comprehensive measures that might be taken as a reliability program to prevent difficulties of the sort encountered by the Wonderful Washing Machine Company.

10

RODUCT FLOW

Production control, together with its sister function, materials control, is a facilitating and coordinating activity concerned with the kind, amount, location, movement, and timing of the various commodities used in and produced by the industrial enterprise. In this chapter we shall explore aspects of product flow: How do product flow considerations fit into the managerial-control process? To whom in the enterprise is this activity entrusted? How are customer orders translated into production requirements? What steps are necessary to interpret these requirements for the manufacturing organization and trigger it into action? How are the work priority and the time sequence of orders established? Today's emphasis is on the word "control." Tighter control is a natural by-product of intense competition. This competition demands flexibility and quick response to customer requirements. There is no room for finished stocks that attract dust instead of buyers, and customers will not tolerate "rubber" delivery promises. What plan will satisfy customers, and what is required to put the plan into effect? How are production orders dispatched and followed up to ensure that the desired routing and scheduling are maintained? What demands are made today on the production control function, and how are these demands being met?

10 PRODUCT FLOW

10-1 THE PRODUCTION CONTROL FUNCTION

We saw in Chapter 3 that, as used in industry, the word "control" invokes multiple meanings. Like other controls, production control not only restrains, curbs, regulates, and checks, but it also stimulates, activates, and galvanizes. Furthermore, it involves the operating tempo and manufacturing teamwork necessary to achieve any desired output of goods with a minimum input of personnel and machines.

The technical, skeptical mind asks: "How does production control achieve this teamwork, this rhythm so essential to the productivity of the enterprise?" For one thing, production control is concerned with eliminating or reducing to a minimum many of the inefficiencies in manufacturing. These may result from performing operations on incorrect equipment or by makeshift, ill-planned processes. Operations may be out of balance, time and effort may be wasted on nonproductive work, and duplications or omissions in planning or executing work may make for confusion and delay. Materials, tooling, and work force may not have been requested far enough in advance to be available when required. Scrap on a particular part or at a certain operation may be excessive. In these and many other ways do losses and waste run rampant where control is lacking. To put it another way, efficiency is born of and fostered by control.

Production control regulates the orderly flow of materials in the manufacturing process from the raw state to the finished product. It takes the influx of sales orders, boils them down into production orders, and feeds them to the plant at a rate and in a sequence that enables the plant to digest them most readily and with a minimum of internal disorder. It aims to produce the right product, in the right quantity, of the right quality, at the right time, and by the best and least costly methods. Good production-control procedure means less work in process, decreased stock inventories, and more rapid turnover, which in turn results in less capital tied up in idle material and greater earnings on money thus invested. As such, production control, like materials control, is a facilitating and coordinating activity which, with the possible exception of additional time and place utility, adds nothing directly to the value of the product (in the sense that work on the product increases its value). Production control involves *both planning and control:* the advance planning necessary to achieve an orderly flow of materials, and the execution of that plan to ensure that the desired control is maintained.

The planning and control of production in most industrial plants are entrusted to a *production-control department* under the direction of a *production manager.* This individual usually reports to the top manufacturing executive, the works manager. The department has functionalized staff authority over the various manufacturing divisions in all matters pertaining to the control of production.

Small plants do not need the elaborate and detailed production-control systems which may be required by their large counterparts. However, the same control principles apply for all plants, large and small. The plant of 50 or so employees, for example, may have a one-person production-control system operating under the wing of the factory superintendent. During the course of his work this one person engages in all the production-control activities—but in a more simplified manner—that are performed by the battery of specialists and clerks found in a large plant.

Briefly, the activities of the production manager and his or her specialists embrace the development and operation of the production-control techniques, procedures, and paper work used in the manufacture of the products of the enterprise. They coordinate the various production-planning activities of the manufacturing divisions and the other staff functions. Since product designs, production methods, manufacturing requirements, and work priority are continually subject to revision, the production-control routine is seldom stabilized for long. Likewise, there are breakdowns in control which have to be patched up and remedied for the future. Thus the work of the production manager and his or her specialists is at times as hectic as it is varied.

10-2 CUSTOMER ORDERS

In some enterprises, production requirements are determined from sales forecasts, and customer orders do not directly affect the production-control system. In others, where products are made either completely or in part to customer specifications, the production-control procedure is set into motion by the customer order.

The first step in processing a customer purchase order in most companies is to register it on an incoming order log. The purpose of this log is to furnish an up-to-the-minute record of incoming business and, where the customer order must be reviewed by people in several departments, to aid in following it en route. A sales-order clerk usually edits the order for completeness and codes it for (1) product category; (2) sales territory; (3) salesperson; (4) class of trade; (5) discount category (if a list-and-discount pricing system is employed); and (6) customer's credit rating. The information in (1) through (4) is used in the preparation of sales statistics, analyses of buying habits, statements showing profitability of product and territories and sales-commission data. The financial data in (5) and (6) are required to price the order and grant the proper credit terms to the customer.

If, in response to sales forecasts, the products involved are *manufactured to stock* or *to repetitive schedule*,[1] the customer order is next checked against the stock records for availability of the items requested. If the goods are available, notation is made on the customer order that they will be shipped from stock on the date requested. Otherwise an entry is made on the inventory records to allocate or apportion the items from a future manufacturing lot or schedule. In this case, the production-control department usually furnishes the sales division with delivery promises on future production planned (as 1,000 vacuum bottles scheduled each week, 5,000 toasters by May 4, 2,000 food mixers by May 11, etc.). The sales-order personnel then apply incoming business against these blanket quantities and automatically quote the customer the promised delivery dates.

Next the sales order, sometimes called the shipping order, is prepared. While procedures vary with conditions encountered, information is provided as follows: (1) to the shipping department for shipping authorization and instructions; (2) to the invoice section of the accounting department for billing purposes; (3) to the customer, accompanying the goods as a packing list; (4) to the inventory-control section for posting the stock records; (5) to the salesperson for notification purposes; and (6) to the customer as an acknowledgment.

Where manufacturing awaits a *specific customer order,* two alternatives are possible: (1) finished or semifinished parts manufactured to stock can be assembled or completed to customer order; or (2) the complete manufacture can be made to specific order. An example of the former is builders' hardware, where special finishes are applied to stocked parts in response to customer request, while a typical illustration of the latter would be the work performed in a job-order machine shop. With either alternative a more complicated order-entry procedure generally is required than where the products are stocked.

If the customer order calls for an item which has not previously been manufactured, the sales-order department must obtain certain information about the item before the order can be processed. The product-engineering division is consulted about product design and specifications. The production-control specialists establish the routing and scheduling. The plant and industrial engineers are brought into the picture to explore machine and tooling requirements and to furnish operation standards or estimates. The cost-accounting personnel estimate the cost of manufacturing the item. Finally a representative of the sales division establishes the selling price.

---

[1]Manufacture of items to stock or to repetitive schedule rather than to customer order is preferable for several reasons. Customers can be given shipments more quickly. Larger and more economical manufacturing quanties are possible. Longer range, more orderly production schedules can be planned. During seasonal and other lulls in demand, the plant can be kept busy building up its stocks. Customer changes in quantities and delivery dates cause less disruption in the plant. However, stock items are generally limited to those for which there is regular, predictable demand. Furthermore, stock balances must be watched closely lest warehousing and obsolescence costs run rampant.

Only then is the customer order ready to·be entered as a sales order. The six-part form described above for the stock order is used here also, except that the copy for the inventory-control section is replaced by one authorizing the manufacture of the item.

If the customer sends in an *inquiry* or *request for quotation,* and the items mentioned have not previously been manufactured, much the same information must be obtained. Once it is at hand, the sales-order personnel then makes the customer a firm purchase quotation. Of course, in the case of repeat orders, the information is readily available, and much of the foregoing procedure for both customer orders and inquiries can be by-passed.

Having been briefed on the manner in which the customer's purchase becomes production requirement, we are now ready to explore in detail the first two, or planning, steps of production control: routing and scheduling.

10-3 ROUTING

Fundamentally, routing determines what work will be done on a product or part as well as where and how it will be done. It establishes the operations, their path and sequence, and the proper class of machines and personnel required for these operations. While routing is a major responsibility of the production-control function, it is also connected with the field of product development in designing a product that can be readily manufactured. Likewise, it is closely allied with plant and industrial engineering in setting up the most efficient operating methods and in establishing a materials flow through the plant for a minimum of handling and backtracking. Thus at one time or another each of these departments may have a hand in product routing.

10-3.1 Routing Procedure

The routing procedure for a new product or part may consist of as many as six separate activities:

1. *An analysis of the article to determine what to make and what to purchase* The decision as to whether to fabricate a component in the plant or to purchase it elsewhere is based primarily on the relative cost involved and secondarily on such factors as technical considerations, purchasing policies, and availability of equipment and personnel. Normally the cheaper method of obtaining the part is employed. However, in some situations the skills, know-how, and plant facilities of a supplier can handle an item that would be difficult to manufacture, and the part is farmed out, even at a higher cost. The need for a second source for the part will sometimes dictate purchase of partial requirements, perhaps at a higher cost than it can be fabricated in the plant. In slack periods there is a tendency to make as much of the product as possible, simply to keep personnel and machines busy. Then in periods of great industrial activity the pendulum swings in the opposite direction, and plants subcontract much more of their product to relieve overburdened

facilities. Thus other considerations at times take precedence over cost in the decision whether to make or to buy.

2. *An analysis of the article to determine what materials are needed* Drawings, specifications, standards of quality, and identification symbols are usually condensed by the routing section into a *parts list.* Frequently combined with the parts list is a *bill of materials.* This not only shows each part name, identification number, quantity required, and application in the product, but also indicates the kind and amount of material required for each part. From this list, the inventory-control section can determine the adequacy of the materials in stock or on order and then initiate the purchase of any additional materials needed.

Another item in routing is the *parts short list.* This form is used for job-order products involving the assembly of many component parts (e.g., a milling machine). It is very similar to the parts list except that it omits those parts which are available either as stock already on the shelf or as purchased items on order. It lists only those parts which are short and hence must be obtained to complete the product.

3. *A determination of the manufacturing operations and their sequence* Next the routing section analyzes the production standards or estimates supplied by the industrial-engineering department together with data on file in the routing section as to machine capacities and characteristics. From these facts it establishes the operations necessary to manufacture the article and lists them in their proper sequence on a *route sheet* or *operation sheet.* This form (see Fig. 10–1) generally shows the part number and description and the material required and then may indicate for each operation its standard or estimated process time or its piecework price, the type or number of machine used, and perhaps the tools required. A copy is issued for plant instruction purposes, another retained in the central production-control office, and a third supplied to the cost-accounting department for cost estimating or preparation of standard and individual-job costs. In some systems the operation sheet has multiple uses. Copies are duplicated and issued to serve as (1) the manufacturing order (authorizing the manufacturing department to perform the specified work); (2) the raw-material requisition (authorizing issuance of the material indicated); and (3) move orders (traveling with the material and authorizing movement to the departments and operations shown).

4. *A determination of lot sizes* The number of units to be manufactured in any one lot or order as established by the routing section depends primarily upon the type of manufacture involved. If the product is to be manufactured strictly to a sold order, the quantity to be made will usually equal that required for the customer's order plus a certain overage or allowance for rejections during the processing (see discussion of scrap factors below). It is customary, where the vendor manufactures quantity products specifically to a customer's order, for the customer to consider that the order is complete if the delivered quantity is within 10 per cent over or under the purchased quantity. Thus if the vendor in his planned quantity allows for normal rejections and other predictable manufacturing losses, he is assured of being able to dispose of the entire lot manufactured.

Where manufacture is to stock replacing depleted inventories, the lot size to be manufactured will usually be based upon the principle of *economic-lot quantities.* Since the subject will be discussed in Chapter 11, it will suffice here to say that

G	OPER	DESCRIPTION	F	SPEED	FEED	DEPT.	GROUP	SCHED. TIME
L	10	CLEAN CASTING				5	5 5 5	0 3 3
		TOOL KIT				5	5 5 5	
M	15	STRAIGHTEN				5	5 5 5	0 1 2
I	18	SPRAY				1 2	7 2 0	0 0 0
M	26	SPRAY PAINT				1 2	7 2 0	0 0 5
I	30	SET UP				1	0 5 1	1 8 0 0
		TOOL KIT				1	0 5 1	
I	30	DR RM SPOTFACE				1	0 5 1	0 9 3
		DR 1 15/64 IN		2 9 5	0 1 4			
		RM 1.250 PL 0005		1 0 0	0 2 0			
		SPOTFACE TO 7/8 DIM		1 0 0	H F			
L	40	BURR				3	6 6 6	0 2 4
K	60	INSPECT				1 4	0 0 0	0 0 0
	70	BUFF AND POLISH				8	0 0 0	0 0 0
K	80	INSPECT				1 4	0 0 0	0 0 0
	81	WASH				5	5 5 5	0 0 0
	82	MASK				5	5 5 5	0 0 0
	83	SPRAY FILL AND SPOT FILL				1 2	7 2 0	0 0 0
84	84	RUB				5	5 5 5	0 0 0
	85	SPRAY PAINT				1 2	7 2 0	0 0 0
	86	REMOVE MASKING TAPE				5	5 5 5	0 0 0
	87	STORES				9	0 0 0	0 0 0

ACME MACHINE COMPANY — PROCESS SHEET
ORDER 6177 QUAN. 0075 DUE 110 DATE 1001 PART 7010 6177
Name: SPDL FEED LEVER ISSUED 05232 SUPERSEDES 05152
Material CODE: MALLEABLE CASTING MTRL. LGTH. / RGH. WGT. 1.3

167   1800

Figure 10-1 Process or operation sheet, used by a machine-tool manufacturer, which is prepared from punched cards by data-processing equipment. It shows part number and name, quantity, scheduling date, material required, operation numbers and descriptions, tooling, feeds, speeds, departments, type of machines ("group"), and standard or scheduled time of each operation or setup for one piece. One copy of this sheet becomes the shop or manufacturing order. Others supply necessary information to the production-control, methods, inspection, and cost departments. (SOURCE: "Manufacturing Control Case Study," p. 17, White Plains, N.Y.: IBM Data Processing Division.)

under this principle the quantity to manufacture is that for which the sum of the setup and other preparation costs and the costs of carrying an inventory of the article manufactured is at a minimum. Naturally this theoretical quantity is frequently affected by such factors as the availability of plant equipment, the breaking off of stock runs to sandwich in customer orders or rush orders, and the unpredictability of seasonal items.

Of course, where manufacture is to a weekly or monthly schedule, the quantity to be manufactured for the period is based on the influx or backlog of sales orders subject to any limitations in the manufacturing capacity during the period.

5. *A determination of scrap factors* In most production processes, it is reasonable to expect that, for any given number of pieces of input at the first operation, a lesser quantity of good units of output will reach the end of the process. The difference, or amount of "shrinkage," depends upon the *scrap factor* encountered in the

process. This factor may be defined as the anticipated normal scrap encountered in the course of manufacturing. Scrap factors are important in the planning of production quantities as a part of the routing functions as well as the scheduling or loading of various machines and work centers. Work force and equipment requirements both are affected by the progressive shrinkage in number of good pieces available at succeeding operations. Particularly is this true in production-line manufacture, where the output of each employee and machine must be balanced for maximum utilization of manufacturing facilities.

It is important to know where scrap is most likely to occur—whether it occurs progressively during the parts fabrication and assembly or all at once after a certain operation or after completion of the assembly. If scrap occurs at but one point in the process, a *single* scrap factor to take care of the anticipated scrap at that point is generally satisfactory. If, on the other hand, scrap is progressive, *cumulative* scrap factors more accurately determine the expected load at each stage in the process (see Fig. 10–2). Note that it is necessary to start with the desired result (finished units) and work backward (toward the raw material).

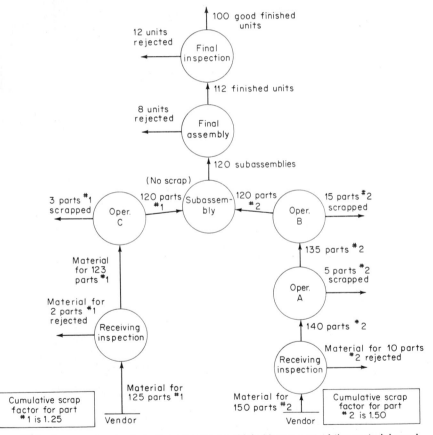

Figure 10-2 An overall manufacturing process in which 20 per cent of the material used for part 1 and 33⅓ per cent of that used for part 2 are lost in rejections somewhere between receipt of the material and shipment of the finished product. The cumulative scrap factors are noted above. Thus is shown the nature of typical cumulative scrap factors or the changing quantity requirements at various points in the line to produce a specified number of finished units.

Best practice dictates the establishment of *standard* scrap factors (either single or cumulative) for use in routing and scheduling. These are based on experience —on records giving scrap history—and, if cumulative, are set for each control point[2] in the process. Actual scrap in each lot or schedule is then recorded at the various control points. From these records, adjustments are made to schedules and to work force and equipment requirements to compensate for differences between scrap anticipated and scrap experienced. Furthermore, if actual scrap is excessive, it may be necessary to initiate replacement lots. Actual-scrap records also serve to localize the responsibility for such scrap and point to areas or operations which should be investigated for cause of trouble. Similarly, such records encourage accurate reporting of scrap figures and localize any investigation of unreported or "covered-up" scrap.

6. *An analysis of the cost of the article.* While the function of *cost estimating* is primarily the responsibility of the cost-accounting department, it also requires contributory efforts of the routing section of the production-control department and plant- and industrial-engineering departments. The estimate is based largely on the routing information obtained in steps 1 through 5 above. Direct material and labor costs are computed, and specific and general indirect expenses are allocated to the product to arrive at the cost estimate. Upon the accuracy of this estimate depend not only the enterprise's opportunity for meeting competition but also the certainty that the expected profit will be realized from the sale.

Of course, for products made on repeat orders, past records and standards furnish data for establishing either an actual or standard cost. Also, in some cases where a new product is similar to a product previously manufactured, the new estimate can readily be projected without complete analysis.

10-3.2 Considerations Affecting Routing Procedures

Routing is affected primarily by the *type of manufacture* employed and hence the manner in which the plant is laid out. This has already been discussed in Section 7-4.1. It will suffice here to say that where the layout is by product, the routing is built into the production line and the flow of materials is virtually automatic. Where the layout is by operation or by stationary material, the discretion and likewise the problems of the routing section are infinitely greater.

Second, routing is affected by the *individual characteristics of the physical equipment.* Similar machines may differ in age, condition, degree of precision, capacity range, speeds, coolants, tooling, and a host of other traits which must be taken into consideration in deciding which machine can best handle a particular job. In such situations it is common practice for the routing section to prepare and place on file a *machine-data card* for each machine, listing its individual characteristics and capacity range. Consideration should also be given to conveyors, cranes, hoists, containers, and other equipment that may be available in one section of the plant but not

---

[2]A control point, as the name implies, is a stage in the process at which production quantities and schedules are recorded. Usual control points are dispatch stations, prior to or following major operations and assemblies, or between departments.

in another. Here again, a card record of such equipment is useful to the routing section.

Third, routing is affected by the *availability of physical plant equipment.* Quite frequently because of machine-load conditions, breakdowns, and absentee operators, the cheapest machine or method cannot be utilized. In such cases it is desirable that the routing section have ready alternative routings to substitute for the standard route. These alternative routings may be in the form of detours around the bottleneck machine or operation or may simply involve a change in the sequence of operations, particularly if the tie-up should be of a temporary nature.

Fourth, attention must be given to the *human factors* involved. Operators vary as to experience and such capability characteristics as visual acuity, manual dexterity, physical limitations, intelligence, and emotional stability. Sometimes the ingenuity, mechanical ability, or general competence of supervision enters the picture. Thus are many routing decisions based largely on the human elements involved.

10-4 SCHEDULING

Scheduling is that phase of production control which rates the work in the order of its priority and then provides for its release to the plant at the proper time and in the correct sequence. Thus scheduling is concerned with *when* work shall be performed on a product or part.

The function of industrial scheduling closely resembles that branch of modern railroading which schedules the use of railroad-track facilities. Similar to the route or path over which materials must flow in an industrial enterprise is the railroad bed with its main lines, detours, sidings, junctions, and switch terminals. Under usual railroad procedure, timetables are established for all passenger trains indicating the precise moment of their arrival and departure from each station and terminal. But trains run at different speeds—some through trains operate on fast schedules; commuter and local trains operate at slower rates. Furthermore, certain feeder trains are geared to the arrival and departure of other through runs, as their passengers, express, and mail loads are transferred either to or from the through trains. And finally, not operating on fixed timetables are the freights, both fast and slow, that must be sandwiched between fixed-schedule trains over the same roadbed.

The aim in railroad scheduling is to run as much traffic over the same tracks as is safely possible without interference or collisions. Similarly the aim in industrial scheduling, within the limits of the customer orders available, is to schedule as great a volume of work as the plant equipment can conveniently handle without similar interference or "collisions" resulting in material stoppages along the route. Naturally, the work of devising railroad timetable schedules is closely allied with that of the dispatchers along the right of way who guide the trains in and out of sidings and spur tracks to permit the passage of faster trains or of trains running in the opposite direction. So also are the fields of industrial scheduling and dispatching closely related, and in many smaller companies both functions are performed by the same individual or group. This fact should be kept in mind as these subjects are herein developed separately.

A production schedule that establishes the starting and finishing dates of all material in process is subject to the limitations of the availability of (1) physical-plant facilities of the type required to process the material being scheduled; (2) personnel who possess the desired skill and experience to operate the equipment and perform the type of work involved; and (3) necessary materials and purchased parts. Failing the adequacy of any one of these three factors, or at least failing the knowledge as to when the missing factors will be made available, no intelligent production schedule can be developed.

10-4.1 Sequence of Scheduling Procedure

Scheduling usually starts with the *master schedule,* a typical example of which is shown in Figure 10-3. This schedule is simply a weekly or monthly breakdown of the production requirements for each product for a definite period of time (as a quarter, 6 months, or a year). As new orders or requirements are received, they are scheduled on the master schedule with due regard for the available plant capacity. Where the requirements noted on the schedule indicate that the plant capacity for a particular week (or month) is absorbed, it is obvious that the new requirements must be carried over to a subsequent period, or the present schedule for the capacity period must be rearranged to accommodate the additional orders.

The type of master schedule shown in Figure 10–3 permits the addition

MASTER SCHEDULE NAME OF PART _Spark Plug_   PART NO. _J-5_

MAX. RUN PER WEEK _10,000_ MIN. RUN PER WEEK _5,000_

Date	Assign. No.	JANUARY Week of 1/2	Week of 1/9	Week of 1/16	Week of 1/23	Week of 1/30	Cum. to	FEBRUARY Week of 2/6	Week of 2/13	Week of 2/20	Week of 2/27	Week of	Cum. to	MARCH Week of 3/6	Week of 3/13	Week of 3/20	Week of 3/27	Week of	Cum. to
For'd		7,968	5,742	3,044	2,221	1,689	12/15	3,520	1,089	786	556		12/15	0	0	332	56		12/15
12/16	33	700	700	700	700	700													
12/18	43							1,100	1,100	550	550			550					
12/19	51	45	68	68	45	45										2500			
12/21	59	1,000	2,000	2,000	2,000	2,000													
		9,713	8,570	5,809	4,966	4,434	12/21												
12/23	76		1,300	2,600	2,600	2,600		2,600	2,600	2,600	2,600			2,600	2,600	1,300			
12/26	81	15	23	68	31														
12/29	87							1,000	1,000	2,000	2,000								
		9,713	9,825	8,432	7,654	7,065	12/31	8,220	5,789	5,936	5,706		12/31	3,150	2,600	1,632	2,556		12/31

Figure 10-3 Master schedule.

of new requirements as they are received and at any time a total can be drawn off in red (as underscored here) showing what is scheduled in advance for each week. In this way it is possible to ascertain when the maximum plant capacity for the article in question has been reached.

The master schedule not only provides a convenient means of keeping a running total of the production requirements but also enables the production manager to plan in advance for any shifting emphasis from one product to another or for a possible overall increase or decrease in production requirements. In addition, the master schedule furnishes the necessary data for calculating the backlog of work or the load ahead of each major machine. Furthermore, once a new order has been entered on the master schedule, it is then possible to furnish the customer with a provisional or perhaps even a definite shipping date for the material on his order. In summary, then, the master schedule provides the information that becomes the basis for all subsequent scheduling activities.

Next, depending upon the type of manufacture involved, a manufacturing schedule or manufacturing order is prepared. The *manufacturing schedule* is used in production-line or semi-production-line manufacture where a single product or a relatively few products are manufactured continuously or are repeated at regular intervals. It serves the purpose of authorizing the plant departments concerned to manufacture the stipulated quantity of parts or product designated within the period for which the schedule applies. In serialized production-line manufacture, such items as shop instructions, routing information, drawings, and specifications ordinarily are readily available in the departments requiring them. Furthermore, since the proper tooling is provided when the production line is erected and since the product is manufactured repeatedly, all tooling equipment would normally be subject to a standard control system which provides automatically for period replacement. Thus, with all the physical equipment available without advance notification, the only information necessary on the manufacturing schedule is the name and number of the part or product plus the quantity to be manufactured each day, week, or other time period, in the department concerned. However, if the product is made in a variety of sizes, weights, colors, types, or styles, the manufacturing schedule will show the quantity of each required and the sequence in which each is desired. The length of the period covered by the manufacturing schedule may be a week, month, or quarter, depending primarily upon the length of the manufacturing cycle of the product involved.

The *manufacturing order,* on the other hand, is generally used for job-lot manufacture or where a variety of products, if repeated at all, are made at infrequent or irregular intervals. Since the manufacturing order invariably contains information required by the plant to make the part or product named thereon—the quantity to be made, specifications, drawing numbers, routing sequence, any necessary shop instructions, and equipment required—it is generally prepared by the routing section and turned over to the scheduling section for a starting or finishing date. When the manufacturing order is finally released to the plant, it constitutes an authorization to each department concerned to start work on the article at the time scheduled.

10-4.2 Scheduling Adapted to Different Types of Manufacture

Just as a chain is only as strong as its weakest link, so the capacity of a serialized production line is limited to that of the slowest operation along that line. Scheduling of serialized manufacture, then, becomes primarily a matter of translating the sales or program requirements into a schedule of the amount of material that can be manufactured on the production line in any given period. The length of time required for the production cycle of a serialized production line is usually established when the line is set up, and material entering that line usually finishes the cycle without change of sequence. Thus, once the starting date of a particular lot of material is determined, the completion date is automatically established, and no intermediate scheduling of operations along the production line is required. The same is true of "batch" manufacture of the type that is so common to the chemical industries. Usually when a batch of material is released for production, it follows through its complete and predetermined cycle, and rarely is its cycle interrupted to permit another batch to pass by.

Semiserialized manufacture, on the other hand, usually does permit some storage and reshuffling of the orders along its production lines, particularly if a range of products or parts with varying process times is fabricated on a single production line. Where several mating parts are involved, it is common practice to interject "matching centers." These are simply storage areas between certain key manufacturing operations designed to take up the slack and to smooth out interruptions and delays caused by parts or materials not being at the right place at the right time. These matching centers serve also as key points for the intermediate rescheduling of material in process.

The scheduling of job-order manufacture, particularly where a range of parts is required for one assembly project, becomes infinitely more difficult, for the fabrication of each part and the assembly of each group of parts must be scheduled with due regard for the availability of equipment, personnel, and materials. Figure 10–4 depicts the factors involved in scheduling a job-order-assembly project. It should be noted that the starting and finishing dates for each part and subassembly are related to the length of their manufacturing cycles. The scheduling of intermediate operations is fully as important as the scheduling of the initial operation. Since little or no progressive flow of material is attempted in job-order manufacture, material not so scheduled soon becomes overlooked or otherwise hopelessly delayed in process. Frequently in job-order plants where the material must be routed through several departments and where the operations in a particular department are not extremely intricate, the scheduling of each operation may be omitted. In such cases the relatively more simple procedure of scheduling the date for the completion of the material in each department may serve to furnish the degree of control desired.

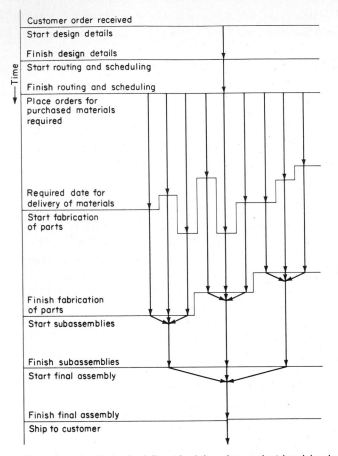

Customer order received

Start design details

Finish design details

Start routing and scheduling

Finish routing and scheduling

Place orders for
purchased materials
required

Required date for
delivery of materials

Start fabrication
of parts

Finish fabrication
of parts

Start subassemblies

Finish subassemblies

Start final assembly

Finish final assembly

Ship to customer

— Time

Figure 10-4 Chart depicting the scheduling of a job-order product involving both fabrication and assembly.

In the scheduling of several component parts of a job-order assembly, each with a different process time, theoretically each part is scheduled so that it will be completed immediately prior to its being required for assembly. In practice, owing to the limitations of equipment, personnel, and materials as described above, it is seldom possible to complete all parts exactly at the time required. Breakdowns, excessive rejections, and inaccuracy of estimates creep in. Also certain standardized parts are made more economically if manufactured not in small lots to a particular order but rather in large lots manufactured in advance to stock. Thus storage facilities must be provided immediately prior to assembly for parts that are being held pending the arrival of those not yet completed.

It is important to remember that schedules are made only to be revised. After all, a schedule is based on the priority or relative urgency of the work involved, and as conditions and customer requirements change, so also does the relative urgency change. A "rush" order may be sandwiched in ahead of a regular or customer order, and even the rush order may be later moved aside to make way for an order in response to a customer's breakdown. A schedule must be flexible, to meet changing conditions.

Short interval scheduling (SIS) is a recent innovation aimed at controlling labor costs. It has been subjected to gross overstatements of its value and to harsh criticism of its effectiveness. Since it is more of a psychological incentive than a formal scheduling technique, its value is largely wrought by the skills and convictions of its practitioners. It can focus attention on increased output and cost reductions, but it also can lead to strained labor relations.

The SIS technique involves assigning batches of work to employees with a time standard for completion. All work at a work center is scheduled by a single individual. This person assigns a batch of work to an employee that will keep him busy for 1 or 2 hours. The worker is told the specified time limit in which his assignment must be completed, and his progress is checked regularly.

Benefits from SIS accrue from the urgency imposed by short-range goals and the activity organization the supervisors are forced to exert. Supervisors must work closely with the employees to know the current status of each batch of work. The frequent checks on progress assure immediate attention for off-schedule operations.

A fundamental difficulty in the implementation of short interval scheduling is the supervisor's responsibility to assign standard times for each batch of work. There is seldom enough time available to develop time standards by formal work measurement methods for every work assignment. Consequently the supervisors utilize work standards based on "reasonable expectancies." Loose interpretations of reasonable expectancies have caused considerable unrest among workers, leading many companies to discontinue or at least question the SIS approach.

10-4.3   Schedule Control Charts

Charts are widely used in industry for control purposes. Sales, production, and financial figures are often more effectively studied when charted. Particularly in the field of production, scheduling charts often constitute the foundation upon which all scheduling activities are based.

Control charts offer a quick, compact, and visual means of recording information, both that which sets forth a plan and that which records what has been done to accomplish that plan. Charts are useful in establishing *control by exception*—the exception in the area of poor accomplishment compared with the original plan readily stands out when charted and thereby points up the need for investigation and possible correction. Control charts are usually dynamic. That is to say, as conditions change, the charts are successively revised so as to furnish a moving force for current as well as for future action.

Control charts used as a tool of production control include the project-layout chart and the load chart.

1. The *project-layout chart* schedules in advance the work ahead of either personnel or equipment, or both, and determines the relative importance of the work and hence the sequence in which it should be performed. Figure 10–4 with dates added along the time axis would be representative of such a chart.

2. The *load chart* indicates by number of hours, days, or jobs the work load ahead of a particular machine, battery of machines, department, or plant (see Fig. 10–5).

Forms of chart construction are (1) the Gantt chart, and (2) mechanical charts. The construction employed in each charting application is determined by the nature of the data and the purpose of the chart.

1. The *Gantt chart* derives its name from the man who developed its format and industrial application, a pioneer in the field of scientific management, Henry L. Gantt. It is an operating chart in that it furnishes information for action. It may depict plans for the future, progress on present operations, and a record of past

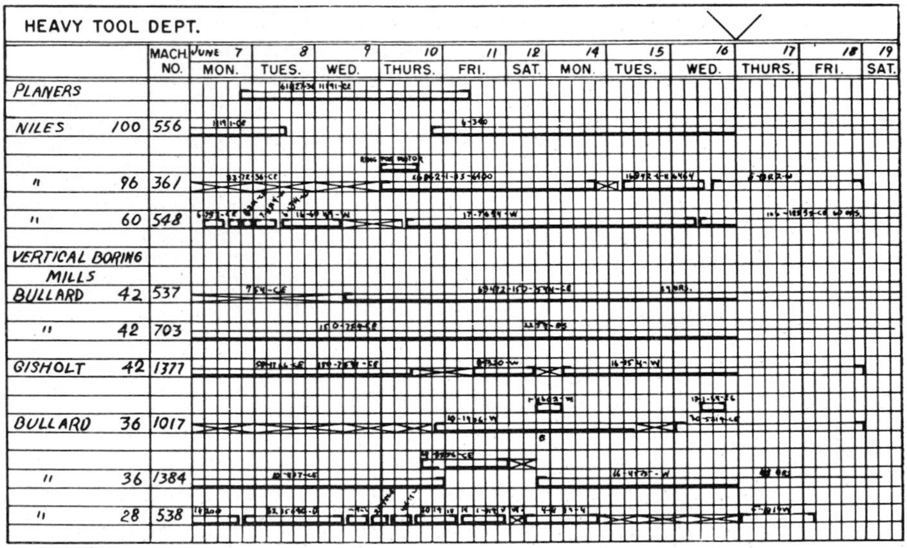

Figure 10-5 Gantt chart showing production planning and performance in a department equipped with two kinds of machines: planers and vertical boring mills. On the first machine, according to the foreman's estimate, part 11191-CE was to have been finished Tuesday noon but had been completed on Monday, and another order was begun, part 61427. (As the case of this machine illustrates, when jobs are completed ahead of schedule, two lines are needed to chart the necessary information.) That job was also finished ahead of estimate, and the third order was begun Thursday afternoon instead of Friday. When the chart was copied on Wednesday, the 16th, the work was just on schedule.

On the second machine, the work was already 3 days behind schedule when it was carried over from the previous sheet. At that time, order X6842 was scheduled to begin Thursday morning and to be completed Monday afternoon, but it was necessary to run in a repair job, a ring for a motor, so that 4 hours had to be allowed for the delay (indicated by crossed lines) before X6842 could be begun. When the chart was copied Wednesday night, the work on the machine was 4 hours behind schedule.

achievements for possible future reference. In the Gantt chart, the horizontal space divisions indicate passage of time (as an hour, a shift, a day), and the light horizontal lines show the amount of work scheduled (or actually done) during the increment of time represented by that space. The heavy horizontal lines indicate the cumulative amount of work scheduled (or actually done) up to a given date or hour. A typical Gantt chart is shown in Figure 10–5.

2. *Mechanical charts* include visible-index files, various wall charts, and scheduling boards that are available from manufacturers of production-control equipment. Usually these charts are enlarged adaptations of a Gantt or bar chart with the addition of mechanical clips, pegs, strings, tapes, and other signaling devices which enable the production-control specialist to visualize and focus attention on situations requiring attention. Figure 10–6 is representative of the scheduling-control boards currently used by industry.

Charts do have certain limitations. The calculations and plotting to keep them continually up to date may require more time than would be involved in simply studying the original table, record, or report. Errors both in calculation and in plotting are hard to detect and are apt to be cumulative; if they are not discovered, the resulting false picture may be responsible for wrong and costly decisions. However, where information in tabular or other written form may defy quick visual and mental analysis, charts do have a definite place in the production-control system.

10-5 DISPATCHING

Dispatching, the initial action element of production control, consists essentially of the issuance of orders in terms of their priority as determined by

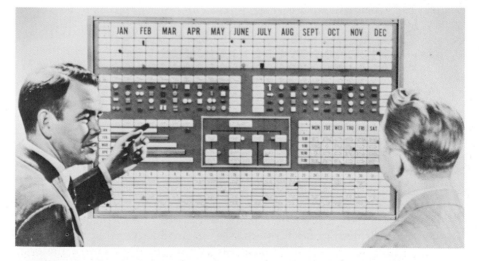

Figure 10-6 In this type of scheduling board, magnetized panels with special symbols are used to aid the scheduling and monitoring of production projects. (Courtesy of Graphic Systems.)

scheduling. It includes the assignment of work to the operators at their machines or workplaces. Thus dispatching in effect determines *by whom* work shall be done.

As there is a close analogy between the scheduling of production orders and the scheduling of railroad trains over a roadbed, so also is there a similarity between the dispatching of production orders and the dispatching of trains over a busy track section. Just as the railroad dispatcher must know every foot of the railroad and the speed of each locomotive, so must the production dispatcher know exactly his routing for each product and the productive capacity of each piece of manufacturing equipment to which he dispatches the work. He must know at all times the position or progress of all orders (trains) under his control. He would prefer to have all items run on a prescribed schedule, but he too is confronted with orders of different degrees of priority, ranging from those which suddenly become classed as "rush," to those on a prescribed manufacturing schedule, and finally down to those which have a lower urgency standing, such as stock orders. Production orders (like trains) move at different speeds as dictated by the dispatcher. If his judgment is faulty, the efficiency or capacity of the plant (railroad) is impaired; if his errors are serious, a production bottleneck (wreck) almost invariably results.

From the foregoing, some of the activities frequently delegated to the dispatcher are apparent. In summary they may be listed as follows:

1. The assignment of work to the machines or workplaces

2. The authority to prepare, assemble, and issue to their point of use the necessary materials, tools, fixtures, and gages

3. The issuance of the orders and production forms necessary to the performance of work and to the reporting of production, payroll, and cost data

4. The responsibility for controlling the progress of material at each operation; for making the necessary adjustments to schedules and work assignments as conditions change or as unpredictable emergencies occur

5. The authority to move work from one operation to the next

6. The liaison function linking the plans of the routing and scheduling office with the performance of the manufacturing divisions

Complexity of the activities of the dispatcher varies with the type of manufacture. The dispatching of repetitive orders, particularly where production lines are involved, is infinitely simpler than is the dispatching of work, materials, tools, and other items for a job-order project that is seldom if ever repeated. In the former case, the productive equipment is predetermined by the line. It is then necessary only to dispatch the materials and supplies required in manufacture. However, for the job-order manufacturer of a product infrequently repeated, tooling and equipment must be checked and missing elements supplied. Gages usually are set for each job as it is run. "Bugs" often develop and must be ironed out. One machine may be used for a variety of operations, generating problems of flexibility. Some machines and operators become overloaded with work; others run out of work. Emergency or rush orders frequently have to be interspersed to the detriment of orders previously dispatched. Seldom can truly progressive flow of materials be completely achieved. Thus, to prevent the foregoing difficulties, the dispatcher in job-order manufacture must exercise considerable planning and ingenuity and keep constant watch on material movement to ensure that there is at all times a reasonable backlog of work ahead of each machine or operator.

10-5.1 Decentralized and Centralized Dispatching

Previously we saw that where line production is involved, the scheduling section prepares a manufacturing schedule for each production item, specifying the quantity to be produced during a given future period. These schedules are issued by the dispatching section to the machines or departments concerned prior to the start of that period. Similarly, in the case of job-order manufacture, individual manufacturing orders for each production item accomplish the same purpose. The manner in which the schedules or orders are issued depends upon whether the dispatching is decentralized or centralized.

Decentralized dispatching consists of issuing manufacturing schedules or work orders in blanket fashion to the foreman or "dispatch clerk" within each department who must then determine the relative sequence in which those orders will be started within that department. It is likewise the duty of the foreman or clerk to dispatch the orders and material to each machine and operator. The only restriction placed on the departmental dispatcher is that the material be completed in the department on or before a prescribed date. Good practice dictates that the foreman be required to acknowledge in writing acceptance of the schedule or order upon its receipt, by which act he subsequently accepts responsibility for completion of the material within the time allowed him. Or, by the same token, he may take exception to the time allotment when the order is issued to him. However, should breakdowns or other unforeseen events subsequently occur to delay completion of the work, he should then be required to notify the central-dispatching division of the production department that a revision of the "finish date" has become necessary.

Centralized dispatching, on the other hand, involves the dispatching of orders from the central-dispatching division directly to the machine or work station. Under this procedure, the capacity and characteristics of each machine as well as the backlog of work ahead of it are known and recorded in the central-dispatching station, and all dispatching is controlled from that point. The foreman merely takes the orders assigned to his machines and runs them as assigned. However, in most cases the foreman has the privilege of objecting to orders dispatched to his machines if he can show cause why it would be difficult or impossible to carry through with the assignment. For example, the operator of the machine in question might not have the necessary experience to perform the operation required, or perhaps the mechanical condition of the machine will not permit the degree of precision required.

The effect achieved by decentralized dispatching is to minimize much of the red tape, the duplication of posting, the elaborate reporting, and the "absentee control" that are usually present in most centralized dispatching systems. Hence it is an inexpensive system from the clerical standpoint. Nevertheless it entails more leg work on the part of the dispatcher, for he must visit the various departments regularly to retain his control and to keep in touch with their difficulties. As for centralized dispatching, it can achieve a greater degree of control—control that is typical of all centralized effort. Also it is more flexible, particularly in peak periods when the plant is running near or at capacity. As changes occur in the relative urgency of orders, they can readily be effected at the central-dispatching station without greatly upsetting the plans and schedules of the individual foremen. As all reporting of production clears through this central station, the progress of any material can readily be ascertained at any time. This makes for less telephoning and running back and forth between the central production office and plant departments.

10-5.2 Dispatching Procedure

Regardless of whether dispatching is centralized or decentralized, it is customary for the department foremen or their clerks to keep themselves informed of the starting date and progress of each order by means of a wall chart, visible-index file, or one of the several types of department dispatching boards. A common type of departmental dispatch board is shown in Figure 10–7. A three-pocket unit is provided for each machine or work station in the department. Orders, job tickets, or prewritten labor cards for each operation scheduled can be filed on such a board against the machine on which they will be run, as follows:

1. In the back pocket, jobs for which material and equipment are not yet available, arranged either in the sequence in which they are to be run or in the sequence of order numbers

2. In the front pocket, jobs for which material is available, arranged in the sequence in which they are to be performed

3. Under the spring clip, the job currently on the machine or in operation

The status of each machine is readily visible, orders are easily arranged and rearranged, and machines for which no future orders are available readily show up as the pockets become empty. Posting of production daily or by shifts to the orders under the spring clips enables the foreman to ascertain at any time the progress of each order.

The dispatching of orders and reporting of work performance in a small plant are generally effected by messenger service, either provided by the

Figure 10-7 One type of dispatch board. (Courtesy of Hyster Company.)

regular intraplant mail deliveries or performed by the dispatchers and expediters themselves. However, in large plants the distances between the central office and the various factory control centers may be so great that communications equipment can provide much more rapid and considerably cheaper service.

Several factors influence the selection of the exact type of communications equipment used. Normally, fast two-way service is essential. In some instances, voice transmission is preferred because the voice can be more personal and persuasive and can explain more clearly than the written word. A written record of what was transmitted is frequently desirable and is a necessity where "posting" or other compilation of data is involved. Versatility in some applications may be a factor, and the favored medium is one that can carry messages, orders, drawings, mail, and even small tools and gages, all with equal ease.

10-6 FOLLOW-UP

Follow-up, or *expediting,* is that branch of the production-control procedure which regulates the progress of materials and parts through the production process. Although it is the agency charged with the responsibility for the production orders after they are dispatched, it is nevertheless closely interrelated with dispatching. Follow-up serves as a catalytic agent to fuse the various separate and unrelated production activities into the unified whole that means progress. It concerns itself with the reporting of production data and the investigating of variances from the predetermined time schedules. As such, follow-up endeavors to see that the promise is backed up by performance.

More and more industrial and other purchasers are turning to *delivery-performance reports* to measure the production reliability of their suppliers. These reports may be prepared weekly or monthly, but either way, cumulatively, over a period of time, they show the number and percentage of each supplier's shipments which were late as received compared with delivery promises. The records then become one of the factors considered in awarding subsequent purchasing contracts to competing suppliers. The result is an increasing emphasis on making shipments "on time" and a focusing of attention on follow-up techniques as the means to improved delivery performance.

10-6.1 Types of Follow-up

MATERIALS   The follow-up of purchased materials is, as will be noted in the section on procurement (Chap. 11), primarily the responsibility of the purchasing department. The original requisition upon which the purchase of materials is based usually specifies the date on or before which the material is required, and it then becomes the duty of the purchasing department to ensure that the material is received so as to be available by that date. However, certain orders for material or for subcontracted items may be extremely vital to the maintenance of delivery promises to the customer, whereas other orders may simply be required to maintain a normal bank of raw material or parts in anticipation of future customer orders. Changed conditions may require that the delivery date of certain material be advanced.

Thus it is frequently advisable for the follow-up section of the production-control department to follow outstanding material requisitions placed with the purchasing department which are deemed vital to the maintenance of preplanned schedules. This follow-up may be accomplished most simply by filing one copy of the requisition in a daily follow-up file or in a tickler file according to the date the material is due to be received. Delivery information as obtained from the purchasing department through this type of follow-up can be transferred to the stock records to supply a ready cross reference for the source of the information.

WORK IN PROCESS   The follow-up of work in process in a layout by product consists primarily of checking the materials required for that process and recording the production accomplished for comparison with preplanned schedules. Once material enters the production line, it cannot easily become sidetracked or dormant. Thus, when the material is put into process in the desired sequence, follow-up of that material is a relatively simple matter. Generally a daily production record or a control chart will reveal any delays in production items along the line. Thus, by use of the principle of exception, late items can be given special attention.

The same cannot always be said for the follow-up of work in job-order manufacture. Where products are diversified and where a number of orders are running concurrently in the plant, it is possible for the order sequence to become jumbled or to be changed deliberately to meet emergency conditions. Hence, follow-up clerks or expediters in conjunction with the foremen must continually reexamine the progress of orders at various operations so that any delayed items can be given the green light through the rest of the process and the lost time can be made up.

As a part of the follow-up activities of job-order manufacture, a record is usually made of the start and completion of each job or operation, as well as of the number of pieces made and those which are defective or spoiled. Allied with such records are those showing the idle time of people and of machines which thus reveal lost-time conditions requiring investigation.

Follow-up of job-order manufacture may be organized either by product or by department. Under the first system, a follow-up clerk is assigned to follow up or "father" a particular product through all its operations and through all departments from the raw material to its completion. However, where the follow-up is organized according to department, a follow-up clerk expedites all products through a particular department, and when each article moves to another department, the responsibility for its control is placed in the hands of another follow-up clerk. The "fathering" system usually operates best when the product represents a complicated assembly requiring numerous component parts all of which must be available before assembly of the product can be completed, for under this system one person is responsible for following all the component parts. However, the disadvantage to this system lies in the fact that frequently several follow-up clerks, each interested only in expediting his or her particular material, hound a certain foreman for the simultaneous use of the same machines and equipment. Thus for less complicated products, it is frequently advisable for the follow-up to be organized by departments so that one follow-up clerk is left with the responsibility of advising the foreman how to make the best use of his facilities.

ASSEMBLY AND ERECTION   Responsibility for assembly and erection of products in assembly manufacture is almost invariably vested in one follow-up clerk using the "fathering" technique. Recognizing that it is virtually impossible always to bring together component parts of an assembly at exactly the right instant, many companies provide matching centers for temporary storage of the component parts awaiting assembly. When all parts are available, the follow-up clerk permits assembly or erection of the product to start.

In the case of large and complicated products, the assembly and erection as well as the subsequent servicing of the product may of necessity take place at the purchaser's plant. This type of erection is frequently required for machinery and for other highly technical articles where the follow-up clerk must be throughly acquainted with the engineering details of the product, with the applications in the field, and with the trouble shooting and servicing of the product after it goes into service.

10-6.2 Preventing Production Delays

As can be seen from the foregoing, the follow-up clerk or expediter is concerned with the delays that creep into industrial production. He learns of the delays through analysis of the production reports and through personal observation. He must not only take corrective action after trouble has occurred but also anticipate and prevent it before it actually develops. An ounce of prevention is far more valuable than a pound of cure where delays in industrial production are concerned.

Common causes of delays for which the expediter can help administer the remedy include:

1. *Errors in Planning*   These are essentially errors of production management whereby equipment is scheduled with work beyond its capacity to produce, setups are excessive as the result of scheduling uneconomically small lots, or work force demands have been underestimated. The follow-up clerk, by his close association with plant conditions, is often able to discover such errors and have them rectified before serious trouble is caused.

2. *Lack of Materials, Tools, or Equipment*   Here the problem may be a basic one of improper planning, or it may derive from a delivery failure which could have been prevented by closer follow-up by the purchasing department or the production expediter.

3. *Equipment Breakdown*   Preventive maintenance and duplication of vital pieces of equipment help minimize delays from breakdowns. However, the expediter can assist in seeing that prompt transfer is arranged to the alternate, or "stand-by," equipment as breakdowns do occur.

4. *Excessive Rejections*   Materials scrapped at any point in the process in excess of the scrap factor allowed subsequently cause a shortage in the finished item. The follow-up clerk is instrumental in setting in motion the machinery to replace the defective material and in expediting the replacement lot so as not to delay the production of the finished item.

5. *Out-of-balance In-process Inventories*   Where the bank of materials builds up to a point of excess between some operations with a resultant starvation of material between other operations, slight spurts or lags in production can cause operators to run out of work. The follow-up clerk must then take steps to level off the float to a point where idle worker and idle-machine time from this cause is eliminated.

10-7   TRENDS IN PRODUCT FLOW CONTROL

Customers are demanding faster, more certain deliveries of manufactured items. Management is demanding better, more positive control of production, with attendant lower costs. How is industry responding to these demands?

First, industry has found that best manufacturing performance can be realized by integrating control of all manufacturing endeavors, from the unloading of raw material to the shipping of the complete product. This vertical control parallels the trends toward vertical integration of processes, plant layout by products, and automation. It is the avenue to complete and most effective coordination of effort in this field.

Secondly, industry is making ever-increasing use of mechanical equipment in production-control systems as the medium for complete, accurate, and speedy two-way information on which the control process depends. It also is the way to reduced clerical costs of this control. Some of this equipment has already been touched on: duplicating machines for preparing forms, commercial control boards for scheduling, and communication equipment for dispatching and follow-up.

10-7.1   Computerized Production Controls

Also coming into more widespread use for production control is *data-processing equipment*—electric tape-punching and -reading typewriters, tabulating-card machines, and electronic computers. A typical production-control system using such equipment would start with sales-order entry, at which point the customer's order is transferred to punched cards. This transfer is accomplished by selecting partially prepunched cards from a reservoir file for standard products and regular customers or sometimes by the automatic punching of cards as a by-product of typing the sales order. In either method, a separate punched card is prepared for each item ordered and for each shipping date specified or promised. Other prepunched cards from a master file can automatically prepare the various routing, scheduling, dispatching, and follow-up forms, as well as those required for wage payment and cost control. The cards are fed into a computer where standard production-time allowances are extended and starting and finishing dates for the order are automatically computed. The computer can be programmed to signal overloaded schedules in any week and to set aside the cards for the jobs affected so that they may be rescheduled. A continuous picture of the plant's backlog is thus available. The cards, or reproductions of them, then become "promise cards" and are used for customer assignment of completed goods for shipment. Work performed and time actually used are punched into cards, and the machines then quickly draw off daily production reports and comparisons with quantities scheduled. The promise cards may subsequently serve another purpose: to prepare on tabulating machines the invoices billing the customer for goods shipped. Furthermore, those cards representing sales orders and shipments frequently made the basis for statistics on incoming business, shipments, cost of sales, changes in product demand, production performance, and inventory position as well as information to indicate profitability of products, territories, and classes of trade.

There is a growing realization in top management that there remains a substantial lag in clerical time which must also be reduced. This lag occurs in many enterprises as an integral part of the production-control system. Customer orders directed to branch sales offices are forwarded to the main office. They are then recorded, edited, summarized, and translated to manufacturing and material requirements. Material is clerically received, recorded, and issued. The manufacturing paper work is prepared, scheduled, and transmitted to the factory. Thus the vicious clerical dragon continues through the entire production process to consume vital time—time used solely to communicate, record, summarize, analyze, decide, and prepare instructions so that action at each step in the process may finally begin. This time lag in many companies runs into a matter of several weeks. How, then, to slay the dragon?

The answer to the clerical delay between cause and effect in manufacturing is linked in part with the second trend considered: that toward the mechanization of production control. Many concerns have found that various combinations of mechanical equipment provide the desired clerical speed. Another approach to the problem is to eliminate all transcriptions by writing or typing the basic data received so as to make subsequent copying unnecessary. Still another solution is derived from regular examinations of procedures and steps in the system to squeeze excess minutes from clerical and communications time—minutes which totaled represent a substantial delay (see Fig. 10–8).

Perspective 10A   COMPUTER-ASSISTED PRODUCT FLOW

The benefits obtained from computerized product-flow control at A. B. Chance Company are described by P. D. Sturgeon:

Nine months after installing an advanced production information and control system (PICS) to support sales forecasting, material requirements planning, and other functions, we:

- Doubled our capability to ship from stock—without corresponding increases in inventory
- Lowered direct labor costs as we balanced inventory
- Decreased set-up costs as a function of direct labor by 10 percent
- Increased product sales from our three plants affected by the system about 20 percent
- Speeded inventory turns by 20 percent.

None of these benefits or the many others provided by the new system should be directly attributed to the computer. . . . All our systems are designed so that *managers* are still in control. We need to react immediately to, say, a storm in Louisiana which will almost invariably affect sales, since Chance is a major producer of electrical utility supplies. But the computer and its programming do provide valuable, time-phased information which can be used as *intelligence* to help a good manager become a better manager.*

*source: "Production Information and Control—A Working System," *Industrial Engineering,* July, 1973.

COMMENT   The quantity and variety of data needed to keep track of the materials, machines, parts, products, and people involved in a production process makes production control an obvious candidate for computerized assistance. Most successful applications, such as the one described at A. B. Chance Company, have evolved from an initial use of punch-card equipment, and the evolution included involvement of all the affected personnel—first- and second-level shop supervisors, industrial engineers, production controllers, and managers. Such participation guards against two main causes of failure in computerized production control: (1) wrong information is provided or (2) correct information is ignored.

10-7.2 Analysis Techniques for Production Control

Another trend is toward more sophisticated control analyses. This trend is closely related to computerized production control; without the data-proc-

Figure 10-8 A Touch-Tone computer system developed by Omark Industries' electronic data processing department is used to keep tabs on thousands of small parts. After each manufacturing operation, a worker feeds details to a central memory bank via a Touch-Tone phone. Status of in-process inventory is known at all times.

essing capability now available to most organizations, the growing number of analytical techniques could not be utilized. The techniques rely on data accumulated to perform the voluminous calculations required to treat complex manufacturing systems.

Some of the techniques are applications of quantitative methods discussed in previous chapters—critical path scheduling, simulation, queuing, linear programming, etc. Other techniques take the form of decision rules such as priorities for dispatching. Assigning starting times or due dates for jobs to be completed within a department is typically a responsibility of the department foreman. When a backlog of orders awaits assignment, he attempts to satisfy many objectives: keeping the equipment busy, serving preferred customers, following inventory and working-hour policies, satisfying rush orders, etc. The traditional first-come, first-served priority rule may be best; or it could be modified to allow priority classes based on dollar value ratings of the jobs; or should the utilization of resources receive prime priority through assignments that minimize operating times? Not all the choices are readily apparent or easy to rate once known. The department foreman does not have time to investigate all the alternatives. Such investigations are usually a staff function and are performed by specialists using sophisticated mathematics, but the outgrowth of the studies are decision rules that can be applied by the foreman on the factory floor.

"Line of balance" is an example of several established graphical techniques combined with data-processing procedures to aid control of assembly operations. It is designed to control logistics in conformance to a contracted delivery schedule and to keep costs within specified limits. The initial step in application is the development of the project plan, a network of activities necessary to complete one unit. Numbered events in the plan show the completion of key activities such as "ordered parts received" or "module B assembled and inspected."

Records are kept of the quantity of items passing each numbered event. These quantities are compared to the amount needed at given dates to meet the schedule of delivery for completed units. For example, in Figure 10–9 the final assembly cannot be completed until 20 days after the subassembly has passed the inspection, designated event 12. The quantity that should be completed at the date "now" is read from the vertical scale of the objective chart at a point set by the intersection of the scheduled delivery curve and a vertical line drawn from the bottom time scale at a date 20 working days in the future from "now." A line connecting expected completion levels for all the events is called the "line of balance." The heights of the bars in the progress chart show how close actual production inventories are to the need indicated by the line of balance. Similar comparisons of budgeted costs to actual costs are shown in the "program expenditures" bar graph.

The inventory and cost comparisons can be made by computer programs without conversion to charts. In conformance with the principle of management by exception, the printout calls attention only to the events in which the difference between the line of balance and actual progress exceeds a

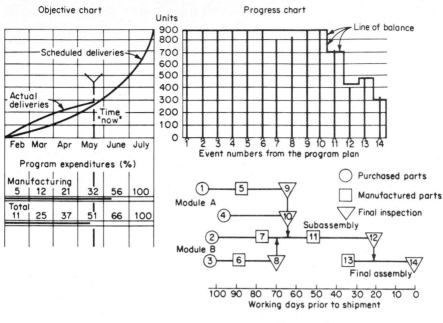

Figure 10-9 Charts associated with the line of balance technique. The program plan details manufacturing steps. The objective chart shows contracted and actual deliveries of finished units. Actual inventory levels of parts or assemblies associated with each event of the program plan are shown by bars on the progress chart. The required inventory levels to conform to the delivery schedule are shown by the "line of balance."

predetermined limit. The aim of both the graphical and the computer versions is to control the manufacturing process by close attention to costs and the progress of current output in relation to known future demands.

Perspective 10B   ASSEMBLY LINE BALANCING

Assembly line balancing is associated with a production process in which products are progressively refined as they pass through a regular series of work centers; an automobile production line is an example. The period allowed to complete operations at each work station is determined by the speed of the assembly line; all work stations have the same cycle time. The objective of line balancing is to minimize idle time while assigning operations to work stations according to a predetermined product flow plan.

The problem of allocating work to stations along the line, in order to minimize either the cycle time or the number of work stations, has been a popular area of analysis since the publication of the first formalized line balancing technique in 1955. Questions about which techniques are actually used are answered by a survey conducted by Dr. R. B. Chase. The major findings from 111 responses to a 44-item questionnaire are given below.

1. Formalized published line balancing algorithms are not being used, primarily because practitioners are not familiar with them.
2. The probable causes for their lack of use among those who are familiar with them are their complexity, the time it takes to use them, and their perceived inflexibility.
3. There is a definite need for usable line balancing procedures, especially in tractors, engines, and auto parts, as evidenced by the large number of major rebalances undertaken each year in these categories.
4. Light manufacturing appears to be the most stable category in terms of its line balancing activities, having the fewest major rebalances per year. It also appears to be the most sensitive to line balancing adjustments, taking substantially more time than other categories to achieve full production after a major rebalance.
5. The most critical problem in assembly line balancing is dealing with multiple products.
6. The use of job rotation and job enlargement is widespread, suggesting a growing concern on the part of practitioners for the behavioral factors affecting assembly line jobs. This interest, in part, may be attributed to the large amount of grievances and high turnover found among the survey respondents.*

*SOURCE: "Survey of Paced Assembly Lines," *Industrial Engineering*, February, 1974.

COMMENT Numerous algorithms designed to optimally balance assembly lines have been forwarded in recent years, perhaps more than the prevalence of assembly lines warrants. Nevertheless, product flow offers a major challenge for analysis because small improvements per unit, when multiplied by the large number of units passing through a typical assembly line, can amount to very significant savings.

10-8 REVIEW QUESTIONS

1. What is production control? How does it aid in securing more economical production?

2. Distinguish between the two types of customer orders. How are specific orders translated into production requirements?

3. What determines the routing procedure of a product?

4. Describe and indicate the use of a bill of materials and an operation sheet.

5. What is meant by "scheduling"? What are the limiting factors in production scheduling?

6. Describe and indicate the use of a master schedule, a manufacturing schedule, and a manufacturing order.

7. What function is performed by the dispatching section in a production control department?

8. What are the two types of dispatching procedures? What are the advantages and limitations of each type?

9. Why is follow-up the real control aspect of production control?

10. Differentiate between follow-up organized by product and follow-up organized by department. Where is each preferable?

11. Describe some of the common causes of delay.

12. What is meant by the line of balance? How and where is the line of balance technique used? Compare the line of balance with line balancing according to their areas of application.

10-9 TOPICS FOR DISCUSSION

1. List 10 examples of products which can be manufactured to a sales forecast. List 10 more which must be manufactured to customer order. What significant differences do you note between products on your first list and those on your second?

2. The modus operandi of some enterprises employs the principle that the production-control department has but one customer, the sales department. What advantages and disadvantages do you find in this operating philosophy?

3. How is the saying "What you can see, you can control" applicable to industrial manufacturing?

4. Automobile companies receive orders from their dealers at regional sales offices. Each order specifies the style, model, paint colors, type and color of upholstery, various accessories, etc. This information then goes to the assembly plant supplying that region.
   In the assembly of a given automobile, the time lag from completion of the body to its start down the final assembly line seldom exceeds one-half hour. During that period of time, the various stockrooms must be notified and must supply the correct color and style of fenders, wheels, tires, steering wheel, and other items specified on the order for that car.
   What communication facilities would most effectively carry order information from regional sales offices through to the various stockrooms in the assembly plant? Give reasons for your selection.

5. A wag has defined "expediting" as "adding commotion to confusion." Suggest steps in the production-control process which can prevent this definition from taking on an element of truth.

6. The competitive advantage of small manufacturing concerns serving other industries is illustrated by the following condensation of the remarks of two purchasing agents:
   The small shops starting out are in an enviable position. They can take care of rush business because they don't have too many customers. If you're in a rush they're willing to work overtime to get a job done for you. You can almost set your own delivery dates. If you want three or four pieces or a gage, they will come to the office, give you a price and have it on their machine in half an hour. There's no red tape and channeling things through departments, etc. When a small firm gets a blueprint for a job, the owner will mark it "make two of these" and hand the print to a mechanic. A large firm will break down the blueprint given them into specialized blueprints for all the individual parts, have different people make these, and then assemble the finished parts. In a small shop it will be a one-person operation, and he will build each section and component to fit with the others. In a big shop with specialization, where one person only grinds, etc., if there are any errors or things don't fit and they must rebuild some of the parts, there may be considerable delay . . . to change any piece may be a very expensive and extensive operation.
   How can large, well-established manufacturing concerns meet this challenge of new, smaller shops entering their industry?

7. One manufacturer of diversified metal products recently installed a data-processing system to control manufacturing functions from raw-material procurement through to the finished product. Among the advantages claimed for the new system is this by-product: machine-setup costs per unit product are now reduced significantly. Suggest how this saving can be derived from an effective control system.

8. Case 10A: *The Clashing Gear Company*
The Clashing Gear Company makes a complete line of gears, some standard and made for stock, others special and made to customer order. The production-control manager of the company has

been under criticism for lateness of shipments made recently to a number of important customers. In an effort to ascertain whether or not the criticism is justified, he has prepared a "delivery performance report" listing all late shipments for a period of a month and noting the reason why each item was overdue. This report was as follows:

1. One hundred gears made for one customer and completed on time were diverted by the sales department to another substantial gear user who previously had not been a customer.

2. An order involving 550 gears was given the wrong operation sequence on the route sheet. Result: all rejected and scrapped.

3. Fifty gears quoted a customer as being in stock were not in stock owing to a clerical posting error which resulted in an incorrect stock balance.

4. One thousand fifty gears were scheduled to be made on a machine which subsequently broke down and had to be overhauled.

5. There was shortage in a customer order owing to heavy rejections over and above that planned for the order.

6. The gear identification number was incorrectly copied in preparing a work order, causing the material to be mislaid in the plant for 3 weeks.

7. Pressure from the sales department on the scheduling supervisor to meet the short delivery request of an important customer led to overscheduling the capacity of certain plant equipment, with the result that two other orders were completed late.

Questions

1. Suggest possible procedural shortcomings which caused each of the foregoing broken delivery promises, and indicate what might be done in each instance to prevent recurrence.

9. Case 10B: *The Ray Company*
The Ray Company's missile division designs and manufactures missile components under direct government contract and as subcontractor for other missile prime contractors. Over a thousand different parts are in various stages of manufacture at any one time. Some of these are critical items which the division engineers decide are to be produced by the Ray Company either because the parts are vital to the proper functioning of the missile component or because the company is best able to meet a close delivery time involved. The remainder of the parts are made outside by subcontractors under Ray Company guidance. The complexity of some of these missile parts can be gauged by the fact that their manufacturing cycle may require up to 3 months for completion of all operations. Manufacture of these parts is further complicated by continual engineering revisions due to the fluid state of missile technology. At times as many as 50 change orders a day have been released.

Control over manufacture of parts produced by the Ray Company has been centered in two groups, the fabrication methods section and the assembly methods section, each staffed with project engineers. Each engineer was assigned to specified parts and their tooling. Data sheets on each part were filed by part number in folders located in filing cabinets. A master materials-list book, about twice the size of a Sears, Roebuck catalogue and weighing almost 30 pounds, was located centrally in the methods department and used repeatedly by all engineers to check such essentials as materials specifications, heat treatments, surface protections, inspection requirements, and the like. Each engineer retained a notebook which he filled with job-data jottings to record the progress of the various jobs for which he was responsible. Because of the individuality of records kept by the various engineers, coordination among them, and particularly between the fabrication and assembly sections, frequently just did not exist.

Questions

1. What principles of good production control appear to have been violated here? Suggest appropriate remedies.

10. Case 10C: *The Rat-A-Tat Tool Company*

The Rat-A-Tat Tool Company manufactures on a job-lot basis 300 models of portable air tools requiring some 5,000 different parts. Production control in the plant is essentially a visual system which operates as follows:

In the center of the manufacturing area is a factory control room. There, as each order is received from the scheduling office, the control-room clerk notes the desired delivery and schedules the required parts by department and operation. Around the room are control boards, each tool having its own board area. For each part number there is a separate factory order which lists operations in proper sequence and which is coded by color to indicate the departments involved.

Periodically during the shift each foreman walks to the control room, looks over the boards, and checks orders bearing the color of his department, noting their priority and progress. A clip placed on his departmental color indicates that the parts are ready for his department. A clip on a particular operation number indicates where work is being performed, and the clip is moved from operation to operation as the order progresses. Color flags show urgency: a red flag calling for 60-day delivery; yellow flag, 30-day; and white flag, rush.

A form of job card known as a "traveler" accompanies the parts and contains all necessary technical information on work to be performed. The traveler also has spaces for posting production of good and rejected pieces at each operation. Twice during each shift the foreman reports to the control room the progress of each order being processed in his department.

Questions

1. Comment on the various features of the foregoing dispatching and follow-up system, noting any advantages and shortcomings you detect.

11

ATERIAL FLOW

Over the broad view, control of industrial materials bears significantly on the nation's economy since cyclical changes in business conditions are heavily influenced by industry's accumulation and liquidation of inventories. More narrowly, materials soak up a substantial portion of the capital invested in the individual enterprise and thus demand a continuing and considerable amount of attention from its management.

Who in the industrial organization is responsible for its materials? What activities are involved in material procurement? What policies and procedures aid in acquiring materials of the right quality and quantity at the right time and price? How are materials best received, packaged, and transported? As we consider material control, we direct our attention to these basic questions: Why does the enterprise require inventories? How are they controlled as to size and storage? How frequently and to what degree should stocks be replenished? What types of equipment are available to handle materials efficiently, and what determines their proper application? These are the questions surrounding the control of material flow.

11 MATERIAL FLOW

11-1 MATERIAL MANAGEMENT

Materials, one of the principal "m's" of industry (money, management, manpower, machines, markets, and materials) worry controllers, annoy sales managers, plague purchasing agents, haunt production managers, and harass stockkeepers. Management at all levels finds itself embroiled in problems which take root in materials. Many business failures are the direct outgrowth of excessive inventories. Too much material causes idle funds, storage and obsolescence problems, and marketing headaches. On the other hand, if materials are not adequate to meet the needs of the operating and distribution segments of the enterprise, efficiency suffers and costs skyrocket. Manufacturing delays are frequent, and broken delivery promises inevitable. Material management, then, is a continual struggle between too much and too little, too soon and too late.

In some companies, materials represent a large part of the sales dollar, affording management opportunity for substantial savings if it can wring dollars from material costs. Materials for which supply and demand occasionally get out of balance and those subject periodically to rising and falling prices are given the constant scrutiny required of any fluctuating-market situation. Never-ending search is conducted for better and cheaper material substitutes. Careful controls are placed on the size of inventories so that the enterprise can be responsive to changes in product and process. Also, the importance of low inventories to the maintenance of operating flexibility and cash liquidity in our rapidly changing economic world is not to be overlooked. Costs of storing, packaging, and transporting materials are such that management is always on the lookout for more efficient methods in each of these fields.

In sum, material management is concerned with *controlling* the kind, amount, location, movement, and timing of the various commodities used in and produced by the industrial enterprise. It starts as an outgrowth of production planning with the "explosion" of the product into materials and parts and with the determination of supply and expendable equipment items required in the manufacturing process. Thereafter it is a partner of production control, becoming the "logistics" branch of that function. Its responsibilities end as the correct, finished product in proper condition and quantity passes to the customer.

11-1.1 Classes of Materials

Industrial materials can be divided into six main classes:

1. *Raw material* Material used in the product which is in an unprocessed condition. Metal bars, tubes, flat stock, castings, forgings, leather hides, cloth, and commercial chemicals are examples of raw materials.

2. *Purchased parts* Items used in the assembly of the product which are obtained from outside sources. In this category are commercial parts such as bolts, nuts, screws, bearings, and gears. Similarly, automobile tires purchased by an automobile manufacturer for its car assemblies and electric switches which find their way into the lamps of another concern are typical purchased parts.
3. *In-process material* Material used in the product upon which work has been performed to change its form, size, or physical or chemical characteristics. Here value in terms of processing labor and perhaps other material has been added to what originally was a raw material. Examples include a machine-tap blank turned from a bar, a shoe upper cut from a leather hide, and a sandblasted and painted casting.
4. *Finished products* Goods completely manufactured and inspected, ready for shipment to a customer. Following through the foregoing examples, we would find the completed machine tap, a finished pair of shoes, and a decorated cast-aluminum vase.
5. *Supplies* Consumable materials used in the manufacturing process which do not become a part of the product. Here we have such diverse items as files, grinding wheels, taps, drills, belting, sandpaper, oils, sawdust, plating supplies, lumber, shipping cartons, stationery, and pencils.
6. *Equipment items* Expendable parts of machines and other physical facilities. Jigs, fixtures, fittings, valves, fuses, and fluorescent lamps are a few of the many repair or replacement items which are not, strictly speaking, materials but which are here considered as such because they are subject to the same controls.

11-1.2 Scope of Material Flow Control

Effective control of materials embraces four phases:

1. *Procurement* Purchasing

2. *External transportation* Receiving, traffic, and shipping

3. *Internal transportation* Material handling

4. *Inventory control* Store keeping

Distinct as are the scope and duties of the four phases of material control, nevertheless, they all serve as links in the chain of action by which that control is achieved. If one link is weak or improperly coupled to the next, the entire chain may fail. Thus the phases must be closely coordinated if they are to operate successfully.

Perhaps this coordination can best be achieved by placing all four phases of material control under the direct authority of a single individual. However, in actual practice it is quite common to find the various phases under separate authorities in the organization structure. Where the purchased materials represent a considerable portion of the sales dollar—as would be the case in the manufacture of tin cans, a fully automatic process in which relatively little labor on the product is required—the work of the purchasing agent is of such extreme importance to the profitable operation of the enterprise that he may be made one of the major executives of the enterprise, often with the title of vice-president. In perhaps a majority of companies, however, the purchasing department is a responsibility of the plant manager, since most of the purchases are made for the manufacturing divisions. Yet it is not uncommon to find the purchasing department working under the direction of the treasurer, apparently because of the purchasing agent's close relationships with the company's purse strings.

External transportation, inventory control, and internal transportation activities are sometimes consolidated under a *manufacturing services manager* who is then responsible to the plant manager. Where these activities are left in separate departments, all external transportation is handled by a *traffic manager,* generally reporting to the plant manager or perhaps to the purchasing agent. Inventory control and internal transportation may function under a *stock-control supervisor* and *material-handling supervisor,* respectively. A host of other titles identify these two jobs, but regardless of title the occupants report either to the plant manager or, where close alliance of these activities with production control is indicated, to the production manager. Thus it can be appreciated that the workable organization structures for controlling materials in an industrial plant are many and varied, and the one that is correct for any particular enterprise depends upon the circumstances and individuals involved. The final test in each case is empirical: Does it work?

11-2 PROCUREMENT

The purchasing function of the enterprise is the liaison agency which operates between the plant organization and the outside vendors on all matters of procurement. The importance of the function to the successful operation of the enterprise ranges from minor, when raw material and purchased parts represent a low percentage of the value of goods sold, to major, when purchases comprise a high percentage of the sales dollar. However, in any company the importance of the purchasing responsibility for getting the right material delivered from vendors on time cannot be overlooked. Even a minor item of low value not available when needed can stop production, put people out of work, and delay deliveries to customers. Also of some consequence to every enterprise is that area of the purchasing function which is concerned with the physical facilities—plant and equipment items and maintenance of them.

11-2.1 Activities of the Purchasing Department

In general, the purchasing agent is made responsible for maintaining the four major procurement factors of *quality, quantity, time,* and *price. Quality,* of course, refers to the kind of goods desired as established by specifications emanating usually from the product-engineering department. The *quantity* of the purchase will generally be determined directly or indirectly from the production and material requirements set forth by the routing division of production control, and the *time* allowed for delivery is linked with the production schedules of the scheduling division. Thus these three factors —quality, quantity, and time—are generally established *for* the purchasing department, and its responsibility in this connection then becomes principally a matter of securing reliable vendors who will maintain the factors established. The fourth factor of *price*, however, is essentially the responsibility of the purchasing department, for that department with its contacts with outside markets is in the best position to determine what is a fair price. Nevertheless, just as any business activity is most effectively carried on through the cooperation of all interested departments, so can the best results be secured where prices—and, for that matter, all the procurement factors—are discussed among and approved by the various departments concerned.

More specifically, as to the activities of the purchasing agent and his staff, they are expected to:

1. Know and maintain records showing possible materials and substitutes, sources of supply, prices, and quantities available

2. Review specifications for possible simplification and standardization of materials or for unreasonable requirements

3. Negotiate with vendors

4. Accumulate and analyze quotations

5. Place purchase orders with vendors

6. Follow up purchase orders for delivery as specified

7. Audit invoices to check compliance with agreed terms

8. Maintain records of all purchases

9. Coordinate with other departments on all matters pertaining to procurement

Likewise a major duty of many purchasing departments is the handling of sub-contracts. Practically all enterprises at one time or another "farm out" the manufacture of some parts or production items. Usually these represent but a small portion of the total purchases of a manufacturing organization. However, during periods of high business activity, subcontracting is frequently the solution as overburdened plants seek to increase their production. Also, it is common practice to farm out dangerous, obnoxious, or expensive operations to other concerns whose know-how and equipment permit them to perform the work better, more safely, or more cheaply. Other instances involve companies desirous of providing competition in costs for their own departments or of escaping royalty payments or burdensome labor agreements. Since the appraisal of a potential subcontractor's productive facilities and questions of product quality are often beyond the scope of the purchasing function, the technical phases of subcontracting are usually turned over to the engineering, production, and inspection groups, while the purchasing agent acts primarily as a liason or contact person between the two or more firms involved.

There is a blurred line between the responsibility of the purchasing department and the product-engineering department for material-quality standards. Both may exercise some jurisdiction, but usually the duty of the purchasing agent is only to see that materials bought meet requirements established by specification or, in the case of items not regularly purchased, entered on the purchase requisition—in either case, the responsibility resting on the engineering department. But where materials are requisitioned without special quality standards, the purchasing agent assumes the responsibility for quality, as is natural for any purchaser.

Last but far from the least of the purchasing agent's duties is that of acting as the eyes and ears of the enterprise in finding new and useful materials or effective substitutes. Large companies may even create a section in the purchasing department to perform this service. In small companies, the purchasing agent and his assistants generally read periodicals dealing with new equipment and materials and interview vendors to find out "what's new." If the proper individuals concerned are thus kept informed, some of these new developments may be applied with attendant monetary savings to the enterprise.

11-2.2 Purchasing Procedures

A prerequisite of any purchasing contract is a meeting of minds as to the exact nature of the material required and to be furnished. Material standards which define the major requirements (i.e., form, size, composition, performance) of the material and also state acceptance terms and shipping conditions are called *purchase specifications.* They are usually established in writing by the product-engineering department with the assistance of the purchasing, production-control, and other interested departments. They are referred to in the purchase order and either accompany the order or have been placed on file with regular vendors. Of course, many standard materials are purchased by catalogue number, description, or name. This practice makes for simplicity, but because specifications of branded or catalogue items are often subject to change, it is not always the wisest policy with major materials.

The actual purchase originates on a *purchase requisition* (see Fig. 11-1). Properly signed and approved, it authorizes the purchasing department to order the material, specifies *what* kind is desired, *how much,* and *when,* as well as *where* it is to be delivered in the plant. Purchase requisitions usually are serially numbered as an aid in filing and follow-up. For items that are ordered regularly, a *traveling requisition* is used. This is a card carrying the usual information on the purchase requisition but with space for repeat orders. Thus it is used over and over again without the retyping of data. This eliminates clerical work and the need for a separate purchase-history record.

```
                        PURCHASE REQUISITION
                                    Dept.........................
                                    Requisition No.................
    To Purchasing Agent:            Date.........................
    Please order the following:     Requested by...................
         Ship to.....................  Approved by....................
         ............................  Checked by....................
              Via............  F.O.B.............  Terms.........
    Date Material Wanted...........
```

Quantity	Description	Material on Hand	Average Consumption	Price

Special Instructions

```
    Ordered from...................  Purchase Order No..............
    Date Ordered...................  Approved by....................
    Purpose........................  Checked by.....................
    Charge to......................  ..............................
```

Figure 11-1   A composite purchase-requisition form prepared by the National Association of Purchasing Agents and based on an analysis of the requisition forms of some 120 companies of all sizes and in all industries. (SOURCE: "Purchase Requisition Forms," National Association of Purchasing Agents, Inc.)

Once authorized to make the purchase, the purchasing agent looks over the sources of supply and asks for *quotations* as to price, delivery, amount, and possibly an exact description of the material each vendor is in a position to furnish. This last is necessary when a vendor's product differs from his competitor's in some respect but may be equally satisfactory for the purpose intended. For example, on such branded products as solvents, oils, and greases, the buyer may require details of each company's brand standard.

Once the quotations are received, the buyer, aided by other interested parties, selects the vendor from whom the goods are to be purchased. When goods vary as to description, price, or delivery, this selection may be virtually automatic. Laboratory or plant tests may show which vendor's product is preferable. However, when all factors are virtually equal, it is up to the buyer to select the vendor.

Materials bought under continuing contract or those purchased repeatedly do not require quotations from the vendors since all necessary information would then be available to both parties. In the case of repeat orders, the purchase order might include the phrase "... as previously furnished on our Purchase Order No. ———." In actual practice, many of the major material items are purchased repeatedly, and it is thus imperative that the purchasing agent develop adequate and dependable sources, preferably two or more, from which to obtain such items, rather than shop around at each repeat order. Of course, the purchasing agent may check the quality, price, and delivery of the usual sources by asking for occasional quotations from other vendors.

When the vendor has been decided upon, the next step is the preparation of the *purchase order* (see Fig. 11-2). This states *what kind* of material is to be furnished, *how much,* and *when* delivery is requested or promised, together with a stipulation as to how shipment is to be made (express, freight,

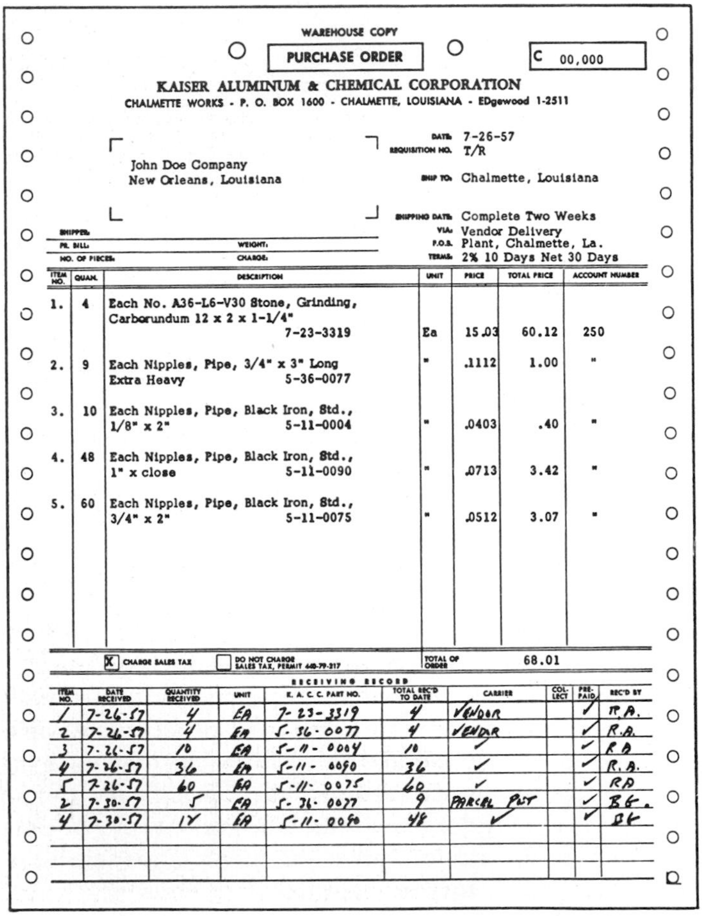

Figure 11-2 Four copies of this particular seven-part purchase order are used in the purchasing and expediting process. Two are sent to the accounting and office files. The remaining "warehouse copy" serves as a master receiving record. Each time a new shipment is received, a photographic duplicate of the warehouse copy is sent to the expediter, accounting, etc., as a receiving notice, thus eliminating much recopying data. (SOURCE: Paperwork Simplification, no. 47, Standard Register Co.)

cheapest way, etc.). The unit price and discount expected will likewise be shown, as will the purchase-order number and that of the originating requisition.

Routine follow-up of vendors is conducted through the use of follow-up form letters or cards on which the order number and other necessary information can be filled in and which request the desired delivery information. More urgent items demand visitations, telephone calls, or telegrams to ascertain the current status of the material on order.

11-2.3 Organization for Effective Purchasing

The industrial procurement function can best be made effective if all purchasing is channelized and centralized through one agency—the purchasing department—and under one head—the purchasing agent. All vendor inquiries and contacts as well as purchasing commitments should then be arranged through the purchasing department. This centralization of purchasing almost invariably makes for more efficient ordering of materials, eliminates much duplication of effort, and simplifies the purchasing procedure and the payment of invoices.

However, there are circumstances which, for reasons of efficiency, dictate a decentralization of the purchasing function. Occasionally plants or points of material use are so widely scattered as to make centralized procurement a hindrance rather than a help. Particularly is this true for high-quality or technical items wherein control over purchases made from a remote point may be difficult to achieve. Also where the materials involved are heavy and bulky commercial items (such as oil products, fuels, sawdust, and paint), transportation costs and speed of delivery may dictate the purchase of these items by each plant from its own local vendors. Nevertheless, small items of fairly high value, such as tool bits, micrometers, and grinding wheels, as well as those for which quantity lots bring discounts, may best be bought by a central purchasing department. Since the transportation costs on such items would be relatively insignificant, such an arrangement might thereby be more economical than would be the case were each plant to make its purchases separately. Furthermore, centralized purchasing may in many cases specify branch-plant delivery and still gain quantity discounts. However, centralized purchasing for scattered plants requires systematized control in each plant over quantity and quality supplied. Otherwise, full value for the company's monetary expenditure may not be realized.

Whereas an incompetent or not too energetic purchasing agent may waste many of the company's dollars, so, on the other hand, will a competent buyer repay his salary many times over. The purchasing agent should be able to deal with vendors on technical details, use, and cost of the materials he is required to buy, and he should be familiar with the markets that supply those materials. An individual with an analytical mind and perhaps with an engineering background frequently makes a good purchasing agent. He should be willing to lean over backward to be helpful to the rest of the plant organization. In fact, "service" is the middle name of any good purchasing agent.

In most concerns where the purchasing agent is considered to be one of the major executives of the firm, he has the power to execute purchasing contracts for the company. Where such power is not granted, generally some other executive such as the treasurer or controller reviews all purchase orders before they are sent out.

Where the purchasing department is large and several purchasing agents are required, it is common practice to divide the duties among the personnel according to the types of purchases made. One buyer may be assigned to purchase the major raw material; another, the supplies; another, plant equipment; etc. This functional division of effort makes for increased specialization and permits each purchasing representative through close association with a particular trade to gain a better "feel" of the market to which he is assigned.

11-2.4 Constructive Purchasing Policies

The reputation of many an industrial organization rises and falls on the policies of its purchasing department. An enterprise wherein the purchasing department is noted for its *fair dealings* with vendors is very likely to gain for itself the respect and confidence of the trade. *Sharp practice,* on the other hand, will breed only sharp practice in return. It is poor policy for a purchasing agent, instead of negotiating and bargaining for a fair price, to use means fair or foul to browbeat the vendor down to an absurdly low price. The person who takes unfair advantage of the vendor in one transaction is likely to find that the difference is recouped in a subsequent deal. Furthermore, a price that is too low may force a supplier out of business and thus be a factor in destroying a sound source of supply for the purchaser.

It is, however, the duty of the purchasing agent to see that a vendor does not take advantage of him in the matter of price. The wise purchasing agent makes it his business to learn everything possible about the vendor's manufacturing processes. By piecing this information together and upon consideration of the vendor's proposals, he generally can determine whether or not the price is fair.

In a sense, the purchasing agent should maintain a judicial attitude on the disposition of all matters between his enterprise and its vendors to see that both parties are dealt with fairly. He should practice at all times the golden rule—not the David Harum version: "Do unto others as they would do unto you, only do it first."

Optimum performance cannot be expected from a purchasing department without close cooperation from other departments, particularly production. *Quantity discounts* are allowed on some materials when the order size exceeds a certain minimum. Purchasing has to know anticipated monthly or yearly usage requirements before the actual economy of quantity discounts can be evaluated. The effect of large orders on inventory holding costs and on operating policy should be forwarded to purchasing from the affected operating units. Similarly, the purchasing department should be informed which orders must be filled immediately to avoid delays in production. It is false economy to negotiate for lower prices when delivery delay costs exceed price discounts.

Everyday *social and business courtesies* apply in the relationships with vendors and their representatives. For example, the practice of either interviewing salespersons promptly or advising them immediately when an interview must be delayed is a small but important consideration in good purchasing relationships. Yet altogether too many purchasing agents are careless in this respect and frequently keep their vendors' salespersons waiting for considerable periods in the reception room.

The *acceptance of personal gifts and favors* from vendors, particularly Christmas gifts, world series or football tickets, and free dinners and entertainment, is a rather controversial issue. Some purchasing agents are not opposed to accepting personal gifts and maintain that in their subsequent relationships with vendors they do not let the gifts influence their decisions. However, other purchasing agents state that ultimately in one form or another their company always pays for the cost of vendors' gifts. Hence they refuse to accept all gifts which are for their own personal use or which cannot be construed as institutional advertising.

Broken delivery promises and the vendor's inability to make delivery on the date specified are continual causes of friction between vendor and customer. The reasons for this lack of performance may be many. The customer may not forecast his requirements sufficiently far in advance to allow the vendor adequate time to make delivery. Or the customer may arbitrarily engage in the efficient practice of specifying "Rush" or "Wanted at Once" on all his orders. Should this happen, the vendor either endeavors to accommodate the customer and make quick delivery—which invariably runs up the prices asked of that customer—or the vendor gets the impression that the customer is "crying wolf" on every order and hence pays no attention whatsoever to any of his urgent delivery requests. Still another cause of broken delivery promises is that which results from the vendor's insufficient knowledge or control of the backlog of orders in his plant. As a result he promises delivery of goods beyond his capacity to produce.

Cancellations of purchase orders violate the purchase contract and are often destructive to good business relationships between vendor and customer. However, cancellations frequently are necessary and may result from design or model changes, improvements in manufacturing methods, or conditions beyond the customer's control. Thus it is customary to permit concerns to make cancellations on purchases, provided that the material has not been placed in process and that no binding commitments (such as for new machines or equipment) have been made from which relief cannot be gained. If, however, the material is in process or such commitments have been made and a cancellation becomes necessary, the purchaser may agree to pay the costs incurred up to that point rather than have the material carried through to completion.

Another and rather interesting purchasing policy is that which determines whether the department is to be permitted to engage in *speculation.* Speculation may be defined as the purchase of materials in excess of normal requirements and in anticipation of a price rise or a market shortage.

Pure speculation occurs when the materials are purchased primarily for subsequent resale at a higher price and hence for a profit. Since manufacturing enterprises are not generally incorporated to engage in such transactions for profit, pure speculation should be discouraged. If, however, it is permitted, the profit or loss resulting therefrom should be segregated from the normal operating profits of the enterprise; otherwise a true picture of the operating efficiency is not obtainable.

Operational speculation is simply advance buying for manufacturing purposes in an attempt to cover the operating needs for some future period. Although it is more readily condoned and more commonly engaged in by industry as a whole, even so, this practice can be somewhat dangerous as it tends to decrease the liquidity of the enterprise by tying up money in more materials than should normally be carried, involves greater storage and carrying costs (space charges, insurance, taxes), and increases the business risk of obsolescence.

Of course, in the purchase of certain commodities, there is the perfectly legitimate practice of *hedging* or the use of the "futures contract" to protect against a price rise. By contracting both to buy and to sell at some future date, the purchasing agent in a sense operates on both sides of the fence and is assured of at least breaking even in the event of a change in price in either direction.

Reciprocity is simply that purchasing policy whereby the enterprise makes a practice of buying from its customers. Some purchasing agents feel that it is not fair to let the prospects of future sales to a customer influence their purchasing decision or to force them into buying from that customer an inferior article or one at a higher price. Others feel that a valued customer is entitled to a fair share of their business and tend to favor their customers if at all possible. The prevailing opinion on this matter seems to be that reciprocity in moderation builds up customer good will. Thus when a customer's product can be used, it is generally believed that he should be given the same opportunity to bid for the business as is given all other vendors. The factors of quality, quantity, time, and price being relatively equal, the enterprise may then justifiably buy from its customer if it so desires.

Perspective 11A   A PURCHASER'S SUPPLIER RATING SYSTEM

Many factors influence the choice of which supplier to buy from. The National Association of Purchasing Agents developed a cost-ratio plan for numerically rating suppliers.

The plan attempts to attach a number to each of four major procurement factors: price, quality, delivery, and service. The supplier who consistently provides the required material at the lowest net value-cost is, in theory, most frequently selected. The steps for determining the rating, supplemented by sample calculations, are summarized below.

1. Net delivery price = list price − discounts + freight cost + insurance, taxes, etc.

2. Quality cost ratio $= \dfrac{\text{material quality costs}}{\text{total value of purchases}}$

The material quality costs are taken from past quality reports on purchases made from each supplier. These expenses include the cost for laboratory tests, incoming inspections, processing inspection reports, handling and packaging rejects, spoilage and waste, and manufacturing losses. Most of these costs are prepared by production and quality-control departments. The yearly trend of the ratio indicates whether quality levels are being maintained or improved by the supplier.

3. Acquisition cost ratio $= \dfrac{\text{acquisition and continuity costs}}{\text{total value of purchases}}$

The denominator of the equation is the same as in Step 2. The numerator is derived by the purchasing department from the cost of sale negotiations, communication tolls, surveys, premium transportation, monitoring, and progress reporting.

4. Delivery cost ratio = acquisition cost ratio + promises-kept penalty
The cost of deliveries later than promised is expressed as a percentage of the total value of purchases delivered.

5. Service cost ratio $= \dfrac{\text{maximum possible rating} - \text{supplier rating}}{\text{maximum possible rating}}$

(A supplier rating below a given level, such as 60, automatically makes the ratio = 1.0.) Service costs are determined from absolute ratings of special considerations which suppliers offer with products and services. These ratings are converted to a penalty percentage and charged against the supplier lacking the considerations. The following list illustrates how a supplier service cost ratio of $(100 - 70)/100 = 0.3$ could be obtained.

Maximum Points	Category	Supplier Rating
	Competence and Ability:	
15	Product development and advancement	11
15	Product leadership and reputation	9
10	Technical ability of staff	9
10	Capacity for volume production	8
10	Financial solvency and profitability	8
	Attitudes and Special Considerations:	
5	Labor relations record	2
10	Business approach	8
5	Field service and adaptability to changes	2
10	Warranty conditions	6
10	Communication of progress data	7
100	Total Points	70

6. Net value cost = net delivery price + (net delivery price X sum of ratios from Steps 2, 4, and 5)

The comparison of suppliers is based on their present net delivery price modified by additional costs expected from the history of their past performance. For instance, a net value cost for one supplier could result in the following price and penalty pattern:

Step 1: Price quote ($114,300) − discount (10% X $114,300) + freight ($600) = net delivery price ($103,470)
Steps 2-5: Sum of ratios = quality cost (2.2%) + delivery cost (1.2%) + service cost (0.3%) = 3.7%
Step 6: Net value cost = $103,470 + ($103,470 X 0.037) = $107,300

Such ratings are then compared for each order to identify the preferred supplier.*

*SOURCE: *Evaluation of Supplier Performance,* a pamphlet published by the National Association of Purchasing Agents, New York, 1963.

COMMENT: An interesting viewpoint is developed by reviewing the rating system as it appears to the supplier. The most pertinent source of information by which a supplier can evaluate his products and services is the response of the purchaser. A purchasing policy is dedicated to maximizing returns from supply expenditures—at least that is what the supplier must believe if he is to use his sales as a criterion for improving his competitive position.

Suppliers recognize that few purchasing agents will give 100 per cent of their orders to one vendor, but there is some maximum percentage they will give. The difference between this maximum percentage and the percentage being supplied is a measure of the opportunity cost for a supplier. Assuming a purchaser will reveal the maximum percentage, the supplier can see what potential sales are available from each buyer. The potential is an indication of how much the supplier can afford to spend to make his product and services more attractive to the purchaser. Then the problem narrows to determining what must be done to improve performance enough to obtain more orders.

11-3   EXTERNAL TRANSPORTATION

The external transportation of materials involves *shipping* (preparation of goods for delivery to the customer), *traffic* (transportation of both outgoing and incoming items), and *receiving* (acceptance of incoming articles). As indicated earlier, these functions are the responsibility of the traffic manager. The everyday activities of a traffic department generally include preparation of goods for shipment; selection of the carriers; handling of all matters pertaining to shipping classifications, tariffs, and rates; weighing, marking, documenting, and loading goods for shipment; handling, documenting, and inspecting goods received; and processing claims for damaged goods. The traffic manager may also take on such special duties as securing transportation for business trips of company personnel, arranging import–export shipments, and handling rate cases before regulating agencies.

11-3.1   Packaging for Shipment

Virtually all outgoing material is packaged, marked, and weighed preparatory to shipment. Packing containers in general are subject to three cardinal rules:

1. They should be designed to minimize breakage in transit.

2. They should make for ease of handling.

3. They should conform to the commodity classification regulations contained in the "Consolidated Freight Classification," the "Official Express Classification," or the "Postal Laws and Regulations" which provide the necessary data for economical shipping by the standards of the type of carrier to be selected. Copies of these publications should be available in every shipping department and consulted whenever there is any doubt as to classification.

Shipping containers can serve purposes besides protection and handling convenience. Cardboard containers frequently display advertising or identification messages. Special measures may be introduced to give added protection from fungi or pests when long storage periods are anticipated. A sad documentary to recent practices is the increased attention awarded to "burglar-proof" containers. Recent developments for bulk shipments, particularly via boat transportation, are designed to thwart outright theft by mass packing and better means of inspecting contents.

Efficiency dictates certain additional rules that apply to packing. Container and package sizes and styles should be standardized as far as possible. Interior closures and dividers can often be utilized for odd-sized items rather than adding to the variety of containers used. Paper waste, particularly old newspaper, can often be used as fill-in material. Multiple wrappings and containers should be avoided through the design of a few standard containers with adequate protective provisions. Cartons, wooden boxes, and other containers can often be reused and should be handled and opened with this thought in mind. Wherever possible, packing should be made an integral part of the manufacturing process to avoid rehandling.

Among the more common types of containers are the corrugated cardboard box and the wire-bound or strap-bound wood shook. *Unit-load* packages have enjoyed ever-increasing popularity in recent years. These are constructed by bundling one or more parts on a standard low-cost wood pallet which is used as the base of the package. For example, a unit package can be made to ship automobile radiators by properly wrapping and protecting 32 of them, building them up in layers on the egg-crate principle, and strapping them to a pallet. Material shipped in this fashion can be readily handled by fork-truck (see Fig. 11-7), which makes for low-cost handling and simplifies the storage problem at both originating point and destination. Furthermore, packaging costs are comparable with other means, and the pallet base permits a nesting of the material so as to reduce the possibility of damage in transit.

However, the advantages of pallets are somewhat offset by the initial cost of the pallet itself, by its adding shipping weight to the package, and by the cost of returning it to the shipper. Many concerns have found that these added costs more than offset the reductions in handling and storage costs. Also, it has not been found practical to standardize on pallet construction and size throughout industry so as to permit interchangeability and reuse. Nevertheless, the introduction of lightweight, low-cost, "expendable" wood and kraftboard pallets for one-way usage only has tended to minimize the afore-mentioned disadvantages.

Containerization is a basic concept in shipping packages that holds promise for the future. "Containers" are large boxlike units into which products may be packed for shipment via truck, rail, or ship. They can be locked for pilferage protection, and those used for perishables can be refrigerated. An extension of the unit-load principle, containers aid both shippers and carriers in faster loading, reduced terminal operations, and less contamination, damage, and loss. They also facilitate door-to-door service and lower rates by combined truck and rail "piggyback" or truck/rail and marine "fishyback" routing. In most cases the containers are owned and supplied by the carriers, who attempt to spot them throughout the country for availability to shippers as needed.

11-3.2 Modes of Transportation

There may be several alternative modes of transportation available for the shipment of goods. Where *boat* transportation is available, it provides a slow but inexpensive means of shipping large quantities of bulk material (see Fig. 11-3). *Railway freight* is perhaps the best means of hauling heavy or bulky goods long distances, particularly in carload lots, where waterway transportation is not available. The U.S. Postal Service and United Parcel Service are fast and handy carriers for small articles but involve considerably greater cost. *Motor freight* is an excellent way of shipping over short hauls, particularly where full carload shipments are not possible and where door-to-door delivery with but one handling is desirable. *Air freight* is suitable for light to heavy items and is finding favor where faster delivery over considerable distances is required.

The method of shipment and the routing over which the material travels may be specified in the purchase contract, but if not they are the prerogative of the shipper. Selection of the mode of transportation frequently involves a knowledge on the part of the traffic manager of the classifications into which all commodities are grouped by the carriers and from which the tariffs are determined.

A number of companies that regularly make shipments to customers over a limited area find it more economical to maintain their own fleet of trucks than to use the common carriers. These concerns argue that they thereby

Figure 11-3 Largest ore carrier on the Great Lakes unloading iron ore taconite pellets. (Courtesy of U.S. Steel.)

can give their customers faster and more dependable service and can likewise simplify their packing and shipping procedures.

The cost of damaged merchandise must be considered in conjunction with the cost of physically moving the material. Excessive shock from rough handling or inadequate tie-downs can mar external surfaces, cause spillage of liquids, or even destroy an item being shipped. Prolonged vibration may seriously damage fragile instruments. Exposure to extreme atmospheric conditions may ruin shipping containers and harm their contents. Other deleterious conditions which contribute to damaged merchandise include salt spray, sand, dust, fungi, humidity, and sunshine. Thus a theoretically correct package gives protection only when subjected to expected exposure and handling.

11-3.3 Traffic Procedures

As each shipment is made, forms are prepared to notify the customer that the goods are in transit and to record the transfer of goods to and from the carrier. When the goods are shipped by common carrier, this record usually takes the form of a *bill of lading,* which not only serves as a promise from the carrier to deliver the goods to the customer (consignee) but also acknowledges the carrier's receipt of the goods from the shipper (consignor). The shipper generally sends the customer a copy of the shipping papers indicating when and how shipment has been made. This information is helpful to the customer's purchasing and receiving departments and also to his traffic manager, should it become necessary to *trace* and *expedite* the shipment en route.

Generally speaking, common carriers guarantee the safe arrival of all goods they accept. When goods arrive in a damaged condition, it is prima facie evidence of the carrier's liability. However, the carrier relieves himself of the burden of proof by asking the consignees to sign a receipt for the goods. A careful inspection of the condition of the goods before acceptance by the consignee's receiving department is therefore important. When goods are received in a damaged condition, the traffic manager files a *damage claim* which starts negotiations toward collecting for the damage done. Also, a wise traffic manager whose own goods repeatedly arrive at their destination damaged asks for an investigation and return of the damaged containers if possible. He then endeavors to fix the blame on the carrier, the design of the container, its packing and sealing, or the loading procedures, so that the difficulty may be corrected.

Demurrage has been defined as the higher mathematics used by railroads to penalize shippers for delays in handling freight cars. Shippers are granted reasonable free time to load and receivers a like amount of time to unload each car. Thereafter, demurrage is charged on a per diem basis. However, by scheduling cars to arrive only as fast as they can be loaded or unloaded, by educating suppliers to send shipping papers to arrive in advance of the material, by better materials-handling equipment, and by holding foremen concerned strictly accountable for demurrage charges, this extra cost can be minimized.

11-3.4 Receiving

The receiving department is responsible for making and checking all receipts for both condition and count, for seeing that the material is delivered to its desired location, and for reporting the receipt to the proper individuals. As discussed above, the receiving department is charged with the nonacceptance of all articles that are visibly damaged. It is also required to report promptly all articles found to be damaged when the container is opened together with any shortages discovered in the shipment.

The purchasing department usually supplies the receiving department with a copy of each purchase order from which the latter department may ascertain the quantity and description of the material on order as well as other pertinent information as to its point of use, vendor, method of shipping, etc. The incoming material may then be checked for completeness against this purchase-order copy.

The receiving department may notify the purchasing department that the material has been received by returning its copy of the purchase order properly marked. Or it may use the invoice memorandum or shipping papers supplied by the vendor to serve the same purpose. Better still, the receiving department may use a *receiving notice,* or "inbound notice," as it is sometimes called. This form usually is serially numbered for easy posting and reference. In general, the receiving-notice form is preferable to the other notification methods mentioned, for several copies can be supplied, and it simplifies the procedure where partial shipments are received. Copies of this notice are usually sent to the purchasing department and to the department or person where the requisition originated. A copy is also included with the material for identification purposes, and a file copy remains with the receiving department.

Where material is sent first of all to a receiving-inspection department for a thorough quality check, the receiving notice may be used also to record the inspection results, or a separate inspection form can be used for those data. The receiving-inspection department is generally a part of the plant's inspection function as it checks the quality of raw materials received and therefore is closely linked with overall quality control. When substandard material is discovered, it is usually reported to the purchasing agent, who arranges with the vendor for its disposition.

11-4   INVENTORY CONTROL

While the desired amount of materials or size of inventories is readily established by management policy, the administration of that policy to achieve the desired results is a considerably more difficult and seemingly endless process. The activities employed in this process are blanketed under the name "inventory control."

Effective inventory control is aimed at ensuring that an adequate but not excessive bank of materials is on hand at all times to meet operating requirements. Under ideal operation, materials would move through a plant in a smoothly flowing stream, and no storage of material would be required at any point. While this ideal is seldom completely realized, some companies with high manufacturing volume approach it by close scheduling (in terms of a few days or, in some cases, even a few hours or minutes) of incoming materials prior to time of use. Then by liberal use of line-production and automation techniques, these companies minimize in-process inventories.

However, for most companies inventories perform two functions. First, they act as "safety stocks" of material, or in effect, short-term insurance against fluctuations in supply, manufacturing, or sales. Material stocks effectively cushion these fluctuations, while normal control procedures become operative. Here feedback control, with its observation of conditions, delayed reactions, and overcorrections is a part of this system and helps explain the need for safety stocks. Second, inventories permit a company to operate with disconnected processes in the manufacturing and distribution cycles. As we saw in earlier chapters, for many companies efficiency is best achieved by progressing from materials supplier to product customer in a series of jumps interspersed with resting points. Were it not for inventories at these resting points, "interruptible" processes would not be feasible and resultant scheduling hardships and inherent delays would cause costs to soar.

The size of the inventory carried is based principally on the relative costs involved. Large quantities of slow-moving materials tie up cash that is thus unavailable for more productive pursuits, and their storage incurs substantial carrying costs. On the other hand, the costs of not maintaining an adequate inventory likewise are great. Low inventories limit the flexibility of production schedules, prevent manufacture of economic-lot quantities, eliminate the price advantage of quantity purchases, and furnish no insurance against vendor and shipping delays. Thus the maintenance of a proper balance between the costs of carrying excessive stocks of materials and those which result from inadequate stocks is one of the principal objectives of good inventory control.

It should be pointed out that high inventories are frequently used to offset managerial incompetence, i.e., as a substitute for good management. If an enterprise is willing to retain large reserve stocks of material, these can often cover up the shortcomings of a weak organization and loose policies and procedures. By the same token, a company which wishes to minimize investment in inventories must demand greater effort on the part of its organization and in general run a tight show.

In addition to regulating material quantities, inventory control is concerned with the systematic receipt, storage, disbursement, and recording of material in a manner that supplies the desired degree of service to the enterprise and minimizes the cost of that service.

11-5 QUANTITY OF INVENTORY

The quantitative control of inventories in most storerooms is accomplished by three kinds of papers: (1) replenishment requisitions; (2) withdrawal requisitions; and (3) perpetual-inventory records.

The use of *purchase requisitions* to initiate inventory-replenishment orders with outside vendors was discussed in Section 11-2.2. Where the material stocked is manufactured in the plant, similar *manufacturing requisitions* are issued by the stores or inventory-control personnel to initiate manufacturing orders with the plant.

Materials are withdrawn from the storeroom only upon receipt of a formal *material requisition.* These requisitions are analogous to bank withdrawal slips or checks and are presented for "payment" in materials at the storeroom. Return of unused or overdrawn goods calls for the use of a *stores credit slip,* which is a material requisition in reverse and is similar in form and information contained.

Perpetual-inventory records are established for each item stocked and show the historical movement of the item in and out of the storeroom as well as the current balance on hand. Practically all such records are prepared in terms of unit quantities such as number of pieces, pounds, gallons, etc. Many also include evaluation data so that the value of the stock carried can be ascertained for factory accounting purposes. Perpetual-inventory records not only provide the information necessary for effective monetary and quantitative control of materials but also are vitally necessary to the scheduling of production. Where the backlog of production orders is great, this backlog must be translated into material requirements which are to be ordered and made available as necessary to meet this backlog. Thus, where this apportionment of material is large in relation to the amount of material carried in stock, it is common practice to provide scheduling information by recording the material "apportioned" with respect to that "available".

Clarification of the following terms commonly used in perpetual-inventory records may be required:

1. *Ordered* or *on order*   Quantity of material on order with the plant through a manufacturing requisition or with the purchasing department through a purchase requisition

2. *Received* or *in*   Quantity of material supplied to the storeroom in response to a manufacturing or purchase requisition

3. *Issued, disbursed,* or *out*   Quantity of material issued to the plant, sent to a customer, etc., in accordance with a material requisition or customer order

4. *Balance* or *stock on hand*   Quantity and/or value of material physically on hand as of the date indicated

5. *Apportioned* or *allocated*   Quantity of material applied on or earmarked for future orders already planned but not yet issued to the plant or to a customer

6. *Available*   Quantity of material available for the plant or customer in the sense that it is either actually on hand or on order but not already earmarked

The minimum, or *min,* refers to the ordering point or flag point at which a new order should be placed to replenish used stock. The min on an item is set so that stock will not be depleted during the *lead time* required for the new order to be processed in manufacturing or with a vendor, as the case may be. When the minimum is reached, sufficient material is generally ordered to bring the stock up to a maximum, or *max.* The max and min are usually stated in terms of number of units, as a min of 30 pieces and a max of 100 pieces. Occasionally, it may be preferable to translate these into time units, as a min of 3 weeks' supply and a max of 10 weeks' supply. Some companies add an *absolute min* below the regular ordering min. This is the danger point below which the on-hand stock balance should never go. However, if the absolute min should ever be reached, it indicates that the on-hand stock is dangerously low and that the material on the replacement order should be expedited for immediate delivery lest the stockroom run out of that material.

There are many types of perpetual-inventory records in use by industry today, the composition and format of each being dependent upon the nature and value of the materials involved and upon the degree of control required. These records may be posted manually, by bookkeeping machines, or on data-processing equipment. Manual posting requires only a pen or pencil, some record cards, and a file. Bookkeeping machines which compute the effect of receipts and disbursements are moderate in cost, while the more automatic data-processing equipment can run into fancy figures. Posting by hand is the slowest method; data processing equipment, generally the fastest and certainly the most versatile. Which of these methods is used depends on (1) the number of items stocked; (2) the value of the inventory and effect of market-price fluctuations and possible obsolescence on that value; (3) the frequency and volume of transactions; (4) the importance of current records to operating decisions; and (5) the degree of integration of inventory control with production control and with sales. In general, the greater the magnitude of these five factors collectively, the greater the mechanization, automaticity, and investment in record-keeping equipment that is warranted.

Data-processing equipment is of particular value in inventory-control work where the daily volume of transactions is great (as in large stockrooms), where a heavy investment in inventories requires a constant, up-to-the-minute check on inventory balances and maximum and minimum limits, and where there are many widely scattered branch warehouses. In the last instance, central control of inventories by item and by warehouse can be effected without costly duplication of hand-posted records otherwise required.

A computerized inventory system can be of major assistance to the production scheduler. Most production involves an end product containing parts supplied by vendors and parts produced in the plant. A scheduler must be concerned with both classes of supplies. More frequent reports of actual inventory levels allow smaller safety stocks to be held because there is less chance an unusual demand will deplete the stock on hand before being recognized. Once a computerized system has been established, shorter reporting intervals do not add much cost. When production rates and demand forecasts are combined with current stock levels in a computer program, different production schedules can be simulated, and their effect on future inventory status can be evaluated.

11-5.1 Ordering Policy

The nature of the material stored determines whether replenishment requisitions are initiated by a centralized inventory-control division of the production-control function or by the storeroom personnel. Production materials hinge on production requirements and schedules and generally are ordered by the production-control department. Replenishment of supplies and maintenance items, on the other hand, is based largely on withdrawals, with the replenishment request originating directly from the storeroom. In the latter case, a store clerk, on posting withdrawals, compares the balance on hand with the min established. When the min is reached, he refers the records to his superiors for determination of the ordering quantity and data required.

Ordering quantities are based on the rate of past consumption, as determined from records together with anticipated future requirements, and are tempered by the company's policy on inventory levels. A simplified representation of material flow is shown in Figure 11-4. The triangular pattern results from receiving an order of material (vertical line) and a steady rate of usage (sloping line) over a replenishment period of time (bottom line). This basic pattern incorporates several principles of inventory analysis. As detailed below, these principles are the basis for economic lot size calculations presented in Perspective 11B.

1. Minima are set so that, when fresh stock arrives, a small reserve of material is still on the shelves. This dormant reserve stock prevents the stockroom from being entirely out of that material should some slight delay in getting the fresh stock develop, but of course this reserve increases the *average inventory* carried.

2. A *stockout cost* occurs when an item is needed but not available. Ordering policies are based on inventory patterns expected from previous experience, but unusual conditions can occur which cause serious consequences. The amount of stock held in reserve (safety stock level) should serve as a measure of the damage that will result if the stock is exhausted. This cost of running out of stock generally is difficult to determine. The direct cost of halting a production line because critical materials are missing is relatively easy to predict, but the side effects such as lower morale or a reduced pace for the work force are awkward to quantify.

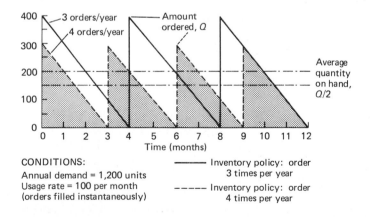

CONDITIONS:
Annual demand = 1,200 units
Usage rate = 100 per month
(orders filled instantaneously)

——— Inventory policy: order 3 times per year

- - - - Inventory policy: order 4 times per year

Figure 11-4 Idealized pattern of material usage and replenishment. In reality, the usage rate for material is seldom constant (straight sloping lines) and the replenishment is never instantaneous (vertical lines). However, a straight line is a reasonable approximation of usage that varies slightly above and below the line. Also by replacing orders before inventory levels reach zero, replenishment is in effect instantaneous because a new order is delivered close to the time the supply on hand is exhausted.

Immediate sales may be lost owing to stockouts, and even more serious, former customers may be lost permanently to competitors when deliveries are delayed.

3. Material in stock incurs certain carrying charges called *cost of possession* which make it desirable to carry a low average inventory:

• Material in stock represents an outlay of the company's cash funds. Money invested in any enterprise is subject to certain interest charges that are based on the business risk factors for the enterprise involved. Unless the money so invested brings a return to its investors, that money will be withdrawn and invested elsewhere, Money spent on idle or dormant stocks of material is not bringing any return on its investment.

• Stocked material occupies space that must bear its proportionate cost of heat, light, taxes, repairs, and depreciation on the building.

• Insurance is generally carried on all material in stock, thus introducing another cost factor.

• Material in stock is always subject to possible deterioration or damage. Also there is the risk of obsolescence as technical advances or changes in methods and materials render the stocked material valueless for the purpose for which it was originally intended.

4. Each time material is ordered, certain *costs of acquisition* are incurred which make it more desirable to order large quantities infrequently than to order small quantities frequently:

• In the case of purchased material, expense is incurred in the preparation and placing of the purchase order, the receiving, handling, and invoice paying.

• In the case of manufactured material, there is the cost of production planning the order, clerical costs, costs connected with the issuance of tools, gages, tickets, work orders, and blueprints. Also a part of this cost for each order is the time required to set up the necessary machines.

From the foregoing, it can readily be seen that costs of possession and of acquisition operate at cross purposes to each other. Low costs of possession point to the ordering of smaller quantities at more frequent intervals. Low costs of acquisition mean larger quantities per order and hence less frequent orders. Economic-lot quantity formulas establish mathematically that the quantity to order for which the possession and acquisition costs added together are at a minimum (see Fig. 11-5).

Actually in any situation there is not one but a family of economic-lot curves which take into consideration the item value and its activity. Fast-moving items are revealed as those for which inventories should be kept low with more frequent orders. Slower-moving items, on the other hand, can have higher stocks and less frequent orders. The net result can be no overall increase in inventories compared with the traditional method in use by many companies of "across-the-board ordering," e.g., ordering for all items, regardless of value or activity, 3 months' requirements at each purchase. This

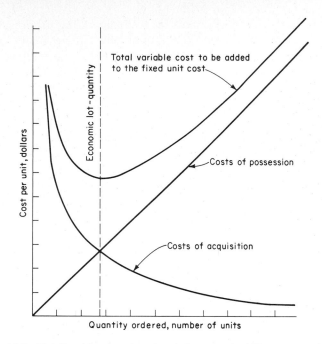

Figure 11-5 Relationship of cost and ordering quantity. Where costs-of-possession and costs-of-acquisition lines cross, the total variable cost is a minimum.

revelation of the ordering differences between fast and slow items is one of the principal uses of economic-lot formulas.

The validity and hence usefulness of calculated economic-lot quantities hinges on many assumptions. For example, withdrawals from stock usually are assumed to be at a constant rate while in actual practice withdrawal quantities may fluctuate violently. In like fashion, manufacturing techniques, operator productivity, and purchase prices all are assumed to bear a direct relationship to storage space and time. Any one or all of these may oversimplify the facts of a particular situation and influence the accuracy of the formula.

Other factors tending to limit the usefulness of economic-lot formulas also enter the picture. Market considerations, such as anticipated rising or falling prices and abundance or scarcity of supply, are important in some situations. From the standpoint of competition and customer good will, it may be desirable to store larger quantities of finished or semifinished goods than a formula would indicate, simply so that sizable orders may be filled promptly from stock. Purchase discounts and transportation costs, particularly where carload lots are involved, both have an important bearing on the lot size. Financial policies, determined, for example, from the company's cash position, must also be considered. Thus in establishing the quantities to order, most companies simply make their top inventory-control personnel aware of the cost factors affecting economic-lot quantities and rely on their judgment guided by such policy considerations as are applicable.

Allied with the question of quantities to order is that of *turnover* of material in stock. Turnover is the rate at which material moves in and out of stock and may be defined technically as the ratio of the value of material used during the year, at cost, to the value of the average annual inventory maintained during the same period, also at cost. Turnover varies with the kind of material, type of industry, and nature of the manufacturing processes. In general, raw materials turn over more slowly than do work in process and finished products. Industries making high-priced goods in volume tend to turn over materials faster than do manufacturers of low-priced off-the-shelf items and those making job-order goods. Continuous-process companies likewise turn over inventories much more rapidly than do companies with variety, layout-by-process manufacture. By a close scrutiny of turnover, a stockkeeper can find, investigate, and possibly dispose of obsolescent materials which might otherwise lie idle in stock indefinitely.

Perspective 11B ECONOMIC ORDER QUANTITY

The relationships between the costs of possession and acquisition, displayed in Figure 11-5, and the usage-replenishment cycle shown in Figure 11-4 can be expressed in a mathematical model. Many simplifying assumptions are made for the sake of workability. The basic inventory model, called the *economic order quantity* (EOQ) formula, is no exception. Though many of the relationships used in calculating the EOQ are idealized, it still provides reasonably accurate figures for practical applications. A host of more refined models are available for closer representations of actual conditions. However, the cost of attaining greater reality in models must be paid in added mathematical complexity.

The economic order quantity is the size of order which minimizes the cost of acquiring and holding an inventory item. The ordering cost and carrying cost vary inversely with each other, that is, when a large order is placed, the ordering cost goes down while the carrying cost increases. The reason is easy to see in Figure 11-4. In the situation shown, one inventory policy is to order material three times a year. Thus ordering costs occur three times. In the other inventory policy shown, four orders are placed to obtain the same amount of material annually. By placing four orders instead of three, the amount ordered each time, Q, is less. A smaller Q yields a lower average inventory, $Q/2$. Since total carrying costs are a function of the average inventory, and total ordering costs depend on the number of times orders are placed, the cost of carrying decreases when the cost of ordering increases.

If we let the symbol O indicate the ordering cost per order and D the annual demand, then the total annual ordering costs equal OD/Q. By letting H indicate the cost to hold one item in stock for a year, the expression for the total annual carrying costs is $HQ/2$. Note that $Q/2$ is the average number of items on hand.

Adding the two cost expressions gives the total basic inventory cost: $OD/Q + HQ/2$. To find the economic order quantity, we can use trial-and-error tabulation, graphing, or algebra. To illustrate each of these methods, they will be applied to a problem in which

D = annual demand = 20,000 units
O = ordering cost = $46.00 per order
H = carrying cost = $0.115 per unit

A tabular solution is shown below. It is a trial-and-error method of solving for the EOQ. Given annual demand, carrying cost per unit, and ordering cost per order, the order quantity is determined by dividing the annual demand (20,000) by the number of orders per year. Then the total carrying costs equal half this value, multiplied by $0.115. Total ordering costs equal $46 times the number of orders per year. Total basic inventory cost is the sum of the ordering and carrying costs. Calculations are continued until a minimum point is identified, the EOQ. Note at this point that the carrying costs equal the ordering costs.

(1) Number of orders per year	1	2	4	5	6	10	20
(2) Order quantity: 20,000 ÷ (1)	20,000	10,000	5,000	4,000	3,333	2,000	1,000
(3) Carrying cost: $0.115 × (2)/2	$1,150	$575	$288	$230	$192	$115	$58
(4) Ordering cost: $46 × (1)	$46	$92	$184	$230	$276	$460	$920
(5) Total annual cost: (3) + (4)	$1,196	$667	$472	$460	$468	$575	$978
				EOQ			

The same solution could be obtained by graphing the data; it would produce the pattern shown in Figure 11-5. The intersection of the lines representing costs of acquisition and possession indicates the EOQ, in units of inventory, on the horizontal axis. Recognizing that ordering and carrying costs are equal at the minimum total cost point, and using the same symbols for the inventory factors, we have the equation

$$O\frac{D}{Q} = H\frac{Q}{2} \text{ (at EOQ)}$$

where D = annual demand = 20,000 units
O = ordering cost = $46.00 per order
H = carrying cost = $0.115 per unit
Q = order quantity

Rearranging the equation to collect the order quantity symbols Q on one side,

$$OD = \frac{H}{2}Q^2 \quad \frac{2OD}{H} = Q^2$$

and then taking the square root of both sides produces

$$Q = \sqrt{\frac{2OD}{H}}$$

which is the formula for the EOQ.

$$Q = \sqrt{\frac{2 \times \$46 \times 20,000}{\$0.115}} = \sqrt{\frac{\$1,840,000}{\$0.115}}$$

$$= \sqrt{16,000,000} = 4,000 \text{ units} = \text{EOQ}$$

By manipulating the basic equation, we can calculate several other conditions associated with the EOQ:

$$\text{Basic annual inventory cost} = O\frac{D}{Q} + H\frac{Q}{2}$$

$$= \$46\,\frac{20,000}{4,000} + \$0.115\,\frac{4,000}{2}$$

$$= \$230 + \$230 = \$460$$

$$\text{Optimum number of orders per year} = \frac{D}{Q} = \frac{20,000}{4,000} = 5\ \text{orders}$$

$$\text{Optimum order interval (calendar days between orders)} = \frac{365\ \text{days/yr}}{\dfrac{D}{Q}} = \frac{365 \times Q}{D} = 73\ \text{days}$$

Perspective 11C   MATERIAL REQUIREMENTS PLANNING

A major innovation in production and inventory management has emerged in the last few years. It is called *material requirements planning* (MRP) and has found a wide and growing acceptance among manufacturers. Its departure from the traditional order-point system (see Perspective 11B) is described by Joseph A. Orlicky:

When it comes to managing inventories, there are two alternative basic approaches, or two sets of techniques, that can be employed in a manufacturing enterprise. They are:

1. Statistical Inventory Control (also called Order Point techniques—I will use these terms interchangeably)
2. Requirements Planning

Order Point is part-based, whereas Requirements Planning is product-oriented. Order Point utilizes data on the historical behavior of a part, while Requirements Planning ignores history and instead works with data on the relationship of components (the bill of material) that make up a product. Order Point looks at the past. Requirements Planning looks toward the future (as defined by a manufacturing master schedule).*

The following is a brief summary of MRP, according to Dr. Orlicky:

This type of inventory management system is a set of procedures and decision rules designed to determine requirements of inventory items on all levels below the end product, and to generate order action to meet these requirements.
    Main input is the product forecast or the master manufacturing schedule, and the two principal files are

1. Product structure (bill of material)
2. Part master (inventory records)

Many versions of Requirements Planning Systems are in existence—crude or refined, gross or net requirements, product lot oriented, time-period oriented, etc. They differ from one another in the scope of the planning horizon they cover and in the size of the so-called time buckets into which they segment the record data. Some regenerate all requirements and allocations in every requirements planning cycle. Some are non-regenerative (called "Net Change") in that they update old data by processing only net changes to the previous master schedule.

These systems also differ in the frequency of re-planning. The most advanced, and most useful, version is a non-periodic, non-batch, Net Change system with time-phased (time series) requirements and an automatic order generation capability.

Because of the high data volume that must be handled by a Requirements Planning System in a company with tens, and sometimes hundreds of thousands of records, as well as because of the high frequency of re-planning, requirements planning represents a job that can only be done on a computer.

It is one of the classic computer applications, enabling us to do a job that would have been impossible, or at least quite impractical, in pre-computer days.*

*SOURCE: "Requirements Planning Systems," *Presentations at APICS 13th International Conference,* 1970. For a more extensive presentation, see Joseph Orlicky, *Material Requirements Planning,* New York: McGraw-Hill, 1975.

11-5.2   Material Identification

Standard industrial practice classifies, through the use of symbols, all materials, parts, and products, as well as operations, departments, machines, factory accounts (for cost-accounting purposes), and occupations or jobs (as a part of job-evaluation analysis). Identification of such industrial entities by means of "shorthand" saves clerical and speaking time—just as abbreviations and nicknames are timesavers in social activities. Further, industrial symbols aid in sorting and segregating items under various classifications or group headings.

At this point we are concerned principally with the identification of materials by means of either *numerical* or *mnemonic* symbols. The numerical method classifies materials by assigning numbers to them much as libraries use the familiar Dewey decimal system to classify and identify books by subject matter. The mnemonic method uses combinations of letters and numbers which are easily memorized. Thus, one manufacturer of expanded-metal partitioning catalogues partition components by such symbols as P48 (panel 4 by 8 feet), WSL (slide wicket), SW37 (single swing door 3 by 7 feet), etc.

Materials in storage may be located either by *symbol* or by *index.* Where the former is used, one row of bins may take only parts carrying, for example, numbers in the 1000 series, the next row of bins, series 2000, etc. Each item in a grouping is permanently assigned to a bin section. Obviously such a system of storage is apt to waste space in one section and make for an overcrowded condition in the next, since the stocks of each item are seldom constant over a period of time. Thus it is common practice under such a material-locating system to provide a bin for each item that is adequate in size to store an average supply of that item and to allow additional space or bins in the same general area for surplus stock when, as, and if required.

A system of indexing, on the other hand, permits material to be stored in any bin that happens to be free at the moment, but of course requires that a record be made of the location or locations in which each item is stored. Under any index system, each bin section is classified in a fashion similar to the designation of houses in a city area. Thus each main aisle (avenue), subaisle (side street), and bin (house) is appropriately labeled with numbers or letters for ready identification. Very large warehouse areas frequently require use of charts or maps of the storeroom layout so that all items may be located quickly. Storage of material by index makes the most effective use of the storage space available but does entail accurate records and postings of receipts and disbursements if material is to be located.

Other systems of storeroom identification make use of paint, tags, or distinctive marks to segregate material. For example, the ends of rods, bars, and tubes or the edges of metal sheets are often painted with identifying colors to aid in segregating them by size, alloy, date of shipment, or vending company. Barrels or wagons used to collect turnings and scrap pieces of various alloy metals are frequently painted distinctive colors as are the machines on which the respective alloys are used, thus aiding in keeping alloy turnings and scrap segregated for resale and remelting.

Most job-order companies have the problem of identifying specific materials for specific production orders. Frequently similar or identical material may be in process concurrently, and the problem then becomes one of identifying and segregating each batch of material through the various operations. This problem has been solved in various ways, depending upon the nature of the material involved. Sometimes paint is used, the color identifying the lot. Tags can be employed, attached either to the material itself or, in the case of small parts, to the container in which they are stored. For machinery parts, the machine or order number may be imprinted or stamped on the part itself. Finally, materials that do not lend themselves to one of the foregoing procedures can often be kept separate by segregation alone as in separate bins, on separate pallets or skids, or on individual material-handling trucks.

11-6 PHYSICAL INVENTORY

An actual physical count of materials on hand is taken periodically so that adjustments may be made to correct cumulative errors in receipts and disbursements, incorrect postings or extensions, and possible omissions. Count of large items is taken manually or by weight; small items are usually weigh-counted on scales. Three methods of taking the physical inventory are in wide use, the application of each depending upon specific conditions involved in each case. These methods are:

1. Inventory at a stated time annually (as on New Year's Day) covering all items at that time. Generally, inventory is taken either at the end of the fiscal year for the enterprise or during a period when the stocks of the inventories as a whole are low. When the inventory is taken by this method, all production generally must stop and a special crew is organized for the job.

2. Periodic physical inventories of all items during the course of the year so that each item is inventoried at least once during the year. This method does not disrupt

operations in the plant and places a steady load on the personnel taking the inventory.

3. Inventory of each item whenever the stock on that item reaches its lowest point. Under this system, items are inventoried irregularly, but the time for the actual inventory is reduced to a minimum because of the small quantities involved.

A form of physical control of inventories takes place where the minimum or stand-by quantity is bonded in stock by tying together the required number of boxes or units, binding them with scotch tape, etc. When the bond on such material must be broken to meet requirements, it becomes a signal to the stores clerk that stocks should be replenished by sending through a new order. This form of control can be used either to supplement and furnish a double check on the perpetual-inventory records or, in cases where only a very elementary form of control is necessary, in place of perpetual records.

Customary methods of pricing inventories for accounting purposes are (1) *first-in-first-out* (fifo); (2) *last-in-first-out* (lifo); and (3) *standard cost.* These methods will be described and analyzed in Chapter 19. It will suffice here to point out that a careful control of inventory quantities; proper determination of material items which should be written off as *obsolete* owing to method, material, or product change; and intelligent pricing of the remaining or active items by one or more of the methods listed above—these all are important to good inventory management.

Not all the items kept in inventory deserve the same amount of care and control. *ABC analysis* is a routine by which different classes of items can be evaluated. The basic assumption is that items which have experienced the highest value should receive maximum attention, and those with lower value should receive proportionately less concern. The procedure is to categorize all items into three classes, A, B, and C, according to individual ratings. The ratings are determined by multiplying the usage rate of the item by its cost. It is typically found that the top category, A, accounts for about 70 per cent of the total dollar volume for the entire inventory while containing only 10 per cent of the items listed. Close physical control over this 10 per cent segment is obviously warranted. Category B might account for the next 25 per cent of the items stocked where the dollar volume totals 20 per cent of the sum. The remaining 65 per cent in category C with a 10 per cent share of the dollar volume receives minimum attention.

Perspective 11D   THE PARETO PRINCIPLE

ABC analysis is an application of a relationship in economics discovered by Vilfredo Pareto, the famous Italian engineer-economist-sociologist. In his attempt to characterize the distribution of wealth, Pareto gathered statistical data from such diverse countries as England, Germany, Italy, and Peru. By ranking personal fortunes in a decreasing order of magnitude, he observed that the greater the personal wealth, the smaller the number of persons who possess it. An equivalent view is that a very small percentage of the total population possess a very large percentage of the total wealth. This distribution pattern became recognized as *Pareto's law.*

The inventory equivalence of Pareto's law is demonstrated in the following tables. Table A shows the annual usage of ten classes of materials ranked according to their dollar amounts. Since classes 101 and 202 account for 70 per cent of the annual expenditures, they constitute the A category. A summary of the ABC analysis is shown in Table B.

Table A   Annual Material Usage, in Units and Dollars

Item	Units	Unit Cost ($)	Total Amount ($)	Cumulative Percentage (%)	ABC Category
101	280,000	0.15	42,000	46	A
202	220,000	0.10	22,000	70	A
303	80,000	0.15	12,000	83	B
404	110,000	0.05	5,500	89	B
505	80,000	0.05	4,000	94	B
606	30,000	0.10	3,000	97	C
707	8,000	0.10	800	98	C
808	15,000	0.05	750	99	C
909	3,000	0.10	300	99	C
111	4,000	0.05	200	100	C

Table B   Summary of the ABC Categories

Category	Class of Items	Items (%)	Amount per Group ($)	Percent of Usage (%)
A	101, 202	20	64,000	70
B	303, 404, and 505	30	21,500	24
C	All others	50	5,500	6

COMMENT   The Pareto (ABC) principle is universal; it is equally applicable to any control function in which attention should be focused on a vital few activities so that the bulk of available resources can be devoted to controlling them. It is also a worthy philosophy to guide personal planning—direct most of your effort toward a few critically important objectives—a strategy called "management by exception." In inventory control, ABC analysis effectively "buys" time for control of A items by overstocking C items.

11-6.1   Storeroom Location and Layout

In general, material storerooms are located close to the point of use. Raw materials are logically stored near the first operation, finished goods in the proximity of the shipping area, banks of in-process materials immediately ahead of the next operation, and supplies and tools in a location central to the personnel and equipment served. Of course, good layout practice usually brings the point of origin, storeroom, and point of use in adjacent and proper sequence for best flow of material. Sometimes, however, the size, weight, or value of the material or the fact that it is perishable or flammable will place definite limitations on where it can be stored.

While centralization of stores is usually desirable for reasons of control, material-handling factors may dictate partial or complete decentralization. One important new plant has decentralized material storage so that all materials are delivered directly to point of use. It is claimed that no material is moved twice in this "factory in a stockroom" and also that a visual form of inventory control can thus replace much of the usual record keeping. Other companies favoring decentralized material storage use "traveling stockrooms." They employ continuous merry-go-round conveyors which hold banks of materials and parts and carry them to and from fabricating and assembly operations.

A well-laid-out stockroom provides space for the receipt and inspection of incoming materials and for making disbursements as well. Materials brought or conveyed into the area may have to be checked, sorted, or inspected, and even stored temporarily before they are placed in the storage racks. Where no provision is made for this temporary storage, the tendency is to use the aisles as receiving areas, which makes for a dangerous and inefficient condition. Main aisles should usually be between 4 and 8 feet wide, depending upon the type of material involved and the amount of traffic to be accommodated. The subaisles between racks and bins may in some cases be a minimum of 30 inches wide.

If portable and salable items are to be stored, the entire store area should be enclosed with wire-mesh partitioning or with a solid-frame structure. An information or service window can be provided as part of the enclosure, and material requisitions and small items may be passed through this window. Thus, shop and operating personnel can be kept out of the store area, a condition absolutely necessary for effective control.

Perspective 11E   IN-HOUSE SUPERMARKETS

Establishing a semiautonomous market within a firm to supply operating departments is a recent inventory wrinkle. It has been effective for housekeeping supplies and repair work.

A quantity of expendable items such as office and janitorial supplies is traditionally issued to departments several times a year. Between issues the departments run out of some items and accumulate a surplus of others. A stockroom operates as a supermarket by displaying items on shelves with the prices marked. Department representatives call on the market and pick out needed supplies. The purchases are charged against the department budget. The system eliminates filling out requisitions and associated processing, reduces delivery time, lowers departmental hoarding of excess items, and still controls the dollar usage of supplies.

A similar procedure can be followed for simple maintenance and repair. Each department has a "charge plate." Items requiring repair are delivered to a maintenance depot accompanied by the charge plate. The time and material required to fix the item are billed on a job order to the plate address. On-the-spot comparison of repair cost versus a replacement can often be made by representatives of the department involved.

In both cases the departments are considered to be customers of an independent "supermarket" facility.

11-6.2 Storage Facilities

The major precepts upon which the selection and installation of storage facilities are generally based may be stated as follows:

1. Allow for easy, quick, and sure receipt, storage, and disbursement of material

2. Provide space and storage equipment adequate as to both size and load-bearing capacity for the material to be stored

3. Protect against damage and deterioration

4. Provide means for identifying and readily locating contents

5. Provide for the selection of the oldest material first

There is available today a wide variety of commercial storage equipment designed to handle the more common industrial materials: tote boxes; standard steel shelving parts which can be erected into bins or racks of length, depth, and height to fit almost any requirement; tiering frame racks; tanks for liquids; and hopper-type bins for finely divided dry materials. Mechanized handling equipment designed especially for storeroom application is now on the market.

Two trends in the use of storage facilities should be noted. One is the current emphasis on "going up"—use of the airspace in the storeroom. The capacity of many a storeroom has been greatly increased in recent years by the acquisition of facilities which permit storing vertically, in some cases right up to the ceiling. The high cost of industrial floor space has furnished an added incentive for better utilization of storeroom airspace. The second trend is a by-product of the increased use of pallets and unit loads in material handling. Where palletized loads are received by or can be created in the storeroom, the trend is to store "without breaking the bulk." Not only does this permit more compact and efficient storage with a minimum of material handling, but it also simplifies the control of inventory quantities and the taking of physical inventories (see Fig. 11-6).

Figure 11-6 This is a view of a 3-aisle, 50-foot high system to store in-process material, mostly consisting of weldments that are used for fabrication and assembly at the John Deere Harvester Works. The operator is located on a mezzanine arrangement whereby he can see all the material inbounding and outbounding from the lower conveyors and can control the retrievers from his upper mezzanine location. (Courtesy of the Triax Company.)

11-6.3   Storeroom Operation

A major premise of stockroom operation is the fixation of responsibility for the operation and control of that stockroom in the hands of one individual. Only this person and his or her subordinates should be allowed access to the stores area; all others should be permanently locked out. Unless this is done, it is hopeless to expect that the records and stocks will be kept in good order.

As pointed out above, the heart of the quantitative control of materials lies in the use of perpetual-inventory records. Hence, it is important that orders, receipts, and disbursements are posted to the records promptly and that a close check is constantly made on the stock balances to ascertain when the minimum is reached. Also when the stock becomes dangerously low, this fact should likewise be made known so that overdue orders may be given special attention. If a constant watch is maintained for those items the consumption of which is unusually high, an investigation may be made to reveal the breakdown of some type of control in the plant. Where slow-moving items are involved, it may be possible to see that these are used up before any new or better substitutes are permitted to be withdrawn.

Prima facie evidence of an efficiently operated stockroom is a well-organized and speedy stores service which prevents as far as is possible idle time on the part of operating personnel waiting for material. Frequently, good arrangement and housekeeping in the storage area will prevent the accumulation of hidden stocks and will greatly reduce the toll of damaged articles. A good stockkeeper is ever on the watch for possible ways in which materials can be simplified and standardized. He likewise carefully watches for potential savings resulting from the purchase of bulk material in place of packaged material and for possible changes in the package size or in the quantity ordered that may enable him to take advantage of a lower price. Packaged material, provided it does not have to be opened for inspection, should ordinarily be stored and disbursed in package-lot quantities to save handling and counting. Regardless of the accounting procedure followed, the oldest material should be used first, and the incoming material should be so segregated that this is possible.

Finally, since standard items often invite theft and are possible of resale, the stock system should be such that petty thievery of this type is soon discovered. Just as a daily balance system relieves bank clerks of any temptation they may have to steal the money they handle, so also are stock clerks and others who handle industrial materials relieved of temptation through the knowledge that pilferage will be promptly discovered. In most enterprises, materials in various stages of usage or completion are in abundance throughout the plant. Where such material can be used or peddled outside the company, pilferage control may be necessary. This may take the form of a daily accounting with each employee for materials to which he, is assigned, keeping pilferable items in plain view of some responsible person, locking up materials when they are not assigned to an individual, and searching employees as they leave work. For such materials, fear of discovery and removal of temptation are the prime requisites of effective control.

11-7 MECHANIZED MATERIAL HANDLING

Internal transportation starts with the material-handling equipment and systematizes the operation of this equipment. Where the transportation is intermittent, as in the case of trucks, development of regular pick-up and delivery schedules for production material; processing of move tickets which record work progress; handling of supplies, minor equipment, and waste within the plant; training of truck drivers for safe and efficient operation of the equipment; and scheduling of maintenance and servicing activities for best utilization of the handling equipment are among the diverse activities required of personnel responsible for internal transportation. If continuous conveyors are used, the transportation system is built around control stations where conveyor speeds may be regulated and material is added or removed.

The development of machines that move materials is not new. Prehistoric man's earliest mechanical implements were those which enabled him to move rocks and other heavy articles. But the application of such machines for industrial use has tended in the past to lag behind the introduction of machines that produce goods. The automotive industry was perhaps the first to realize that the extensive use of material-handling equipment should be an integral part of manufacturing. World War I led to some notable advances in the application of such equipment, but it remained for World War II to demonstrate to industry once and for all that a production machine is only as efficient as is the machine supplying it.

Production people now realize that material-handling equipment is not merely a substitute for a person with a strong back and a weak mind, but instead is a vital element in the continuous flow of goods through a plant. True it is that production machines make the goods, but it is equally true that, were it not for their servants, the material-handling devices which wait on them hand and foot, congestion of materials in the work areas and delays in the supplying of materials would be such that their full productive capacity could not possibly be realized.

A sound plant layout frequently can reduce or even eliminate the need for materials handling. Conversely, well-organized material handling can smooth out a troublesome plant layout. There is no question but that today a greater opportunity for reducing industrial costs lies in the direction of better handling and transporting materials rather than in better manufacturing processes.

Such a wide variety of mechanized handling and transporting devices is now available that most industrial materials can be moved mechanically about the plant. The advantages of mechanized handling properly integrated with processing may be summed up as follows:

1. The manufacturing-cycle time can be reduced by the elimination of much nonproductive time in the manufacturing process. Authorities have calculated that at least 30 per cent of the total time required in manufacturing is consumed by material handling. Mechanical devices permit more rapid handling and movements of material and often can slash this waste of time.

2. Human fatigue in lifting and handling manually can be reduced and in some cases eliminated. Thus, much of the hard physical labor associated with many industrial processes is gone forever.

3. Idle machine and employee time can be brought to a minimum. Most of the waiting for work that occurs where intermittent and nonmechanical delivery of

materials is involved can be eliminated by equipment that ensures a steady, constant flow of materials.

4. The productivity of employees working on the product is increased by a reduction of the time they would otherwise spend in handling materials.

5. Increased safety of handling results where materials are not "man-handled." Mechanical equipment never suffers back injuries, hernias, or toe accidents.

6. Storage space is conserved, particularly where mechanical equipment is used to stack materials vertically. With the initial cost of industrial floor space falling in the neighborhood of $22 per square foot, this space conservation is often a major consideration.

7. Nonproductive, indirect labor can be released for more productive, direct-labor activities.

8. Certain types of mechanized handling equipment tied in with automatic machine controls open up vast possibilities in the field of automation.

11-7.1 Types of Material-Handling Equipment

Functionally, there are two general classes of handling equipment: the *floor type* and the *overhead type.* Under the first classification there are:

1. *Hand trucks* These include the four-wheel hand-lift truck used for transporting skids and platforms; the four-wheel wood-stake truck used for all-purpose carrying; the stock-handling cart or "tea wagon" type of truck for handling small, light items of all sorts; and the general-purpose two-wheel truck. In addition there are special-purpose hand trucks designed to accommodate beer kegs, barrels, carboys, etc.

2. *Truck tractors* These are generally small but powerful gas-powered tractors used with trailers. Frequently they are of the single-wheel-in-front, short-wheel-base variety to provide a small turning radius and all-round maneuverability. Although they are generally employed in outdoor applications, with suitable exhaust equipment they may be used to advantage inside as well. Their high-draw capacity makes them a useful tool for moving machines and other equipment as well as heavy production materials.

3. *Power lift trucks* A very useful type of equipment in any plant, these trucks are gas or electrically powered and are provided with either an elevating platform, a set of tiering forks, a ram, or a crane, depending upon the application for which they are intended. Either they may be low-lift for simply transporting and low-stacking materials, or they may be of the telescoping high-lift type to permit stacking all the way up to the storehouse roof. Tiering forks are used in conjunction with wood pallets, which are inexpensive and may be carried and stacked in much the same manner as the conventional skid on the platform truck. The ram is used with special classes of materials, such as coils of strip steel and wire which may be handled by their hollow interior. For small loads, generally under 1 ton, a powered hand-lift truck, likewise made with either a platform or a fork, low- or high-lift as the occasion demands, is an economical vehicle for transporting and stacking (see Fig. 11-7).

Figure 11-7   A high-lift fork truck is shown stacking palletized loads. (Courtesy of Hyster Company.)

4. *Stackers*   Being only moderately mobile, the stacker is used primarily for the vertical stacking of heavy or bulky articles. One common type is the barrel stacker for handling standard oil drums and other barrel products to and from a barrel stack rack wherein they may be stored vertically as high as desired. In recent years, semiautomatic and fully automated stackers have been developed to load and unload racks in warehouse areas more rapidly and with a minimum of human energy (see Fig. 11-6).

5. *Gravity-roll conveyors*   Constituting perhaps the most widely used conveying means employed in industry today, gravity-roll conveyors are used to convey materials on ball-bearing rollers down a gentle grade by utilizing the natural force of gravity. The articles moved on roll conveyors may range in size from a few ounces to 20 tons or more. For example, department-store roll conveyors take packages of hosiery weighing only a few ounces. In steel mills, roll conveyors are used to handle many tons of sheet and bar steel. Between these two extremes, almost all kinds of commodities in a wide variety of containers are conveyed on the various types and sizes of roll conveyors now available. The length of such conveyors may vary from a few feet between machines or operations to several hundred feet between departments. Conveyor manufacturers stand ready to provide a variety of standard curves (to permit material to turn corners or go around objects) and roller spirals (to accomplish a considerable vertical drop in a short distance). They will also provide storage decks of conveyors (to facilitate storing a "float" of materials between operations), gate-hinge mechanisms (to permit the lateral passage of employees), and power boosters (to provide increased elevation).

6. *Power conveyors* Power conveyors are frequently used in applications where gravity-roll conveyors are not practicable, as would be the case where small individual parts are conveyed separately or where vertical or sloping changes in elevation as from one floor to the next are required. The exact type of conveyor will depend upon the application (see Fig. 11-8). Belt conveyors are in common use and generally consist of powered endless belts traveling over rollers. Slat conveyors, apron conveyors, and push-bar lifts are simply adaptations of the belt type. Oscillating trough conveyors, consisting of flat-bottomed metal troughs which are given an upward and forward vibratory motion, can convey such items as coffee, steel chips, sand, and even small metal parts. Vertical-lift conveyors of the finger type and of the "dumb-waiter-elevator" type have wide application. Hoppers and chutes, frequently provided with electric vibrators, are used for handling coal, ores, and other bulk materials. Grain, pulverized coal, and chemicals are

Figure 11-8 Thousands of paper movements per day are conducted on a 32-channel conveyor system which connects order-processing stations at U.S. Steel's centralized facility. Twenty-five channels provide two-way movements to specific customer order-entry stations and seven color-coded channels run to transmission, file, and control rooms. (Courtesy of U.S. Steel.)

types of materials that are sometimes lifted pneumatically through pipes or in bucket elevators to the tops of storage silos (see Fig. 11-9).

The most widely used varieties of *overhead-handling equipment* include:

1. *Chain conveyors*   These are of a number of types but usually employ an overhead monorail on which run trolleys attached at regular intervals to an endless chain. Under each trolley is placed a hook or other carrying device. The principal advantages connected with these conveyors are that they are located overhead and out of the way, that they thereby do not take up valuable floor space, and that they can be used to preposition the material at the level and at the point in the plant where it is desired for use. Many continuous-process conveyors are of the chain type. Some, instead of being located overhead, are placed underneath the floor (see Fig. 11-10).

2. *Cranes*   There are so many varied types of cranes that any generalization as to their characteristics is somewhat difficult. However, all of them, whether they be classed as traveling, locomotive, tractor, jib, or gantry, both pick up and transport the material. Their application is generally for extremely heavy materials sporadically handled.

3. *Tram-rail and monorail hoists*   These are simply standard chain, electric, or pneumatic hoists mounted to a single rail by means of a trolley. Horizontal movement

Figure 11-9 Pipes are frequently used to convey chemicals. Shown is a portion of an Esso Standard Oil Company refinery. (Courtesy of Esso Standard Oil Company.)

Figure 11-10 This jungle of overhead chain conveyors is part of a well-organized system that moves automotive bumper parts from presses to plating, to polishing, and finally to storage at the Rheem Automotive Company Division of Rheem Manufacturing Company.

may be controlled electrically or by hand. Such an arrangement adds mobility to what would otherwise be a stationary hoist.

11-7.2 Selecting the Equipment

A decision about whether or not to buy new mechanized handling equipment or to replace old is subject to the same equipment-replacement policy as the company would use for other productive equipment (see Chap. 5). The criteria for evaluation are direct costs of operating a piece of equipment, indirect costs, and intangible factors. Most of the direct costs are easily measured. Indirect costs are less observable for such factors as their effect on taxes, changes in overhead, effect on inventory control, changes in quality, and modified physical or mental demands on the work force. Possible intangible savings include increased customer good will because of a reduction of the in-process cycle time, fewer handling accidents, less fatigue, and better working conditions. There is no universally accepted rule

Figure 11-11   This is a view of the wood chip and sawdust handling area of a pulp-paper-tissue mill. The trailer truck at far right arches into the air, discharging its load of chips or sawdust. Conveyors deliver sawdust to silo at left, chips to outside storage. (Courtesy of American Can Company.)

about how the intangibles should be weighed with respect to the direct and indirect cost figures. It is highly possible that an alternative with higher measurable costs will be selected over a competing alternative with lower cost figures when intangibles are considered. The difference in measurable costs is, in effect, a quantitative evaluation of the intangible factors.

Perspective 11F   HANDLING MATERIAL-HANDLING NEEDS

There is a large array of material-handling equipment on the market today, ranging from back-saving lifts for individual operators to completely computerized, automatic sortation, storage, and retrieval systems. Considerations for improving existing facilities by utilizing new material-handling designs to stretch the capacity are described by K. E. Lanker:

In evaluating a "stretch" program, the first and foremost consideration is to determine the various building obstructions, obstacles and limitations within which a system must operate. Once these are known, various types of handling systems should be critiqued as to their practicality within a restricted environment. Some of the major issues that first must be evaluated are the restrictions and limitations placed upon the system by the existing building and a determination of what alterations can be made. Some of the major factors to be considered are: floor and ceiling load limitations, existing processes too large to move, column size and location, clear height under all obstacles or obstructions, multifloor transfers and interconnections between noncontiguous buildings. . . . Air rights offer several effective means to improve product handling and storage and provide much needed floor space. Two techniques in this area are the use of pallet racks for higher level storage or monorail conveyors for an off-floor delivery system.

Wheeled vehicle systems are available today that furnish a wide range of versatility, from a low-lift walkie pallet mover to a sophisticated high-rise wire-guided, computer-controlled vehicle. The degree of sophistication depends on the means and the economic advantage that the system demands. As an example, for a small parts picking operation it is possible to have a complete computer-controlled wire-guided vehicle where the operator is given hard copy documents listing his instructions and he commands the vehicle to the next desired pick location. The operator may perform parts consolidation or packaging while enroute with on-board computer or card reader controls. A more simplified system of picking is to use a small people-moving cart similar to a golf cart for low-level order picking at a safe speed. . . . If the facility restrictions are such that wheeled vehicles are impractical and mechanizing the operation is practical, one sport-type people mover is roller skates. This is being done today in some plants."*

*SOURCE: "Improving Productivity Through Material Handling," *Proceedings,* Systems Engineering Conference, 1975.

COMMENT   The ideal material-handling situation would require no material handling at all, because the handling of products does little to enhance their value; it mainly adds cost. The best alternative is, therefore, to handle materials with minimum expense. And it must be remembered that costs accumulate not only from labor and capital investments, they also include charges for damaged products, orders inaccurately filled, transportation delays, and misplaced materials.

11-8   REVIEW QUESTIONS

1. Define the purchasing function. How is it related to other major plant functions?

2. The function of purchasing is to "buy more than price." Comment.

3. Define centralized purchasing and decentralized purchasing. Give an example of their application.

4. Comment on the purchasing policies of hedging, speculation, and reciprocity.

5. Describe the functions performed by the receiving and shipping sections of a company.

6. What are (a) demurrage and (b) a bill of lading?

7. What is the objective of inventory control? What types of costs have to be considered in controlling inventory?

8. Explain the ABC control policy.

9. What is economic lot size? What are the limitations in determining the basic lot-size formula?

10. Given the data below, determine the minimum-order quantity by graphing the total inventory cost (vertical axis) versus the order quantity (horizontal axis). Use 400, 800, and 1,200 units for the amount ordered. What is the EOQ? Check your answer by using the EOQ formula.

    - Price per unit: $10
    - Annual usage rate: 12,000 units
    - Ordering cost: $60 per order
    - Carrying cost: 20 per cent of the value of the average number of units in the inventory

11. Dandy Duds, Inc., has analyzed its inventory costs to determine that its administrative cost per order is $32 and its carrying cost for cloth is 8 per cent of the average inventory value. Dandy Duds expects to order $200,000 (100,000 yards at an average price of $2 per yard) from one supplier during the coming year. What is the dollar amount of the EOQ?

12. What criteria are used in the selection and installation of storage facilities?

13. Assume that you are trying to justify an investment in a new piece of material-handling equipment. What types of savings could be considered in the justification?

11-9 TOPICS FOR DISCUSSION

1. Some observers see an evolving form of organization for material control which in large companies will appear in an organization chart about as indicated in Figure 11-12. The top person in the chart reports directly to the chief operating executive. Smaller companies, these same observers point out, will have essentially the same form of organization except that there will be fewer key persons with each wearing more than one hat.
   a. What objectives of good managerial control are found in this form of organization?
   b. What possible difficulties do you foresee with this form of organization and why?

2. A director of automotive purchasing has stated:
   "For productive material, we issue a blanket, no-quantity commitment purchase order for each part number which is to be fabricated and shipped in accord with quantities and shipping dates specified on Planning Department releases subsequently issued against each purchase order."
   This is a practice fairly common among large industrial purchasers. Evaluate its merits compared with standard purchasing procedures from the point of view of the purchaser; then from the point of view of the supplier.

3. Who in the organization should be made responsible for checking receipts of the company's products returned from customers and claimed to be defective? Why?

4. Inventories are carried on the corporate balance sheet as a current asset. Since inventories turn over several times a year, they are considered to be a liquid, short-term investment that is quite devoid of risk. However, some observers point out that inventories are really comparable with fixed assets (e.g., buildings, machines) in that they represent a permanent investment of capital. As soon as some part of the normal inventory is liquidated, the cash thus released is quickly reinvested in new stock, these observers point out, causing a permanent tie-up of capital. Comment on the liquidity of inventories and their degree of risk, indicating factors and situations encountered in different industries which bear on liquidity and risk.

5. Many companies in national distribution maintain widely separated finished-product warehouses strategically located throughout the United States. At any given time, some warehouses invariably find themselves with peak stocks of items on which other warehouses of the company are currently out of stock. On other items, reverse situations may prevail. This results in waste space in each, maldistribution of product, and unnecessary duplication of stocks, not

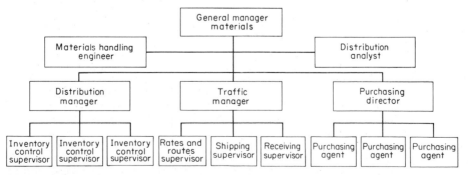

Figure 11-12

to mention high warehouse capital investment, operating expense, rehandling costs, and maintenance charges. In this day of rapid air freight to all parts of the country, how can companies justify continuance of such warehouses?

6. Case 11A: *The Budd Company, Hunting Park Plant*[1]

Over 85 per cent of the production at the Budd Company Hunting Park Plant is devoted to automotive body and chassis parts, the balance being concentrated on space-atomic devices and welding controls. Six thousand people are employed, and annual purchases run in excess of $50,000,000, mainly for automotive and chassis items purchased in substantial quantities. Because the automotive industry traditionally approaches a feast-or-famine pattern of activity, major peaks and valleys are a normal part of Budd's requirements with its vendors.

Budd has developed "eight vital points" which any vendor should stress in pointing up his sales presentation to Budd to match the areas of interest of the Budd purchasing staff:

1. The products offered by the salesman
2. The corporate status of the vendor and his financial and economic strength
3. The mechanical and production facilities of the vendor and his production capabilities; production "follow-through"
4. The engineering and technical facilities and capabilities of the vendor and his technical-services record
5. The vendor's quality-control and quality-management capabilities
6. The vendor's prices and price-quotation methods and policies, and performance
7. The vendor's geographic location and shipping and delivery facilities and record
8. The vendor's "Budd Company consciousness" and real understanding of Budd Company products, production, and service

Questions

Assume the point of view of a purchasing agent of a company comparable with Budd. Apply Budd's "eight vital points" to the following situations, describing how you would act and why:

1. A small vendor with excellent financial rating in competition with a large vendor with equally good rating, both of whom have bid on a large contract with substantially equal quality, price, and delivery
2. A vendor whose price is considerably lower than that of his competitors, but whose mechanical and quality reliability on past orders has left something to be desired
3. A new vendor with whom your company has not previously done business and who offers a product for which your company has had for many years one completely satisfactory, exclusive source of supply
4. A supplier of good-quality Japanese-made products stocked in a United States warehouse whose prices are 15 per cent lower than those of domestic manufacturers of comparable products

7. Case 11B: *The Grits and Grinds Wheel Company*

The G and G Wheel Company supplies abrasives and abrasive grinding wheels to various industrial metalworking companies. Many of its products are ordered repetitively. The G and G Wheel Company carries a stock of such items to offer rapid customer service (a competitive factor in the abrasive industry) and to permit processing larger quantities than would be the case were items made to specific customer order. The production-control department replenishes this inventory on the following formula:

[1]The facts in this case, including the "eight vital points," are taken from an article prepared by the Budd Company purchasing agent, "Eight Keys to Buying at the Budd Company Hunting Park Plant," *Automotive Industries,* p. 61, Aug. 15, 1960.

1. At a stated time each month for each item the scheduling clerk examines records of stock on hand and the rate of sales (i.e., shipments) for the past 2 months.
2. He works to a replenishment lead time of 5 weeks, equaling the time to complete the manufacturing cycle on a new lot of material.
3. He then enters an order for the factory to make an amount equaling the projected sales for the coming 2 months, based on sales for the past 2 months less amount of stock on hand.
4. Weekly checks of violent changes in sales and inventories are made to prevent running out of stock between normal monthly reviews.

This very logical ordering formula is producing rather illogical results in that the company's manufacturing requirements from month to month take on the appearance of a roller coaster. Top management has now directed the production-control department to recommend ways and means of correcting this situation.

Questions

1. What basic faults do you find in the inventory-replenishment policy employed? Suggest a new formula which corrects the situation.

8. Case 11C: *The Smooth Paint Co.*

The Smooth Paint Co., when setting up a series of automotive refinish warehouses, found itself faced with an unusual storage problem.

Each warehouse served local automotive-parts distributors and body-refinishing shops. Each was to stock in quart and pint cans more than 3,400 paint items—all the colors on cars made by automobile manufacturers during the previous 4 years. Quantity carton lots of each paint item were to be shipped from the central paint-manufacturing plant as required to meet the needs of each warehouse. Items as received in and ordered out were to be identified by paint number.

The volume of business done in each warehouse would require sizable inventories of full-carton lots. This fact, linked with the great variety of items carried, would make it desirable to concentrate the storage of a maximum of 12 cans and a minimum of 5 cans of each paint item and size can in as compact a storage area as possible. Then as orders from distributors or refinishing shops were received, stock clerks could fill them rapidly and with a minimum of walking. Another important consideration in paint warehousing was to provide a method whereby the oldest stock would always be issued first.

Questions

1. Recommend to the Smooth Paint Co. a warehousing arrangement that best solves its problem, indicating also how you would control quantities.

9. Case 11D: *In Order to Save—Save in Orders*

"I propose that we apply EOQ calculations to all our inventory procurements. At the present time we have one all-purpose purchasing agent who operates in a very informal manner, so informal that we don't even find out how much it costs us to place an order. We know he gets paid $10,000 a year, occupies an office that we figure costs $2,000 a year, has a telephone bill averaging $300 per year, and annual incidental expenses of about $200. Since our small company has no major material requirements, he just circulates around the building to see what supplies are needed. Then he phones the orders to local merchants and writes out the checks himself to make all the payments. Apparently he places about 2,500 orders each year, ranging in size from a few dollars to 300 or 400 dollars. That comes out to about $5 ordering cost per order. We can probably cut the number of orders down to 1,500 which means a savings of (2,500 − 1,500 orders) X $5 per order = $5,000 per year."

Questions

1. Identify and discuss three attributes of the present system that should receive consideration before changes are made to formalize the inventory policy.

12

QUANTITY CONTROL

There is always a better way, and it often can be found! In industrial methods improvement the continued effort is to find that better way. Those seeking to improve methods pose these questions about every product, every process, and every job: Why is it done? In this way? Using this machine? Can it be combined? Resequenced? Simplified? To answer these questions, aimed at improving the process, managers use a variety of techniques. What are these techniques? How do managers use therbligs, general process charts, man–machine charts, right-and-left-hand charts? What are some of the rules of motion economy? To what extent can methods-improvement techniques be applied to office operations? What means make it possible to enlist employee cooperation and participation in methods improvement?

How is the efficiency of plant and equipment maintained? When should a facility be scrapped or sold and replaced? What principles and practices are utilized to minimize the impact of industrial accidents? How can waste be controlled?

12 QUANTITY CONTROL

12-1 THE SEARCH FOR IMPROVED METHODS

About 150 years ago, when Charles Babbage made the first systematic survey of manufacturing plants in England and Europe, trying to find one capable of manufacturing the automatic computer he had designed, he found many method improvements in use. Some factory workers used special tricks; others were not aware of them. Methods were not then a responsibility of a separate methods engineer. In the United States today they are. From a definition of methods engineering by the American Society of Mechanical Engineers Work Standardization Committee, it appears that the field embraces the technique that subjects each operation of a given piece of work to close analysis in order to eliminate every unnecessary element or operation and in order to approach the quickest and best method of performing each necessary element or operation. It includes the improvement and standardization of methods, equipment, and working conditions; operator training; the determination of standard times; and occasionally devising and administering various incentive plans.[1]

The search for better production methods probably originated with man's earliest inventions of the lever, wheel, and inclined plane. It continues both as personal invention and through the use of techniques to be described. We are separating motion study, treated here, from time study, treated in Chapter 16, because methods improvement can stand alone without incentive payment. Neither is more important, and together they may be most effective, especially as applied to the industrial enterprise. The merger of general improvement in industrial management with the systematic approach recommended by Babbage formed the scientific-management movement about the start of the twentieth century.

Taylor, whose name is a historical synonym for scientific management, was an assistant foreman in a steel-plant machine shop who tried to decide on a fair day's work for his people. He found that each had worked out for himself a different method and that some methods were more effective than others. He gradually developed by *research, standarization, control,* and *cooperation* what seemed the best composite method and taught it to his people. The results were spectacular. Taylor rose to chief engineer, then became a consultant and trained or influenced most of the industrial engineers of his day.

To Frank B. Gilbreth and Lillian M. Gilbreth goes the credit for the origin of *motion study* through emphasis upon the nature of movements. They also sought the "one best way." Among their contributions were the use of

---

[1]Not all practitioners have responsibilities exactly as defined here. Many work where industrial relations handles training, and not a few where equipment is supervised by the plant engineer. Problems of automation, operations research, integrated data processing, and controlled creativity also exist. The area considered here is also known as work simplification, methods study, motion study, and broadly, as methods control.

micromotion photography in preparing process charts and the identification of 17 basic elements of motion, dubbed *therbligs* (Gilbreth rearranged). The Gilbreths counted time in *winks:* 1/2,000 minute. Present-day motion analysts use a decimal time compilation for ease of addition and computation. Time as used in motion study is essential for durational knowledge but is not necessarily preliminary to establishing the *work task* as it is in time study.

There have been several additions and variations developed in the original Gilbreth basic elements. As presented by the Methods Engineering Council the basic elements are broken into three groups, and within each group careful classifications are made of each possible variation. The basic breakdown is shown in Figure 12–1. A further discussion of methods and time studies is included in Chapter 16.

Group 1. Useful elements which usually accomplish work, although not always in the most effective way:	*Group* 2. Elements which retard work usually by slowing down group 1 elements:	*Group* 3. Nonaccomplishment elements in which operator adds nothing to complete task:
Reach	Change direction	Hold
Move	Preposition	Unavoidable delay
Grasp	Search	Avoidable delay
Position	Select	Rest to overcome
Disengage	Balancing delay	fatigue
Release	Plan	
Examine		
Do		
Action: Study to uncover possible improvements in performance using the laws of motion economy and corollaries.	*Action:* Eliminate first five by better workplace layout. Reduce plan by supervisory preplanning, go-no-go gages, and workplace layout.	*Action:* Substitute mechanical holding devices for human action, rearrange motion sequence, and improve workplace layout to eliminate first two. Reduce last two by improved supervision, adequate incentives, and removing causes of fatigue.

Figure 12-1 The three groups of basic-motion elements of which every human performance is composed. These are grouped according to the productivity of the action comprising the element. Recommended steps for increasing accomplishment are given.

Perspective 12A   TAYLOR-MADE MANAGEMENT PRINCIPLES

Frederick Winslow Taylor (1856–1915) was a catalyst in the turn-of-the-century revolution in labor-management practices. His message was that scientific investigation and knowledge should replace individual opinions. Acceptance of the message required a new mental set for both employees and employers. Taylor summarized his objectives as follows:

First. The development of a science for each element of a man's work, thereby replacing the old rule-of-thumb methods.

Second. The selection of the best worker for each particular task and then training, teaching, and developing the workman, in place of the former practice of allowing the worker to select his own task and train himself as best he could.

Third. The development of a spirit of hearty cooperation between the management and the men in the carrying on of the activities in accordance with the principles of the developed science.

Fourth. The division of the work into almost equal shares between the management and the workers, each department taking over the work for which it is better fitted; instead of the former condition, in which almost all of the work and the greater part of the responsibility were thrown on the men.*

*SOURCE: F. W. Taylor, *The Principles of Scientific Management,* vol. 1, New York: Harper & Row Bros. 1929.

COMMENT The four aims listed by Taylor do not seem very startling today. The originality of his contributions can be fully appreciated only by recognizing the environment from which they emerged. For instance, when Taylor began his work in steel mills, workers were expected to put in 10-hour days 7 days per week, while today we are experimenting with 4-day work weeks and job democracy as epitomized by workers on the company's board of directors.

12-2 METHODS-IMPROVEMENT PRACTICES

The major responsibility for methods improvement rests with the *industrial engineering department.* Its scope of activities in recent years has been broadened in many enterprises to cover other factory and nonfactory aspects. These include safety engineering, operations research, nonincentive wage and salary administration, organization planning, office practices and equipment, communication devices, and systems analysis and evaluation. When so broadened, the function assumes a hat with a "management-engineering" label, although seldom is it called that unless performed by outside consulting firms. The department generally reports to the top manufacturing executive, since the emphasis on its endeavors is in the realm of manufacturing. Less frequently, as in smaller companies, where the top financial or industrial-relations executive may have encompassing interests and responsibilities beyond those normally assigned to the function, the industrial-engineering department may be found associated with either of these divisions.

A well-managed enterprise does not view methods work as the prerogative of the industrial engineers only. Methods analysis pervades the organization. Plant and product engineers, controllers, cost accountants, production- and quality-control specialists, purchasing buyers, industrial-relations personnel, and line supervision at all levels spend a significant portion of their time on methods.

Rank-and-file employees frequently are called upon to contribute. When methods-improvement techniques are taught to employees, the term *work simplification* is often used to designate the cooperative project. Employee acceptance of methods-improvement activities is essential to any program. If their enthusiastic participation also can be obtained, results and savings can skyrocket. While in some quarters work simplification is restricted to improvements in manufacturing-employee motions and effort, actually it can cover all phases of work in the industrial enterprise, including procedures, systems, equipment engineering, tooling, maintenance activities, and office work.

Companies which fail to call on employees for improvements overlook the fact that the person who spends 8 hours a day on a job is perhaps the one best informed about and most interested in that job and how it is performed. Frequently he can suggest changes that would elude even the trained methods person. The more people in the organization who are thinking about methods, the better.

12-2.1 Charts Used in Methods Study

Many processes, operations, and work elements are best analyzed by charting observed practices and work patterns. Investigation can be made by personal observation at the scene or, where close study of details is required, by analysis of motion pictures (sometimes involving a closed-loop of film which will repeat the work cycle endlessly). The study is recorded on one of three forms of charts. The *process-flow chart* (see Chap. 7) is used to study a part or product through its process. The *man-machine chart* gives in detail actions, simultaneous or sequential, of the operator and equipment operated. This chart points up idle time of either the man or the machine, which can be eliminated by a change in work pattern. The third, the *right-and-left-hand chart,* is illustrated in Figure 12–2. When this chart is carried further and all parts of the body are charted in greater detail, it is called the "simomotion" chart. Used in micromotion study, perhaps with line patterns of the motions involved, such charts become exceedingly complex. In function, the right-and-left-hand operation chart makes it easy to spot idle time on the part of either hand. Once the waste is discovered, its prevention is often simple. Experienced methods engineers frequently dispense with charts. For them bad practice stands out. Charts are used, however, in training new methods analysts and in selling a proposed process to management, immediate supervision, and employees. Also, where it is desired to record exactly how a job is performed, charts are indispensable.

12-2.2 Principles of Motion Economy

It is possible to discover "rules to be followed in trying to improve performance at the workplace." Frank Gilbreth first named these "principles of motion economy." Maynard, Mogensen, Barnes, and others have modernized the list, until Close stated them according to five areas of improvement summarized here.

1. Rules affecting the human body:
   a. Use both hands for productive work.

Job No. _844_ Part No. _1974-16_ Dept. _89_ Date _3-6-55_

Part Name _Forming Pin Bar_ Chart by _H. Stackman_

Operation _Closing Two Rivets in Opposite Side of Flat bar_ Chart No. _107_

Chart Type _Left-Right Hand_ Method _Present_ Time Unit _2000_ of _Min (winks)_

~~Summary~~	~~Man~~	~~Machine~~		Summary _Single cycle_
~~Use~~				Simultaneous Motion Chart
~~Idle~~			Best Cycle	
~~Total~~			Ideal Cycle	
~~% Efficiency~~				

LEFT HAND ~~MAN~~	Therblig	CLOCK OR METER READING	Therblig	RIGHT HAND ~~MACHINE~~
Reaches for rivets	Transp. empty	4 / 8	Transp. empty	Reaches for flat bar
Selects and grasps two rivets	Selects grasp	10 / 4	Select grasp	Selects and grasps one bar
Carries rivets to bar	Transport loaded	12 / 10	Transport loaded	Carries bar to modified arbor press
Positions two rivets in prepared holes	Assemb.	5 / 5	Hold	Holds bar in place
Assists right hand in placing piece in fixture	Transp. loaded	8 / 12	Transp. loaded	Carries piece to fixture in modified arbor press
Moves hand to clamp and grasps clamp handle	T.E. grasp	6		
Clamps piece	Use	6 / 12	Position release load	Inserts piece in fixture and releases it
Holds clamp in place	Hold	12 / 4	Transp. empty	Reaches for and grasps lever
Opens clamp, releases clamp handle	T.E. release	6 / 10	Use	Closes first rivet
Moves hand to fixture	T.E.	6 / 6	Release	Releases lever
Grasps bar, turns it around and releases	Grasp position release	16 / 8	Unavoidable delay	Waits for left hand
		8	Transp. empty	Reaches hand to fixture
Moves hand to clamp and grasps clamp handle	T.E. grasp	6		
Clamps piece	Use	6 / 16	Position	Assists left hand in reversing bar in jig
Holds clamp in place	Hold	4 / 16	T.E. grasp	Reaches for and grasps lever
		10	Use	Closes second rivet
Opens clamp, releases clamp handle	Release	4 / 6	Transp. empty	Releases lever (drops delivery)

Figure 12-2 Right-and-left-hand chart. Note: Therbligs are only approximate. Chart form may be used as either right-and-left-hand or man-machine chart.

b. Both hands should move simultaneously in opposite and symmetrical directions, beginning and ending their motions at the same time.
c. Smooth continuous curved motions of the hands and arms should be developed.
d. The work should be arranged to allow rhythmic and automatic performance.
e. Within the limits of the operation, move the shortest distance possible and use the lowest practical motion class.
f. Use the body and momentum to the best mechanical advantage.

2. Rules affecting the workplace:
   a. The workplace should be designed so that the motion path of the hands and arms is kept within the normal work area.
   b. Work requiring use of the eyes should be maintained within the field of normal vision.
   c. Tools and materials are best located at fixed work stations.
   d. The height of the workplace should preferably be designed to allow working from either a standing or a sitting position.
   e. The work area should be confined to minimize walking.
   f. Good working conditions at the workplace lead to good work performance.

3. Rules affecting tools and equipment:
   a. Tools and equipment should be prepositioned to facilitate pickup or grasp.
   b. Use foot pedals and fixtures to relieve the hands for other useful work.
   c. Provide ejectors to remove finished work.
   d. Locate machine controls for ease of operation.
   e. Apply special-purpose tools and combined tools.
   f. Consider the use of a machine to perform the operation.

4. Rules affecting material handling:
   a. Design the work for easy grasp.
   b. Arrange gravity-feed hoppers, separators, counters, bins, and conveyors to deliver the material close to the point of use.
   c. Preposition and identify materials and parts for the next operation.
   d. Make use of drop delivery in releasing finished work.
   e. Transfer all heavy lifting to mechanical devices.

5. Rules concerning time conservation:
   a. Question all hesitations or temporary ceasing of motion of worker or machine.
   b. The motion pattern that requires the fewest steps or elements usually gives the shortest time.
   c. Work should be performed while the machine is running, and the machine should be running while work is performed.
   d. Two or more parts should be processed at the same time.

12-2.3 Methods Improvement in the Office

To the extent that much modern office work resembles factory routine, the same techniques apply. Modifications introduced as systems and procedures work, which is sometimes originated in the industrial-engineering department, are compounded by changes caused by integrated data processing and the introduction of computer techniques. Those changes are discussed more fully in the office-management chapters. Office motion study makes use of the same analysis techniques, charts, and approaches as the factory. Special chart forms include work-distribution charts for the analysis of task or duty lists and multicolumn flow-process charts for following the interlocked actions of several office workers simultaneously.

Physical motions, including walking, are treated much the same. A much greater use is made of suggestions from office-machine manufacturers, professional associations, and office-management experts. The National Office

Management Association and the Systems and Procedures Association have been especially productive of usable ideas. Such a list would stress such useful "small office tools" as gathering racks for collating, calculating charts, and "out markers" for removed file folders. The office area is often a neglected gold mine for moneysaving suggestions from employees.

12-2.4 Suggestion Systems

One of the most successful bridges between methods-improvement efforts and good industrial relations is the use of a suggestion system in which employees may offer ideas to save time, effort, cost, or injury for prizes or money rewards.

Industrial-relations departments promote suggestion plans to improve employee morale. Employee cooperative spirit may be estimated from the attitude shown in the suggestions made. Suggestion systems have operated continuously since the closing years of the nineteenth century in such companies as Yale and Towne, National Cash Register, Eastman Kodak, and Bausch and Lomb. The labor-management committee (LMC), a type of suggestion system operated with employee participation, developed as a part of the World War II drive to increase production. Most such committees were discontinued in 1945, but a nucleus of the most successful carry on, largely because of the methods improvements and savings they contribute. Company-tailored systems complete with blanks for recording ideas (numbered stubs for anonymity), display boards with monthly posters, and plant mailboxes can be purchased from several sources. The important part of the installation must originate within the adopting company. This consists of demonstrating to employees that their ideas are given full consideration, of actually making changes suggested promptly, and of rewarding contributors.

Since the most common reward is 10 per cent of the expected savings during the first year, an idea of savings made can be obtained from the awards paid. A giant company like General Motors will pay out millions and has—4 million in the first 6 years of its plan. The Illinois Central Railroad paid out half a million over the first 10 years. Smaller enterprises have made proportionate payouts. Altogether the total in awards is over 2 million a year —and could be 30 million if all plants had suggestion plans (reported in *A.M.A. Production Series* 165). In RCA's electron-tube division a prize contest for employees not usually eligible for suggestion awards brought savings totaling $7,000,000 for a $72,000 cost of drive, 200 employees submitting 3,000 ideas.

Patent protection is usually given to employees whose ideas are good. Often the methods-engineering laboratory staff helps the employee with the perfection of a half-formulated idea. It is important in all cases that the employee, the foreman, and others who made a contribution be given full credit, even though the engineers perfected the improvement.

12-2.5 Value and Limitations of Methods Study

Work simplification for its own sake is desirable. In a profit-driven business, however, certain limitations must be kept in mind. It does little good to study in detail, with camera, charts, and "brain sweat," a process of short duration. Savings realized on small orders take a long time to add up. The methods engineer must, therefore, decide whether or not the probable savings will pay for the cost of the investigation proposed. Short-running jobs should receive cursory examination. Long-running and bottleneck operations should be given "the works." Among the considerations that should appear on the balance sheet of a proposed methods-study project are:

1. The capital required to produce results: buildings, machines, equipment

2. The working force required and labor relations: wages, working conditions, training required, union restrictions, ratio of labor costs

3. The duration of the job: Will the company continue to make this part? Is it a high-demand, good-profit item or a marginal product? How many pieces like this were made last year? How many months has it been running?

Methods study can pay for itself. Indeed, it can show a bigger "profit" than any other single staff endeavor. Because of natural human resistance to change, it is often necessary to draw up a brief balance sheet proving without doubt that the innovations suggested are savings. Labor-union alertness to possible worker displacement requires that these proposed changes be considered from the employee's viewpoint as well as from a pure "costs-and-savings" angle. An employee-relations-minded methods analyst will introduce participation of employees early, make improvements gradually, and give special attention to changes which may adversely affect workers' status.

12-2.6 Job Design

Job enlargement or *job enrichment* is the name given to a reversal of a job specialization trend. The motive is to make jobs more interesting by adding variety. Although the implementation of this goal may seem contrary to motion economy, it need not be. Adding variety to a job does not mean adding unnecessary motions. The enlargement is more mental than motor. Sequential tasks performed by, say, two or three workers can be grouped so that each worker performs all the tasks. When the final task in a sequence is an inspection or packaging function, the worker sees the end product of his effort and assumes more responsibility for a successful completion. The regrouping of jobs also allows method changes that might otherwise be difficult to initiate.

Motivational advantages of job enlargement are discussed in Chapter 16. Not everyone agrees with the morale-building claims of the proponents, but from a methods-improvement viewpoint it is generally agreed that a properly designed program can emphasize craftsmanship and improve worker identification with his work while maintaining or even improving the efficiency of operations. The practical limitations of job enlargement are the extra training and facilities required to accommodate the modular arrangement.

The concepts of work simplification as described earlier in this chapter have been around a long time. Formal "work-simp" programs are of a more recent vintage. Many of the contemporary programs are conducted by agencies outside the organization or are abetted by services brought in to freshen interest. The typical aims of the programs are still to effect changes and to improve working methods, although some agendas are designed to improve managerial decisions.

Numerous gimmicks and variants are employed to enliven interest: contests, professional movies, testimonials, annual or more frequent newsletters, alumni bulletins, reunions, town-hall meetings, etc. The justification for the tricks is that they seem to work. It must be admitted that motion principles in themselves may seem too obvious to be very exciting. Continued exposure to any repetitive theme breeds monotony. Since boredom is not a setting conducive to method changes, innovative efforts directed toward worker participation and cost reduction do not deserve disdain. After all, creativity is a hallmark of methods improvement.

Perspective 12B PARTICIPATION IMPROVES PRODUCTIVITY

Attempts to improve productivity may seem contradictory to efforts to improve the quality of working life. They need not be so. Ways to upgrade jobs are to make the work more interesting and to give the worker more responsibility. These actions may also contribute to greater productivity. Three examples follow:

1. In 1969 the New York Telephone Company had a serious problem of subscriber discontent with service. The 15,000 operators, whose main job was to help phone users, were unhappy too; 600 operators a month quit or were fired. Changes were initiated that allowed 10,000 operators to handle a higher volume of traffic, yet the turnover dropped from almost 50 per cent a year to about 4 per cent.

   The employees who take telephoned complaints of service malfunction used to write down the name, address, and nature of complaint on a slip that they then passed along. Now the complaint taker quickly conjures up on a screen quite a lot of relevant information: The last complaint about that number, how the trouble was dealt with, whether it was in the subscriber's home or elsewhere in the system, whether the repairman reported an "access problem," for instance, an intimidating dog.

   An employee on the complaint desk can also press a button that produces a computerized diagnosis of whether the trouble is in the home or outside. With all that information, the complaint taker is no longer a passive receiver of squawks, but can engage in a significant conversation with the caller.*

2. Productivity at a General Motors plant rose after the workers were given greater responsibility.

   In one plant, glass breakage rose to 46 per cent of the glass handled. In vain managers tried all the traditional methods to make the employees more careful. Nothing worked. Frustrated supervisors quit in disgust. Finally, the problem was turned over to the employees themselves. They began to identify causes of breakage. For instance, a window might break because the car's body was improperly aligned. The window installers would talk to the body workers about the problem. As a result of this improved communication among workers, glass breakage in that plant has almost ceased.*

3. A management principle at Texas Instruments (T.I.) is that "employees at all levels participate actively in the planning and control, as well as performance, of the job."

Seventy-three per cent of T.I.'s manufacturing employees and 49 per cent of other employees form teams of four to ten members each. Each team tries to produce a "method improvement." In a warehouse, for example, a team worked out a new way of handling, inspecting, and recording incoming material. The flow time from receiving dock to warehouse was reduced from 3 weeks to 3 days, the value of material tied up in the flow at a given time was cut from $960,000 to $430,000, the jobs of several workers were eliminated, and the warehouse group's productivity improved by 25 percent.*

*source: Max Ways, "The American Kind of Worker Participation," *Fortune,* October, 1976.

COMMENT   Over the many years since Taylor introduced scientific management, specialization has certainly raised efficiency and productivity. It also created problems. In recent years it has been proven that better technology alone cannot produce all the needed solutions. More reliance must be placed in people.

12-3   WORKER SAFETY

Safety in industry may be considered from the mechanical side or from the legal angles of workmen's compensation, or even as a matter of training in and motivation toward safe work practices for employees. These last responsibilities are often assigned to the industrial-relations department. The immediate supervisor, however, has the active responsibility. He must see that the workplace is properly arranged and maintained, that equipment is in safe operating condition, and that employees do in fact follow safe work habits. One of the long-standing controversies in safety work concerns a belief that 85 per cent (or 90 per cent) of industrial injuries result from unsafe acts, while only 15 per cent (or 10 per cent) result from unsafe conditions.

Regardless of the exact percentage relationship, influencing human motivation to work safely is an important responsibility of the supervisor as well as of the industrial-relations department. A study conducted in hazardous U.S. Army installations found that while employees at all levels recognized the same hazards as professional safety personnel, they worked more safely after an opportunity to "report to management" the hazards on the job.

12-3.1   Safety Engineering

Safety begins on the drawing board. In the original design of a set of tools or the layout of a workplace, accident hazards may be built in or eliminated. A safety-minded building designer will make adequate provisions for aisle and local storage space to minimize materials-handling hazards, will locate control and fuse panels where they can be reached safely, will install permanent ladders for all overhead controls, will insulate all surfaces heated above 200°F and screen high-pressure heating areas, and will adequately guard belting and line shafting even if it is normally inaccessible. A safety-minded machine designer will include in his specifications limit switches, overload devices, overspeed tripping mechanisms, deadman controls, gear guards, and whatever positive-action safety devices seem indicated to protect the operator. A safety-minded engineer changing a process will permit no unsafe process to be used, will provide workplace protective clothing and equipment where necessary, will consider work-movement hazards, and will specify mechanical handling in the safest form.

The safety engineer is one representative of management whose interest is primarily in safety and only secondarily in production or costs. He needs a sound mechanical-engineering background to enable him to hold his own in the arguments for job reengineering. He may report to the production superintendent or plant manager, but is often a part of the industrial-relations department. For full success, he needs, as do all staff men, the absolute confidence and enthusiastic support of top management. His field of work is far more extensive than may be suggested by the term "safety" to the uninitiated. It often includes plant housekeeping and industrial sanitation.

In addition to accident prevention, a complete safety program has to do with promotion of employee health, with prevention of such occupational diseases as silicosis, and with fire prevention. State and municipal labor departments and unions have waged successful battles against fire and industrial health hazards. Fire protection as a safety function is highly important, for while modern factory structures are usually fire-resistant, the materials used may be inflammable. In one memorable and disastrous fire, an oil-base cleaning compound ignited by a repair welder's torch wiped out a modern metalworking plant in a matter of minutes. Years ago, panic and lack of fire escapes forced a number of young women to jump from upper-story windows in the notorious garment workers' fire. The Textile and Garment Workers' unions diligently police present-day establishments to prevent a repetition. Most factories have regular fire and civil-disaster drills, often supervised by municipal fire inspectors. Few employers intentionally risk fire, but careless supervisors may permit workers to block fire doors or limit free access to fire exits. Regular inspection is the only prevention.

12-3.2 OSHA

The first phase of the safety movement involved a legalistic tangle over a master's liability for injuries suffered by his servant in employment, as distinct from liability to public persons. Around the turn of the century, some progress was made by the passage of employers' liability laws by the various states. Interest in liability was succeeded by emphasis on workmen's compensation laws. Recently, however, liability problems again came to the fore in civil suits by employees attempting to exceed award maxima in workmen's compensation laws.

State workmen's compensation laws came into being early in the 1900s for the most part. However, a few Southern states held back, with the last (Mississippi) passing a workmen's compensation law in 1948.

These laws contained the basic principle of employer "liability without fault" on the assumption that accidents were one of the natural hazards of factory employment and therefore a legitimate cost of production to be passed on to consumers. Also removed were the defenses of *contributory negligence, carelessness of fellow servant,* and *assumption of risk* known to exist. When the employer paid damages regardless of who was at fault, he quickly took steps to limit hazards. The former liability insurers quickly shifted to providing compensation risk coverage and developed advisory service. The National Safety Council was founded in 1913, and much recent work has been on a cooperative basis, headed by that council.

The *Occupational Safety and Health Act* (OSHA) became effective in 1971. It applies to more than 5 million businesses involved in or affecting interstate commerce. Over 60 million workers are covered by the act. Its aim is to ensure "so far as possible every working man and woman in the nation safe and healthful working conditions and to preserve our human resources." Among the rights provided for workers are opportunities to

1. Request an inspection by the Department of Labor when there is suspicion that a job safety or health violation exists which threatens physical harm

2. Participate in inspections

3. Participate in the hearing when an employer protests a fine or abatement period resulting from an OSHA violation

4. Request a determination "whether any substance normally found in the place of employment has potentially toxic effects in such concentrations as used or found"

The U.S. Department of Labor is responsible for enforcing occupational safety and health standards. Inspections are made by OSHA Compliance Officers located in offices throughout the country. These inspectors work with state authorities in some areas. They may issue citations that result in fines or court actions that could, in extreme situations, shut down operations.

Safety research and education functions are handled by the National Institute for Occupational Safety and Health (NIOSH). It is authorized to conduct necessary research to identify hazardous substances and to set tolerance levels as parts of the OSHA standards. NIOSH may require employers to measure, record, and report on employees' exposures to health-endangering substances. Lists of toxic substances and the levels at which toxic effects will occur are published annually.

12-3.3 Accident Costs

Accidents can be very costly to the injured individual, but they are also costly to the employer. Medical and hospitalization costs and payments to employees for temporary or permanent disability resulting from industrial accidents are generally covered by each employer's workmen's-compensation insurance policy. However, some larger companies prefer to "self-insure." Either way, in the final analysis, the "insured" pays the bill. His insurance premium or his rate of replenishment of his own insurance fund depends primarily on how much or how little has been paid out to cover his accident experience.

Yet these direct costs represent only one-fourth of the total costs of an accident in industry. Such indirect cost items as machine stoppage, material spoilage, machine and tool damage, idle time of nearby machines and operators who stop to help or watch, time lost taking the injured to the hospital, lowered production by the substitute worker, legal costs, and management time in compensation hearings—some or all of these can add greatly to the cost of an accident. It is to avoid these costs, as well as to meet its moral responsibility, that a company is interested in the safety of its employees.

12-3.4 Safety Devices

Safety devices are included in modern equipment by the manufacturer but sometimes must be added to out-of-date equipment by the user. Where mechanical guards cannot be added, or for nonmachine hazards, special protective clothing may be supplied by the employer to the employee. Examples are protective eyeshields or goggles, rubber boots, aprons, and gloves. An example of the range of safety devices which can be applied to a single problem will be provided by considering the power press used in metalworking, where a hazard to the operator's hands is created through the need for serving the machine by putting metal sheets or cups under the punch or die, which then descends. The original safety device was a sweeping arm which brushed the operator's hands aside. More recently positive-action "safety handcuffs" have been used. With these the operator straps his wrists to a cable, which in turn is fastened through pulleys to the mechanism so that, whenever the punch descends, the operators' hands are withdrawn. A similar result is obtained by requiring the operator to press two operating levers simultaneously, one with each hand. The RCA Victor Division at Camden, N.J., has successfully employed an electronic safety guard on presses. A curtain of light, reflecting across the front of the machine and returned to the phototube by means of two mirrors, automatically—if interrupted—locks the machine safely. A different solution is shown in Figure 12–3.

Perspective 12D   SAFETY STATISTICS

The first step toward control is measurement. You have to have an indication of magnitude to know where to start corrective action and to find out if the actions are successful. One of the problems in safety management is assessing the seriousness of damage owed to safety violations. Classical criteria for measuring safety performance are exemplified by the following standard measures:*

1. Disabling injury frequency rate F:

$$F = \frac{disabling\ injuries \times 10^6}{employee\ hours\ of\ exposure}$$

2. Disabling injury severity rate S:

$$S = \frac{lost\text{-}days\ charged \times 10^6}{employee\ hours\ of\ exposure}$$

3. Average days charged per disabling injury $= S/F$

*SOURCE: "Methods of Recording and Measuring Work Injury Experience," ANSI Z16-1-1967, American National Standards Institute, New York, 1967.

COMMENT   Critics of the conventional measures of accident data claim the standards direct attention to existing problems instead of prevention and control of future problems. Alternative approaches include the following:

1. *Error Analysis*   Defines job-related activities and classifies the kinds of errors the job holders could make. This technique is likely to reveal the types of operator-error exposure in advance of an accident.

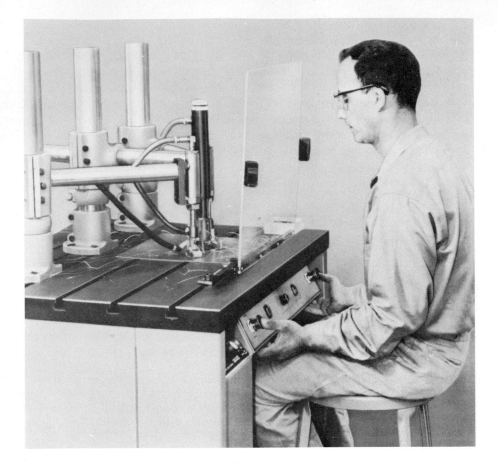

Figure 12-3 Safety features on this welder used for high-speed assembly operations include a plastic shield to protect the operator from sparks and two-part activating controls which force the operator to keep his hands out of the way when the welding unit is discharging. (Courtesy of Omark Industries.)

2. *Task Engineering* Uses techniques associated with systems and human-factors engineering to evaluate human mental and motor performance in designing a work environment that has minimal accident potential.
3. *Critical Incident Technique* Operators subject to hazardous conditions are interviewed to determine any near-misses they have experienced. A "near-miss" is an event where human error could have caused an accident. The seriousnesses of the errors are rated and then ranked according to frequency and severity. The intent is to correct hazardous situations before accidents occur.
4. *Safety Rating Formulas* Mixtures of quantitative data and subjective evaluations are included in formulas that purportedly measure significant safety parameters. One example is a formula by W. T. Fine for evaluating the risk of an accident and justifying the correction of the hazard:**

$$J = \frac{(C)\ (E)\ (P)}{(CF)\ (DC)}$$

where C = Consequence of accident
E = Exposure to hazard
P = Probability of occurrence
CF = Cost factor for correction
DC = Degree of correction

Fine provides factor listings with associated points by which accident situations are subjectively rated. For example, points for the C factor (consequence of accident) run from 100 for a catastrophe to 1 for minor cuts. The inclusive J rating is used for deciding which hazard to correct first.

**SOURCE: W. T. Fine, "Mathematical Evaluations for Controlling Hazards," *National Safety News*, October, 1971.

12-4 WASTE CONTROL

Industrial waste control is accomplished most effectively by a twofold program of (1) *waste prevention,* which endeavors to eliminate or reduce the causes of waste; and (2) *salvage,* which attempts to utilize, reclaim, or dispose of all waste that does occur. These two functions are separate in organization and approach. Waste prevention is a Hydra-headed program in which everyone in the manufacturing organization, from plant manager to sweeper, engages. In spite of all efforts, manufacturing processes do generate a variety of waste which must be disposed of so as to bring the greatest financial return—or the least financial loss—to the enterprise. Here, then, lies the *raison d'être* of the salvage function. Contrasted with waste prevention, which is everybody's business, salvage is generally the responsibility of a section or department reporting to the plant engineer or allied with the maintenance function.

12-4.1 Waste Prevention

Types of industrial waste and preventive measures include:

1. *Unusable Production Material* This material generally results from such causes as errors in engineering and drafting; defective purchased materials; improperly made or sharpened, worn, or wrong tools; defective or poorly set-up equipment; poor workmanship; damage in handling and transporting; and surplus, spoiled, or obsolete materials. In all the above the element of carelessness stands out as the prime cause. Since to err is human, it cannot be entirely eliminated, but it can be minimized by the application of controls. For example, a system for the careful checking of engineering drawings, the systematic inspecting of purchased materials, proper inspection controls of in-process material, improved handling techniques, and better production- and inventory-control methods—these are indicative of the ways in which industry can overcome human failings and reduce its waste production materials.

2. *Residue Material from the Process* This category includes "skeleton scrap" or filigree metal remaining from punch-press operations; "butt ends" or short pieces of the original material; and chips, turnings, remnants of fabrics and plastics, and other items left from production processes. While much of this waste can be

classed as legitimate, some residue materials can be kept to a minimum by altering the process so as to reduce the resultant waste (e.g., die-cast to size instead of sand-cast and machine to size), specifying purchased material sizes to leave a minimum of waste (e.g., slit sheet-metal and cut-fabric widths to leave a minimum of edge waste), improving layout use of material (e.g., "nest" irregularly shaped designs on a metal sheet to obtain the maximum number of blanks per sheet), and checking product design for changes which reduce waste (e.g., design for standard mill widths, thicknesses, and lengths of wood).

3. *Dormant Equipment* Here we consider worn-out, obsolete, or broken machine parts, tools, dies, fixtures, jigs, and gages as well as plumbing and electrical parts, partitions, conveyors, and the like. Careful use and maintenance and controlled issuance and storage are typical of the preventive measures which prolong the life of such items. Once worn out, they should be relegated to the scrap pile and not allowed to clutter up the plant interior.

4. *Supplies* As in the spoilage of production material, carelessness also dominates the wastage of shop supplies. The answer to this type of waste is generally to be found in educational and control measures which militate against carelessness and neglect by employees.

5. *Power and Fuel* Unnecessary use of lights and failure to shut down motors or machinery not in use are two common ways in which power is wasted. Steam, gas, or air leaks likewise are sources of waste. Here the solution is prompt detection and correction of the condition. Other wastage results from technical difficulties or poor engineering of equipment. For example, improper combustion in the plant's boilers and failure to counteract boiler-scale-producing salts are common sources of wasted fuel. Also, oversize motors installed on machines and power-distribution systems with excess line losses contribute to the amount of power wasted.

12-4.2 Salvage

The salvage section collects waste from its point of occurrence and sorts, segregates, grades, and stores it as necessary. Then this section earmarks it for (1) utilization as is; (2) reclamation by repairing or reprocessing; or (3) disposal in the form of scrap. Shipping containers from received goods, dismantled piping, electrical wiring and switches, and used oil drums are typical of waste which can be utilized as found.[2] The filtration of dirty solvents or coolants, welding or brazing of broken tools and machine parts, dry-cleaning of soiled work gloves, and reworking of a defective product so that it passes inspection are examples of how items can be reclaimed to be "as good as new." Whatever cannot be utilized or reclaimed must then be disposed of as scrap. Here we find such activities as the sale of metal chips

---

[2] A similar situation develops with off-standard products which can be sold as "seconds." Here, however, the salvage is placed in the hands of the inspection division and is governed by a merchandising policy prescribed by the sales department.

or machine turnings, the burning of scrap paper, and the dumping as "fill" of scrap that cannot be sold or burned.

When scrap is sold, it is frequently handled through a scrap broker, the actual in-plant arrangements being made jointly by the salvage section and the purchasing or sales department, whichever by custom handles such miscellaneous sales. Finally, the duties of the salvage function include a continual search for other uses of waste, either in the plant or elsewhere, and encouragement of efforts to find ways of handling and processing all forms of waste which will reduce costs and bring in a greater return.

Perspective 12E   WASTE CONTROL CAN SAVE ENERGY AND CUT POLLUTION

The traditional incentive to control wastes has been to reduce production costs. That is still a major incentive, but other concerns have reinforced the need for closer waste controls—rising prices for raw materials makes material recovery from wastes more attractive, potential energy shortages justify investments to convert wastes into fuels, and increasing alarms about pollution bolster efforts toward better waste treatment.

Control of oil wastes is a priority effort because of its energy-saving and pollution-reduction potentials. Control starts with the calculation of an *oil balance* for the operation. The procedure is described by T. F. Dalton:

> Essentially, it involves the determination of all types of oils that come into the plant from any source, such as fuel oil, cutting oils, lubricating oils, quench oils, hydraulic oils, gear oils, etc.
>
> Once the amount has been fixed, as to what comes into the plant, the next procedure is to determine how much and by what means the oil leaves the plant. This involves the calculation of how much oil is separated and recycled back to the same system, how much fuel oil is burned through the combustion process, how much soluble oil or cutting oil leaves the plant in the form of an emulsion, and how much of the various other types of oils are collected for reclaiming purposes. After this approximate quantity has been determined, the difference between these two figures represents the amount of oil that is being lost from the plant or that which remains behind in the system. Of course, the most important value is how much oil is leaving the plant in an unspecified form or undetected form.
>
> Once an oil balance has been made, and a quantitative determination on all types of oils has been ascertained, it is important to see how much of these various types of oils can be treated, recycled, or disposed. Certain oils, by unique segregation, lend themselves towards complete recycling. They include soluble oils, which can be reprocessed and recycled with a great deal of economic benefit. Other oils such as tramp oils or quenching oils may have more use in other forms, such as a fuel oil.*

*SOURCE: T. F. Dalton, "Cut Your Oil Waste," *Industrial Engineering*, August, 1974.

12-5   PLANT AND EQUIPMENT MAINTENANCE

In Oliver Wendell Holmes' narrative of an earlier century, "The One-Hoss Shay," we find a twofold lesson for modern industry. First, nothing is "so built it couldn't break down," and, second, unless a constant watch is kept for the evidences of "a general flavor of mild decay," disaster inevitably befalls. Applied to industry, these two principles lead to but one conclusion:

Effective maintenance of a plant and its equipment is prerequisite to efficient plant operation and uninterrupted production.

Plant buildings deteriorate because of (1) the effects of the weather—sun, rain, cold, heat, wind—and (2) wear and tear resulting from general use, vibration, fumes, etc. While deterioration cannot be stopped, it can be greatly retarded by maintenance.

Machines and equipment likewise are subject to wear and tear from use. Furthermore, machines gradually tend to go out of adjustment not only as the result of use but also because of temperature changes, vibration, "seasoning" of machine parts, settling of floors, and a host of other causes. Time is likewise a factor as corrosion forms in pipes and on vital parts, moisture seeps into electrical windings and breaks down insulation, and dirt gradually finds its way into many types of equipment. To arrest or counteract the effects of all these diseases in its equipment, the only wonder drug at industry's disposal is proper maintenance.

12-5.1 Scope of Maintenance

Industrial maintenance activities generally cover building exteriors, interiors, installations, and servicing equipment; yards and yard equipment; power-plant and power-transmission equipment; electrical equipment; and productive equipment. Also functions of the maintenance department are the stocking of repair parts, piping, wiring, and other materials of maintenance; the introduction or installation of measures to reduce factory waste (e.g., self-closing water faucets, proper dispensers for powdered soap, heat exchangers to permit reuse of cooling water); the responsibility for maintaining safe working conditions for plant employees (discussed previously in this chapter); and the guidance or education of plant supervision on ways of reducing the maintenance required in their respective departments.

Most large maintenance departments today have one or more specialists skilled in each of the major maintenance trades. Smaller plants usually hire outside tradesmen for specific maintenance jobs, principally building repairs and painting, laying roofs, and cleaning windows. These tradespeople operate under the supervision of the maintenance supervisors or all-round handy man, depending on the size of the plant.

Even the larger plants possess some complicated equipment which must be serviced by outside specialists. Automatic elevators with their self-closing doors and various safety devices often call for the attention of trained elevator service personnel if they are to function properly. Complicated office equipment, such as calculators and payroll machines, likewise defy diagnoses by regular maintenance personnel. Many manufacturers of such equipment offer contractual arrangements for periodic servicing by trained specialists.

The apparent trends toward more automatic machines and complex electronic equipment for manufacturing mean that maintenance will become even more important than it is now. And it will be more difficult. Malfunctions must be detected and corrected quickly because an outage in one part of an integrated system can shut down the entire system, and a loss of control can result in a huge number of defective products in a very short operating period. It is reasonable to expect that more refined maintenance equipment will be developed to treat the more elaborate production systems. Such equipment will require greater technological competence to operate. The maintenance personnel of the future will have to be intensively trained. They will likely form a highly selective and respected segment in tomorrow's industrial society.

12-5.2 Planned Maintenance

Planned maintenance is an organized attempt to prevent sudden breakdown in equipment and emergency shutdowns for repairs. It is accomplished first of all by *preventive maintenance*—a definite program of periodic cleaning, servicing, inspection, and replacement of worn parts for vital plant facilities. When a failure does occur, investigation is made of the cause, and statistical records are kept to indicate whether or not the preventive program really is effective.

Such preventive maintenance has long been an economic necessity for enterprises which must operate continuous processes: chemical and cement plants; paper, steel, and brass mills; and oil refineries because of start-up costs. Today many intermittent-process plants invoke planned maintenance, as the high rates paid to employees for down time make equipment failures very costly. Also the prevalence of serialized manufacture and automation, wherein a breakdown of one machine in the production line causes stoppage of the entire line and idleness of personnel, puts a premium on preventive maintenance.

Continuity of operations demands that the following general procedures be carried out:

1. Down time of each item of production equipment for servicing should be planned in advance, and the maintenance department notified.

2. Important items of equipment that require regular cleaning and maintenance or are liable to sudden failure should be installed in duplicate. Included in this category are pumps, compressors, transformers, and power lines.

3. Where (2) is not possible, spare units, parts, assemblies, controls, etc., should be at hand for rapid substitution for an item that fails or shows signs of approaching failure.

4. Records should be kept and analyses made of repetitive failures.

5. Regular and prescribed inspections should be made for signs of approaching failure.

Virtually all plant engineers agree on the first four of the principles defined above; the fifth is debatable. A number of engineers feel that in the long run the cost of regular inspections of equipment exceeds the cost of failures that are thereby prevented. They point out that many breakdowns occur suddenly and without warning, hence the impossibility of predicting the approach of such failures. How does one foresee a fractured drive shaft, a sticky hydraulic valve, a limit switch which suddenly fails to operate, a transformer which blows up, a press die which breaks? These are only a few of industry's breakdown headaches which are difficult if not impossible to cure by the inspection medicine. Thus, each case of preventive-maintenance inspection must be weighed on the balance scale of cost. Does an ounce of prevention really effect a pound of cure, or does a pound of prevention result in only an ounce of cure?

Several mathematical routines have been developed to compare different maintenance plans. The basis for an evaluation is the time distribution of breakdowns. Where machines have been in operation for a considerable period of time, records of the timing and extent of failures are available. Knowing the probability of breakdowns and their associated costs, the expected expenses of different maintenance policies are calculated. One of the best-known examples is the economic comparison of a policy of changing all street lamps at one time and replenishing between blanket replacements with a policy of replacing each lamp whenever it burns out. Similar evaluations are applicable to maintenance policies where the costs of performing overhauls at various fixed periods with repairs made as required between periods are compared to repair costs incurred when no overhauls are scheduled. The wide acceptance of preventive maintenance is indicative of the value of calculations which reveal the interval between overhauls that minimizes maintenance costs.

Of course, economic reasoning frequently must bow to other considerations. In the case of plant buildings, for example, only through regular and thorough inspections can buildings be preserved. No plant engineer worth his shingle waits until the floor caves in before he decides to fix it. On some items of equipment, failure is prohibitive from the standpoints both of property damage and of employee safety. Consider the result of a major elevator failure or an explosion attributable to improperly grounded electrical equipment. Here the consequences dictate careful and frequent inspections which will prevent failure.

The frequency of inspections will depend upon the nature of the facility or item being checked, its importance to the continuity of operations or to the safety of the plant and employees, and the time interval from the first indication of trouble to the actual failure. Safety guards on productive equipment are customarily checked at every setup and at the start of each shift. Certain items of plant fire equipment are checked daily or, at the very minimum, once a week. General inspection of machinery can be scheduled at intervals of perhaps 3 months. Building exteriors generally receive a going-over in the spring and fall of each year.

The second phase of a planned maintenance program is concerned with *long-term maintenance.* Machine-tool manufacturers in recent years have begun to meet industry's demand for machines that require little maintenance or at least are easy to maintain over a long period of time. The moving parts of many machines are now covered with "streamline" metal housings or covers, for not only is such equipment safer to operate but also dirt is prevented from finding its way into working parts. Removable panels and maintenance openings with doors that hinge or snap in place facilitate the work of repair personnel. More and more machines are equipped with semiautomatic or fully automatic lubricating equipment, which make use of either pressure-feed oilers or simply "splash" lubricators. Some bearings and other moving parts are prelubricated for life and require absolutely no attention. Furthermore, motors, controls, and auxiliary equipment often can be standardized with that already in the plant to keep down the variety of spares required.

12-6 PLANT AND EQUIPMENT REPLACEMENT

A sound program for replacing plant buildings and equipment is of long-range importance to any industrial enterprise interested in remaining in business. Wear and tear gradually take their toll on plant facilities, and even the most carefully maintained building or machine eventually becomes prohibitively expensive to maintain further. Today's accelerated rate of technical change brings such a stream of new concepts in construction, design, and materials that with increasing frequency plant facilities "become old before their time" and must be replaced for reasons of quality or operating efficiency. Management cannot "fly blind" on the matter of capital-asset replacements. It must have a planned program which insures that it is spending enough—and not too much—on its facilities in order to stay competitive and produce a quality product at reasonable cost. Before taking a look at industry's replacement patterns, let us first gain an understanding of how funds become available for asset replacements.

12-6.1 Obsolescence and Depreciation

Obsolescence is the decrease in usefulness of existing plant and equipment due to the invention of new and better processes or equipment. Machine-tool manufacturers and other industrial-equipment producers are constantly improving the mechanisms available to the industrial enterprise. Today many items of relatively new manually operated equipment are being made obsolescent by automation. Others become obsolete because they are unable to hold today's close tolerances, meet the needs of miniaturization, or cope with new, harder, and tougher materials. Obsolescence, then, is really a dollar-and-cents measure of the degree to which the productivity and efficiency of existing facilities have fallen behind the productivity and efficiency of those now available.

From an accounting point of view, *depreciation* is an annual charge reflecting the decline in value of an asset due to such causes as wear and tear, action of the elements, obsolescence, and inadequacy. Instead of charging the cost of an expensive piece of equipment to one year's expenses, the charge is spread over the number of years during which the equipment is giving service. It is thus an arbitrary figure entered as a part of the cost of doing business each year, designed gradually to "write off" the financial investment in the plant's assets (see Chapter 19).

From the operating standpoint, depreciation in effect sets aside from each year's income enough money so that funds will be available to purchase a new item of equipment when the present one is worn out. Industry's depreciation system, which is founded on law and Internal Revenue Service regulations, fails to provide for a replacement item of equipment that is high-priced by reason of inflation. It does not provide for replacement equipment that is more costly due to accessories and technological improvements for increased productivity. It likewise does not support additional items of equipment required by company growth. Inflation, productivity, and growth must be financed out of profits or through the introduction of new capital into the business, not from depreciation. The only leeway permitted under today's laws is for a company to use a system of accelerated depreciation by which the enterprise is enabled to retain more of its cash (pays out less in taxes) during the early years of the life of its equipment. With this retained cash, the enterprise theoretically is in a better position to modernize and expand its facilities. However, the tax dollars saved in early years bring a day of reckoning in later years in the form of heavier taxes, the end result being tax deferral, not tax avoidance.

Yet some companies favor small depreciation figures as the way to show greater annual profits on the company's books—for the short-term period at least—and for these companies long depreciation life and slow replacement of present equipment are thus encouraged.

Some industrial owners and conservative controllers hesitate to junk obsolescent equipment on the economic theory that it still retains some undepreciated, useful life on the company's books. Others with an eye on their company's income statement oppose modernization simply because the company still is doing all right financially with old equipment. While their managements may not admit to such a policy, some companies have a tendency to put off buying new equipment until the old is ready to fall apart. In other instances semimonopolistic conditions tend to retard the introduction of new processes and equipment. Fortunately these attitudes, practices, and conditions do not apply to industry as a whole, but they do serve to explain why some segments of industry have been inclined to drag their individual and collective heels on the matter of replacing equipment.

For many years industrial spokesmen have been urging governmental action to relax Federal laws relating to depreciation for tax purposes so as to permit faster write-offs of moneys invested in equipment. They have argued that by shortening the allowable life over which equipment can be depreciated and/or increasing the amount of depreciation that may be taken during the early years of equipment life, thereby increasing retained cash by deferral of taxes, industry will be spurred to modernize its facilities. They have noted how neglect of equipment replacement almost proved disastrous to British industry and how depreciation changes in tax laws helped rectify the situation.

Long-term government opposition to any changes in the tax laws has now swung around to approval, primarily because of the concept that economic activity can be controlled or at least influenced by tax legislation. In the early 1960s, several modifications in the tax laws allowed the use of more rapid, early write-off methods for production resources and encouraged production improvements through investment credits. The tremendous increase in industrial growth as measured by the gross national product in the late 1960s tended to confirm that tax incentives could indeed spur the expansion and renovation of production facilities. After the 1973–74 recession, tax laws were modified again to encourage more capital investment in production facilities as a means to boost the general economy.

12-6.2 Criteria for Plant and Equipment Replacement

How can management decide between the alternatives of continuing with the old facility or replacing it with the new? The general approach is to prepare a cost estimate for each alternative, indicating operating costs over a stated time, usually a year. Each cost figure is then divided by the expected production over the period from that alternative to arrive at a cost per unit of product. Finally, a comparison of the results helps determine whether the return from the new item justifies the expenditure. But what cost factors are considered? What rate of return justifies an investment?

Several replacement methods have been developed as a guide in these matters. The simplest is the method that divides the initial investment by the saving in out-of-pocket operating costs and then applies the rule of thumb, "We'll buy if it will pay for itself in X years." But what is X? One, three, five, or ten years? Should the payoff period for machinery also apply to short-life equipment? To tooling? To office equipment? These questions have found no universal answers, but individual companies have determined answers which fit their own situations, and companies are using this method.

Discounted cash-flow analysis is the most widely used method for evaluating important investment and replacement decisions. A comparison among available alternatives is made by discounting all the cash flows involved to a single point in time. For instance, the purchase price of a machine, its lifetime operating costs, relevant taxes, and final salvage value can all be stated in terms of today's dollar value by discounting the amount of each transaction to the present time. The obvious name given to this evaluation is "present worth comparison." The alternative with the most favorable equivalent present worth, an asset now in use or a proposed replacement, is preferred. Similar discounting procedures yield an *equivalent annual cost* or *rate of return.* All three comparison methods are very sensitive to the accuracy of cost estimates, particularly forecasts of operating costs. Given the same data, the three methods will point to the same conclusion. The rate of return calculations are a bit more tedious, but they produce a rating in the form of a percentage figure which is generally conceded to be the most easily understood criterion (see Figure 12-4 and Perspective 12F).

It is important to note that indirect and in some cases noneconomic considerations not found in any formula also have a bearing on replacement policy. Relative safety of operation, quality levels possible, ease of setup, plant housekeeping considerations, flexibility of the equipment, Internal Revenue Service rulings on allowable depreciation, local taxes affected by asset changes, probable technological developments, unfavorable cash position of the enterprise—these are a random review of other considerations which may stuff the ballot box for or against an otherwise logical policy on equipment replacement.

Of course, a fine balance must be maintained by progressive management to obtain the maximum of use from already purchased equipment while not falling too far behind the march of technological progress. Often, "bugs" present in new equipment designs are worked out during the period of initial adoption by an industry or company, and those enterprises which delay installation slightly obtain more satisfactory equipment in the long run and at lower overall cost than do firms that pioneer in equipment adoptions.

12-6.3 Equipment Rental

In very recent years there has been a significant swing toward the rental of capital equipment by industry as opposed to outright purchase. This trend has found particular favor in rental plans for plant buildings, interplant and delivery trucks, materials-handling trucks, and office equipment. Renting offers the advantages of no capital outlay, no maintenance or servicing worries for the user, and rental cost fully deductible for income-tax purposes as current business expense. Whether the long-range cost of such rentals compared with ownership is lower is a debatable point which each company must decide on the merits of its own case.

Perspective 12F INVESTMENT ANALYSIS

Literature is loaded with recommendations for investment analyses. Various methods of evaluating proposals place emphasis on different investment considerations; for instance, the payback method stresses the flexibility of capital—if the money spent on plant or equipment is recovered rapidly, the funds can be allocated again to other desired projects.

The investment-analysis worksheet in Figure 12–4 leads to dual criteria, the rate of return and payback period. Its use is explained in the following application:

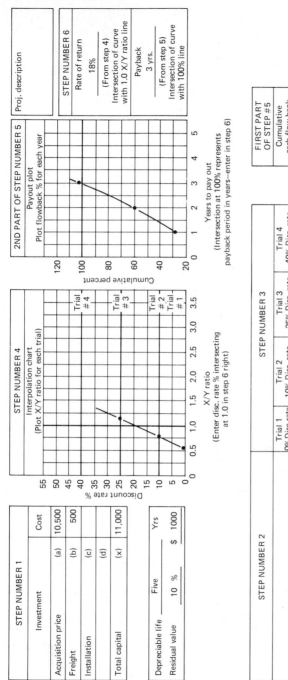

Figure 12-4 Completed worksheet for determination of the rate of return on invested capital and the payback period for a profit-sharing organization.

SITUATION

A proposed replacement requires an initial outlay, including freight charges, of $11,000. It is expected to produce cost savings of $5,000, $7,000, $9,000, $8,000, and $6,000 over the next 5 years. At the end of the fifth year it will have a salvage value of $1,000.

The company has a profit-sharing plan by which 35 per cent of before-tax earnings are distributed among employees. This proportion of earnings is thus an operating expense to the company.

A "capital investment evaluation" worksheet is used to analyze proposals. It is based on straight-line depreciation, a 50 per cent income-tax rate, and interest rates for discrete compounding periods. The proposal is to be evaluated by the six-step procedure given in Figure 12–4.

ANALYSIS

In Step 1, the purchase price and associated costs are recorded. The $11,000 total is the amount X used in Step 3.

Cost savings, lease payments avoided, and other net benefits are entered in column P at Step 2; nonrecurring expenses are deducted in the year they occur. Depreciation in column D results from

$$\text{Annual depreciation} = \frac{\text{total capital cost } X - \text{residual value}}{\text{depreciable life}}$$

This charge is deducted from amounts in column P to obtain net cost benefits C. The portion of these benefits available to the company for capital recovery is 65 per cent, E. After-tax earnings A result from applying a 50 per cent effective income-tax rate to the company's profit share. The after-tax cash flow B is earnings A plus the depreciation charges D.

In Step 3 the after-tax yearly values B are multiplied by single payment present-worth interest factors to obtain the equivalent cash flow at different interest rates. The sums of the discounted values (Y_1, Y_2, Y_3) are the present worths of the net benefits and are the denominators for X/Y ratios representing each interest rate. The X/Y ratio is simply

$$\frac{X}{Y} = \frac{\text{investment at time zero}}{\text{PW of net benefits}} \quad \text{at } i = ?$$

The rate of return is determined graphically in Step 4. At the point where the line connecting X/Y ratios crosses the vertical line at $X/Y = 1.0$, the value of i that makes $X = Y$ is identified.

Similarly, for the graph in Step 5, the cumulative values of the after-tax cash flow at $i = 0(B)$ are divided by the investment X to obtain ratios to plot. The payback period is interpolated from the crossing point of the line connecting the plotted ratios and the horizontal 100 per cent line.

Resulting interpolated values for the return on investment, 18 per cent, and the payback period, 3 years, are recorded in Step 6.*

*SOURCE: J. L. Riggs, *Engineering Economics,* New York: McGraw-Hill, 1977.

12-7 REVIEW QUESTIONS

1. Define motion study. How is it related to methods study?

2. What reactions to methods-improvement programs can be expected from employees and unions?

3. In what fields can the techniques of methods improvement be applied?

4. What is the significance of job enlargement or job enrichment in work design?

5. What effects has OSHA had on employers and employees?

6. How can accidents be reduced? What is the relationship between direct and indirect accident costs?

7. Briefly describe the classes of waste. What is behind the increasing attention given to waste control?

8. What is the difference between breakdown maintenance and preventive maintenance? Where should each be used?

9. What is meant by *obsolescence* and *depreciation?*

10. What is the "payback period?" What significance does it have for managers in equipment replacement?

12-8 TOPICS FOR DISCUSSION

1. In its historic setting, why do you think the scientific-management movement came about just at the time that it did? When else could it have occurred?

2. A definition of methods engineering is proposed consisting of several distinct responsibilities. Which of these seems to you to be the most important? Why?

3. Many suggestion systems started by well-meaning managers have tough going the first year or so. Some even fail and are abandoned. Why should this be? Can you list some approaches which should aid early success?

4. Certain political economists have held that "conspicuous waste" is a hallmark of our civilization. Methods improvement is just the opposite. Which do you think is most characteristic?

5. In recent years, certain equipment-rental companies have become very profitable businesses. On the strength of this fact, the economic basis for the industrial trend toward rental of capital equipment has been questioned by some observers. How do you feel about the justification for this trend? Give reasons for your answer.

6. In what conceivable ways can a company dispose of the following industrial wastes:
   a. Skeleton scrap from punch-press operations
   b. Used and contaminated oils
   c. Water solutions containing cyanide
   d. Worn and broken alloy-steel tools
   e. Radioactive wastes

7. Both of the accidents described below are typical occurrences in everyday operations and both could have been prevented. Assuming you are responsible for safety in each of the situations, what would you suggest to avoid a recurrence? Begin by classifying the incident as due to an unsafe act or unsafe conditions. Then place the cause and responsibility for the injury. Finally, state what action you consider practicable to reduce the possibility of recurrence.

   a. *Incident 1*   A carpenter framing a house was making a cut with an 8-inch electric saw when a fellow employee passing by playfully tickled him in the ribs. He lost control of the saw when it jumped the groove he was cutting. The saw sliced across three fingers of his hand holding the board.

The carpenter was known to be "jumpy." That is why other employees enjoyed tickling him.

b. *Incident 2* A newly hired janitor was pressed into service to run a small power truck when the regular operator was on leave. The truck was used to transport small units of materials from one part of the plant to another on call. The ex-janitor had no training in the operation of the truck but was quite familiar with the factory layout. He piled too many packages on the truck attempting to save time on his trips. On one occasion a box fell off unnoticed and came to rest in the middle of an aisle.

Another worker was walking backwards in the aisle, contrary to instruction, as he wheeled and balanced a handcart loaded with breakable material. He fell over the box lost by the untrained power truck operator, sprained his ankle, and broke half the load he was transporting.

8. Case 12A: *Everyman, Inc.*

In the home office of Everyman, Inc., a great many mimeographed instruction sheets and reports are prepared for the field sales organization. These range from 3 to 35 pages and require collating and stapling. Since a deadline must be met, there is always a rush for completion and often overtime expense. The usual collating method is to place each page in order around a table. The collating people then walk around the table, each picking up one page from each pile, stapling on a large-size stapling machine (able to penetrate 35 pages) at the end of the walk, and depositing the completed reports in a final pile.

Questions

1. Can you suggest improvements in this procedure which may save time and cost?

9. Case 12B: *Small Bolt and Nut Works*

The Small Bolt and Nut Works has a subcontract from General Motors to supply replacement assemblies for auto air conditioners. Each set consists of three envelopes shipped directly to installation garages at automobile dealers throughout the country. One envelope contains a bolt-like rod 6 inches long. The second envelope contains two rubber seals purchased in bulk from another company by the Small Bolt and Nut Works. The third envelope contains two steel washers, a 1-inch coil spring, two brass washers, and a threaded locking cap which acts as a nut on the bolt. When used by the garages, the parts, of which all but the threaded parts are loose fits, are assembled to customers' cars one piece at a time: one brass washer, one rubber seal, one steel washer, the spring, one steel washer, one rubber seal, one brass washer. The bolt is then slipped through and the nut tightened. It can be removed without damage. You are employed as an industrial engineer to reduce the packing and packaging costs on this contract. General Motors does not care how the unit is shipped, so long as it arrives at the garages in good shape. The envelopes are purchased outside at a cost of ½ cent each.

Questions

1. Suggest ways in which savings can be made on orders for 1,000, 100,000, and 500,000. Prepare a complete report of the methods you recommend, showing savings to be attained.

10. Case 12C: *The Bright Shoe Polish Company*

At the plant of this company the final assembly and packing operation is as follows: A steam-jacketed mixer empties the mixed completed polish into 2-inch-high prelabeled jars placed on a conveyor belt. One operator controls the outlet and measures by eye the amount poured, reaching across to fill approximately three jars riding abreast. When the jars have traveled some 20 feet, they reach a final inspector, who notices if the cooled polish has settled level in the jar, drops on the cooled surface a paper disk containing advertising information, adds a felt applicator disk, and spins on the lid, loosely. Three girls, called packers, beside the conveyor, then pick up the jars, complete the lid tightening, and drop the jars into a packing case arranged with space, "egg crates," and corrugated packing shelves. The company is experiencing two difficulties. First, because the jars will hold somewhat more polish than the contents label specifies, there is a tendency to overfill jars. Second, when the weather is warm, the liquid polish has not cooled enough by the time it reaches the final inspector to "float" the paper disk, so the felt disk is saturated. When a purchaser opens such a jar he feels it is only partly full and, in addition, finds the paper disk a nuisance to remove. Furthermore, the hot jars are difficult for the packers to remove from the conveyor belt and they sometimes are spilled, messing up a packing case as well as necessitating refilling.

Questions

1. Can you suggest how this work-station series may have originated as well as why it seems now to be a problem?

2. Assuming that the work load is now balanced and that no change can be made in the jars, packing, or the case for shipment, can you suggest methods improvements in this company?

11. Case 12D: *The Air Strainer Co.*

Foreman Tom Hickey looked as bewildered as could be. How could he get production out of the crimping machine with it fixed the way it was? In his mind he reviewed the history of his dilemma. First Sara, who had run the crimper for 8 years, hung onto a strip too long, and she was now in the sample-preparation room, jocularly called the "hospital" because partly disabled workers were put on light work there. With the machine fixed with a sweep guard Mary worked for just 3 days before she pinched her hand so badly that she quit. He thought that the photoelectric cell guard put on next would solve everything, but the girls were upset. It had taken all his persuasion, and a couple of promises he hated to remember, to get Jane to try it, and when she was hurt the plant manager really got excited. The two-handed operating levers the plant manager had welded on would probably keep anyone from getting hurt, since both had to release air brakes before the crimper could turn over but with both hands on the levers how could an operator make any time feeding? With regret he remembered how Sara used to take six strips at a time and feed one after another without touching the machine.

Questions

1. What suggestions can you make to help Tom Hickey? Outline a series of actions to be taken, and tell by whom each would be done. Which are the most important?

2. Is a long accident-free period of operation necessarily evidence of safe machines? What else may contribute?

3. Would a safety engineer have helped in this plant? How?

12. Case 12E: *Corporation X*

Corporation X is a metalworking firm of fair size and with an established financial reputation in the metals industry. The major share of its investment in equipment lies in its machine tools.

After the first 7 years of successful operations, the nature of the company's business began to change. Old customers faded out; new ones entered the picture with different work requirements. With the company facing new operation problems, the chief plant engineer advised his superiors that $100,000 in new machine tools should be purchased to handle the new production on a low-operating-cost basis.

However, the controller of the company argued that the existing machines were being depreciated at the rate of 5 percent per year and were supposed to be good for 20 years. He presented figures as follows:

Original cost of existing machines $80,000
Current book value at 5% depreciation rate for 7 years $52,000
Estimated secondhand-market value of machines if they were to be sold $20,000
Difference between book and market value or loss on existing equipment $32,000

Of course, in a profit year, the loss on the sale of the old equipment could be deducted from earnings for the year as an expense, but, the controller insisted, a $100,000 investment in new equipment plus a $32,000 loss on the old was a $132,000 transaction.

As a result, no new machines were purchased and the company no longer made the same profit. During years when the old equipment had been profitable, the low rate of depreciation served to keep down the cost of doing business and thereby increased the profits and hence the dividend payments to stockholders.

Now again, several years later, the character of the firm's business has changed. This time new machine-tool equipment is a "must." However, in view of the fact that the high profits of the earlier years have gone largely into dividend payments and the profits of recent years have been low, no cash reserves are available to buy the needed equipment. Efforts to borrow money now have failed because the company's equipment is too old to justify a loan. The company finds itself in the position of having either to raise new capital or to declare bankruptcy.

Questions

1. What was wrong with the policies of Corporation X?

13. Case 12F: *The New Machine Co.*

The New Machine Co., a large machinery manufacturer, has used an old model Herald Internal Grinding Machine to grind the bore and adjacent face of steel countershaft gears. Major restorative repairs are now required on this machine, and a replacement analysis has been requested. The new model Herald machine recommended for this operation costs $30,000 installed. It will produce approximately 2.6 pieces in the time required to produce 1 piece on the present machine. Expected period of use in the manufacture of this gear is 8 years, at the end of which time the estimated value of the machine would be $5,000.

Current sale value of the present machine in its existing condition is $500. Restorative repairs now required on it are expected to total $4,000 and would place it in satisfactory operating condition for the anticipated 8-year period of use. At the end of this time, the restored machine would be expected to be worth $100.

Direct labor cost per year on the present machine is $13,300; on the new machine it is estimated at $5,100. Estimates of other comparative annual costs for the present and the new machine, respectively, are power, $430 and $200; property taxes and insurance, $45 and $550; and normal maintenance, $840 and $500.

Questions

1. What is the payback period for the new machine? What is the rate of return on investment? Would you recommend replacement on the basis of either payoff or rate of return? Why?

13

QUALITY CONTROL

As consumers we all have experienced "products that do not work": items which do not stand up under normal expected usage, are sold with parts missing, or contain poor workmanship. Product reliability—or the lack of it—applies not only to consumer products but also to such items as jet engines, missiles, and nuclear reactors—in fact, to everything industry makes.

How, then, can a company be certain its products will be of adequate quality to stand up in use? What is meant by the term "quality"? Who determines that a product is of acceptable quality? When and how is such determination made? In what ways can statistical techniques aid in controlling and assuring quality? How are measuring instruments used in the quality-control program? These questions define in a general way the nature of management's responsibilities and activities in the field of quality control and hence the scope of this chapter.

13 QUALITY CONTROL

13-1 QUALITY IN MANUFACTURING

Any manufacturing process introduces variables which affect the excellence of the end product. These variables result from the application of materials, workers, machines, and manufacturing conditions. All materials are derived either directly or indirectly from the land, sea, or air and, being thus subject to the caprices of nature, differ greatly as to composition and physical characteristics. People vary in their degree of skill, proficiency, and application to their work. Machines are built by people using the materials of nature, and the interaction of their variables on the machines thus made introduces an entirely new set of variables. Furthermore, machines, equipment, and measuring instruments are subject to wear and tend to go out of adjustment with use. Manufacturing conditions—temperature, humidity, building vibration, composition of coolants, dust and dirt in the air—are likewise factors that of themselves admit certain variations. Only when these variables are regulated to the extent that they do not detract unnecessarily from the excellence of the manufacturing process as reflected in the quality of the finished product can the control of quality be said to exist.

Quality is never absolute—it is always relative to certain other considerations. For one thing, the word "quality" is meaningless unless the *end use of the product* is also stipulated. The term "good quality" means that the article is good for the purpose for which it was intended. For example, a high-quality automobile tire jack might pass every test for quality required of tire jacks, but if it were subjected to tests given jackscrews designed to raise buildings, it would fail miserably. Its quality is adequate only for its intended end use, that of supporting 2 tons—not 20. Also, quality is an abstract word unless related to *definable and measurable characteristics of the product* involved. Thus the quality of a piece of metal should be stated in terms of its chemical and physical properties; a paint in terms of its viscosity, color, drying time, resistance to foreign substances, etc. Quality is likewise related to the *economics of manufacturing.* The degree of quality that can be maintained under a designed manufacturing process, the percentage of imperfect goods, if any, that is acceptable to the producer and/or to the consumer—these are typical of the economic considerations linked with quality control. Furthermore, quality has a bearing on *manufacturing costs* and on *selling price.* High quality generally results in high cost of manufacture, whereas a relaxation of quality standards often permits costs and hence prices to be lowered. Finally, quality bears a relationship to *quantity.* The higher the degree of quality demanded, the tighter become the controls imposed on the manufacturing process and the more difficult it is to achieve quantity output.

In the past two decades industry has seen a tremendous advance in the preciseness of its quality standards. Quality has changed from a generic art to a specific science complete with definite standards and devices for measuring product characteristics against those standards. Instruments now available and in use measure in millionths of an inch. The degree of accuracy involved can be appreciated when it is recalled that one-millionth of an inch is the equivalent of the human hair split 2,500 times! Other characteristics such as color, hardness, surface finishes, and noise, to mention only a few, have in recent years become measurable to great exactness on specially designed instruments. Thus has industry been required to adapt itself to rapidly developing quality standards, measuring equipment, and control techniques. Furthermore, its manufacturing technology has time and again been taxed to keep pace with the ever higher degree of precision demanded by advances in the science of quality.

13-1.1 Scope of Quality Control

Today quality *control* is taking on the emphasis of quality *assurance*—the means to achieving true product reliability. Reliability cannot be inspected into a product; it must be designed and built in. Furthermore, quality control must do more than simply see that products meet specifications. It must follow through to see that products perform in service and, in some circumstances, that they perform in the end product of a customer. When quality control adopts this *systems concept* of reliability, it becomes a factor in every decision in engineering, in manufacturing, and in application, from product development to shipment to end use.

Methodical control of quality can be achieved by means of four principal tools of the trade. These nicely define the scope of quality-control activities and hence are the major topics to be considered in this chapter:

1. *Standards* and *specifications* that establish the quality objectives to be measured or evaluated

2. *Inspection* of materials, parts, and products to compare them against the established standards and to separate good quality from bad

3. *Statistical techniques,* including sampling, analysis, and charting, to indicate whether or not quality is under control

4. *Measuring instruments* or inspection devices used for objective and measurable comparison of actual quality against the established standards

It should be noted in passing that in actual shop parlance the terms "quality control" and "inspection" are often used interchangeably. This, no doubt, is the result of the historical concept of inspection as the principal tool of quality control. Important though inspection is, we must remember that, whereas a program of quality control by bringing variables under control enlarges the production pile, inspection, by separating the good from the bad, merely enlarges the scrap pile.

13-1.2 Organization for Quality Control

Before viewing the tools of quality control, we may logically ask: How does quality control fit into the plant organization?

The administration of quality control in most companies rests with the inspection department. The program is usually headed by a quality manager who, in the case of precision products, operates directly under the top manufacturing executive, usually the plant manager. For manufacture in which precision is not a major factor, the lesser importance of quality permits subordination of the inspection department to the divisional or plant superintendent. Although inspection has been known to operate effectively under the wing of an operating foreman or other supervisor charged with the maintenance of production schedules, this practice is definitely risky. When rush orders arise or when the pressure is on quantity, an operating foreman has a tendency to sacrifice quality in favor of quantity. Best practice dictates setting the people responsible for quantity and for quality on a par with each other and under impartial authority.

A good way to obtain an unprejudiced view of the quality control organization is to look at it as a representative of the customer. The objective of most firms is to satisfy its customers. Customers seek assurance that the firm's products provide a certain level of quality. If the quality control effort is treated as if it was being conducted by the actual customer, operating departments in the firm cannot exert pressure for relief from performance standards. An independent position for the quality control organization allows it to perform whatever activities are necessary to maintain quality standards expected by the customer, even when the activities are unpopular with other departments within the manufacturing system.

Education is an important function of the quality control organization. On the policy-making level, the production-oriented departments may have to be convinced that certain practices or equipment must be installed to raise or maintain quality levels. Since these operating departments often have their own budgetary restrictions, quality representatives frequently have to develop plans, substantiate costs, and present arguments to top management for greater allocations for quality improvements.

Perspective 13A   ZERO DEFECTS

Completely automated factories may eventually become a universal reality, but it seems reasonable that quality control will still be a needed discipline because customized output and services will still be rendered by people. And whenever people are involved there will be variations in performance. Cries of "Craftsmanship is dying" and "Nobody cares about quality anymore" are heard repeatedly. There is no question that the factory system has depersonalized production. It is difficult for workers to take pride in an individual contribution that is scarcely visible in the finished product. Attempts to relieve the "It's just a job" feeling have taken many forms in the last decade. One method that focuses on quality is called " 'zero defects.''

The *zero defect* (ZD) program introduced in the aerospace industries in 1962 has been notably successful in obtaining involvement and higher output quality. The aim of the program is aptly described by its name: ZD means *no* defects. It emphasizes prevention instead of cure to get a job done correctly the first time, every time. It relies on the pride of the workers to identify error-prone situations with the assumption that the people best prepared to eliminate errors are those who create them.

Error cause removal is a key feature of a ZD campaign. Employees are encouraged to sign pledge cards signifying an intent to reduce errors. Suggestions are solicited to help identify areas where mistakes can occur. Supervisors quickly follow up each suggestion to investigate its worthiness and to provide a remedy when necessary. Pins, plaques, dinners, and certificates honor those who contribute the most. ''Days without errors'' scorecards are posted. Top managers speak at mass meetings, and supervisors report on progress at group get-togethers. The high motivation promoted early in a ZD program is difficult to sustain, but the recognition given to the importance of quality production has lasting benefits.

13-2 STANDARDS AND SPECIFICATIONS

The subject of manufacturing standards was discussed at some length in Chapter 9. However, it is important here to consider how the establishment of standards relating to quality affects the maintenance of a program of quality control.

There is a well-known axiom in industrial circles to the effect that *perfection in manufacture is impossible to attain and costly to approach*. We have seen that imperfections are caused by the variables in a manufacturing process and that, through control, the effect of these variables can be minimized to reduce the imperfections. However, the economic law of diminishing returns applies to quality control as it does to everything else: as perfection is approached, costs rise disproportionately.

13-2.1 Tolerances

To be salable, a product must be acceptable to customers as regards both quality and cost. Somewhere along the scales of quality and cost there is a point of compromise at which the quality meets the customer's minimum requirements and the cost fits his pocketbook. At this point, then, is established what might be termed the "basic standard" of quality. In practice, however, there is no such thing as an exact standard, for such a thing is as difficult to attain as is perfection itself. So, recognizing that while it is impossible to avoid variations from any basic criterion it is possible to restrict such variations, industry usually states each standard in terms of a *tolerance* or permissible deviation from the basic criterion. This tolerance defines by means of limits the *zone of acceptability*—a zone of variation that may be permitted without altering the functional fitness of the article involved.

In order that we may better understand the principles underlying the establishment of standards of quality, we must explore further the nature of the manufacturing variables that make tolerances necessary. Basically, manufacturing variables can be grouped into two classes:

Chance variables These include all variables which are inherent in the manufacturing process and which, even if located, cannot be corrected except by a significant change in the manufacturing process itself. They are "chance" in the sense that they are sporadic and may have no regular or predictable effect on the product. Such variables include materials that are not entirely homogeneous, imperfections inherent in the design of the machines employed, natural inaccuracies of inspection instruments, the "feel," eyesight, or judgment of the production operators—all variables that cannot be removed without a major change in materials, equipment, or methods.

Assignable variables These are the variables not inherent in the manufacturing process. Generally they result from such extraneous causes as improper operation of a machine, incorrect sequence of manufacturing operations, machines or inspection instruments worn and in need of repair, room temperatures that vary during the day or in different parts of the same room, vibration of the plant building affecting the performance of the machines—all variables that can be assigned and controlled without altering the manufacturing process.

The chance variables in a manufacturing process generate what is known as the *process capability:* that range of variation in part or product quality that is created by the manufacturing process. Obviously, then, the quality tolerance or zone of acceptability must be set at least wide enough to include within its limits all the variations singly or compounded that are caused by the chance variables in the process. If this is not done, part of each lot of goods is almost certain to be rejected as not falling within the acceptable zone for reasons impossible to control under the existing process. However, where the tolerance is broad enough to embrace the process capability, variation beyond the limits can be assumed to result from assignable variables. These may be detected and located by statistical techniques (described later in this chapter), and corrective measures may be applied.

The tolerance permissible often depends upon whether interchangeable manufacture or selective assembly is involved. *Interchangeable manufacture* is the making of parts to such tolerance that all mating parts will assemble without selection or fitting and will function properly in the finished product. *Selective assembly,* on the other hand, is the sorting of parts into classes according to dimension and the matching of units from corresponding classes and/or the fitting of matching parts so that they will assemble and function properly in the finished product.

Interchangeable manufacture requires close tolerance and calls for precision manufacture of parts so that they will match properly without selection and fitting. Its advantages are cheaper and faster assembly and the interchangeability of replacement parts—an important factor in servicing the product in the field. Of course, interchangeable manufacture is closely linked with standardization and is the *sine qua non* of mass production.

Selective assembly permits looser tolerances and hence requires less exacting manufacturing methods. This reduces the cost of fabrication but may well result in higher assembly costs as each part must be selected or fitted in the matching process. Servicing of the article with replacement parts is complicated, if not impossible. Thus any decision favoring either interchangeable manufacture or selective assembly rests on the relative ease of fabrication and assembly, comparative costs, and field-servicing requirements.

13-2.2 Setting of Standards

In general, standards establishing the quality of products determine standards of engineering, design, process, and material. Quality standards should be reasonable, measurable, available, and understandable. Best practice dictates that they be reduced to writing, possibly on the product drawing, as part of the product specifications, or in standard-practice instructions to the plant. Quality standards are generally set by the product-engineering department in cooperation with the sales, production-control, cost, and inspection departments. The product engineers are guided in setting these standards by the findings of product, process, and material research. As we saw in Chapter 9, the consumer, in the last analysis, sets such standards by his decision to buy or not to buy the product of the enterprise. The product engineers must not only satisfy the customer by pretesting the product for engineering design and utility; they must also consider problems created for the manufacturing organization as it attempts to meet the desired quality standards and the resultant effect on manufacturing costs and selling price.

Under no circumstances should standards be established by the inspection department. The job of that department is simply to interpret the standards for the manufacturing organization and to see that they are observed.

13-3 INSPECTION

Inspection serves the following two main purposes in any quality-control program:

1. *To segregate defective goods and thus ensure that the customers receive only goods of adequate quality.* This type of control is of paramount importance, for upon its success rests the good will and satisfaction of the users of those goods. The principal objective of all "final" inspection (the inspection of finished products) as well as much of the inspection of raw and in-process material is to ensure that no, or at the most very few, defective goods leave the plant.

2. *To locate flaws in the raw material or in the processing of that material which will cause trouble at subsequent operations.* This phase of quality control is purely a tool of manufacturing in that it is designed to anticipate and prevent manufacturing difficulties that might occur. For example, by such inspection, oversize or undersize parts of an assembly are located and segregated before the assembly operation, at which stage such defective parts would cause trouble.

13-2.1 Inspection Responsibility

Authority to pass or reject raw material, purchased parts, in-process material, and finished products is vested in the inspection department. Another part of this department's duties generally is the inspection of critical supplies, tooling, and equipment items. It is also responsible for the issuance, control, and inspection of all gages, instruments, and other measuring devices used by both inspectors and production operators. Joint or possibly complete supervision of the salvage of rejected work and the disposition of scrap to ensure that no defective material is returned to the production flow may be within the province of the inspection department.

Who is responsible for quality—operating personnel or inspectors? One school of thought reasons that foremen have enough to do supervising people, caring for equipment, and getting out production without also taking on the complete quality assignment. Independent inspectors, this reasoning continues, should pass on the process before actual production begins (setup acceptance), then decide periodically during the run whether the process may continue (process acceptance), and finally determine whether the resultant product is passable (product acceptance). The responsibility of the foreman here is simply to see that causes of difficulty with the process and product are promptly corrected. The other school of thought argues that the foreman is as responsible for quality as he is for quantity. Setup acceptance and process acceptance are here placed squarely in the lap of the foreman and his subordinates, and only product acceptance is left with the inspectors. Responsibility for defective work rests solely with the operating personnel. Actually, industry seems to be about evenly divided on this question of responsibility for quality, and both methods are operating with apparent success today.

13-3.2 Inspection Practices

Set forth below are practices which tend to maximize the effectiveness of inspection in controlling quality:

CONTROL RAW MATERIALS AND PURCHASED PARTS The quality of purchased items usually is established through definite, written standards and specifications agreed to by both vendor and purchaser. Thereafter, frequent personal contacts and consultation may be necessary to resolve questions of interpretation, deviation, and substitution.

Raw-material inspection is aimed at two objectives: (1) elimination from the purchaser's plant of those materials that do not meet the quality specifications and could thus cause manufacturing or finished product difficulties; and (2) evaluation of the vendor's general quality performance and ability to furnish acceptable material. This inspection may take place either before shipment of the material by the vendor or after its receipt by the purchaser, as dictated by relative costs. Important raw materials purchased in large quantities and involving high transportation costs (such as wood, steel, and coal) are most economically inspected by the purchaser's resident or itinerant inspector at the vendor's plant. Similarly, because delays due to poor quality may be costly, purchasers often check important subcontracted parts and assemblies before shipment by the vendor. Other materials on which quality failures do not generate major expense problems usually are given a receiving inspection immediately after receipt in the purchaser's plant.

Throughout the production process it may be desirable to retain the identification of the material, its vendor, order number, and data received, particularly if such processing often reveals previously undetected defects. Colored paints, etched or inscribed symbols, or tickets accompanying the material through operations furnish this identification. The practice of identifying raw material and purchased parts makes assignable and hence controllable variables out of what otherwise would pass for chance variables. It also forms a good basis for discussing with vendors the quality of their material.

LOCATE IN-PROCESS INSPECTION STRATEGICALLY Effective in-process inspection prevents (a) a defect from being concealed in the end product (as might happen where the next operation involves assembly or painting); (b) a defect from affecting a subsequent operation (e.g., discovery of a crack in a forging which would break tools and ruin the setup of a machining operation or discovery of an oversize or undersize part that would cause trouble at assembly); and (c) additional work from being performed on rejectable material. In-process inspection is mainly a tool of manufacturing designed to anticipate and prevent subsequent production difficulties that otherwise would occur. The proper locations for such inspection, then, are at points in the process where these objectives are most effectively and economically achieved.

The question of *floor inspection* vs. *centralized inspection stations* also must be resolved. Floor inspection located at the machine or in the production line catches rejections as they are produced and permits immediate corrective measures to prevent further rejects from being made. Centralized inspection stations or colonies of inspectors located outside production centers may not permit this close coupling of manufacture and inspection and require greater transportation of material. However, they facilitate complete segregation of good from bad pieces and improved supervision and control over the output of inspectors.

CHECK END-PRODUCT QUALITY The primary purpose of inspection of finished products (final inspection) is to make certain that the customer consistently receives products which are at a quality level acceptable to him. For most products this involves one or more inspection operations immediately prior to packing for shipment. As we shall see later in this chapter, sampling and statistical techniques play an important part in final inspection.

The military services generally require resident inspection at the plants of their major vendors. Regular calls are also made at the plants of smaller producers of military goods. The assignments of such inspectors include the inspection of raw materials, in-process work, and finished products for adherence to contract specifications. They likewise review inspection practices and procedures in the plant to ensure general inspection competence and check compliance with packaging standards.

PLAN THE INSPECTION OPERATIONS The tasks of each inspector must be clearly established in advance. He must be told exactly what defects he is to look for, the relative importance of each, and the acceptable quality level for each defect so that he may determine when the process is out of control (see Fig. 13–2).

Inspectors should be provided with measuring instruments which as far as possible eliminate the visual, hearing, tasting, and feel methods of inspection. Inspection involving judgment on the part of any of the human senses is far from reliable. These vary with the weather, the reaction of the inspector's digestive system to his breakfast, his mental attitude, home problems, like or dislike of his work, and similarly nebulous chance variables. Thus, wherever the nature of the inspection permits, it is most desirable that comparators or other yes-no mechanical devices be substituted for human judgment. In most enterprises, the production operator is provided with inspection instruments at his or her machine or workplace. These should generally be of the same type as those used in the subsequent inspection operation, so that borderline cases of quality will give comparable readings on both instruments.

INSPECT FOR DEFECTS PROMPTLY Prompt inspection of work has several advantages. Most important, it prevents a machine or process which has gone out of control from continuing to produce defective work. When a float of material is waiting for inspection or when the inspection is performed only after the run is completed, operators are not apprised of their mistakes for some time, and close control is impossible. Also, what otherwise would be simply a sampling inspection for control becomes a 100 percent inspection to separate good from bad pieces. Prompt inspection aids in fixing responsibility for defects. Furthermore, when quantity inspection is tied in with the production-control system and the amounts are compared with those issued to the workplace, it becomes quite difficult for material to be scrapped or stolen without detection.

Tools and gages should be inspected in the tool or gage crib immediately prior to issuance and also directly after use, the latter inspection being designed to discover any damage at once, fix the responsibility for that damage, and segregate the article for repair or discard.

RELATE THE AMOUNT OF INSPECTION TO THE DEGREE OF QUALITY   Inspection is one of the indirect costs of doing business. It is nonproductive in the sense that it adds nothing directly to the value of the product. Wherever an inspection operation can be eliminated or the amount of inspection reduced without interfering with the control of quality, the cost of manufacturing the article in question is reduced just as surely as if an improvement in the manufacturing methods were consummated. Thus the answer to the question of how much to inspect is: the least amount to furnish the control required.

For some requirements, 100 percent inspection furnishes the best, if not the only, means of achieving control. Complete inspection of finished goods, for example, is common practice in many industries. Visual inspections for finish, appearance, condition, or other surface defects, those to control dimensions and to check performance (e.g., testing of electric motors, calibration of thermostats)—in such *nondestructive tests* as these, 100 percent inspection is often inevitable.

However, for other types of control, "sampling" or percentage inspection may be desirable and, in the case of *destructive tests,* the only procedure possible. Typical of such tests are those for longevity (electric lamps), for performance (electric fuses, ammunition), and for ultimate physical properties (tensile strength of metals, ductility of plastics, strength of welding joints, and flash points of oil products). Thus it can be seen that the nature of the inspection has a bearing on the amount of inspection required.

CONTROL INSPECTION OUTPUT AND ACCURACY   Inspection competence is dependent first of all upon the careful selection and training of inspectors. An inspector should be conscientious, thorough, exacting about details, and not averse to routine. Keen eyesight and manual dexterity are requisites for some inspection jobs. The inspector must be carefully instructed not only in the techniques of the inspection operation but also as to its relation to the end product.

In general, there are three means by which inspection output may be controlled. The first and perhaps the most common method is that whereby a standard rate of inspection is established for each inspection element or operation. For example, it may be found that a visual examination of a particular part should be made at the rate of 700 pieces per hour, a micrometer inspection at 500 pieces per hour, etc. These standards should be definitely stated, be reasonable, and not tend to encourage inspectors into slipshod work. The actual performance of each inspector can then be recorded over a period of time and compared with the predetermined standard. In a sense this procedure reveals an inspector's efficiency, and when this efficiency is used over a period of time as a basis for wage increases, the system is essentially one of measured daywork.

Occasionally piecework, or one of the other direct forms of wage incentives, is used as a stimulus for inspection output, but unless carefully controlled, it may be a risky practice, for inspectors become so conscious of their output that quality is bound to suffer. Some concerns, rather than pay inspectors directly for quantity, have devised bonus schemes based on the percentage of defects located. Even so, any inspection on incentive wage payment requires the use of checkers or superinspectors who reinspect a percentage of material handled by the regular inspectors just to ensure that their work is satisfactory. One electric-clock company has found it practical to pay a bonus to its packers for every clock discovered in packing with a visual defect that has escaped its regular line of inspectors.

The third method of controlling inspection output—one which has gained wide favor in line production—is that whereby the inspection operation is geared directly into the line. By setting a standard rate of output for that inspection and balancing out the inspection station against the desired production, as are all other operations in the line, inspection output is thus automatically regulated.

As indicated above, the accuracy of inspectors is determined by reinspection on a sampling basis. An objective measure of accuracy is *the ratio of defects discovered by the inspector to the defects in the original lot.* Whether or not the pay of inspectors is related to their output, good practice dictates the principle that some measure of their accuracy be obtained.

SET UP A PROCEDURE FOR HANDLING BORDERLINE MATERIAL The disposition of borderline material or that where the product quality is just outside the tolerance is often a debatable issue. Should the article be automatically relegated to the scrap heap or can it be passed if the defect is deemed to be so slightly beyond the tolerance as not to be serious? Some quality-control experts contend that if inspectors are permitted to use judgment and to pass some slightly off-color material, the standards and specifications that have been set up for that material are of no avail. If slightly off-color material is satisfactory, it is argued, why not broaden the tolerances and then adhere to them?

The practice of exceeding tolerances can become dangerous unless skillfully handled, for otherwise inspectors tend to disregard standards at will. Many companies permit inspectors to pass only material strictly within tolerances. All off-color material is then set aside for reinspection by special inspectors or a *quality review board,* persons qualified by knowledge of the article and its application to pass or reject it, depending upon the importance of the defect to further processing of the article or to its ultimate service. Sometimes it is necessary to obtain the customer's consent to a *deviation from standard* before shipping him "off-color" material.

MAKE USE OF INSPECTION RECORDS Standard inspection records start with inspection cards or tickets showing the quantity inspected and the number rejected, together with the individual reasons therein. These cards or tickets are customarily made out in multiple, and copies may be supplied to the foreman or superintendent concerned, to the production operator in charge of the work, to the production-control department for posting to production records, to the accounting department for payroll purposes, and to the inspection division as a basis for its records. When these cards are summarized and analyzed over a period of time, they indicate points in the manufacturing process at which control has been breaking down. Assignable causes of past defects can be located by this analysis, responsibility for them fixed, and their recurrence prevented. Furthermore, points in the process at which there has been a dearth or an excess of inspection are indicated. Finally, this analysis can prove or disprove the manufacturing practicability of the product design, reveal quality standards which have been set too high and show up processes that are set to a point of excellence where they are uneconomical to the manufacturer. This sort of investigation, which makes use of past records for future control, frequently employing the statistical techniques described below, can be labeled *quality research.*

Where large, highly complicated, or technical products are involved, it is frequently advisable to retain all inspection records, keyed to the individual product by serial number, for a definite period so as to fix responsibility and to locate sources of trouble that may subsequently develop in the field.

Perspective 13B   QUALITY CONTROL CIRCLES

In Japan a unique movement has united millions of employees in a common pursuit of quality control. It is called the *QC circle,* QC standing for quality control. The first circles were started in 1962 and they now number over 400,000 with greater than 4 million workers participating. A QC circle is composed of a group of production workers and foremen who voluntarily cooperate to solve production-quality maintenance problems. No one is forced to join a circle. After one is formed, it is officially recognized and becomes part of the national organization. Though circles have a grass-roots outlook, top management provides substantial backing and encouragement. Companies help their QC circles actively participate in regional and national conferences.

A first-line supervisor usually leads a QC circle. Meetings are typically held once or twice a month in the evening. During the meeting common problems are discussed, plans are made to solve the problems by collecting data, and recommendations based on the analyzed data are prepared for presentation to appropriate managers. Circle members use control charts, cause-and-effect diagrams, histograms, and other quality-control techniques to develop solutions. A poll of 1566 companies in Japan showed 91 percent have QC circles.

COMMENT   The concern by Japanese workers for quality, as exemplified by the QC circle movement, is compared to American practices by the following commentaries:

Of the utmost importance is the fact that through the QC circles, the Japanese have made a clean break with tired, outworn theory that plagues the West. This is the theory that the company's quality troubles are due to operator indifference, blunder and even sabotage. Under this theory, the operators could solve the company's quality problems if only the right motivational level could be found. . . . All this is in refreshing contrast to the painted, noisy spectacles which characterize all too many of our (Western) motivational programs. The speeches are made, the posters go up, the pledge cards are signed, the hot potato is thrown into the lap of the operators. Yet, except as a show for customer relations, what good is it if the basic assumptions are defective?*

*SOURCE: J. M. Juran, "The QC Circle Phenomenon," *Industrial Quality Control,* January, 1967.

The QC Circle also provides a door in the industrial organizational structure, between labor and management, through which the experience of bringing about technical change is shared by both.
   While the Japanese are gathering their work force's talent, we seem to be going the other way. Hundreds of managements and labor unions are negotiating contracts designed to sustain their workers' material needs. At the same time, all kinds of supplementary schemes are going into contracts to give workers time off the job and compensating them for it.**

**SOURCE: J. F. Hird, "Japan's QC Circles," *Industrial Engineering,* November, 1972.

It is probably not possible for all countries to follow exactly the same approach the Japanese have developed so successfully, but their example has many features worth considering.

13-4 STATISTICAL TECHNIQUES

The application of statistical techniques to the field of quality control is one of the leading advances in industrial technology of the present century. Originally introduced and perfected in the Bell Telephone Laboratories and the Western Electric Company in the 1920s, statistical quality control did not find general acceptance in industry until the 1940s. By that time, workable shop tables eliminating most of the statistical calculations were published, and, as charting techniques became popular, statistical quality control really "caught on" in industry. It has brought startling reductions in inspection costs and permitted a more fundamental control of quality than previously was possible. Proper tolerances for a process can now be set scientifically. Needless inspections and production interruptions (e.g., machine adjustments when the work is well within control) can be eliminated. A reduction in scrap and in material to be reworked, together with an improvement in the plant's average quality level, almost invariably results. Definite assurance of incoming or outgoing quality is obtainable. For the future, as the statistical techniques are improved further and as their application becomes universal, quality control should be virtually freed from its bonds of empiricism.

13-4.1 Fundamentals of Statistical Control

Essentially, statistical quality control regulates the quality of materials, parts, products, and processes by scientific techniques of sampling inspection, analyses of results, and charting devices. It relies on the *theories of probability* originally developed three centuries ago in connection with problems of a dice game and subsequently made respectable by mathematicians who absorbed the theories into their lore. One of the basic premises of probability is that there is a natural variability of things, both man-made and in nature, according to a definite pattern. "Identical" products made in the same lot under stable manufacturing conditions if measured with sufficient accuracy actually are found to vary from piece to piece in each characteristic measured. Sorting and stacking the pieces according to their measurement or plotting the results reveals a definite and predictable variation pattern. Ideally, without any disturbing influences, the pattern would be a completely symmetrical, bell-shaped form known as a *frequency-distribution curve*, in which more pieces tend to locate centrally than are scattered above or below this central *mean* or average (see Fig. 13–1). Any variation in the symmetry of this pattern may represent disturbing influences requiring investigation (see Fig. 13–2).

Furthermore, the chance that measurement of a portion of a lot (sample) will reveal the true condition of the entire lot (population) is also developed from the probability theories. In evaluating the quality of a lot, therefore, it is possible to select a sample of specified size, analyze its condition (usually determining the mean and a measure of dispersion, as the *standard deviation*, or the *range*), and predict from it with calculated *confidence* the condition of the entire lot.

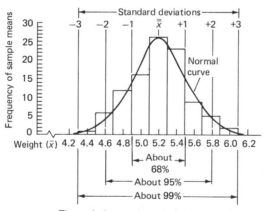

Theoretical percentages under the normal curve

Figure 13-1 The bars in the chart form a histogram that records the means of samples ($\bar{x}$) obtained during inspections. Assuming the sampling is undertaken to check the weight of a product, it is apparent from the chart that the average weight of all units sampled ($\bar{\bar{x}}$) is 5.2, and the means vary from 4.4 to 6.0. The superimposed curve shows the frequency of weights that would occur if the process exactly followed the theoretical normal distribution. The base of the curve is divided into six equal segments, each representing one standard deviation. About 99 per cent of the process observations represented by the normal distribution should fall within three standard deviations on either side of the process mean, $\bar{\bar{x}}$.

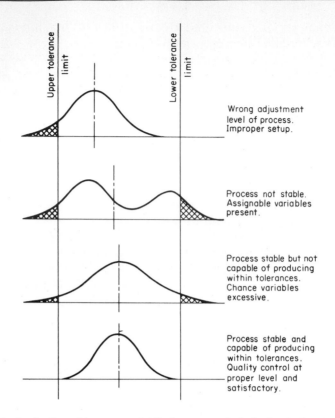

Figure 13-2 Application of frequency-distribution curves to indicate whether quality is under control.

13-4.2 Acceptance Sampling

This is a statistical sampling technique widely used for receiving and final inspection. In either application, the quality characteristics of the product are classified as *critical, major,* or *minor.* A critical defect is one that could result in hazardous conditions for those using or maintaining the product, or that could prevent proper performance of a major end item in which the product is used. A major defect is any defect, other than critical, that could result in failure of the product or materially affect its usability, operation, or performance. A minor defect is one that does not materially affect the usability, operation, or performance of the product. An *acceptability quality level* (AQL) is determined for each defect characteristic and expressed in terms of *per cent defective* (per cent of defective units to number of units inspected) or *defects per hundred units* (number of defects in 100 units, one or more defects being possible in any unit of product). A factor in acceptance sampling is the *process average* or average percent defective of the product as supplied by manufacture for original inspection, i.e., before removal of any rejects. Whether or not the product is being manufactured under satisfactory controls as indicated by the process average determines whether normal, reduced, or tightened sampling inspection is necessary to ensure the desired outgoing quality level.

Let us now see how acceptance sampling is applied in industry. Consider the problem of testing delicate springs for initial tension. We can assume that the lot size is 1,500 pieces, the current process average is 1.1 per cent defective, and an AQL no worse than 2.0 per cent defective is desired. Published tables show that, under a single sampling plan, a random sample of 65 pieces should be taken from the lot and that if two or fewer defects are found, the lot of springs is acceptable. If more than two springs are bad, the entire lot should be rejected and corrective measures initiated. Similar tables present like information for double and sequential sampling methods by which very good or very poor lots are quickly disposed of and more attention is devoted to lots showing evidence of borderline quality.

Many companies now use acceptance sampling in *quality-level certification* whereby the vendor certifies to the customer that the quality characteristics in each lot are within specified limits. Initially the customer analyzes the product for critical, major, and minor defects, as discussed above, and customer and vendor together determine the AQL which can be allowed and achieved for each quality category. They then enter into a "quality-level certification agreement" whereby, in return for assurance from the vendor that each lot will meet the AQLs prescribed, the customer agrees to accept all defects found, provided that the number of defects is within acceptable limits. Both vendor and customer check lots by statistical sampling, and thus control is arrived at economically for both parties. Furthermore, some users of such agreements have found that they tend to eliminate arguments over quality and thus improve relations between the vendor and the customer.

Perspective 13C SAMPLING PLANS

Acceptance sampling is conducted to give assurance that internally generated or externally supplied products meet specified expectations. The products may be packed in boxes, barrels, trucks, rolls, or any other natural division of quantity. The divisions are a measure of lot size. Each lot is sampled to judge its conformance with requirements. The result is a recommendation to accept or reject the entire lot.

Different types of sampling plans have been developed to produce realistic appraisals at a reasonable expense. To select a sampling plan we must answer four questions:

1. What is the maximum percentage of defectives in a lot that makes it definitely unacceptable (*termed the lot tolerance percentage defective*, LTPD)?
2. What is the maximum percentage of defectives in a lot that should be accepted (known as the *acceptable quality level*, AQL)?
3. What probability of accepting an actually nonacceptable lot is the consumer willing to risk (known as the *consumer's risk*)?
4. What probability of rejecting an actually acceptable lot is the producer willing to risk (called the *producer's risk*)?

Answers to these four questions lead to the development of a curve like that shown in the accompanying chart.

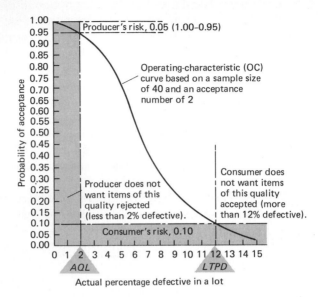

Actual percentage defective in a lot

Every sampling plan can be represented graphically by an *operating characteristic* (OC) curve, as displayed in the chart. The shape of the curve depends on the ratio of the sample size to the lot size and the desired consumer's and producer's risks. The given OC curve is designed for sampling lots with a large population by using a sample size of 40 items. A lot is rejected when more than two defectives are discovered in a sample. The discrimination of this plan (its ability to accurately detect good or bad lots) would be increased by increasing the sample size with a proportionate increase in the acceptance number (the maximum number of defects that can be found in a sample which still allows the lot to be accepted). This increase in discrimination affects the OC curve by moving it to the left in the chart and making it steeper.*

*SOURCE: Two government documents on sampling have become accepted standards for industrial use: Military Standard MIL-STD-105D, *Sampling Procedures and Tables for Inspection of Attributes,* April, 1963; and Military Standard MIL-STD-414, *Sampling Procedures and Tables for Inspection of Variables for Per Cent Defective,* June 1957. Both are available from the Superintendent of Documents, Washington, D.C.

COMMENT In the plan shown, the probability of accepting a lot with 12 per cent defectives is 0.10 and the probability of rejecting a lot with 2 per cent defectives is 0.05. While the design of the plan is undeniably important, the success of the sampling operation depends more on how well it is managed. "What, when, where, and how" to inspect is more critical than "which way" to sample.

13-4.3 Limitations of Sampling

It is important to remember that, where sampling is involved, some defects invariably are passed. However, not even 100 per cent inspection catches all the bad pieces. Such inspection, because it must rely at least partly on the human element and because it is a monotonous operation breeding "inspection fatigue," does not guarantee perfection.[1]

In any percentage inspection, the sample must be selected at random if proper control is to be achieved. Liquids are seldom homogeneous throughout. Tools machining metal parts are subject to gradual wear. Grinding wheels processing precision parts continually break down. Thus, samples taken from only one part of the lot are not always representative of the whole. A representative sample from a tote pan of parts is one that contains pieces selected at random from the top, middle, and bottom of the billet. Tests on coal for heat-unit properties usually require repeated quartering processes to ensure that a representative sample is obtained. Randomization is likewise subject to the honesty of production operators. In more than one instance on record, a not too honest operator, observing that inspectors were checking only material on top of each box, has succeeded in getting defective material passed by simply placing the rejects at the bottom of the box.

13-4.4   Control Charts

The statistical control of process quality is usually accomplished with the aid of control charts. They are a form of inspection record that indicates the need for investigating conditions, processes, or workers for causes of defective work beyond that caused by chance variables. These charts keep a running record right at the machine or workplace to indicate when production is driving down the paved road of good quality, when it is wandering off onto the dangerous soft shoulders of borderline quality, and when it is definitely in the ditch and out of control. Control charts are used for testing tight tolerances, selecting preferred vendors, clarifying disputes between vendor and customer, and improving process quality (by the prompt location of assignable variables). Applied to a specific machine, they show the effects of tool wear, point to changes in methods or equipment, and indicate when to adjust or reset the machine. A typical control-chart application is shown in Figure 13–3. Some companies now include their control chart with each shipment of goods to the customer to certify its quality level.

13-5   MEASURING INSTRUMENTS

Measuring instruments furnish the means for performing delicate and exacting inspections required in today's precision manufacturing. If we had

---

[1]An interesting experiment has been repeated many times to prove the unreliability of 100 per cent inspection where the defects are not entirely obvious. A known number of defects are mixed with a batch of good items and then the entire lot is inspected. Typically, after a 100 per cent inspection only about 70 per cent of the defects are picked up. Even after submission to reinspection three more times (400 per cent inspection), about 2 per cent still may be undetected.

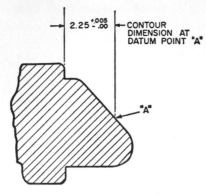

QUALITY CONTROL CHART

DEPT. AUTOMATIC	OPER. 952 1005 922	PART NO. 1234
MACH. NO. 214-5	INSPEC. 821 106 1010	CHAR. CONTOUR DIM.
SAMPLE SIZE 1234	GAGE READING 2.25=0	SPEC. 2.25 +.005/-.00

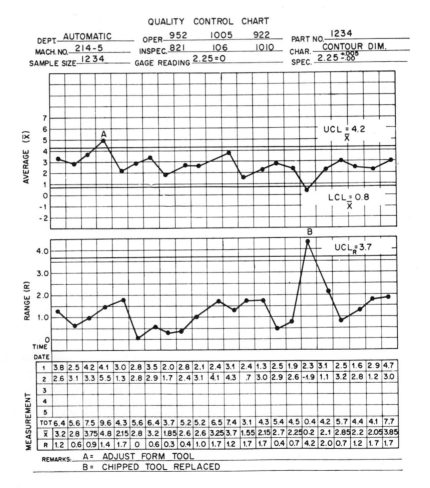

UCL $\bar{X}$ = 4.2
LCL $\bar{X}$ = 0.8
UCL R = 3.7

MEASUREMENT																					
1 3.8	2.5	4.2	4.1	3.0	2.8	3.5	2.0	2.8	2.1	2.4	3.1	2.4	1.3	2.5	1.9	2.3	3.1	2.5	1.6	2.9	4.7
2 2.6	3.1	3.3	5.5	1.3	2.8	2.9	1.7	2.4	3.1	4.1	4.3	.7	3.0	2.9	2.6	-1.9	1.1	3.2	2.8	1.2	3.0
3																					
4																					
5																					
TOT 6.4	5.6	7.5	9.6	4.3	5.6	6.4	3.7	5.2	5.2	6.5	7.4	3.1	4.3	5.4	4.5	0.4	4.2	5.7	4.4	4.1	7.7
X̄ 3.2	2.8	3.75	4.8	2.15	2.8	3.2	1.85	2.6	2.6	3.25	3.7	1.55	2.15	2.7	2.25	0.2	2.1	2.85	2.2	2.05	3.85
R 1.2	0.6	0.9	1.4	1.7	0	0.6	0.3	0.4	1.0	1.7	1.2	1.7	1.7	0.4	0.7	4.2	2.0	0.7	1.2	1.7	1.7

REMARKS: A = ADJUST FORM TOOL
B = CHIPPED TOOL REPLACED

Figure 13-3 Control chart used at the Mueller Brass Co. to control the dimension indicated on the part shown at left above. Note the out-of-control points A and B on the chart, which required corrective action.

to rely on the human senses alone, precision would be a myth. Instruments supplement, and in some cases supplant, the human element in inspection operations. Generally, they magnify and/or compare physical or chemical characteristics of the item being inspected against the desired standards or against a sample of known characteristics. It can be truly said that our high-volume precision manufacture is possible today largely as a result of the tremendous strides made in recent years in developing and applying instruments for inspection.

Decision as to the best measuring instrument for a particular application is influenced by the degree of precision required, the volume, continuity, and value of production, the amount of inspection, and the cost of alternative instruments and their rate of operation. Also, characteristics of the various instruments under consideration, such as their reliability, maintenance and servicing problems, stability without adjustment, and flexibility to meet changes in product or production, are important factors in this decision.

13-5.1 Types of Measuring Instruments

Many instruments of inspection are classified as gages. A gage may be defined as a device for investigating the dimensional fitness of a mechanical element in relation to its predetermined dimensional standards. Gages may be either *absolute* measuring instruments capable of establishing dimensions directly or *comparator* types of instruments which are *calibrated* by absolute instruments. Among the more common absolute gages are fixed-size gages (i.e., plug gages for checking internal holes, ring gages for external diameters) and micrometer gages which use the screw principle for magnification. Comparator gages employ mechanical, electronic, or air magnifying devices to compare the object with a predetermined standard. Comparator gages frequently are used in combination to check a variety of dimensions in one setting or are made automatic, checking hopper-fed items or segregating good from bad parts as they leave a machine. If desired, automatic gages can regulate the machine. Some automatic gages function at incredible speeds and inspect many thousands of parts per hour. Air gages operating on the principle of air escapement between a known diameter and the part being inspected check with great accuracy internal and external dimensions. Optical comparators are flexible and accurate instruments widely used for checking the profiles of exterior shapes and forms and for measuring the dimensions of contours.

Not only has progress been made in the field of dimensional-control instruments, but the materials from which such gages are made have also undergone marked improvement. Various sintered-carbide plug gages, gage points, and gaging surfaces have been developed and are in demand because their remarkably long wear means freedom from gage adjustment and replacement. Chrome-plated gage surfaces are also in favor in some applications because of their wear-resistant qualities.

Electronic inspection devices perform an increasingly large number of industry's quality tests today. Typical applications include the electronic testing and sorting of fruit; testing of milk for pasteurization; gaging of paint for thickness; matching of colors and finishes; and measuring, controlling, and recording of pressure, temperature, humidity, smoke, and acidity. Automatic electronic sorters reject defective, oversize, undersize, and off-color articles. Furthermore, the electron tube is used to inspect the insides of articles which the eye cannot possibly see. Still other electronic instruments convert the noise made in rotating devices into graphic displays of frequency and amplitude of the causal vibrations and inspect the lips of bottles and jars faster and better than can human inspectors. Closed-circuit industrial television (ITV) is employed to see around corners, provide extra eyes for simultaneously monitoring several different points in the process, and peer into equipment where the working conditions are such as to make human attendance impossible. For the future, ITV promises to become increasingly used as a watchdog for controlling process quality and lowering inspection costs (see Fig. 13–4).

Figure 13-4 Television is utilized for quality control. Saw chain parts are projected on a calibrated screen 103 times their actual size. This allows the inspector to get a precise reading on how well the parts have met specifications. (Courtesy of Oregon Saw Chain Division, Omark Industries.)

Industrial radiography is also playing an important role in the field of inspection. Powerful X-ray equipment can photograph the interiors of metals, welds, castings, armor plate, and molds without injury to the item tested. Betatron and radium equipment is used for similar nondestructive testing. A very sensitive and rapid "beta gage" measures the thickness of paper and metal sheets and strip. Here the number of beta rays that can pass through the material determines its thickness. Radioactive isotopes, being much less expensive than radium and X rays, are coming into their own in industrial-inspection applications as tracers and as radiation sources for flaw detection.

Ultrasonics is assuming considerable importance in inspection equipment. Ultrasonic impulses reflected from surfaces or defects in the object under test (similar to the echo principle in radar) are used to measure thicknesses of paper and metal (where only one side is accessible); detect porosity, subsurface cracks, and varying grain structures in metals; and calculate volume of fluids in closed tanks. Another ultrasonic device detects internal defects in the rubber-to-cord bonding and air bubbles in the rubber layers of automobile tires.

Widely accepted as inspection techniques for disclosing hidden flaws in ferrous metals is *magnetic particle inspection.* By magnetizing the item to be inspected and permitting iron filings to be distributed over its surfaces, this process indicates any flaws in the metal as an interruption in the magnetic flux pattern of the filings. Similarly, nonmagnetic materials can be inspected under "black light" through the use of a fluorescent penetrant and developing powder.

Magnetic testing devices have been developed to inspect the hardness of steel parts and to show up cracked articles. The testing of stressed parts is accomplished by a *lacquer coating* which is sprayed on the article to be tested and which breaks up under localized stress, thus revealing cracks and structural weaknesses. The *profilometer* and other similar instruments are widely used for measuring surface finishes in terms of microinches (millionths of an inch). Finding application in the textile, dye, and paint industries is the *spectrophotometer,* a device for checking and matching colors. One instrument measures the moisture content of paper, another indicates leaks in products which must be free of liquid or gas leaks, another measures the shock resistance of a product, and still another determines the adequacy of lubrication. Few product characteristics by now have not succumbed to some form of measuring device. Those mentioned here are typical of the many inspection instruments found in industrial plants today.

Much attention is being devoted today to the integration of inspection devices with production machines as part of the swing toward automation. Inspection devices are used for *in-process control,* i.e., to prevent faulty parts from being made by the production machine, or for *post-process control,* i.e., to inspect parts at a station on or adjacent to the machine and to segregate parts (as O.K., oversize, or undersize). An example of an automatic inspection station is shown in Figure 13–5.

Figure 13-5 This 12-station solid-state testing carousel automatically makes a complete electrical checkup of electric or gas clothes dryers as they come off the assembly line. The test carousel puts dryers through 15 different test functions. When a dryer passes all tests, a green light comes on, indicating ACCEPT. Should it fail any tests, a red light comes on to indicate where the malfunction occurred. The 12 stations are independently controlled by microcomputer. The operator establishes the model number, and by use of thumb-wheel switches, codes the microcomputer. Test parameters are automatically set up. All decisions on acceptability are made within the software program. (Courtesy of General Electric Company.)

13-5.2 Control of Measuring Instruments

All measuring devices, whether used as work, inspection, or master gages, must be under systematic inventory control and undergo periodic inspection. As already noted, such control is properly the function of the inspection department. The usual procedure is to issue portable gages from enclosed gage cribs only to operators and inspectors presenting gage tickets or job cards properly authenticated. Each gage may then be charged out to the employee, either through the use of a ticket-record system or by means of a metal tool check.

Good practice dictates that gages be checked at least once each shift— and, in the case of some gages, even more frequently. Some companies catalogue every gage to find out how long it takes to wear off-limits. On gages subject to progressive wear, the exact dimensions of each may be recorded at every check-in. Then, as wear approaches the fixed limit, the tool-stores department can be advised so that it can plan for repair or replacement.

Process and inspection comparator gages are checked in a "gage room" against such absolute devices as gage blocks of known and carefully maintained fixed dimensions. Some companies requiring very precise measurements establish *metrology rooms,* constant-temperature, relatively dust-free areas, in which gage blocks and other measuring devices are referenced against master sets or are measured to a millionth-of-an-inch accuracy by *interferometry,* utilizing wavelengths of light. The National Bureau of Standards also is utilized by industry for the calibration of master gage blocks.

Perspective 13D CAUSE AND EFFECT DIAGRAM

Cause and effect (C&E) diagrams have evolved from one-sided cause analysis, or a single-sided diagram, developed and widely acclaimed in Japan. Its creator was Professor Kaoru Ishikawa who devised this form of analysis in 1953 while doing quality-control consulting. He used it to communicate with managers who felt the complexities of quality problems were overwhelming when explained orally. Today nearly all Japanese quality control texts contain a section devoted to the Ishikawa diagram.

A C&E diagram is composed of interlocking arrows leading into and out of a problem symbol. The main shafts to the left of the symbol represent principal causes; those to the right represent main effects. Smaller arrows directed toward the major shafts relate control parameters of the cause factors or detail the results of the basic effects.*

The "cause" half of a C&E diagram is shown below. Four main causes have been identified for the "measuring equipment problem." Smaller arrows provide additional information about the prime factors. In a fully developed C&E diagram, the sub-factor arrows would convey specific data, such as the measurement units appropriate to the control of each factor.

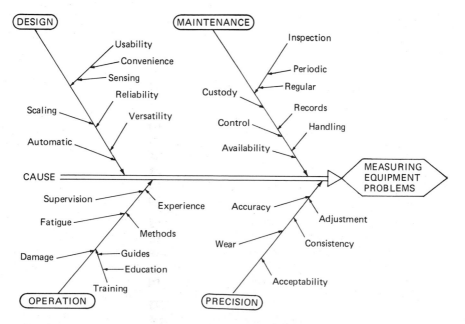

*source: M. S. Inoue and J. L. Riggs, "Describe Your System with Cause and Effect Diagrams," *Industrial Engineering,* April, 1971.

COMMENT The C&E diagram displayed above is one-sided to draw attention to the causes, not the effects, of troubles associated with measuring equipment used for quality control; a complete C&E diagram would have a comparable branching structure to the right of the center hexagon that defines the problem. The purpose of constructing a C&E diagram is to identify and show the relationship of factors influencing a situation. The act of diagramming tends to make the investigation more thorough by exposing what has already been discovered to further questioning, both as to accuracy and completeness. And, like most graphical presentations, it improves communications.

13-6 REVIEW QUESTIONS

1. What is the objective of industrial inspection? How is the objective achieved?

2. Distinguish between chance causes and assignable causes.

3. What factors should be considered in deciding where inspections should take place in a production process?

4. What is statistical quality control? How does it differ from inspection?

5. Describe a control chart and indicate how it is used.

6. Explain what acceptance sampling is and how it can be used.

7. Compare a zero defect program with the QC Circle movement.

13-7 TOPICS FOR DISCUSSION

1. "Once in my life I would like to own something outright before it's broken. I'm always in a race with the junkyard! I just finished paying for the car and it's on its last legs—They time those things. They time them so when you finally paid for them, they're used up."[2]
   How can industry combat a public attitude similar to that expressed by Willy Loman?

2. This advanced age of mayhem, in which armory has been replaced by rocketry, propellers by propellants, and human and divine guidance by inertial and celestial guidance, has given cause to dissect the inch into a million parts. In this new realm of precision, such apparently stable materials as metals, ceramics, and plastics exhibit very unstable tendencies. Let the inspector's hand approach a part or a gage, allow a ray of sunlight to fall on them, open a door and cause a breath of air to enter, permit the part to remain untouched overnight, or give it a ride in the baggage compartment of an airliner, and our immobile, unyielding material appears to be but putty under an instrument that measures millionths.
   What steps can industry take to stabilize the materials it must use so as to give meaning to dimensions expressed in millionths of an inch?

[2]Lament of Willy Loman in Arthur Miller's play "Death of a Salesman," New York: The Viking Press, Inc., 1949.

3. A common industry practice is to require machine operators to work within tolerances shown on blueprints. Then, to allow for slight gage inconsistencies and to take care of the "borderline-quality" problem, inspectors are permitted additional leeway (as blueprint tolerance ±0.001 inch) in accepting or rejecting the item. What do you think of this practice and why?

4. One quality-control practice involves charging the department or employee responsible for scrap. In plants where the department is charged, the cost of scrapped material is charged to the foreman's cost record. Where the employee is "charged," usual procedure is simply not to pay him for pieces he is responsible for scrapping.

   A recent survey of the practice indicated that about 85 per cent of machinery, electrical-equipment, and transportation-equipment plants use a scrap-charging system whereas only 60 per cent of the manufacturers of instruments (for aircraft, missiles, industrial equipment, etc.) use such a system.

   Comment on the pros and cons of the practice. Suggest reasons why it is not so prevalent among instrument plants.

5. Analyze each of the following quotes. State two views on each statement, one supporting the quote and one in opposition or expressing a weakness in the logic. Which view agrees most closely with your personal opinion?

   a. "We don't dare use any statistical techniques for quality control in our business because we can't afford to send out a single defective product to our customers."
   b. "The only thing important to me in a sampling plan is the amount of the consumer's risk. I couldn't care less about protecting the producer. I'm the customer and customers are always right."
   c. "It's misleading to say 'quality is everybody's business.' You should say it is the manager's business to get everybody involved with quality. When a job belongs to everybody, it can easily become a job that nobody does."

6. Case 13A: *The R. Manufacturing Co. and A. Parts Co.*
Magnetron vacuum tubes produced by the R. Manufacturing Co. for use in the U.S. Air Force airborne radar transmitters recently began to be rejected by the Air Force in alarming quantities because of malfunctioning or short-life operation. Engineers checked production runs and final test procedures and established the fact that the magnetrons left the R. Manufacturing Co. plant in excellent condition.

   The company then asked and obtained permission to investigate performance of its magnetrons in actual field service. The investigation revealed that steel tools were being used to install them and steel wool to clean them. (The magnetic properties of the tube must be protected constantly, and the presence of ferromagnetic articles near the tube can cause demagnetization.) Pencil marks made for identification purposes during installation appeared on the ceramic surfaces of the tubes. (Graphite on the ceramic face of the tube could cause a path of arcing and irreparably damage the tube.) Failed magnetron installations showed evidence that the oil used to insulate the cathode bushing in the equipment was contaminated. (Contaminated oil hastens tube failure.)

   The A. Parts Co. supplies gas gages to one of the car divisions of the automotive "Big Three." Recently, customers of cars made by this division complained that their gas gages indicated a full tank when the tank actually was one-quarter empty. The car division blamed the A. Parts Co. for supplying faulty gas gages.

   Intensive investigation made by the A. Parts Co. finally revealed that on this model car the small vent from the gas tank became obstructed by frozen moisture in winter. Then, as the fuel pump continued pumping, a partial vacuum resulted which partly collapsed the tank. The end result was that the operation of the gas-gage float in the tank was restricted and the gage read incorrectly.

Questions

1. What responsibility does a company have for quality once title to its product passes to the purchaser?

2. How can the R. Manufacturing Co. and the A. Parts Co. each prevent recurrence of problems similar to those described?

7. Case 13B: *The Alexander Aircraft Co.*
A prominent manufacturer of aircraft equipment obtains "aircraft-quality" material (raw material and component parts) from many outside vendors. On all incoming material, this manufacturer maintains a quality rating on which a monthly report is sent to vendors.
   The rating formula is as follows:

$$\text{Rating} = 100 - \frac{100 \ (\$ \ \text{material review} + \$ \ \text{source rejects} + \frac{1}{2} \ \$ \ \text{vendor CAD})}{\$ \ \text{inspected}}$$

The item "$ material review" refers to dollars of material rejected at the manufacturer's receiving quality-control check. The item "$ source rejects" involves rework or replacement of parts rejected at the vendor's plant by the manufacturer's "source" inspector. CAD stands for "conditional acceptance deviation," involving borderline materials outside of tolerance but accepted for specific use by the manufacturer.
   When a monthly report for any vendor is construed by the manufacturer as unsatisfactory, the vendor is required to forward a statement showing action taken to improve his quality.

Questions

Comment on the general applicability, inherent fairness, and specific advantages, or the lack thereof, of this particular vendor quality-rating procedure.

8. Case 13C: *Quality at Wanabetcha Company*
The Wanabetcha Company recently discovered that the costs due to the shipment of defective items had risen to an alarming level. To remedy the situation, they decided to implement a quality assurance program (QAP). Previously, all inspection was done by workers on their own work. Since none of the present employees or managers had any formal education in quality assurance, they decided to compose the QAP team of recent college graduates.
   When the team was formed, the company's president told them he expected the percentage of defective items being produced to be halved within 1 month. With this formidable introduction the team went to work.
   Problems, however, began to plague the program immediately. Conflicts arose between the inspectors and the workers. Some of the older employees felt they were being insulted whenever a quality problem was traced to their work. This resentment often resulted in their work deteriorating further rather than improving. Other workers felt they were being wrongly accused of shoddy workmanship. Some even accused the inspectors of actually making defects in their work so that they could claim they had found a problem spot and look good in the eyes of the QAP manager.
   Monitoring reports after the first month showed that the quality level had actually worsened. Management felt that perhaps they had introduced the quality assurance program improperly.

Questions

1. What errors do you feel the Wanabetcha Company made in its implementation?

2. What remedial actions would you take to improve the present situation?

14

HIRING AND TRAINING

If we consider all employees and all employers, the most prevalent industrial-relations function is the act of hiring. Hiring is not always a simple process. Those responsible for personnel management must answer such questions as: What is the significance of company employment policy? What laws apply? What functions does this manager perform? What questions are asked of someone applying for a job? What can be expected of employment tests? What is the employment interviewer trying to find out? Is the problem of maintaining employee records different from other office-management techniques? Can excessive turnover and absence from the job be curtailed?

The first job experience of the new employee is apt to be training. Throughout his employment life occasions requiring retraining recur. One of the phenomena of recent years has been the increase in college training programs for already successful business executives. What, then, constitutes industrial training? What must the manager know about this function of employee relations? Are the methods used the same as they have always been? Who conducts what industrial training? Which employees are trained? What special types of industrial training need be considered?

14 HIRING AND TRAINING

14-1 HIRING

Many preparatory functions may occur in a business enterprise, but until an employee is hired, there can be no industrial relations. Before that it may be a working proprietor or simple partnership. The advent of the first employee starts the personnel director (sometimes called employment manager) through a series of complex activities. These activities are listed as steps in Figure 14-1.

During periods of unemployment, as during a recession, the personnel manager would seem to have little to do except to turn away eager applicants as diplomatically as possible. Conversely, when business picks up, the employment office bears the brunt of sudden pressure to supply needed work force. Requisitions pour in faster than they can be filled, and the few people hired must be the best available.

To help ease the pressure of these periods of slack and rush, a labor market is developed. The labor market for a given enterprise is often considered to be all those nonemployees within convenient travel distance. One desirable action when travel is difficult is to extend the labor-market area by improving available transportation. Since not all such area residents find the company pay scale inviting, its required skills compatible, and its working conditions and status socially acceptable, the personnel manager must first inform the working world of job openings. Then she must select and persuade. Even during a period when there are many applicants, there may be a real shortage of men or women with specific skills.

In certain companies applicants appear voluntarily at the employment office or are "pulled in from the street" by a "Help Wanted" sign or by telling present employees to bring friends. In many, however, each employee must be sought out through the initiative of the company employment manager.

14-1.1 Sources of New Employees

The personnel manager's usual first step in recruiting is to inform the employment service maintained by the several states. At various times these employment offices have been under Federal supervision. The United States Employment Service (USES) still supplies funds, technical service, and interoffice clearance. The state unemployment-compensation system is usually a parallel organization, often sharing offices with the employment service. An original reluctance to use the state employment offices on the part of the best applicants and most employers has been partially overcome. Since the state unemployment-compensation systems require registration at the state employment offices, even skilled employees who formerly felt "the best jobs aren't listed there" now sometimes register. As the public offices

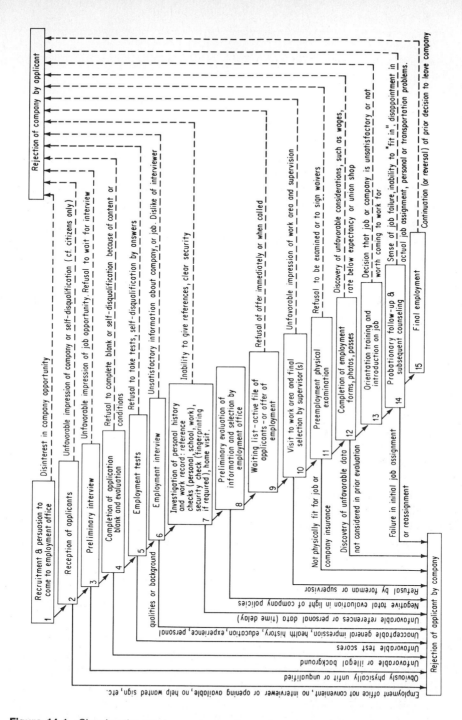

Figure 14-1 Showing the employment procedure as a series of screenings in which the applicant is either rejected or passed along to the next step until "final employment." The applicant may refuse to go to the next step at any point and thus reject the company. At any rejection point a formal or informal "exit interview" completes the procedure. (Based on a shorter chart by R. S. Uhrbrock, *Personnel,* vol. 12, no. 4, p. 231.)

do a better selection job and nondiscrimination becomes more widespread, employer acceptance is growing.

Most private employment agencies are operated on a fee-charging basis and are licensed by the city or state in which they operate. The most common fee is one week's salary paid by the employee during the first month. Some "gold-plated" agencies legally charge 25 per cent of a year's salary for high-paying jobs. In some cases the employer pays the agency's fee, particularly when a labor scarcity exists. In the last few years there has been a great increase in "search agencies" which work for and are always paid by the employer. These are often connected with management-engineering consultants and specialize in finding and evaluating executive applicants.

Other sources of applicants which many employers use are schools, churches, local community leaders, political or national-group clubs, and such groups as the 40-Plus Clubs which help each other get jobs. School and colleges often have free placement services. Company policy may limit referral by present employees. Referrals by unions may be regulated by law or by labor contract. Many employment managers condemn such informal methods but spend large sums on job-opening publicity in newspapers, trade journals, or on radio and television advertising. Local employers usually condemn such "labor-pirating" advertisements, but when recruiting from distant points is limited to excess workers or those employed below their highest skill the general economy may be expected to benefit.

14-1.2 Employment Policies

Before an employment manager can start hiring he must know both the written and the unwritten employment policies. Does the company attempt to maintain a balance of the minority groups in the community in its company population? Does the company employ all religious groups? Is the particular opening suitable for members of all races? Are the sexes considered equal? Are there promotional policies that make physically or mentally handicapped individuals unemployable? Are local residents given preference? Must housing or availability of transportation be considered? Are there preferences for or against relatives of present employees? Are there government security requirements? Are those in reserve units avoided to prevent company disruption in some future mobilization? Are left-handed or glasses-wearing employees subjected to unusual safety risks? Must the oil-allergic or chemical-sensitive be limited to specific departments? What about the color blind? The illiterate? The foreign-speaking only? Veterans? Former employees? The answers to such questions constitute a company's employment policies.

Perspective 14A   WOMEN IN THE WORK FORCE

The proportion of women in the U.S. work force has increased rapidly in recent years. As indicated by the chart on page 385, the upsurge started during World War II, and

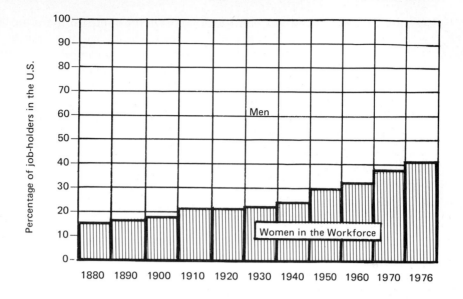

SOURCE: U.S. Department of Labor.

by 1976 reached the level where 41 per cent of all jobholders were women. This total, 39,719,000, accounted for 48 per cent of all U.S. women and girls then 16 years old or over.

Many developments have contributed to this accelerating rise in female employment. Changing social values and attitudes have led more older women with grown children and mothers with young children to seek full- or part-time work. Lower birth rates and an orientation toward industrial careers, fostered by the "women's liberation" movement, have encouraged more young women to become jobholders. They are better prepared for professional industrial positions as a result of acquiring college educations in business, law, medicine, engineering, and pharmacy. Federal laws, particularly the Civil Rights Act of 1964, have increased hiring opportunities. And probably the greatest incentive is the desire for a higher standard of living which is available to families with two incomes.

Despite Federal laws specifying equal pay for women and men, the difference in wages between female and male employees is widening in favor of men. According to the Howe report, financed by the Ford Foundation, the median earnings for women working full time were 63 per cent of those of men in 1956, but dropped to 57 per cent during the next 20 years. However, it has been estimated that 41 per cent of the professional jobs in the United States were held by women in 1976, an increase of 5 per cent over a decade.

14-2 EMPLOYMENT-OFFICE FUNCTIONS

The basic purpose of an employment office is to hire desirable employees for specific company openings. A good employment interviewer does a lot of public-relations work in "selling the applicant the company if not the job" and may even give surprisingly good vocational guidance, but basically he is trying to find the best person for an existing job as promptly as possible. "Best" quality depends not only upon aptitude and experience qualifications for the present job, but also upon potentiality for growth into possible promotions. The selection and placement of the new employee, following the steps in Figure 14-1, are the first opportunity for a company to start to forge ahead of its competitors by having a better work force.

The cultivation of the labor market and recruitment have been mentioned. The other successive employment functions will be discussed in order. Employment offices may have functions other than initial employment. Common additions are employee counseling and operating the seniority system, including posting job openings and calling back laid-off employees.

14-2.1 Reception

The reception of applicants and preliminary sorting may be helped by the use of a brief application blank, often called a "Request for Interview." Containing little more than the applicant's name and address and the type of work sought, such a record card will break the ice and speed up applicant sorting. The brief form will also let the impatient applicant "leave his name" without writing a laborious life history, and will enable the company diplomatically to point out employment requirements such as citizenship.

14-2.2 Application Blanks

Most modern employment offices make use of formal application blanks. There has been a deplorable tendency among many companies to copy established application blanks and to include numerous insignificant and prying questions. In recognition of antidiscrimination laws, questions having to do with race, color, religion, or national origin cannot be asked until after the employee is hired.

Separate application blanks are commonly used for specific employee groups such as office, sales, shop, or supervisory applicants. Each request for information on any blank should be carefully evaluated:

1. Is the question permissible under all applicable Federal, state, or local legislation? Will applicant give reliable answers?

2. Will the information be used to identify the applicant at some stage of employment?

3. Will it assist in applying company employment policies?

4. Will it help match the applicant's ability, experience, etc., to the hiring specification established on the basis of job-evaluation research?

5. Is the application blank the best place to ask for this information, or would it be better obtained during the interview or after hiring at induction or even later?

14-2.3 Employment Tests

Tests are simply a rapid way of obtaining samples of behavior to help the employment interviewer form a judgment to hire or not to hire a given individual. Employment tests are never infallible. A test can, however, determine aptitude, interests, personality, or a specific job skill much more objectively and faster than can an employment interviewer. Several types of tests are in common use.

- *Performance tests* are those which require the applicant to produce results on a job sample. A typist might be asked to copy a page of text, or a plumber to cut and thread a pipe.

- *Personality tests* are those which measure self-action or knowledge of other people's behavior. If personality tests are answered honestly, they measure person-to-person behavior. They are commonly used in selecting salespersons and supervisors.

- *Aptitude tests* explore inborn tendencies to perform well in particular fields. In industry, mechanical aptitude is necessary to success as a machinist, toolmaker, or other tradesman. Finger dexterity may be measured for assemblers.

- *Intelligence tests* are used for many different jobs requiring adaptability or learning ability.

- *Interest tests* may measure similarities in preferred activities among certain occupational groups and the applicant.

By report, the most popular tests are those of general intelligence, although factor-analysis research is casting doubt on any general problem-solving ability. Rather, there seem to be many specific abilities, all affected by the interplay between social conditioning (attitude toward taking the test and degree of motivation to do well in it), physical health, and cultural environment. The net result of this interplay is a "personality," and the second most popular group of tests attempts to measure this either by checking up on reported interests or behavior samples. In this area the greatest disagreement is between those interviewers who constantly seek overly simplified "types" and those attempting to describe the individual as falling at some point on many scales, making up a multidimensional structure.

When an industrial psychologist starts out to build a test for a specific industrial application, he follows seven simple steps. (1) He finds out what job is to be filled, e.g., an operator, or a setup-and-operate person. (2) He determines how management tells how well that job is done. This is the problem of *criteria* and may involve production records, foreman grading, customer reports, etc. (3) He studies the present job holders, seeking to identify characteristics which differentiate good performers from poor performers. He may use standard tests for this or build special new ones. (4) He seeks to hire more people with the characteristics of the good producers and avoid those with the characteristics of the poor producers. (5) He follows up the performance of those so hired to see if those in the new group with the desired characteristics also give good results on the job. (6) If the good performers are alike, he recommends to management the future use of the selection device. (7) If the good performers in the new group do not have the characteristics of the good performers in the old group, he repeats the process, thinking, "What went wrong?" Perhaps the criteria are faulty. Maybe some item on the application blank already differentiates. Is there some standard test that was not tried? Can a new test be developed with greater similarity to the job? Possibly a finer statistical treatment will yield results.

Hundreds of tests are available today. Not all these have satisfactory reliability and validity, and very few have been related to job success satisfactorily. Test results can rarely be transferred from company to company but must be tailor-made as described above. Even when the test fits the company, perfect results cannot be expected and some mistakes will be made. The best that can be hoped, at this stage, is that selections guided by test results will include fewer mistakes than selection made otherwise.

14-2.4 Employment Interviewing

Psychological tests and application blanks supply valuable information to the employment interviewer, but his own skill must finally determine his success. Many researchers have demonstrated that interviewing results depend heavily on the interviewer's ability, since different interviewers get different results interviewing the same job applicants. Efforts to improve interviewing results have centered around developing the "patterned interview" and improving interviewer training, using recorded playbacks and follow-up of results. Accuracy of interviewing is improved by using objective data—past records, physical exams, weighted application blanks, timed applicant response—as well as training of interviewers.

1. For the employment interview privacy may be provided in crowded quarters by railings, glass partitions, or by a wise use of space, but the relationship of confidence is essential.

2. The employment interviewer must discount his own prejudices and should practice taking the interviewee's point of view and listening objectively.

3. The employment interviewer should try to make each interviewee feel at ease and express himself. This aim is served by permitting the interviewee to become accustomed to his surroundings, by a pleasant greeting, by starting out talking about something of interest to him, and by letting him talk, but not dawdle.

4. The employment interviewer should keep control of the interview and keep it on the subject, but should not rush. He should watch for additional information through casual remarks, especially at the close.

5. The employment interviewer must avoid impertinence and not preach or teach during the interview. He should avoid asking leading questions, those that provoke negativism, or more than one question at a time.

6. The objectivity will be improved if the interviewer works from a prepared outline, holds guiding questions in mind only long enough to get answers, and makes the interview as factual as possible by interpreting answers as given and permitting opportunity to qualify replies. Data should be recorded as soon as possible and checked for error.

OBJECTIVE-INTERVIEW AIDS   Many efforts have been made to make the "oldest and least scientific of personnel selection methods" more objective. Some of the earliest "cures" were worse than the "disease," and resort was made to such pseudo sciences as astrology, phrenology, graphology, and physiognomy. Disillusionment with such false prophets led to an understanding that interviewing errors may spring from sparse sampling of a restricted population, from the applicant's ability to control behavior during a short interview, and most importantly from interviewer bias. If the interviewer is prejudiced by well-brushed hair or dirty fingernails, he may find "halo" forcing his ratings up or down. If he subtly condemns drinking, he will discover considerable temperance. If he falls for such false stereotypes as the jolly fat person or the weak-chinned Milquetoast, he may find himself hiring "sales types" instead of persons who can sell. If he is misled by extraneous factors, all the clerks will wear glasses.

Some employers also use the *stress interview* which puts the candidate under severe emotional strain to observe his reaction, the *selection board* or group oral test in which the candidate appears before a committee of interviewers or "examiners" to answer verbal "qualification questions," and the *group interview* or leaderless group discussion where six or eight candidates are observed simultaneously. Some employers have tapped the "in-group perception" of a group of candidates by asking for "buddy ratings." These are judgments as to which of the group is wanted for a "buddy" or team member. Results suggest that group members can pick out potential leaders more accurately than can even the experienced interviewers not so closely associated with the group.

Closely related to these is the use of *trade-test questions,* which have been standardized by having them answered by successful tradesmen, and *situation tests* (also named psychodrama or sociometric tests) calling for the applicant to show how he would meet a job problem. For example, a salesperson might be asked to make a sales presentation.

POSTINTERVIEW CHECKS   The experience claims made will need to be checked with previous employers. About nine out of ten companies make such reference checks and will report the quality of work by former em-

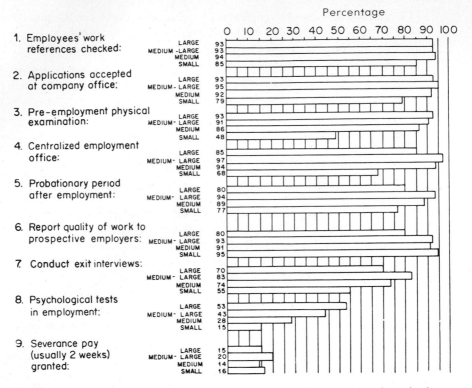

Figure 14-2   The prevalence of common employment practices among various-sized industrial establishments. (SOURCE: Data procured from *Studies in Personnel Policy,* no. 145, National Industrial Conference Board, Inc.)

ployees to prospective employers (see Fig. 14-2). Although personal-history details may be confused unintentionally, and personal references rarely are anything but laudatory, a complete check is wise. Often a telephone check or personal visit will elicit information not available by letter. In important hirings, such calls may be made while the applicant is still being talked to by other company members. Both credit agencies and private detective services have established an employment investigative service which may be cheaper than making home visits to distant points. The information obtained is rarely as good, however, since the "investigator" may depend on local gossip.

Certain government contracts require "security checks" including finger-printing, but forms for this are usually completed after actual hiring, and the new employee is kept on nonrestricted work until clearance comes through. Sometimes reference checks for lower level jobs will also be made after hiring.

14-2.5   Preliminary Selection and Job Offer

The end step in all this factual data collection as shown by Figure 14-1 is evaluation: the decision to reject the applicant (keeping him as a friend of the company), or to make him a job offer. Often if no opening is immediately available, the applicant is put on a waiting list and called when an opening does occur. The evaluation of selection data—application, test scores, interview records, reference checks, etc., is the most difficult and important task of employment. Common danger signals include unexplainable gaps in job history, falsified information, a show of temper or irritability, too many jobs, lack of respect for the company or for self, and unrealistic money demands.

The employment manager's preliminary selection and tentative job offer must usually be confirmed by the immediate supervisor who has the final choice among qualified applicants for the specific job. For simple jobs, this is often only an empty formality, for the supervisor accepts anyone the employment office sends to him, but the supervisor retains a veto exercisable any time during the probationary period (usually 30 to 90 days, and often a union-contract provision). Since, as Figure 14-1 indicates, the applicant may reject the company at any stage, he must visit the work area and meet the supervisor while still an applicant. Otherwise, he may simply "not come back" when he does see the job, thus contributing to the very high turnover which occurs in the first two weeks. If the supervisor wants to hire the applicant, Figure 14-2 shows that most larger companies will require a physical examination while only about half of the small companies will.

14-2.6 Physical Examination

The physical examination of employment applicants is commonly on a service basis by the industrial hospital. In some factories the physical standards of employment are set by the plant physician or industrial surgeon in consultation with the safety and health engineer. The employment interviewer attempts to select applicants who look healthy and who have an employment record indicative of the physical stamina required. The interviewer's judgment is checked by an examination and medical-laboratory testing of indications of general health; by a carefully established medical and health history; and by specific tests of ability to lift heavy weights, read at usual distances, identify colors, hear normally, and for any requirements particularly applicable to the job in question, such as oil allergies or chemical sensitivities. Entrance examinations are given applicants for their own protection so that they will not be required to do work for which they are not physically equipped, for the protection of present employees from contagion and the product from contamination, and for the protection of the company from compensation court claims because of subsequent injury or disablement. Such conditions as unusual noise sensitivity are becoming increasingly important as compensation commissioners hold employers liable for cumulative damage, and in some states even when no loss of earning capacity is demonstrated. In addition the physical examination may be a prerequisite to membership in a group-insurance-benefit plan. Many employers require employees with physical disabilities to sign waivers with the compensation commissioner. Although these may have only limited legal standing, they may deter an unscrupulous suit.

Perspective 14B REALITIES OF PHYSICAL LIMITATIONS

Tests can measure an applicant's mechanical capability, mental alertness, and physical suitability. Of these, the physical qualifications would appear to be the easiest to determine. Still, each job must be evaluated separately to delimit the physical handicaps that actually influence job performance. It is not enough to merely say that the applicant should be "healthy."

The suitability of an applicant's physical qualifications for operating lift trucks is discussed by N. H. Wells:

Where hundreds of thousands of dollars of products and goods, equipment, real estate, and human life are at stake, you can't afford to put just anybody aboard a lift truck. Therefore, you must consider the capabilities and health of the employee. Unfortunately, there are various physical and mental conditions that could eliminate a driver, or severely limit his duty.*

Wells lists several abnormalities that could disqualify a potential material handler:

- *Vision*   Problems of focus, field or sight, color detection, and other eye diseases lead to collisions.
- *Cardiac diseases*   Effects of heart attack, high blood pressure, chest pains of cardiac origin, and some types of valvular heart disease limit operator ability to work, at the very best.
- *Hearing*   Wax in the ear and chronic middle ear infection cause hearing loss or dizziness; the result is inattention.
- *Psychiatric disorders, emotions, attitudes*   These affect judgment, reaction. Drugs and alcohol complicate the situation.
- *Neurological diseases*   These cause needles-and-pins sensations, numbness, paralysis, muscle wasting, lack of coordinated movements, vision loss or visual eye muscle impairment, difficulty with speech or swallowing, or poor urinary or bowel control. To a driver, these are distracting.
- *Joint and bone diseases*   Arthritis, rheumatoid arthritis, and osteoarthritis cause pain, swelling, and limitation of joint movement and may affect motions. The result is loss of production and tendency to accidents.
- *Major amputations*   These often limit important functions, although corrective appliances help overcome many limitations.
- *Convulsive disorders*   Epilepsy and similar seizure-type abnormalities can overtake a sufferer very rapidly, rendering him incapable of movement or mental function or judgment. Blackout may occur without warning.
- *Pulmonary (lung) diseases, or a tendency to them*   Chronic bronchitis, asthma, emphysema, and sometimes tuberculosis. All may reduce effective breathing capacity, causing sufferers to cough, gasp, or wheeze, impairing function.
- *Excessive overweight*   This is an abnormality that may be associated with an emotional problem. Obesity reduces agility, decreases work capacity, and interferes with seating and control arrangements.*

*SOURCE: N. H. Wells, "Trained Lift Truck Operators? You Can Do It!" Allis-Chalmers, Milwaukee, Wisconsin, December, 1977.

COMMENT   Since perfect physical specimens are rare, personnel managers must be wary of setting standards too high. After listing the consequences that could result from hiring an unqualified operator, they should be critiqued closely to determine which ones are serious enough to truly disqualify an applicant, and what specific level of physical incapacity triggers the disqualification.

14-2.7 Employee Records

If the employee applicant has passed all hurdles up to this point, the employment manager may "sign him up." This is not mere clerical routine but is the original source for many important company records. First among these records is the application blank already used by the interviewer. Certain items may be completed after hiring, especially those dealing with race, religion, and national origin. Included with the application is often the original employment requisition describing the job to be filled. In some organizations there may also be collected during the hiring process employment test scores, interviewers' report sheets, foreman acceptance sheets, hospital or medical record, induction training record, and receipts for employee handbook, identification, keys, etc. All these records are kept in a central file of personnel records, often in a special personnel-record envelope or folder which also contains a master record card to which is posted a running record of employment history as it occurs through promotion and transfer. Figure 14-3 shows one form of master record card.

The variety of employment-office records which an establishment will maintain depends upon its size, the nature of the employment it offers, and the importance the management attaches to facts about employees. Plants employing largely unskilled labor will need records different from plants employing many precision machinists. Companies with large office and sales

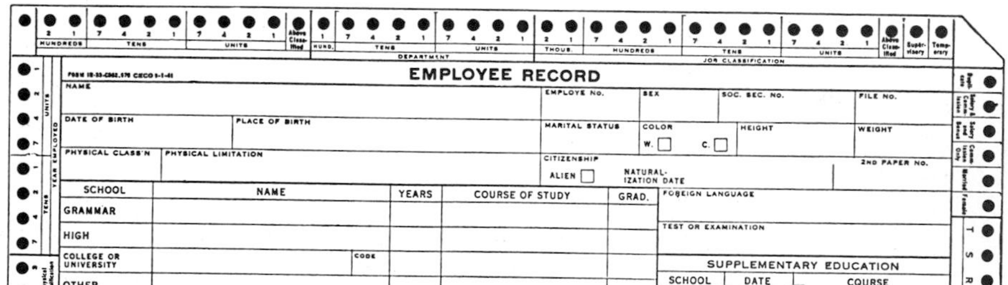
EMPLOYEE RECORD

NAME | EMPLOYE NO. | SEX | SOC. SEC. NO. | FILE NO.

DATE OF BIRTH | PLACE OF BIRTH | MARITAL STATUS | COLOR W. ☐ C. ☐ | HEIGHT | WEIGHT

PHYSICAL CLASS'N | PHYSICAL LIMITATION | CITIZENSHIP | ALIEN ☐ | NATURALIZATION DATE | 2ND PAPER NO.

SCHOOL	NAME	YEARS	COURSE OF STUDY	GRAD.
GRAMMAR				
HIGH				
COLLEGE OR UNIVERSITY	CODE			
OTHER				

FOREIGN LANGUAGE

TEST OR EXAMINATION

SUPPLEMENTARY EDUCATION

SCHOOL	DATE	COURSE

INTERVIEWED BY | DATE | REMARKS | CODE

OCCUPATIONAL EXPERIENCE

1.

2.

3.

4.

HUNDREDS | TENS | UNITS | DEPARTMENT | THOUS. | HUNDREDS | TENS | UNITS | JOB CLASSIFICATION

TRANSFER POS

Figure 14-3 A cumulative employment record using the McBee Keysort patented-edge marking. Data posted are keyed around the margin by V-punching the card edge. Sorting needles pushed through the indicated holes of a packet of cards hold back the cards with solid edges but permit cards with perforated edges to drop out. Speedy sorting in all four directions soon identifies the employee with the desired characteristics. The back of this card provides space for the service and job-classification posting.

groups will need records showing employee experience in those fields. Union seniority clauses and pension plans require a careful accounting of employee service. During wartime, draft and alien status becomes important.

PERFORMANCE RECORDS   Employee merit ratings are discussed in Chapter 16. These may be kept in the employee's record folder. Even with a formal merit-rating system, but especially when the employer does not maintain a formal system of merit rating, he will usually find it expedient to maintain two closely related employee records: (1) *disciplinary and warning records,* and (2) *promotional or advancement records.* Discipline records are maintained largely to provide a record of previous warnings in case of dismissal for violation of company rules. Almost the only defense an employer has, when charged with dismissal of an employee for union activity, is proof of a "bad record." In recent decisions it has been stressed that proving the dismissed employee has a bad record is not enough. The employer must also prove that other retained employees have a "good record" and that the offending employee has been adequately warned. A carefully kept record of all disciplinary action taken makes such a defense possible.

Promotional records justify the promotion of the most qualified individual. The employer must be able to prove that he has considered all candidates and selected the best. Hiring employees from outside the organization and over the heads of equally qualified present employees is not conducive to sound employee relations. Any savings that may result from not having to train several people in a chain promotion are lost through disgruntled performance. The problem of finding the person for the job inside the company, to carry out a policy of promotion from within, is greatly simplified by an understudy system and by keeping up-to-date records. Any school courses the employee may complete should be entered on his master record card for consideration in promotion.

SIMPLE EMPLOYMENT SYSTEMS   Cardinal aims of any work with records are keeping them simple, active, and useful. A periodic review of all personnel forms should be made regularly to determine whether any duplications may be eliminated or if any portion of the system in use may be abandoned. One form of abandonment should be avoided, however, i.e., the elimination of basically sound and useful records on the grounds that maintaining them is a needless luxury since almost no promotion or hiring is occurring. Systems thus dropped always cost more to reconstruct during periods of increased employment than they do to continue.

14-3 TRAINING PROGRAMS

The field of training in business is the oldest centralized industrial-relations function. As the industrial-relations specialty developed, management first centralized training responsibility. Recently there has been a pendulum swing back toward line responsibility for training, but most formalized training activities in the United States are the responsibility of the training section of the industrial-relations department.

To understand the position of the training director, a quick review of the "who, what, why, when, and how" of training may help. Briefly, industry trains all its employees. Almost none come fully equipped for immediate employment. Even the professional specialist requires a "shakedown period," during which he learns company policy, specialized vocabulary, and a working camaraderie with his fellow employees. Perhaps the most difficult initial learning problem is to determine a hierarchy of importance among tasks. Each employer puts first things first. But what are "first things" for a specific company? Middle management, clerical workers, and factory-production operatives require training because each job is unique. Even though two adjacent metal manufacturers use the same automatic screw machine, each will use it differently and the mechanic's skill must be oriented to company intentions.

The question is often asked: Why train? The simple answer is: growth and change. In certain situations some business firms claim that they find it more economical to "pirate" trained employees from competitors. This does not add to the supply of trained people. Ultimately a point is reached where skilled employees with a knowledge of company procedures and intention (which can be gained only on the job) must be created. In terms of time, basic job training usually takes place within the first few days after hiring. During periods of great labor shortage, employees may be hired for enrollment in a "vestibule school," where they learn in a training situation to do the job before reporting on it. Hiring for learning is also characteristic of skilled trades and scientific-technical pursuits. The machinist, electrician, and cracking-still attendant learn their art in a period of 2 to 7 years of observation—helping highly skilled practitioners. The intern approach is also characteristic of electronic-data-processing programmers, technical salespersons, and medical detailers. Virtually every company has an orientation training program conducted with varying degrees of formality, during which the employee is given some acquaintanceship with company history, operating rules, and other essentials.

The most elementary training process is the instruction of an individual worker to accomplish a limited task. This situation commonly occurs for work of a simple and repetitive nature which is suitable for unskilled labor. A supervisor may describe or demonstrate the task to the prospective operator. The workplace can be color-coded to assist training. When large numbers of operators are to be trained as in seasonal hirings for knitting mills and canneries, motion pictures or other training aids may be utilized. Operators then perform the task over and over again to attain competence.

A typical "learning curve" for an individual operator's performance plotted against time has been well established. The shape of the curve is shown in Figure 14-4 where the improvement of a worker is represented by an increasing production rate per unit of time. The important feature of the curve is the plateau region. An operator customarily progresses through at

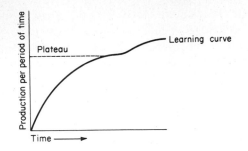

Figure 14-4 A typical learning curve for an individual operator during training.

least one period where his performance levels off before a subsequent spurt. The number and lengths of training plateaus for a task depend on the skills required, such as eye-hand coordination, mental alertness, depth perception, and muscular control.

There is no consensus about the best training techniques, but there is general agreement about a preferred approach to designing a training program. A fairly typical plan is described by the following six steps:

1. A job analysis on site to record exactly what is done.

2. The determination of what to teach. What skills, what understanding, what facts will help do the job better? How can these be field-tested to show training success?

3. The organizing of a training plan for teaching what is needed. This will include subject matter and method as well as teaching aids, audio-visual material, etc., all aimed at creating a change that can be measured.

4. Conducting an "experimental group" through the new teaching plan.

5. Evaluating the results of that training on the job, often by comparing field performance of the experimental group with the performance of a group trained in some other way. Performance is measured in terms of the test originally devised, and nothing that cannot be tested is "taught."

6. Modifying the training plan to yield still better results, often through discussion with the trainees, who report what lessons were particularly effective and suggest ways to make all lessons better. In the language of the industrial trainer: "If the learner hasn't learned, the teacher hasn't taught!"

The six-step training-project-planning method is especially effective at supervisory and higher levels when it starts with a set of performance standards for each job. On the basis of standards originated by the employee and his or her boss, a training plan is organized and individually performed. The standards themselves contain their own performance measures, and success is evaluated on the grounds of desired changes occurring.

14-4 RESPONSIBILITY FOR TRAINING

Industrial training is especially important in modern industry because of the great increase in both skilled and semiskilled workers with a resultant decrease in unskilled workers required. Today's industrial workers are often hired without specific skill and are trained on the job to perform skilled industrial operations. As technology changes, those same workers are retrained for different operations. Without effective training our complex industrial society could not operate. Much industrial training is actually retraining older employees in newer methods or subjects developed after those employees were out of school. New laws, new technology, new machines and methods, and new managerial procedures make training a never-ending task. Industrial training again reconfirms "lifelong learning."

Employers accept the moral obligation to retrain the technologically unemployed and have done so since mechanization of industry began. They also retrain their own help because no public agency could do the job so well. There is an increasing understanding, however, of industry's need by professional educators. The vocational-guidance and training programs of many cities and states are slanted toward the needs of possible employers to an increasing extent. Industry is benefiting from this. Especially effective have been the work-study programs of the cooperative community colleges and technical institutes. Federal assistance has been effective in helping students through joint university-industry programs by low-interest loans, work-study wages, subsidies, scholarships, and stipends for veterans.

All of the various types of training programs are usually guided by a training director, who is part of the industrial-relations division. He works with the company supervisors to discover training needs, often by means of the six-step training-project-planning method. He often teaches training classes and encourages managers of all levels to use a teaching approach in supervision.

A training committee is often used to advise or assist the training director, or in small organizations may substitute for a full-time training director. Training committees help select trainees, help adapt training to company needs, and help evaluate results. Such committees often consult with executives of "cooperative" colleges in adapting the college offerings to specific company needs. Under the committee's direction (with the aid of a full- or part-time director) a training course is prepared in cooperation with experts in the field to be treated, or with a "cooperative" college possessing the facilities and technical staff essential to a basic attack on the training problem. The approved course is then taught by committee-approved discussion leaders to committee-approved trainees. If only a few trainees come from a single company, they may be combined with students in an area-wide joint program. Those trained, and such training assistants as the company may have, will pass appropriate material along to others in the organization. It is in this "passing along" that the committee of operating supervisors performs its most valued function—that of assuring the new methods and material a ready welcome!

In carrying out his responsibilities, the training director must help supervisors learn to teach. Many supervisors are too much concerned with supposed difficulties in "teaching old dogs new tricks." The only essential of adult pedagogy is to treat adults as adults, i.e., teach informally, don't talk down, avoid meaningless frills and mannerisms, and keep the learner's interest with fresh examples, daily-life tie-ins, and alert discussion. Learning is influenced by the physical condition, natural aptitudes, past experience, and "habits of learning." Involvement, participation, and motivation are desirable, but too intense motivation (especially fear, pain, frustrating anxiety) leads to distraction. That which makes the strongest pleasant emotional impression is learned most readily, and a record of success is essential to tolerating failure. What the learner understands is retained better, and those understandings he reaches himself transfer best. Nothing beats practice, and spaced practice is best, although knowledge of results seems essential.

Perspective 14C EDUCATED DATA PROCESSING

As electronic data processing (EDP) enters its second quarter century, it becomes increasingly evident that many managers have to learn more about EDP to stay effective, and DP people need to know more about management to be efficient. Bob Knight identifies four facets of the training challenge:

1. *Organizational training* Training in corporate objectives and how they are really met, and how departments really interface—or fail to interface—with one another can provide the analyst the perspective necessary to gather all those other answers needed: Who has the right information at which level of what department? Who is responsible for what file? Who is maintaining what report? Is there duplication of effort in some areas, or no effort at all in others?
2. *Communication training* How can management hope to learn anything about information processing if the people in electronic data processing are unable or unwilling to translate what they are doing in terms managers can understand? The answer is nested in the question. The DP professional must eliminate the jargon that serves so well in communicating with other data processors and explain the situation in terms the user manager will grasp.
3. *Information management training* The computer has brought management the opportunity and power to make decisions and forecasts undreamed of in the precomputer era. But that opportunity, that power, will be lost to the manager untrained to use it. There might be a wealth of information tied up in the computer that managers may be dying to get at. DP people themselves might have pure nuggets of data for which no one has asked them to provide.

   But until managers train themselves to ask the right questions, they will have to be satisfied with a hit-or-miss method of extracting the nuggets with which they can purchase the best decisions.
4. *Marketplace training* Management can no longer afford to depend on either their own DP people or vendors to decide what hardware and software the organization needs. Both can provide unlimited technical data from which the decision can be made, but the decision now must be management's alone. The delegation of that decision can only mean an abdication of responsibility, at a cost to the organization.*

*SOURCE: Adapted from Bob Knight, "Management Needs DP Training, Too," *Infosystems*, May, 1977.

COMMENT Most specialists decry management's unfamiliarity with their specialty. Lawyers, engineers, accountants, and other professionals feel that every manager should be able to talk their language and understand their viewpoint. Ideally they would. Practically, few managers have the opportunity or capacity to do so. Yet computers deserve extra attention, because they are at the heart of information flow and the brain center of corporate decision making.

14-5   TRAINING TECHNIQUES

The training director will use a variety of training techniques depending on the material to be taught and the abilities of those to be trained. These techniques will include occasional lectures with coordinated demonstrations and possibly recitations to impart new information. Whenever possible training will emphasize "learning by doing" and participation. Audio-visual aids such as sound motion pictures, closed-circuit TV, posters, flip charts, flannel boards, tape recorders, and working models will help. Small group participation is encouraged by the conference method, by case studies, by "buzz sessions," and by role playing. Larger groups may use the forum, panel discussion, or dramatic skit and may get buzz session results by forming small informal discussion groups among those who chance to be seated close together in a larger audience.

The following sections will give special attention to three of the many training methods: the *conference*[1] *method,* the *case study,* and *role playing.*

CONFERENCE METHOD   This is by far the most popular method with trainers for exchanging information and ideas among experienced adults. Where the conferees lack experience, however, there is danger of "sharing the ignorance." Group discussion may often seem to be time-consuming, but more can be *learned* in "bull sessions" than in twice the time spent at a prepared lecture. The ability to lead a conference is an important skill, usually acquired primarily by practice in a conference group. The conference method is increasingly used at all levels. Aside from training purposes, conferences are used for business meetings, civic hearings, and all sorts of joint action. Often the training-conference method used in a supervisory situation grows almost imperceptibly into a method of management. There are perhaps five types of problem-solving conferences, and the results desired dictate the type used. In the *exploratory conference* such as might be held between management and union representatives prior to formal negotiations, the leader *spars* to get acquainted and investigate the subject matter. In the *creative conference,* sometimes called "brainstorming," the leader seeks

[1]The term "conference" is sometimes used to mean any business meetings but here refers to a small group, sitting facing one another, considering a formal proposal or set of ideas. It differs from the larger meeting, sitting facing the speaker and listening to a lecture, perhaps with discussion encouraged afterward. A conference for training purposes differs from a seminar (advanced original research group discussing a topic under guidance of an expert), a forum (open public discussion of a general-interest topic), a symposium (round-table discussion by scholarly specialists), debate (tour-de-force oratory between opposing speakers), or panel discussion (four or so specialists exploring a problem before informal audience participation), although these may deal with the same topics and involve the same individuals.

to *ignite* the group and to capture ideas, not evaluate them. In the *informational conference,* also called "directed discussion" or "determinant discussion," the leader seeks to give his own beliefs and opinions as well as to expose those of an invited "resource person" and to lead the group to a predetermined conclusion. In the *developmental conference,* also known as "indeterminant discussion," the leader acts as a suction pump for the group's ideas and avoids openly contributing ideas of his own. In the *reconciliation conference* the leader helps to integrate differences in viewpoint held by individuals in the group. Usually a problem-solving conference is held around a table to help face-to-face communication. The leader breaks the ice, tosses out a discussion question, encourages participation, and lists the conclusions the group reaches on a blackboard or wall tablet. In some cases he may control the overly active, keep the group on the subject, and draw out those who do not take part easily. It is his responsibility to diagnose and treat the "hidden agendas"—those hip-pocket solutions and private purposes that hold back progress—and above all to build a bridge for carrying out the decisions made.

CASE METHODS AND BUSINESS GAMES   This training technique has been taken over from use originally in legal and medical education and more recently in engineering and the social sciences. It seems first to have been used in management training some forty years ago at Harvard University. In practice it consists of two parts: the case history and the case discussion. The success of the discussion depends upon the leader. He must keep the group on the subject, cut off digressions, and teach his students to dig for facts from which they can draw significant conclusions. When those discussing the case have similar backgrounds and are of equal rank, case discussion can result in significant changes in on-the-job behavior. Many training directors believe that the case method develops the ability both to think logically and to work more effectively with others. Various ways of presenting the case history are as follows:

1. The *Harvard approach* provides long and detailed case material, not all of which is relevant to the particular questions asked. It is prepared from a real business situation by a case-writing specialist and is often documented with company financial data and statistics. Careful analysis is required to sift out significant facts. There is no "right answer" to a case problem, and the aim is to develop the ability to think broadly about business problems.

2. The *briefed case* starts out with the same data in the professor's files, but a skilled executive presents objectively only the high points needed. The executive-student who briefs the case gains a great deal more than the rest of the class. The class spends only a limited amount of time on preparation, since the "most correct action" is usually apparent, with only key factors identified and all facts presented in an orderly manner. Its critics claim that the "brief" is not true to life, no matter how "real" the original case may have been.

3. The *recorded case* is used to start discussion without requiring any prior reading

of case material, since all necessary facts are recorded. This method is used especially with foremen and in human-relations cases. The recording may be on film or tape. This case method may offer role-playing participation as a related technique.

4. The *incident process* requires the group to seek out required facts. All that is given is a news-flash "incident": "The Wigget Works went on strike!" The group then cross-questions a leader to obtain additional information. After the group has elicited what it believes are the key issues, it decides on action to be taken. Its decision is then compared with "what really happened." Student involvement is often extensive, and sessions using the incident process may become heated.

5. The techniques of *simulation* are used to add life to training cases and show promise of helping make "generalists out of specialists." One approach is by means of the "in-basket" technique, also used to evaluate executive capacity. This approach usually assumes a business situation such as a sudden promotion and, instead of telling the student about the facts, lets him "experience" them. An example is the in-basket case study given at the end of Chapter 15. The experience may be with a group or alone.

6. A different approach is by using the *business game.* Essential features of the business game are the establishment of a dynamic model and the creation of competition and effective response to feedback of information. A business model is often a series of mathematical assumptions. One assumption might be that a salesperson will average one sale for every ten sales calls made, i.e., a 10 per cent probability of a sale. The model may be simple, attempting to teach only one facet of inventory control, or it may be complex, interrelating such variables as selling cost, product development, production planning, and the state of the economy. Competition may be created by dividing the students into teams—with team names, colors, separate meeting rooms—which play the game simultaneously. The actions of competitors often have an important and realistic interplay with the actions taken by competing teams. Feedback is arranged by reporting such results as comparative profit, market position, and operating costs to the teams, so that each can compare the effectiveness of its decisions.

Critiques presented by instructors and participants of actions taken are an important training feature. A surprising sense of reality develops, and even experienced businessmen report a new understanding of the interrelationships between business variables such as finance, production inventory, and sales. A special kind of interaction between people being trained, mathematical models, and machines is possible when an electronic computer is used to simulate the economy or that portion reflected by the business game.

To overcome the artificial rigidity and ultrasimplification necessary to create a business-game model, the "dynamic business-game case" has been developed. This adds to the usual business game or computer simulation even more dynamic objectivity. All the rules of the game are not specified in advance. Since players are given information as they ask for it, different teams may get different information. Financing is made more realistic. Public relations, labor negotiations, and other human problems are introduced. Emergencies arise within the continuous play, and human referees react to decisions made by the team. Creativity is nurtured. Many future developments may be expected in the more than 100 business games now available, but this will remain only one method of business training.

ROLE PLAYING A development growing from efforts to make the case method more realistic is the introduction of the group-dynamics technique of role playing. One member acts out the part of an employee, and another answers his grievance, acting the part of a foreman in unrehearsed dialogue. The two may then reverse roles, or other "actors" may repeat the case. This training method is an excellent way of releasing individual tensions and may actually change human behavior out in the shop, where so many other lessons are quickly shrugged off. Role playing developed from the psychodrama.

14-5.1 Foreman Training

The training of foremen, like that of senior executives, many times is both an induction for newly appointed supervisors and a refresher for those who already know the rules but occasionally forget. As a matter of objective study the foreman has all the problems that higher level administrators have. In a setting slightly different from the top executive's, the supervisor, whether in factory, office, store, service center, or government agency, has problems which may be listed in eight groups:

1. Human relations: selecting, training, discipline, and morale

2. Work production: control of quality and quantity, control of costs, improving methods

3. Accident prevention

4. Supplies and equipment

5. Record keeping

6. Compliance with labor laws

7. Carrying out the provisions of the union contract

8. Working with other departments (cooperation, tact, fairness, firmness)

Solutions to these problems will be found throughout this book as the problems of management are discussed. The supervisor today has a more difficult job than the supervisor in the past. As industrial units grew larger, as factory production became more precise, as workers increased in skill and obtained representation, and as government rules became more numerous, the supervisor's job became more complex. Today's industrial leader must consult subordinates for their opinions, respect the rights of others, and obtain workers' intelligent cooperation because they understand the reasons. It is this transition which turns foreman training into management development.

Unions, too, recognize that leaders must be developed. They often conduct seminars, institutes, and summer-vacation schools in negotiating, shop leadership, economics, and political action. Local sessions may be held at the local union hall. Slide films, motion pictures, role-playing outlines, and conference topics are often supplied by national headquarters. Sometimes local educational institutions are requested to offer needed classes.

14-5.2 College-Graduate Training

Another group for which both orientation and refresher training is provided is the recent college-graduate trainee group. Many of today's business leaders came up from the ranks. Only a few were prepared by college training for the jobs they fill, and even these had the additional advantage of on-the-spot experience as small plants grew to giant industries. As a substitute for this irreplaceable experience, many enterprises are turning to planned recruitment and training of college graduates.

Such trainees are often selected with the cooperation of the college placement officer, who arranges interviews. In recent years there have been shortages of new graduates, especially those with highly technical preparation. Some companies offer working-experience opportunities during school vacations; some schools require the accumulation of specific working experience as an internship before graduation.

Once the new college trainee enters a company he may have "training experience" added to his regular job or he may be rotated among jobs for several years, largely as an observer. The company training director usually acts as supervisor of the trainees while they work in real jobs where they must produce results to succeed. The training director also encourages useful experiences outside the company, prolonged orientation courses, and coordinated training classes. The training director and the general manager of the company face the need for balancing a number of conflicting considerations if the company is to receive the greatest possible overall benefit from this type of training. Among these are:

1. New college graduates need to develop real maturity before they are ready for any responsibility other than as "general assistant" or as working head of a small clerical unit, yet many have been led to expect rapid advancement and quick professional responsibility.

2. Everyone starts as a specialist, but the greatest management shortage is in general management, which combines the many specialties into an effective operating team. Overabsorption in a specialty may actually limit advancement.

3. Many of the trainees and most other employees, including noncollege supervisors, are apt to expect that the chosen few will automatically advance to the higher level jobs. The "crown prince" attitude is bad for both groups. The training director must limit advancement to earned promotion and foster up-from-the-ranks advancement. Even success cannot provide continual upgrading past the first few steps of the organizational pyramid, and no amount of planning can assure an exact match between trained work force and opportunity.

14-5.3 Management Development

Larger companies have been giving increasing attention to the training and development of management members above the foreman level: department heads, staff assistants, and officers. The basic goals of such training are listed in Figure 14-5. Many companies have a policy "to fill higher level jobs by promotion from within whenever possible." This means that specialists promoted must have general-management training if the company is to have broad-gage executives. Most companies bring in enough "new blood" to

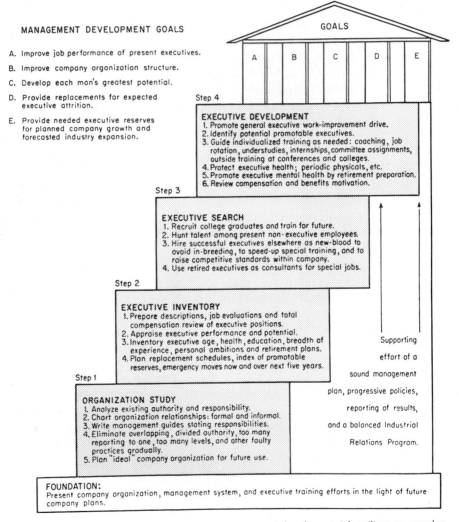

MANAGEMENT DEVELOPMENT GOALS

A. Improve job performance of present executives.

B. Improve company organization structure.

C. Develop each man's greatest potential.

D. Provide replacements for expected executive attrition.

E. Provide needed executive reserves for planned company growth and forecasted industry expansion.

GOALS

A B C D E

Step 4

EXECUTIVE DEVELOPMENT
1. Promote general executive work-improvement drive.
2. Identify potential promotable executives.
3. Guide individualized training as needed: coaching, job rotation, understudies, internships, committee assignments, outside training at conferences and colleges.
4. Protect executive health; periodic physicals, etc.
5. Promote executive mental health by retirement preparation.
6. Review compensation and benefits motivation.

Step 3

EXECUTIVE SEARCH
1. Recruit college graduates and train for future.
2. Hunt talent among present non-executive employees.
3. Hire successful executives elsewhere as new-blood to avoid in-breeding, to speed-up special training, and to raise competitive standards within company.
4. Use retired executives as consultants for special jobs.

Step 2

EXECUTIVE INVENTORY
1. Prepare descriptions, job evaluations and total compensation review of executive positions.
2. Appraise executive performance and potential.
3. Inventory executive age, health, education, breadth of experience, personal ambitions and retirement plans.
4. Plan replacement schedules, index of promotable reserves, emergency moves now and over next five years.

Step 1

ORGANIZATION STUDY
1. Analyze existing authority and responsibility.
2. Chart organization relationships: formal and informal.
3. Write management guides stating responsibilities.
4. Eliminate overlapping, divided authority, too many reporting to one, too many levels, and other faulty practices gradually.
5. Plan "ideal" company organization for future use.

Supporting effort of a sound management plan, progressive policies, reporting of results, and a balanced Industrial Relations Program.

FOUNDATION:
Present company organization, management system, and executive training efforts in the light of future company plans.

Figure 14-5 Interrelationship of common management-development functions as growing out of a foundation of present company practices and plans supported by balanced programs and aimed at the stated goals.

avoid any feeling of "complacent heir apparent," and these also need training.

Almost all the training methods mentioned as foreman and college-graduate training techniques are used in management development. In addition, the methods of job rotation, junior boards of directors, and guided experience (or coaching) are used. Job rotation may include interchange of jobs between employees of about equal position or temporary promotion to higher jobs on an acting basis. The junior board is best represented by the McCormick Company multiple-management plan. Under this plan several committees of supervisory employees, originally designated by the company and self-perpetuating thereafter, meet regularly to discuss management problems. Their recommendations are passed along to the company management and are usually accepted.

The 1970s have seen an upsurge in management training/development courses offered by professional societies, consultants, and universities. There are innumerable opportunities to attend 1- to 5-day institutes, seminars, and workshops in college centers, as well as several "traveling conferences" which repeat the same institute sessions in widely scattered industrial centers for local groups. Many of the larger corporations have set up their own management-training schools. Others conduct conferences at headquarters for managers assigned across the country and in foreign countries. These have sometimes been conducted by colleges or by management consultants but are more often planned, staffed, and taught by the company training department.

Perspective 14D   SENSITIVITY TRAINING

Some rather exotic approaches to management development have emerged in recent years. One controversial technique is sensitivity training. This training is usually conducted at some location other than the normal place of work. For a most effective group, the organizer gathers a small number of people with generally common interests. They need not be from the same job level of their organization. Each member of the T group (training group) examines how he affects and is affected by other persons in the group. This assessment is made in a free exchange of opinions and frank views which has no agenda and no formal focus. Sessions are designed to make participants more sensitive to themselves and to others. The basic assumption here is that lack of sensitivity causes poor task performance in work that requires group effort. Correspondingly, high sensitivity can supposedly reinforce motivation individually and for teams. Collateral characteristics of T groups are discussed by R. A. Luke, Jr.:

As sensitivity-training techniques matured, researchers generally agreed on what people could expect from a T-group experience: (1) self-insight, or some increase in self-knowledge, (2) an understanding of the forces that inhibit or facilitate group functioning, (3) an understanding of the interpersonal operations in groups, and (4) an opportunity to develop skills for diagnosing individual, group, and organizational behavior. . . .

A number of organizations served as clients, and for a time, T groups were a popular managerial innovation. The results of these experiments are mixed, and it would be stretching the point to say that T groups have made a substantial dent in the managerial philosophy of U.S. organizations.*

*SOURCE: R. A. Luke, Jr., "Matching the Individual and the Organization," *Harvard Business Review,* May–June, 1975.

COMMENT   The ultimate test of any form of training is whether or not it increases the desired skills of the trainees. And these skills should be applicable at the place of work; in the case of sensitivity training, a participant returns to the same work surroundings and coworkers he had before the training, an environment where the behavioral insights found in his T group may not be accepted or wanted by those without the special exposure.

14-5.4   Sales-Force Training

All employees recruited for sales are in need of training. Since each company has its own peculiar requirements for successful selling, each company will have something to teach to even the most experienced person hired. A new salesperson needs to know the background of the company, its production methods and capacities, its services, and its sales policies and procedures, as well as the basic principles of salesmanship. He or she will need to build the necessary confidence, enthusiasm, and selling skill. This training is provided through on-the-job training, in home office or branch schools, and through related outside education. Many work-study programs in community colleges provide sales training.

The sales supervisor is a personnel supervisor and will use the industrial-relations methods discussed in this book to select, train, and motivate the sales force. We no longer believe a "salesperson is born, not made" and proceed to train and supervise even unpromising material into an effective force. An increasing number of companies include potential salespersons in the college-trainee group and working salespersons and sales supervisors in the management-development programs already discussed. After field analysis of each salesperson's current record, the sales supervisor, with the assistance of the training director, will coach each salesperson in better utilization of working time, including covering the territory more effectively; better planning of sales presentation, including actually closing sales; and a more complete knowledge of the sales points of the product.

Many sales supervisors, recognizing that the salesperson who usually works alone at a distance from the home office and close supervision, poses a special training problem, feel that *sales training should never end,* and they regularly conduct refresher courses and review field performance to make sure the salesperson continues to operate within the framework of company policy and makes contacts or presents sales points as planned. Some companies use closed-circuit television presentations, or especially filmed movies in either black and white or color, to add impact.

14-6   MAINTAINING THE LABOR FORCE

Once the applicant becomes an employee, emphasis shifts from selection to the prevention of turnover and absenteeism. It does little good to select outstanding employees unless they are kept on the job. Orientation or induction training is usually the first step in maintenance. Probationary follow-up and subsequent counseling on the job may be viewed as extended induction making for stable maintenance. This kind of employee counseling involves a discussion of the employee's problems of adjusting to the job (and possibly to the community, transportation, housing, schools, etc.) in such a way that the solution becomes apparent without the company dominating the employee's life.

14-6.1   Exit Interview

A termination interview with employees who are quitting or have been discharged is used by many companies. Three large aircraft companies found exit interviews effective in salvaging about 15 per cent of those who intend to quit. Other companies say that exit-interview reports returned to the supervisors have a salutary effect in reducing discharges and attempts to quit. In any event, a leaving employee may feel more free to criticize the company than one who must depend on the company for income.

Not too much credence should be given to the reported reasons for quitting, although higher management, as well as the immediate supervisor, usually reviews the tabulated reasons. In the first place, workers are often prevented by custom from complaining or giving the emotional reasons behind what may seem irrational acts. In the second place, accurate exit interviewing requires an extremely skilled interviewer.

The unemployment-insurance termination slip is usually prepared during the exit interview. The employee may also be required to return borrowed tools and clear up outstanding company debts. Exit interviews provide a central clearance to avoid layoffs in one department of a large company at the same time that new employees are needed in another department. They also help to protect the employee and the company from arbitrary discharges.

14-6.2   Cost of Labor Turnover

Employers attempt to avoid turnover because hiring and training a replacement are expensive, because certain states use experience rating (industrial merit rating) under which the payroll tax varies with turnover experience, and because the community often finds short-residence citizens undesirable. An undesirable employee even on leaving can often destroy a carefully nurtured public-relations "company image." The cost of finding, selecting, hiring (badge, photograph, reference checks), and training a new employee may vary greatly, depending on the complexity of both the job and the employment procedure. Any company should make an effort to avoid such costs. Supplemental unemployment payments and annual wage plans also result in additional costs, which may be lowered by reducing turnover. The employee who changes jobs may also lose both wages and job satisfaction.

Although personnel managers differ as to the proper mathematical formulas for calculating labor turnover, the methods of the U.S. Bureau of Labor Statistics are most widely accepted. One such formula is

$$\text{Labor turnover} = A + S \div \frac{P_1 + P_2}{2} \times \frac{365}{M}$$

Where A = *accessions* or hirings and additions to the payroll

S = total of all *separations* for whatever reason, including quits, layoffs, discharges, deaths, permanently disabled, retired on pensions, etc.

P_1 = total number on the payroll at the beginning of the month

P_2 = total number on the payroll at the close of the month

M = number of days in the month for which the figures were obtained

---

Perspective 14E TRAINING TRENDS

A fast-changing technology requires and is supported by flexible technical and professional training. Examples vary from system analysis, an offshoot of the space program, which requires skilled clerical personnel to operate computers and office machines, to prefabrication, a technology being developed to meet rising housing needs, which radically affects the demand for construction skills. Many of today's standard skills will be obsolete by the end of this decade. In the past two decades the former ratio of production to service jobs, 55/45, has been reversed. The trend that now has 55 per cent of the labor force engaged in nonproduction activities will apparently continue as a result of rising social expectations, and will breed new organizations to provide new services. Employers will continue to train new workers, but an increasing number will receive vocational education and develop practical skills in post-high-school training programs.

Retraining will be a major concern in years ahead. The recruits for retraining will come from young workers who chose the wrong field for their initial training, experienced workers with skills no longer needed, women who enter or reenter the labor force after rearing families, and professionals who periodically return to school to keep up with technological advances. Such training will be a vocation itself where both public and private agencies market educational opportunities.

Industrial trainers are involved in the battle of learning theory and educational technique every bit as much as are educators at other levels. Some insist that training teaches the student only "what" to do, whereas education explains "why." Others adopt the philosophy that their function is to teach employees what to do in given circumstances, with specific materials, to achieve a predesignated end.

One example of the industrial approach is found in the use of teaching machines, those self-instruction devices of automated teaching, which created a furor in educational circles during the early 1960s. Amid the horrified cries of those who criticized the dehumanization of the teacher and the mechanization of education, farsighted educators, industrial trainers, and the electronics companies went quietly ahead, developing means for imparting industrial (and educational) information by feedback and reinforced-learning methods. Teaching machines have been used in industry to train keypunch operators, radar troubleshooters, symbolic logicians, and complex assemblers.

14-7 REVIEW QUESTIONS

1. What are the major sources of new employees?

2. What are some of the company employment policies a manager should be aware of before hiring?

3. What are some of the different types of employment tests? What part do they play in the selection of an employee?

4. Of what value to a company are (a) employment interviews, (b) references, and (c) physical examinations?

5. Why is it important for a company to maintain performance records?

6. Why is industrial training important? "Almost none come fully equipped for immediate employment." Comment.

7. What six steps should be considered in planning a training program?

8. How is the case method different from the role-playing method?

9. What are the training needs of the four groups of workers discussed in the chapter?

10. What is the purpose of an exit interview?

14-8 TOPICS FOR DISCUSSION

1. Assume you are in charge of a medium-sized employment office. What procedures would you use in filling an office position, a production-machine-operator job, and two positions for a scientific technician? Explain why the three procedures differ, if they do.

2. Small-town familiarity and years of acquaintance with an applicant help an interviewer. As factory size increases, however, more objective means are commonly employed. How would you make your interview more objective?

3. When the excessive cost of labor turnover is considered, the employment office can be fully justified. Yet it is one of the places where the force-reduction ax most commonly falls. Explain why this may be so.

4. Compare the use of employment tests with the psychological tests used in clinical psychology and explain the difference. If you feel that clinical methods would be an improvement, defend your position. If you feel that they have little to add, explain why.

5. Certain old-line executives have challenged the defensibility of spending company funds for extensive training, especially for what may be classed as preparatory rather than job-perfor-

mance training. Why do you think profit-minded investors might not accept training expenditures? Should they?

6. Many people feel that sales work calls for younger persons, but some older salespersons do very well, both in field sales and upon promotion to management positions. How do you feel that this disagreement can be lessened?

7. Case 14A: *"Take It Easy, Sneezy"*

Burke Herndon was distracted! He took no pleasure in the important papers awaiting his signature. The report was damning! In so many words it proved that his future son-in-law—the man to marry his Marcy next week—did not measure up! It was a good report. Jed Tame knew how to write.

For a moment Burke had an irritating thought. Had he made Jed his industrial-relations manager because Jed could write reports the way he, Burke, wanted them? Was Jed only a "yes man"? But the job had grown too big. Burke recalled how he used to enjoy getting the facts out in the big plant firsthand. Now it was reports. He wouldn't even have this report if he hadn't chanced on that "Take It Easy, Sneezy" poster, which his future son-in-law George Height had ordered prepared. When no one could explain the crudely lettered slogan that seemed meaningless to Burke, he demanded to know why the department was protecting George Height! Protecting an incompetent who didn't follow policy just because George was going to marry the boss's daughter? Was his whole staff shot with cowardice? Burke felt queasy as he now saw evidence of nepotism.

His desk would wait. He would go down Jed's list item by item. A walk through the plant would do him good. Marcy's happiness was too important, the marriage too close. At the compensation office the company lawyer confirmed the first item. George, although only a trainee, completely without authority, had compromised the company's legal position by calling on an injured employee. Now his expression of sympathy was being used by an ambulance chaser as proof of company negligence. Such interference was completely outside the policy book. And George had defended himself to the lawyer, citing the injured person's fine work record, saying no malcontent would have reported to work in the first place while ill with a virus just to complete a rush job.

At the cafeteria George's violation was even more flagrant. Burke himself had forced through the "no private dining-room" rule, so officers and workers shared the same tables. George was undemocratic to want to move in portable partitions for departmental celebrations. The fact that a "wedding shower" under way at the time of his investigation terminated suddenly raised but little suspicion in his mind.

Checking the third "mistake" in the employment office, Burke was greatly disturbed to find that he too liked the young scientist whom George had hired there. When the hiring supervisor stressed how George disregarded test results and chose this person on the basis of a National Science Fair award, Burke let his irritation show—but he wasn't sure why.

It was the last straw when, after seeing the wife of the compensation case and finding her angered with the company lawyers but very much on George's side, Burke found he couldn't get into a remote plant site without a badge. George Height was running a dance there. The plant guard was adamant in enforcing the pass and badge rules but seemed willing to bend them if George would identify his boss. It was as he turned away after refusing to be identified that Burke wondered why the people liked George so much. Then he discovered that the poster that started it all was really an employee catch phrase, one that said in that plant "Work Carefully" better than the safety ad people had been saying it.

Questions

1. Should George be fired for these failures?

2. What would you do in Burke Herndon's shoes?

3. Can nepotism ever be defended in business? How do people in general react to evidence that family members are given special treatment?

4. Take each one of the items on Jed Tame's list and prepare both Jed's condemnation and George Height's defense of the acts in each situation.

5. Should industrial-relations trainees be given as much freedom as this case suggests?

8. Case 14B: *The Central Pipe Company*
The main industry of a small farm town is manufacturing at the Central Pipe Company, whose 400 employees come from farm families within 20 miles of the plant. Employment is centered in the hands of the sales manager as a part-time function on the theory that "he meets people." All employee data except rate of pay are posted on a 5-by-8 card from the employee's verbal statements during or shortly after the interview. Employment requisitions are made by telephone or informally when the supervisors happen to meet sales manager Ted James around the plant. Changes in addresses, married names, and other changes in employee record are sent in by employees on mimeographed forms and are filed in 5-by-8 open-end envelopes. The employee's name and address are posted on the outside of the envelope, and the "active" envelopes constitute an alphabetical employee file. Changes in rate of pay are sent to the paymaster by the shop foreman. The employee's earning record and legal financial records are maintained, along with the record of hours worked calculated from timeclock cards, by the paymaster. Records of employee suggestions are kept by the plant engineer, who operates a suggestion system with emphasis on safety.

Questions

1. Assume that you have been hired as assistant sales manager and asked by your boss to take over industrial-relations responsibilities. What changes would you recommend to Ted James in the light of the steps described in this chapter?

2. After your new system has been in effect 1 year, a labor union is certified by the NLRB as bargaining agent. What changes would you now suggest?

3. A few months later the year-end report shows that the company had a prosperous year and the owner asks you to suggest what activities and benefits should be added to help win back the loyalty of the employees. What would you suggest?

9. Case 14C: *The Roland-Stone Corporation*
The research and development department of the Roland-Stone Corporation has expanded from 30 to about 140 employees in 10 years, most of it in the last year. The supervisory staff of the department has increased from 2 to about 15 now. Of this group about 7 are young persons, inexperienced from the standpoint of supervision. The rest are "of the old school" and are still living in the past. In ordinary times they would never be made supervisors and might be happy if left to function as scientists. Close supervision of the research department is essential because the company does delicate work and must employ many employees who are inexperienced.

Management recognizes the need for training, as evidenced by its recent expenditure of large sums of money for a supervisory training course purchased from an outside consultant. Although this course had good content and should have met with considerable success, it was not well received. Supervisors attended the classes only because management requested it. They are not in a receptive mood toward further training. Yet there is ample evidence supporting the contention of management that the research and development department is badly in need of training on such topics as job evaluation, induction procedures, and methods improvement, which are commonly accepted in other parts of the Roland-Stone Corporation.

The problem of training research supervisors is somewhat different from that of training shop foremen or supervisors. The people supervised are different. They have different expectations. Results are different. The scientist's mind has been developed to analyze problems, to get the facts, and to use those facts to solve the problems.

Questions

1. Suggest a possible approach to the continuation of training for the research and development supervisors of the Roland-Stone Corporation, recognizing that *effectiveness* is dependent upon voluntary *acceptance.*

2. Should the old and the new supervisors be trained by the same methods and in the same classes?

3. Suppose you were leading the classes for the purchased training course. What means would you use to gain better acceptance of the course? How would you get participation? What problems might you meet? List three "overhead" questions which you might use to get the discussion started on each of the topics mentioned.

10. Case 14D: *Maintenance Department Case*

Electrician Bill Endicott looked up from replacing a burned-out motor when he heard footsteps. It was his boss, maintenance chief Paul Sands.

"C'mon," said Sands crisply. "There's a breakdown on the new mill. I'll show you how to fix it."

The two walked silently toward the center of the plant. The giant mill was quiet. Anxious-looking production guys stood around. Endicott had seen the mill often, but he had not been there when it was installed. He didn't even know where to start looking for trouble on this monster—so different from those he was used to. In 17 years' experience he had never seen one like it.

As they approached the mill, Sands broke away and sought out Harv Warren, the production foreman. The two talked rapidly for a few minutes. Sands turned back to Endicott, who had felt he shouldn't eavesdrop. "Bill, this is Harv. We got to look at his control box. It must be a relay," Sands said confidently.

Sands led the way to the rear of the machine. He removed a panel facing and handed it to Bill, who looked about for some place to lay it. Thirty seconds later a motor started. "We'll need to replace that relay soon," Sands said. He looked pleased with himself. "Bill, put that panel back on. I have to get back to the union negotiations." Bill turned to find the panel, muttering to himself.

It was a week later. Sands was at a plant-equipment show out of town. Bill Endicott was burning off some insulation in the yard when Harv Warren dashed up. "Hey, been expecting you back. The new mill is down again. Quit just like it did last week. Got a rush order, and I guess I overloaded it. Come on, get us back in production."

Questions

1. What do you expect to happen next?

2. Can you suggest why Bill Endicott muttered to himself at the end of the first breakdown?

3. Outline in simple terms the steps you should take if, like Paul Sands, you had to teach a skilled man a new task which you fully understood.

4. Write out what Paul might have said as the two men stood before the motor panel behind the giant mill.

15

LABOR-MANAGEMENT RELATIONS

No manager today can afford to neglect the employees of the enterprise and the industrial relations, which, by increasing their satisfaction, raises the productivity of the people associated with the organization. Nor can the consumers be neglected. And the general public deserves attention. Public opinion demands that a higher level of labor-management statesmanship be attained to provide the leadership in collective bargaining, which means labor-relations peace.

To do justice to employees, an industrial manager must be able to appreciate the answers to such questions as these: What are the historical antecedents of present-day industrial relations? How can public relations be fitted into the organization structure? What force does human relations exert in management? Does the impact of electronic data processing on management affect future industrial relations? Do all levels of management have equal responsibility for the success of industrial relations? What are the main responsibilities of the director of industrial relations?

To help provide labor-management statesmanship, the industrial manager and union leader must understand such questions as these: How do employees look upon membership in unions? How did the present labor movement develop? How does union organization occur? What are the steps in collective bargaining? How does grievance procedure work? What are the interests of union members? What responsibilities and problems do industrial managers, employees, and union leaders together face?

15 LABOR-MANAGEMENT RELATIONS

15-1 INDUSTRIAL RELATIONS

No one can question the fact that people constitute a major element of any industrial enterprise. A company operates, grows, and prospers through creative, dynamic leadership cooperatively applied to capable employees—from the president down to the lowest sweeper. This truth has been recognized, but sometimes it has been overlooked in the hustle-bustle of the marketplace, the technology of the factory, and the pressure of competition. Industrial relations is that part of management which is concerned with the manpower of the enterprise—whether machine operator, skilled worker, or manager.

The director of industrial relations[1] supervises as direct line head a number of service functions such as the cafeteria or hospital, but his most important task is to advise all levels of other managers on problems of selection, training, and supervision. In the smaller company regular line supervisors may have to solve such problems for themselves, and in all companies the most important industrial-relations work is that done as part of the day-to-day supervision of employees.

Supervision may be termed faulty in industrial relations when it fails to elicit the wholehearted cooperation of employees. This sometimes happens because there is a sharp contrast between the enlightened management philosophy of top officers, the human-relations codes of company advisers, the carefully detailed procedures prepared by staff specialists, and the things superiors do when dealing with employees. Even with the best possible follow-through from philosophy to practice, however, industrial relations cannot be perfect because it is one of those areas of management that is most in need of facts upon which to base its decisions.

One of the main reasons for management's concern with industrial relations is its influence upon the competitive position of the enterprise. No business organization can long continue unless it remains competitive. While many elements influence competitive position, a successful company finds its industrial relations a major help. Success results from the wise blending of the elements of management. It is not equally easy to maintain an advantage in every area.

---

[1] Sometimes called the personnel administrator, personnel manager, manpower manager, management-relations coordinator, employee-relations director, or assistant to the president. In some companies this manager may perform all the functions but carry the title of only one part, as employment manager, labor-relations director, or community-relations head. Sometimes company history excludes functions which might be included, as when labor relations is handled by the legal department. Public relations especially may be a separate activity tied in with sales or advertising. We shall make no attempt to include all the variations but shall detail only some of the best current practice.

Organized programs of industrial relations are relatively new to business. Only 120 years ago organized efforts of workers to improve their conditions were viewed as illegal conspiracies. At the time of the war between the States workers in factories were often regarded as mere *productive machines*—only not requiring so much care as mechanical equipment—or as a *commodity* necessary to production.

Isolated companies boasted specific functions before the turn of the century, but coordinated programs as a specific staff function were virtually unknown until World War I. By the early 1920s the first professional and research associations were formed, the first college conferences were held, and the first textbooks written, but the function was most often considered at the supervisory level. Industrial relations were elevated to the policy-making level and accepted widely as a top-management function only with World War II.

The first glimmerings of present-day industrial relations took the form of employee-welfare programs established by feudalistic employers. Such paternalism, based on the idea that "papa employer knows what's best," seldom met employee wants and was not popular with workers who felt that their lives were being dominated. Some employers provided housing, hospitals, company stores, and schools. Others introduced lunchrooms and recreation centers. These reforms were condemned by other employers as "mollycoddling," and were resented by first-line supervisors as destroying the "will to work."

As factories increased in size, the need for centralized employment services became apparent. Foremen, who in many cases were "dictators" in their own departments, were spending too much time at the factory gate "hiring on help." The same misfit was hired and fired by several foremen in succession, if he "looked strong."

Following the central employment office, with its early efforts at standardizing records, came physical examinations, first aid, and safety work prompted by workmen's compensation laws. Complex production jobs filled by immigrant labor called for employee training and company schools. A growing recognition of the need for leadership in supervision encouraged foreman training. Growing union activity led companies into labor relations. Public interest in large corporations gave public relations its start. Various federal and state laws changed the employment relationship. No one company added these functions in this exact order. Many functions in their early days were not as we know them today. The pattern of growth, however, from single, unrelated functions to integrated programs, was characteristic.

Today's professional industrial-relations director no longer views his job as "personalizing management," "social work in the factory," or "union busting." He is apt to think of his department as an adjunct to management supervision at all levels, keeping other executives informed of new discoveries, program trends, and needs, while providing efficient service in the operation of numerous centralized systems.

15-2.1 Human Relations and EDP

Industrial relations continues its historical development from such management pioneers as Babbage, Robert Owen, Taylor, Gantt, and the Gilbreths, subject to two forces that tug in somewhat different directions. They are not opposed forces, but in reacting on each other, they may generate a new direction. The resultant first force can be characterized as the *human-relations* approach, if it is understood not to include any paternalistic or "do-gooder" elements. This force continues to battle a dark-ages concept that included these beliefs: that industrial man is incapable of directing his own work, that his only goal is to satisfy subsistent needs, and that the "management lords" must plan work methods in detail, direct "factory serfs," and motivate them like the proverbial donkey with a carrot in front and a stick behind. The human-relations precepts are just the opposite: the worker can direct himself if given a chance, has a capacity to grow and assume responsibility, and must be self-motivating. In the words of one advocate, "Instead of setting up and administering its organization for workers whose inherent capacities are to be led, directed, and motivated, let management assume a new leadership role of creating conditions (technological, sociological, psychological, and through its own behavior) whereby workers can realize their own goals best by directing their own efforts toward organizational objectives."[2] This school cautions managers not to expect human material with which they work always to fit a standard or remain the same. To do so is as fallacious as assuming that H_2O will always be a gas, a liquid, or a solid, regardless of temperature and pressure, and planning for its manufacturing use in disregard of these differences.

The second force affects industrial relations along with all other aspects of management. It is the impact of electronic data processing and the use of computers in business. These are used in employee record keeping and in manipulation of records for layoff, seniority, and skill registers. They are used in research in job evaluation, wage administration, merit review, employment-test evaluation, and union-contract negotiations. Also, research is made more significant in morale surveys, public-opinion polls, and in the determination of "community climate" or attitudes toward the company, labor-relations issues, and political activity.

Fresh employee dissatisfactions seem to have been generated needlessly in some cases when data-processing installations were made without the necessary regard for employee expectations, fear of disruption of familiar routines, and demand for security that must guide all changes in business procedure. Some EDP managers have preferred to centralize personnel functions in their own departments rather than use central industrial-rela-

[2]Douglas McGregor, *The Human Side of Enterprise,* New York: McGraw-Hill Book Company, 1960, p. 421.

tions services, but this seems a matter of personal preference, since other managers have successfully used central services. Just what will be the final effect of EDP on industrial relations depends on its final effect on management in general. Present trends suggest changes in the composition of the work force and distribution of the manager's time to increase the importance of supervision and of attention given to industrial relations by the individual manager. Less staff work in general and fewer lower level supervisors will intensify the need for specific industrial-relations functions in such areas as executive development. Finally, the intensification of "systems thinking" and the necessity for all managers to consider an operation as a whole will force some managers who have preferred in the past to delegate industrial-relations responsibility to do their own industrial-relations thinking and decision making.

15-2.2 Range of Industrial-Relations Specialization

Workers in industrial relations are often specialists in some staff function among the many shown in Figure 15.1. These specialized functions are often centrally supervised by a director of industrial relations. As suggested by Figure 15-1, he may have several assistants and may report directly to the president. In multibranch enterprises the pattern of headquarters functional supervision is often duplicated at the operating locations by directors reporting to the local operating head. In the top organizations of giant corporations the tendency is toward grouping all nonoperating activities into control and service categories.

No single function in management today is as diversely organized in different enterprises as is industrial relations. This is not to say that it is badly organized in any specific instance where local conditions may dictate a specific pattern, but does suggest that alternative arrangements are possible. At the same time broad changes across many establishments do occur. An example is found in relation to retirement age.

Perspective 15A   LENGTH OF WORKING LIFE

The accustomed retirement age of 65 is being questioned. On one hand, workers in many industries are retiring well before their 65th birthdays as a result of improved retirement benefits. On the other hand, contemplated legislative actions would push the mandatory retirement age from 65 to 70, freeing many employees to continue employment if they so desired. Previous legislation to protect the working rights of older workers was passed by Congress in 1967; the Age Discrimination in Employment Act bans job-related bias against persons between the ages of 40 and 65.

The impact of outlawing mandatory retirement before age 70 would be felt throughout the economic system. The size of the nation's work force would immediately grow, as would unemployment, at least until the employment pattern stabilized. The financial burden on the social security system would be eased a bit as workers stay longer on

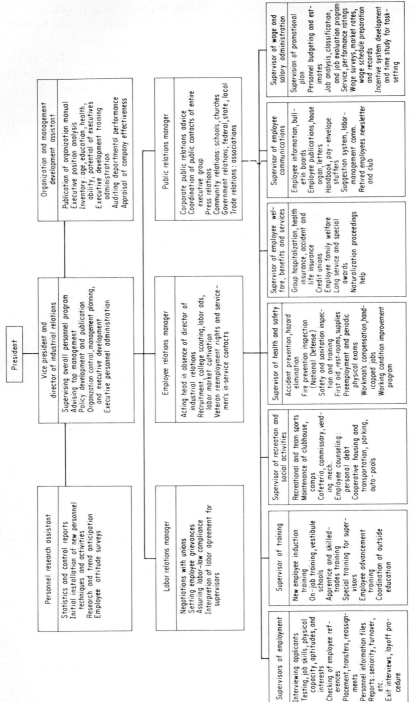

Figure 15-1 Composite industrial-relations program showing the functions found in the typical industrial enterprise.

a job, but younger people would have to wait longer for promotions because those ahead of them would not be moving out as fast. Many company-pension plans would have to be renegotiated.

Long-term effects of increases in the mandatory retirement age are cloudy. Some businesses might decide to release marginal workers in mid career, in anticipation of being locked into a less than desirable employment contract. More rigid objective standards of work performance might develop to define when older workers can no longer perform their duties effectively. Executives might be prone to stay on the job longer than those in subordinate positions, thereby frustrating advancement opportunities.

Surveys differ about how many employees would opt for the added worklife beyond age 65. Sears, Roebuck, & Company concluded from its poll that one-third of its nonmanagement employees would work past 65 if the firm's mandatory retirement age were raised. Officials of General Motors Corporation indicate that in 1977 only 2 per cent of the firm's 450,000 hourly paid workers planned to work all the way to their mandatory retirement at 68. Inland Steel Corporation, which has no forced retirement for production workers, found that just 41 of 18,243 workers at its Chicago mill are over age 65.

15-2.3   Functional Requirements

Since the industrial-relations program is an essential portion of a sound management plan, it is well to consider the basic requirements upon which a successful program is based. Five functional requirements may be stated: (1) top-management understanding and interest; (2) sound personnel policies; (3) adequate practices developed to effect these policies; (4) supervisory training in carrying out those personnel practices; and (5) control or follow-up of industrial-relations results. Each of these will be discussed in turn.

TOP-MANAGEMENT SUPPORT   Since industrial relations is a functional staff service, it must derive authority from the line organization. This is accomplished by having the industrial-relations director report at the top of line authority—usually to the president or executive vice-president. But simply reporting to the president is not enough. The members of top management must set an example. The individual foreman is much more sensitive to example than to admonition. He has learned to repeat what he sees as success. He will use advanced industrial-relations methods when and if he is convinced that "the boss means it." One of the surest ways of convincing all levels is for the head person to use the personnel viewpoint in his or her daily actions and never "let down" in his or her regard for employees as people. Perhaps the greatest danger is that top executives will subvert their own good intentions by appearing to be more interested in budgets and production goals than in the employees—thus putting untenable pressure for "results" on lower level supervisors and causing them to sacrifice long-term goals for short-term results. This is not to imply that executive quality is only human relations, for the successful executive must first get the job done.

Another weakness is creating the impression that all the many industrial activities exist *only because they produce a profit.* They are profitable! Company after company has demonstrated that, but industrial relations must also increase human dignity, must help every employee identify himself with the enterprise, and must create a public image of the enterprise so that the employee at whatever level, from operator to manager, finds lasting satisfactions in being identified with the enterprise. Otherwise, much of the profit potential is lost. An equal weakness is in pretending that money hardly counts at all—that all modern motivation of employees is by good industrial relations. In disproving the "economic person" of classical economists some managers have substituted an "emotional person" who has no financial interest. This view of human-relations values and monetary rewards as an either–or proposition misses the fact that one cannot be substituted for the other, but both must be in balance.

SOUND PERSONNEL POLICIES   These are statements of management intention in regard to industrial relations. They constitute a business philosophy for the guidance of the human-relations decisions of the enterprise. The purpose of any business policy is to decide ahead of emergency need, in the calm light of ultimate effect, what shall be done with the multitude of bothersome daily problems. Too many so-called company policies, particularly of the unwritten variety, are badly misunderstood, or even unheard of, at the working level. No policy can be considered clear until it is followed at all levels of management. No company-minded executive can continue to violate the stated rules of company conduct once he understands them. Superintendents, foremen, and line supervisors need only to be informed of company intention—then they can make their own applications. An executive or supervisor operating within policy has greater freedom of decisions, since he or she knows what actions management will stand behind. Most managers in America today try to give equal treatment. Even with the best intentions, however, equal treatment cannot be guaranteed to every employee under the same circumstances without a set of rules to guide the several supervisors consistently.

ADEQUATE PRACTICES   A third requirement is the provision of adequate practices developed by professionally minded staff assistants to effect the policies of the company. A system of procedures is necessary to translate intention into action. The procedures and practices of industrial relations are the "tools of management" which keep the supervisor ahead of her job: the daily paper work of timekeeping, rate adjustments, grievance reporting, merit rating, etc. It is in the thoughtful development of working rules and detailed operating plans that the professional staff touch is most useful. A knowledge of what has been tried elsewhere will often prevent a needless mistake.

DETAILED SUPERVISORY TRAINING   To carry out the policies and practices developed by the industrial-relations staff, the job supervisors must be trained in detail, and the significance of the policies must be *communicated to the employees.* Supervisors must be trained in leadership and in communication. Discussion conferences and role-playing sessions by the industrial-relations staff supplement coaching by superiors. Ideally, the training starts at the top and follows the line of authority downward. Communication flows both downward and back up from the employees. Supervisors must learn that upward communication from the employee is the best evidence available that the employee has an acceptable idea of what the job is, what company goals are, and how one's contribution will be rewarded. Supervisors must accept the lack of effective communications as a failure on their part.

FOLLOW-UP OF RESULTS   The industrial-relations director has no "police power." As a functional staff person he has only "the authority of his ideas," but to measure his own success in carrying out the policies he has helped top management to establish, he must keep a running record of industrial-relations matters in the departments he services. As he reports these results to line authority, the "control over industrial relations" is exercised. Follow-up of turnover, absenteeism, departmental morale, grievances, employee suggestions, wage administration, etc., must be supplemented with continuous research to make certain that the policies pursued are those best fitted to company needs and employee wishes. Hints of problem areas may also be found in exit interviews, in union demands (in or out of the company), and in management meetings, as well as in formal social-science research.

To make this follow-up more effective as well as to test results in the program of industrial relations, managerial attention has been turning to yardsticks for evaluation of existing practices. General Electric Company has given an appropriate name to the measure it has developed for this purpose—*employee relations index* (ERI). The company has found this index a useful means for spotting trends within plants and for comparing managerial performance among plants. What it amounts to is the development of statistical measures that bear a yardstick relationship to such aims of the enterprise as productivity, quality, and profitability. Some of these measures are the increasing rate of suggestions offered in the suggestion system; participation in the employee insurance plan; falling rate of absenteeism, disciplinary suspensions, separations, work stoppages, job accidents, and grievances; and other measurable conditions which lend themselves to construction of a statistical index.

15-3   PUBLIC RELATIONS

In many enterprises, the public-relations function is a part of the industrial-relations division. In other equally well-known, profitable, and popular managements, the function reports elsewhere. Perhaps the most common alternative locations are as a parallel to the company legal counsel or as a part of sales or advertising. Among top corporations, three out of four do have an internal public-relations department, although most also use the services of the public-relations counselor, who operates much as an advertising agency does.

Much of the confusion regarding public relations derives from its historic roots in advertising and press relations. This confusion continues because most of the large advertising agencies have established public-relations departments to serve clients and because a head count among workers finds many who have been newspaper reporters.

That public relations differs from advertising (even institutional advertising) is recognized by most. In general, advertising is paid for directly as an aid to sales, immediate or future. Public-relations counselors, while they may use the same media, are interested not primarily in sales but in "the corporate image"—that impression of the company which makes it easier to hire desirable employees, prevent union trouble, cause voters and legislators to think twice before restrictive legislation, and help administrative law enforcers believe that any apparent violation may have been unintentional.

There need be no conflict between industrial relations and public relations since both seek a more sympathetic ear for the employee's problems. Too often, however, the public-relations person outside the industrial-relations department forgets that the employees *are* the company, not just another public.

WHAT IS PUBLIC RELATIONS? The activities of company public-relations managers and outside counselors have one purpose, an established process, four functions, and unlimited media for activity. The purpose of public relations is "to make the enterprise look good" to all people in all its actions. Perhaps its greatest contribution is the general cleanup of corporate activities and policies that customarily precedes a concerted public-relations program.

The four functions of public relations are:

1. To aid top executives to determine the overall purpose or goals of the enterprise

2. To keep managers at all levels informed of the current status and of changes in the opinions of the various publics

3. To warn of unfavorable reaction which company action (or lack of action) may have and, conversely, to suggest desirable "good public relations" activity

4. To communicate by way of all established media and means the company policy and actions

Many of the procedures used are shown in Figure 15-2, which analyzes seven active campaigns.

Many governmental units, service associations, and labor unions use public-relations techniques. Trade associations may publish well-written presentations of a whole industry's story. Labor unions use this tool of management as they do most others appropriate to their size and purpose. Such devices as union teaching kits, visual aids, pamphlets, and news releases are made available to the external public. Union leaders treat their internal public (members) to such devices as comic strips, air shows, sound films, and truly original means of their own.

The benefits of a sound public-relations program are very evident in the other aspects of industrial relations. More applicants of all kinds hear about the company. Better applicants are more apt to seek work at the "good" company. Applicants do not feel so frightened or mystified at the prospects of employment if they have heard of the company. New employees stay long enough to "season." Expensive turnover is reduced. Employee morale and, hence, productivity are raised. Union relations are apt to be on a higher plane. Strikes and unrest are reduced. Customers sign fewer restrictive sales contracts. Suppliers are more attentive. All parts of the company work together better in improved understanding. The greatest gain, however, is often the completely objective review of company policies and procedures which must precede turning on the spotlight of publicity.

Perspective 15B   CORPORATE INPUTS TO PUBLIC AFFAIRS

Many millions of dollars are spent each year by corporations to improve their public image. Expenditures range from mass media messages on TV and in newspapers to the funding of local projects that promote good-neighbor feelings. The traditional approach to public relations has been low-profile—sponsoring educational programs, supporting civic issues, donating to art shows, developing recreational areas, etc. A more aggressive approach has been used by Mobil Oil Corporation:

Mobil deploys every weapon in the p.r. armory, but its views come across clearest in its weekly "op-ed" ads in the *New York Times* and several other newspapers. With the program now in its fifth year, Mobil has become the most accomplished practitioner of what is known as "issue" or "advocacy" advertising. Few organizations of any kind can rival Mobil in the artfulness and sophistication with which it presses its opinions, whether it is advocating a national energy policy, resisting congressional proposals to end vertical integration in the oil industry, or championing the cause of mass transit.

With strong advocacy goes bristling resistance whenever Mobil encounters unfairness, or what it regards as unfairness, on the part of the media. This is remarkable, for most large corporations prefer to minimize controversy if at all possible; faced with media attack, they avoid a strong counterthrust lest it prolong the unpleasantness and result in more unfavorable publicity. . . .

Energetic advocacy and a willingness to trade blows in public are only one side of Mobil's distinctive p.r. approach. The other side involves an effort to generate goodwill by financing a variety of cultural projects—public-television shows, outstanding dramatic works on commercial TV, all manner of art books and exhibits. Mobil was a pioneer among corporations in funding public television, making its first grant in 1970 to launch "Masterpiece Theatre," a notable success.*

*SOURCE: Irwin Ross, "Public Relations Isn't Kid-Gloves Stuff at Mobil," *Fortune,* September, 1976.

COMMENT   Public relations work differs from advertising in that specific products are not pushed, but public relations may still produce sales dividends. Mobil's motivation,

Programs	Representative Activities Included	General Purpose of Program
Attitudes surveys	Opinion polls, "Why I Like My Job" contests, door-to-door check, public complaint meetings	To find out the causes of employee dissatisfaction, supervisory ineffectiveness, or public lack of good will
Employee communication	Plant magazines, letters to employees, employee meetings addressed by president, annual reports to employees, posters, pay-envelope stuffers, handbooks, booklets, public-address system, dramatization	To supply adequate information to employees, to counteract false rumors heard elsewhere, to give employees a sense of "belonging" and of their improtance to the enterprise, i.e., to build team spirit and develop morale
Civic activity	Reports to community on jobs furnished, products bought, or taxes paid; plant tours for civic leaders; company speakers at local club meetings; public exhibits	To gain understanding of neighbors, voters, and elected representatives in plant locations; to improve tolerance of noise, smoke, and necessary wastes; to lessen excessive charity demands
Press relations (including all types of magazines, trade journals)	News releases; photographs; cartoons; personal contacts with editors, reporters, columnists; interviews; arrangements to answer all critical editorials, "Letters to the Editor," etc.; informative "ads"	To keep newspaper readers and, indirectly, employees informed; to combat false charges; to increase "friendly" news, limit derogatory stories, by furthering understanding by editors and reporters of industry

Radio; television; films	Paid programs, include news commentators as "press," industrial film shorts, educational film strips, recordings, plays	To improve understanding through visual aids and auditory effects in contacts with employees and public; to treat "new" outlets like "press"
School programs	School library, research units, teaching guides, exhibit booths, trade class "samples," booklets, films, company speakers, plant visits, annual schoolday; sponsor clubs, sports, contests, scholarships	To give teachers full story, counterbalancing misinformation; to prepare new employees in advance; to attract future managers, engineers, and skilled workers; to build future community understanding
Employee family contacts	Open-house programs, family picnics, father-son nights, recreation centers, children's clubs and programs, home-improvement campaigns, gardens	To "let family know what Daddy does," to build job pride; to add to family acceptance of necessary overtime, dirt, nightwork; to lessen radical influence
Professional group communications (clergy, lawyers, physicians, dentists, pharmacists, etc.)	Plant tours, welfare cooperation, informative brochures, "questions and answers," suggested sermons, safety and health literature; "gift" decorations; personal contact of company "professionals"	To provide additional employee information indirectly through community "thought leaders," to counteract false information, to crystallize acceptance of social responsibility and company position

Figure 15-2 Public-relations program activities and purposes. (Based on analysis of campaigns conducted by American Iron and Steel Institute, Society of American Florists, U.S.V. Pulpwood Campaign, and New York, New Haven, and Hartford Railroad Co.)

according to company officials, stems from a sense of corporate responsibility. Its public affairs department had a budget of $21 million in 1975, none of which was used to advertise Mobil products. To avoid complaints that it editorializes at the expense of taxpayers, the company does not take a business deduction on ads involving an expression of opinion.

15-4 LABOR RELATIONS

Day-to-day labor relations are primarily a problem for line supervisors, although collective-bargaining direction and service in connection with organization, negotiation, and grievance procedure are usually provided. Because top management is often preoccupied with matters of finance and technology, this service is occasionally less than both line supervisors and employees desire.

Labor relations, even in those cases where a company's employees are not union members and discipline in groups is better referred to as joint relations, now occupies an increasingly large part of the line supervisor's time. Formerly, under individual bargaining, each employee made his own agreement regarding wages, hours, and working conditions very quickly, often simply by accepting the employer's terms. Today, collective bargaining takes more time. It is probable that it will continue to be difficult and time-consuming. This will be true whether the tendency is back toward individual bargaining, toward industry-wide agreements established by trade-association bargaining, toward greater worker participation in management along socialist government patterns, or toward some as yet unsuspected bargaining arrangement.

It has been increasingly pointed out by students of our economic system that the power of giant employers and the matched power of giant unions are so great, their disagreement so bitter, and the impact of their disagreement on the public so sharply felt as to virtually invite government control. Management and labor leaders must find ways of working together if our present free collective-bargaining system is to continue.

The second way in which government influence is felt by management is in the necessary compliance with other laws not having to do with unionism but affecting the employer–employee relationship. These are legion. Examples include workmen's compensation laws mentioned in the safety section, wage and hour laws, the Social Security Act of 1935, and the Employment Act of 1946. In addition many state and local ordinances, such as sanitary codes and fire laws, are controlling. In specific circumstances regulations of the Interstate Commerce Commission, Civil Aeronautics Board, Federal Communications Commission, Maritime Commission, and the Federal Bankruptcy Act must be followed.

As has been indicated, the problem of legal compliance can no longer be left to the company lawyer or to top management except in the small company. Each department head throughout the organization must know and comply with the regulations that govern his operations. Thus the employment manager must set up procedures for obeying such laws as unemployment-compensation regulations, minimum working-age laws, and the antidiscrimination codes found in some states. The plant hospital and safety engineer must know state sanitary codes, rules governing the handling of explosives, workmen's compensation, etc. The company social-service workers must know Social Security and local "poor laws" and coordinate with the operations of local welfare departments. The wage administrator must keep the company in compliance with minimum-wage laws, the Fair Labor Standards Act, the Walsh-Healey Act, and equal-wage-for-equal-work requirements. The list is so long, the coverage so great, and the growth of administrative interpretations so uncertain that no industrial-relations department can be sure it is always in step with the law, but the conscientious try to be.

15-5   THE LABOR MOVEMENT

If recent decades are a reliable guide, many hours of the future manager's time will be spent in meeting demands of employee representatives. The difficulties of joint relations arise primarily because employees are people, making demands on the job not made by inanimate machines and materials. In this sense there is a resemblance to the problems of marketing and other "people relationships," although not all of these will be discussed here. Joint relations contrasts with individual bargaining and covers arranging the conditions of employment between the employer and groups of employees. Contact occurs at three levels: at the *organizational* level, where a spokesman attempts to obtain recognition for a unit of employees; at the *contract-negotiation* level, where the rules covering "wages, hours, and conditions of work" are established; and at the *employee-grievance* level, where individual-worker complaints are settled. Joint relations at all three levels may exist either with or without a union. *Collective bargaining,* since Federal control was established in 1935–1937, is a kind of negotiation that can legally exist only between an employer and the freely selected representative of his employees.

About a third of the labor force in the United States are trade-union members. It is because of this relatively low density that we must study joint relations without unions, as well as legal collective bargaining. The bulk of industrial wage earners are employed by a small number of very large companies, although most companies are small. The average size of a company varies greatly between industries, but in certain industries at least, the day of relations between the independent, individual worker and the small-shop owner is rapidly passing. Large blocs of workers, acting through vigorous labor organizations, have taken their place. In a great many other industries, however, the small shop still prevails. Individual relations between worker and small-shop owner predominate, but the status of such labor is increasingly becoming a problem to both small-shop owners and to the large labor unions.

The attitude of American society toward unions has been derived from

English common law. The roots of unionism can be traced back to American colonial days but are generally several decades behind English developments. In Great Britain during the sixteenth and seventeenth centuries the state regulated wages and conditions of labor as well as prohibited unions. During the eighteenth century many of the controls fell into disuse, but trade unions were still viewed by the courts as conspiracies to raise wages and as combinations in restraint of trade. American courts held to the view that unions were conspiracies until about 1840. During the quarter century until the war between the American states, unionism grew gradually with many radical and utopian offshoots.

15-5.1 Employee-Representation Plans

Employee-representation plans, or joint relations plans, are found in several areas. They are distinguished from collective bargaining in not being required by law. Some employers had voluntarily organized employee-representation plans before 1935. Since traditionally some of these were employer-dominated, they were all declared illegal by the National Labor Relations Act. A few, following local elections under the act, continued as legal collective-bargaining agents. These, and the few locals organized since, which are not affiliated with national unions or federations, are called "independents." They usually restrict their membership to the employees of a single company and may be very successful in pushing local demands.

Most "unorganized" employers, having no union machinery, receive employee complaints via the "open door." The employee takes his complaint "right up the line" from his foreman to the company president. The open door is often locked tighter than many employers imagine, since the flow upward is often throttled by lower levels of supervision. Some employers without unions use industrial-relations-department representatives to settle grievances, while others have multistep appeal machinery. With or without a union, the successful manager will strive to keep open the channels of communication upward from employees to top management.

Consultative management, or discussion of management decisions in advance with various levels of employees, is planned to give employees a sense of real participation in the enterprise. It is not a substitute for collective bargaining. The method may be used with or without a union, although in nonunion plants care must be exercised to avoid matters of collective bargaining. Consultative management is actually supplemental to collective bargaining in the same sense that state government is supplemental to Federal government.

15-5.2 Labor Organizations

The Knights of Labor, a social-reform group which enrolled others besides workers, flourished in the 1870s and was gradually replaced by the American Federation of Labor. This federation was first formed by a group of craft unions in 1881 and reorganized along a city-council and state-federation plan in 1886. Its growth reached a peak during World War I, with a severe decline in membership in the 1920s. During these years the AFL followed a policy of "business unionism." Unions kept out of political entanglements, except for using votes "to reward your friends." In fighting employers, the leaders tried to improve wages, hours, and physical surroundings.

In 1935 a group of the more industrial-minded unions split off from the craft-dominated AFL to form the CIO and organize the mass-production industries. Twenty years later the two again merged to form the AFL-CIO. This is a federation of some 188 national unions. (Some call themselves *international* to cover locals in Canada.) These national unions charter hundreds of local unions. Some locals in large cities have thousands of members. The foundation of the trade-union movement is the local union offering leadership to the working members. The new AFL-CIO federation attempted to exercise stronger central control over its affiliates than either had previously. The second AFL-CIO convention in 1957 implemented the ethical-practices codes by expelling for corrupt practices the Laundry Workers', Teamsters', and Bakers' unions. New national charters had been issued by 1960 for the Laundry Workers and Bakers.

In the AFL-CIO the old distinction between affiliates organized on the craft principle (workers of a single trade regardless of employer) and industrial unions (taking in most employees of an employer regardless of trade) began disappearing. Such industrial unions as the United Auto Workers began giving office employee and skilled trades members new autonomy, while such craft groups as the Carpenters and Machinists increased organization efforts in industrial organizations. By 1961 the mergers of state and local labor councils of the old AFL and the old CIO into unified AFL-CIO councils were largely completed. Many, although not all, jurisdictional and "no-raiding" disputes among affiliates were also on the way to agreement. Periodically some of the more than 50 national unions outside the AFL-CIO consider joining or taking cooperative action.

In early 1968 the United Auto Workers broke away from the AFL-CIO because of policy differences and leadership struggles. Later in 1968, the Alliance for Labor Action (ALA) was formed as a partnership of the auto workers and teamsters unions. The ALA became a definite rival to the AFL-CIO when the 110,000-member Chemical Workers Union split from its AFL-CIO allegiance to join the ALA. It remains to be seen whether the results of such factionalism will have a deleterious effect on the public image of unionism or whether the competition will benefit the rank-and-file worker.

All national union officials are concerned about the falling density of membership among the working population. Three trends are blamed. One is the loss to the industrial unions of workers replaced by further mechanization of manufacturing. A second is the industrialization of the South, which has had fewer union members than Northern industrial centers. The third is the growing number of workers employed in white-collar occupations. The unionist answer as to this loss is to step up organization drives in these areas and intensify political activity. The early AFL leaders, observing that prior union movements had floundered on the political shoals, tried to follow a policy of using votes "to reward your friends, punish your enemies," but avoiding party endorsement. Since the New Deal, labor-union political activity became more direct. The CIO started COPE (the Committee on Political Education), and after the AFL-CIO merger, political action intensified. In world politics the AFL in 1919 was instrumental in providing for the creation of the International Labor Organization in the World War I peace treaty. The ILO has been particularly effective in aiding workers of many countries affected by industrialization. In 1949 labor representatives from 60 countries formed the new world-wide labor organization, the International Confederation of Free Trade Unions (ICFTU), which has fought the spread of communism.

Unions as organizations are largely led by elected leaders who, since they are elected, respond mainly to the demands of the membership. Because those demands change, especially at the local level, it is entirely incorrect to speak of "what the unions want," or "what the unions will do." Occasionally, some union social planner will state a union demand that catches on with the members, but if that demand does not articulate the grass-roots beliefs of the membership, it cannot support a bitter negotiating battle and "fighting strike." In this connection, the *wildcat strike* deserves attention.

Although such action may sometimes be instigated as a deliberate negotiating tactic to "soften up" the opposition, the wildcat strike is by definition a work stoppage by union members occurring without the sanction of the union's leaders. As such, a wildcat strike or "quicky" (which lasts for a prescheduled time, usually less than one day) is most often a protest by the rank and file against union leadership thought too complacent (management might call such leaders responsible and mature) over company neglect of specific group grievances. Unauthorized strike action may also result from continuous work isolation or other frustrating conditions. Sometimes it is a pressure tactic to obtain undeserved special treatment for the strikers. Under such conditions, the responsible union leaders may be temporarily helpless against the mob leaders.

Perspective 15C INDUSTRIAL IMPACT OF LABOR LAWS

The U.S. Congress enacted the Wagner Act (National Labor Relations Act) in 1935. Its purpose was to stimulate collective bargaining. It also created the National Labor Relations Board (NLRB), which is concerned with administering the law and providing relief from unfair labor practices by employers. The Taft-Hartley Act of 1947 amended the Wagner Act by putting restraints on unfair labor practices by unions; for example, provisions in the act prohibit union labor from refusing to bargain, coercing an employer to pay for services not rendered, and forcing an employer to enter into a "hot cargo" agreement (where an employer agrees to take no action against employees who refuse to work when any goods or services are supplied by nonunion sources). An amendment to the Taft-Hartley Act in 1959 established minimum standards of responsibility and ethical conduct for internal union affairs.

In the early 1960s union membership was diminishing until Executive Order 10988 opened the untapped reservoir of potential union membership among public employees. These employees are now swelling the membership ranks of the labor unions —federal workers, teachers, firemen, police, professors, etc. In 1974 another amendment to the Taft-Hartley Act removed the exemption for not-for-profit hospitals. As a result, many hospitals administrators were faced for the first time with the collective bargaining process. Their responsibilities are described by C. L. Packer:

Collective bargaining is not a game. It is problem solving in a conflict situation; and negotiations between a health care provider and a union often generate highly emotional discussion, a certain amount of name calling, and a continuing crisis preceding the strike deadline. Through all this, the management team must represent the operational supervisor and not tie his hands, the fiscal director and not overspend his revenue potential, and the community, optimizing the use of its health care dollar. At the same time, it must reach a settlement that is equitable and salable to both the bargaining unit membership and hospital management.

Although financial failure can swiftly result in the collapse of an organization, so, too, the forfeiture of noneconomic issues can steadily erode management rights until the organization can no longer function. Therefore, no proposal made at the bargaining table should be looked on as insignificant. Each should be studied to determine its short-range and long-range impact on the organization, and the management position should be established on the basis of logic, cost, and relevancy of the proposal.*

*SOURCE: C. L. Packer, *Preparing Hospital Management for Labor Contract Negotiations,* Chicago, Ill.: American Hospital Association, 1975.

15-5.3 Organizational Effort

An earlier paragraph of this treatment stated that labor relations had three stages: organization, negotiations, and grievances. The organization campaign for a specific plant resembles any sales campaign. Leaflets and handbills are passed, corner speeches made, meetings held, and members signed up. In some cases, the enthusiasm of untrained organizers suggests violence, threats, and intimidation, but these illegal actions are more typical of a strike situation.

The organization effort is now usually abandoned if a substantial interest is not shown by employees, although in times past economic warfare often raged. Strikes were called, or if no members were present to strike, pickets were posted to enforce sympathetic boycotts to force the employer to bargain. Sometimes employers fired union organizers, or "locked out" union employees before they could strike. Under the Labor Management Relations Act, when an organizer has signed authorizations from 30 per cent of those in the unit, or expects the employer to "consent" to an election, he may request the NLRB to hold an election to certify his union as exclusive bargaining agent. Organizers from different unions are usually in competition, and some of the most severe jurisdictional difficulties arise from that

conflict. A development in 1960–1961 was the Philadelphia combined organizing drive. Four large national unions, normally in jurisdictional conflict,
selected about 100 small plants without unions, settled possible conflict of
jurisdiction in advance, and shared organizers to "knock them off one at a
time." Some of the high cost of organizing these small plants was borne by
national headquarters, which also supplemented the common pool with
organizers from the organizing department.

15-5.4 Negotiation

After an NLRB election certification, the employer is presented with union
demands and asked to bargain. After the initial agreement is reached, the
provisions are renegotiated at periodic intervals, which in recent years have
tended to be at 3-year intervals. Some of the provisions commonly included
concern rates of pay, hours of work, seniority benefits, and grievance procedure. There is often a tendency toward identical contracts, although usually
there are local applications and interpretations even when an industry-wide
contract is negotiated. To help reach agreement, the parties may resort to
mediation, conciliation, and, rarely, to arbitration. Then outside experts
interested in avoiding continued disagreement try to get the parties to
agree.

The relations between a union and an employer will depend on the
organizing stage, the past experience of the parties, and the maturity of the
respective representatives. The variations can be seen most clearly at the
collective-bargaining level. On the union side this may range from a deliberate attempt to put an undesirable employer out of business to a concerted
effort to help a good employer by promoting his product. Often the union
helps the employer by means of the union label; the union label is generally
used to promote the use of union-made products and, when demanded by
customers (or secondary union users in production), can be very effective.
The union can also help the employer by reducing his costs and even at
times by lending him money. Union policy toward the employer is sometimes confused by conflict between rival factions within the union or between rival international leaders. Union leaders generally are elected to
local office for short terms and must often make fantastic promises to retain
office in the face of insurgent demands. The wildcat strike has been mentioned as a form of protest. Even presidents of international unions have
been known to resign or have been unseated by insurgents when the membership no longer supported them. The newspapers and magazines published by unions are often an important source of information for bettering
relations, but scanning out the trends may prove difficult. A recently developed aid is the University of Michigan Index of Labor Union Periodicals,
which attempts to summarize monthly the prevailing opinion of leading
unions.

On the management side, collective-bargaining policy is less influenced
by immediate political considerations, although the company negotiator too
must keep his job by getting a contract that he can sell to other company

officers. Company union policy may cover a wide range of contrasts, from successful cooperation with union leaders in reducing production costs and increasing profits to avowed "industrial warfare." Most company negotiators vary their position and appear to operate without policy, although they may be very systematic about trading concessions for benefits to the company, protecting essential management functions, and keeping up with new collective-bargaining developments.

15-5.5   Grievance Procedure

When the working rules of the enterprise have been established by negotiation or by employer statement of policy, individual employees may have complaints, called "grievances." The procedure for settling such grievances is an important part of labor relations. Good grievance procedures are essential whether or not a plant is organized. The grievance machinery enables management to discover and correct the sore spots in working conditions and employee relations. If no systematic way exists for bringing complaints to the surface, small unseen grievances may grow until an inevitable explosion occurs.

An effective grievance procedure must provide (1) a series of steps or hearings on the complaint from the immediate supervisor through his superiors to the highest management authority; (2) a systematic procedure for promptly remedying the conditions complained of; and (3) recognition that, in making complaints, the employees may be letting off steam over workplace frustrations and a lack of participation in decisions affecting their daily life. Thus, the surface grievance may not be the true complaint. Grievances which were serious enough to go to arbitration, the final step in most procedures, are listed in Figure 15-3.

15-6   LABOR-MANAGEMENT STATESMANSHIP

The demands of the public, i.e., American consumers, stockholders, all citizens, seem to be forcing decisions upon management and labor leaders. The public would seem to be on the verge of taking away the traditional voluntary system of collective bargaining unless the leaders involved can find a solution. John P. Citizen seems little interested in joint relations until he finds his train will not run or that construction of his house must be delayed for lack of materials. In response to public pressure, one suggestion is government-sponsored conferences. Over the years, government-sponsored conferences in the United States seem not to have provided an answer. Even under the pressure of wartime or postwar emergencies, only partial results were achieved by the 1918 War-Labor Conference Board, the 1919 Industrial Conference, the 1941 Labor-Industry Conference, and the 1945 President's National Labor-Management Conference. Better labor-management statesmanship seems required.

BASIC DIFFICULTIES   While issues between labor and management in joint relations, as distinct from local plant or industry collective bargaining, can

Issue*	Number of Cases
Discipline and discharge	456
Seniority advantage	301
Job evaluation (usually changed material or conditions)	223
Incentive plans	107
Overtime	82
Vacations	61
Holidays or holiday pay	50
Wages	46
Welfare provisions or application	42
Arbitrability of issue (as sole issue)	41
Foremen and supervisors (appointment or authority)	31
Hours of work or work schedule	29
Guaranteed employment (applications of agreement therefor)	26
Transfer of worker to or from job	26
Union security provisions	22

*Other issues with fewer than 20 occurrences each were observance of grievance procedure, pay for time not worked, probationers, call-in or reporting pay, merit increases, subcontracting, leave of absence, pensions, severance pay, and miscellaneous.

Figure 15-3 Grievance issues which were serious enough to go to arbitration in 1,183 cases before the American Arbitration Association.

be stated, they hardly go to the heart of our industrial society as do actual difficulties.

1. *Inability to Communicate*   Labor leaders and industrial managers do not seem to talk the same language; the same words seem to have different meanings for each group. Often the give-and-take of collective bargaining forces the participants into a position where communications break down.

2. *Prerogatives*   When traditional means of management control (often called management prerogatives) run counter to the politically oriented union leader's need to expand services to the electorate, there is frequently little understanding of the purposes behind management control. Yet we know also that past procedures are often continued for no good reason.

3. *Foreign Competition*   When European, South American, and Asiatic suppliers can lay down industrial products in American ports at lower prices than the cost of raw materials in the United States, workers lose jobs and employers lose markets. In their dilemma, they tend to wrestle with each other instead of with the problem. This problem is closely related to the inflationary spiral which has become so familiar. Management sees that inflation as wages, while union members find it in prices. Both must find other solutions than lengthy picket lines and smokeless chimneys.

4. *Work Rules and Plant Practices*   Many strikes are ostensibly over work rules. Railroad featherbedding, which requires unneeded workers, is a continuing consternation. Management condemns the archaic practices of the unions, while labor leaders condemn the mechanistic approach to the human element.

5. *Responsibility of Management and Labor to the Public*   There is grave doubt whether any one group of private citizens in a country, be they either management or labor, should rightfully have the power to create a national emergency. Strike actions by government employees, who are restricted by law from unauthorized work stoppages and are often involved in activities or services vital to public safety, have caused particular concern. The dramatic power plays of strike negotiations damage both parties in the eyes of society. Little is gained by painting the leaders of either side as villains.

15-6.1   Union-Leader Responsibility

In democratic unions the leaders hold their positions only through their persuasiveness and the gains they make for the members. Like some political leaders, union leaders are always in competition with "rising young people who promise more to the electorate." Many leaders are sincerely interested in the future of the organized labor movement as an institution of which they are a part. They may willingly sacrifice their own interests for the good of the cause. Some of the best known union leaders are active crusaders for social welfare. Most respond in kind to the position taken by the management members with whom they deal. Both responsible management and higher levels of union leadership have been cultivating a greater sense of social responsibility for the whole economy among labor leaders. The march into union contracts of such provisions as pensions, guaranteed annual wages, supplemental unemployment benefits, and the like may be credited to leaders who feel the obligation to help the underprivileged. The AFL-CIO position on racial integration and Fair Employment Practices springs from these roots.

Of increasing importance to management is the participation of unions at the stockholder level. Some unions are in a position to invest very large sums of money accumulated from benefit funds, and most of them invest in industrial stocks—often of the same companies with whom they bargain. At least one union owns a bank, and several own private insurance companies. In a recent stockholders' proxy battle, the union announced it had voted its stock for the incumbent management.

However, many local unions recently have been charged with discriminatory practices toward Negroes and women. The Civil Rights Act of 1964 prohibits unions from excluding individuals from membership because of race, color, religion, sex, or national origin. Most charges are aimed at local levels where discrimination takes the form of closed apprenticeship programs and inaction on applications for membership. At the national level, unions have forwarded equalitarian principles such as nondiscrimination clauses in contracts and internal education programs designed to reduce discrimination against minority groups.

15-6.2   Responsibility of Industrial Managers

Managers, as the representatives of their employer, may be assigned the legal responsibility for collective bargaining with unions. As designated management representatives, supervisors must exert effective leadership toward company goals. This leadership is needed whether or not the employees supervised are union members. The supervisor can sometimes use fellow workers to "whip" recalcitrant workers into line. The future effectiveness of management leadership may well depend on the manager's ability to take an active role in the dynamics of improved joint relations. Management has been criticized by labor leaders for a somewhat reluctant acceptance of this new responsibility. Management philosophers have emphasized that managers must *manage* or give up claim to the right. Experience with European codetermination has indicated that much the same results are obtained whether the "bargaining" takes place with trade-union members on the board of directors or around the contract negotiation table. Moreover, managers who give first attention to the motivation of their employees rather than to traditional productivity, profits, and costs excel in these areas also.

Employers have now largely abandoned a passive wait-and-see approach in joint relations and, both by improved public relations and by initiative in seeking contract changes (usually aimed at improved work rules or lower costs), are becoming more aggressive. Some have collaborated more closely with other employers through joint committees (basic steel), through "parallel bargaining" (autos), by exchanging information (aircraft), and by developing "strike insurance," as did the airlines.

Union aims are not necessarily in conflict with successful management. The National Planning Association in its series on the causes of industrial peace named, among others, these reasons for success: (1) the company uses the constructive potential of unionism; (2) the foremen and stewards have become effective conduits of upward and downward communications; and (3) the union has felt institutionally secure and has respected management's control over hiring, firing, and directing the labor force. The success which will result from such mutual understanding will proceed on the three levels of organization, negotiation, and grievance handling.

Perspective 15D TO OVERCOME JOB DISCRIMINATION

A blunt version of recent legal interpretations of actions demanded by the Civil Rights Act of 1964 is given by Dr. S. M. Zimmerman:

If your management policies still discriminate either intentionally or unintentionally, it is going to cost you money. If you have not yet fully integrated formerly segregated employees you are breaking the law. Your progress towards full integration will be measured by how the formerly segregated employees are progressing up your promotion ladder. The procedures you have developed to move your formerly segregated employees rapidly up your promotion ladder will be examined with a critical eye. Your only defense is business necessity and it's not very effective when the statistics are against you.*

Zimmerman describes the setting in which efforts to overcome job discrimination must occur:

One way which workers (through their unions) have developed to stabilize relationships between themselves is called a line of progression (LOP). A line or sequence of ever increasing dollar value positions is established. An individual is supposed to start in the lowest job and as higher positions become available move up the line. A constant order between individuals is maintained. Only the exceptions are those who decide to "sign out" and to remain at a given level. This action changes the sequence established by the starting date of each individual into the line.*

The concept of a line of progression is not a discriminatory tool, but the procedures of implementation can be discriminatory. Tactics to eliminate LOP segregation advised by the courts include the following:

- *Rightful place concept*   Placing individuals in the LOP where they would have been if there had been no discrimination
- *Red circling*   Allows an individual to start at the bottom of a new LOP without sacrificing pay; present wages are circled in red and carried over
- *Advance entry*   Payments to compensate for insufficient progress in remedying discriminatory practices
- *Business necessity*   Positions should be filled on the basis of the minimum standards necessary to do the job, not the most qualified applicant willing to take the job.

*SOURCE: S. M. Zimmerman, "The Law Says—End Race Discrimination Now! And it Means It!" *Proceedings*, AIIE, 1977.

COMMENT   Two groups have industrial-relations managers sandwiched between them. One group, composed of individuals who have suffered discrimination, expects remedial action, and soon. The other group, which has enjoyed privileges in the past, expects fair and consistent treatment in the future. Only in rare situations can both sides be satisfied fully. And whatever course of action is selected will cost a company extra money. But the price must be paid now, in dollars and unrest, or it will surely get worse ahead as the movements (age, sex, race, and many minority causes) for equal treatment widen and intensify.

15-7 REVIEW QUESTIONS

1. What is industrial relations? Why is it important to management?

2. Trace the pattern of growth of the industrial-relations function.

3. What are the requirements of a successful industrial-relations program?

4. What is public relations? What are its four functions? Where does "advocacy education" fit into public relations?

5. What are the benefits of a sound public-relations program?

6. What are the three levels of joint relations between employees and employers?

7. What is meant by "collective bargaining"? How is it different from joint relations?

8. Of what importance is negotiating in union-management relations? What are some of the provisions included in typical negotiations?

9. Why is a grievance procedure necessary? What must an effective procedure provide?

10. What issue of joint relations between labor and management has caused considerable public concern?

15-8 TOPICS FOR DISCUSSION

1. Some writers have in the past placed "Taylorism" and the efficiency movement in the industrial-engineering field in one corner for a bout with human relations in management. Now there seems to be a battle royal shaping up, with the Scanlon plan (see Perspective 16B) for union group cooperation and the use of electronic data processing as a force also entering the ring. Which do you think will win the battle royal, and what will happen to the others?

2. Are most of the differences in industrial relations in different industrial segments, like rubber and steel, the result of different unions? If so, why do the unions differ by segments?

3. In the discussion of government-sponsored conferences five basic difficulties resulting in issues are suggested. Select any of them and state your understanding of the position of the two parties. Then explain why you agree or disagree with one or both.

4. How can the strength of the local union and its function as champion of the interests of the local members be maintained in the face of the concentration of policy, decision making, and bargaining at the top of national unions often dealing with giant multiplant corporations or industry-wide associations?

5. Billion-dollar reserves are building up in trusteed "pension and welfare funds" collected from employers for employee benefits. Like the insurance company reserves which they resemble, these amounts are so large that investment becomes a problem. What should be the primary guide for such investments: a safe income and conservation of capital or the social desirability of the investment, such as in community improvements or low-income housing?

6. Some have eyed with apprehension the increased productivity of factories improved by automation and identified the distribution of goods as the most pressing problem of the next 10 years. Dozens of alternatives have been proposed. How best can full employment be achieved: (a) by a continuation of the decrease in working hours which have gone down from 60 through 54, 48, and 40 to 36 or 30 hours; (b) by a reduction in the 75-year compulsory retirement age to 60 or 65 years; (c) by a limitation on married women working; or (d) by increased production and trade aimed at development of economically backward areas of the world?

7. Do industrial workers want a shorter work week as some union leaders have claimed, or would they use the extra time off to work on second and third "moonlighting" jobs? In an industrial society with periodical ups and downs of employment in specific factories, is multiple-job holding a wise or an unwise precaution against unemployment?

8. Case 15A: *The Viso-Audit In-Basket*
Assume you were hired as an industrial engineer and systems analyst by the Viso-Audit Company. As part of your orientation course you accompanied the director of industrial relations on a tour around the company's seven plants located in the Midwest and on the Eastern seaboard, with one plant in Los Angeles. The director of industrial relations was a friendly, assured traveler, who talked to you mostly about eating establishments and housing accommodations during the trip, but you met many important plant managers and operating executives. You returned to New Jersey headquarters on Wednesday afternoon. Mr. Dearth remained in Los Angeles. Friday afternoon, after quitting time, a report is received by the president from California of Mr. Dearth's death from a heart attack. Since he had no assistant, the company president then asked you to

occupy Dearth's office and take whatever action was necessary until a successor could be selected. His instructions to you were: "George, you have been in close contact with Bill Dearth during this last swing around the country. You have met our plant managers and know our operating problems. There are many pressing industrial-relations matters which cannot wait until Jim White comes back from Europe. If he is willing to shift from international operations to industrial relations, he will be our new vice-president. If he is not, I will have to find another one. For the next 60 days I want you to consider the job yours. Take whatever action seems necessary. Call me if you need help. I don't want the details and know that all of our executives will work with you. Bring your first report of the staff meeting next Wednesday. We usually hold that meeting at the Country Club over a late breakfast about 9:30."

You go into the office Saturday morning, although the plant is not normally open, to find the following situation:

1. All your new staff, consisting of Bill Coffee, director of personnel and employment, Tom Jones, head of salary and wage administration, Ed Ward, training manager, and Julia Smith, benefits chief, are attending a branch plant picnic which has been scheduled for some time. They are not expected back until Monday morning, when a regular staff meeting is scheduled for 9:00 AM.
2. The only other person working in the office is the elderly female clerk in charge of personnel records. She knows the location of keys, files, and reports, but has not heard of Mr. Dearth's death.
3. She reports that your secretary, Alice Denny, left on vacation Friday and is not expected back for 2 weeks. The substitute, Kathryn Bishop, is drawn from the company stenographic pool and has only passing familairity with the department operation.

Questions

Mr. Dearth's in-basket contains the following items. Indicate for each one by number what action you would take. Remember that you must attend Mr. Dearth's funeral on Tuesday, the personnel department staff meeting Monday morning, and the corporate staff meeting on Wednesday morning. According to your own information, both you and Mr. Dearth were expected in Canton, Ohio, at the opening of plant union negotiations on Thursday.

Item 1

MEMORANDUM

To: Mr. William Dearth   From: Carlton Smith
    Industrial Relations   Director of Economic Studies

Subject: Preparation for long-term change in the company labor force.

As you will see in the attached diagram, we can look forward in 1985 to a considerable change in the proportion of women in the national labor force. But this is part of the general change which we can expect as the distribution of the labor force becomes excessive in the younger and older categories, with a shortage of middle-aged workers. We may expect this to be particularly significant in regard to managerial and highly skilled trades.

Viso-Audit Company does not now have in its employment a proper balance of female workers. I would like to talk to you about your plans for the future.

A Larger Proportion of Women, Especially Older Women, Will Work
Percentage of Women in Each Age Group
Who Will Be in the Labor Force in 1985

Age Group	Per Cent 1985
14–19	28.1
20–24	52.2
25–34	45.7
35–44	47.6
45–54	59.0
55–64	41.1
65 and over	16.9

Item 2

Letter to William Dearth

Dear Bill:

As you know, we have been having a lot of trouble with old Charlie, our plant guard. He has been hitting the bottle again, but hard. I hate to dismiss a man with 30 years of service, and I had hopes that Alcoholics Anonymous could keep him dry until he retired. He drove the plant jeep into the snow ditch at the far end of the parking lot while on duty yesterday and is now in the hospital. I understand he will be released tomorrow, having only minor injuries. I have given him an additional 3 days to recover before reporting back to work, but I would like to have you solve this problem. As I explained to you before, I have done all I can, and it is in your lap now.

Charles Wilson
Plant Manager

Item 3

Union demands at Canton, Ohio, plant

1. An across-the-board increase of 48½¢ per hour for all production and maintenance employees represented by the union
2. A fifth week of vacation for all employees with 15 years of service
3. Free access by union stewards to all personnel records, arrangements to be made by steward with personnel file clerk as required
4. Seniority for demoted foremen to be calculated on the basis of length of service in the bargaining unit and not to include any time spent as working foremen or department supervisors
5. Reclassification of blacksmith-mechanics into labor grade-III

Item 4

MEMORANDUM

To: William Dearth   From: Byron Johnson
                                                                              President

I know you have been busy recently preparing for union negotiations, but I need some facts for the Chamber of Commerce Integration Committee. I understand that the state blacklisting law prevents our recording certain information on our employment records, but the Chamber is particularly interested in the recent influx of Puerto Rican workers. Can't you make a quick rundown of our situation, in the main plant particularly, and get the figures to me for my meeting next week?

By

Item 5

MEMORANDUM

To: William Dearth   From: Ham Baxter
Subject: Request for reclassification of assembler job
As you know, we have had the job of assembler restudied several times. I seem unable to convince your men that I am unable to hire female assemblers at $5.50 an hour. This is a complex job and it sometimes takes us 3 days to bring a new girl up to the production rate, although it helps if she has factory experience. I know that there are unemployed workers around and need immediate reclassification of this job to get them into the plant and get the new contract delivered to the Navy on time.

Ham

Item 6

Note from Helen Adams, Chief Nurse, to William Dearth, Director, Industrial Relations
This will remind you that it is now time for the members of your department to have their flu shots, inasmuch as the last ones were administered 1 year ago. If you will arrange for each member to schedule himself through the infirmary during the first part of next week, this will enable us to complete the immunization program.

Item 7

Minutes of Hearing in Compensation Case

Finding of fact: Phil Gross, crane operator, while climbing the ladder to his cab, slipped and injured his back and knee. He was hospitalized and is now released. Light work is recommended. He should do no climbing for 2 years. Disability award will be based on job assignment.
Testimony of Phil Gross: "While performing my job at the start of the shift last July 6, I slipped and injured myself. My doctor says I should do only light work and cannot climb. Operating the crane requires that I use my arms and back continuously. Besides, I cannot climb into the cab. I am willing to take any company job on the same shift which pays my crane operator's rate."
Summary of testimony by foreman, Phil Gross case: "This man was a probationary crane operator who had not yet become accustomed to the stairs. His fall was as much his own fault as anyone's. I have no openings in my department for light work, since all foundry work is heavy. The old crane operator, whose position Phil Gross was filling during a leave of absence, has now returned and I would not need him even if he were able to work."

Item 8

Letter from East Chester Community Improvement Association
Dear Mr. Dearth:

As you have in the past, I would like to have you loan our Association one of your dump trucks to aid in our clean-up campaign at the Children's Recreation Park next Sunday. One of our regular drivers is chairman of our Grounds Committee and he can bring the truck from the plant if you will authorize this usage.

Our Association has appreciated your company's cooperation in past years and hopes to continue our good work.

Item 9

MEMORANDUM

To: Bill Coffee   From: Philip Wright
    Director of Personnel and Employment

Subject: Phil Gross case

As you requested, I attended the compensation hearing for Phil Gross and feel that it will be necessary for us to find him a job some place in the plant. He does not have much ability and probably was beyond his depth in the crane-operator assignment. He did, however, exceed the probationary period and is now a regular employee. The union has not taken up his case, but I am sure from his mentioning the steward's name that we can expect a grievance if satisfactory adjustment is not made. The compensation commissioner indicated that he would hold off final judgment until we had had an opportunity to do all that we could. I gather that no one in the foundry department has any particular regard for Phil Gross or his ability.

Item 10

MEMORANDUM

To: William Dearth   From: Carl Andrews
                                                         Sales Manager

I will want to take up the attached outline for a sales training program at our staff meeting next week. I have not been satisfied with the orientation program your training department has provided for new sales candidates. Consequently, I have talked to Edward Peale of Peale Associates and want to hire his expert trainers for this delicate task. The outline which they have used successfully at some of our leading competitors is the one enclosed. Unless I hear from you by Wednesday, I will announce this program to our Regional Sales Managers' Convention.

Note: No outline attached. A.D.

Item 11

To: Director Industrial Relations
From: Labor-Relations Manager—Plant "XYZ"

I need immediate advice as to arbitration on the following issue—Holiday Pay for Frank Roach. The issues are as follows:

Frank is a machinist in our washing machine section. He took a leave of absence for 10 days to re-roof his house after the recent windstorm. Leave was granted under Contract Provision 104, which permits leave for personal business at company convenience but requires that all such leaves shall be without pay.

Frank Roach returned to work on June 3, as scheduled, and worked his regular shift. He now demands pay for Memorial Day on the basis that he worked his last scheduled day before and after the holiday. This is true, but we did not pay him on the basis that leaves of absence are without pay. Had he been laid off for lack of work, he would not have been paid. Had he been present May 29 and 31, he would have been paid. This grievance has gone through all steps in our procedures and has now reached arbitration. The submission will be on the basis of the conflict between the "Leaves of Absence" clause and the "Holiday Paid" clause.

Please advise immediately as to whether we wish to fight this one through?

9. Case 15B: *Frank Roach*
Refer to Item 11 in the in-basket case.

Questions

Put yourself, alternately, in the position of Frank Roach arguing for your Memorial Day pay and of the plant manager who has refused it as: "Inasmuch as all leaves of absence are without pay, Frank doesn't get paid for the holiday that occurred between such absences. If he wanted a 10 days' leave and holiday pay, he should have arranged so that the leave did not include the holiday."

1. Indicate in your reply both the argument and the reason for the argument as you understand it.
2. Assuming that you were the arbitrator in this case, what would your decision be and how would you support it?
3. If you had knowledge of some previous arbitrator's decision on a case similar to that of Frank Roach, would this influence your decision? State why.

10. Case 15C: *Image Merchants*
The Image Merchants Agency planned a promotional public-relations campaign for its client, New School Suppliers. The first step was a survey of school principals on the use of New School Company supplies. The plan was that those administrators who praised the products would be credited in a booklet incorporating the ideas and suggestions made. If no school administrator mentioned some useful idea, the information would nevertheless go into a "synthesis of many recommendations." The results of the survey were printed by the "Committee for Better School Administration." This was a "front" group originated by Image Merchants. Six months later, New School Suppliers "discovered" the report of the committee and, as a public service, reproduced it and mailed it to a wide range of school personnel. The brochure was also quoted in a series of informative articles sent to legitimate educational journals and magazines.

Questions

1. Criticize the campaign planned by Image Merchants from the viewpoint of a public-relations procedure. Is it likely to attain the results desired?

2. Public-relations counselors do, on occasion, use false-front organizations. There is no law against it, and propagandists have employed the technique since Euripides. Discuss the ethical aspects of New School Suppliers.

3. Eleven months after the survey at the time of the appearance of several of the educational-journal references, a highly respected school administrator, whose contribution had been quoted, protested at a national meeting on this series of activities. As a result of his complaint,

an ethical-practices committee revealed the whole chicanery. What effect would you anticipate on New School Suppliers' sales position?

11. Case 15D: *The National Production Company*
There are several different unions with separate jurisdictions in the company. The training director has been operating a job training program for the technical employees covered by Union A of the Technical Engineers. Employees of the company who belong to Union B of the Production and Outside Engineers are considered professional workers and no training is given in the work which they perform. Both unions have contracts in force which give them the right to use test stands under certain conditions. In September Union B claimed exclusive jurisdiction over test stands and refused to work if Union A members operated any test-stand equipment. Delivery of the company's products depends on the operation of test stands for final inspection. This is normally done by Union B, but the members are not working, and no other employees are trained for final inspection.

Questions

1. If you are required to meet with Union B for negotiations, what would you propose to them to get shipments made?

2. Union A feels that its members are being discriminated against by Union B and calls upon the company to live up to the written contract in force. What answer will you give?

3. The dispute is not settled, but the Union B members go back to work and then ask management to renegotiate their contract to grant their exclusive claim to operate test stands. Would you grant the demand, and if you did, how would you handle Union A negotiations later?

12. Case 15E: *Union Demands at Viso-Audit Company* (Refer to the in-basket case, 15A, Item 3)

Questions

1. If these demands were presented to you as a company negotiator, which ones would you accept, which ones would you wish to discuss, and which ones would you refuse?

2. What would you want to know about demands 2, 4, and 5 before granting each demand?

16
JOBS
AND WAGES

Of the many responsibilities a manager faces, problems connected with jobs and wages are among those most important to the continuity, profitability, and social contribution of the enterprise. Much depends on the fairness of the wage payment plans and how well job performance is evaluated. We may then ask such questions as these: What are the logical procedures available in wage and salary administration? Is there an industry-wide wage policy? What factors affect the income of wage earners? What are the several methods of payment in common use? How are wage surveys used? What is the basic theory behind the payment of different wages for different jobs, and how can it be defended? What effects do automation and job enlargement have on job-skill levels? Are clerical and salary jobs evaluated similarly to factory jobs? What qualitative and quantitative job-rating methods are in common use? Can management's evaluation be made more flexible? Can credit unions, guaranteed annual wages, profit sharings, and executive performance standard be made useful tools of management, benefiting the participants, the specific enterprise, and the economy?

16 JOBS AND WAGES

16-1 SOURCE OF JOBS AND WAGES

The payment of rewards for working is not new. Popular writers about primitive people assume the arrowmaker traded his work for the game of the hunter. The Book of Genesis (29:15, King James) records that Laban asked Jacob, "Tell me, what shall thy wages be?" and Jacob said, "I will serve thee seven years for Rachel, thy younger daughter." Among the earliest written records of civilization are references to work and earnings. The mass-production movement identified by specialization of product and concentration of workers which started in the sixth and seventh centuries B.C. also extended the practice of paying wages. All through history the problem of suitable reward for work has presented difficulties.

The managers of the enterprise face the problem discussed in Chapter 1 of combining natural resources, accumulated capital, and human effort in just the right way to create more capital or wealth. What is created can be divided. That portion paid as rent goes to the suppliers of land and buildings. That portion paid as interest goes to those who lend money to the enterprise. The major portion usually goes to workers as wages. Part of this is the portion paid as salaries to hired management. There is no fixed rule for apportioning the shares. The theories of economic philosophers can help explain certain current wage trends, but such theories apply mostly to past conditions, and managers today had best consider wage and salary administration as an orderly procedure having as its aim a minimum of dissatisfaction to all parties. That this aim is not always achieved is evident, and if the foregoing takes more wealth than has been created, the enterprise is insolvent. If income exceeds the claims of rent, interest, wages, salaries, and certain arbitrary taxes (such as that on real estate), pure profits exist. These belong to the equity owners of the enterprise. Part of these profits is subject to income taxes (often exceeding what is paid out as dividends). Part may be used to expand the business or kept in liquid form for emergencies. Part may be turned back to consumers through lowered prices in the future. Periodically, extra dividends may be declared. Some may provide extra inducements to attract exceptional management ability.

The managers of the enterprise, although in modern days usually themselves hired labor, make most of the decisions concerning allocation of the income portions. In recent years workers, through their unions, have been gaining a greater voice both in the division of earnings and in other management functions. While the function of management to arrange wage payments is recognized by all concerned, the area subject to negotiation with labor unions is constantly enlarging. State and Federal officials also claim a voice in the payment of wages, for instance, by way of workmen's-compensation laws and minimum-wage laws.

16-2   WAGE ADMINISTRATION PROCEDURES

Disregarding the historical origin and the parties of interest, the management procedures connected with wage administration may be considered as shown in Figure 16-1. These are six logical steps toward a pay relationship mutually satisfactory to the employee and employer. Regardless of job structure or union relationships, the company intentions are expressed in wage policy, written or unwritten. The next step is job analysis, a finding of the facts by research on the job. These facts may be recorded in terms of qualifications, responsibilities, and job conditions, or they may simply be held in mind while the next step of job rating is taken. Job rating establishes the interrelationship among jobs and arranges those jobs in a hierarchy of status and payment. The job-pricing step, along with task setting, regulates how much pay will be given the worker during a given period of time or for a given quantity of satisfactory production. The final step of wage control is usually supervised by the accounting head, as service to line managers.

Decisions having to do with wage policy and practice are important. The wage level in relation to productivity determines the profit margin and,

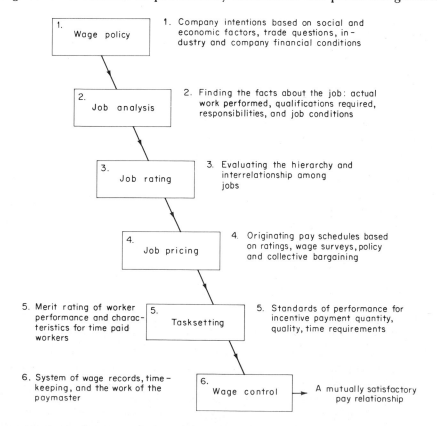

Figure 16-1 In six steps, the major activities of the wage and salary administrator. All steps are interrelated, with no fine line where one stops and another begins.

hence, the competitive position of the enterprise. Wage matters are also basic to the employer-employee relationship. Whether the employment contract is signed as a step in collective bargaining or understood informally in individual dealing, wages constitute a major portion of that contract.

Wage administration is so important to the enterprise that it can never be completely delegated. Such procedures as job evaluation, rate setting, and merit rating are usually supervised by the industrial-relations or the industrial-engineering department, carrying out through foremen and the line organization the policy decisions made by top management. These decisions, which are often much more detailed than policy decisions in the areas of sales, design engineering, or accounting, must cover such broad economic sweeps as are suggested in the introduction to this book. Furthermore, the detail of paying each employee every week (or other period) and of living up to top-management policies, labor laws, and union contracts makes wage control very complex. For these reasons, many companies employ a wage administrator. He usually operates as part of the industrial-relations or the industrial-engineering department but may be attached to the controller's staff or the organization-control section. In the smaller company, the plant manager may perform the function. In any event, his job is to originate wage schedules, job-evaluation plans, merit-rating plans, incentive systems, and the related controls. To guide management in its policy decisions, he will make periodic wage surveys of prevailing rates, fringe benefits, and innovations in the wage and salary field. He has also the responsibility for assuring company compliance with the various wage and hour laws.

The wage administrator or industrial-relations manager may, after consultation with line management, reduce desirable action to writing for top-management publication. Many considerations such as productivity, profit margins, supply of labor, cost of living, living standards of employees, climate, and cultural factors will enter into the determination of a company's wage policy. A company may have a policy of making quick adjustments to changes affecting wages, or it may choose to act relatively slowly. Where industry and regulatory standards permit and where better workers may be attracted thereby, a company may have a policy of paying higher than average rates. Other common policy provisions include decisions on the productive standards to be expected, provisions for changing standards, a payment method for nonproductive time, and a means of appeal from wage decisions.

Weekly income differs widely among different industries. Some of this industry contrast results from differences in the profitability of industries. Other contributing factors are differences in availability and use of raw materials, power and transportation, "foreign" and technological competition, degree of investment, seasonal stability, extent of mechanization, and industrial history including unionization.

The personal income of individuals within an industry will also vary widely. Some of this variation results from the interplay of aptitude, education, trades training, mental and physical health, as well as from differences in effective personal effort. Employers customarily pay different employees different wages. The greatest part of the difference is because of varying duties. The wage administrator uses job analysis, job evaluation, and wage surveys to set these gross differences. Within the same job, however, different rates may be paid to different employees. If they are paid incentive rates, their wages rise or fall day by day (even hour by hour or minute by minute) as their productivity changes.

Many of the methods of calculating employee pay may be included in one of two major classes: those based upon satisfactory performance of duties during a period of time, and those based upon the successful completion of a unit of work. Time-payment methods are still commonly called "daywork," although the most usual time interval used for calculation is now the hour of working time. Time wages may be figured by the week as is customary for lower paid clerical and sales employees, by the month as for higher ranking supervisory and governmental employees, by the term of three or six months as for teachers and seasonal workers, or by the year or a longer contract period for managers and technicans. In any event, the actual earnings are customarily delivered weekly or biweekly.

Although daywork is the simplest method of paying wages, it may be more costly in the long run. The clerical expense of careful production, time, and earning records necessary for incentive payment is saved. The salaries of incentive engineers are saved. Less supervision may be needed. This is not all gain. The records kept for incentive payment are so useful for other management-control purposes that they may have to be kept anyway. The industrial engineers necessary to an incentive system may improve operations in general through scientific management, especially methods improvement. The more numerous supervisors may be better supervisors—more competent technically, better able to enlist employee cooperation—and, under greater pressure from the employees, may do well management's job of planning, scheduling, and controlling. In addition productivity of operators may be increased, since when a company installs an incentive system it commonly reports a 20 to 50 per cent increase in productivity on the same equipment with consequent higher employee earnings and lower unit-production costs.

16-3 JOB ANALYSIS

The key mission of job analysis is to determine how long it should take workers to perform the tasks for which they are being paid. It is particularly important to the success of incentive wage plans that the units of work be carefully evaluated and monitored, less the payment schedule discourages rather than encourages greater productivity. The following conditions are essential to the success of wage incentives:

1. Standard conditions and procedures must be established for the performance of each operation. These procedures must be the best methods possible, must be followed completely, must be recorded in easy reference form, and *must be revised* when new or alternative methods are used.

2. Management must establish a sound wage policy for the guidance of its members in wage matters.

3. The company wage structure must be established by logical means such as job evaluation and community wage surveys.

4. Careful time studies must be made by intelligent trained observers, devoting sufficient time to each study for recording an accurate performance *standard.* Where elemental data are available, the timing may be set synthetically, but even greater care is then required.[2]

5. These time-study standards must be uniformly translated by simple understandable methods into task rates permitting worker earnings in keeping with established wage policies.

16-3.1 Time Study

Although in past years the foreman or plant manager often set rates, this is now the function of the industrial engineer or a technician helper. With his observation sheet attached to a clipboard, which is specially shaped for ease of recording while standing and which holds his decimal timer (a special decimal-dialed stop watch), the industrial engineer or technician observes the job and records results. He may let the decimal timer run continuously, or he may stop and start the timer with each operation in the "snap-back" technique. The steps of his observation will include:

1. A thorough study of possible ways of improving the operation and determining the quickest and best methods.

2. A careful recording of observations made on a selected average worker. See Figure 16-2 and 16-3 for a typical time-study record sheet.

3. Leveling the observation to correct for minor variations and bringing the results closer to that expected from the average worker (also called "speed rating" or "normalizing"). The Society for the Advancement of Management has attempted to establish industry-wide performance standards so that all time-study persons will level to the same standard.

4. Apportioning allowances for personal needs, delays, and overcoming fatigue. These should permit the normal employee to work on that operation regularly without exceptional fatigue and perform the task set in the standard time.

[2]Although the terms have an exact meaning, *time study* and *rate setting* are commonly used to mean "putting a price on a job" by means to be discussed. In the same way *piecework* is used to mean any method of pay which gives the employee more money for more production, including production *bonus plans* and other *incentive systems.* The specialist in this field is known variously as an *industrial engineer, time-study engineer, incentive engineer, rate setter, time-study person,* or *standards person.*

STOP 8:27.04 PROD 36 pcs
START 8:02 PCS PER LB 67
ELAPSED 25.04 min.
SHIFT 2nd
SHEET NO. 1
OF One

Element descriptions (read across):
1* H pick up fixture, insert RH piece in press. RH trip press.
2* RH press to flare fixture. RH remove part from fixture. Inspect.
3* LH open fixture, position RH cover, remove part. LH position, remove.
4* RH position, tissue, cover, assemble, insert. Repeat remove.
5* Repeat wrap. Repeat wrap cover. Repeat remove.

Main time-study data (T = elapsed; R = continuous watch reading):

NUMBER	1*	2*	3*	4*	5*	1*	2*	3*	4*	5*
1	.49/.49	6/.55	5/.60	8/.68		48/1.16	6/1.22	5/1.27	8/1.35	
2	45/1.80	7/1.87	6/1.93	7/2.00		47/2.47	6/2.54	7/2.60	7/2.67	
3	48/3.15	6/3.21	6/3.27	7/3.34		46/3.80	7/3.87	6/3.94	6/4.00	
4	47/4.47	6/4.53	6/4.58	7/4.65		47/5.12	7/5.19	6/5.25	5/5.30	
5	45/5.75	6/5.81	6/5.87	8/5.95		48/6.43	6/6.49	9/6.58	7/6.65	
6	49/7.14	8/7.22	6/7.28	7/7.35		49/7.84	6/7.90	8/7.98	7/8.05	4/8.09
7	49/8.58	6/8.64	8/8.69	8/8.77		52/9.29	6/9.35	5/9.40	8/9.48	
8	48/9.96	7/10.03	4/10.07	8/10.15		48/10.63	6/10.69	5/10.74	9/10.83	
9	52/11.35	6/11.41	5/11.46	7/11.53		45/11.93	5/12.03	5/12.08	A	
10	46/12.68	6/12.74	5/12.79	8/12.87		48/13.35	5/13.40	5/13.45	9/13.54	
11	46/14.00	6/14.06	6/14.12	7/14.19		46/14.65	6/14.71	6/14.75	9/14.84	
12	48/15.32	7/15.39	5/15.44	6/15.50		48/15.98	6/16.04	6/16.10	8/16.18	
13	50/16.68	6/16.74	6/16.80	8/16.88	5/16.93	47/17.42	6/17.48	5/17.53	8/17.61	
14	49/18.10	6/18.16	4/18.20	8/18.28		47/18.75	5/18.80	5/18.85	10/18.95	
15	48/19.43	7/19.50	5/19.55	8/19.63		48/20.11	6/20.17	5/20.22	8/20.30	
16	48/20.78	6/20.84	5/20.89	8/20.97		47/21.45	6/21.51	5/21.56	7/21.63	
17	47/22.10	6/22.16	5/22.21	8/22.29		46/22.75	6/22.81	5/22.86	8/22.94	
18	51/23.45	6/23.51	6/23.57	7/23.64		53/24.17	6/24.23	7/24.30		
19	48/24.78	6/24.84	6/24.90	8/24.98	6/25.04					
20										
21										
22										

FOREIGN ELEMENTS

	R	T	DESCRIPTION
A	12.22 / 12.08	14	Dropped piece, assembled under economy
B			
C			
D			
E			
F			
G			
H			
I			
J			
K			
L			

NOTES: New work place layout somewhat disturbing to operator →

SUMMARY

	1	2	3	4	5
TOTAL TIME	17.71	2.27	2.03	2.74	.15
NO. OF PIECES	37	37	37	36	3
AVE. TIME	.4786	.0614	.0549	.0761	.05
BASE TIME	.45	.05	.04	.05	.04
LEVELED TIME	.52	.08	.09	.10	.06
	.5073	.0651	.0582	.0807	.053
FL. TIME/(PCS)	.5073	.0651	.0582	.0807	.0044

FINAL CYCLE TIME .7157

Rating tables:

SKILL
+0.15	SUPERSKILL
+0.13	
+0.11	EXCELLENT
+0.08	
+0.06	GOOD
+0.03	
0.00	AVERAGE ✓
-0.05	FAIR
-0.10	
-0.16	POOR
-0.22	

EFFORT
+0.13	KILLING
+0.12	
+0.11	EXCELLENT
+0.08	
+0.05	GOOD
+0.02	
0.00	AVERAGE
-0.04	
-0.08	FAIR
-0.12	
-0.17	POOR

CONDITIONS
+0.06	IDEAL
+0.04	EXCELLENT
+0.02	GOOD
0.00	AVERAGE ✓
-0.03	FAIR
-0.07	POOR

CONSISTENCY
+0.04	PERFECT
+0.03	EXCELLENT
+0.01	GOOD ✓
0.00	AVERAGE
-0.02	FAIR
-0.04	POOR

+0.09 TOTAL -0.03 LEVELING FACTOR 1.06

* Continuous recording in hundredths of a minute on decimal-minute watch, from which alternating columns of elapsed times are obtained by successive subtractions.

Step 1: Obtain elapsed time by subtraction from continuous watch readings. This provides the values in columns 1 to 5.

Step 2: Summarize these values to obtain total time spent on each element during the study. Foreign elements such as A are discarded in this summarization (shown in bottom quarter of page, top line, under Summary).

Step 3: Count the number of usable recordings of each element (second line under Summary).

Step 4: Calculate average time by dividing values obtained in steps 2 and 3.

Step 5: Record minimum time for each element. Observe this in columns 1 to 5. If this time is illogically different from the average, some foreign elements may not have been caught and certain readings may have to be discarded. If this is done, steps 1 to 4 must be repeated. Discarding readings without recording reasons is undesirable, and if it occurs often, the whole study must be repeated. This is a matter for the judgment of an experienced time-study man.

Step 6: Repeat step 5 for the maximum time recorded. (Workers will object vehemently to the discarding of "long times.")

Step 7: Calculate the level factor. This is obtained by totaling algebraically the successive judgments under "skill," "effort," "conditions," and "consistency" with regard to the specific time-study observation made. In Fig. 23-4 we wish to add 6 per cent; so the level factor is 1.06.

Step 8: Level the average time found in step 4 by multiplying each average by the level factor. Record this leveled time.

Figure 16-2 Time-study record sheet.

451

CARD NO. 2192   PART NO. 745-77   OPERATION Assemble

Radio base, flare base, inspect, wrap and pack

DEPT. Radio   DATE March 15, 1944   OBSERVER H.A.S.

ARTICLE Aircraft Radio connector base

OPERATOR Ⓔ Mary Jane M   CHECK NO. 145576   MUST STAND ☐ CAN SIT ☒

SERVICE Floorman brings work in pans to left side of press, wrapping tissue and boxes to right side; removes finished work from pile to operator's right. Operator fills own work holders, polishes punch once each day. No other maintenance.

MACHINE DATA
TYPE Horton
Bench Press
NO. 89
SAFETY Horton 2 hand and sweep
DRIVE Belt
R.P.M. 168
FEED Hand
LUBRICANT None

TOOL DATA
TYPE Single action
SIZE 1/8 x 6 x six

PROD. DURING STUDY 36 pcs.

EARNINGS DURING STUDY $.364 or $.688/hr.

TOTAL CYCLE TIME .7157 min. per unit

PERSONAL TIME 5 % Polish

MACHINE DOWN TIME 1% punch

FATIGUE 2 %

ADJUSTED % 100 − 8 = 92 %

ADJ. CYCLE TIME .7157 ÷ .7779 = .7779 min. per unit   92%

INCENTIVE 20 %

FINAL ALLOWED TIME .9335 min. per unit

STD. PROD. 64.27 per hr.

STD. HRS. 15.56* per 1000

CODE 23-40

DISPOSAL DATA
Packed after wrapping in dozen box. Left piled

MATERIAL DATA
ALLOY 706-pins
FINISH Nickel-pins
TEMPER ✓
GAUGE ✓
SIZE 1/8 x 1

DATE EFFECTIVE 3-15-74

PERMANENT ☒   TENTATIVE ✓

OLD STD. HRS. None DATED ✓

REMARKS Initial order in this size

Fiber base-purchased

REFERENCE RATES
See 745-75
745-76

* 15.56 x 65¢ base rate = $10.114 per 1000 or .010114 each

Diagram labels: Belt drive · Hand trip · Horton Bench Press (89) · Fixture · Fibers-Pins · OPERATOR · Tissues · Completed work · Incoming work · Hand trip · Boxes · Incline feed on boxes · Box in process of packing piled else where on skid after filling

Step 9: Record the number of times each element occurs in production cycle. Note that element 5, "cover," (which in its use of the next box top to close the previous box is a good example of work simplification), occurs only three times in 36 complete readings—only one-twelfth of a time per cycle.

Step 10: Find elemental time per cycle by multiplying leveled time by occurrences per cycle.

Step 11: Total the values found in step 10 to record total cycle time. Turn over sheet and enter this in center column.

Step 12: Decide and record allowances to be made for personal time, machine down time, fatigue, etc.

Step 13: Total allowances and subtract from 100 per cent to obtain adjusted percentage.

Step 14: Divide total cycle time by adjusted percentage to obtain adjusted cycle time. This is the time it takes an average operator to assemble, wrap, and pack the radio connector base when we consider necessary time lost.

Step 15: Apply the "incentive" (necessary only if a low base rate is used and high earnings are expected) to arrive at the final allowed time.

Depending on the incentive system used, the timing calculated may be carried through several alternative final steps. Standard production per hour, standard hours per thousand, price per thousand, price each, or expected earnings per day may be used to express the final value.

Figure 16-3 Reverse side of time-study record sheet of Figure 16-2.

5. Calculating the time to do the task from the observation. The actual steps are outlined in Figures 16-2 and 16-3 as applied in a straight piecework incentive system.

The steps of establishing a standard-performance requirement are the same whether followed by a time-study engineer to pay employees or by a controller to estimate potential labor costs where no incentive payment is used. The production scheduling, budgeting, and "manning" functions of management require similar accurate information about worker output.

When time study is used in the payment of unionized employees, the most common objection is to the leveling or normalizing of the observation in an effort to reach average expectancy. Time-study engineers themselves seem to be most concerned with the adequacy of the original sample, and have applied statistical methods to determine the number of observations required.

16-3.2 Predetermined Elemental Time Standards: Alternative to Stop-Watch Recording

As a substitute for recording times actually taken by operators, averages from many previous observations may be used. In any industry where the same operation is repeated many times on different products, elemental timings may be used to build time standards which will be of considerable use in estimating, production and cost control, and under circumstances where a timing cannot be made, as on a single casting in a job factory. The essential steps in establishing predetermined elemental time standards are (1) to make accurate time studies in the usual fashion over a considerable period of time, exercising care to select elements of like nature whenever timings are made of similar operations; (2) to accumulate data from separate time studies on the same element into a statistical table; (3) to evaluate the several contributing parts and arrive at an average time value for the element; and (4) to test this average time value statistically and to determine its usefulness. Finally, if the average time values prove statistically sound, they may be used to make elemental time studies.

Method Time Measurement (MTM), one of several predetermined time systems, analyzes human work into such fundamental actions as foot motion, leg motion, turn body, stoop, kneel, sit, stand, walk, and hand-arm motions. The hand-arm motions (the most frequently occurring in industry) are further broken down into such designations as reach, move (object), turn, apply pressure, grasp, release, position, and disengage (See Fig. 16-4). A basic time allowance (predetermined by research) is credited for each basic motion (plus an additional allowance for such modifications as distance reached). Adding these derived time units gives an estimate of probable time required to perform any work task. This estimate is then treated as an observed average performance to establish the standard task and set an allowed rate. Advocates claim that this method makes the use of the stop watch unnecessary, thus letting new standards be set away from the job or even before new equipment to be used is in operation. Unit results are also said to be faster, less subject to variation, and easier to explain to workers. Naturally, the accuracy of the results depends on the accuracy of the original observations, proper statistical reduction of those observations to standard data, and skill in synthetically constructing a motion pattern that actually reflects the average worker's movements.

Distance moved, inches	Time TMU				Hand in motion		Reach description
	A	B	C or D	E	A	B	
3/4 or less	2.0	2.0	2.0	2.0	1.6	1.6	A. Reach to object in fixed location or to object in other hand or on which other hand rests.
1	2.5	2.5	3.6	2.4	2.3	2.3	
2	4.0	4.0	5.9	3.8	3.5	2.7	
3	5.3	5.3	7.3	5.3	4.5	3.6	B. Reach to single object in location which may vary slightly from cycle to cycle.
4	6.1	6.4	8.4	6.8	4.9	4.3	
5	6.5	7.8	9.4	7.4	5.3	5.0	
6	7.0	8.6	10.1	8.0	5.7	5.7	
7	7.4	9.3	10.8	8.7	6.1	6.5	C. Reach to object jumbled with other objects in a group so that search and select occur.
8	7.9	10.1	11.5	9.3	6.5	7.2	
9	8.3	10.8	12.2	9.9	6.9	7.9	
10	8.7	11.5	12.9	10.5	7.3	8.6	
12	9.6	12.9	14.2	11.8	8.1	10.1	
14	10.5	14.4	15.6	13.0	8.9	11.5	D. Reach to a very small object or where accurate grasp is required.
16	11.4	15.8	17.0	14.2	9.7	12.9	
18	12.3	17.2	18.4	15.5	10.5	14.4	
20	13.1	18.6	19.8	16.7	11.3	15.8	
22	14.0	20.1	21.2	18.0	12.1	17.3	E. Reach to indefinite location to get hand in position for body balance or next motion or out of way.
24	14.9	21.5	22.5	19.2	12.9	18.8	
26	15.8	22.9	23.9	20.4	13.7	20.2	
28	16.7	24.4	25.3	21.7	14.5	21.7	
30	17.5	25.8	26.7	22.9	15.3	23.2	

Case	Time TMU	Grasp description
1A	2.0	Pickup grasp — Small, medium, or large object by itself, easily grasped.
1B	3.5	Very small object or object lying close against a flat surface.
1C1	7.3	Interference with grasp on bottom and one side of nearly cylindrical object. Diameter larger than 1/2".
1C2	8.7	Interference with grasp on bottom and one side of nearly cylindrical object. Diameter 1/4 to 1/2".
1C3	10.8	Interference with grasp on bottom and one side of nearly cylindrical object. Diameter less than 1/4".
2	5.6	Regrasp.
3	5.6	Transfer grasp.
4A	7.3	Object jumbled with other objects so search and select occur. Larger than 1"×1"×1".
4B	9.1	Object jumbled with other objects so search and select occur. 1/4"×1/4"×1/8" to 1"×1"×1".
4C	12.9	Object jumbled with other objects so search and select occur. Smaller than 1/4"×1/4"×1/8".
5	0	Contact, sliding, or hook grasp.

Figure 16-4 Examples of basic-motion data, codes, and time values used in the methods-time-measurement system. One TMU (time measurement unit) = 0.00001 hour. (Courtesy Methods Engineering Council, Pittsburgh, Pa.).

16-3.3   Work Sampling

Another application of statistical methods is work sampling. This method produces facts about machine operation or worker activity by means of random observations. Irregularly spaced samples are substituted for continuous observation both to save time for the observer and to get a more accurate sample of true expectancy. This method may be used with typical production operations but is more commonly used to set standards for work which varies greatly, such as maintenance.

Related applications of statistical methods important to the time-study person include studies of machine loading and interference (based on worker time per machine and number of machines assigned), tool utilization, machine and tool efficiencies, machine capability and tolerance studies, as well as quality control.

In office management, considerable use has been made of time-study statistical methods to reduce the costs of procedures and to set standards of production. The very great increase in the ratio of clerical and administrative help to production workers in recent years has resulted in the drafting of the industrial engineer into office management where he has set production standards as well as assisted in mechanization, office layout, and procedure simplication. Incentive payment remains uncommon in the office, but predetermined elemental time standards have been used by many companies and sold by several consultants.

Both time-study and predetermined-elemental-standard data are used but rarely to set tasks for sales persons and management executives, although both commonly have an incentive element in their commission and bonus method of payment. Work-sampling and standard-data techniques have been used to evaluate executive performance.

16-4   Wage Incentive Methods

Different segments of industry use incentive-pay plans to a varying extent. The variation in prevalence results from differences in the type of work performed, as well as from differences in the attitude of both management and labor organizations in the specific industry segment. Statistics reported by the Bureau of Labor Statistics indicate that there has been little change in the prevalence of wage-incentive payment since the end of World War II and none is anticipated in the immediate future. There is variation by industry and by geographical region.

Several plans representative of many different kinds of incentive systems used by American management are described in the following sections. The plans can be judged by the general principles cited below.

1. Both employers and employees should feel that the incentive plan is fair. The plan should be tailored to the jobs to which it is applied.

2. A plan must be thoroughly understood before it can be effective. More complicated plans have to be explained repeatedly so that each worker knows exactly how his earnings are determined.

3. Plans with guaranteed minimum earnings are generally preferred to those with no minimum base. Gains to be earned by better workers should range from 15 to 30 per cent for the plan to be effective.

4. The means by which standards are set should be open to inquiries. Procedures should be incorporated for fair hearings of injustice claims and for modifying rates when conditions change or errors are recognized.

STRAIGHT PIECEWORK   Under this system, management establishes a price that it will pay for each unit of production, say, 6/10 cent for each hole drilled. Then for drilling 10 holes the worker gets 6 cents, for 100 holes 60 cents, and for 1,000 holes $6. For a day's pay of $48, the employee would drill 8,000 holes. It is customary to guarantee at least a minimum hourly earning rate, usually much below the average incentive earnings.

In rate setter's parlance such a minimum guarantee is often called a "Manchester guarantee" after Manchester, England, where the practice originated. Because of minimum-wage laws, the practice of paying workers only what they earn at piece rates with no minimum guarantee has now been virtually abandoned under all incentive systems in the United States. If the difference between the average earnings expected of the average worker—called the "task rate"—and the lowest wage customarily paid for the type of work involved—called the "base rate"[2] —is large, the system is known as a low-base system; if it is small, as a high-base system. In terms of incentive wage theory, the low-base system, which requires continuous application to approximate usual earnings, provides the greater urge to the worker to sustain production. In practice, it is sometimes found that a worker who gets off to a bad start or for some reason is delayed in his work is discouraged by the large gap between his usual earnings and the earnings he may then receive.

The standard hour system of calculating costs is often used with straight piecework, and then the employee earns hours (possibly 10.5 hours in an 8-hour day) at a standard rate instead of money per piece, but it makes little difference to the worker who invariably figures the price he will be paid as so much per 1,000 pieces or dozen workpans.

The straight piecework system has been called the highest type of incentive and certainly has many advantages to both the employee and employer. Any objections that may be made to it are summarized later under labor objections to incentives in general. Certainly straight piecework is the fairest of all incentive plans and often appeals to workers for this reason. Ambitious workers are able to earn high wages and are equally repaid at all steps of

---

[2]"Base rate" may in some cases be below the "guaranteed minimum" especially in old piecework installations that have been modernized piecemeal. In such cases the base rate is only a mathematical factor used in calculating expected earnings. Workers in factories having incentive systems often confuse "base rate" and "task rate."

effort. Straight piecework stimulates a sense of fair treatment and simplifies record keeping and earnings explanation. Production output is more constant, and cost or scheduling planning may be done more accurately. Cooperation is furthered both between workers and between management and workers.

Inasmuch as overhead costs remain relatively fixed, the employer benefits through lower overall costs per piece produced, although his unit labor costs remain the same. Because payment is the same for each unit produced, straight piecework is called "100 per cent premium" or "100 per cent sharing plan." This contrasts with plans such as the Halsey plan described below.

HALSEY (50-50) CONSTANT SHARING PLAN   This type of incentive developed from independent work at the Yale and Towne Manufacturing Company and at the Rand Drill Company and has also been known as the "Towne-Halsey gain sharing plan" or, in England, the "Halsey-Weir plan." Its chief value is the sense of partnership which it sponsors, since increased profits through greater production are supposed to be split.

The foreman or rate setter judges the time necessary to complete a given task and offers the worker a premium over his or her day wage for completing the task on time, or ahead of time. The premium offered is commonly 50 per cent of the time saved because that appeals to the worker as an equal and just partnership. If expected production were set at 24 pieces per 8-hour day for a $24 per day wage, about $1 would be paid for each piece produced at that level. If 48 pieces were produced in an 8-hour day, the production rate would be 200 per cent and would result in a saving of 8 hours. The saving is shared with management 50-50, however, and a $36 wage is paid. This is about 75 cents paid for each piece produced. Here a constant sharing plan contrasts most sharply with a straight piecework plan. In defense it should be noted that it often pays a greater per piece price at lower production levels than can be justified by selling price, and makes up the loss by the lesser price per piece paid at higher production levels.

The owners gain more from a production increase under a Halsey plan than under straight piecework, since under straight piecework 100 per cent of the gain goes to the worker. This feature has been attacked by labor but, since production tasks are usually low and workers do get higher wages, the plan sometimes works. For the initial lift from lower production, a premium plan is usually more generous than piecework to the operator, but it soon loses its generosity as higher production levels are reached.

A Halsey premium plan often pays a portion of the gain to foremen and supervisors. This has the effect of interesting these people in increasing production and thereby the earnings of their subordinates. A premium payment plan is especially well adapted to job manufacturing (and to indirect labor or maintenance jobs) since premiums can be set on the basis of estimates. Bickering is apt to develop through workers' efforts to be assigned to jobs on which generous estimates have been made.

Many of the varieties of incentive payment have developed through modifications of straight piecework and premium systems. Common modifications include (1) the introduction of bonus steps instead of the smooth ratio curve relation between production and earnings; and (2) various plans for accelerating or retarding the slope of the earnings curve at various levels of production.

GANTT TASK AND BONUS   H. L. Gantt, the associate of Taylor in the development of scientific management who showed the greatest appreciation of the human problems involved, developed what has come to be called the "task and bonus" system of incentive payment. It differs from other incentive systems in three main particulars:

1. It pays the employee a high relative hourly rate which he gets whether he makes his time on the job or not.

2. It pays him a higher rate if he does complete the job in the time allowed and continues this higher rate just like straight piecework for all work produced beyond the standard.

3. As originally developed by Gantt, the plan provides for showing the employee graphically and daily just where he stands in relation to other workers, his own previous records, and the standard set.

An early advocate of much that has become standard in personnel management, Gantt stressed the worker's individuality and pride of achievement. He stressed the "habits of industry" to be ingrained in the worker so that he always made a high rate of pay. The combination of a high guarantee and of nonsharing increment makes this plan a particularly good installation where an old piecework system is redone.

In terms of application, suppose the expected production had been set at 24 pieces per day for which $28.80 would be paid. Then, for 14, 16, 18, 20, or any number up to 24 a wage of $24.00 might be paid. For 27 pieces (a saving of about 1 hour of production time) $32.40 would be paid, and for 32 pieces (a saving of over 2 hours production time) $38.40 would be paid. Earnings below task are hours worked times rate; at task a bonus of 20 per cent is added; above task the bonus is 20 per cent of standard hours earned. In effect this plan awards a prize for reaching task, then pays straight piecework above task, on a standard-hour basis.

MEASURED DAYWORK   This is a system of paying production workers job rates based on job evaluation plus an added inducement determined by merit rating at 30- to 90-day intervals. The merit-rating system used considers such factors as dependability, potential, and versatility along with quality and quantity of work measured against a time-study standard. This system is extensively used by paper and chemical companies.

Advantages claimed for measured daywork over simple daywork are: The pay rates of production workers can be reduced if their production level falls through their own lack of effort (supervision under daywork can usually only dismiss low producers, not reduce rates), production is measured more closely against more accurate production standards, job evaluation and merit rating are more accurately administered, and workers are imbued with a spirit of "high pay for high production."

Advantages claimed for measured daywork over other incentive systems are: Improved cooperation in attaining low-cost production between supervisors and workers, since methods changes which reduce costs do not reduce worker earnings; greater security and higher morale for production workers since their income is not subject to hourly ups and downs; less expensive standard setting and record keeping; and greater ease in making machine changes and temporary "production experiments."

There are also disadvantages: Success depends on accurate records, a high quality of continuous supervision, and the complete understanding of employees as to how the system works. Since the amount paid by merit rating is usually only a small percentage of the assured rate, this is a "weak incentive," and workers may refuse to try to meet the standard set, preferring slightly less pay for a much lower level of production. In addition, although the system is supposed to provide for wage reductions if production falls, such reductions strain the supervisor-employee relation so greatly that they are rarely made. Inasmuch as production records are considered after a lapse of time, no one may remember why production was lost. Unless workers are aware that production interruptions "cost them money" and insist that they be quickly remedied, the system may lack what some incentive engineers explain as the chief reason why incentives increase production, i.e., the pressure brought on supervision by interested workers to keep all machines in repair, tools sharp, material handy, quality acceptable, and work flowing through the department steadily.

Perspective 16A INCENTIVE PLAN SURVEY

A 1977 survey* of 1,500 industrial organizations compares the use of work measurement and incentive plans with a similar survey conducted by *Factory* magazine in 1959. In the new survey, 89 per cent reported that they are using work measurement, and 44 per cent say they have wage incentive applications. Eighteen years earlier, the *Factory* survey reported 71 per cent used work measurement and 51 per cent had wage incentive applications. Thus it appears that the use of work measurement for production operations has increased greatly, but its application to incentive plans has declined slightly. Replies to several other questions in the 1977 survey reveal the nature of work measurement efforts and wage incentive applications. (Percentages in the tables add to more than 100 because of multiple uses.)

Question: For what purpose do you use work measurement?
Response:

	Percentage
Wage incentives	59%
Estimating and costing	89%
Performance measurement only	41%
Production scheduling	55%

Question: If you have wage incentive plans, what types?
Response:

Type of plan	Percentage
Straight piecework	35.9%
Standard hour	61.1%
Sharing plan	18.6%
Plantwide bonus plan	5.4%
Profit sharing	8.4%
Measured daywork	3.0%
All others	6.0%

Question: What effects are your wage incentives getting?
Response:

	Direct Labor		Indirect Labor	
	Yes	No	Yes	No
Improved productivity	95.1%	1.9%	43.2%	5.6%
Reduced costs	94.4%	1.2%	42.6%	5.6%
Improved employee morale	60.5%	21.0%	28.4%	13.6%
Better supervisory effectiveness	58.6%	27.8%	26.5%	18.5%
Improved quality of output	25.3%	50.6%	2.5%	
None of the above (ineffective)	3.7%		4.3%	

Question: What is the nature of wage incentive administration when the employees are represented by a union?
Response:

	Yes	No
Are employees on incentive represented by a union?	61%	39%
If "yes," are standards or piecework rates subject to collective bargaining agreement?	45%	55%
Are new standards reviewed, but not necessarily approved by union representative?	55%	45%
Does the union review time studies and standard data?	46%	54%
Does the union make independent time studies?	29%	71%
Are standards subject to grievance?	88%	12%
If so, are they a legitimate strike issue?	32%	68%

*source: R. S. Rice, "Survey of Work Measurement and Wage Incentives," *Industrial Engineering*, July, 1977.

16-4.1   Plant-Wide Incentive Plans

Most incentive systems apply to the productivity of an individual worker or a small group, all working on a measurable product: if they produce more pieces, they are paid more money. Another class is the plant-wide incentive, where everyone benefits from total output instead of from individual effort. The keynote is teamwork, and the most common type is profit sharing. Other plans pay off for savings above standard costs or for production beyond a plant-wide standard. Perhaps the two best-known names in plant-wide incentive plans are Rucker and Scanlon. The plans are similar, although Rucker advocates claim greater statistical accuracy and that it provides for built-in control of upsetting variables. Scanlon plans have been changed by negotiations to overcome the same variables: such things as rising costs of materials, changes in make–buy ratio, increasing wages, changed sales price, variable product mix, etc.

   The Scanlon plan was originated by a union leader who worked at MIT the last 10 years of his life. Emphasis is on management–worker cooperation, and in most successful applications the plant has a powerful union. In using this plan the first step is to negotiate a "norm"—the physical output per unit of labor input. Originally any savings below that norm cost went to the workers, with management getting its gain through volume and lower unit costs. In recent applications 75 per cent of the saving goes to the workers—all workers, shop, office, sales, etc.—and 25 per cent to the company. It might work like this: Suppose in the base year labor costs had been 38 per cent of the dollar value of shipments from the plant; so that was taken as the norm. Now in a given month suppose shipments totaled $70,000 and inventory increased $30,000, so total production value for that month was $100,000. Applying the 38 per cent normal would yield a payroll expectancy of $38,000, but if actual payroll costs for the whole plant were only $35,000 that month, the difference of $3,000 would be divided among all the employees, usually after laying aside a "reserve" for possible "excess months."

   In practice, firms using the Scanlon plan have a "screening committee" to take out the effects of unforeseen variables as well as to act as a "productivity committee" to consider possible laborsaving and cost-reduction suggestions. The average plant seems to show an average productivity increase a little over 20 per cent. The average earned bonus is about 17 per cent above gross pay in the base year.

Perspective 16B APPLAUSE FOR THE SCANLON PLAN

Many of the livelier concepts of management lore seem to be regularly recycled. The Scanlon plan is one of them. Critics have riddled the Scanlon concept with abuse, yet it keeps getting rediscovered. Robert J. Doyle, a personnel and organization development manager at Donnelly Mirrors, where the Scanlon plan had been in effect since 1952, wrote in 1970:

The Scanlon Plan has been called a labor management cooperative plan, a labor cost savings plan and a group incentive plan. But it is actually a Better Management Plan, it is a better way to manage a firm. Its application is not too complex. Perhaps it is so simple, we do not trust it.

Competition has never been kind to the mossback manager or to the company that has developed hardening of the managerial arteries, but it would seem that in 1970 with profit margins slimmer than in 1928, with younger, better educated, more mobile employees, with more complex technology and distribution, it could be even more unkind. Change can be delayed for a while, but not resisted forever. The Scanlon Plan is a good change, because it is constructive in economic and human terms. It is not an easy change, but it is worth the effort.*

*source: R. J. Doyle, ''A New Look at the Scanlon Plan,'' *Management Accounting,* September, 1970.

The plant manager of the Victor Products Division of Dana Corporation, J. Lee Hess, also has kind words about his experience with the Scanlon plan:

As a manager, the challenge of trying to achieve productivity grows larger every day, and my way of meeting that challenge is through the Scanlon Plan. This is a plan which offers something different. It is a means of achieving recognition for a worker whose ideas no one had previously asked for. It makes a believer out of young and old and is especially effective in reaching the worker who may have spent many years under a system of alienation. It is an excellent motivator, leads to improved quality, helps eliminate boredom on the job, creates better income for both company and worker, and fosters understanding, cooperation, and better relations between Union and Management. There is a great deal in this plan for the labor unions and they are not unaware of the benefits a competitive, well-run operation has for their membership. And best of all, *this plan WORKS.* **

**source: J. L. Hess, ''Productivity—People Participation,'' *Proceedings,* AIIE, 1977.

COMMENT Incentive plans, in common with most methods of motivation (as discussed in the next chapter), seem to burst on the business scene with a flourish of testimonials and then slowly fade from attention, only to rise again. The apparent moral is that most acclaimed methods have merit, and their successful application depends more on the competence of their use than on their inherent qualities. One approach fits a certain situation better than another, or fits a certain manager's style better than another. That is the reason we have so many different management plans, each with its dedicated advocates.

16-4.2 Incentive Compensation of Executives

A world-wide shortage of effective administrative executives persists. Many people want the privileges, compensation, and prerogatives of leadership. Few can exercise administrative leadership effectively.

High personal tax rates and the growing shortage of qualified executives in recent years have led to renewed emphasis on incentive plans for executives. Some of these have been introduced to ''keep up with the Joneses'' but others have been an effort to get executives to work as hard as they used to when they owned the business they managed. Although high-salary workers respond to the same financial and nonfinancial rewards as other workers, special care must be taken to get the incentive effect desired. Many ''gimmicks" or special pay arrangements, originated primarily as tax dodges, have yielded undesirable results, and incentives cannot be expected to replace sound management at any level. Incentive payment must follow careful selection for jobs, effective training, individual recognition, wise organization, including delegation of responsibility with adequate controls of performance, and an otherwise fair and equitable wage and salary system. Among the incentive plans for executives, a bonus plan, usually tied to company profits and based on a preagreed formula or higher management discretion, is most common. About half the companies reporting to the American Management Association use some kind of bonus plan for middle- and top-management positions.

Other supplementary compensations include profit-sharing plans (which seem to provide a greater incentive for executives who can influence profits more easily than can individual employees), and such fringe benefits as pension plans (often on a deferred-payment basis to lower taxes), thrift and stock-investment plans (including executive stock option plans which permit executives to exercise an option to buy below market prices after their efforts have contributed to raising company stock prices), life and health insurance, and such extra privileges as paid family vacation trips; club memberships; free use of a company boat, lodge, or airplane; and other nontaxed expense-account benefits. However, many of these privileges are under close scrutiny by the U.S. Internal Revenue Service and their legality is being questioned.

Perspective 16C DO EXECUTIVE INCENTIVES MOTIVATE?

According to Arch Patton, a Director of McKinsey and Co., most executive incentive plans fail to produce the expected performance improvement:

A complaint from a director I chanced to meet recently led me to review an executive incentive plan that was failing to provide the motivational life expected of it. It did not take long to locate the source of the problem.

The company's new chief executive, only 18 months on the job, had decided to allocate bonuses as a percent of salary without regard for individual performance. Unlike his predecessor, who had launched the incentive plan and was a firm believer in performance-based bonuses, the new president felt that in his company's particular industry it was unrealistic to attempt to judge the short-term performance of individuals. So he switched to equal percentage allocations—in effect, notifying the best performers that mediocrity would receive the same rewards as excellence. This obviously led to a disenchantment with the plan among executives as well as among directors.

And this case is not unusual. In fact, I have concluded that at least one half of the 100-odd executive incentive plans with which I have had experience over the last two decades provide no more motivation than could be expected from straight salary remuneration. In other words, the shareholders of these companies received little return on their incentive program investment. And this is no small sum, for companies with bonus plans are known to pay their executives 20% more, on the average, than do comparable nonbonus companies.*

*SOURCE: A. Patton, "Why Incentive Plans Fail," *Harvard Business Review,* May–June, 1972.

A survey of compensation earned by 53 top executives, who were in office for six or more years during the period 1960–1974, tends to support Mr. Patton's contentions:

For 66% of the executives studied there was no statistically significant relationship between changes in their compensation (salary plus bonus, whether deferred or current) and changes in their company's return on equity.
  For 40% of the executives there was no significant relationship between changes in compensation and earnings per share.**

**SOURCE: K. R. S. Murthy and M. S. Salter, "Should CEO Pay Be Linked to Results?" *Harvard Business Review,* May–June, 1975.

COMMENT   If the prospects for profits do not appear to be related to executive incentive pay, why have incentives? Apparently most companies feel incentive plans are better than anything else, because two-thirds have them. Also, it is believed that the hard-driving, competitive types who often reach top management positions appreciate and respect the challenge of incentive pay. It would appear then that the design of the incentive package is the critical determinate of success.

One way to make incentives more effective is to tie payments to readily measurable criteria of achievement (return on investment, earnings per share, etc.), but make provisions to distinguish good local management from general industry trends. For example, if the average increase in ROI for related industries is 15 per cent, while one company in the group earns just 4 per cent, the managers of that company do not deserve a bonus even though the company did show a profit gain for the year. Bonus formulas which persistently overreward or underreward an executive group do not provide effective motivation; the executives either feel exploited or become complacent.

A classic case of a simple criterion of success was Harold S. Geneen's promise to double profits within 5 years after he became chief executive of IIT Corporation. He did it, despite the company's previous history of lackluster performance. Then he publicly promised to double profits again during a second 5-year period. And he did it again. He also became the highest paid executive in the United States.

16-4.3 Mathematical Control of Incentives

The basis of much of the mathematical and statistical control which is growing in importance in modern management is a careful initial time study. Where this time study is used for incentive payment, sound statistical control of standards is essential. Employee relations, cost and material control, and production engineering can all be improved by a sound knowledge of what production the average worker can be expected to turn out in a workday. A neglected set of performance standards can be dangerous, whether used as the basis for incentive payment or not. If new standards are not set when new methods of manufacture are adopted, unit costs will increase. Neglect of incentive standards once installed may force their subsequent abandonment when earnings get out of line, and later trouble may result.
  The two extremes between which the incentive controls must be maintained are runaway earnings and excessive restrictions of output by either the workers themselves or the first-line supervisors. Earnings of individual

incentive workers which exceed the expected earnings by too large an amount are a constant source of employee unrest. Few other workers are willing to believe that the high earnings result from extra effort, and many demand that their rates be set looser so that they can earn the same high earnings; other workers demand that their job-evaluation rates be raised to compensate.

Where lax supervision permits, excess work completed by one worker may be taken from him and credited to a slow comrade. Often the group exerts pressure by means of ostracism, "wolf calls," painting lockers or lunch boxes yellow, etc., to make the fast worker or "rate buster" take on group service tasks that interfere with individual production, such as making coffee, getting additional material, or writing reports.

Incentives for executives should also be monitored regularly to determine whether they are serving their intended function. One approach, depicted in Figure 16-5, is to itemize executive duties and place performance standards on their accomplishment.

16-5 JOB EVALUATION

The essence of any employment contract, oral or written, is that an individual will receive payment for job performance. How much will be paid for a standard unit of production or period of time is a matter of job evaluation. In common industrial usage, job evaluation includes an analysis of job duties expressed in standard terminology as well as arranging the jobs in order of importance or payment. It is one of the series of basic steps in the

---

THE STANDARD OIL COMPANY (OHIO)—PRODUCTS PIPELINE
Standards of Performance
TriState Division Area Supervisor

Safety
Performance is satisfactory when:
    a. Frequency of serious injuries is less than 10.0 per million man-hours.
    b. Frequency of lost time injuries is less than 4.0 per million man-hours.
    c. Frequency of vehicle accidents is less than 0.35 per hundred thousand miles.
Operations
Performance is satisfactory when:
    a. Gaugers required to run 1,000 barrels per day are less than 0.90.
    b. Tickets written by one gauger per month are in excess of 174.
    c. Cost of gauging supplies is less than $300 per year per gauger.
Public Relations
Performance is satisfactory when:
    a. At least two planned visits per year are made to operating offices of other pipeline companies in the area.
    b. At least two stories pertaining to SOHIO are carried by local newspapers each year.

Figure 16-5 Excerpt from a managerial standard developed through consultation between the position holders and their immediate superiors at the Standard Oil Company, Ohio. The original listed nine principal areas of responsibility: safety; personnel administration; operations; communications; general administration of accounting records; purchasing procedure; engineering; crude-oil purchasing and records; and public relations. Most such standards will be less quantitative but will use verifiable qualitative standards.

systematic wage administration described in the last chapter as an essential function in a sound management plan.

Historically, job evaluation was taken over from the civil-service movement. A start at job classification before the turn of the twentieth century was supplemented in 1910 with formal job analysis and job rating. An installation about that time by the Commonwealth Edison Company broke the ice in industry. Early installations in manufacturing companies were found at the United States Rubber Company in 1922 and in large electrical companies before 1930. The practice grew apace with the more systematic practices of modern management and had a rapid rise during World War II. Not all the fast installations were satisfactory, and in 1947 a survey by Princeton University found 20 to 30 per cent of those companies using job evaluation somewhat disenchanted. A management consultant's survey in 1960 of large national companies found only 10 per cent of the users then dissatisfied and 97 per cent saying they would install a job-evaluation program if they had it to do over again. That survey also revealed the importance of union acceptance (somewhat easier to obtain in the West and Midwest than in the East) and of training for all levels of management.[3] Today most industrial establishments will have some form of job evaluation. Many follow the procedures described hereafter, although the smaller ones adhere to a more informal approach.

16-5.1 Common Job Profile

One of the most extensive methods of describing jobs in standard language is the common job profile developed by the United States Employment Service and shown in Figure 16-6.

I. Education
II. Specific vocational training time
III. Aptitudes: intelligence, verbal, numerical, spatial form, clerical, motor coordination, finger dexterity, manual dexterity, eye-hand-foot coordination, color discrimination
IV. Temperaments: variety and change; repetitive, short cycle, under specific instructions; direction, control, planning; dealing with people; isolation; influencing people; performing under stress; sensory or judgmental criteria; measurable or verifiable criteria; feeling, ideas, facts, set limits, tolerances, or standards
V. Interests: things and objects; business contacts; routine, concrete; social welfare; prestige; people, ideas; scientific, technical; abstract, creative; non-social; tangible, productive, satisfaction
VI. Physical capacities: strength; climbing; balancing; stooping-kneeling; reaching-handling; talking-hearing, seeing
VII. Working conditions: inside-outside, cold, heat, wet-humid, noise-vibration; hazards, fumes, odors, etc.

Figure 16-6 Basis of comparisons between the worker-trait requirements for over 23,000 different jobs being made by the United States Employment Service classification system in the search for common job profiles. It is on such variables as these that jobs may be rated.

[3]"Job Evaluation," *Factory*, vol. 118, no. 10, October, 1960.

16-5.2   Wage Theory and Cluster Theory

Even the casual observer can see an apparent lack of logic in many wage rates. An explanation is sometimes found in a history of applicable legal controls, general wage and market conditions, and the specific history of a given area or industry. It is on the basis of that lack of logic that some union leaders resist job evaluation. A Wharton School group of labor economists spent the equivalent of 36 man-years establishing a defensible wage theory to guide industrial management. The essence of this proposed explanation is that any given wage structure constitutes a tightly balanced system containing (1) a job cluster, (2) a wage curve, and (3) a wage contour.

The *job cluster* is a fairly stable job family within a company plant. The rates within a cluster are related to each other. Those employees who belong within a cluster tend to be more concerned about overpayments and underpayments within their own cluster than with those outside of the cluster. Each cluster is built around a "yardstick job." This may be either the highest ranking job or the most commonly held job. The *wage curve* is seen by cross-plotting wage rates and drawing a progression line through the rates for related successive job clusters. The rate of key jobs in each cluster linked together across a reasonably wide range forms the company wage curve. A given *wage contour* results from combining the wage curves of several related companies. In most cases this grouping is a labor market. Trade or regional wage differentials are seen by comparing wage contours. In some cases, especially when industry-wide union contracts are found, a contour group may be a whole industry.

In a wage contour the rates of a leading company act similarly to a key job, with others grouped around it. This wage theory offers an explanation of the great influence job evaluation has upon the economy in general. The interests and identification of union members with a specific job cluster are at times in conflict with the responsibility of the union-local leaders for considering the whole wage curve and with the responsibility of the national union leaders for considering the whole wage contour as well as the interrelationship between contours.

16-5.3   Automation and Job Design

Two important influences in the operation of a job-evaluation plan are automation and job design. Both have positive and negative influences, raising or lowering the jobs in a given enterprise as they act upon it. When automation was first considered, it was thought to be a force which removed the skill from the job and naturally lessened job importance. The average result seems to have been otherwise. In both factories and offices where automation has been introduced, it appears to have eliminated the least skilled jobs. This raised the average skill level and actually increased the number of skilled, control, and inspection jobs.

For many years the most common way to design factory jobs was to simplify them. The intent was to reduce the chance of error inherent in a given job and thereby to allow the hiring of minimally qualified employees at lower rates. The process has begun to backfire. Workers frequently become bored and apathetic in conducting their simple routines. When active resentment emerges, the company is openly vulnerable to work slowdowns or stoppages.

Reasons for discontent are many and varied. During periods of high prosperity, jobs are plentiful and workers do not have to work in undesirable situations. When they find themselves in such situations they speak out. With the work force increasingly better educated, workers expect more challenging work. Again, when work fails to meet expectations, workers have the outlets, education, and inclination to have their views aired. The present social environment which refutes most authoritarian measures tends to pay attention to the expressed views.

16-6   METHODS OF JOB RATING

Job rating, or the process of slotting jobs into a hierarchy, has taken many forms. Organizationally, the process usually includes the foreman and a representative of the industrial-relations department, commonly called the wage administrator. In some enterprises the employees' representative is included on the committee. Union representatives have made the program more acceptable to employees in some cases, and in others, through the exercise of their legal right to knowledge of the wage structure of the bargaining unit, have forced the adoption of a more easily understood system. Most of the job-rating methods in common use are some combination of two qualitative and two quantitative forms. The simplest of these four is position-to-position comparison, or simple *ranking*. This means arranging jobs in order from low to high on the basis of general-knowledge comparison. The other qualitative method is *job classification*, which introduces intermediate steps into the ranking. These steps, or grades, within the job ranking simplify installation, but comparison is still made of jobs, according to unnamed qualities, on an overall basis. The two quantitative methods are *factor comparison* and the *point system*. Most job-rating installations contain elements of all four systems. They are distinguished here only to make a greater contrast possible.

JOB-TO-JOB COMPARISON   The old-fashioned way of rating a job was to compare that job in its entirety with all other jobs without putting any details of the comparison in writing except the final conclusion. The records would then show "what" but could not show "why." In a small plant accurate results are possible with this method, although it is usually difficult to find a rater or committee of raters who know all the details of any considerable number of jobs. One method is to list the highest and the lowest jobs to be considered, then to pick out several jobs of average difficulty to place in the middle of the list. Each job to be rated is then compared with the jobs on the list. As the list becomes longer, more and more comparison is necessary to locate successive jobs accurately. Ease of arrangement is sometimes increased by putting the job titles on individual cards.

JOB CLASSIFICATION This method is thought to be somewhat simpler to maintain than job ranking. A new job to be added to the schedule simply needs to be put "in grade" with a group to which an established minimum and maximum pay rate applies. The job-classification system used in the United States Civil Service has 18 grades in the general schedule (GS) and 10 grades for craft, protective, and custodial (CPC) jobs. Grades are not interchangeable between GS and CPC. Many state, county, and municipal civil-service systems also use this qualitative method. Most other installations have many more grades than the 18 Federal grades. The greater number of grades facilitates the establishment of pay differentials on a prevailing rate basis. The simplest factory classification may have only two grades (and two pay rates) for all production workers. Usually some rating system other than classification is then used for skilled, maintenance, and clerical workers.

FACTOR COMPARISON Some of the directness of job-to-job comparison is carried over in this method, but the comparison is made factor by factor instead of on an overall basis, i.e., all jobs are arranged in order of their possession of certain characteristics such as skill, effort, responsibility, and working conditions. Points are assigned to each factor, and the factors are then totaled and converted to a money scale. The points are assigned in a continuous series by one-digit steps, which results in easy recognition of slight variations between jobs. This system, in common with other point systems, is subject to a basic difficulty in weighting the several factors equitably. If a toolmaker ranks first in the skill factor but far down the list in undesirable working conditions and a coal-car unloader ranks first in undesirable working conditions but equally far down the list in skills, how are the two factors to be added together to a logical summation? This is the problem of weighting. Comparison among large numbers of different jobs for even one factor is a laborious process. The factor-comparison method seldom defines exact degree steps. Those who use this system establish the degree steps by the use of key jobs. Thus a first-class toolmaker (highest skill) may be granted 37 skill points, a shop machinist 29 skill points, and a common laborer 3 skill points. Points are then assigned to other jobs by reference to these. After points are assigned to other factors, such as effort, responsibility, and working conditions, these are totaled and reduced to a class indicating the hourly rate of pay. When wage rates change, this total must be treated with a conversion factor to price the new scale. A key-job list is very useful when additional jobs are rated or when rating committee actions must be defended to workers or union.

POINT SYSTEMS OF JOB RATING   The most commonly used method of job rating employs one of the several different point-system scales. These point systems presuppose that a *descriptive scale* can be prepared for each job-rating factor. The entire range from the least amount found in a factory to the greatest amount probable is broken into approximately equal degree-steps. Definitions are written for each degree, and sometimes key jobs selected as typical of the degree. Equal point values are commonly assigned to each degree-step of a factor. Some systems assign an exact point value to each degree; others provide a range. Jobs to be rated are compared with this scale instead of with each other. The point values derived from the degrees selected for each factor are customarily grouped into brackets called "labor grades" or "wage groups" for ease of administration. Thus all point values from 110 to 130 might be grouped into one labor grade. This grouping partly destroys the false sense of accuracy which the use of numbers in the rating imparts. A point system having wide acceptance is that advocated by the National Electrical Manufacturers Association and the National Metal Trades Association. The essential steps in this application are:

1. A point system of job rating based on 11 factors, each described by five degree definitions. The factors and their weightings are those shown on the job-substantiating data sheet (Fig. 16-7). Other point systems use slightly different weightings, and some introduce other factors.

2. A substantiating data sheet which is prepared for each job rated. These often follow one of a series of master write-ups prepared in advance.

3. A job-by-job and factor-by-factor comparison between each job rating and all others to assure consistency between jobs, departments, and plants. All jobs must be logically rated in the light of company policy, local labor-market conditions, union classifications, worker expectations regarding "clusters," and supervisory opinion.

4. A graphic display of the job-rating points and the wages earned. Any out-of-line pay rates or questionable ratings may then be quickly spotted. It is on such a display that overpayments are often "red-circled" as out-of-line situations which will be permitted to "die out" or be corrected gradually over a period of time by job transfer, upgrading after training, etc. The need for keeping a rating up to date once it is installed has been mentioned. A rating system cannot be left to run itself—it must be *administered and controlled.* Four conditions are essential to successful operation: (1) a carefully established plan, i.e., one "sold" to employees and supervisors; (2) full approval of all members of management; (3) union acceptance—if there is a union; and, most important, (4) adequate administrative controls. These include centralized coordination, systematic evaluation of new or changed jobs, and regulation of rate changes in accordance with job rating.

JOB RATING – SUBSTANTIATING DATA

Job Name _____ Lathe Operator – Engine (Up to 30") _____   Class ___A___

POINTS PER DEGREE	FACTORS	DEG.	BASIS OF RATING
14	EDUCATION	3 (42)	Use shop mathematics, charts, tables, handbook formulas. Work from complicated drawings. Use micrometers, depth gages, indicator gages, protractors. Knowledge of machining methods, tools, cutting qualities of different kinds of metals. Equivalent to 2 years' high school plus 2 to 3 years' trades training.
22	EXPERIENCE	4 (88)	3 to 5 years on wide variety of engine lathe work, including diversified setups.
14	INITIATIVE AND INGENUITY	4 (56)	Wide variety of castings and forgings of complicated form. Close tolerances. Difficult setups of irregular shaped parts. Considerable judgment and ingenuity to plan and lay out unusual lathe operations, select proper feeds and speeds, devise tooling, for varying materials and conditions.
10	PHYSICAL DEMAND	2 (20)	Light physical effort. Setups may require handling of heavy material mounting on face-plate. Machine time greatest part of cycle. Most of time spent watching work, checking, making adjustments.
5	MENTAL OR VISUAL DEMAND	4 (20)	Must concentrate mental and visual attention closely, planning and laying out work, checking, making adjustments. Close tolerances may require unusual attention.
5	RESPONSIBILITY FOR EQUIPMENT OR PROCESS	3 (15)	Careless setup or operation, jamming of tools, dropping work on ways, jamming carriage, may cause damage seldom over $250.
5	RESPONSIBILITY FOR MATERIAL OR PRODUCT	3 (15)	Careless setup or operation may result in spoilage and possible scrapping of expensive castings, forgings, shafts, etc., *eg.*, machining below size, inaccurate boring of diameter and depth. Probable losses seldom over $250.
5	RESPONSIBILITY FOR SAFETY OF OTHERS	3 (15)	Flying chips may cause burns, cuts, or eye injuries. Improperly fastened work may fly from face plate or chuck. May injure another employee when setting work in machine.
5	RESPONSIBILITY FOR WORK OF OTHERS	1 (5)	None.
10	WORKING CONDITIONS	2 (20)	Good working conditions. May be slightly dirty, especially in setups. Some dust from castings. Usual machine-shop noise.
5	UNAVOIDABLE HAZARDS	3 (15)	May crush fingers or toes handling material or from dropped tools or clamps. Possible burns, cuts, or eye injury from flying chips and particles. Finger or hand injury from rotating work.
	Total	311–4	

Figure 16-7   Master sheets like this have been developed to expedite the actual task of rating jobs. (SOURCE: *Factory,* vol. 97, no. 10.)

Perspective 16D   RATING JOBS AND ESCALATING WAGES

The survey cited in Perspective 16A also revealed information about methods used for rating jobs. Sixty-nine per cent of the respondents reported that they use a job evaluation plan; presumably the rest negotiate wage rates or follow wage patterns established by industry-wide trends. As shown in the table on page 472, 50 per cent of those using job evaluation plans have adopted a point rating system.

Related to wage payment plans is a cost-of-living allowance. This feature of multiyear wage settlements has become increasingly prominent as annual inflation rates stay high. Of the 1,500 industries surveyed in 1977, 36 per cent have a cost-of-living factor built into their wage agreements. Adjustments are made most frequently on a quarterly basis. About 60 per cent base their "adders" on popular indices, either the cost-of-

Type of Job Evaluation Plan	Per Cent Using Plan
Point rating	50
Ranking	8
Factory comparison	16
CWS	3
Metal Trades and Electrical Manufacturers plan	16
Others	7

living index or the consumers price index. Escalation adjustments are utilized to keep the basic wage rates from eroding due to general inflation.

16-6.1 Clerical and Salary Evaluation

Evaluation of clerical, technical, professional, and supervisory jobs is handled by most companies as a function independent from the evaluation of production jobs. Production employees are usually studied from without; other employees usually assist in their own job rating either by filling out questionnaires or by answering questions about the job. Items such as "confidential information" must often be added to the clerical rating, while such factors as "physical effort" and "hazards of the job" lose their significance. Office progression from starting job to supervisor is usually much more identifiable than are similar lines of progression from factory job to foreman. Office ratings are harder to maintain, because most office operations are unstandardized and may add or subtract functions periodically.

16-6.2 Managerial Job Rating

The systems used for evaluating managerial and professional jobs may be similar to those used for production or clerical jobs, but to the extent that the customary job-rating characteristics do not measure management-level jobs, other factors must be selected. One system evaluates jobs on seven functional responsibilities. In essence, these are for planning ahead, for keeping abreast of a field, for creative work, for contacts within the company, for influencing people outside, for direction of others, and for creating profits and preventing losses. Applied with a flexible approach, these factors establish a defense for justified differences in executive salaries.

Perhaps the most significant difference is that the individual is helped to establish standards by means of which he can evaluate his own job performance. No one does this for him. No one plans to call him on the carpet. A usual approach is a group discussion with the immediate boss for administrative functions common to all and an individual interview on technical aspects of the job, during which accepted standards are agreed upon. The subordinate executive now has objective means for knowing how well he is doing his job. These are for his use, not for outside appraisal. A few companies do use similar standards as a part of the appraisal to the executive himself.

In practice, two basic steps are followed: first, breaking down the job into the major areas of responsibility; second, setting up standards for stating *how well each task is to be done.* These require (1) an up-to-date executive-job description; (2) a separate statement describing each principal task; (3) agreements written for each task, saying both what is to be done and how well it needs to be done to achieve satisfactory performance (best provided as ranges); (4) acceptance on the part of superior and executive of straightforward, reasonable, equitable, and balanced criteria of quality and quantity for performance. Old-line supervisors, many of whom feel they "own their job," often scoff at the idea of establishing formal standards of performance for managers at any level. Higher ranking executives and those who have successfully filled several positions in succession are apt to defend standards. These executives suggest the following advantages:

1. Formal performance standards give higher management a more logical basis for promotions, dismissals, wage changes, organization planning, or executive hiring. These actions will occur, and the same logic that defends formal procedures at lower levels applies here.

2. Managers themselves are given a greater sense of inner security when they know what their job is and how it is measured. Real self-confidence depends on this. Nothing is so frustrating as to be assigned a new executive position with no statement of responsibility or function. Almost equally bad is to be assigned the supervision of other executives for whom no standards exist. Then all training, motivating, and supervision must be done "in the dark," or according to assumed standards actually applicable to other jobs.

3. Training and development needs are more easily identified by staff departments, the individual, and his superior. Without standards to determine where performance falls short, it is difficult to train for better performance.

4. The tendency is to try to disguise decisions based on expediency, preconceptions, and deals, as sound job evaluation.

16-7   MERIT RATING OF EMPLOYEES

Job rating, discussed so far, has dealt primarily with the job performed as if it were an entity in itself, without the necessity of a person doing that job. We turn our emphasis now to merit rating, which deals with how well the job holder performs the job. The origin of merit rating is credited to Robert Owen, the Scottish millowner who in the early nineteenth century kept "character books" for his employees and displayed a colored block indicative of merit on each worker's bench. Development was halted until the rise of the personnel movement a hundred years later. Its growth was sporadic then but an NICB survey found 11 plans started by 1918 and 16 more by 1923. By the mid-sixties over half of the large companies had a formal merit-rating plan, while over a quarter of the small companies did. The most common rating interval is twice a year. New employees are often rated at shorter intervals. Many companies report rating results to employees, and some discuss the ratings with employees and use them as part of a personnel-development program.

16-7.1 Why Merit Rate?

Merit rating is most commonly used to justify wage increases, but it has many other industrial-relations uses.

1. Merit ratings are used as a part of the *selection* process itself in deciding whether probationary employees are to be retained by the company or not.

2. Merit ratings are used for the purpose of *guiding* new employees by identifying their defects. This kind of merit rating forms the basis of supervisory inspirational conferences with the employee for the employee's benefit.

3. Merit ratings are valuable as aids to the analytical study by the supervisor of the employee for purposes of correct *job placement* in line with the individual employee's personal peculiarities.

4. Merit ratings help in the identification of *promotional* and *transfer* candidates. Such ratings are an excellent tool for determining those individuals who are not making a success of their present assignment and therefore would benefit by a substitute assignment or for selecting those individuals most deserving of additional opportunities.

5. Merit ratings may be used as a *criterion* by the employment office to judge the effectiveness of its own selection of new employees. They may be used in the same way by the industrial-relations director as a measuring stick of employment-office-selection effectiveness.

6. Merit ratings (considered for the benefit of the employee previously) may also be a useful tool for the *benefit of the supervisor,* who learns through rating the employee more about his own job.

7. The quality of the merit-rating job that the supervisor does may form the basis for *rating the supervisor* himself in terms of his supervisory capacity.

8. The merit ratings may be used as part of a seniority system for *layoff purposes.* Where ability is considered along with length of service as a part of seniority, a defensible selection between two individuals for layoff may be made on the basis of merit ratings. This type of record will be different from the usual increase or promotional merit ratings.

9. Merit ratings may be used as a part of the employee's *disciplinary record* to protect the employee, the supervisor, and the company from discrimination, favoritism, or charges of such unfair labor practices. It should be remembered in this connection that a given individual can be proved "bad" by a merit rating only to the extent that other merit ratings prove other employees to lack the defects and therefore to be "good."

10. The merit-rating record of an employee may be collected simply as part of the whole background story about the employee. No immediate use may be at once apparent. Future uses are sure to develop. In this sense, merit rating is actually a *"stand-by" record* which by its existence tends to improve morale. The regular collection of merit ratings will also help to systematize the handling of all personnel matters.

16-7.2 Methods of Merit Rating

Merit rating may be considered from three viewpoints: from that of the personnel worker who constructs a rating scale, from that of the rater, and from that of the ratee. Constructing a good merit-rating system is one of the most complex industrial-relations functions. Some 11 different ways that have been used are shown in Figure 16-8. This also shows what the rater does to use the scale. It should be remembered that the rating scale is much less important than a qualified trained rater making an objective judgment. We shall discuss as examples the graphic rating scale and the forced-choice method.

Both the *forced-choice* and the *weighted random check list* shown in Figure 16-8 are statistically weighted on the basis of rating group action rather than the constructor's opinion and, as such, are examples of the greater use of statistical verified facts in modern industrial relations. In the forced-choice method, the raters are made to choose which of several statements are most like or least like the individual being rated. One example might be: Blows up under pressure vs. treats employees fairly vs. definitely interested in his jobs vs. argues overlong when given orders. Another: Selfish in his interests vs. shows ingenuity and initiative vs. makes excuses for his mistakes vs. works slowly.

Figure 16-9 shows a portion of a graphic rating scale used by Ditto, Inc. It represents a budding conviction that the most important purpose of merit rating is not to give an employee a grade but to cause the supervisor to have a constructive talk with the employee. A new feature of this form is the "return coupon" on the bottom. The Ditto Company says that almost 95 per cent of their employees send this in, and that about 90 per cent say the ratings were fair.

All the merit-rating methods which have been developed to date share certain weaknesses: (1) the *halo effect,* or the tendency to rate a person who is high on one trait high on all others; (2) *different standards among raters,* recognized by a tendency to rate high or low; (3) *lack of discrimination,* so that everyone is rated "exceptional"; (4) *lack of agreement* among raters who rate the same employee, unresolved because no two raters see the same performance; and (5) *lack of significance,* because ratings do not always agree with results obtained on the job or such measures as incentive earnings. Although the ideal rating system has not yet been developed, there is great promise in merit rating. The industrial-relations worker, or supervisor, will find employee relations improved by the development of good merit-rating plans. The individual employee benefits greatly from sound merit rating.

Name of Method	How Constructor Develops Scale	What Rater Does to Use Scale
1. "Character books"	Provides convenient recording space	Keeps record of good and bad actions
2. Rank-order classification	Provides list of names of those to be rated (ratees)	Ranks individuals on list from best to worst
3. Man-to-man comparison	Determines and defines traits to be rated; directs rater to select from his experience representative key individuals at top, bottom, and in between points in each trait	Matches ratees to key individuals in comparison groups
4. Graphic scale, linear, alphabetical, numerical, defined distribution	Determines and defines traits to be rated, composes a continuum for each trait, and provides scale steps along each trait continuum	Marks where each ratee falls along each trait continuum; may also give reasons
5. Check list	Collects extensive list of behavior statements and traits; may pair opposing statements or use spiral arrangement	Marks those statements which do or do not apply to each ratee
6. Forced choice	Collects statements concerning work; establishes criterion measure on basis of rating-group opinion; selects final items statistically for differentiation value; evaluates alternatives chosen by rater	Marks alternatives as "most like" and "least like" ratee
7. Paired comparisons	Compiles pairs of ratees with each name paired with every other name	Chooses the better ratee of each pair
8. Weighted random check list	Collects descriptive statements; has group of judges rank these behavior statements; assigns scale values statistically; weights rater notations	Determines which items apply to ratee to what degree
9. Field review	Interviews each rater personally and records descriptive rating given; evaluates behavior reported	Describes ratee behavior on job
10. Critical incident	Collects incidents in which ratee good or bad performance had a critical effect; presents samples and provides for reporting situations; evaluates reports	Reports occurrence of critical incident
11. Committee nomination	Selects appropriate rating committee; acts as recording secretary during sessions; reports committee decisions	Nominates and defends to committee ratees who are outstanding

Figure 16-8 Different methods of merit rating in terms of operations required by the scale constructor. (SOURCE: Some of this material is from E. B. Knauft, "Personnel Rating Methods," *Journal of Applied Psychology*, vol. 31, no. 6.)

The written record protects him from discrimination, and discussions of the rating with sympathetic supervisors help him to adjust to and grow with the job. Valid objections to merit rating which have been raised by unions have usually referred to abuses which would be equally condemned by the managements under which they occurred.

MERIT RATING REPORT

Ditto Incorporated   Instructions

Name
Job Title
Date
Rated By

RATING IS TO BE ACCOMPLISHED BY CHECK MARKING THE BOX ABOVE THE DESCRIPTION WHICH MOST NEARLY DESCRIBES THE QUALITIES OF THE INDIVIDUAL BEING RATED. CONSIDER EXPLANATION OF FACTORS INVOLVED CAREFULLY.

Comments

1. Punctuality and Attendance

CONSIDER GENERAL RECORD OF ABSENTEEISM AND TARDINESS; PROMPTNESS IN RETURNING FROM REST PERIODS AND LUNCH.

| UNSATISFACTORY | COULD IMPROVE CONSIDERABLY | SATISFACTORY | VERY DEPENDABLE | OUTSTANDING |

2. Initiative and Creativeness

CONSIDER ABILITY TO THINK WITH ORIGINALITY; FIND BETTER WAYS OF DOING JOBS; OFFERS SUGGESTIONS.

| VERY FEW OR NO IDEAS | RARELY OFFERS NEW IDEAS OR SUGGESTIONS | OCCASIONAL NEW IDEAS | FREQUENT NEW IDEAS | UNUSUALLY ORIGINAL AND CONSTRUCTIVE IN THINKING AND IDEAS |

6. Quantity of Work

CONSIDER AMOUNT OF SATIS-FACTORY WORK PERFORMED UNDER NORMAL CONDITIONS

| LOW OUTPUT | SLIGHTLY BELOW AVERAGE OUTPUT | SATISFACTORY OUTPUT | GOOD OUTPUT | CONSISTENTLY HIGHEST OUTPUT |

7. Knowledge of Job

CONSIDER FAMILIARITY WITH REQUIREMENTS OF JOB GAINED THROUGH EXPERIENCE, EDUCATION, OR SPECIALIZED TRAINING.

| INADEQUATE KNOWLEDGE TO PERFORM JOB REQUIRES EXCES-SIVE SUPERVISION | REQUIRES MORE THAN AVERAGE SUPERVISION AND INSTRUCTION | ADEQUATE KNOWLEDGE OF JOB | VERY GOOD KNOWLEDGE OF JOB, SELDOM NEEDS INSTRUCTIONS | RECOGNIZED EXPERT ON JOB |

IN DISCUSSING THIS RATING WITH THE EMPLOYEE, WHAT WAS HIS GENERAL REACTION?

DOES THIS PERSON HAVE QUALIFICATION FOR PROMOTION? YES   NO   IF YES, TO WHAT TYPE OF WORK?

WHAT CAN YOU SUGGEST THAT HE MIGHT DO TO IMPROVE AS AN INDIVIDUAL OR EMPLOYEE?

REMARKS:

(DETACH AND GIVE TO RATED EMPLOYEE TO COMPLETE AND FORWARD IN SEALED ENVELOPE TO INDUSTRIAL RELATIONS DEPT.)
DO YOU BELIEVE YOUR MERIT RATING WAS FAIR AND IMPARTIAL? YES   NO
IF "NO" PLEASE EXPLAIN.

DO YOU THINK YOU WERE HELPED BY THE MERIT RATING AND DISCUSSION WITH YOUR SUPERVISOR?   YES   NO
WOULD YOU LIKE TO BE CONSIDERED FOR A DIFFERENT TYPE OF WORK?   YES   NO
IF "YES" WHAT TYPE OF WORK?

REMARKS:
NAME: DATE   DEPARTMENT

Figure 16-9   A portion of the merit-rating form for graphic rating used by Ditto, Inc. The removed portion included adjective degree scales covering (3) cooperation, (4) ability to learn, and (5) quality of work.

16-8   WAGE-PAYMENT DEVELOPMENTS

Criticism of wage-payment systems, time study, job evaluation, and merit rating abound. Persistent demands of unions and nonunionized employees for increased security, motivation, and participation have helped create many new fringe benefits. Original efforts by employers created some, while still others originated in legislation. This section deals with a select few: credit unions, guaranteed annual wages (GAW) or supplemental unemployment benefits, profit sharing, and stock ownership.

The history of *credit unions* (a common personnel practice supervised by the industrial-relations manager) is a good example of industrial-relations growth. From a self-help impetus in Germany founded on famine in 1849, the first credit unions reached North America at the turn of the century and moved from Canada to the United States 9 years later. The initial support was from Boston merchant Edward A. Filene, who in 1921 established an educational bureau to promote credit unions. As a part of the New Deal in 1934, a Federal Credit Union Act was passed placing supervision in the U.S. Agricultural Department. The Filene bureau (Credit Union National Extension Bureau) was merged into CUNA (Credit Union National Association) for further self-help within credit-union management. By 1959 there were 19,825 United States credit unions with over 11.3 million members and over $4.8 billion assets. More than half of these are located in industrial establishments, with another 5 per cent in labor unions.

The guaranteed annual wage (GAW), or *stabilized-employment,* idea is 70 years old in America and much older in Europe. Unemployment-insurance provisions aimed at stabilizing income became United States law more than 30 years ago. Managements of such diverse companies as Nunn-Bush Shoe Company and Armstrong Cork Company used market research, the master sales budget, subcontracting, warehousing during off seasons, product diversification, lengthening or simplifying the line manufactured, working longer or shorter work weeks, and regulated introduction of new machinery in an effort to avoid boom hiring and seasonal layoffs.

In one sense an appreciable proportion of the long-term employees of major companies already enjoyed an annual guarantee through the operation of seniority provisions when the United Auto Workers and the large automobile manufacturers agreed to an unemployment-compensation supplement and the Steelworkers were granted an employment or wage guarantee in 1955 negotiations. These agreements and those signed by the Electrical Workers, the Teamsters, and other unions provide a wide variety of solutions at the contract level. Their actual administration, and the regular flow of productive work upon which their success depends, has not proved so simple. Most state unemployment-compensation laws had to be reinterpreted to permit supplemental unemployment benefit (SUB) payments by an employer. Some states still bar unemployment compensation payments to workers receiving SUB. Since some union contracts contain SUB provisions which require the employer to make supplementary payments to bring unemployment income up to some specified level, an alternative plan must be negotiated in these states. The most common alternative is for the employer to make lump-sum payments, either after the worker has been recalled from layoff or after the unemployment compensation payments are exhausted.

Any plan of employment stabilization, whether GAW or SUB, must face such questions as: Is the guarantee for 30 or 40 hours a week, for 36 or 52 weeks a year, at three-fourths pay or full pay? Are all employees eligible or only the most senior? Is the plan supported only by an ear-marked reserve or the full credit of the employer? What happens when the reserves are gone or the business faces bankruptcy? These are only a few of the problems facing company management and employees (unionized or not) as they mutually endeavor to regularize employment and income. The problem has always been the customer, who, while he makes the business possible, insists on snapping up bargains, switching brands, following fads and "style," and buying seasonally.

Profit sharing is one of the most controversial ways of supplementing payments to both workers and executives. There are no more fervent evangelists than the managers (commonly owner-managers) of companies that have profit sharing. While some local unions accept profit sharing and a few actively promote profit-sharing plans, most national unions have condemned the way such plans are operated. They claim that profit sharing is too often found in companies that oppose union organization. They ask why the earnings of workers should go down (i.e., no profits to distribute) when company earnings go down because of management mistakes in buying materials or in engineering and selling the product.

The annual report of the Council of Profit Sharing Industries each year stresses such favorable results as higher total earnings for employees, greatly increased productivity at lower unit labor costs, and "the spirit of mutual understanding" between employer and employees. A successful profit-sharing plan, like the incentive-payment plans with which it was grouped in a prior discussion, seems to depend upon good industrial relations generally, plus an understanding by employees of the connection between their efforts and the company's profits.

Employers sometimes make company stock available to employees through *stock ownership plans* as an incentive to help make the company more successful. This may be done by outright sale (sometimes by installment payments) or by the "restricted stock option." Under a stock option, the individual is offered a number of shares of stock at a specified price with delivery to be made at some time in the future. If the option is exercised, deductions begin immediately. When the delivery date arrives, he may accept either the stock at the original agreed price (which may be below the current market price) or get his money back. The tax laws may make buying stock in this way advantageous, especially in high-income tax brackets.

Employee-stock-purchase plans attained widespread popularity in the twenties, but most collapsed with the market in 1929. Interest has been growing again steadily since World War II, however, with the new plans attempting to avoid the defects of the earlier experience by completing purchase rapidly, diversifying investments (stock purchase plus thrift plans), and educating employees in the fact that a free market also goes down, as has been very evident in the 1970s.

16-9   REVIEW QUESTIONS

1. Is the determination of a wage level a policy decision? Why? What are the six steps of a satisfactory wage administration procedure?

2. What is a predetermined time standard? How and why are such standards used?

3. What prerequisites should be met before an incentive system is installed?

4. What is work sampling? Of what value is it to management?

5. Which incentive plans are suited for individuals, and which for groups? What are the relative merits of each version?

6. What is job evaluation? How does it help determine the worth of an individual job?

7. Briefly explain the comparison method and the classification method of job rating.

8. What is the factor comparison method of job rating? Which factors are commonly used? How does the point rating method differ from the other methods of job rating?

9. What is meant by ''merit rating''? What is the distinction between job evaluation and merit rating?

10. What is a particularly important point to consider in using merit ratings? What are some of the weaknesses of merit rating methods?

11. Explain some of the ways management has attempted to provide supplemental benefits to its work force?

16-10 TOPICS FOR DISCUSSION

1. Discuss the alternatives that might govern employment if wages were not paid. Refer to both ancient and modern history for examples.

2. There are many reasons why different workers may take home different-sized pay checks. List as many different reasons as you can on the basis of this chapter and explain each in a sentence.

3. State the most important step in time study and be prepared to defend your selection.

4. Why do you think there will be (or will not be) an increase in the popularity of predetermined elemental time standards as manufacturing management turns increasingly to mathematical control methods?

5. How do you account for the glowing endorsement of the Scanlon plan given in Perspective 16B and its general lack of application as indicated by the survey reported in Perspective 16A?

6. A union leader said, ''That job rating jazz I don't dig. You are confusing us when we want to bargain on a wage increase for the machine operators.'' Comment on his position and why management might feel otherwise.

7. Certain weaknesses in job evaluation have been pointed out. Which of these do you feel is most serious? Why?

8. Several of the more recently developed merit-rating systems ask raters to supply facts which are evaluated by statistical methods from weights calculated by computers. No supervisor using the system is supposed to know the significance of the facts fed into the machine. Should this sort of control be extended to other industrial-relations practices? Why or why not?

9. Social thinkers have stressed the undesirability of creating an especially favored group of employees enjoying the advantages of low-cost credit through credit unions. Similar attacks

have been made on guaranteed annual wages and profit sharing. Indicate whether you feel that each of these attacks is equally justified from the viewpoint of those who do *not* enjoy the benefits. Be specific.

10. Case 16A: *Wide Wear, Inc.*

Two large manufacturers, one of men's apparel and the other of women's wear, merged to combine their retail stores for national distribution. Before the merger each of the two companies serviced its stores directly from its factories. Now, however, the increased number of stores, the expanded territory, and the broader line of purchased merchandise resulted in the establishment of a strategically located distribution center.

Some time after operations at the new center had settled down to routine performance, costs were found higher than expected. At an executive conference Harold Gold, vice-president in charge of manufacturing, suggested, "Let's get Oscar Videlli up here from the factory and have him install some operating standards. If he gets time records of what's happening now, we can control costs." Videlli came and, using modern industrial-engineering techniques, found these operating costs:

Administration and supervision	$244,000
General expenses	$700,000
Merchandising centers	$240,000
Clerks: shipping and receiving, and stockkeeping	$516,000

Administration and supervision included managers, secretaries, accounting, and all office expenses associated. General expenses included interest, rent, insurance, supplies, and packing materials, but no salaries or labor.

The merchandising centers are in effect five replicas of the original factory distributing department. These were created by the manager to handle the complexity introduced by multiple lines. Each of five merchandisers has a small group of helpers in a separate office and a separate area for actual stockkeeping. They analyze sales tabulations and reorders within each merchandise line. The work is primarily routine record keeping but requires categorizing styles as to color, design, trim, and accessories. This requires merchandise knowledge and aesthetic judgment in selecting assortments. Considerable difference in record keeping existed between the different merchandising centers.

The "clerks" are of two different classifications. The first consists of employees engaged in shipping and receiving; clear-cut manual work amenable to standardization. The second is the stockkeeping classification. These clerks work in the five separated stockkeepers areas. In addition to the physical work of putting goods into stock and taking it out for shipment to stores, the work entails some degree of merchandise knowledge gleaned from running contact with the merchandisers. The stockkeepers take the final step in making assortments in style, color, and size within the categories allocated. The inclusion of merchandising judgment in the operation stood in the way of standardizing stockkeepers operations. In recognition of their higher status the stockkeepers are granted 15 minutes extra wash-up time, mostly to travel to a centrally located coatroom used by all the executives and office workers.

Oscar Videlli proceeded to set standards to as great a degree as feasible. The total coverage turned out to be only $210,000. Even this small coverage required an inordinate amount of standard data. Videlli felt that to properly maintain and administer the standard would require a time-study person full time. The projected yearly savings from the application of these new standards amounted to $30,000.

To utilize the standards more fully, a wage-incentive system was also proposed for individual productivity. When the incentive system was being worked out, it was reviewed with the union representative, George Mudd. The national policy and practice of this union called for wage payment on a time basis. Since the new wage-incentive plan was contrary to this policy, strenuous opposition to its use was voiced by George Mudd, who warned of difficulties ahead if the new system were used.

Questions

1. Which of the factors that make the installation of an incentive system in the Wide Wear, Inc., more difficult are the most important?

2. Are we to conclude that if Oscar Videlli cannot install incentives, the use of standard-operations time records is inappropriate in a merchandise distribution center of this type? Why?

3. If Harold Gold, the vice-president, insists on having the standard-operations time records collected, what should the approach be to make best use of them?

11. Case 16B: *Wide Wear, Inc., Revisited*

The stockkeepers described have to combine a considerable amount of physical work, similar to that of receiving and shipping clerks, with a degree of merchandising knowledge and judgment. The two kinds of work were used there to show the difficulty of setting standards.

Questions

Describe the kind of job-rating system which would have application in this company if no methods change were made. Would this have made easier the setting of applicable standards?

12. Case 16C: *Viso-Audit In-Basket Explored Again*
   See Item 3—Union Demand

Questions

See item 3—Union Demand

1. In relation to demand 1, across-the-board increase for all production and maintenance employees, would it make any difference if production employees were paid on an incentive basis? What else would you want to know?

2. How would demand 5 affect the pay scale if it were accepted?

See Item 5—Reclassification Request

Questions

1. Would you grant the request which Ham Baxter makes? If so, what do you assume would be the results? What other things would you like to know before acting on this memorandum?

13. Case 16D: *The Midwest Roadbuilding Co.*

The chief construction engineer for the Midwest Roadbuilding contractors, George Kelly, called a meeting of the six project engineers. The "call order" gave the purpose as establishing performance standards. Although George was relatively new in his position, he wanted his people to develop an understanding of their responsibility in terms of standards. All six were experienced people and equally balanced between three recent college graduates and three old-time construction workers. During the meeting it was apparent that one old-timer, Ed Johns, was not cooperating in the project. He did not raise objections, however, and a few realistic standards were mutually agreed upon. The other five men seemed to be participating sincerely. The new boss was so pleased with their participation that he assumed that Ed Johns was just quiet by nature. All in all, George Kelly felt it was a successful standards-setting meeting. When the construction job was under way, George Kelly sat down with each of the project engineers to review achievement of standards. All went well until Kelly talked to Johns. Johns was impatient and told Kelly: "I sat around while you wasted almost all day in fooling around with all that standards stuff, but I didn't know you meant it for me. We got a highway to build. That's my job. I know it. I do it. Right now I'd be doing more good by planning now for tomorrow, not wasting time hashing over last week's stuff."

Kelly replied, "Ed, you sat in our meeting 2 months ago and didn't object when we set up these performance standards. They apply to you as well as the others. I noticed then you didn't say much. Now I take it you think we wasted a lot of time."

"As far as I'm concerned, we wasted a day," said Ed. "I've been around, George. I know what

I'm doing. If I don't do it to suit you, say so. If you can't tell how well it's done, that's your problem. I've got eight foremen under me. I don't have to waste time on standards with them. They know what I want because I've told them. If they goof off, I tell 'em quick. If they do O.K., they know it.''

''I appreciate that, but maybe you might even find ways to do better, if you regularly reviewed these standards with me,'' countered George.

''Could be, but I don't get the point in going at it this way. Now don't take this personal. I've gotten a fair shake so far. But believe me, this standards business is a waste of time. We can't waste time gabbing about what we're going to do, then hash it all over when we don't get it done. After all, I've been doing pretty good for the past 5 years building roads without it,'' said Ed.

After blowing a smoke ring at the ceiling, George Kelly asked, ''How do you know? Can you prove it, Ed?''

Questions

1. In your opinion, was this a good answer? If Kelly made a mistake, where was it? If Ed was wrong, how so?

2. What points concerning executive-performance standards might Kelly have made to help Ed understand the use of executive-performance standards in the supervision of executives?

14. Case 16E: *Real County Foundry*

Carl Malitis was manager of the Real County Foundry, a department of a large manufacturing concern. The foundry employed some 50 people. Many of these workers prided themselves on the importance of their work. Most had long service. The foundry workers had comprised four job classifications: molders, casters, knockout men, and chippers and grinders. Each group had its own pinochle parties. In the molder group three or four old-timers controlled the rest quite rigidly. In 1979, in line with the general company policy, all foundry employees, except molders, were put on group piecework under a single classification, ''foundry hand.'' Until 1979 the casters, knockout men, and chippers and grinders had been on straight individual piecework. The molders were paid daywork. It was Carl Malitis's belief that defects would be reduced by making all employees responsible for turning out good work. He also felt that earnings would be distributed more equitably. After 6 months, total output, instead of having increased, was lower. Instead of less scrap, there was more. Each group blamed the other for causing scrap. The casters felt that they were not getting what they earned. Individual operators in each group with high outputs felt they were carrying the less efficient colleagues. Workers who had previously earned around $7.00 an hour now averaged $5.50. This was not intended. All earnings were expected to be above the old classifications since a ''penalty charge'' was eliminated. A quick investigation indicated that the new rates on group incentive were not in any way tighter than the old rates. A review of the job descriptions indicated that the workers were all doing jobs as described in some part of the foundry-hand description. Carl Malitis now faced the difficulty of increasing production as planned. There were other management complications at this time, involving human relations, patents, and financing, as well as supervisory difficulties. The situation in essence, however, seemed to be dissatisfaction with job classifications, assignments, and pay received.

Questions

1. What seems to you to be wrong in the Real County Foundry?

2. Should Carl Malitis reverse himself and go back to the old classifications and piecework system? Why? Why not?

3. If you were a caster, how would you feel about this change?

4. If your earnings had been reduced, what would you do?

17

MOTIVATION

Most workers find work a social experience. It occurs in the presence of others and occupies much of waking life. The spirit and willingness with which that work is done constitute job morale. Without high morale work is drudgery, and supervision is near slave-driving. For most managers the question of chief interest is: What can I do within the organization to improve employee motivation that encourages greater cooperation, enthusiasm, and productivity? A good question! Answers are sought. Which factors in the work situation lead to job satisfaction? Which to dissatisfaction? What problems are created by different responses to the same motivation factors by different individuals? What theories have been advanced to explain how motivation works? What procedures have been developed to translate motivation theories into improved employee morale?

17 MOTIVATION

17-1 EMPLOYEE MORALE

In recent years there has been a change in attitude concerning the importance of employee morale. No thoughtful manager says that morale is not important. High production can result only from the cooperative and enthusiastic efforts of willing employees. What has been challenged is the "treat-them-nicely" approach of an outmoded paternalistic human-relations effort. Studies of the work relationship clearly indicate the effectiveness of employee-centered rather than work-centered supervision. Recent management critics, however, have pointed out that employees do not need to be extremely happy to be productive on the job. Some research evidence suggests that the "gripers" may also be more productive than the completely placid. One study at the University of Pittsburgh seems to have indicated that morale is made up of two sets of elements, one set containing those which help to make a person satisfied with his job and a second set containing those which tend to make him dissatisfied when they are lacking. Correction of conditions leading to dissatisfaction does not yield satisfaction but rather a sort of neutral willingness to be satisfied. This does not suggest that employers should abandon their efforts to improve employee morale. It simply indicates that the tools of social control in employee–employer relations should be used thoughtfully.

17-1.1 Employee-Attitude Survey

An effective way of measuring employee morale is by means of an audit or a study of employee satisfaction. In its simple form, an attitude survey or opinion poll may be a series of informal questions asked by a company personnel counselor. At its best, it is a matter for experienced social scientists requiring careful preparation and pretesting of questions, experienced administration, and skilled interpretation.

An employee-attitude survey develops a statistical morale index for the company as a whole, but its greatest value lies in pointing out "trouble spots" in specific departments. "Sore spots" may develop because of unskilled supervision, faulty company policy, ineffective staff work, or peculiarities in the specific work group. Some of the questions asked in a typical survey are shown in Figure 17-1.

Among industrial-relations workers, it is almost a cliché that employees do not express their true wants. Workers ask for more money or for bigger benefits when what they really want is a chance to participate in matters that affect them. Many managers with a mechanistic approach to administration bewail the unstandardized nature of the people whom they must supervise. They seek in people the uniformity they experience in a steel alloy. The whole lesson of individual differences cries out against expecting uniformity

1. *What do you think of your job?*	3. *How would you describe your supervisor?*
2% I do not like it	4% He is a very poor supervisor
13% I am not very well satisfied	12% He doesn't know much about being
51% I like it pretty well	a supervisor
34% I am very well satisfied	54% He's a pretty good supervisor
	30% He's the best I've ever worked for
55. *Do you feel the company offers you the opportunity to get ahead?*	56. *What do you think of the discipline in your department?*
11% Opportunities for advancement are very poor	8% It is very poor; there's too much playing around
22% It's pretty hard to get ahead here	21% The discipline is just fair
53% The chances for getting ahead are fairly good	48% It is quite good
14% The chances for advancement are excellent	23% It is very good

Figure 17-1 Percentage of Standard Register Company employees who checked specific answers on a confidential questionnaire submitted anonymously; 81 per cent of the employees also added comments. (SOURCE: *Factory,* vol. 106, no. 8.)

and hence expecting any other individual to respond exactly as you would. That is where the straightforward approach falls down. What seems entirely logical to the individual supervisor may be anything but logical to one or more of the workers supervised. Supervisors sometimes fail to understand the worker's need—to know and be known by the "big boss" as well as by the fellow at the next bench. This fact accounts for the good employee relations that commonly exist in the small shop where all the workers call the owner-manager "Bill." Many small-shop managers are astounded to discover, when once they have expanded beyond the one-person management stage, how quickly they can lose contact with the working force.

17-1.2 Current Conditions

Above all else, today's industrial worker wants a share in the management of the enterprise of which he is a part. The same may often be said of non-policy-making levels of management. This *sharing,* this mutuality of interests, is what the worker is really after in his attempts to know the boss. Oh, yes! He likes the feeling of "being somebody." He gets a kick out of association with the great. He wants someone in authority who will listen sympathetically to his human troubles and problems. (That's why the counselor policy succeeds.) He wants all that. But, he wants *something more* as well.

In the old days when the worker dealt with "Bill," the small-shop owner-manager, he felt he was *in* on things. He shared Bill's problems, too. The confidences were mutual. He knew Bill's wife, heard when Bill's kid got measles, sympathized with Bill when the bank called a loan unexpectedly, *worked out with Bill* the cost and sales prices of products. In other words, in the small shop, the worker was a participating member of the team, as well as a fellow human being and friend of the boss. No gap existed between boss and worker. This was a status that allayed distrust.

Today, there is a gap, a wide gap, between impersonal corporate owners and employees. This is understandable. There is no excuse for a gap, however, between the hired manager and the worker. Too often the worker is regarded impersonally. He has no sense of fellowship with the boss, no companionship, no confidences, and no pride in the final product because he makes only part no. 758. He does not *participate* in the enterprise.

The worker today is seeking, often subconsciously and perhaps without himself ever having been a member of a small-shop family, the old familiarity, the old sense of belonging, the full confidence of participation. That is what the worker wants. That is the desire that management is trying to satisfy with dead committee memberships, with collective bargaining at arm's length, with canned morale builders, with empty counseling, and with welfare activities. So long as these pale imitations alone are offered, so long will the worker remain mysteriously dissatisfied. So long as management does not go the second mile, so long as the worker does not have that sense of full sharing, that sense of responsibility in the enterprise as a whole, just that long will there be suspicion, distrust, and trouble between workers and management.[1]

Perspective 17A SWEDEN HAS PARTICIPATION PLUS

Worker participation in the management of companies is more extensive in Sweden than in any other country. While "participation" in the United States is generally geared to activities of production, the Swedes give it a much deeper meaning that implies classless cooperation between workers and management. The following report exemplifies the differences:

In 1974 the Ford Foundation took half a dozen production workers from U.S. auto assembly lines and placed them in self-managing work groups at Saab-Scania in Sweden. For 3 weeks, they worked as Swedish workers do, assembling complete engines in 30-minute stints instead of doing 2-minute tasks. Subsequently, newspapers were full of the report that five of the six Americans didn't like the Swedish style as well as their own.

Many Swedes are still upset because the Americans' reaction seems to cast aspersions on Swedish advances in work patterns and industrial democracy. "Of course the workers didn't like it," expostulates Pehr Gyllenhammer, president of Volvo. "They come from an entirely different work culture. Our people have grown into these patterns gradually, for reasons that are essentially Swedish."*

Swedish industry is characterized by low unemployment (about 2 per cent), high unionization of blue-collar workers (90 per cent), mostly private ownership (97 per

---

[1]Some industrialists feel that workers, particularly organized groups of workers, have not demonstrated that they really desire to participate in management, i.e., workers do not show a willingness to study problems of production and marketing, understand comparative financial statements, nor be realistic in their economic demands. Those who hold this view state, "Workers don't want to take over the management of a plant, don't want the headaches and problems. They only want to be assured that their interests are considered." Certain union leaders feel much the same. Thus the "U.E. Guide" says in effect: *Management's job is to run the plant. The local union's job is not to be drawn into management problems but to protect the interests of its membership.* Neither of these views considers the broad desire of the individual worker to identify himself with his work and find it interesting, purposeful, and worthy of his effort.

cent), and a national dedication to improving the quality of working life. This thrust has taken the direction of an ever-louder voice by workers in the management of company affairs. It has been a legal requirement since 1946 that employee-elected representatives (works councils) deal with all shop-floor matters. A 1972 law makes it almost impossible to fire an employee after 6 months on the job. Since 1975 companies are required to give works councils full access to all financial data. Additional laws have been proposed that would shift the "right to manage" from management to a coalition of employers and employees, with a tilt toward the workers.

The highly publicized Volvo program, similar to the one in which the six Americans worked, has employee involvement throughout. New plants have been specially designed for group work rather than assembly line operations. Plants are small, usually under 600 employees. Teams decide how to rotate jobs and who should do different types of tasks. The roles of production engineers and managers are more advisory than autocratic. Top managers operate in a large, nonpartitioned office area instead of private offices.

*SOURCE: N. Foy and H. Gadon, "Worker Participation: Contrasts in Three Countries," *Harvard Business Review,* May-June, 1976.

COMMENT   Trying to import intact the Swedish form of participation would be futile, but importing concepts and experiences that would be adapted for local use could prove very beneficial. There are many managerial methods and techniques in use around the world that could be successfully transplanted with minor modifications. That is why those everywhere interested in management need to communicate. There is much to share. Just the drive of modern managers to provide an environment that encourages worker involvement has resulted in many forms of employee participation, ranging from workers on the company's board of directors to worker councils that elect the plant manager. Although the approaches vary widely, they share the common quest for greater productivity in industrial organizations.

17-2 THE HAWTHORNE EXPERIENCE

Discussions of the social aspects of management usually start with the 50-year-old Hawthorne experience.[2] In this experiment the Western Electric Company initiated a study under the sponsorship of the National Research Council with the guidance of Harvard scientists:

the aim of which was to determine the relationship between intensity of illumination and efficiency of workers, measured in output. One of the experiments made was the following: Two groups of employees doing similar work under similar conditions were chosen, and records of output were kept of each group. The intensity of the light under which one group worked was varied, while that under which the other group worked was held constant. By this method the investigators hoped to isolate from the effect of other variables the effect of changes in the intensity of illumination on the rate of output.

[2]National Research Council, "Fatigue of Workers and Its Relation to Industrial Production," New York: Reinhold Publishing Corporation, 1941. A recast of this experiment is H. A. Landsberger, "Hawthorne Revisited," Ithaca, N.Y.: Cornell University Press, 1958.

In this hope they were disappointed. The experiment failed to show any simple relation between experimental changes in intensity of illumination and observed changes in rate of output. The investigators concluded that this result was obtained, not because such a relation did not exist, but because it was in fact impossible to isolate it from the other variables entering into any determination of productive efficiency. This kind of difficulty, of course, has been encountered in experimental work in many fields. Furthermore, the investigators were in agreement as to the character of some of these other variables. They were convinced that one of the major factors which prevented their securing a satisfactory result was psychological. The employees being tested were reacting to changes in light intensity in the way in which they assumed that they were expected to react. That is, when light intensity was increased they were expected to produce more; when it was decreased they were expected to produce less. A further experiment was devised to demonstrate this point. The light bulbs were changed, as they had been changed before, and the workers were allowed to assume that as a result there would be more light. They commented favorably on the increased illumination. As a matter of fact, the bulbs had been replaced with others of just the same power. Other experiments were made, and in each case the results could be explained as a "psychological" reaction rather than a "physiological" one.

The obvious conclusion drawn from rising output unsupported by environmental improvements was that soaring production was owed to the unusual attention given to the workers during the study. A powerful, dormant motivator had been ignited. Exact workings of the motivator could not be determined, but several causal conditions were noted. One factor was that interviews with the workers conducted by the study teams allowed employees to ventilate their feelings and thereby obtain a more objective attitude toward their work.

Another cause was the influence of informal worker associations. These groups proliferated despite management's effort to nullify them. Groups hostile to management could hold productivity to the minimum level that was still tolerated. Social pressure was exerted to defeat the "bribery" of management's incentive proposals. Attempts to "get tough" were met by silently organized output restrictions.

Sometimes the worker groups associated themselves with management goals, and productivity rose higher than expected. A high output rate was interpreted as an expression of the group's mastery of its own job. The alignment of management and worker objectives was attributed to more personal concern evidenced by managers and recognized by workers.

Perspective 17B AFTER HALF A CENTURY, WESTERN ELECTRIC'S MOTIVATION EXPERIMENTS CONTINUE

From 1924 to 1933 the Western Electric Company conducted its now-famous experiments at the Hawthorne Works to determine which factors in a work situation affect the morale and productive efficiency of workers. Studies aimed at the same subject area continue to this day. At Western Electric's Merrimack Valley Works, a program called "motivation and enrichment trial" (MET) seeks answers from today's workers about what type of work conditions are most satisfying to them.

In the planning phase of the program, the following set of goals was established:

1. Improve performance, including such things as earnings, efficiency, and attendance.
2. Change work lives so as to be more compatible with the social environment of the seventies.
3. Test some of the principles of the participative style and determine if some of these things should be introduced into other shops.

After several group meetings attended by supervisors and employees, the following actions were implemented:

- Workplace rules were changed to allow employees to move around at will, keep radios or tape decks at their work stations, and decorate their stations with potted plants and other decorative items in good taste.
- Section chiefs could abandon neckties, and most did so.
- Suggestions and comments were actively solicited. A peer-group committee received and responded to every input within a week.
- A prominent bulletin board displayed the more interesting responses from the suggestion system and progress reports about the program activities, including its effect on wage incentives.
- Training programs featured topics such as "transactional analysis" and incentive arrangements.
- Where appropriate, job contents were enriched to make them more interesting.
- Employees participated in certain promotion and production decisions.

Some of the promising results from the MET program were improved production performance and better attitudes, as implied by employee statements such as:

"A manufacturing shop like this can be almost like a prison sometimes. But now, if you know you're free to get up and walk around or go to the water fountain, it makes a difference."
"We hardly see a supervisor any more. It used to be that when the boss left for a meeting or something, everybody would relax. That just doesn't happen now."*

*SOURCE: B. N. Heath, "The Motivation and Enrichment Trial," *Industrial Engineering,* November, 1974.

COMMENT   A revelation from the Hawthorne studies is equally applicable today: Physical change does not lead to a direct, automatic result when people are involved; change affects a person's attitude, which in turn affects the result. And basic attitudes fluctuate in tune with the social values of each era. It is said that today's better educated workers want more meaningful work and more opportunities for personal development. If so, many of the conventional jobs in industry will leave them unsatisfied; yet it is still uncertain just how jobs should be redesigned to meet expectations. For such reasons, the motivation experiments begun at the Hawthorne Works may never be complete, because as solutions are found, the problems mutate to send the searchers in new directions.

17-3   NEEDS, DEEDS, GOALS, AND GAINS

From the viewpoint of psychology, motivation is anchored by (1) *needs* that operate within an individual; and (2) *goals* in the environment which the individual moves toward or away from. In one way or another (and many of them are very subtle) all human behavior can be linked theoretically to the needs people feel, and the way they go about satisfying those needs. As pictured in Figure 17–2, the motivation cycle starts when a need is felt. This felt need leads to the identification of a goal that will supposedly satisfy the need. Behavior is directed toward achieving this goal. Successfully attaining the goal may satisfy the original need which allows another need to take its place as the impetus for the next motivation cycle.

Since needs and goals are considered by many to be the fundamental source of behavior, we shall examine some of the theories proposed to explain their influence. Generally speaking, psychologists assume we learn what goals are relevant by a process of trial and error. This learning starts very early in life when a baby thrashes around, seeking means of contentment. Results of the thrashing can be successful, unsuccessful, or may even increase discontent. In the jargon of experimental psychology, these instances respectively represent reinforcement, nonreinforcement, or negative reinforcement of need-to-goal relationships.

The trial and error process is a life-long ritual. Just as an infant learns that actions which bring success are valuable, adults accumulate experiences gained in attaining past goals that should be valuable in the future. The message to managers here is to try to help workers attain their goals through appropriate deeds. In other words, when an employee is seeking a goal, assist him by recognizing through reinforcement, nonreinforcement, or negative reinforcement the approved means of goal achievement.

A need creates a tension in a person. The amount of tension is a function of how strong the need is. When a person has been deprived of something for a significant period, the tension is greater. The longer someone has been

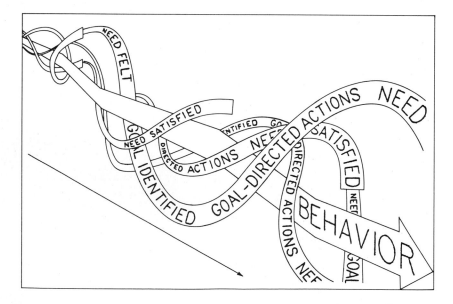

Figure 17-2 Human behavior is motivated by the needs an individual feels and the goals he seeks to satisfy his needs. Many needs of varying strengths vie for attention and influence actions. Needs, goals, and reactions to motives change with time.

deprived of water, the more the tension for a drink increases. Goal-directed behavior is the thirsty person's actions to obtain a drink. Once a good long drink has been downed, the need has been satisfied and the goal diminishes in importance. Drinking more liquids is not as satisfying because the driving tension has been relieved.

A need with a high expectation of achievement is generally more motivating than one with only a remote chance of being satisfied. This concept reveals an interesting connection between human behavior and history. In primitive societies personal needs focused on simple goals of subsistence. As the basic needs for survival were satisfied, goals became more personal. We still need food and shelter, but now we tend to specify what foods we want, the style of clothing, and the type of house. Relief from the strife of gaining physical security has extended the scope of needs to include goals unthought of in the past. The accumulated effect of this freedom is apparent in the rapid advances in science and technology which characterize our present society. The new freedom has also altered the management methods in today's industrial scene.

17-3.1   Theory X and Theory Y

The distinction between management policies based on control over the physical needs of workers and policies inspired by more indirect forms of motivation has been captured nicely by Douglas McGregor's theory X and theory Y.[3] The old-fashioned, traditional management approach is titled theory X. It depicts a harsh attitude toward employees based on the following beliefs:

1. Employees inherently dislike work and will resort to all kinds of self-serving and disruptive practices to avoid it.

2. Since employees cannot be trusted to do the work expected, most of them must be strictly watched, controlled, and threatened with punishment if the desired work is to be accomplished.

3. Strict controls and threats produce desired results because most employees actually appreciate rigid leadership that lets them avoid job responsibilities. They react to threats because they prize security above all other factors in their job.

Although the points in theory X may sound to us like a satire on unenlightened management, the theory does call attention to prejudices that led to labor unrest in previous generations. And there is just enough logic twisted into theory X to make it appeal to some intolerant managers today. Figure 17–3 diagrams the evolution of management practices that has drawn employers closer to employees.

Theory Y is the counterpart to theory X. The difference between the two views is the emphasis on the human element in theory Y. Employees are

[3]Douglas McGregor, *The Human Side of Enterprise,* New York: McGraw-Hill Book Co., Inc., 1950.

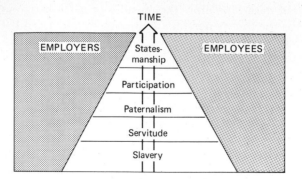

Figure 17-3 Modes of management are changing to bring employees and employers ever closer. The age when a "master" could dictate to his subjects without challenge has vanished. The "father image" of the organization head watching over the affairs of his flock of employees is fading. The modern leader is distinguished by his ability to bring about cooperation among reluctant factions, to see and understand both sides of a question, and to act diplomatically.

treated as feeling, principled individuals, not just as numbers to be manipulated. The assumptions underlying theory Y are:

1. Employees do not inherently dislike work. They are anxious to use their abilities if given a fair opportunity.

2. Employees do not need to be supervised closely or threatened with punishment in order to get work done properly. They will direct themselves toward self-accepted goals, and the pursuit of these goals can produce the desired work.

3. Responsibility and self-direction are sought, not shunned, by most employees. They value security but also actively seek other goals that use and reward their creativity and intellectual potential.

Management's mission in the application of theory Y is to establish work conditions that foster cooperation and enthusiasm. Cooperation is required to align employee goals with employer needs. Enthusiasm encourages employees to commit their diverse talents to objectives without promises of specific rewards. High employee morale does not ensure high output, but it increases the chance of realizing the advantages promised by theory Y.

Perspective 17C   THE LAST CHANCE TO BOOST MORALE

To most managers the next worst thing to being fired is to fire someone. The ordeal for both parties is relieved by a relatively new service. Specialized counseling firms offer to assist an executive who has to wield an ax and to ease the victims' distress by helping them adjust to a search for a new job. In the doublespeak slang of personnel placement, employee recycling is handled by "out-placement" or "de-hiring" firms.

Corporations hire de-hirers for humanitarian and economic reasons. Managers that must fire as well as those who are fired are spared psychological abuse. The de-hirers advise managers who have to do the firing how to make it less painful—deliver their termination message quickly (10 minutes at most) and never do it just before a week-end or holiday. Counseling starts as soon as the terminated employee hears the decision. Professional out-placement guidance tends to provide a job faster and with less mental anguish than a self-search. The shorter period of unemployment may save the client firm money on severance pay and likely leaves a less bitter employee who might vengefully run down the reputation or sell secrets of his former employer.

17-3.2 Need-Ranking Theory

The backdrop of theory X, theory Y, and most contemporary views of motivation is the concept that humans are motivated by many needs which can be grouped categorically in order of relative importance. Psychologist A. H. Maslow has developed a widely adopted framework for a *hierarchy of needs*—needs arranged in order of importance under the assumption that a lower level need must be satisfied before the next higher need becomes a motivating factor.[4] This ladder of needs is shown in Figure 17-4 and is expanded upon below. The needs are listed in ascending order of importance.

1. *Physiological Needs*   The body needs food, water, shelter, and sex. Since these needs are largely provided for at this time in our culture, they are not significant motivators.

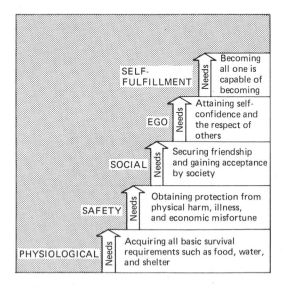

Figure 17-4 Factors affecting motivation.

[4]A. H. Maslow, *Motivation and Personality*, New York: Harper & Brothers, 1954.

2. *Safety Needs* The needs for protection from physical harm, sickness, economic disaster, and unexpected emergencies. An example of the transition from physiological to safety needs as motivators is the way demands of labor unions have changed. In earlier years, the unions demanded greater pay. Recent negotiations emphasize accident prevention, guaranteed annual wages, job security, and other fringe benefits.

3. *Social Needs* The needs for companionship, affection, and a feeling of belonging. From the managerial standpoint, this level of needs marks the departure from essentially economic goals to a quest for mental health. Satisfied social needs are apparent in a work situation when an individual becomes so much a part of the group he is working with that he sees the group's efforts as his own. When he identifies closely with the group, he is more likely to contribute to its progress, which he terms "our" progress rather than "their" progress.

4. *Ego Needs* The needs for self-esteem and the respect of others. In an occupational setting, ego needs involve a personal feeling that the content of the job is worthwhile and that others recognize this worthiness.

5. *Self-Fulfillment Needs* These needs Maslow defines as the "desire to become more and more what one is, to become everything one is capable of becoming." They are entirely an individual choice; the individual sets and attains his own goals to his own levels of satisfaction. Full personal potential can be realized in any occupation. It matters not whether a person is a lawyer, secretary, corporate president, janitor, professor, or mother when seeking self-fulfillment. What counts is the drive to be effective in that endeavor.

While need theory assumes that lower needs are the most primitive and urgent, it also implies that attaining higher needs is indicative of growth and development by the individual. The passage from one level to the next is not automatic. On occasions an individual may be forced to forfeit safety to fight for food or to sacrifice social needs in order to ensure safety.Such backsliding or even being stuck at a level below expectation leads to frustration. Reactions to frustrations range from trying harder to giving up. In either case, until the obstacle is overcome and the need tension is relieved, a person remains emotionally stunted. Thus need theory suggests that a role of management is to assist employees in achieving (and recognizing they have achieved) their level of need maturity, and that the manager's reward is a more competent organization plus his own maturity.

17-3.3 Two-Factor Need Theory

Another explanation of how needs influence behavior has been advanced by Frederick Herzberg.[5] This theory is often referred to as the *two-factory theory of motivation* and is more job-oriented than Maslow's need hierarchy. Herz-

[5]F. Herzberg, B. Bausner, and B. Snyderman, *The Motivation to Work*, New York: John Wiley & Sons, Inc., 1959.

berg suggests that factors influencing behavior on a job can be classified into two categories: *maintenance factors* and *motivational factors*. The elements involved in each of the factors are displayed in Figure 17–5. According to the theory, the factors have the following characteristics:

1. Maintenance factors are needs which do not increase motivation when they are satisfied, but do detract from motivation when they are not satisfied. They are associated with general conditions in the work environment, not the work itself. For example, for most people, a clean place to work and air conditioning are appealing enough to be maintenance factors.

2. Motivational factors are high-level needs which contribute to strong motivation when satisfied, but do not necessarily lower morale when not fulfilled. They are closely related to a job, its work content, and its position in the organization. Example: a chance for promotion within the organization will appeal to most people. Also, a challenging assignment such as having to survey an entire marketing area and write a report would be motivational to a marketing major.

3. An individual whose behavior is influenced by motivational factors is likely to be content with less than complete satisfaction of the maintenance factors, but the reverse is not true. Example: let us take the case of the person, again, who is motivated by a chance for promotion. As long as he feels that he has an opportunity to be promoted, he will not be unduly concerned about whether or not the air conditioning is there or whether it works at 100 percent efficiency if it is there. On the other hand, the person who cares only about air conditioning and a clean place to work and has no ambition to be promoted within the organization may be very unhappy if these conditions are not met.

Thus, a highly motivated person will continue to be productive when some of his work relationships are not ideal, while a person striving to satisfy just his maintenance factors is easily bothered by any deficiencies in the work environment.

MOTIVATIONAL ↑ 1. Achievement
FACTORS   2. Advancement
(Factors that   3. Recognition
increase mo-   4. Responsibility
tivation when   5. The work itself
satisfied)   6. The possibility of growth

MAINTENANCE   1. Company policies and administration
FACTORS   2. Interpersonal relations with supervisors
(Factors that   3. Interpersonal relations with subordinates
cause dis-   4. Interpersonal relations with equals
content when   5. Job and financial security
not   6. Personal life
satisfied)   7. Quality and competence of supervision
                   8. Salary level
                   9. Status associated with work environment
↓   10. Working conditions

Figure 17-5 Positive and negative factors affecting motivation.

17-4 FROM THEORY TO PRACTICE

Theories provide a framework by which we can view happenings around us and better understand the reasons behind the happenings. Need and goal theories direct attention to certain aspects of behavior that otherwise would be overlooked or deemed unimportant. They help explain some actions that seem awkward or hard to understand. Not everyone agrees completely with the theories, however, particularly the two-factor motivation concepts. Lack of agreement is surely not serious. It is quite predictable for a subject so open to appraisal. But it does serve to remind us that we do not have all the answers. Need and goal theories may seem to be so simple and logical as to not require explanation. While this very simplicity appeals to many people, ways of converting the theories to practice are not directly apparent nor simple to undertake.

In addition to setting a reference framework, theories should also serve as a foundation for erecting operational plans. In the following sections we will consider several motivational methods that draw on needs and goal concepts. Just as the theories have been questioned, so the plans designed to implement the theory concepts have been criticized. Again, criticism should not condemn the plans; it should serve only as a precaution.

To get an idea of the difficulties involved in motivation, try to solve the age-old problem of how to inspire students to learn. The theories about motivation help but do not fully explain students' behavior. It is obvious that studying is difficult with an empty stomach, under uncomfortable conditions, or in sickness or fear. The importance of social contacts with other students is also apparent. These observations could be classified as satisfying the physiological, safety, and social needs or the maintenance factors. Yet we know that when these needs are met many students still balk at education. Perhaps theory Y should govern the thinking of teachers as they relax rules and encourage pupils to see the advantages to be gained and the challenges of education. Maybe more emphasis should be given to recognition for high achievement, the fulfillment gained from knowledge that extends personal horizons, or the satisfaction and growth obtained from the act of studying. But how?

When you think back over your own schooling you can probably recall instances when most of these motivational techniques were tried on you and your fellow students. Some got through and some didn't. Which ones got through differed among individuals. The motivating impact varies with the situation at the time and the state of maturity of the individual. What works once may fail on the next application. The same irregularities plague all motivation methods. What works for one manager fails another. Each of the following plans has enthusiastic advocates and each has disillusioned detractors. The art of management includes knowing what is available and then adapting it knowledgeably to fit the given situation.

Perspective 17D   DO CHANGES IN WORKING HOURS MOTIVATE?

Two responses by American industry to the perceived desire of employees to have more control over their destinies are the 4-day work week and adjustable work schedules. The pros and cons of both work patterns are still debated, but it appears that the use of flexible working hours is increasing, while the 4-day work week is losing popularity.

Attention to the *four-day, 40-hour workweek* (4/40) picked up in the late 1960s and may have peaked in the seventies. A report by the American Management Association in 1972 predicted that a sizable proportion, if not a majority, of workers would be working a 4-day week within 10 years. Since then, other surveys have indicated that the popularity of a 4/40 arrangement may not be as great as originally expected. Some advantages and disadvantages are listed below.

1. *Advantages*
- The 3-day "off" periods promote improved morale and physical health.
- Extended days allow overlapping between shifts to provide double manning during the busiest periods.
- Actual productive time is increased because a longer period exists between start-up and shut-down activities.
- 4-day weeks reduce commuting time and energy usage. Absenteeism is also reduced by the extra day off to take care of personal business.
2. *Disadvantages*
- Unavailability of particular personnel during the "fifth" day.
- Longer workdays may cause lower efficiency during the last hours of each 10-hour period. Also, some businesses are geared to 8-hour service requirements.
- Shorter evenings limit participation in certain activities.
- Extended "off" periods encourage many workers to seek second jobs, thereby canceling any morale and health advantages. Also, overly ambitious 3-day weekends may detract from work performance.

Flexible working hours, or *flextime,* allow individual workers to determine within limits the hours they will work each day. Typically, an employee can decide when to arrive at work within a two-hour period—say, between 7:30 AM and 9:30 AM in winter and 7 to 9 AM in summer. He will then be on the job for the next 8¼ hours, which includes 45 minutes off for breaks and lunch. Start times may vary from day to day.

The advantages to employees arise from being able to work according to their own rhythm. Morning rush hours can be avoided, guilt feelings from tardiness are eliminated, and time can be arranged to participate in activities of personal importance. Companies receive the benefits associated with a happier work force—lower absenteeism and turnover, decrease in overtime pay required, and an increase in productivity. And best of all for the companies, the benefits are gained at very little expense—some administration costs for scheduling or time keeping and supplementary heat or light bills.

The move toward flexible working hours has been underway in Europe for several years. An estimated 40 per cent of Switzerland's work force and about a quarter of the workers in West Germany use flextime. In the United States, government workers are the main users. One difference in the U.S. and European flextime systems is that European workers are usually allowed to build up overtime hours and "bank" them for extended vacations from work at full pay. Few U.S. companies allow workers to decide when they want to work overtime stints in order to build up a reserve of worked hours to trade for future absences.

17-4.1   Job Enlargement/Enrichment

Job enlargement has been successful in combating boredom in many repetitive work situations. It is not an automatic cure, but it is an alternative that has often proved capable of improving motivation and productivity with a modest investment in facilities. A token effort is seldom rewarding; a job enlarged by just having a worker fill a larger crate of melons than he had filled previously is a frivolous application. True job enlargement seeks to enrich a job in variety, interest, and significance.

In outward appearance jobs may be expanded horizontally and/or vertically. A horizontal expansion increases the number and variety of operations assigned to an operator to provide him with "a natural unit of work," one that reveals his contributions. Vertical enlargement brings the operator into the planning, scheduling, organizing, and inspecting responsibilities associated with his work. Less apparent, though still important, aspects of job enlargement include attention to group activities of operators and individual indoctrination of how each person's work is part of the total productive process. A worker may be taught how to do several related jobs besides his own, partly so that he can swap or fill in and partly so that he can know the other job responsibilities. While the focus of job enlargement is on the scope and content of work, the thrust is toward worker satisfaction.

Job enlargement, particularly vertical enlargement, embodies many of the concepts of job enrichment. Both methods seek to involve workers more intimately with their work. The difference is one of emphasis; job enrichment attempts to bring the job content up to challenge the skill level of the worker hired to do the job.

Herzberg, a strong proponent of job enrichment, stated the following in his article "One More Time: How To Motivate Employees," *Harvard Business Review,* January-February, 1968:

Not all jobs can be enriched, nor do all jobs need to be enriched. If only a small percentage of the time and money that is now devoted to hygiene (motivational factors), however, were given to job enrichment efforts, the return in human satisfaction and economic gain would be one of the largest dividends that industry and society have ever reaped through their efforts at better personnel management. The argument for job enrichment can be summed up quite simply: If you have someone on a job, use him. If you can't use him on the job, get rid of him, either via automation or by selecting someone with lesser ability. If you can't use him and you can't get rid of him, you will have a motivational problem.

17-4.2 Managerial Grid

The style of leadership employed by a manager undoubtedly affects motivation and employee behavior. Just how physical and mental traits or different styles of personal behavior affect leadership has long perplexed both management scholars and practitioners. As with motivation, many theories have been proposed. We will consider just one approach of recent vintage that has been widely applied for training individuals and groups.

The *managerial grid* concept is based on research into the personal behavior of leaders and is best known for its application to management development programs.[6] Part of its success is due to the graphic format used to focus attention on different styles of leadership. The appropriately named managerial grid is depicted in Figure 17–6. Each intersection represents different leadership characteristics. Descriptions of leaders classified by the four extreme positions and the center of the grid are shown in the diagram.

Leadership can be defined as the process of influencing followers to accept direction and control. In the grid, leaders are classified as to what degree they are production-oriented and people-oriented. Research has suggested that higher production can be expected from groups led by an employee-centered manager—one who builds effective groups with high performance standards by fully communicating work objectives to subordinates and then allowing them considerable freedom in the way the work is

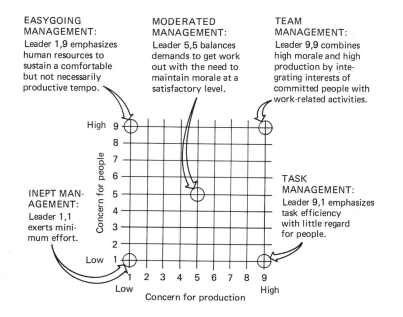

Figure 17-6 The managerial grid.

[6]R. R. Blake and J. S. Mouton, *The Managerial Grid*, Houston, Tex: Gulf Publishing, 1964.

to be accomplished. It appears, then, that a leader who exhibits 9,9 characteristics is the ideal person for any supervisory position. Assuming that an ideal leader should indeed devote high concern simultaneously to both people and production while concurrently satisfying both superiors and subordinates, it is obvious that such leaders are rare. Proponents of the managerial grid suggest that programs based on the grid can assist leaders to move toward a 9,9 classification.

Participants in a managerial-grid program study ways to improve individual effectiveness for one-to-one relationships, team skills for getting maximum results from joint efforts, intergroup relations for solving problems between organized groups, and corporate culture for analyzing work and introducing changes. Much of the success of these programs comes from using company personnel, not outsiders, to run the programs. The training must involve all levels of management. The conceptual framework provided by the grid tends to encourage a common reference theme for discussions.

17-4.2 Management by Objectives

Management by objectives (MBO) is a managerial motivation technique that has received worldwide attention. It has acquired a legion of advocates from all types of industries and government agencies since Peter F. Drucker first introduced the concept in *The Practice of Management* (New York: Harper & Brothers, 1956), saying, ". . . management by objectives and self-control may legitimately be called a 'philosophy' of management. It rests on an analysis of the specific needs of the management group and the obstacles it faces. It rests on a concept of human action, human behavior, and human motivation."

According to Drucker, MBO is especially valuable to managers because it allows them to control their own performance. This feature contributes to stronger motivation by satisfying higher motivational factors.

George Odiorne, another speaker for MBO, suggests that the MBO process aids motivation of all participants through having superior and subordinate managers jointly identify common goals, carefully define them, and together monitor progress toward achieving results.[7] Need satisfaction is theoretically simplified when a goal is distinctly evident and progress is obvious to all. Intuitively we can sense that a person is more enthusiastic when he can plainly see his goal and how fast he is progressing toward it. By coordinating personal goals with the aims of the administrative unit, participants gain added incentive to improve work performance.

The implementation of an MBO program includes the following operational steps:

1. A meeting between a superior and subordinate is arranged to discuss goals for the subordinate that conform to the organization's goals as explained by the superior.

[7]George Odiorne, *Management by Objectives,* New York: Pitman Publishing Corp., 1965.

2. The subordinate takes the lead in establishing priorities for his duties that will support the organization's priorities. The superior and subordinate jointly agree to what is expected during the operating period, what criteria will be used to measure accomplishments objectively, the need to acquire any special resources, and dates for review of accomplishments.

3. Subsequent meetings between the subordinate and superior are held to discuss progress on the goals and any modifications that might be necessary due to changes in other parts of the organization.

4. All agreements on objectives and performance appraisals are mutually committed to writing for use in reviews and merit evaluation procedures.

Figure 17–7 shows both the way objectives are integrated and the flow of information in the MBO process. A superior draws his objectives from the organization's policies. The tactics required to implement his objectives involve actions by his subordinates. Their accomplishments then are his accomplishments and, correspondingly, his goals are their goals. These linkages between goals and accomplishments carry through all managerial levels of the organization, becoming more detailed and output-oriented as they approach the firm's actual production levels.

Management by objectives, in common with other techniques designed to improve leadership and motivation, has plus and minus aspects. Looking at

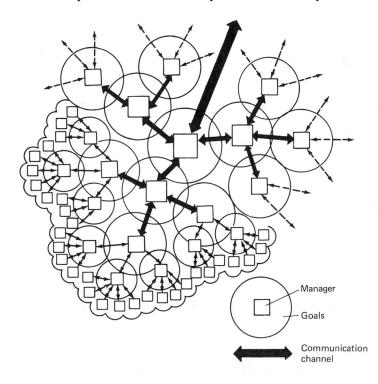

Figure 17-7   Relationship of goals to channels for communicating guidelines and results.

the negative side first, MBO programs prove unproductive if the higher levels of management are not sufficiently convinced of its value to devote the time needed to make the superior-subordinate exchanges useful. And the exchanges, including preparation and reviews, do consume substantial blocks of time. The associated paperwork also adds to the administrative burden.

Points on the positive side for MBO programs include:

1. Improved personnel development through setting goals at the limit of current capabilities to encourage growth

2. Improved communications resulting from scheduled appraisal sessions where key aspects of the work are ensured consideration by the previously agreed-upon agenda for performance reviews

3. Improved perspectives for both superiors and subordinates as a result of counseling that purposely looks at both sides of each situation

4. Reduced anxiety by subordinates about their jobs because they are kept up to date about how superiors feel toward their work performance

5. Greater objectivity in rating work performance because the identification of goals includes establishing quantitative means to measure progress

6. Higher morale resulting from the opportunity to help decide what is included on a job and from recognizing how the job content contributes to meaningful objectives

Drucker got right to the core of the implementation issue when he stated, "And yet the ultimate test of management is business performance." Motivation is a difficult concept to grasp, as we noted at the beginning of this chapter, yet it continues to preoccupy managers because its effects always influence business performance.

17-5 REVIEW QUESTIONS

1. What is morale? Is high morale always desirable in the working force of an organization?

2. What is the purpose of employee attitude surveys? How can they be used to improve morale?

3. What are the conclusions that can be drawn from the Hawthorne experience?

4. Which factors do you personally believe cause particular satisfaction or dissatisfaction in working at a job?

5. In theory X, what are the assumptions a supervisor makes about his workers? Are these assumptions realistic?

6. What are the two factors of the two-factor need theory? Which of the two is usually more influential to work performance?

7. In what ways do 4/40 or flextime schedules contribute to higher morale?

8. What is the difference between job enlargement and job enrichment?

9. What are the two ingredients which characterize a supervisor's behavior in a managerial grid context? What do grid values 1,9 and 9,1 mean?

17-6 TOPICS FOR DISCUSSION

1. The viewpoint which Douglas McGregor calls theory X seems all too common in industry. Relate an experience during which you were supervised on a job (or in class) by this method and report your feelings. Did the supervision experienced give you the reactions McGregor reports? How would you have supervised?

2. Most writers assume that the individual person will have difficulty in expressing what he really wants from his job. With regard to the first job you expect to hold after completing this course, express those conditions which you expect to find which will make you dissatisfied, that is, your negative wants. What could be done about them?

3. Why do you think some surveys of workers' wants report wages and security most important while others by equally competent research directors report these of little signifance when compared with growth opportunity and chance for advancement?

4. Most motivation and worker-sentiment treatments in current management manuals make liberal reference to the Western Electric studies which were discontinued in 1932. Are these 50-year-old results still valid? What influences may have changed worker sentiments?

5. Case 17A: *Nowheresville*
An experimental nuclear plant is to be built on a small isolated island. The purpose of the installation is partly to produce power, but mostly to investigate new methods of power generation and new techniques for using hot waste water from the nuclear reactors. The technically sound but unproved power-generating process is not considered dangerous. Innovations to dispose of unwanted cooling water include using it to heat large ocean pens for raising fish and trying other means of aquaculture. Both endeavors require scientists to conduct and evaluate the experiments plus a skilled staff to operate the installation.

The plant will be of the latest design, and living facilities will be constructed on the island for all staff and their families. No expense will be spared in providing comfortable homes and other conveniences, such as a small shopping center and recreation hall. Children, however, will have to be boarded at schools on the mainland.

It is apparent that the salaries will have to be considerably higher than the industry average to attract and hold qualified people. Probably additional incentives will be necessary to get and keep these people on the island.

Questions

List additional incentives that might be offered to attract and maintain a satisfied work force.

6. Case 17B: *The Cost of a Pinch of Motivation*
A personnel manager and a manufacturing manager became spokespersons for two factions in an executive conference. The original question dealt with the preparation of budgets and justification of expenditures. The production manager argued that all activities and every program should be evaluated strictly on dollar and cents, benefit to cost ratios. He contended that other departments in the organization were spending too much on frills and were reluctant to accept real accountability controls because they could not substantiate their expenses in terms of money saved or money earned.

Counter arguments came from many support departments. They claimed that their activities were necessary to sustain the manufacturing operation, but the benefits could not be measured directly, as could be done in production activities. The personnel manager mentioned the activities designed to build morale such as the company newspaper, recreation program, occasional parties, and payroll fringe benefits. He said it was not possible to measure these factors but that they assuredly contributed to better production. He challenged the manufacturing manager to get along without such features as the newspaper, the landscaping and care of the lawns and grounds, the new rug in the president's office, and the company-sponsored golf tournament that the manufacturing manager had just competed in.

Questions

1. Prepare a reply by the manufacturing manager.

2. Prepare a rebuttal to the manufacturing manager's reply.

7. Case 17C: *Measuring Morale*
Eliot D. Chapple and Leonard R. Sales discuss management's interpretation of morale in *The Measure of Management*, New York: The Macmillan Co., 1961:

The relationship between productivity and human relations was conceived very simply as the presence or absence of this morale factor.

Security Factors: A decent living, a safe future
Job security, employment stabilization (45%)
Compensation (base pay) (28%)
Benefits: insurance, pensions (24%)
Profit-sharing plans (16%)
Vacations and holidays with pay (16%)
Company medical aid programs (10%)
(Lower ratings for frequency and method of paying, dismissal compensation, extra
   compensation (bonuses), savings plans, accident prevention programs, etc.)

Opportunity Factors: A chance to get somewhere
Opportunities for advancement (31%)
Promotion from within company (11%)
Employee merit-rating procedures (10%)
(Lower ratings for suitable placement, training and education, job-evaluation
   plans, employee suggestion systems, etc.)

Human Relations Factors: Recognition and communication
Supervisor's temperament and personality (16%)
Company attitude toward employees (14%)
Quality of supervision (10%)
[Lower ratings for contact with company executives, type of union leadership, per-
   sonnel counseling, social and recreational activities, music on job, smoking privileges,
   information services (bulletins), friendly attitude among employees, etc.]

Human Dignity Factors: Doing something worthwhile
Informing of success and failure (20%)
Type of work (19%)
Working conditions (14%)
Working hours per day or week (12%)
Employee eating facilities (11%)
(Lower ratings for rest periods, company's reputation with public, tools and equipment
   furnished, employment of mixed races, transportation to work, leaves of absence,
   location of plant, etc.)

Thus, morale was used to explain good or bad organizational results, much the same way physicists once used the concept of the ether. Not knowing how electromagnetic energy was transmitted, it was satisfying, if not very useful, to assume that some mysterious element—ether —provided the medium. Not understanding why employees fail to do their best, it was reassuring to speak of "low morale."

When it came to measuring this elusive but potent factor, management turned to some of the traditional assumptions of the labor economists, e.g., the employee derives certain quantities of satisfaction from each of the elements in the work situation: wages, working conditions, supervision, coworkers, type of work, etc. Added together, it was assumed, these satisfactions made up his or her morale. . . .

Attitude questionnaires developed by both companies and consultants as measuring scales have been produced in numbers to take these readings. Vast sums are expended annually in their processing, although systematic, impartial analyses of the results fail to show any correlation between these attitudinal scores and employee job performance.

Excerpts from an attitudinal survey made over 35 years ago (1944) by the National Industrial Conference Board are given in the table on page 506. The data were collected from six large companies whose employees were asked to give the five most important factors concerning job satisfaction. Only categories receiving a response of more than 10 per cent are included.

Questions

1. Comment on the value of the attitudinal survey displayed in the table with respect to the views expressed by Chapple and Sales.

2. Compare the results of the survey with Maslow's and Herzberg's need theories.

3. Do you think the same results would be obtained today using the same survey? Why?

8. Case 17D: *Office Electronics, Inc.*
This well-known New England manufacturer of automatic office equipment felt that a great deal of time was being wasted by machine operators waiting for setup people to adjust machines, by setup people waiting for supervisors to read blueprints, by supervisors waiting for staff specialists to provide service, and by general management in acquiring and using operating reports. As an experiment, operators' jobs were enlarged to include machine setup from blueprints, gaging, and final inspection. Each operator was trained to run several different kinds of machines. Assistant foremen took over difficult machine adjustment and complex inspection. Foremen did all planning, designing, hiring, training, and grievance settling. A clerk-dispatcher took over all paper work to free the foremen for team-building personal contacts. Most workers now understand the purpose of their team—to build a unit of the Office Electronics machine—and have learned enough of the operation to make their own decisions. Workers sharpen their own tools, maintain their own machines, keep their own inventory and parts stock, and help "supervise" the rest of the team.

Questions

1. Would you expect this experiment to produce lower cost machines?

2. Would the average worker be more satisfied? How about the former setup people, inspectors, maintenance personnel and staff specialist?

3. What training would have to be given to the foreman, and what kind of incentive system could be set up to encourage him?

4. If this experiment is successful, should it be extended to the other three plants of the corporation which manufacture shoes, greeting cards, and zippers, respectively?

9. Case 17E: *The Round Chain Co.*

A new general manager has been hired by the owners of the Round Chain Co. For five years the profit ratio of the company has been falling. He finds it is a marginal producer in a highly competitive, very mechanized industry. The past year the plant operated at a loss. Maintenance has been neglected, the plant is dirty and in some ways dangerous. Wage scales are lower than the industry or area averages, although because of 6-day, 10-hour operation, employees have taken home satisfactory pay checks. Employees are resentful of this overtime and show very little interest in their work. There is no training course, employee magazine, or recreation program. Most of the foremen have risen from the shop. There is no union.

A banker approached for an operating loan states that it would be best to close down the operation, and the owners are inclined to agree, since they feel the property can be sold profitably. The new general manager believes that if he can raise employee morale, productivity and profits will increase. This may enable the plant to continue in business. Suggest a course of action for the general manager, indicating the timing of the moves to be made. Comment on the probable costs of your proposed action and the results to be expected.

Questions

1. Will there be time for a full-scale industrial-relations program, or can a temporary makeshift program save the plant?

2. Can employee morale be raised in the face of logical reductions in take-home pay?

3. Should the new general manager put this plan into effect himself? If not, who should?

18

MARKETING

Since the effectiveness of an industrial organization is to be judged by its ability to serve and with reasonable profit, the climax of the company effort comes in its marketing activities. Within a few years a company may experience a change of relative position from top rating in the market to one of obscurity. Conversely, it may rise to a point of dominance in its competitive field. This is not mere happenstance nor an act of fate. Every company is faced constantly with the problem of improving its organization consistent with radical and rapid changes of its market and the competitive environment in which it operates. What is the nature of these changes? How can a company equip itself for early detection of changes in market demands? By what alternatives may it seek to meet competition in new-product development and improved effectiveness in distribution and servicing of product? Can ethical and legal standards in advertising be established and enforced to ensure constructive benefits to our society? What principles and procedures can be established by an enterprise to evaluate advertising? These are some of the questions, together with organization of functions, to which attention will be directed in this chapter.

18 MARKETING

18-1 INCREASING PRODUCTIVE POTENTIAL

As technological developments increase the productive potential of people and machines, as discussed in previous chapters, companies look also to scientific research for new products and new markets by which sales volume may be expanded. In this way only can the general economy of the country be maintained. Each company and each employee is a part of this economy. The general economic health of all will be maintained only if technological progress and market expansion go hand in hand.

Many illustrations have been cited to show how American industry has put improved production technology to work for the improvement of the economy and for the welfare of all people. Much of this benefit has been made possible through the lowering of prices and, thereby, the expansion of the market potential. The effective exploitation of this potential, however, requires much different marketing organization and marketing procedures than would be required in serving a smaller or a more geographically restricted market. Consider, for example, the case of a small manufacturer of hardware specially designed to customer specifications. The production of this hardware involves a large amount of handwork operations. The company operates under a conservative marketing policy directed toward the continuance of a small group of customers who want individualized design and high quality and are willing to pay a premium price. Now assume that this manufacturer explores the possibilities of expanding his production through the use of automatic production equipment and the adoption of standard lines of products. He immediately faces an entirely new marketing problem because he must now enter intensively a wide field of distribution geographically and must compete with others for the mass market if he expects to dispose of his increased volume of products. The policies and practices of his competitors will be a strong determining force in the establishment of his own marketing policies. To continue with "small-market" procedures in selling with "big-production" volume will only sound the death knell for the once prosperous small business. This is one of the hazards in the transition from small to large. It is one reason why some businesses elect to remain small.

Fortunately, many manufacturers have elected to put automation to work in service to a mass market and in doing so have brought a larger number of products within the financial means of a larger number of people. It has been estimated, for example, that an automobile of today, built by 1908 methods at today's wages, would cost $150,000. The fact that we can produce it and sell it today at $5,500 is due only in part to improved production methods. This price is also dependent upon a high volume of sales through a national network of sales agencies. Compare, for example, the price of special or experimental models with the price of standard models. One anticipates limited sales; the other is priced to sell in large volume.

As any company looks toward the adoption of automation to improve production, it is faced with the possible alternatives of increasing volume, which in turn calls for increased sales, or of maintaining previous volume but with fewer man-hours of labor. As previously indicated, the second alternative is frowned upon by forward-looking management and by labor unions. Where possible, the first alternative of increased volume is chosen as the one that will reap the greatest long-term benefit. Therefore, the predominant question is: How much can we sell and by what means?

18-1.1 Analysis of Consumer Wants

Marketing executives are recognizing that it is the public that determines product trends. It is becoming increasingly hazardous to invest in high-pressure sales programs unless first it has been determined that people want to buy. We are now in a period where the level of formal education is significantly higher than it was a quarter of a century ago. In some states two-thirds of the college-age population are enrolled in some form of post-secondary education. What does this mean to marketing? We know that with knowledge comes confidence and that confidence breeds individuality. This means that the better-informed customer will be more selective in terms of his own wants, taste, and feelings and less susceptible to "follow-the-leader" psychology.

It is not easy to find out what people want. We cannot depend upon asking them because experience has shown that people cannot be expected to be articulate about what they want. Instead, the consumer analysts search for indirect cues. It is known from studies of history that current consumer taste and feeling in the design of exterior appearance follows a common pattern in the popularity of contemporary artists, architects, interior designers, and fashion designers. Therefore a manufacturer of furniture may study the work of the leaders in these other fields, find the common elements of such factors as line and color, and take his cue for his own product development and marketing plans. The trend toward the compact car, with its simple clean lines, could have been anticipated much earlier had the big-three automobile manufacturers studied architectual trends in home building and interior design of homes and furnishings. To be sure, these cues are checked by various types of consumer surveys at the points of sale, but largely for purposes of verification and the clarification of details.

The 1980s may be recorded in business history as the decade of the consumer. Spurred by the bold efforts of Ralph Nader in his crusade for automobile safety, public attention in the late 1960s was focused on the products offered by manufacturers. Packaging policies and deceptive advertising claims were questioned. Service industries were brought into the fray by attacks on shoddy workmanship and certain practices such as credit policies, which culminated in "truth in lending" legislation. Finally, the nationwide concern for environmental protection unleashed critical reviews of almost all phases of the supplier-consumer interface. Chemical contamination from pesticides and certain food additives resulted in bans on some products. Public sentiment forced other products off the market, and the power of the consumer was felt as never before. If the passion for "consumerism" does persist beyond the seventies, all industrial organizations will feel the pressure, and the reaction will assuredly affect marketing policies.

Greater individuality of expression on the part of the informed consumer also results in the demand for greater diversification in products. Retailers are finding that they must stock greater variety of products within the same category in order to satisfy individuality in taste. This greater variety plus rapidity of change results in difficulty in mass production. As a consequence, some manufacturers in some fields are going counter to the general trend of the mass-production line and instead are turning to general-purpose production setups or to specialized production facilities.

Perspective 18A IS THE CUSTOMER ALWAYS RIGHT?

According to Philip Kotler, the United States is in the third wave of consumer movements. The first was fueled by rising prices and culminated with passage of the Pure Food and Drug Act and the Meat Inspection Act in 1906, and the creation of the Federal Trade Commission in 1914. Rising prices again sparked a consumer movement in the 1930s that resulted in the Pure Food and Drug Act being strengthened and enlarging the powers of the Federal Trade Commission. The third and current movement is championed by Ralph Nader with assists from many grass-roots organizations and consumer-oriented Federal agencies. Kotler defines "consumerism" as follows:

Consumerism is a social movement seeking to augment the rights and power of buyers in relation to sellers. To understand this definition, let us first look at a short list of the many traditional rights of sellers in the U.S. economic system:

- Sellers have the right to introduce any product in any size and style they wish into the marketplace so long as it is not hazardous to personal health or safety; or, if it is, to introduce it with the proper warnings and controls.
- Sellers have the right to price the product at any level they wish provided there is no discrimination among similar classes of buyers.
- Sellers have the right to spend any amount of money they wish to promote the product, so long as it is not defined as unfair competition.
- Sellers have the right to formulate any message they wish about the product provided that it is not misleading or dishonest in content or execution.
- Sellers have the right to introduce any buying incentive schemes they wish.

Subject to a few limitations, these are among the essential core rights of businessmen in the United States. Any radical change in these would make U.S. business a different kind of game.

Now what about the traditional *buyers' rights?* Here, once again, are some of the rights that come immediately to mind:

- Buyers have the right not to buy a product that is offered to them.
- Buyers have the right to expect the product to be safe.
- Buyers have the right to expect the product to turn out to be essentially as represented by the seller.

What additional rights do consumers want? Behind the many issues stirred up by consumer advocates is a drive for several additional rights. In the order of their serious challenge to sellers' rights, they are:

- Buyers want the right to have adequate information about the product.
- Buyers want the right to additional protections against questionable products and marketing practices.
- Buyers want the right to influence products and marketing practices in directions that will increase the "quality of life."*

*source: P. Kotler, "What Consumerism Means for Marketers," *Harvard Business Review,* May-June, 1972.

COMMENT   Most people in industry feel that they are honestly serving the best interests of their customers. They are often defensive about the claims of unfair or improper practices aimed at them by consumer advocates. A more progressive attitude is to listen to the demands and treat them as opportunities for improved product development and marketing.

This challenge is made difficult by the need to serve both the immediate and the long-term interests of consumers. Current customers' desires determine which products will sell immediately, while long-term interests determine which products will satisfy future consumers. For instance, in the early 1970s many customers wanted large, expensive automobiles, but it was apparent to some planners that concerns for energy conservation, pollution control, and total transportation expenses would soon create a demand for smaller, more efficient cars. Other long-term marketing considerations include more nutritional value in foods (while maintaining taste appeal), more informative packaging (while upholding design appeal), and trouble-free machines of all types (while retaining price appeal).

Successful marketers are well aware that "the customer is always right" for immediate selling prospects, but long-term consumer confidence depends on satisfying societal expectations.

18-1.2   Controlling Marketing Costs

Marketing costs are made up of such items as advertising and general sales promotion, transportation, packing charges, overhead expenses of various sales offices, service costs, installation costs, and the salaries, commissions, and expenses of salespersons. Until a few years ago, little attention had been given to the analysis and reduction of distribution costs. Since distribution does comprise such a large part of the sales dollar, it is worthy of careful attention and study.

Today, however, management faces a cost problem that is far from academic. No longer is the problem only one of answering the public cry regarding distribution costs. The big issue now is how to reduce total costs in order to bring the price of a product within the reach of a larger market. When a top executive looks at total costs, his eye dwells on the distribution portion because it represents one of the larger portions. He knows that for many years the plant has been driving hard toward the reduction of labor costs through methods improvements. It has made improvements in materials for cost reduction. Has it made the same scientific approach to the reduction of distribution costs? Too frequently the answer is "no." Here, then, lies opportunity.

It is recognized, of course, that management is concerned primarily with *unit costs* rather than total costs. Thus it is found often that increased total sales expenditures that open new markets or further develop old markets may actually reduce unit cost through increased sales volume.

The following points represent some of the means for cost reduction that have been revealed by scientific analysis and experimentation:

1. Concentration of sales calls on the larger potential customers.

2. Reallocation of geographical sales territories for more economical use of salespersons' time.

3. Establishment of financial incentive systems for salespersons.

4. Simplification of internal and external sales orders, particularly if small orders' risk of loss is less than cost of detailed handling controls.

5. Simplification of product lines for reduction in number of variations, thus reducing inventory requirements, packaging, and shipping costs.

6. Closer control over advertising and sales-promotion activities through evaluation as to actual sales effectiveness of these specific activities. For example, advertising copy that shows good results may be repeated at designated intervals, while less effective copy may be discarded.

The control of sales costs is especially difficult because of the wide geographical scattering of sales offices, warehouses, and individual salespersons in the field. As personal contact between supervisor and salesperson or local offices and regional offices becomes by necessity more infrequent, greater reliance must be placed on written reports and forms of communication. These should be two-way communications to serve the felt need of all parties concerned. They should be used as a means of coordination of goals and efforts and as guides to effectiveness rather than tools for mere restriction and discipline. For example, travel-expense reports should be looked upon as information to be used to improve future planning of travel time and expense to produce the greatest possible units of sales with the least possible expense.

A partial list of sales-coordination reports includes:

1. Sales developments as measured against budgeted market objectives

2. Market-research guides to design, price, and customer demand

3. Comparative analysis of sales volume by product, geographical area, and type of customer for the purpose of charting trends and potential growth

4. Comparative profit and cost analyses by products, areas, etc.

5. Analyses of expenses such as advertising, sales promotion, travel, and salaries

6. Routine work and progress reports from salespersons, offices, and districts

The above listing is only a sample to show types of reports. Each company will vary in its report requirements according to its particular needs.

18-2 PRICE-REGULATION CONTROVERSIES

A manufacturer is constantly faced with the problem of maintaining equitable prices for all customers while also attempting to meet the prices of competitors in particular localities.

One of the problems in meeting competition is the difference in freight costs. The buyer considers total cost, including delivery. A purchase by a buyer for a Detroit firm from a seller in California obviously involves higher freight costs than a purchase in Detroit or nearby. The question arises whether the California seller can legitimately reduce his price to the Detroit buyer in order to absorb the extra freight costs.

The problem is complicated by the interest in preventing monopolistic practices and price discrimination on the one hand, and permitting fair and reasonable competition on the other. The element of "intent" plays a part in the decisions on individual cases and further complicates the development of a clear-cut settlement with universal application.

For example, In November, 1956, a Federal Trade Commission examiner ruled that Anheuser-Busch, Inc., of St. Louis, engaged in unlawful competition by lowering its prices in the St. Louis area below those charged in other areas and thereby committed regional price discrimination. The examiner claimed that Anheuser-Busch lowered its prices below those of competitors in order to punish competitors for not raising their prices in the St. Louis area following a general round of wage increases. He claimed a violation of the Robinson-Patman Act in that the intent of the regional discrimination was to lessen competition and create a monopoly. This ruling of the examiner was not a final decision but illustrates the difficulties involved in the application of the law. Regional wholesale price differentials to retailers in the sale of gasoline is common knowledge. Yet all companies, whether beer, gasoline, or capital goods, are faced with the problem of meeting regional competition on the one hand and dealing with all geographic regions equitably on the other.

Another problem of pricing revolves around the practice of manufacturers who attempt to establish minimum prices for the resale of their products by dealers or retailers. The practice was originally advocated by manufacturers of highly individualized, trade-marked, or branded products as a protection against unrestrained price cutting among dealers to whom the products were sold. In some localities now, however, dealers are pressing manufacturers to establish minimum resale prices when the manufacturers would prefer to leave prices open. On the other hand, resale price fixing places severe restrictions on retail distributors who seek through efficiencies to meet the demand for lower distribution costs with consequent lower prices to the public.

18-3 FUNCTIONS OF THE MARKETING DIVISION

The functions of a marketing division are to plan, price, promote, and distribute goods and services to consumers and industrial users. Depending on the structure of the firm, its size, and the nature of its business, the marketing functions include different activities, several of which are described in the following sections.

18-3.1 Market Research

Mention was made in previous chapters of the importance of market research in the development and improvement of a product. Research regarding the technological aspects of a product conducted in the product-engineering section may indicate that it can be produced without undue technical difficulties and with reasonable assurance of satisfactory performance. The next step is to find out from potential users the extent of the demand for the product. This is done through the *preliminary survey.* Then as plans materialize for the actual production of the product, an intensive *market study* is conducted to discover the location of the market and the steps required to sell the product in the face of competition. Many new products and enterprises fail because they are launched on a "guesstimate" of the potential market which is never realized. The cost in time and money of a careful market study is relatively cheap insurance for the larger failures it helps to avoid.

In many instances it may be desirable to have an outside agency do the work. Many professional organizations—marketing specialists, advertising agencies, business-engineering firms—perform this service. Newspapers, magazines, radio and TV networks, and other advertising media make surveys of markets tapped by their circulation coverage; such surveys may be of very great help if adapted to the needs of the manufacturer. Or the company may wish to make its own survey. In that case it may be done by the sales department, a special research department, or by a "task force" of management personnel delegated to do the work.

The immediate object of the study is to arrive at a *sales estimate* on which to base actual production schedules, materials commitments, price and sales terms, and financial requirements. Likewise, it will form the basis for determining the scope of advertising and the nature of the sales campaign. An illustration of the unusual types of problems that can be encountered in market research is the introduction of detergent cleaners to replace laundry soaps. Initial sales were disappointing. An investigation revealed women did not feel their clothes were getting clean because detergents produced no suds. When a redundant ingredient was introduced to produce some suds, sales increased dramatically.

The data provided by the preliminary market survey showing the potential market are widened and deepened through the intensive study to develop the minute details that will be required in the plans mentioned previously. Every effort is made in the study to identify the prospective buyers, learn their circumstances and characteristics, chart the conditions under which they are likely to buy, determine the type of effort necessary to sell to them, discover if and how they are being served by competing firms or with comparable products, and what obstacles the firm will encounter in attempting to distribute the product in the market outlined. No "assumptions" or guesswork in an inquiry of this kind can substitute for the patient collection and study of the most detailed information that can be found.

Perspective 18B   THE OLDEST MARKET

The purchasing potential of the population can be categorized in numerous ways—by occupation, sex, region, marital status, ethnic origin, etc. Age is another obvious one. The youth market receives a lot of attention because of its wealth and faddish nature. The senior-citizen market receives less attention, although it is the fastest growing segment of the population.

During the decade ending in 1977, the over-65 group in the United States increased by almost 20 per cent to 22,000,000, and it will continue to increase to 26,500,000 by the mid 1980s. In evaluating the market potential of this group, several characteristics are prominent:

- Women outnumber men 1.3 to 1.0.
- It is less well educated than younger groups, about two-thirds did not complete high school.
- Incomes are well below the national average.
- Less than 20 per cent of its members are counted in the labor force.
- It exhibits higher than average expenditures for medical supplies, transportation other than automotive, household maintenance, and food consumed at home.

While the characteristics of the oldsters are rather easily identified, the means to tap this market are elusive because its members resist advertising directed to "old people." Part of the reason is that they apparently do not want to be patronized and many of their buying habits are ingrained. However, some marketing strategies are reasonably clear. These include packaging smaller quantities of food in recognition of reduced appetites, smaller households, and limited budgets; labels that use bold graphics and larger than normal print for directions and ingredients; and convenient ways to open containers to assist those who are weak or infirm.

18-3.2   Sales Forecast

The market research conducted by a company plus the analyses of current sales experience and trends form the basis for the construction of a *sales forecast.* This forecast estimates sales volume for each product line by sales territories and for specific periods. Usually, the forecast is projected for a year and then is broken down into quarters or months or even weeks. This forecast represents a commitment on the part of the sales department and each of its divisions of expected sales. It becomes the goal against which the effectiveness of the department will be measured. Furthermore, each sales division and each salesperson of a division has his own share of this goal against which his own performance will be measured. Consequently, each salesperson and his division has a part in planning the forecast. If estimates prove to be too high, he will be censured for inefficient estimating. If estimates are too low for the profitable operation of the company, the management will attempt to determine whether the salesperson, the division, and the entire department are fully exploiting the market potentials in their estimates. It will do this by comparison with its competitors, by the study of general business trends, by considering evidences of consumer expendable income, and by various other means available. The forecast must be documented with adequate research and comparison so that there is reasonable evidence that the estimates are sound (see Chap. 4).

It is expected that circumstances will arise that will necessitate changes in estimates from time to time during the year. Political developments both at home and abroad affect sales. A threat of war may create increased demand, or the same threat may create a scarcity of materials, thus delaying production. Unseasonable weather may affect the demand for seasonal clothing. Developments by competitors may either increase or decrease customer demand. Such changes may cause a revision of forecast with a new 12-month projection broken down into smaller time intervals.

As indicated previously, this sales forecast tells how much income the company can expect. Thus it forms the basis for all planning by the company. For the sales department, it is the key to the planning of all advertising and sales promotion; to the recruitment, transfer, or discharge of sales personnel; to the reallocation of sales territories; to the planning of plant and warehouse facilities; and to all other activities of the department as described in the following pages.

18-3.3 Advertising

Advertising may be divided into two principal types: advertising intended to promote the sale of a particular product and advertising intended for the promotion of an idea. The first type is the one most commonly used over a period of years. It is the type that conveys information regarding quality, price, and general desirability of a named product. It is a direct approach to the customer in an attempt to induce him to buy. This type of advertising is particularly important in introducing a new product to the market.

The second type of advertising which proposes to promote an idea is a more indirect approach to the customer. In many instances it may be intended as a means of keeping the name of the company before the public. Some have termed it "good will" or "institutional" advertising; others call it "publicity"; while the more severe critic may call it "propaganda." Many companies have developed special services, as part of their sales-promotion activities, through which they carry on this kind of work. Lecturers are sent out to appear before women's clubs, service clubs, and various groups of community and business organizations to speak on topics of general interest, content if the only advertising that they get is the announcement that the lecturer is a member of the X Manufacturing Company. Many large organizations, including railroads, the General Electric Company, General Motors, and others, have carried on this type of advertising very extensively for the past number of years.

The selection of media for the promotion of an idea or product is a highly technical matter that should be based on careful, scientific research. Consideration must be given to the geographical area to be covered, the type of buyer to be reached, his habits and customs, and his psychological reactions. Because of its complications, the selection of the media usually requires the services of special research organizations which are equipped with experience and special facilities. Each medium has its special advantages. Newspapers, being a daily custom of the mass of people, are excellent avenues for obtaining immediate action. Consequently they are especially good in the advertising of consumer products such as food and clothing, these being items that are bought frequently and with relatively limited forethought. Magazines, as contrasted with newspapers, hold the attention of the reader and potential buyer for a longer period of time. Consequently they are more appropriate for idea advertising where sustained thought on the part of the reader is required. Outdoor advertising is favored for its geographical selectivity in that it automatically comes to the attention of many of the people who pass it.

There appears to be a growth in the spread of legal and ethical responsibility regarding advertising to a larger number of people in different phases of the work—the manufacturing or retailing sponsor, the advertising agency, the media, and even the professional participants in advertising programs. Fears were voiced that freedom of the press might be endangered by new legal rulings. Various groups claimed immunity for one reason or another. But the really biggest fear arose from the feeling that the scandals and the confusion would stimulate additional legal controls and increased Federal "bureaucracy" in the field of advertising.

The trend toward policing advertisements and sales promotions are exemplified by events in 1969. The center of controversy was cigarette advertising. In the previous year, the five leading cigarette companies had spent a total of more than $186 million on television advertisements and $20 million on radio commercials. Rather than face government regulations, cigarette companies agreed to remove all cigarette commercials from the airwaves by 1971. This decision was called unfair by radio and TV interests because it hurt their revenue while leaving newspapers and magazines untouched. In turn, publishers assured Federal regulators they would not accept a massive shift of tobacco advertising to the print media. Similar concerns occurred in the areas of packaging, labeling, and food additives—especially after the partial ban by the Department of Health, Education, and Welfare on the use of cyclamates. The Federal Trade Commission also clamped down on the lottery game promotions by imposing restrictions to avoid "rigging" and demanding that the astronomical odds against winning the top prizes (often over a million to one) be publicized. Such examples illustrate the legal and ethical problems facing the advertising profession, and they underscore the significance of its responsibilities.

18-3.4 Sales Promotion

Sales promotion as a specialized function may be established as a separate department or it may become a part of the advertising department. The scope of the function itself may vary greatly between companies. For example, in some companies the sales-promotion function may include specialized service and maintenance, or the handling of complaints and adjustments. In other companies where the amount of such service is large, a separate department may need to be established.

Usually sales-promotion materials are thought of as special booklets for distribution to customers, window and counter displays for dealers, and souvenirs and samples. In some instances companies may find it advisable to seek the services of outside agencies for some of these highly specialized materials. This will depend somewhat upon the volume produced and the availability of specialized personnel. In the case of special promotion booklets where copy is the important element it is almost imperative that it be prepared by the advertising department. The Johns-Manville Corporation, for example, prepares instruction books for customers. The material for these booklets must necessarily come from the engineering department working in cooperation with the advertising department. The Cleveland Rock Drill Company produced at one time a small booklet answering questions regarding trouble experienced in operating tools. This is an effective means of attempting to train the users of the tools in proper care and maintenance, thus avoiding complaint and dissatisfaction and consequently promoting future sales among satisfied customers.

Many customers consider it a sales-promotion responsibility to assist dealers in providing service for customers. The automobile industries have, for many years, conducted training courses for repair mechanics. Other companies, particularly those dealing in the manufacture of production machinery, have developed special courses for the purpose of training the maintenance and engineering staff in the proper use and care of the equipment.

The advertising department may carry full responsibility for its sales promotion, or it may share in it as a cooperative undertaking. For example, in the case of training courses for dealers, the advertising department may have the responsibility of preparing the instruction manual for use in the courses, while the sales department or training section of the industrial-relations department may carry the responsibility for the actual conduct of the courses.

Advertising and sales-promotion activities require the assistance of specialists skilled in the techniques of research and promotion within their particular fields. To serve this need, agencies have been organized consisting of groups of specialists—specialists in research, in the preparation of copy, in art, in production, in the selection and contact with media, in radio, and in other specialized functions. To the agency, the manufacturer delegates all or a part of the responsibility of his advertising and sales-promotion campaign. Needless to say, no specialist can properly carry on an advertising campaign for a manufacturer without obtaining close and continued cooperation from the personnel of the various departments in the manufacturing enterprise. Usually the manager of the advertising department in the company acts as liaison officer between the company and the agency. He provides for the services that must come from the engineering department regarding the technical phases of the product to be advertised, from the production division regarding process and operations through which the product passes, and from other departments that can supply specific information needed by the agency to develop effective copy.

In addition to acting as liaison between advertiser and media, the modern agency renders services of both a creative and an advisory nature. These services, standards, and ethics are considerably advanced from the original advertising agencies, which were principally dealers in advertising space. In those days the agent merely bought space from the media and sold it at a higher rate to the advertiser. In fact the form of agency compensation in use today, whereby the agent draws a commission of 15 percent from the media, is a carryover. This usually represents his full compensation except where special advisory services are involved.

The agency in most cases assumes responsiblity for the recommendation of media, the preparation of copy, the making of engravings, arrangements for radio and television programs and talent for those programs, and all other special technical phases.

Recognizing the valuable specialized service that may be obtained from an advertising agency, one might be led to question whether the function of an advertising department can be justified. However, most advertisers go on record proclaiming that an advertising department is essential for efficient operation.

In general, the functions of the advertising department may be classified as follows:

1. Preparation and control of the advertising budget

2. Liaison with the agency

3. Supervising advertising and marketing research

4. Keeping in touch with representatives of important media

5. Cooperation with the sales department and with other departments

6. Distribution of advertising material

7. Production and supervision of sales-promotion material

8. Supervision of copy

9. Merchandising the advertising

10. Administration

18-3.5 Evaluation of Advertising and Sales Promotion

The age-old questions are: How far shall we go with advertising? Where is the point of diminishing return—with a new product and in the maintenance of an established product?

It does not seem possible to give a generalized answer to these questions. First of all, the answer will vary with different products, and with the breadth and type of market selected. Second, the answer must take into consideration the amount of advertising conducted by competitors. Nevertheless, these are items that must be considered. Often the manufacturer will use every means to the fullest in launching a new product, but then he asks, "How much must I continue in advertising to maintain the established volume? If I drop a million dollars of advertising, will I drop more than a million in profits? If so, how long will it take for this loss to occur? What will be the rate of decline in momentum of established sales?"

A large hosiery manufacturer sought answers to these questions through experimentation by geographical regions. It introduced a new brand of hosiery with an extensive advertising and sales-promotion program. The program was conducted by geographic regions in sequence. Every possible means was used to saturate the region with knowledge of the new product. Then all advertising was eliminated for the region, and volume of sales was watched closely. In the first region, sales continued to climb for the first few weeks following the elimination of advertising. The momentum had been established and kept rising. Then after a time the decline started as competitors' advertising moved the customers away. Another splash of advertising was then released and sales again turned upward.

In other regions the company experimented with variations in time span, in amount expended, and in the degree of curtailment. Although, for competitive reasons, the results are not available, this experimentation suggests the interest that exists in testing the benefits from advertising and the points of diminishing returns. With growing competition and smaller profit margins, companies are becoming more unwilling to spend blindly for advertising and sales promotion. These activities must be scientifically evaluated specifically in terms of sales volume.

There are, of course, many ways of checking specific advertising, copy, and promotion activities in terms of customer response. Give-away items and service offers announced in advertising are one way. Code numbers which the customer is asked to use in ordering are another. There are many others. These are especially good in making comparisons of the relative value of different copy, media, and sales-promotion activities.

A nagging dilemma is whether advertising increases the retail price of products without a corresponding increase in product utility. A misdirected or ineffective advertising campaign obviously adds to the cost of a product if it fails to increase sales. Is this added cost passed on to the consumer by higher prices or does the producer bear the loss with lower profits? A successful advertising campaign creates similar questions. High sales should allow savings in production through economies of high volume. When the final balance of production savings to advertising costs favors savings, lower prices might be forwarded to the consumer. However, net savings for one company do not mean that the entire industry has benefited from a particular sales effort; perhaps the increased sales for one company came at the expense of another company rather than by raising industry-wide sales. Roles could be reversed by subsequent campaigns. Thus the question becomes very involved. And it is probably more academic than practical because advertising is firmly established as a fundamental tool of business competition.

Perspective 18C   ADVERTISING IMPACT

From a large-scale economic study of 25 markets in eight European countries conducted over a 10-year period, the following broad conclusions emerged:

1. The economic effects of advertising can be fully understood only in relation to the entire marketing mix. Marketing competitive behavior is a more relevant perspective to be adopted in the analysis of industrial competition. The distinction often made between price and nonprice competition does not seem to accurately reflect actual situations in large-scale markets.
2. Both hostile and friendly analysts of advertising have overestimated the economic power of advertising per se; socioeconomic forces have a more decisive influence. Advertising in general has limited capacity to stimulate total market growth, and purely persuasive advertising is even less effective. Advertising is powerful only when it accompanies more objective tasks, and the content of advertising is more important than the total amount spent on it.
3. In nonexpandable markets, an increase in advertising competition hurts the consumer. The reason stems from a built-in mechanism: since competitive brand advertising causes a reciprocal cancellation effect and since corporate advertising policies tend to be interdependent, advertising expenditures escalate. The objection is not so much that competitive advertising is duplicative, but that it does not benefit the consumer in the long run, as price and quality competition do.
4. Consumer buying behavior is more rational than advertisers assume. In advertising-intensive markets, consumers respond more readily to copy that incorporates tangible persuasive advertising. This kind of response suggests that factual and informative advertising content is welcomed in consumer markets, precisely the point stressed by the consumerism movement.*

*SOURCE: Jean-Jacques Lambin, "What is the Real Impact of Advertising," *Harvard Business Review,* May-June, 1975.

COMMENT   Although generalizations cannot answer specific questions about advertising strategies for a given product, they do expose critical considerations for economic evaluation of advertising effects. Big gaps exist in our knowledge of how advertising works in diverse, large-scale consumer markets: how it affects market share, competition, and consumer buying habits. Until these factors are adequately measured, advertising will retain its mystic image and remain a controversial contributor to the free-enterprise system.

18-3.6 Inquiries and Orders

A significant function of the central and branch sales offices is the handling of inquiries coming from customers by mail, telephone, or telegraph. These inquiries request information regarding a particular product, the date on which delivery can be made, points regarding installation and maintenance, complaints, and many other points of a similar nature. The sales offices usually designate responsibility for this function to a group of specific individuals, frequently referred to as sales correspondents. They must become familiar with the products manufactured and the sales policies pertaining to the distribution and servicing of those products, in order to deal intelligently with inquires received. It is expected that technical questions must frequently be referred to the engineering department for an answer. However, the person receiving the inquiry may assume responsibility for following it through to completion. Many of the inquiries will be directed to a branch office or to a salesperson in the field for a more personal follow-up. In other instances, the sales correspondent may respond to the inquiry, sending a copy of her response to the salesperson assigned to that particular territory.

Frequently the sales correspondent will be responsible for the actual handling of the order. On the other hand, some companies establish a separate order division. The advantage of the correspondent's handling the order is that it centralizes contact between the office and the customer in the checking of specifications, establishing credit, setting delivery dates, and other special problems that may be peculiar to the order. These matters will require clearance with many different departments, such as engineering, manufacturing, credit, and shipping. From the standpoint of efficiency and customer relations these clearances must be centralized.

18-3.7 Servicing

Industry is rapidly adopting the principle that service is an essential part of the sale itself. A manufacturer of production machinery finds it essential to see that his products are properly installed. This not only is a service to the customer but is protection against complaint and general dissatisfaction on the part of the customer, which in the end would operate to the detriment of the manufacturer and his products. Once the equipment is installed, the manufacturer may assume responsibility for instructing the maintenance crew of the customer in the proper care of the equipment. He may also provide a maintenance service over a designated period of time through his special maintenance staff located either at the home office of the company or through its network of branch offices.

At times it is possible for a manufacturer to provide this maintenance service through his salespeople if the product is not so complicated that an unusually large amount of skill is required. For example, typewriter salespeople are frequently trained as repairmen. Typewriter manufacturers' sales offices may extend a 12-month service with each machine sold. Any repairs required during this period are usually minor in nature and can be made by anyone familiar with the parts of the machine. It has been found that customers appreciate the continuity of service on the part of the salesperson and the personal interest that he or she demonstrates through service after the sale.

In the case of more complicated machinery, it is a common practice for a manufacturer to maintain a staff of skilled engineers and mechanics who serve the customer through making necessary repairs and adjustments at the point of installation.

18-3.8 Channels of Distribution

The problem of selecting routes or paths by which the product goes from the manufacturer to the actual user is becoming increasingly complex and will vary in terms of the nature of the product. The manufacturer may choose a direct channel with the consumer. He may go through intermediary trade, known as middlemen, who in general are specialists in the resale of products to consumers. The middlemen may be at several points in the channel—manufacturers' agents (independent of the manufacturer), wholesalers, jobbers, brokers, etc.

In the case of consumer goods, manufacturers have relied almost exclusively upon resale agencies. In some instances a manufacturer may have a limited number of retail stores operating under the name of the company. There appears to be a growing trend to establish distribution centers, owned and operated by the company, by which a central warehouse or distribution pool will service retail outlets of the given geographic area. These outlets may be owned by the company, they may be operated independently under franchise and often with financial backing from the manufacturer, or they may be completely independent of the manufacturer. Several advantages are being sought by these means: (1) The manufacturer is attempting to procure greater emphasis and attention at the retail level toward the sale of his particular line of products, rather than be mixed with his competitors and without special emphasis. (2) He attempts to reduce distribution costs by cutting out some of the middlemen. (3) He seeks to improve the servicing of the product through centralization in a specialty outlet within the community, e.g., Midas stores operating under franchise become specialists in 15-minute installation of automobile mufflers. (4) He strives to establish better control over inventory and speed of delivery with his warehouse centers and their clusters of stores. (5) He is attempting a better programming of distribution to the consumer. The inclination toward this type of operation is brought on not only because of increased competition, but also because of the growing complexity of products, increased variety of products, and increased reliance on the manufacturer for the servicing of products. For example, few general retailers can afford to maintain a staff of service people trained in the intricacies of the great variety of home appliances on the market today. Even the stocking of replacement parts becomes impractical for the average retailer. To return the appliance to the factory for repair may take weeks or months and is a nuisance to the customer and the retailer.

The operation of outlets by the manufacturer, however, is no panacea for all his ills. First of all, the establishment of factory-owned retail outlets cuts him off from independent retailers, who resent his entering the retail field. If he adopts such a plan, generally he must expect to go all the way with it. Many of the consumer goods, especially those of the luxury class, are purchased not on the basis of need, but more by whim or fancy. Selling to this market is considered the job of specialists. The product must be dramatized and demonstrated; a desire for the product must be created since it is not prompted by need. To accomplish this, direct personal contact is an important advantage. Also, the market for consumer goods may be as large, potentially, as the population itself. To contact this vast market, the manufacturer who is first a specialist in production usually prefers to rely upon other agencies for distribution. Needless to say, capital investment is also an item that must be considered in attempting a direct channel between the consumer and the manufacturer. Where volume and inventories are large and prices irregular, manufacturers may wish to free themselves of this financial uncertainty.

Another method of approaching this problem is through the establishment of *manufacturers' branch offices.* These branches are owned and operated by the manufacturer in order to facilitate the distribution of his products through direct contact with the industrial purchaser or the retailer or consumer. The sales branch may have its own warehouse, or several branches may be served by one warehouse or directly from the plant.

Perspective 18D MULTIMARKETING

Producers are always anxious to find new markets for their products. Robert E. Weigand discusses his concept of "multimarketing" to explain the benefits and limitations of selling through multiple channels:

Business people often allude to "my product" or to "the market," suggesting a far more monolithic view of business than is warranted. Companies vary products and marketing channels in order to accommodate real or perceived differences either in markets or in the laws under which businesses must operate. Most businesses sell a variety of products through several channels and to various customers, who may differ in type, in volume purchased, in location, and in other characteristics. . . .

There is an almost unlimited number of ways in which a multimarketer can sell. Unfortunately, the social benefits of multimarketing are difficult to assess, because the views of most business people are profoundly affected by whether they benefit from a particular practice. Some look upon multimarketing as "the free enterprise system working at its best." Others who may be looking at exactly the same data—middlemen are a good example—declare it to be "unjust enrichment by confiscation of markets that rightfully belong to others."*

*SOURCE: R. E. Weigand, "Fit Products and Channels to Your Markets" *Harvard Business Review*, January-February, 1977.

COMMENT Because greater production volumes tend to decrease the per-unit cost of products, marketers scramble to develop more ways to present their wares to potential customers. Countering promises of expanded markets are dangers that limit the practice of multimarketing. Customers may find out that essentially the same product is offered at different prices under different names, and buy only the cheaper version. Distributors may balk at carrying a certain product if they believe that a competitor is getting a better deal from the supplier, or if they feel that the supplying company itself is competing with them.

18-4 ORGANIZATION FOR MARKETING

Attention is now directed to the consideration of possible organization structures by which a marketing department may coordinate and direct its activities in such a way that there will be a continuing stream of orders and services in accordance with the planned sales program. Consideration must be given not only to the functions and personnel of the sales department, but also to the interrelationship of the department with other departments of the company.

18-4.1 Responsibilities of the Marketing Executive

The responsibilities of the marketing executive may be divided generally into three parts: (1) formation of policies; (2) interpretation of policies; and (3) administration of sales activities. The nature of sales activities and the policies governing them will vary widely depending on type of product, diversity of product, nature of the market, size of the company, and economic conditions. Thus it is important that the sales executive be experienced not only in the industry but in the specific company.

MARKETING POLICIES First, policy must be established for the selection of channels of distribution. Will the company sell directly to the users of the product or distribute its products through wholesalers or jobbers? Will it employ its own sales force or use representatives and agents? Second, what price policies will be established? Will discounts be offered? If so, under what conditions? Third, what credit terms will be offered to customers? Fourth, what service policies are to be established? What responsibility will the manufacturer assume for installation and for repair and replacement of parts? Will such service, if offered, be performed from the home office, from regional offices, or through wholesalers?

These are all policy matters requiring thorough investigation and consideration by the marketing executive, who is primarily responsible for the formulation of marketing policy and consultation with others in the division. These will include both staff specialists and salespersons who are in direct contact with the customers and who know their desires and complaints.

The marketing executive will also be expected to seek the counsel of policy-level executives of other divisions directly concerned with sales policy. For example, a toy manufacturer established a credit policy whereby customers would be billed October 1 of each year for orders placed and delivered between January 1 and July 1. The suggestion for this policy originated in the production division as a possible means toward the more equal distribution of production throughout the year, at the same time relieving the storage problem. The business is highly seasonal, the Christmas trade being the predominant market. It was proposed that the cost of this unusually liberal credit policy would be more than offset by savings through equalized production and less storage requirements. This was, primarily, a marketing policy decision. This policy consideration required consultation, however, with the production division that originated it; with the finance division that would be concerned with the working-capital requirements and the possible losses through cancellation and bad debts; with the legal department regarding the extent of legal commitment by both buyer and seller under such arrangements; with the personnel department regarding the effect on the labor force of more equalized production; with the industrial-engineering department regarding the possible utilization of floor space released by reduction in storage requirements; and with the various departments of the marketing division for a prediction of customer acceptance of the proposed policy.

A marketing policy so widespread in its effect on the various segments of the company would obviously be carried to the executive committee of the company for final review. So, while the marketing executive is responsible for the formation of sales policy, he performs in consultation with all who may be concerned.

POLICY INTERPRETATION   New policies and changes in policies require explanation, illustration, and provision for handling exceptions. It is of primary concern that the administration of these policies shall be fair and consistent in relation to those directly affected by them. The issuance of a handbook or manual stating these policies is probably essential, but it is not enough. Each policy must be discussed and elaborated down through the several organization levels of the division. Each of these levels becomes the interpreter to the next level and subsequently to the customer through written material and personal contact. Such communication and interpretation furnish a means toward accuracy in the application of policies, recognition of exceptions that require separate action, and an avenue through which weaknesses in policies may come to the attention of the marketing executive and result in appropriate policy revision.

ADMINISTRATION OF SALES ACTIVITIES   When we think of sales activities we tend to think only of the salespeople in direct contact with the customer.

We may overlook the fact that even in a retail department store the ratio of salespersons to others who assist them may be 1:2. The nonselling people are assisting in procurement, storage, display, advertising, sales promotion, market research, credit, accounting, handling of complaints, adjustments, servicing, transportation, and other activities essential to effective selling, but they are often overlooked by the casual observer.

It is the responsibility of the marketing executive to promote the coordination of these activities for the greatest possible service to the customer and profit to the company. But it must be remembered that to coordinate is to assist, not merely to control and restrain. For example, Pabco Products, Incorporated, of San Francisco found upon investigation that "only about 30 per cent of salespeople's time was being spent in the actual presence of customers. The remaining 70 per cent was spent, some of it necessarily, of course, in traveling, waiting, answering correspondence, and attending to paper-work details." The company found that salespeople received as much as 18 pieces of mail per day. The result was that the salesperson hastily skipped over correspondence that deserved careful attention and spent needless time on the relatively unessential. But most important was that they were being robbed of valuable customer-contact time. After investigation, the sales administration came to the aid of the salespeople by eliminating or simplifying some of the correspondence and providing office assistance in the sorting and screening of mail. This is only one of many possible illustrations of how administration may help or hinder. Coordination is essential, but its primary purpose is to *assist*.

Another responsibility is sales control. The best marketing policies are of little value unless the sales force applies them. Assuming the salespeople are convinced of the worthiness of the policies, the need still exists to see how well they are followed. Devices such as sales reports, quotas, and compensation reviews are indicators for the control system.

Reports of sales activities are the easiest to evaluate. Quantitative data include expense accounts with the ratio of expense to sales, number or cost of calls with the ratio of customer contracts to sales volume, reports of customer complaints and adjustments, ratio of salesperson's time to order size, and profit or gross margin per sales territory. Less tangible considerations include salespeople's conduct, generation of good will, initiative in developing new approaches, and timely reporting of customer trends or competitors' activities. In evaluating such information it should be remembered that report preparation must be subtracted from the salesperson's actual selling time.

18-4.2   Organization of the Marketing Division

Mention has been made of the levels of organization established for the effective coordination of marketing activities. This organization in its simplest form is shown in the line sales organization of Figure 18–1. Here the manager works in a liaison relationship with other divisions; carries the

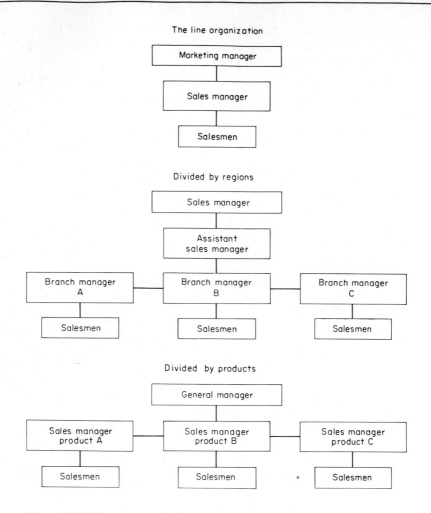

The line organization

Marketing manager

Sales manager

Salesmen

Divided by regions

Sales manager

Assistant
sales manager

| Branch manager A | Branch manager B | Branch manager C |

Salesmen   Salesmen   Salesmen

Divided by products

General manager

| Sales manager product A | Sales manager product B | Sales manager product C |

Salesmen   Salesmen   Salesmen

Figure 18-1 Three types of sales organizations.

responsibility for sales promotion, advertising, market investigations, and contact with selected customers; and through his assistant coordinates the work of salespersonnel.

Figure 18–1 also shows a division in the organization of salespeople by geographic regions, each region or branch headed by a branch manager. As a company grows in its geographic coverage, these branch divisions are established to facilitate the speed and effectiveness of service to customers and to supervise and assist salespersons of the region.

Another type of organization makes division by products. The theory of this organization is that a salesperson specializing in the sale and service of one product or line of products is more effective than a salesperson responsible for several different products or lines. This type of organization is particularly appropriate for the company producing equipment of a complex nature or to customer specifications—equipment requiring extensive knowledge and experience on the part of the salespeople. It is also appropriate for the company producing highly diversified lines for distinctly different markets. Ordinarily this organization would not be adopted by a company that serves a single market. Obviously, to have several salespersons from one company, but with different products, calling on the same customer could lead to confusion.

Chapter 2 described the·need for and development of staff departments to aid the line organization in the many management functions. In the same way the marketing division must have specialized assistance in advertising, market research, customer service, sales promotion, exporting, and various other special functions, some peculiar to a given industry.

Figure 18–2 shows the decentralization of staff departments by branch or product. Each branch or product manager has his own staff departments in addition to the staff departments that report to the sales executive. Some companies have *only* branch staffs or at least do not duplicate in the home office the staffs established in the branches. As shown here, the home-office staff departments carry on service activities for the branch staffs, have liaison with them, but do not have authority over them. They also carry on research development and company-wide programs that can best be centralized in the home office.

In most instances we shall find the advertising manager responsible to the head of the marketing division, although there has been a strong attempt on the part of advertisers to encourage the establishment of a separate advertising division with the advertising manager reporting directly to the president or the general manager. The reason given is that the functions of advertising are expanding to the extent that it includes functions pertaining not only to the sale of goods, but also to other activities such as the promotion of better employer-employee relations and the improvement of the coordination of personnel throughout the internal organization of the company. The advertising department is also being given a great amount of responsibility in public relations. The extent to which the advertising department is given the responsibility in areas other than the direct promotion of sales will carry a direct influence in the decision as to whether the adver-

Figure 18-2 Decentralization of staff departments.

tising department should be a section of the distribution division, whether it should establish direct contact with the policy-making group, and whether it should be in a more independent position to work with the various departments or divisions of the company.

In the organization of the advertising department it is important, so far as possible, to separate the work according to functions, placing individuals in charge of one or more functions. A few illustrations will show how this division and assignment of functions may vary. Figure 18–3(a) makes a very simple division between advertising distribution and advertising production. Figure 18–3(b) groups the functions into three divisions: publicity, sales promotion, and production.

Figure 18–3(c) makes a somewhat different division of functions. Here the division is made in terms of publicity, sales promotion and miscellaneous, and trade service. The trade-service division assumes responsibility for working with dealers and jobbers and for all special exhibits and industrial

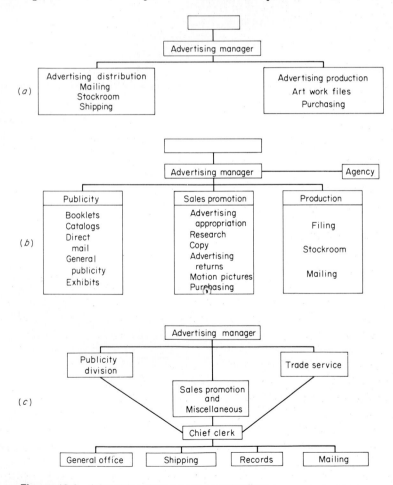

Figure 18-3 Advertising-department organizations.

shows. Serving all three of these divisions is a centralized division operating under a chief clerk and broken down into four subdivisions: general office, shipping, records, and mailing.

18-5   REVIEW QUESTIONS

1. Why is management tending to place greater emphasis on marketing?

2. What are distribution costs? What are some of the means of reducing distribution costs?

3. What are some of the problems faced by a marketing department in the pricing of products?

4. What functions are performed by the marketing department? Of what value are the results of a market research?

5. Of what importance is advertising to the introduction and maintenance of sales for a product in the competitive market?

6. Comment on the following statement: The results of experiments to evaluate the effect of advertising on product sales indicate that advertising is a necessary evil.

7. What are two types of advertising?

8. How is a product distributed? What factors favor the trend toward factory-owned outlets? What are its limitations?

9. In the line type of organization, what are the two ways of structuring a marketing department? Where is each form used?

18-6   TOPICS FOR DISCUSSION

1. What basic changes or trends in marketing policies and practices can be expected to result from accelerated change in products and the greater variety of products demanded by consumers?

2. Since the cost of distribution at the wholesale and retail levels constitutes such a large portion of total cost, manufacturers may be expected to give increased attention to possible distribution-cost reductions. Suggest some of the points in typical distribution processes where certain specific changes might be contemplated in the cost-reduction effort.

3. Indicate your opinion of the appropriateness of minimum-resale-price maintenance as a principle in our American economy. What possible economic and social changes in the future might tend to influence the success or failure of attempts at price regulation?

4. "Officials of an office equipment manufacturer troubled by narrowing profit margins recently made a careful study of a list of the company's customers. Then they placed each customer in a category numbered from 1 to 26, corresponding to the volume of business normally obtained from the account. The number indicated how often salespersons should call on customers—once a week for those in the first category, which contains the largest customers, for example, and only twice a year for those in category 26.

   "The purpose of this elaborate screening process: To facilitate concentration on the big accounts that bring in the bulk of sales and to avoid wasting too much time and money on small accounts whose orders don't amount to much and contribute little to profits."[1] Comment on possible variation in conditions affecting application of these conclusions.

5. Comment on the probable relative effectiveness of voluntary vs. government control of ethical practices in advertising. What have been the experiences in other fields? What are the principal points of difficulty in attempts toward enforcement?

6. Critics of advertising claim that advertising increases the cost of distribution and consequently increases the price that must be paid by the consumer; that advertising is an uneconomic practice from a broad social point of view; and that, if the cost of advertising were converted into the improvement of quality of the product or if the cost of advertising were eliminated with a resulting reduction in the price of the product, the consumer would benefit and the manufacturer would gain through increased sales.

   Advertisers contend that history does not support these claims of the critics. They point to instances where advertising has over a period of years increased volume with resulting decrease in price.

   Both of these opposing points of view appear logical, but how can they be reconciled if true? Can other means be suggested for the dissemination of information that will promote the necessary volume in the sale of products but with less economic waste?

7. In consideration of the huge advertising appropriations of larger companies, how can a small company hope to compete for attention in the presentation of its name and its products to the public? Will advertising eventually eliminate the small manufacturer? Is it possible that advertising of "name" products may hinder the introduction of new competing products? What recourse does the small manufacturer have against this possible development?

8. Case 18A: *Sears, Roebuck and Company*[2]
The following case is presented as an application of the merchandise center (or pool) form of distribution and to call attention to the probable advantages and disadvantages connected therewith. Although in this case the application is to factory-retail relations in distribution of consumer goods, the general plan is also applicable in many ways to the distribution of all forms of merchandise.

Sears, Roebuck and Company is one of the largest distributors of consumer merchandise in the United States. Most of its merchandise is procured either on the open market or by contract with independent manufacturers. Some is produced by company-owned plants, although this by policy is held to a minimum and is used only when adequate supply of given quality and cost cannot be procured elsewhere.

The company has developed five merchandising pools for the decentralization of distribution of a large percentage of the fashion (apparel) merchandise to its stores in the more heavily populated areas of the United States. Each pool serves from 70 to 80 stores in a territorial area, e.g., the Southeastern area of the United States, extending from the Southern border of Virginia to the Gulf of Mexico.

The five centers distribute many millions of dollars' worth of merchandise annually. Each has its general manager and four department managers divided according to classification of product. Each department has an assistant who studies the merchandise wants and habits of the stores of the region and requests merchandise accordingly from the parent buying staff. Apparel is highly seasonal, and style changes are frequent and difficult to predict.

The merchandise center is responsible for the disbursement of the proper type of merchandise for each store, although the store does have the privilege of issuing a "stop order" or special request on any particular item. However, the stores do not buy anything direct from source in these merchandise classifications.

[1]*Wall Street Journal,* Sept. 29, 1960, p. 1.

[2]Presented with permission of Sears, Roebuck and Company.

Each department head in each retail store is expected to complete a sales and stock report every Saturday showing sales for the week and stock on hand. He also reports comments on the selling trends in regard to items in the department—color preferences, styles, etc. These reports are supposed to be mailed on Saturday to reach the pool on Monday, thus enabling the pool to replenish the store stock within the week.

A number of problems have arisen. Since these weekly reports are prepared by hand, they are very time-consuming and subject to human error. As a result, the department managers on busy Saturdays are at their desks counting tickets and doing the mathematics of the weekly sales and stock reports, when they more profitably should be supervising the selling floor. It is estimated that about 8 hours' time of the department manager is required for the preparation of these reports even without major problems and discrepancies.

The inaccuracies to be expected from human error distort the stock and sales picture, resulting in under- or overshipping to the retail store. Even a small distortion in a single store, when multiplied by hundreds of stores, can do serious damage to the profit picture.

The company currently is experimenting with several basic changes which it hopes will result in significant improvements, some already proved in one of the territories.

Questions

1. Enumerate the probable advantages the company hoped to achieve through the original establishment of the merchandise centers.

2. Referring back to Chapter 3 on Managerial Controls and Chapter 11 on Inventory Control, offer suggestions as to how the problems in regard to the sales and stock reports might be minimized.

9. Case 18B: *Distribution Costs of Product X*

It is difficult at times to understand how distribution costs of the manufacturer, the wholesaler, and the retailer accumulate, and are calculated into a total percentage of retail value. For example, assume that product X sells at a manufacturer's recommended retail price of $98. Assume also that this allows a markup for the retailer of 40 per cent of retail value and a markup for the wholesaler of 20 per cent of wholesale value. The manufacturer's analysis in this case shows that his own distribution costs of product X amount to 10 per cent of his factory price.

Questions

1. What is the factory price of product X to the wholesaler?

2. What is the total cost of distribution (in amount and as a percentage of retail value) including the distribution costs of the manufacturer and the markup of the wholesaler and the retailer?

10. Case 18C: *The Coles Manufacturing Company*

The Coles Manufacturing Company for many years has been engaged in the manufacture of electrical appliances for the consumer trade. At one time the company converted 75 per cent to the manufacture of various types of insulated wire under subcontracts with manufacturers of aircraft and communications equipment.

Later the company returned to its appliance business to take advantage of the new consumer demand. However, its product-development division continued to experiment in the development of new manufacturing processes and with new materials that might reduce the cost of production of insulated wire. As a result of this developmental work the company is now ready to return to the wire business with the announcement of a new product which it feels can undersell the market.

Distribution of electrical appliances manufactured by the company has been entirely through a separately owned and separately organized distributing organization specializing in electrical appliances of several different manufacturers. The Coles Manufacturing Company is now faced with the necessity of decision regarding the distribution of insulated wire to the manufacturing trade on a job-order basis.

Questions

1. What, if any, changes in channels of distribution would be necessary in the marketing of insulated wire as contrasted with the line of electrical appliances?

2. What new selling and service functions would be introduced?

3. What variations in advertising methods and media would be necessary?

19

INTERNAL CONTROLS

An organization is kept on course by its system of internal checks and balances. Unusual variations in operations are detected and investigated. Standard procedures are developed and utilized to guide routine activities, while special departments and staffs handle different financial functions, such as auditing, payroll, taxes, and cost control. Certain analysis techniques and costing practices are associated with internal controls. What are they and how can they be implemented? What is the nature of the principal control functions necessary in relationship to finance? How can these functions be organized for greatest effectiveness? How does organization for the control of costs vary, and what are some of the reasons for these variations? What are some of the alternative plans by which we can make equitable distribution of costs that are not directly and exclusively associated with any one product? What is the nature of the relationship between cost and price?

19 INTERNAL CONTROLS

19-1 FINANCIAL CONTROLS

The usual control functions for the management of the internal finances of an industrial organization are shown in chart form in Figure 19-1. In the large organization, these controls are usually centralized under the direction of a controller who may report to the treasurer, to a financial vice-president, or to the executive vice-president. In a small organization, the treasurer usually assumes the controller functions.

The concept of controllership has been defined as the coordinating, planning, and control of profits. By this concept the controller should be in an investigative and advisory position on sales and production control as they relate to the finances of the business. The controller has been referred to by many people as the right hand of management and the chief adviser on all internal financial affairs. On many occasions he is the budget officer, a position through which he may exercise the breadth of function inherent in this concept.

Preceding chapters have mentioned the trend toward decentralization. In such cases the managers of divisions are held responsible for much of the direct control of operations such as payroll, cost accounting, and certain of the general accounting functions. Each plant or division has its own financial staff responsible to the plant manager. The records of each plant become subsidiary to the central control records in the headquarters offices. Regular reports are transmitted to headquarters summarizing the financial activity of each plant or division for designated periods. The headquarters staff, in turn, submits consolidated reports to the plants in order that they may be informed regarding the operations of the entire company.

19-1.1 The Auditing Function

Most large companies maintain an internal audit procedure as a function of the general accounting department or in a separate department under the controller. This function includes the checking of payroll, inventories, and the general books of the enterprise. The importance of this function is emphasized where the enterprise maintains a large number of branch plants and subsidiaries scattered over a wide geographical area. Traveling auditors provide a check on accuracy, but perhaps their most important function is

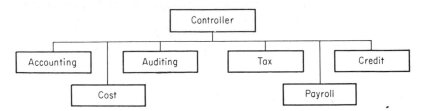

Figure 19-1 Typical control functions in internal finance in a manufacturing enterprise.

to promote the standard accounting practices that have been adopted by the enterprise. Naturally, in such matters as payroll and inventory, a check of a sample of not more than 50 per cent is practical. In the case of payroll, the auditor checks the worker's account card, which shows the number of hours worked, against time-clock readings, wage payment, etc. He also checks on alterations within the wage system, and the time studies which may have been used as a basis for such changes, in his attempt to verify the adequacy of method and the results obtained.

The internal audit is entirely a company proposition, as contrasted with the annual audit by an independent firm of accountants, which is for verification of the financial records of the enterprise in the interests of its stockholders.

19-1.2 Payroll Department

Although the volume of work of the payroll department has become greatly expanded as the result of federal and state wage regulations and various deductions such as Social Security, group insurance, union dues, and income taxes, the introduction of modern office machinery has actually simplified and expedited the operations of the department.

The actual details of the records of the department will naturally vary with the enterprise and in terms of variations in wage systems as described in Chapter 16. Now that the data in these records can be sorted and tabulated by automatic machinery, they carry significant importance in the planning and control of costs and in research studies regarding such subjects as absenteeism, employee earnings, and effects of training programs.

19-1.3 Tax Department

Accounting for taxes has become one of the major functions of the controller. In a small company, this is handled in the general accounting department; in a large company, a special department is organized, as shown in Figure 19-1. It is the responsibility of this department to calculate all taxes on the basis of the general accounting records, including reports of payroll deductions for taxes, the taxable earnings of each employee, the excess profits tax of the corporation, and all other taxes or deductions subject to state or federal regulations. A significant part of the function of the tax department lies not only in the mere recording and reporting of taxes but in advising the controller relative to action that should be taken in anticipation of taxes.

For example, federal regulations permit a company to purchase a reasonable amount of life insurance for employees. If the company is paying a tax on its profits of 52 per cent, the net cost of such insurance would be only 48 per cent of actual premiums. Management might well consider that present and future values of such action are well worth the relatively small investment. As another example, contracts with educational institutions for the organization of training programs for the company can be purchased covering a period of several years, yet arranged in such a way that payment chargeable to operating costs can be made in one year, since the value of benefits in subsequent years cannot be calculated. Projects such as these not only are permitted but are expected of a progressive management that looks toward continued improvement in benefit to the enterprise and the society in which it operates.

One of the major concerns of a company's tax department in recent years has been the policies and procedures governing the accounting for the depreciation of the company's properties. These are the policies which predetermine the "useful life" of equipment, buildings, and other assets that by their nature depreciate in value through use and the expiration of time. A portion of the original cost of such assets is charged or "written off" each year by the company as an expense item. The funds accumulating from these "write-offs" are placed in "reserves for depreciation" for future years for the replacement of these assets as they become obsolescent.

It is to be expected, of course, that companies are not given a free hand in determining depreciation policies. For many years the bible of the Internal Revenue Service, in establishing the useful life of industrial properties for tax purposes, has been its somewhat unrealistic Publication 456, *Depreciation: Guidelines and Rules.* This assigns arbitrary lives for various types of machine tools, equipment, and buildings in a number of industries. Actually this publication has now become a starting point from which companies may depart where shorter life can be proved appropriate.

Prior to the Internal Revenue Act of 1954, companies, unless they could justify a different approach, were required to use the *straight-line method* of depreciation. Assume a $10,000 asset with 20-year life. Under straight-line depreciation, 5 per cent (or $500) could be written off yearly. The 1954 act, recognizing industry's argument for permission to accelerate depreciation to more nearly reflect the useful and profitable life of the property, permits as options the *double-declining-balance method* and the *sum-of-the-digits method.* The former writes off about two-thirds of the original costs of the asset during the first half of its tax life, and the latter about three-quarters of the original cost in the same period. According to IRS Bulletin 534 (revised October, 1974), "Any reasonable method that is consistently applied may be used in computing depreciation. The three most generally used are: (1) straight line; (2) declining balance; and (3) sum-of-the-years digits."

The double-declining-balance method applied to the $10,000, 20-year asset allows 10 per cent (twice the straight-line rate of 5 per cent) annual depreciation applied to the undepreciated balance each year: thus $1,000 (10 per cent X $10,000) the first year, $900 (10 per cent X $9,000) the second, etc. For the same asset, the sum-of-the-digits method adds the successive number of years of tax life for the asset (1 + 2 + 3, etc., up to 20 = 210) and divides the total into the remaining years of tax life. Thus the first year the charge is $952 (20/210 X $10,000), the second year $905 (19/210 X $10,000), etc.

Although in any one accounting period the write-off method used affects the amount of income taxes the enterprise pays, if its profit level and the tax rate are unchanged, total taxes paid over the life of the property are the same under all methods. The principal advantage claimed for all the accelerated-depreciation methods is that the enterprise can retain more of its cash (pay out less in taxes) during the early years of the property life and thus is better able to modernize and expand.

19-1.4 Credit Department

Practically all sales in an industrial enterprise are made on a credit basis as contrasted with over-the-counter cash sales of a retail establishment, thus emphasizing the role of the industrial credit department. The credit manager in charge of the department is responsible for the establishment of policy and procedure which will enable the enterprise to maintain and possibly expand in sales volume, yet at the same time to avoid unnecessary losses through bad accounts and to avoid an undue drain on working capital. This means that the credit department must establish effective sources of information regarding the financial status of its present and potential customers. It also means that it must work very closely with the sales department and with the financial heads of the enterprise.

There are numerous sources of financial information regarding customers. Financial houses, such as Dun and Bradstreet, publish listings of credit ratings and, upon request, will prepare special reports regarding a specific enterprise. Trade associations may also maintain a credit bureau as a service to their members. The salesperson is perhaps one of the most valuable sources of information. Through his contact with the customer he can obtain pertinent credit information, such as a copy of the current balance sheet, profit-and-loss statement, and other financial statements which may reveal the current operating status. Care should be taken to view such statements critically, making sure that they present an accurate picture of the present, since the financial condition of an enterprise may change rapidly. If the salesperson is receiving a large order, he may ask the customer to prepare a special statement of specific information of existing liabilities, advance production orders, etc.

There is a very close relationship between the certification of credit and the administration of collection procedures. Care in the first step will greatly facilitate the second. Customers may be classified roughly into three groups: (1) those who always pay their accounts promptly when due; (2) those who are considered good risks but are slow in payment; and (3) those who are questionable or poor credit risks. Unfortunately, it is not easy to classify an enterprise into any of these three groups and be assured that the classification will remain permanent. Circumstances beyond control may force the customer into a situation where it is not possible to meet accounts promptly. There are always those customers who appear to sway back and forth between two classifications. These are the customers who require the careful and personal attention of the credit department, lest misjudgment result in the loss of a potentially good customer or overconfidence in him result in a loss through a bad account.

Perspective 19A   CAPITAL BUDGETING

The flow of funds in an organization has to be watched and scheduled as rigorously as materials and labor. Most demands for capital arise from plans for expansion, a need to replace existing facilities, and operating expenses. Most organizations face the same problems for operating capital plus the strategic need to ration funds for new investments in machines and buildings, promising research projects, enticing advertising campaigns, bargains in raw material procurement, and many other attractive but cash-consuming proposals. Someone has to decide which ones to nourish and which to starve. One way to make the decision is with a "capital inventory" as described below.

The *capital-inventory* approach for selecting which proposals to fund matches the cost of capital to the returns expected from investments. As portrayed below, the shaded blocks form a ladder of investment proposals promising various rates of return; RR_1 is a smooth curve representing the blocks. Curves RR_2 and RR_3 represent other configurations of investment opportunities that might become available during a budgeting period. The cost of each additional dollar acquired for purposes of making capital expenditures is given by the bold MCC *(marginal cost of capital)* curve. This curve is relatively flat up to an amount which exhausts the normal sources of capital; beyond this point, it rises sharply as more expensive sources are tapped.

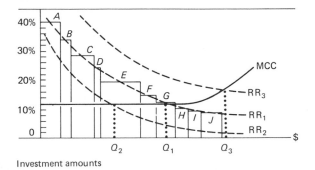

Investment amounts

The capital-inventory graph shows the marginal cost of capital (MCC) and three investment-proposal schedules (RR_1, RR_2, RR_3). The smooth-curve schedules represent discrete investment projects as indicated by the lettered ladder of proposals represented by RR_1.

If all proposals that promise a rate of return greater than the marginal cost of capital are funded in schedule RR_1, capital allocations would be made to proposals A through G. These investments total Q_1. The same criterion would indicate investments in the amount Q_2 for the RR_2 schedule; Q_2 is smaller than Q_1 because the investment opportunities of schedule RR_2 are not so lucrative as those of RR_1. A wealth of proposals with high rates of return might induce the firm to secure additional capital to allow the Q_3 level of investment for the RR_3 schedule. Any proposals that have a rate of return smaller than the marginal cost of capital are rejected by the investment-inventory criterion.*

*source: J. L. Riggs, *Engineering Economics,* New York: McGraw-Hill Book Co., Inc., 1977.

COMMENT Most proposals for modest investments in physical assets or special projects originate in the operating departments. Each department collects the facts and figures to support its proposals. Guidelines are normally available to ensure a complete description and substantiation. Both limits on the amount of money that can be requested and a minimum return expected from the investment screen out the less promising or unrealistic proposals. A committee of department heads, with advice from appropriate staff officers, frequently conducts another screening. Selected proposals are then submitted to higher offices where the final budget is set by consolidating all requests and evaluating their total effect on operations. This final selection budgets available capital to the most promising proposals from all parts of the organization.

19-2 COST CONTROL

Cost accounting is a part of the total accounting organizational procedure. It concerns itself with the accumulation of facts pertaining to expenses of the enterprise which are chargeable to a particular period of operation, to a given department, to a specific product, or to a single manufacturing operation. No attempt will be made in this brief space to offer a description of the cost-accounting processes. Attention will be confined to (1) purposes of costing procedures; (2) organization for the control of costs; (3) cost standards and estimates; (4) means toward cost reduction; (5) methods of expense distribution; and (6) the relationship of cost to price.

There are three primary purposes of costing procedures. Such procedures serve as:

1. An important element in determining the selling price of a product

2. A measure of the efficiency of operation

3. A check on whether certain lines of products are profitable to the operations of the enterprise

4. A basis for evaluating inventories on financial statements of the enterprise

It has been stated that the primary purpose of an industrial enterprise is to make a profit. That profit is interpreted as a return on the investments of the stockholders. Stated another way, a manufacturer sells time of buildings, equipment, and personnel. This time is used in transforming material or products into items of greater utility to the buyer. The cost of the time allocation to a particular product plus a reasonable profit determines the selling price of the product. It therefore becomes apparent that the manufacturer must have some means for determining cost in order that he may determine selling price.

19-2.1 Organization for the Control of Costs

Obviously, since the function of cost control is so vital to successful operation of an enterprise, it must be coordinated through some central division of the organization. The natural division for this coordination is, of course, the finance division. However, this function is one which is also highly dependent on the willing cooperation of all divisions and departments. Historically, such cooperation has been difficult to obtain. One reason is the negative attitude which most people have taken toward requests for cost estimates and commitments to budgeted allowances.

A second difficulty in coordination has been caused by the very nature of the subject, i.e., the necessity for close acquaintanceship between the work of the shop and the work of the financial offices. Effective coordination is dependent upon adequate records. This is especially true in finance and the accumulation of statistical data. Someone must know what information in the shop is procurable and significant. At the same time, there must be knowledge of how to systematize the information for effective use. This combination of knowledge is seldom found in one person. Even with experience in both plant and office, a single individual would need to keep in constant touch with changing circumstances. The better alternative, obviously, is a working team representing the different phases of operations but having as much company-wide contact as possible.

Some companies have established coordinating cost-control units under the jurisdiction of industrial engineering with responsibility for collecting cost information from operating departments, consolidating such information, and transmitting it to the finance division. Such a unit serves as a "go-between" with shop and finance. It is advantageous also in that industrial engineering is responsible for other functions, such as methods and time study, that have a significant relationship and influence upon cost control.

19-2.2 Elements of Cost

The costs of an industrial enterprise may be divided into three principal elements: (1) material, (2) labor, and (3) expense (see Table 19-1). These elements vary in terms of their application to a chargeable cost unit—product or service.

The cost of material may be either *direct* or *indirect*. If the material in question is used in the manufacture of a specific product and becomes a part of that product, it would be considered a direct material charge. Material which does not become a part of the product but which is essential to the manufacture of the product is considered indirect material. This classification includes such items as sandpaper for the sanding of the brushes of electric motors, fuel oil for the operation of heat-treating furnaces or for the heating of the plant, and chemicals for the cleaning of water-heating units. These are materials essential to the operation of the equipment which manufactures the product but are difficult to allocate to a specific product unit.

Labor costs are classified in much the same way as material costs. Labor which is applied directly to the manufacture of a product and which changes the shape, form, or nature of the product is considered *direct labor* and is

Table 19–1   Illustrating the Classification of Cost Items

Direct Costs	Indirect Costs		
	Factory Expense	Administrative Expense	Selling Expense
Direct material	Superintendents	Salaries of chief	Salaries and
Direct labor	Salaries of foremen	executives	commissions
	Factory office	General office	of salespersons
	salaries	salaries	Salaries of ser-
	Wages of mainte-	Office supplies	vice and
	nance staff	Professional fees	installation
	Material and parts	(general)	personnel
	for repair of plant	Telephone, telegraph,	Salaries of sales
	and equipment	and cable	office clerks
	Factory supplies	Loss on bad accounts	Advertising
	Insurance on plant	Depreciation of	Rent on branch
	and equipment	office equipment	sales offices
	Depreciation	Insurance on office	Traveling ex-
	Light, power, and	equipment	penses of
	heat		salespersons

charged directly to the product unit. Labor which has a more general and less direct application is considered *indirect*. Salaries of janitors, carpenters, electricians are usually considered indirect labor charges.

As in most rules of classification, there are instances where it is difficult to determine whether a cost should be considered direct or indirect. For example, material used in a finishing or plating operation may become a part of the product and actually change its appearance. Yet it is difficult to measure the exact cost of this material that is used in one particular product. Many different products may pass through the same vat or spray. Many factors may operate to bring variations in the amount of material used per product. In such case it may be considered more appropriate to make a proportionate indirect charge instead of attempting to calculate the exact charge that should be made direct. The same principle applies to labor. A member of the maintenance staff may be assigned exclusively to the cleaning and repair of equipment that is used in the manufacture of one product. In such case her salary would be chargeable directly to the cost of that product. In general it may be said that where the amount of material or labor that has gone into a given product can be precisely identified, it should be considered a direct charge to the cost of the product. Otherwise a proportionate indirect charge should be made.

Costs other than labor and material costs are classified as expense. This cost is frequently referred to as *overhead* or *burden expense*. Items such as taxes, interest, rent, utilities, depreciation, and insurance are included in the classification. A portion of the total of these expense items is charged to the cost of a given unit.

A division of expense is usually made in terms of (1) factory expense composed of items wholly chargeable to the actual operation of the factory;

(2) administrative expense which includes such items as general office salaries and professional fees; and (3) selling expense including advertising, salaries of salesforce, and other expenses connected with distributing the product.

19-2.3 Problems in the Control of Costs

Pick up almost any industrial publication today, and you will find at least one article devoted to means toward cost reduction. Such emphasis usually is the result of a "buyer's market," increased competition, uncontrollable increases in specific costs such as labor and material, or the anticipation of any of the three. Wise management, however, keeps its eye on the cost picture at all times. A manufacturer is constantly faced with the problem of meeting the demands of three groups:

1. The buyer, who requires quality, service, and a favorable competitive price within the limits which he can afford to pay

2. The worker, who demands wages commensurate with the changes in the cost of living and community wage standards

3. The stockholder, who expects a reasonable return on his investment

In facing a necessary decline in price the manufacturer must choose between lower profits and reduction in costs. In granting an increase in wages he must accept a decline in earnings, an increase in selling price, or reductions in other costs. The result is that he searches constantly for present or possible future opportunities to reduce costs.

Once the selling price is quoted, the manufacturer must find means of controlling his costs in order to keep them within the bounds of his price quotation. He must obtain data on the waste of material which may be occurring through spoilage, poor planning of operations, faulty workmanship, or many other possible circumstances that may increase costs and consequently reduce profits. He must develop a continuous source of factual information regarding the man-hour efficiency of personnel—is production conforming to the man-hour requirements that have previously been estimated or experienced through previous periods? And so we might go on through all the elements of costs, showing that for each there must be a means for control if the enterprise is to operate efficiently and profitably.

It may be that an analysis of cost data will show that a given product or line of products is unprofitable to the enterprise. This may be due to the price of material, competition of other companies manufacturing a similar product, or other circumstances peculiar to this particular product. In such case the manufacturer must consider the total advisability of continuing the product at a loss or comparatively small profit, or discontinuing it from production.

19-2.4 Cost Allocation

Indirect costs are those applicable to the business in general; they cannot be easily identified with a specific product. Indirect costs are often referred to as *overhead* or *burden expense.* Since they are not directly chargeable to any one product, methods are sought whereby they may be distributed equitably over all products, making possible the calculation of the total costs (direct and indirect) of each product unit.

There are four principal methods used in the distribution of factory expense. All the methods aim to base the expense-burden rate on a factor that is common to all products and varies in direct proportion to the amount of the burden that should be charged to any one of the products. One hundred per cent accuracy can, of course, never be attained universally over all the products. For this reason most companies have found it more practical to use different methods in different departments or with different products.

1. *The direct-material basis*   This method charges a burden rate commensurate with either the weight or the cost of the direct material going into the product. This method is limited in its application to companies or departments of a continuous-process type, and where the material and method of manufacture are common to all products. If, for example, either of two materials (steel or aluminum) is used in the manufacture of the products in a company, it might be relatively simple to chart the expense-burden rate in terms of the variation of weights and manufacturing operation of each material. In a job-order plant, however, variations in materials and production operations would limit the practicability of the method to those operations which were of a repetitive nature for most production orders.
2. *The direct-labor basis*   This method uses the cost of direct labor charged to a particular product as a basis for setting the expense-burden rate for the product. Based on past experience, if the total direct-labor payroll of the plant is $50,000 as compared with $10,000 general factory expense for the same period, the expense-burden rate would be 20 per cent of the direct-labor charge. Therefore, if the direct-labor charge on an order is $5,000, the expense burden would be $1,000.

   The cheif fallacy of this method is that it ignores variations in equipment used in different production operations. Thus, a highly skilled filing operation requiring only hand tools might carry a heavier burden rate than a hydraulic-press operation requiring large and expensive equipment. Under normal operating conditions this method might be quite satisfactory. Assume, however, that the trend of production orders results in an increase in semiskilled machine operations and a reduction in skilled hand operations. Expense distribution will at once be thrown out of balance and an undistributed expense balance will remain to be deducted from profits at the end of the period.
3. *The man-hour basis*   Variations in pay that cause confusion in the direct-labor cost basis are eliminated in the man-hour basis. By this method hours instead of cost of direct labor form the basis for determining the expense-burden rate. It still does not recognize variations in type and size of equipment.
4. *The machine-rate basis*   The machine-rate basis attempts to base the expense-burden rate on a study of the actual overhead expenses of the equipment used.

Factors such as capital investment, average maintenance and repair expense, depreciation, proportionate charge for floor space, and power consumed are calculated.

A burden rate is then established on an hourly basis. A product is charged in terms of the number of hours of operation required on each of the various machines.

It can readily be seen that this method is applicable to a larger number of different situations than the methods previously described. There are, however, two principal criticisms: (1) considerable additional record keeping is required; and (2) the accuracy of the method is dependent upon the accuracy of predetermined estimates of the hours of operation for each of the various machines. Estimates are very difficult to make in abnormal times, yet these are the times when accuracy is needed most.

Any of the methods for distributing expense is dependent upon estimates of time, volume, quality of production, and many other factors which may affect the number of units passing through the plant within a given period and to which a portion of the expenses may be attached. It also depends upon estimates of the total amount of expense that will be incurred during a budgeted period. It is to be expected that either a plus or minus balance will remain in the manufacturing-expense accounts at the close of the periods. If the expense for any period exceeds that forecast or if the volume of production is lower than budgeted, a balance will remain in the manufacturing expense accounts which has not been charged off to the costs of the products manufactured. On the other hand, if expenses have been overestimated or if production volume has been underestimated, the manufacturing expense will have been "overdrawn," i.e., too much would have been charged off. The means for caring for this plus or minus balance has been termed "manufacturing-expense absorption."

There are two principal means of effecting this absorption: (1) it may be apportioned to the cost of the products manufactured and in turn be reflected in the profit or loss on the products; or (2) it may be applied to the surplus account. The latter method is favored because it forms a more stable basis for the fixation of burden charges to each product, from one period to the next, that are not disturbed by temporary variations in the general or manufacturing expenses. Also, a special report of unabsorbed expense that is to be withdrawn from surplus will draw the attention of the management. This special attention may cause steps to be taken to correct the causes in order that similar results will not occur in future periods. It may be that poor planning resulting in idle man- and machine-hours has contributed to the situation. Undue waste of materials or other factors previously mentioned may be in need of study and correction. It is true, of course, that these factors could and should be studied if the unabsorbed expenses were charged to the products manufactured. There would be a tendency, however, for them to become lost in the total cost picture.

19-2.5 Standard Costs

From the data procured through cost accounting of past performance, most companies are now able to establish cost standards in much the same way as they establish material standards or engineering standards. In other words, an analysis of previous experience makes it possible to establish a normal cost for material, labor, and overhead or general expenses for a product or for a production unit within the organization. The establishment of cost standards has two principal benefits:

1. It reduces much of the need for detailed and continuous cost analysis, procedures which are time-consuming and which have a tendency to slow up the avenues of control and correction. Standard costs tend to bring about a more systematic and thorough analysis of costs and discourage reliance on separate job-by-job studies as a basis for cost estimates on new products.

2. Standard costs have a tendency to reduce to a minimum the variations in price or job quotations. Once costs are thoroughly studied and selling price is established in terms of cost standards, only major changes in circumstances, such as cost of material or labor, should necessitate a change in the selling price.

It is to be expected that standard costs would operate best in serialized production of standard products where there is a continuous flow of materials from one operation to the next and where there is a minimum of variation in operations required on different production orders. Standard costs become less applicable as diversification of production orders increases. Companies operating on a job-order basis are usually organized on a functionalized department or production-center basis. In cases where the operations of a department or production center are the same for all or most of the production orders passing through that department, it may be possible to establish cost standards for that department.

It is possible at times to establish standards for the elements of costs that are constant in a given operation. This is quite frequently true in departments engaged exclusively in the processing of materials. Usually basic material of a type that would be processed within a department can be placed in one of a few classifications as to grade, quality, etc., in the raw stage, and also as to processing required. For example, impregnated wood used in many industrial products is made by compressing wood under a very high pressure and impregnating it with urea or other chemicals that soften the gluey lignin and make it resistant to oil, water, and fire. Added strength can be obtained by making it into a plywood of crisscross grain, the layers glued with a resin glue of tremendous strength. Classifications are established in terms of such requirements as strength and pliability. The standards of each classification form the basis for processing. Naturally, variations in the requirements of processing will vary the costs. By careful analysis of the process required of each classification it is possible to segregate the basic cost elements of direct material and direct labor and establish cost standards for them.

Many job-order plants make a special effort to establish cost standards for direct labor. There are two purposes to be served through the establishment of standard labor costs or time standards: (1) it is a check over the quantitative efficiency of labor; and (2) it forms a basis for the scheduling of production orders through the plant. Because of this second purpose, the planning department usually keeps a record of the time requirements of all types of operations. This record becomes the basis for the establishment of time standards on specific operations. When a production order is written up, specifying the operations to be performed, the standard time is marked beside each operation for which standards have been established. If the details of the operation are different from any previous operation ever performed in the department, a time estimate is indicated. The operator may be paid a bonus for performing the operation in less than the estimated or standard time, thus providing an incentive for the improvement of efficiency. Time standards must, of course, be subject to change, especially on relatively new operations. The aim, however, is to avoid frequent fluctuations after a period of thorough analysis and experience with the operation. Recognizing that actual costs will vary from standards, special variation accounts are used for under and over amounts, finally being cleared into the profit-and-loss statement. If a consistent variation persists, the job must be restudied and new standards established, or the causes of excessive cost eliminated.

19-2.6 Methods of Pricing Materials

The importance of materials in the total cost of a product has been discussed in Chapter 11. One of the problems that arises in the proper control of material costs is the determination of policy to be followed in the pricing of materials. An appropriate and consistent policy is essential to the accumulation of cost data referred to in the preceding pages.

There are three methods of pricing materials in widespread use:

1. The *first-in-first-out method* (fifo) is based on the premise that almost invariably the oldest material is disbursed first and should not continue to affect the value of the remaining and more recently received material. As soon as the oldest lot on hand is used up, the price of the material disbursed then reverts to that of the next oldest material. Under this method, since the material disbursed to the plant is charged into the current operating cost at the oldest price available and since the material in stock is valued at what most nearly approximates current market values, operating profits are exaggerated on rising prices and minimized on downward trends.

2. The *last-in-first-out method* (lifo) is the reverse of fifo, since it is assumed that material most recently received is disbursed first, and hence the material is charged out accordingly. The underlying theory in this case is that in stocking

materials for normal manufacturing operations a reserve bank of materials must be maintained which, in a sense, represents a fixed asset that is seldom if ever taken out of stock. Therefore, the theory continues, this reserve should be valued at a more or less constant figure,[1] and any fluctuations in the prices of new materials received should be absorbed currently in the cost of operations. This method tends to reduce profits (and hence income taxes) on the upswing of prices and to accentuate them on declining price trends.

3. Under the *standard-cost method,* a standard cost is established for each material. This standard may be actual current or replacement cost or a cost estimate, or it may represent an average of the cost of that material as taken from past purchases. All disbursements are charged out as an operating cost at the standard value, regardless of the price actually paid for the material disbursed. As the price of receipts of new material varies from lot to lot, this overage or underage is debited or credited to an inventory-variation account which is finally cleared at the end of the year into the profit-and-loss account. Only as a seemingly permanent change in the price of that material appears to have been made is the standard-cost figure revised to more nearly approximate the new price.

Which of the above methods is applicable in any specific situation depends upon the type of material, its price-fluctuation pattern, and the manner in which it conforms to the overall accounting procedure followed by the enterprise in question. No one method is the best for all situations. However, in all cases the method followed should be consistent from year to year and should be acceptable to the U.S. Internal Revenue Service if it is to be used in the computation of Federal taxes.

Perspective 19B   COSTS OF WHITE-COLLAR CRIME

Crimes committed against a company by its employees are reaching alarming proportions. The U.S. Department of Commerce estimated the following business losses from crime in 1976 as:

	Annual Cost
"Ordinary" crimes: burglary, robbery, shoplifting, employee theft, bad checks, credit-card fraud, and arson	$21.7 billion
Bribery, kickbacks, and payoffs	$ 7.0 billion
Fraud against firms and banks	$ 4.5 billion
Insurance fraud	$ 1.5 billion
Total	$34.7 billion

---

[1]The Internal Revenue Code requires under lifo that the reserve inventory be valued at cost. Thus where lifo is adopted during a period of high prices and a deflationary period follows, inventory values, profits, and hence taxes all are unjustly inflated. Furthermore, lifo is adversely affected by improvements in manufacturing methods which reduce costs and by new and cheaper substitute materials, both situations in which lifo tends to overvalue inventories.

In addition, another $5 billion was spent for crime prevention, making the total bill for crime amount to $39.7 billion in one year! That is $185 for every man, woman, and child in the nation.

No business is safe from losses due to theft by customers and employees. The breakdown by type of business for the "ordinary" crimes is

Retailing	$ 7.3 billion
Services	$ 5.2 billion
Manufacturing	$ 3.7 billion
Wholesaling	$ 2.7 billion
Transportation	$ 2.3 billion
Arson victims	$ 0.5 billion
Total	$21.7 billion

The President's Commission on Crime reports that white-collar theft is increasing at a rate of about 10 per cent per year. It is estimated that 9 per cent of all employees steal on a regular basis, and profits for many department stores and food markets are cut in half by "inventory shrinkage," believed to be caused mostly by theft. Firms may pass on their losses to customers by marking prices up, typically by as much as 8 per cent in big city stores and near 2 per cent in suburban stores.

COMMENT Reasons given for stealing from employers include:
- "It's a fringe benefit. No one will miss a few items."
- "Everybody else rips off the company. Why shouldn't I? It's so easy to do."
- "Stealing adds a little excitement to a boring day, and it doesn't really hurt anyone either."
- "I'm just taking things to make up the difference between what I'm being paid and what I'm really worth to the company."

Although there are no easy remedies to thwart theft, a dual attack has helped many organizations: (1) change the work environment to make jobs more personal, thereby encouraging employees to identify with the goals of the company; and (2) tighten internal controls to make thievery more difficult. The former approach helps create the attitude "don't spoil it for the rest of us," and the latter discourages casual crime, especially when the bulk of the workforce actively backs the crime-prevention program.

19-3 RELATIONSHIP OF COST TO PRICE

The accounting department, if it is a centralized department, is responsible for the accumulation and determination of cost information pertinent to price setting. This does not mean that accounting sets price or that cost plus the addition of the desired margin of profit is the sole determinant of price. Many other factors must be taken into consideration. Most of these have been mentioned in earlier discussions but will be reviewed in this section in order to assist in the integration of the total price picture.

Fundamentally, price is set through the joint consideration of expected *volume at designated price levels* and the *cost per unit* at each level. The market survey, as described in Chapter 4, is expected to supply information regarding the first part, i.e., how many items can be sold at different price levels such as $14.95, $16.95, $19.95, or $24.95. Competition, of course, is a significant factor. A strong *quality* competitor may make the lower price field more attractive. Or the survey may show strong competition in both the $14.95 and the $24.95 fields but a gap of supply in the middle- or medium-price bracket. In the latter case the survey may show a demand for a product better in quality than existing lower priced competition but yet at a lower price, and consequently lower quality, than the existing higher priced products.

The company is interested not only in the fact that a demand exists but in the extent of the demand, i.e., how many it can sell at this price in contrast to either a higher or a lower price.

The accounting department is responsible for the second part of the basic consideration of price, namely, the cost per unit at a designated volume. The company has indirect costs, explained in preceding pages, which in general would be expected to reduce per unit as volume increases. Direct cost of labor per unit may be decreased through methods improvements if justified by increased potential sales volume. Substitution of lower quality material required by the lower or medium-price bracket should cause reduction in direct material costs per unit.

During a period of inflation, a manufacturer may set prices in anticipation of future increased costs, e.g., anticipated increase in wage rates in the next union contract. On the other hand, there may be organized pressure by governmental, union, or consumer groups to encourage him to reduce price as a stimulant to a reversal of the inflationary trend.

Distributing costs, as discussed in Chapter 18, may make up 50 per cent, more or less, of the selling price. The market survey may show the percentage of the selling price which must be allowed as a margin for the wholesaler and retailer. Such margin will include customary discounts.

The more common forms of discounts are (1) quantity discounts, legal under the Robinson-Patman Act when probable savings from the quantity order result; (2) trade discounts, where differentiation is made between classes of dealers such as wholesalers, agents, and retailers; (3) cash discounts, established by the credit policy and influenced considerably by competitive practice; and (4) special discounts, usually in the form of "extra" goods or for distributor advertising. Such discounts must be for a specific and justifiable purpose.

The manufacturer's distributing costs, including advertising, sales promotion, sales office expenses, sales service, and other expenses connected with getting the product into selected trade channels, must be added as a part of the unit cost.

From these and other considerations the accounting department is able to report the expected cost per unit at each of the quality and quantity levels in question. These are then translated into profit per unit multiplied by expected volume. All other things being equal, a unit profit of $1.00 with an expected volume of 500,000 units is to be preferred to a profit of $1.50

for 250,000. The purpose of the survey and analysis is to show at what point of quantity, quality, and price the company may expect the largest net return.

Aside from these fundamental price considerations, other factors have been mentioned which in the end might be the determinants in the selection of the price level. The survey may show that dealers are unreceptive to the lower price brackets because of lower dealer profits per unit. They may prefer to handle competing lines where returns per unit are larger. In such case the manufacturer must either establish new outlets, perhaps his own, or resurvey the project for possible adjustments better calculated to meet dealer demands.

The manufacturer may consider that the new product at the lower price may be injurious to some of his other products in the line.

The long-term forecast of economic conditions may provide warning of risks that make inadvisable the capital investment needed for increased production.

These are only a few of the many considerations that at times may cause the manufacturer to select a price bracket which to the casual observer would not appear to be the most profitable.

Perspective 19C   BREAKEVEN CHARTING

The interaction between costs, revenue, and levels of output is conveniently visualized on breakeven charts. The essential pattern of a breakeven portrait of operations is shown in the accompanying chart. The vertical axis of the chart is scaled in dollars, representing revenues and costs. Across the horizontal axis is a scale of operational activity, possibly in units of output, volume of business, or percent of total capacity. Entries in the chart depict receipts or disbursements as a function of operating volume.

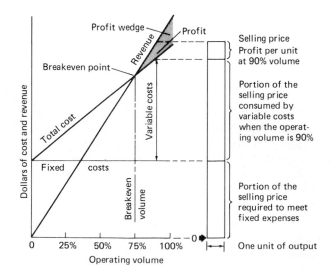

The rectangle to the right of the graph shows the profit gained from selling one unit when the firm is operating at approximately 90 per cent capacity; it also reveals the proportion of cost attributable to direct and indirect expenses of production.

The center of interest in the chart is the *breakeven point,* the intersection of the total cost and revenue lines that defines the operating volume required just to meet expenses. The area between the two lines beyond the breakeven point is the *profit wedge.* In addition to knowing the position of the breakeven point, it is important to recognize the shape of the profit wedge. A rapidly opening wedge, as opposed to a narrow taper, indicates greater profit on each additional unit made and sold, once the breakeven volume is attained. However, the same condition causes greater losses when volume fails to reach a breakeven position. The opposing wedges thus represent graphically the frequently encountered situation where the chance for greater gain is accompanied by a corresponding risk of larger loss.

Breakeven charts are useful in profit planning and cost control to visually show current cost–volume–profit relationships. Over the long run, the relationships are altered by internal factors (new products, different production facilities, improved work methods, etc.) and external impacts (competition, state of the general economy, etc.). Thus, a breakeven analysis is like a medical checkup; the examination reveals the current state of health and provides clues about what should be done to become or stay healthy.

19-4   CONTROL THROUGH RECORDS AND REPORTS

Records form the basis of action. But those records in the hands of a busy executive are worthless unless the pertinent information contained therein is summarized and directed to the problem in question. A report may come as a result of records that reveal exceptions in terms of the "exception principle." It may present the findings resulting from a long period of research and experimentation, or it may merely be a segregation and condensation of material drawn from various sources but requiring not more than a half day's time to prepare.

Thus we find that reports will vary considerably in scope and in subject matter. They will also vary as to type and presentation.

19-4.1   Types of Reports

One of the many possible classifications characterizes reports as either *periodic* or *special.* A periodic report is one that forms a part of a regular system. It may be presented daily, weekly, quarterly, or at any other regularly designated period. A monthly financial statement is an example. Sales reports may be presented daily, weekly, monthly, or quarterly. Various reports are presented by executives to the board of directors at regular intervals. These may include income statements, balance sheets, tax accruals, orders by product division this year and last, and the number of employees classified by department, by shifts, by method of wage payment, by function, etc.

A *special* report is one that is presented upon request of an executive or upon the initiative of anyone in the plant. In either case it is submitted in reference to a specific problem or idea. It is based on analysis of data secured upon special investigation. Because of the nature of its purpose it usually includes not only facts but conclusions and recommendations. This may vary somewhat in terms of the position and prestige of the individual submitting the report or the dictates of the person requesting it. Special reports may arise automatically as the result of the showing of a danger signal in the accumulation of records. Examples of this are reports on the causes of excessive scrap, absenteeism, and idle time of machines.

19-4.2 Principal Financial Reports

Among the various financial reports that must be prepared, two stand out as basic summarizations which are widely used by anyone seeking to study the financial condition of an enterprise. These statements are the balance sheet and the profit-and-loss statement.

THE BALANCE SHEET   The balance sheet presents a statement of what the company is worth, expressed in terms of dollar value. This statement is divided into three major parts: (1) the assets (what the company owns); (2) the liabilities (what it owes); and (3) net worth (the difference between the dollar value of assets and liabilities).

The balance sheet may report the assets and liabilities of the current year only, or it may make a comparison between 2 or more years, listing the assets and liabilities, and net worth, for each year or parts of years in separate columns. This is known as a *comparative balance sheet.*

Where an industrial organization is made up of more than one corporate unit, the financial condition of any one unit is dependent, of course, upon the condition of the other units. In order that an observer may obtain a financial picture of the complete organization, *a consolidated balance sheet* may be issued. This practice has become so widely established that it is considered imperative where multiple units are involved.

Figure 19-2 is a consolidated balance sheet of the Union Carbide Corporation and subsidiaries. Note that current assets are classified separately. These are assets that are fluid and easily converted into cash. Other assets are classified as more permanent in nature and more difficult to convert into cash.

A significant problem in the reporting of assets is the determination of true value. As a general principle, only those assets are included in the balance sheet for which value can be determined with reasonable accuracy. Note, for example, that in the Union Carbide statement care is taken to show how value of land, buildings, machinery, equipment, and tools is determined.

In the reporting of liabilities, it is considered good business to include even those liabilities which may be doubtful. These may be set up in the form of contingencies or reserves. For example, if the company is being sued for a patent infringement, an estimated liability should be included

CONSOLIDATED BALANCE SHEET
Union Carbide Corporation and Subsidiaries

Assets

	Dec. 31, 1960	Dec. 31, 1959
CURRENT ASSETS		
Cash	$75,362,000	$75,066,000
United States Government and Other Marketable Securities at cost (Market Value 1960—$49,937,000; 1959—$95,604,000)	49,933,000	95,165,000
	125,295,000	170,231,000
Receivables (After Allowance for Doubtful)		
Trade Notes and Accounts	163,369,000	171,073,000
Other Notes and Accounts	44,783,000	38,892,000
	208,152,000	209,965,000
Inventories (Cost or Market, whichever lower)		
Raw Materials and Supplies	104,023,000	111,740,000
Work in Process	91,351,000	88,551,000
Finished Goods	144,805,000	117,156,000
	340,179,000	317,447,000
Prepaid Expenses	14,749,000	17,024,000
Total Current Assets	688,375,000	714,667,000
FIXED ASSETS (At Cost)		
Land, Buildings, Machinery, and Equipment	2,176,770,000	1,974,346,000
Deduct—Accumulated Depreciation and Amortization	1,206,016,000	1,102,349,000
	970,754,000	871,997,000
INVESTMENTS (Cost or Less)		
Affiliated Companies	9,381,000	6,453,000
Foreign Subsidiaries	32,447,000	32,503,000
Other	1,596,000	828,000
	43,424,000	39,784,000
DEFERRED CHARGES		
Unamortized Debt Discount	5,553,000	—
Other	4,832,000	5,802,000
	10,385,000	5,802,000
PATENTS, TRADE MARKS, AND GOODWILL (Carried at $1.00)		
	$1,712,938,000	$1,632,250,000

Liabilities, Capital Stock, and Retained Earnings

	Dec. 31, 1960	Dec. 31, 1959
CURRENT LIABILITIES		
Accounts Payable	$52,528,000	$58,558,000
Installments due within one year on Long-Term Debt	13,418,000	12,459,000
Accrued Liabilities		
Federal Income and Other Taxes	119,597,000	135,802,000
Interest	3,851,000	2,001,000
Other Accrued Liabilities	56,533,000	48,384,000
	179,981,000	186,187,000
Total Current Liabilities	245,927,000	257,204,000
LONG-TERM DEBT (Note 2)	484,332,000	446,791,000
CAPITAL STOCK		
Union Carbide Corporation		
No Par Value—not including 413,264 shares held by the Corporation		
29,787,916 shares (29,672,401 shares at December 31, 1959)	246,511,000	241,676,000
314,292 shares (425,542 shares at December 31, 1959) held by the Corporation as collateral under the Stock Purchase Plan for Employees (Note 5)	28,946,000	33,399,000
30,102,208 shares (30,097,943 shares at December 31, 1959)	275,457,000	275,075,000
Less present amount of Agreements	27,892,000	32,314,000
	247,565,000	242,761,000
RETAINED EARNINGS	735,114,000	685,494,000
	982,679,000	928,255,000
CAPITAL STOCK AND RETAINED EARNINGS	$1,712,938,000	$1,632,250,000

Figure 19-2 Sample balance sheet (Courtesy of Union Carbide Corporation).

in the reserve for contingencies if there is a possible chance that damages may be allowed.

PROFIT-AND-LOSS STATEMENT   The profit-and-loss statement (or income statement) summarizes the operations of the enterprise for a given period in terms of the effect on profit or loss. To do this, it reports the income for the period and deducts from that the costs of operations. This statement is particularly important in analyzing recent operations. Where the balance sheet reports the financial condition at a designated date and compares it with the financial condition on a previous date, the gain or loss between those two dates stands unexplained. The profit-and-loss statement attempts to offer explanation of this change.

Figure 19-3 is the companion statement for Figure 19-2. This, like the balance sheet, is a greatly simplified statement with the items grouped into broad classifications. The complete report submitted to stockholders included a commentary on the principal points of the statement and any points that might in any way be questioned.

Stockholders, investors, and creditors are always concerned regarding the details of changes in the surplus accounts. To serve this interest, a special report showing a reconciliation of surplus accompanies the balance sheet and profit-and-loss statement. This report merely presents a summarization of the factors resulting in the change in the surplus between the beginning and the end of the designated period. Usually the report states the earned surplus at the beginning of the year, lists any special adjustments in the net income for the year as taken from the income statement, subtracts cash dividends, and shows the earned surplus as of the end of the year.

OTHER REPORTS PREPARED BY THE CONTROLLER   Most routine periodic reports are usually the responsibility of the controller. The records maintained by his department contain the information essential to the operating reports for departments throughout the organization. These departments are usually held responsible for the control of their own budgets, adjusting their activities as necessity dictates. Therefore, it is exceedingly important that reports to department heads must come at frequent intervals of not more than a month. The kind and number of reports prepared by the controller must naturally vary in terms of the requirements of a particular enterprise.

19-4.3   Controlling the Budget

Any budget, regardless of how carefully it may have been prepared, must be followed up in operation if it is to achieve its full purpose. Too frequently the budget is prepared and then forgotten until too late to remedy or remove the factors that are blocking progress as planned. Of course it is quite possible that these conflicting obstacles cannot be altered, but instead the budget must be changed in consideration of them. The important thing

CONSOLIDATED STATEMENT OF INCOME AND RETAINED EARNINGS

Union Carbide Corporation and Subsidiaries

	Year Ended December 31, 1960		Year Ended December 31, 1959	
INCOME				
Gross Sales—Less Discounts, Returns, and Allowances........	$1,548,168,000		$1,531,344,000	
Other Income (Net).......................	29,740,000	$1,577,908,000	25,589,000	$1,556,933,000
DEDUCTIONS				
Cost of Goods Sold...........	1,001,188,000		952,358,000	
Selling, General, and Administrative Expenses............	142,288,000		130,784,000	
Depreciation and Depletion...............	117,611,000		101,851,000	
Amortization.......................	11,640,000		19,763,000	
Interest on Long-Term Debt............	16,630,000	1,289,357,000	17,000,000	1,221,756,000
NET INCOME BEFORE FEDERAL INCOME TAXES..........		288,551,000		335,177,000
Provision for Federal Income Taxes.............		130,571,000		163,540,000
NET INCOME..................		157,980,000		171,637,000
Net Income Per Share—On 30,097,943 shares outstanding.....		—		$5.70
Net Income Per Share—On 30,102,208 shares outstanding....		$5.25		—
RETAINED EARNINGS AT JANUARY 1...............		685,494,000		622,202,000
		843,474,000		793,839,000
DIVIDENDS DECLARED.................		108,360,000		108,345,000
RETAINED EARNINGS AT DECEMBER 31...............		$ 735,114,000		$ 685,494,000

Figure 19-3 Sample profit-and-loss statement (Courtesy of Union Carbide Corporation).

is for changes and variations to be called to the attention of the budget committee as soon as possible in order that their effect may be anticipated and adjustments made to counteract them.

The machinery for the control of the budget in operation is planned in conjunction with the preparation of the budget as previously explained. Each department or division is organized with responsibility allocated for the control as well as the preparation of the budget. The various divisions are then coordinated through the budget director and the budget committee of the enterprise as a whole.

RECORDING OF OPERATIONS   Good budgetary control requires that accounting procedures be established that will provide a recording of actual operations in terms of sales, production, income, expenditures, or other budgeted units within a department. These recordings form a basis for the authorization of operations and the comparison of actual results with those which had been budgeted. This enables the budget director and each department to have a constant check on operations. Unusual variations come immediately to the attention of the departments concerned.

OPERATING REPORTS   Regular reports to the budget director showing comparison of actual and budgeted figures, and the reasons for variations are prepared for each department. Frequently the reasons for variations are not immediately explainable, but at other times they may be quite apparent. For example, failure to meet a production schedule may be directly attributable to a shortage of labor or the unavailability of material.

Variations between actual and budget and the reasons for them, however, may frequently require more thorough analysis by the budget director and his staff. He should seek to determine why the employment department has not been able to obtain sufficient labor, what methods have been used in the attempts, what other methods should be explored. Herein lie the means for control and coordination of all departments throughout the plant. Because of the inevitable interdependency of departments, all must be kept, if possible, to at least a point of minimum effectiveness if the total operations of the enterprise are to stay within reasonable limits of the budget as planned.

The various department reports are summarized and consolidated by the budget director in his regular reports to the budget committee. On the basis of his report the budget committee may recommend revisions in the budget. The budget director may also submit supplementary reports regarding special points of variation upon which he asks for action regarding policy and procedure.

Perspective 19D   PLANNING, PROGRAMMING, AND BUDGETING

A modified approach to government budgeting was inaugurated in 1965 when President Lyndon Johnson required each large Federal agency to set up a planning, programming, and budgeting system (PPBS). The purposes of PPBS were spelled out by the original government directive, a portion of which is quoted below, where the reasons for an improved budgeting system are noted.

. . . Objectives of agency programs and activities have too often not been specified with enough clarity and concreteness; accomplishments have not always been specified concretely; alternatives have been insufficiently presented for consideration by top management; in a number of cases the future year costs of present decisions have not been laid out systematically enough; and formalized planning and systems analysis have had too little effect on budget decisions.*

The process by which a PPB system operates is described in a very general fashion by the following four phases:

1. *Identifying objectives*   The basic goals of the organization should be stated as explicitly as possible. Even when goals cannot be defined precisely, they should at least be clear enough to evaluate alternate methods of accomplishment.
2. *Relating goals to specific programs*   It is not unusual to find programs built around the historical mission of traditional organizational units. These missions may be related only remotely to the objectives of the central entity. By assigning organizational units to specific programs designed to achieve overall objectives, economies of operation often accrue. A program may require the cooperation of several complementary units before the end objective can be obtained.
3. *Relating programs to resources*   Since there are seldom sufficient resources to carry out all the desired programs, a means of evaluating the efficiency of alternative courses of action is needed. It is important to consider the time span over which the expenditures take place. A resource deployment plan could be attractive for a short-range venture but very uneconomical if the venture extended beyond the period considered.
4. *Relating resources to the budget*   The final phase of a PPB application is the conversion of resource inputs into dollar values. Once the budget dollar figures have been generated, specific allocations to operating units direct activities toward the organization's goals; the budget implements the program.

The phases listed above are a continuing process as objectives are reappraised to determine how money was spent and what benefits were obtained. At each review the current programs are questioned to see whether they could be accomplished at lower cost. Success guides future planning and programming.

*SOURCE: "Planning-Programming-Budgeting," Bureau of the Budget Bulletin 66-3, October 12, 1965.

COMMENT   PPBS is certainly not a panacea for all the ills of budgeting. It tends to systematize the thinking involved and may lead to an overdue reorganization which will facilitate longer range planning and more efficient utilization of resources, but it does not make a budget cut any easier to accept or budget making any less of a chore. Too frequently too much is expected of a system of budgeting. It should be recognized that no budget is better than the people who operate it and that people cannot be changed in their habits and interests overnight. The idea of budgeting must be sold, and, furthermore, it must be demonstrated. As previously mentioned, many will consider the budget only a negative control, something to be resisted. Budgeting, as an instrument of planning, control, and coordination, must be cooperative budgeting.

19-5 CONTROL OF SUPPORTING OFFICE OPERATIONS

Control reports and their supporting records as discussed in this and preceding chapters make necessary a tremendous load of paper-work activities,
including the computation of statistical data, preparation and duplication of
reports, preparation and handling of sales and productions orders, incoming and outgoing mail, and the systematic handling of records of operation
of all departments.

In recent years the volume of such activities has grown along with the
complexity of the geographical scope of business, increased government
control with its resulting multitude of reports, and increased emphasis on
coordination of departments and divisions. In many companies these activities have become so burdensome in time and expense that a major effort has
been directed toward simplification and improvement of their effectiveness.

The larger or medium-sized organization finds it expedient to organize
some of these functions that are common to most of the divisions of the
company into the following departments:

1. A mail department which opens and distributes incoming mail

2. A filing department for the maintenance of the principal records of the organization

3. A duplicating department for the duplication of reports for distribution inside or
   outside the organization

4. A method department, in a staff relationship, with the function of assisting in the
   simplification of office activities and in the promotion of an even and effective flow
   of work

5. A central stenographic department for handling correspondence

Each department is under the supervision of a department head. Frequently these department heads report to a person who may be known as
an office manager. All of these departments are specialized service departments for assistance to other departments and divisions of the company. For
example, the centralized stenographic department supplies stenographers
on call from any department; the duplicating department receives copy from
any and all departments and prepares duplicates according to instructions
from the person originating the copy.

The office manager should also serve as an aid to all offices of the company through the performance of certain specialized staff functions, including (1) the selection and transfer of office personnel; (2) training of
personnel; (3) improvement and standardization of office methods; (4) form
analysis; (5) job analysis and classification; (6) salary administration; and (7)
the standardization of office regulations or personnel practices.

Many companies may allocate these staff functions to appropriate staff
divisions of the company or, at least, provide for service to the office man-

ager from the staff departments. For example, the industrial-relations division should be prepared best to provide services in hiring and training personnel. There are differences, however, in the requirements for office personnel in contrast with plant or engineering personnel. Differences also occur in the training of personnel. A combination, therefore, of the specialized knowledge of the office manager regarding office jobs and requirements and the specialized knowledge and resources of industrial relations regarding the techniques of recruiting and training should operate more effectively than either performing separately. Other staff divisions, such as industrial engineering, may assist also in the performance of other staff functions.

Perspective 19E   CONTROLLING COMPUTER OPERATIONS

The performance of all the functional units of an organization should be checked regularly to see whether the services they provide meet current needs and, if so, whether they provide them economically. Even a highly profitable firm needs to evaluate its individual units because its overall success may hide shoddy performance of small units that, if left undetected, could eventually hurt other units by providing inadequate services or consuming revenue that could be better spent elsewhere.

For example, EDP services are utilized by many different parts of an organization. Tardy or insufficient service can detract from a variety of operations. According to Professors Scriven and Hallam, three methods commonly used for computer evaluation have the characteristics shown in the table on page 564.*

COMMENT   Most personnel-intensive operations are subjected to some type of performance appraisal system. The key features of such systems are a set of standards that establish the objectives of the operation, a schedule for observing the operation and rating performance according to the specified criteria, recording the ratings, and regular management reviews of the results to spot unsatisfactory performance or variations that portend future problems. The performance of capital-intensive operations is somewhat easier to evaluate, since cost data are usually available from accounting records, and the ratings are more objective than personnel appraisals. Both approaches can be applied to the control of EDP costs.

When a performance evaluation indicates that savings would likely result from operational changes, high-cost and high-volume activities are prime candidates for change. Robert C. Chomko* believes the ABC concept of inventory control (see Chapt. 11) should be applied to computer operations to point out the most promising areas for closer control. His studies suggest that 20 per cent of the computer programs control 80 per cent of the data processing, and 20 per cent of the peripherals control 80 per cent of the total time. Thus, analysis time should be shortened by concentrating it on the critical 20 per cent of the computer activities or equipment.

*SOURCE: R. C. Chomko, "ABCs of Improved Computer Performance," *Infosystems,* October, 1976.

Comparison of Traditional EDP Evaluation Methods

Computer Performance Evaluation	Computer Audit	Computer Feasibility Study
Continuous sampling	Regular, periodic sampling	Occurs only when hardware change is contemplated
Uses evaluation hardware of software; little staff time required	Internal auditor or "outside" auditor examines records, procedures — limited interviews with staff	Entire study conducted by staff; requires substantial staff time
Provides numeric measurement of hardware utilization	Provides judgmental opinions on accuracy of records and processing procedures	Provides substantial documentation of all systems and procedures together with alternatives for processing
One-time cost for hardware or software monitors. Price range is $5,000–$10,000 each.	Repeated cost for each audit. Price range is $10,000–$20,000 for each audit.	Cost for each study is basically the staff time devoted to the study. Cost range is $25,000–$50,000.
Evaluation data collected during daily running time	Requires approximately 4 calendar weeks	Requires approximately 4–6 calendar months for complete study
Results not valuable due to lack of utilization standards	Results reflect accountants' viewpoint of recordkeeping and reporting	Results emphasize best hardware to meet needs

SOURCE: "New Approaches to Computer Performance Evaluation" by D.D. Scriven and S.F. Hallam, *Infosystems,* October, 1976.

19-6 REVIEW QUESTIONS

1. What is meant by "controllership"? In an organization, to whom does a controller report and what are the duties of the position?

2. What is the purpose of capital budgeting? How does a capital inventory assist decisions in allocating resources?

3. Which are the accelerated depreciation methods? Why is an accelerated depreciation method used?

4. Explain the reasons for having costing procedures.

5. Distinguish among direct labor, indirect labor, and material costs.

6. Explain the benefits of established cost standards. Describe three methods of pricing materials and their effects.

7. What are the four methods of allocating indirect cost to a product?

8. What factors influence the price level of a product?

9. Why is the analysis of budget variations of primary importance?

10. What are the objectives of PPBS and the four steps of planning, programming, and budgeting?

19-7 TOPICS FOR DISCUSSION

1. Comment on the adequacy of present-day accounting procedures to furnish management the information it needs for proper coordination and control of the enterprise.

2. It is contended that good financial budgeting must be done cooperatively with the various departments of the company and cover all elements related to potential income and expense. What are some of these elements, and how is each specifically related to the financial budget?

3. The trend toward automation in industrial production tends to reduce direct man-hour costs per unit of production. At the same time it tends to increase the indirect and burden costs involved in equipment and maintenance and in administrative personnel. How will this affect the application of the variable-budget principles and the benefits to be derived therefrom? How can industry seek to offset these negative influences?

4. The determination of selling price involves much more than a standard unit cost of production plus the desired margin of profit. Summarize the factors that may be involved in price determination.

5. Consider the rationale used to justify stealing given in Perspective 19B. Also consider the dangers from computerized crooks discussed in Perspective 3F. What managerial actions can you suggest to counter this growing threat from crime?

6. It appears, at times, that the pressures and "drives" for better quality, larger volume of production, special services for customers, and cost reduction may be in direct conflict. The foreman, in such a situation, may tend to concentrate his efforts where the pressure is the greatest and without regard for the interrelationship of these "drives" in their effect on the total welfare of the company. Explain how you would attempt to avoid this tendency yet recognizing that there must be organized effort for adequate promotion of quality, quantity, service, and cost reduction.

7. Case 19A: *The J. P. Jenkins Company*
The J. P. Jenkins Company manufactures a wide variety of builders' hardware. Although well established in the market from successful operation for more than 50 years, it is now feeling increased pressure of price competition. Much of the company's production is in standard miscellaneous hardware, but specially designed hardware for large customers has always been a feature of the business.

The management of the company has called in a firm of management engineers to analyze its operating costs in an attempt to devise more accurate cost estimates to be used in pricing.

The practice has been to estimate costs from standard data gathered from experience and classified as stand-by or variable, as discussed in this chapter.

In consultation with the engineering firm, management is convinced that the theories of *learning curves* and *manufacturing-progress functions* may have appropriate application.[2] These theories apply operations research to the measurement of progress in productivity. The assumption is that as production of a given item continues, as measured either by time or by number of units, improvement in production effectiveness results. Many factors contribute to this progress in effectiveness. One of the most obvious is operator learning through repetition. Recent studies suggest, however, that there may be other equally important changes, resulting from experience on the product, that will bring about cost reduction. Furthermore, it is suggested that this anticipated deduction can be charted.

[2]These were discussed in Chapter 8.

Questions

Indicate some of the during-production factors that should be studied by the engineers in their analysis of progress in production effectiveness.

8. Case 19B: *The Cameron Hardware Company*

The Cameron Company, manufacturers of builders' hardware, is seeking an internal reorganization in order to give more responsibility for financial control and productivity to the superintendents of the three operating divisions. These divisions are organized on a product basis, each making a distinct line of noncompetitive hardware items. All are located at one central point in a group of four buildings.

The company has the usual centralized staff department such as those described in earlier chapters. Currently, the superintendents are responsible only for "productive" or "operating" personnel. The company retains a total employment of 2,000 on a relatively stable basis. It has a national market served by a sales force organized on a geographical basis. The volume of business and the diversity of products have caused the company to look with disfavor on suggestions of sales organization by product.

The chief executives of the company recognize that, in order to obtain the interest and cooperation of the superintendents and their foremen, they must provide opportunity for the divisions to exercise control over those functions which have the greatest effect on the operating costs and total productivity. Yet they realize, also, that it would be a mistake to attempt too large a transition at one time. The company plans to announce soon the establishment of financial incentives for superintendents and foremen of the operating divisions by which a bonus would be payable each month based on the volume of orders shipped.

Questions

1. Indicate the staff functions which you feel are most clearly related to operating costs and productivity and which should be placed under the control of the operating superintendents.

2. Show the probable points of gain and loss from such decentralization of functions.

3. Indicate other staff functions which you feel might be left temporarily on a centralized basis but in which superintendents should have the opportunity to *share* in the formation of policy. How would you provide for this sharing?

9. Case 19C: *The Equitable Manufacturing Company*[3]

The Equitable Manufacturing Company has attempted to increase the scope of authority and responsibility of its production divisions as a means toward more effective on-the-job control. Consistent with this, it has sought to move more items of cost from the *fixed,* or *noncontrollable,* category into *semifixed,* or *variable,* category (controllable). One such item was plant equipment and physical facilities. The idea was to establish the division plant manager on a semi-independent basis. In effect, the company would supply plant and equipment, for which the manager would pay rent (depreciation). The marketing of the division's products however, was handled by a separate division of the company and not by the production divisions. The marketing division had responsibility for new-product development and for removing or adding products to the line, subject to the approval of top management.

Top management of the company judged the effectiveness of its production divisions by the rate of return on capital investment in the division. It rewarded the administrative personnel of these divisions according to this measure of effectiveness. This encouraged the division managers to keep capital investment at a minimum and productive utilization at a maximum. They had authority to scrap obsolete or unused equipment, remove it from their capital-investment accounts, and reduce depreciation charges accordingly.

[3]Fictitious name. This case is adapted from John Dearden, "Problem in Decentralized Profit Responsibility," *Harvard Business Review,* vol. 38, no. 3, May/June, 1960.

One day the manager of a production division observed idle testing equipment occupying about 200 square feet of floor space. Upon investigation with his own personnel he was told that this equipment was not usable on the current products being manufactured and that it would not be used unless there was a change in product. He then consulted the marketing division and was informed that a new product had replaced the old one on which this testing equipment had been used and that they saw no possibility of its present or future use. The equipment had a gross book value (original cost) of $200,000, with an annual depreciation charge to the production division of $20,000. The production division manager, finding no resale outlet for the equipment, ordered it scrapped.

Two years later further change in product design reintroduced the need for this testing equipment, which then had to be purchased new at a cost to the company of $300,000, although identical with that scrapped 2 years before.

Let us now examine the results of these scrapping and purchase transactions for their effect on the company and on the production division in question, assuming that all other factors remained constant.

	Division's Profit	Division's Investment	Rate of Return (%)
If equipment had not been scrapped	$600,000	$3,000,000	20
With equipment scrapped ($20,000 less depreciation charge)	$620,000	$2,800,000	22.14
Benefit from scrapping equipment	$ 20,000 (increase)	$ 200,000 (decrease)	2.14 (gain in percentage points)

Thus we see that the production division gained in its rate of return on investment, yet in the long run it cost the company $300,000 to replace the equipment that had been scrapped. Of course, if the equipment is now continued for its estimated 10-year life, the division will be penalized to the extent of $10,000 per year in extra depreciation charge—a total of $100,000. But it benefited from a decreased charge of $20,000 per year for the 2 years that they operated without this equipment (total of $40,000). So the net penalty, even if now carried for the full 10 years, will be only $60,000, while to the company the loss is $300,000.

Questions

1. Referring back to previous chapters on the discussion of equipment replacement (Chap. 7) and on budgeting and rate of return (Chap. 5) and considering the emphasis given in the current chapter on the sharing of knowledge, responsibility, and authority in profit and financial control, how would you change the policies and procedures of Equitable Manufacturing affecting the issues in question in this case?

10. Case 19D: *Breakeven by the Numbers*
Breakeven charts are commendable for summarizing and displaying data, but they are not very convenient for analyzing the data. Precise points in a chart are better identified by numerical expressions. By letting N = number of units, p = selling price per unit, v = variable cost per unit, and FC = fixed costs; then, revenue $R = pN$, total variable costs TVC $= vN$, and profit $Z = R - (\text{TVC} + \text{FC})$ or $Z = pN - vN - \text{FC}$.

Using these symbols, several relationships can be pursued. The breakeven point BP is by definition located at the output level where the profit is zero, $Z = 0$. Therefore, at BP the revenue equals the total cost: $pN = vN + \text{FC}$. Solving for N,

$$N_{BP} = BP = \frac{FC}{p - v}$$

A salesperson occupied the lonely hours he spent in hotel rooms while on selling trips by writing a book, naturally entitled *How to Be a Successful Salesman Without Really Trying.* After his manuscript was rejected by all the trade-book publishers, he recalled one of the themes of his book, "believe you are a winner and you will be," and decided to publish it himself. Preparation costs (artwork, editing, typesetting, plates, etc.) amounted to $12,000. For each 1,000 books printed, the variable costs (paper, printing, binding, etc.) would be $2,000. Being a salesperson, he was well aware of the importance of the price selected for the book. He figured he could sell 5,000, 10,000, or 25,000 if the selling prices were, respectively, $7.95, $4.95, or $2.95.

Questions

1. What profit could be expected at each selling price?

2. If the salesperson-author could double his sales at any of the listed prices by investing $30,000 in an advertising campaign, would you advise him to do so? Why or why not?

20

CHALLENGES TO INDUSTRIAL ORGANIZATION AND MANAGEMENT

Having developed in previous chapters all phases of industrial organization and management, there remains the problem of bringing them to bear upon the coordination of the enterprise. In summary, what does this entail? People set up businesses and industrial enterprises for many reasons, but the prime motive is to gain profits. Real profits come only from the production and exchange of goods and services. The goal of an enterprise is to maximize these profits within the framework of management responsibilities to stockholders, labor, and public. In many respects a business or industrial enterprise is like a machine, consisting of such parts as land, buildings, people, equipment, and materials. Materials of many kinds and forms flow into it, are processed by the workers and equipment within the plant, and then flow out of it in different forms designed for other manufacturers to use or for consumers. These parts must be carefully selected and arranged. They must fit together and operate in harmonious and reciprocal relations. At the same time the enterprise must be fitted to serve in the world outside factory doors. This larger world includes interactions with governments both at home and abroad. It exposes an enterprise to critical questions about the use of natural resources and energy; protection of the environment; responsibilities to consumers, employees, and the general populace; and participation in programs to bolster the national economy. Answers to such questions are the 1980s' challenges to industrial organization and management.

20 CHALLENGES TO INDUSTRIAL ORGANIZATION AND MANAGEMENT

20-1 IMPORTANCE OF COORDINATION

The business executive is familiar with the coordination problem in its most practical aspects. From the inception of an enterprise there is a continuing challenge to balance the need for and use of land, labor, plant, equipment, and capital. High costs with low profit margin may result in financial difficulties that sicken or destroy the enterprise. If the production department turns out more goods than the sales department can sell, inventories pile up, costs rise, and losses set in. If sales exceed production capacity in the time set for delivery, customers may be lost. If equipment is not properly maintained and if the flow of production is not well planned, waste, stoppages, and breakdowns result. If personnel is poorly selected or improperly placed in the enterprise, disharmony and inefficiency weaken performance. If finances are not carefully planned, the enterprise may fall into distress. These and a thousand more detailed experiences may hamper efficient production and consequently cut down profits. If harmony and a sound working balance are not achieved, the enterprise will be weak and may ultimately fail.

As will be seen, a considerable amount of coordination is achieved as a routine part of good management. If the company is soundly organized and if officials merely carry out their regular departmental functions in an alert and intelligent manner, a certain amount of coordination can be expected as a matter of course. This is because a well-organized enterprise gains functional unity from the very nature and operations of its specialized parts. Certainly this is true in the case of internal coordination of the enterprise; it is also true, in part, in the external coordination of the enterprise; with its whole industrial field.

Beyond that point, coordination is less a by-product of the routine functions of management and more a process which must be pursued as a conscious policy if management is to be successful in the modern world. First, management must have the vision to see the value of coordinating its activities with events and conditions in the broader field outside the company's special sphere of operations. Second, it must adopt a deliberate policy embodying the will to coordinate. Third, it must encourage company officers and department heads to engage in coordinating activities. Fourth, it must utilize the company organization—the board of directors, special committees, and channels of communications—for the discussion of the ways and means of coordination.

In the small proprietorship, partnership, or corporation where most of the routine functions of management rest upon the owner, manager, or company president, the responsibility for coordinating the enterprise falls upon a single individual and possibly a few assistants. In such small concerns a fairly high degree of unity is achieved because the scope of the enterprise is small and one person makes most of the guiding decisions, but the area of coordination is limited by the capacities of that one person. As we examine companies of increasing size and departmental organization, the area of coordination widens and the number of people participating in the coordinating processes increases until, in the very large corporation, several dozen may be involved. For the large company, coordination today covers such a broad field and includes so many methods and channels that teamwork of all management personnel is essential for success. Such teamwork will develop naturally if the company follows a policy of coordination, encourages its officers to participate, and utilizes the company organization for that purpose wherever possible. But, in addition, many leading companies charge some top officer—probably chairman of the board, president, or vice-president—with overseeing the effort to coordinate all phases of the company operations.

Unifying the enterprise as a producing mechanism may be approached as a problem of *internal coordination;* and as one of *external coordination,* fitting the enterprise into the outer world. Separating the problems thus for convenience of discussion should not obscure the fact that there is constant interaction and interralation between them.

20-2 INTERNAL COORDINATION

Although often difficult and complex, the problem of internal coordination is a manageable one. Every industrial enterprise is something of a little world of its own. It is an independent unit, has functional completeness, and controls its own activities. Although outside forces of various kinds do affect the internal operations of an enterprise, a large degree of control over company operations is exercised by management. Company executives determine policies and objectives. They know that success depends upon revenues exceeding expenditures. This is the simple rule of profit and is itself a guiding hand and unifying element for the enterprise. Company executives deal with a simple operational structure—production, sales, and administrative departments; all other parts of the organization are elaborations and refinements of these. Within certain limits, executives can plan production, speed up or slow down operations, and change the quality, nature, and style of the product. They can rearrange departments and change the sequence of operations. They can change working conditions, hire better people, carry on in-factory training, and discharge incompetents. They can study the market and adapt their products to it. They can originate sales policies and advertising campaigns for the wider distribution of their product. Executives can budget finances and plan future operations. They can set up administrative and operations committees and establish a system of interdepartmental memoranda, records, and reports.

Attention to all these things is involved in the problem of internal coordination. Its essence lies in constant experimentation with all phases of company organization and operations. The object is to bring all the parts to the highest perfection possible and to weld them into a smooth-working, efficient organization of the enterprise as a whole. It can be said fairly that management is thoroughly familiar with this problem of internal coordination and that it strives constantly to solve it by study, planning, and experimentation.

What practices are followed? There are, of course, the usual meetings of the board of directors, periodic meetings of department and division heads, meetings of special personnel, such as the home and field sales forces, and meetings of parent and subsidiary—company plant and production personnel. Most of these meetings are rather formal, relatively short, and often devoted to special problems of policy and operations. They are not alone sufficient to build intimate teamwork. Supplementary devices are required. One of these devices is a weekly *management newsletter* which should deal with executive matters and not be allowed to change into a general company bulletin or magazine. Another is regular *progress reports* from top officials to the board. The same device can also be used in reverse—*from* the board to other management personnel. These reports should deal with policies, problems, special features of operations, and "what goes on," and may be digested for the management newsletter. A third device is to appoint *special committees* from time to time to review and report on organization, finances, sales problems, production problems, expansion plans, and other special features. A fourth device is to have *regular luncheon meetings and bull sessions*, with questions freely encouraged. At times these meetings may be organized around some special topic of general management interest. Frequent meetings of this kind should be especially encouraged between directing personnel whose work has a special correlation with the work of other directing personnel, in such combinations as research–product engineering–production, or sales–credit–finance. Operations research, bringing together teams of experts whose different techniques are utilized in the solution of all problems of management, promises to be a potent tool of coordination (see Chaps. 3 and 8). Many such groupings are possible in the large firm. Many leading companies have one or more *circulating or roving officials* from top management whose main job is to bring management personnel together, to find out what is going on and what problems exist, and to circulate intelligence among the different departments and divisions. Alert management can use all these methods and probably devise many others. The objects should be to foster communication, to encourage conferences, to circulate information, and to build the intimate relations among the management personnel on which successful cooperation and coordination are based.

Perspective 20A   CAN RISING COSTS OF PAPER WORK BE CONTROLLED?

Managers in both government and industry are familiar with the paper work plague. President Carter was aware of it when he stated that the paper work demanded by the federal government "is too often duplicative, unhelpful, and sometimes unread. The cost is staggering."

The estimated annual cost of federal mandated paper work is $40 billion. Government agencies print about 10 billion sheets of paper a year just to be filled out by U.S. businesses. The government spends $15 billion a year to process its own paper work, $1 billion for forms, another $1 billion for directives to accompany these forms and explain how to fill them out, and $1.7 billion to file and store them.

A study by the Council on Wage and Price Stability disclosed that the steel industry is subject to more than 5,000 separate regulations stemming from 27 agencies administering 57 major programs. The effect, concluded the study, is to transfer the critical decisions from the private sector to the public: "With few exceptions, company executives scarcely can move without federal approval. Ostensibly, the company managers are running their plants; for practical purposes, the bureaucrats are."

COMMENT   Two rather frightening extrapolations can be drawn from these statistics: (1) paper work generation and processing will consume ever-greater resources without contributing directly to manufacturing productivity; and (2) federal regulations will increasingly tell industry what it must do, rather than their traditional message of what industry should not do.

Although changes in company paper work policies could cut internal communication costs, actions at the federal level will be necessary to reduce the larger costs of reporting to the government. A commission on federal paper work has been set up to suggest paper work reforms, but a fundamental shift in public policy would be required to limit expanding government regulations, with their consequent paper work proliferation, on industrial operations.

20-3   EXTERNAL COORDINATION

External coordination deals with problems which are generated in the world outside factory doors and which vitally affect the conduct of every industrial enterprise. No company today can be operated in disregard of the influence of labor organization. No company can remain aloof from developments in its industrial class or from the influences of the wider economy. Every enterprise must keep abreast of advances in science and technology. Industrial management today is vitally affected by government operations and by the demands that complex community life makes upon private enterprise. If management fails to understand and to take account of these forces and conditions, the success of the enterprise is likely to be jeopardized. It is the aim of external coordination to tie the individual company to its industrial group and to the national economy; to fit it into life in the community and in the nation; to bring it into contact with the international economy; in short, to provide for a two-way passage of information between the industrial enterprise and the outer world and to bring about mutual understanding of the problems in each sphere. To do this, it is necessary to understand the complete setting in which every enterprise must function.

Perspective 20B CAN ANYONE GRASP THE BIG PICTURE?

Each executive views the world that surrounds the corporation from a different perspective. Hershnen Cross, senior vice-president at General Electric, observes it from the purchasing angle:

The new element in today's buying and selling equation, I think, is the interconnectedness and interdependence of nations and people. If we imagine the future as a series of concentric circles surrounding the purchasing function, the most distant circle might be the long-range availability of natural resources; moving inward would be the international trading arrangements which are under renegotiation at this very moment; closer in, and occupying the years between now and 1980, would be the trend in domestic productive capacity, inflation, and rate of growth of Gross National Product. The inner circle would represent the ring of suppliers in direct and continuous contact with you.*

*source: H. Cross, "Purchasing Through Centuries and Cycles," International Purchasing Conference, May 17, 1976.

COMMENT As the interplay of economic forces around the world becomes more complex, planning and forecasting difficulties increase correspondingly. We know that the traditional relationship between employment and inflation no longer seems to apply, and that conventional supply-demand relationships can be warped by cartels established by cooperating nations. It is hard to develop strategy when the rules keep changing; the big picture is always in motion.

20-3.1 The Setting of the Industrial Enterprise

In addition to his own interests, every person has interests connected with his family, his community, and the nation. He has contacts and relations in each sphere. From each of them he receives certain benefits and to each he owes certain responsibilities. Rarely can he live his life uninfluenced by conditions in these other spheres. In the same way a single industrial enterprise can function only in relation to its industrial family, the community, the nation, and to other areas of thought and action. In each of these spheres certain forces and conditions are present which differ from those in the other spheres. For that reason and for convenience of explanation, we treat each sphere as something of a "world" of its own. We try to see what transpires in each sphere, how it affects the industrial enterprise, and what management can do about it.

Entering the factory door, so to speak, are the many worlds with which managers must maintain relationships (see Fig. 20-1). Suppose we look first at the picture as a whole and later describe its parts in detail. We start at the focal point with the XYZ Company, which is a small world of its own. Passing to the ring first removed from the company, we find the *industrial world* with which the company is closely related. Here, we find the industry, associated industries, service organizations, and markets functionally related to the company. The second arc is the world of the *national economy*. The company and the industry of which it is a functional part comprise a small section of the larger field of "manufacturing," which is itself a small

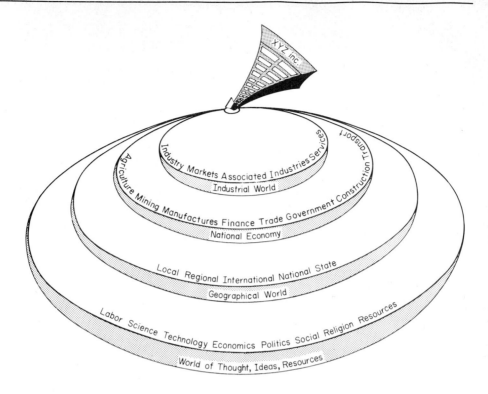

Figure 20-1 The scope of relationships between a single enterprise and the world outside its doors.

branch of the whole national economy. The third ring shows the *geographical world* which is the physical setting for every enterprise. Every company has some practical relation with various areas: the local community, the state, the United States regional area, the nation, the world regional area, and the international community. In the fourth, outermost ring we find the *world of thought, ideas, and resources.* What goes on in the many fields here influences the industrial enterprise profoundly. The world external to the enterprise is thus not a simple, single universe, but a complex series of many worlds with which the single enterprise must maintain contact.

In the discussion to follow, it will be seen that the company can approach and solve some of its problems in each ring of its external relations by direct and immediate action of its own. But there will be other problems in each area which the company cannot solve by its own efforts. To make headway on such problems, the company must act indirectly and with others in group operations. To avoid repetition, these latter channels of coordination are treated in section 20-3.2, Network of Coordinating Channels for Group Action.

COORDINATING THE ENTERPRISE WITH THE INDUSTRIAL WORLD The industrial world immediately surrounding the individual company is the world best known to it because the company is a functional part of it. Here, we find other enterprises producing the same and similar products and competing with the company. We also find the vast network of associated industries and activities which cooperate with the company and with which the company cooperates in turn. These are the materials and equipment suppliers, the sources of labor and services, and those who provide outlets for the products of the enterprise.

Although these enterprises and activities lie in an area outside and surrounding the individual enterprise, they are so essential to it that they are, in fact, but external parts of it. The individual company cannot function without coordinating its activities with theirs. The production and purchasing departments of a company, for example, establish relations with those who supply raw materials, machinery, other equipment, and production services. Employment and industrial relations departments maintain contacts with the labor supply and with labor organizations. The sales department makes contacts with the various outlets for the products of the enterprise and, through advertising and other methods, attracts the attention of others in the industry. The shipping department coordinates its activities with transportation agencies. The managing officers of the company build up relationships with insurance, banking, and other service agencies. This natural coordinating process is aided by a large and varied literature pertaining to the industry—catalogues, directories, statistical reports, and other material issued by government and private organizations. In this manner and as a routine part of its own functions and operations, each enterprise surrounds itself with a network of coordinating lines which tie it in with others who serve and complement it. These connections are supplemented by organizations serving the particular industry in which an enterprise is classified, and by coordinating channels within the economic system as a whole.

COORDINATION WITH THE NATIONAL ECONOMY   Each department of the enterprise is linked with the national economy through function, specialization, and such *institutional coordinators* as the great networks of finance, marketing, transportation, the price system which regulates the relationships among commodities, producers, sellers, and buyers, and all other economic activities. In addition to these direct, functional means of coordination, the alert enterprise will use many of the other channels of coordination for group action (see Section 20-3.2).

COORDINATION WITH THE GEOGRAPHICAL WORLD   Every enterprise has a physical setting in a local community and relationships with other geographical areas in which the company is active. Some of the problems which arise from these relationships are local and can be solved by the enterprise locally. Others require wider action. By studying the nature of its interests in relation to the geographical setting, the company can determine how best to approach the problems that arise.

For example, take the question: How best can a company work with the local community in which its plants are located? The problems here usually have to do with local taxation; with ordinances bearing upon the conduct of business; with health, safety, and morals of the population; with housing and community improvements; with relief of workers in time of unemployment; and with local charities. In other words, the company is a member of a local community and is expected to play a part in solving community problems.

There are many ways by which to bring about coordination between the company and the community. Almost every official of every department of the company finds it necessary to keep informed of conditions and events in the local community. In many instances it is part of the daily routine, just as are relations with the industrial world. But community problems go beyond the technical relation with plant operations; and in these instances coordination has to be brought about by other means.

A wide variety of channels are open for this purpose. Officials of the company often serve in various capacities in local government bodies. They participate in community organizations which deal with general problems. They become members of local service clubs where they meet officials of other enterprises and where local problems may be discussed. They take part in political groups where most community problems are focused. They make friends in other influential quarters of the community. Many of the associations previously mentioned as coordinators in the industry and in the national economy have local branches in the community, through which company officials often work. Not only should the company seek to solve its local problems through community action, but it should strive to see these problems through the eyes of the people and public officials in the locality. This may result in some temporary inconvenience to the company, but it is likely to be the best policy in the long run.

Perspective 20C   WHAT IS THE COST OF POLLUTION AND THE PRICE FOR CONTROL?

Critics of our technological society claim that we are destroying our environment and setting the stage for social upheaval. This view is dramatically described by Alvin Toffler:

The psychic pollution is matched by the industrial vomit that fills our skies and seas. Pesticides and herbicides filter into our foods. Twisted automobile carcasses, aluminum cans, nonreturnable glass bottles, and synthetic plastics form immense middens in our midst.*

*source: Alvin Toffler, *Future Shock,* New York: Random House, 1970.

COMMENT   Vivid writings such as Toffler's directed attention toward a long-neglected resultant of industrial growth. They spurred actions to correct ecological damages that had accumulated for years. Great accomplishments have been made. More remains to be done, but the priority is being questioned. The trade-off between energy and resource consumption versus a cleaner environment is a difficult decision when both sides have serious long-range consequences for neglect.

COORDINATION WITH THE WORLD OF THOUGHT, IDEAS, AND RESOURCES

At the outermost arc of the external relationships of the industrial enterprise lies the world of thought, ideas, and resources. Here, we find the forces of science and technology at work. Here, too, we come upon the broader problems of labor and resources. It is also the world of frontier thinking in the fields of economics, politics, social relationships, religion, and ethics.

Every field in this outer arc has its concrete practical aspects, which directly affect the individual enterprise, and also its abstract aspects, which seem to lie beyond practical affairs. There is not much trouble about coordinating the little world of the enterprise with the concrete aspects of this outermost world. This is because they enter the immediate world of the industry and directly touch the interests of every industrialist and business person. Take, for example, the idea of social security. So long as this remained a dream of a world of "plenty for all," it was an abstraction to be fondled by dreamers, philosophers, and humanitarians. But when the abstract ideas began to take concrete form, as pension and retirement plans, industrial accident and health insurance, unemployment compensation, and laws regulating working conditions and levying taxes for social ends, the once abstract idea became a part of the practical world of the industrialist.

Whether we look into the distant past or scan the promising future, ideas generated in the "intellectual climate" seemingly remote from practical operations bear fruit of enormous importance to practical business. If industrial enterprise is certain to be vitally affected by these problems, it ought to know about them, participate in the discussion and solution of them, and learn how to adapt its policies and operations to them. It is a fair conclusion that enlightened managers are rapidly tending to this view.

Perspective 20D   WILL WE RUN OUT OF RESOURCES?

The writings of E. F. Schumacher are a rallying point for conservationists and critics of our "wasteful technology":

A businessman would not consider a firm to have solved its problems of production and to have achieved viability if he saw that it was rapidly consuming its capital. How, then, could we overlook this vital fact when it comes to that very big firm, the economy of Spaceship Earth and, in particular, the economies of its rich passengers.*

*SOURCE: E. F. Schumacher, *Small is Beautiful,* New York: Harper and Row, 1973.

COMMENT   Schumacher identifies three categories of irreplaceable capital being consumed for industrial growth: fossil fuels, the tolerance margin of nature, and the human substance. He suggests the concept of "intermediate technology" to reduce the consumption of fuels, maintain the regenerative capability of nature, and humanize work; it is characterized as "production by the masses instead of mass production."

20-3.2 Network of Coordinating Channels for Group Action

In our discussion up to this point we have seen that the single enterprise has varied means of direct coordination of its activities and interests with each of the spheres external to the enterprise. But there is a limit to what it can do for itself. Beyond that limit it must join with others in collective action to solve its problems. To deal with all these broad problems there is an elaborate network of coordinating channels for *group* action, ranging from the single-industry trade association to international organizations.

TRADE ASSOCIATIONS AS COORDINATORS Among the organizations directly serving particular branches of industry, the trade associations are by far the most important. A trade association is a voluntary nonprofit organization of business competitors established to look after the common interests of all member firms in an industry or particular branch of an industry. Business units such as corporations, partnerships, and individual enterprises, rather than individuals, make up its membership. It does not itself produce, buy, or sell goods for profit. The trade association assists its members in matters of accounting practices, business ethics, commercial and industrial research, standardization, statistics, trade promotion, and in relations with government, labor, and the general public. It may issue periodic bulletins on these interests and often conducts a trade magazine. It arranges frequent conferences and annual conventions for members of the industry. It often represents the industry before legislative bodies and in public relations. The trade association, in short, is a powerful instrument directly concerned with coordinating the firms in a particular industry and relating them to all other industries.

REGIONAL AND SPECIAL-INTEREST ASSOCIATIONS AS COORDINATORS Those industrial enterprises whose problems involve regional and special interests will find many associations at hand whose purpose is to coordinate these interests and assist in solving problems by group action. Examples selected at random are the New England Council (sponsored by states, cities, and individual companies), the Mid-West Shippers Advisory Board, the 70 commodity exchanges, the Western Petroleum Refiners' Association, and even organizations dealing with different types of a single commodity such as the American Sugar Cane League, Inc., of Louisiana and the U.S. Beet Sugar Association of Washington, D.C.

NATIONAL BUSINESS, SERVICE, AND TECHNICAL ORGANIZATIONS AS CO-ORDINATORS Looking beyond the associations connected with specific trades, industries, regional and special interests, there is a wide range of other organizations whose functions include the coordination of common interests of their members for group action. The range of organizations in this group includes business and industrial interests like the National Association of Manufacturers and American Association of Small Business; service clubs like Rotary, Kiwanis, Lions, and others; professional organizations for men and women like the Society of Manufacturing Engineers, National Association of Accountants, American Management Association, and American Institute of Industrial Engineers. The range also covers educational and scientific associations, charitable and research foundations, cooperative societies, foreign-trade associations, foreign government agencies, associations of many racial minorities, political and religious bodies, recreation and social-welfare groups.

Too often in the past these organizations represented a blur in the distance as the factory executive looked out of his office window. Interested in the technical problem of getting out a product for profit in the face of lively competition, industralists found little time to examine the activities of nonbusiness groups. In some cases, they permitted their publicity departments to use these groups for propaganda purposes favorable to industry alone. Industrialists began to take closer notice, however, when these associations grew larger and began to line up behind such demands as those for pure food laws, workmen's compensation acts, social security provisions, protection for investors in securities, honesty in advertising and grade labeling, abolition of commercial frauds, fair employment practices in regard to women and racial minorities, conservation of natural resources, prosecution of monopolists, governmental regulation of private enterprise, slum clearance and better housing, and other matters of interest to the welfare of the people.

20-3.3 Industry Relations with Government Agencies

In addition to working with scientific, commercial, and social organizations, practical business people might also make better use of government agencies at their disposal. Where the agency is close at hand or serving the direct functional needs of the enterprise, company officials do make contact with them. But for the most part, individual enterprises leave relations with government agencies to their group associations. By such indifference they overlook many aids that would be of distinct advantage to them.

All governing bodies, from the smallest local community to the federal government, are organized primarily along functional lines. This means that there are government departments and officials responsible for specific activities bearing upon many phases of the private economy, such as public works, finance, industry, domestic and foreign trade, and national defense. Each of these broad fields is further divided and subdivided until we find specialists at work on every detail of problems that touch industrial enterprise. Except where political appointments have lowered standards, government employees possess high qualifications and gain their posts through competitive Civil Service examinations. It would be impossible to set forth in detail all the departments and agencies on the three government levels. It can only be pointed out that they exist, that they develop a vast amount of information valuable to industry, and that they are eager to cooperate with businesses on the problems of the economy. Officials in charge of functional activities within the company might well maintain continuing contacts with government agencies whose work bears upon company operations. By correspondence, direct personal relations, use of government literature, and by willingness to aid and to receive aid from government departments, individual companies may go a long way toward the coordination of industrial interests with those outside of factory doors.

This does not mean that a company must go to the extreme of making itself an unofficial branch of government departments. Yet the contacts between government and industry have steadily increased over the years, and the trend is likely to continue. Industry collects excise, social security, income, and other taxes for the government. In this and other connections, industry's services to government go far beyond the simple tax-paying relationships of the past.

20-3.4 Broader Difficulties in the Problem of External Coordination

Where problems are technical and closely connected with the functional operations of industry, the channels of external coordination appear to serve adequately. But where the problems are social; where they concern improvement in the general welfare of the people; where benefits have been sought for such groups as consumers, wage workers, the aged, and the underprivileged; or where changes have been sought in the established ways of business in the interest of full employment of work force and resources with the object of higher standards of living for all the people; in matters such as these, the channels of coordination seem to work imperfectly. That such coordination is lacking seems to be amply proved by frequent economic crises of increasing severity, by bitter controversies between industry and labor and between industry and government, and by prolonged resistance to social betterment.

Why is this so? Despite the vast network of coordinating channels, is machinery lacking for the purpose? If so, what kind of machinery is needed to do a better job? If present coordinating channels are ample, why do they fall so far short of success? Why do management and labor so often deal with each other at arm's length, with the implied threats of lockout and strike in the back of their minds? Why are the solutions of so many social problems sought by law (compulsion) in the place of being worked out in harmony through the voluntary cooperation of industry with all other interests in the outer world? If machinery is not lacking, is there something wrong with the methods employed or with the people who operate the machinery?

In a large populous country like our own and in modern times, it is perhaps inevitable that special-interest groups will be formed. That these groups disseminate one-sided propaganda and exert pressure upon government and others in order to obtain laws and conditions favorable to their members seems equally inevitable and understandable. The practice is not objectionable; each group is entitled to make the most of its special case and to protect the interests of its members. The struggle between self-interested groups is not altogether unhealthy in a free economy *if it leads to compromise and balance in the direction of social peace and progress.*

It is precisely at that point, however, that serious objection must be entered against self-interest groups. The struggle between them does lead to compromise, but compromise is too long delayed; the price in terms of social peace is too high, and the compromise is not always in the direction of social progress. Delay in adjustments is permitted until the struggle between self-interest groups either approximates domestic warfare, as in strikes and lockouts, or reaches the arena of politics and government. Either consequence is likely to be bad. Domestic, economic, and social warfare leaves deep scars on all participants, and the victory of any one group over another is a brief one before the struggle breaks out anew. If struggles in the private economy are carried into the field of politics and government, then the compromise takes the form either of a coercive law or of a transference to government of functions that might have been better performed by private enterprise.

Perspective 20E   CAN WE AND SHOULD WE CUT ENERGY CONSUMPTION?

Energy is the food that keeps industry alive. It is also a necessity for the way of life now enjoyed by most Americans. How much energy will be used by whom and where it will come from are the critical questions. EXXON's projections for U.S. energy demands and probable energy supplies up to 1990 are shown by the charts on page 583:

COMMENT   Every critical question has many facets. An article in the London Economist reveals the optimistic side: "The present energy 'crisis' is about the fifteenth time since the war when the great majority of decision-influencing people have united to say that some particular product is going to be in the most desperately short supply for the rest of this century. On each of the previous occasions, the world has then sent that product into large surplus within 5–10 years."

The gloomier side of the energy situation is evident from the EXXON charts, particularly when demand is related to proven energy reserves and their location.

Between these two views are pragmatic outlooks that balance energy conservation against personal inconveniences of efforts to conserve, value of new energy sources against R&D costs, and development of alternative energy supplies against environmental damages incurred during development.

The question, "Can we afford the actions needed to solve the energy problem?" is ambiguously answered by another question, "Can we afford not to?"

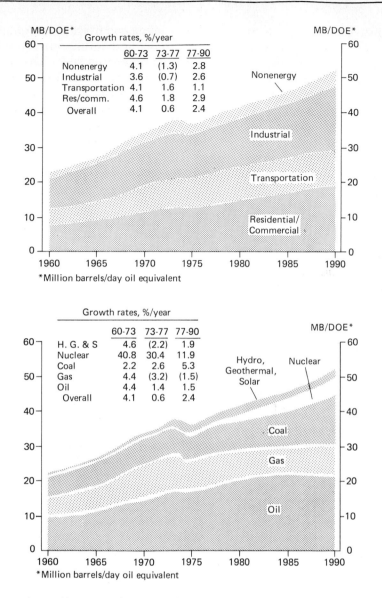

U.S. energy demand by consuming sector. (SOURCE: "Conserving Today's Energy for Tomorrow's Need," *EXXON U.S.A.,* vol. XVI, no. 4, 1977.)

20-4 MULTINATIONAL OPERATIONS

The initiation and operation of worldwide branches of U.S. businesses provide striking examples of the difficulties and opportunities of external coordination. American business enterprise overseas has steadily widened into a multiplicity of forms. Where once the movement was limited mainly to arrangements for distribution and sales abroad of American exports, to a few enterprises concerned with the exploitation of natural resources in foreign countries, and to a few American branch plants abroad to manufacture distinctive American products, it is now concerned not only with these developments, but also with industrial and business enterprises covering the whole field of economic activity. The organizational forms include whole international divisions of diversified activities, branch plants and subsidiaries, international corporations, trade and product royalty licensees, acquisitions by Americans of foreign corporations in whole or in part, contracts for the production, distribution, and sale of products abroad, and arrangements between American companies and foreign governments.

Perspective 20F   UPS AND DOWNS OF THE MULTINATIONAL MOVEMENT

U.S. corporations began their overseas moves in the 1950s. Initially intended to surmount trade barriers erected by dollar-short countries, the overseas operations proved to be very profitable. Combining advanced U.S. technology and marketing skills with cheap foreign labor allowed multinational companies to earn more abroad than they could at home. Host countries sometimes accused the companies of unfair practices. Distrust occasionally led to takeovers and often to restrictive laws and regulations by the host nations.

In the 1960s, multinational expansion was encouraged by the overvaluation of the dollar, which made exporting difficult and importing profitable. Manufacturing plants were set up in foreign countries to supply those markets and, in some cases, to supply U.S. markets. American labor accused the multinationals of exporting jobs.

The book value of U.S. foreign direct investment rose from $12 billion in 1950 to over $50 billion by 1966. The estimates for 1977 varied between $140 and $150 billion. This flow has been criticized as draining needed capital from the United States. But the direction may have changed. From 1971 through 1975 the number of American overseas subsidiaries decreased by almost 10 per cent. Some of the reasons for the decline are:

With the passage of time, the glamour of foreign investments has disappeared, along with many of the substantive reasons for going abroad. The dollar is no longer overvalued; its worth is largely determined by the movement of market forces. So U.S. exports are not artificially overpriced. There is no longer any need for a company to invest abroad merely because it can't find export markets for U.S.-made goods.

And while cheap labor still attracts many U.S. companies to developing countries, European labor is clearly not cheap at all. Says Alfred Moccia, senior vice president of Sperry Rand: "European wages are quite high and productivity is slipping badly. Absenteeism in Holland, in particular, is an unbelievably serious problem. The high wages, together with actual or potential restrictions on management's freedom to hire and fire workers, are discouraging U.S. foreign investments while at the same time encouraging local firms to move to the United States, where the labor climate is much more congenial."*

*SOURCE: Sanford Rose, "Why the Multinational Tide is Ebbing," *Fortune,* August, 1977.

COMMENT   U.S. multinational corporations have endured attacks both at home and abroad. Changes in U.S. tax laws, expropriation by host countries, and a trend to restrict free trade worldwide threaten their continued existence. Yet, some areas of overseas investment and operation remain attractive.

One area is the United States. It is "overseas" for parent companies in Japan, Germany, and other countries. Construction of auto plants and other large factories on U.S. soil have somewhat reversed the historical flow of multinational money. The newest entrants into multinational business are the oil-rich countries and, surprisingly, Russia; bidding to capture new markets in the West, Russia ran 40 international companies in 1977, with subsidiaries in 13 non-Communist countries.

20-4.1 Selecting the Type of Organization for Overseas Operations

The American company seeking to locate abroad has to select and adapt a form of organization appropriate to a wide variety of operating conditions. In general, for each country, it has to consider tax and trade regulations; market and competitive conditions; problems of specific location; currency-exchange problems; and whether to build and maintain independence facilities, to operate as a branch of the parent company or as a foreign corporation, or to affiliate with an existing foreign company. Production and equipment problems may influence the choice, and all risks in the venture will have to be appraised. The emergence of common markets and other common tariff arrangements among foreign countries add new inducements and new problems to these considerations.

Location of the overseas operation, for example, calls for a careful consideration of many factors. An appraisal of political and economic factors must be made. There has to be existing or potential demand. Government regulations have to be checked to determine what capital equipment, materials, and parts can be brought into the foreign country. The cost and availability of land and facilities are always matters of prime importance. There must be some guarantee from foreign countries that profits can be transferred into dollars and capital repatriated. Tax considerations are important not only in the foreign country but for the parent company in the United States. Finally, there are the comparative costs of production involved in any choice of a foreign location. Here wage differentials alone are not the determining factor, but merely one of many factors which enter into the choice of location, just as they do in locating domestic enterprises.

In the earlier days of expansion abroad, the customary form of operation was mainly through foreign distributors and sales agents. The vitality of this method still continues, but as foreign expansion broadened and accelerated, the forms of organization broadened and became more specific. Today they are tailored to a wide variety of operating conditions. In the main, two distinctive groups emerged: the *international division* and the *international corporation.* They are distinguished chiefly by the relationship they bear to the originating company. Thus the international division is an integral part of the American parent company, while the international corporation is a separate entity with extensive authority and operational freedom.

20-4.2 Managing the International Operation

In many areas of management, there is no difference in principle or practice between domestic and foreign enterprises. Basic principles of management are universal, but when a domestic company and its foreign affiliates are related in one enterprise, certain differences become apparent. Perhaps the greatest difference lies in the fact of remote control. The domestic company is physically far removed from its overseas subsidiaries and affiliates. It has to expand its organization and personnel to include management of the overseas enterprise, and instead of dealing with them directly, it must do so by varied means of longer range control. The result is that international division managements enjoy a high degree of autonomy. In general, the wider the scope of overseas operations, the greater is the degree of autonomy according to international division management. Decentralization of control is thus an outstanding feature of overseas operations. The international division management tends to become a link between the overseas line-and-staff executives and their counterparts in the domestic company. Carrying decentralization farther along the line, the local management of units in foreign countries usually has wider latitude in making decisions, with referrals limited to regional executives. Here it is not inconsistent to say that one characteristic feature of overseas management is that considerable reliance is placed on one or a very few strong individuals, who exercise the ultimate power of control. This traditional Old World paternalistic attitude, however, has been receding as specialization in management becomes better understood. Control varies in degree in different companies, but in the case of two areas of management responsibility—financial and legal—a tight rein is held by the parent company because of the importance of its commitments in these areas.

Another area in which international management differs from that of domestic enterprises is in the types of problems encountered in overseas operations. Managers of domestic enterprises are familiar, of course, with federal–state relations in the United States economic system and the problems which arise in these relations. To some extent there are similarities in management across state lines and management across foreign-country boundary lines, but the analogies cannot be pressed too far. Points of departure appear in language difficulties, in legal jurisdiction over enterprises limited by national boundaries, currency-exchange problems, tax regulations, and tariff and trade restrictions. Many businesspeople operating abroad are insufficiently aware of their rights in overseas operations. If common markets continue to grow, many of these differences will be reduced or eliminated, and to that extent the conduct of enterprises in those areas will become closely similar to experiences with Federal–state relations in the United States. But developments along this line are for the longer-range future.

Acceptable managerial behavior in a foreign country is a difficult and demanding art. The actions and routines that worked well on home soil may not work in a foreign land; they may even be damaging. It is easy to advise the new manager going abroad to be sensitive to political trends and to abide by prevailing social conduct, but he may not possess the background to recognize trends, or he may be incapable of adapting to the new culture. For example, a manager in the United States is accustomed to face-to-face confrontations to settle differences. He may not be prepared for a culture in which employees are not expected to get too near to or look directly at a supervisor. Although such behavior may appear trivial when taken individually, its total effect can frustrate anyone unprepared for the exchange.

The movement toward broader and improved management of international business enterprises is also accompanied by activities to improve international public relations. A good public-relations program helps sales, attracts capable employment and managerial personnel, helps improve productivity, and wards off government interference. According to Charles E. Allen, director of international operations for Hill & Knowlton, Inc., American business overseas faces five broad public-relations problems: (1) the fear that American companies are displacing foreign local industries; (2) the suspicion that United States companies are exploiting the economic growth of other areas for American rather than local citizens; (3) the feeling that American companies exert political influence for preserving the *status quo* and thereby frustrate popular demands for economic and social progress; (4) the resentment of high-pressure American business methods abroad and the fear of "Americanizing" traditional foreign cultures; and (5) the widespread criticism that most American personnel do not assimilate well with foreign communities in matters of language, local customs, and personal relations. In meeting these problems, it is pointed out, Americans may have to create an acceptable degree of national participation in an overseas enterprise, make a contribution toward the host country's aspirations, such as locating processing and other operations in the foreign country, develop an effective program for selecting and training Americans sent abroad, and manage its relations with the host government so as to improve political, economic, and social conditions.

20-4.3 Competition at Home and Abroad

The rebuilding of European and Japanese industry following WWII eventually led to a much more intensive competitive climate for American industry at home and abroad. Overseas markets for booming European and Japanese enterprises have been rapidly increasing. Many of these industries were either built or modernized with American money and equipment. Many are as well organized and as efficiently operated as are American companies. In many cases, they enjoy markets better protected by tariffs, quotas, licenses, and exchange restrictions than does the United States. Their wage levels are often less than American wage levels for comparable work, and related costs are lower in proportion. They enjoy lower shipping costs. With the passing of the "dollar gap," foreign competitors attained a surplus of dollars and other hard currency, which now enables them to extend lower interest and credit terms to expand sales abroad. The development of common markets has intensified many of these conditions.

The result has been to increase European competition with the United States in world markets and to increase competitive imports in the American home market. In the industrial field most of the imported products come from France, Great Britain, West Germany, Italy, Sweden, Switzerland, Japan, and Canada. To the older invasion of the American market by such products as glass, china, pottery, watches, leather goods, textiles, and a wide variety of handmade specialties, there has now been added automobiles, tires, bicycles, typewriters and office machines, steel, steel cutlery, nuts and bolts, barbed wire, machine tools, hand tools, farm machinery, electrical and electronic equipment, sewing machines, photographic equipment, optical instruments, radios, hardboard, and clothing. Some of these products, like sewing machines, zippers, typewriters and office equipment, and the like, are coming from American factories established abroad.

Perspective 20G   WHAT PROBLEMS DO MULTINATIONAL CORPORATIONS FACE?

Lee A. Iacocca, former president of Ford Motor Company, comments on the climate for multinational corporations:

Ford Motor Co's recent investment in Spain is an example of what a multinational company can do. It took us just three years to the day to build an industrial complex 2½ miles long and half a mile wide, with 55 acres under roof. To get from farmland to an annual capacity of 250,000 cars and 400,000 engines, we drew on the experience of 75 years in the automotive business, utilizing personnel and technological resources from all over the world.

In the course of those three years, we invested close to $800 million—$500 million in Spain and $300 million more for the expansion of related facilities in Europe. In addition, we contracted with and coordinated the efforts of more than 200 Spanish suppliers, who provide 65 percent of the content of production, under very specific quality controls that we continuously monitor. The plant itself now employs 9,000 workers. They are all local people and all well paid by local standards.

You might assume all nations would welcome investments like this. But the malevolent multinational of the exploitation myth dies hard, and many governments actually discourage such massive infusions of capital and know-how, unwittingly or otherwise. Bureaucrats dictate how much a company can export, what local materials and parts it must use, what prices it can charge and how much money it can take out of the country to finance operations elsewhere in the world. Worse yet, the uncertain investment climate is being further clouded by the proliferation of codes and guidelines now under study by various bodies in the United Nations, primarily at the urging of the developing nations.*

In testimony before a U.S. Senate subcommittee in 1973, executives of Citicorp, a multinational holding company with 1241 installations in the United States and in 103 other countries, presented their corporation's international code of conduct:

CITICORP'S INTERNATIONAL CODE OF CONDUCT

1. We must never lose sight of the fact that we are guests in foreign countries. We must conduct ourselves accordingly. We recognize the right of governments to pass local legislation and our obligation to conform.
2. Under these circumstances, we also recognize that we can survive only if we are successful in demonstrating to the local authorities that our presence is beneficial.
3. We believe that every country must find its own way politically and economically. Sometimes we feel that local policies are wise; sometimes we do not. However, irrespective of our own views, we try to function as best we can under prevailing conditions.
4. We have always felt free to discuss with local governments matters directly affecting our interests, but we recognize that they have final regulatory authority.

In an interview with the *Harvard Business Review* staff, William I. Spencer, president of Citicorp and Citibank, answered the question "What do you consider to be the most important threat to the future of the world economy?"

Nationalism, provincialism. There's bound to be unevenness in wealth and trade. How does a country cope with it? The way of nationalism is to put a circle around its business and try to protect it by tariff barriers. "All we need to do is keep imports down" is the attitude. It's very easy, then, for the attitude to spread to other countries. "Well, if they're going to do that to us," they say, "we're going to do the same to them." So artificial price levels are created, and production and distribution become uneconomic. Imagine what would happen to the United States if Michigan started to put tariffs on goods made in New York!**

*SOURCE: L. A. Iacocca, "Myth of the Big, Bad Multinational," *Newsweek,* September 12, 1977.

**SOURCE: "Who Controls MNCs," *Harvard Business Review,* November–December, 1975.

20-5 ADAPTING THE ENTERPRISE TO CHANGING CONDITIONS

Change is the one indisputable law of the universe. With the passing of the moment, nothing remains the same as we have seen or known it. Change is growth; it is decay; it is the constant mutation of living things and inanimate matter into different forms and qualities. In some instances, change is slow and barely noticeable; in others, it is rapid and violent.

Ours is a generation of revolutionary change. War has compelled the country more than once to make the drastic shift from peace to war and back to peace again. The greatest economic depression in modern history compelled us to make the most fundamental alterations in our lives and work. The world as our fathers knew it has been completely remade by electric power and nuclear energy; air travel, television, and computer technology; synthetics; electronics; assembly-line production and automation; and other products and processes. Our productivity has brought us to the brink of the greatest achievement since the dawn of civilization—the abolishment of poverty. Society has been shaken to its foundations by Nazi, Fascist, and Communist systems, by the demand of suppressed peoples, as in China, India, and Africa, for control over their own destinies, and by the rising insistence upon the part of working men and women at home that things be ordered in the interest and general welfare of the many rather than of the few. A thousand times a day the meaning and effect of these great developments knock at factory doors and make themselves felt in every department of the enterprise. No enterprise can ignore them. How can it adapt itself to changing conditions?

The enterprise has to become as dynamic and as fluid as is the world in which it functions. It cannot sit complacently on an established routine. It must be ready at all times to cut out, trim, and make over its organization and operations. Many of the great changes today revolve around the problem of reconciling the freedom and interests of the individual person and enterprise with the welfare of the people generally. This means that each enterprise will have to reexamine its policies and operations to see how best it can serve all the people—stockholders, workers, consumers. Every tool of management must be employed to appraise changing conditions and to make the most of all opportunities for efficient and profitable operation of the enterprise for the benefit of all who have direct claims on the enterprise, as well as to serve society as a whole. Where the problems come from outside factory doors, there is the extensive network of channels for coordinating the efforts of many enterprises. Finally, every chapter of this book is aimed to bring industrial enterprise abreast of modern developments and to provide management with tools for adapting it to future conditions.

20-6 CHALLENGES OF THE IMMEDIATE FUTURE

In a dynamic society the future will always raise broad challenging problems for management, and solutions will be sought to suit changing times. These problems are important to the reader because they are typical of those now facing or shortly to face the leaders of industry. No one can read the future so as to say with certainty that these are the most important problems, or that other and different problems will not arise. However, listed below are some of the important challenges facing industrial organizations.

1. TO RECOGNIZE LEGITIMATE INTERESTS DIRECTLY AFFECTED BY THE OPERATIONS OF AN ENTERPRISE

No industrial enterprise today concerns only its owners. Its formation, its financing, the conduct of its operations, its product, its gains, and its losses affect many others as well. What you do in your own back yard may be your own business up to a certain point; but when what you do affects your neighbors, they will soon want a voice in controlling your operations. Industrial operations today are at a stage where they seriously affect others. This is the basis on which labor, government, and the consumer claim a share in management along with stockholders and hired managers. What forms can this share in management take, and by what methods can it be brought about?

The earnings of many large corporations today are distributed over a wider range of interests than in the past. They cover lower prices to consumers, wage increases and welfare benefits to employees, compensation and bonus plans to management officers, dividends to stockholders, and corporate contributions to public education and social causes. The determination of the proportions of each interest has been the result of a wide array of influences: legal requirements, economic pressures, collective-bargaining pressures, desire by the corporation for public good will, decisions of corporate officers on matters of their own rewards, etc. *Should management study this problem with a view toward establishing some rational guides and formulas?* What share of national efforts to eliminate poverty should be borne by private enterprise?

2. TO RESPOND APPROPRIATELY TO DOMESTIC SOCIAL ISSUES SUCH AS EMPLOYMENT FOR THE DISADVANTAGED, ELIMINATING DISCRIMINATION, AND FINANCIAL SUPPORT FOR SOCIAL CAUSES

Business leaders have been accused of being out of touch with today's youth and the ideals of the younger generation. Executives have been asked to do more than defend their financial management at annual corporate meetings; they are questioned about the broad range of affairs concerning their companies and society. *Should company spokesmen express their views on political issues that do not directly affect their business?* Should the resources of a company back activist social movements? *What can the private business sector do to improve its image and counteract the criticism of young people?*

3. TO RESPOND APPROPRIATELY TO INTERNATIONAL ISSUES SUCH AS ALTERING COMPANY POLICIES TO CONFORM TO THE POLITICAL STRATEGY OF THE NATION

Should corporations cease to deal with countries that follow policies contrary to current world opinions? Alliances and allegiances shift according to the political interactions between nations, sometimes very rapidly. Multinational companies have been criticized for activities that were applauded just a short time previously. What response is appropriate?

Unmistakable signs of a world-wide trend toward economic expansion and investment in developing countries seems to be in progress. Competition for the world market, as well as for our own market, has risen substantially. *Is the United States responding adequately to these challenges by increasing efficiency, by keeping costs competitive, and by seizing the opportunities now opening before us?*

4. TO CONDUCT RESEARCH AND DEVELOPMENT LEADING TO IMPROVED PRODUCTION METHODS AND PRODUCTS

Efforts to reduce energy usage and develop new sources of energy have high priority. Similarly, conservation efforts directed toward the more efficient use of the earth's natural resources are a growing concern. *How can private enterprise contribute to these goals?* By improving its products, an enterprise strengthens its competitive position and probably increases productivity at the same time, thereby serving consumers and employees alike. Research expressly dedicated to improving productivity and inspired leadership to implement productivity improvements are vitally needed. To do so, can private enterprises improve upon their cooperation with universities, technical schools, government agencies, and other bodies engaged in such research?

5. TO IMPROVE THE QUALITY OF WORKING LIFE

Should a policy be devised by industry, labor, and government to further increase automation and mass production? What effect would such a policy have on unemployment, on the morale of workers (both blue-collar workers affected by automated production machines and white-collar workers affected by automated data processing), on the economy of the nation, on international trade, and on social changes such as early retirement, special skills required for employment, and extra free time resulting from shorter working hours.

Great strides have been made in making the work environment safer and more pleasant. More can be done, but in some industries continued improvements, particularly in process safety, are becoming very expensive. *How safe is safe enough?* Similarly, the use of more machines to do unpleasant tasks and provisions for further enhancement of the workplace requires capital that could instead be spent for other useful purposes. *How should available capital be budgeted?*

6. TO SUPPORT AND OPERATE ACCORDING TO THE HIGHEST STANDARDS OF BUSINESS ETHICS

The U.S. public has long shown some distrust of big business. In recent years the distrust has apparently increased due to investigations of international bribery, scrutiny generated by the consumer movement, and carryovers from disclosures of political corruption. The need has never been greater for industry to show that it believes in and pursues ethical behavior.

How can essential honesty be more completely secured in economic life? Is the brand name a completely satisfactory method for guaranteeing the quality of merchandise? How can the public be protected from the confusion of like products, each one claiming to serve a need better than all others? How can deceit, fraud, and plain hokum be eliminated from advertising and selling? Is it possible for industry to plan a system of national laboratories to test products in the interests of consumers and to induce producers to improve the quality of their products? How can the wasteful use of people and resources in making useless or inferior goods be eliminated? Much progress on these lines has been made, but infinitely much more needs to be done. A new business moving into a community is usually welcomed as a good neighbor until proved otherwise. *How can companies maintain this attitude of acceptance?* Should business leaders who enjoy good community relations speak out against industries that detract from the environment? Can private industry police itself, or must the public turn to government aid which means government regulation of industry?

How can monopolistic practices of all kinds be eliminated, or, where monopolies are permitted for justifiable reasons, how can we be assured that they are devoted to public rather than private interests only? What can the individual enterprise do about the patents it owns to avoid censure for abuse of its privileges? How can prices be cleared of the monopolistic elements contained in them in recent years, which competition has been powerless to remove? If prices can be arbitrarily fixed (administered prices) by corporations producing the bulk of a given product, by what methods can consumers be assured that such prices are fair? How can corporations owning large national resources assure the public that such resources are being used in the public interest?

7. TO ACT IN THE BEST INTERESTS OF CONSUMERS

What reaction should industry make to the growing concern for consumer protection? It is no longer respectable to hide behind the old adage "let the buyer beware" because the complex products now on the market shelves are beyond the understanding of most layman buyers. *How can shoddy service be improved?* Is there any way to increase the pride of workmanship in today's machine-supplied society?

How can "sticky" prices be made more flexible? There are signs that the price level is too high to give consumers the full advantage of mass production; *are pricing policies in need of overhauling?* What can be done about the rather ridiculous byplay that now surrounds "list" prices, net prices, discounts, and other tactics of the "I-can-get-it-for-you-wholesale" complex? Should productive efficiencies and increased output be reflected in price reductions as well as in wage increases? What responsibilities do companies have to react to pressure for price rollbacks by political "jawbone" tactics from elected officials?

The costs of getting goods from factory producers to ultimate consumer (distribution) are today considered excessive. How can they be reduced? How can wasteful crosshauls be eliminated? What suggestions can be offered in the way of coordinated air, water, and land transportation? What new transportation devices offer possibilities for increased efficiency and lower costs?

8. TO PROMOTE ACTIVITIES THAT SERVE THE TOTAL POPULACE

It is doubtful if the public will ever again permit the outrageous spectacle of the great depression during the 1930s in which factories operated at half and even quarter of normal capacity while people walked the streets looking for work and the public suffered for want of the goods these factories could have produced but did not produce. This is as much a problem of the individual enterprise as it is of the economy at large. It concerns the future of the free-enterprise system. What is meant by "full employment"? What steps can be taken in each enterprise to contribute toward the goal of full employment?

Points have been made in the text that industry today is closely interdependent; that disruption of production results in considerable loss to investors, workers, communities, and consumers, and endangers the economy. *In the light of these circumstances, has the time come when industrial disputes should be settled by means other than strikes? What means do you suggest?*

The conservation of natural resources and battles against pollution are highly emotional issues which too often tend to pit conservationists against industry. *What are the responsibilities of private enterprise in preserving or improving the environment?* What can a company with a sincere desire to cooperate do beyond making sure it does not contribute to pollution? Should earnings be allocated to projects which do not benefit the financial status of a company? If so, how much and on whose authority can sums be allocated?

Industry is in partnership with federal and local governments to maintain and improve the many factors that contribute to a high standard of living for all citizens. Together they must plan and implement programs to protect the environment, eliminate discriminatory practices, provide fully rewarding work experiences, and sustain a strong economy. Each has certain limitations and special capabilities that must not be ignored during emotionally charged periods. Industry may therefore serve the total populace by resisting efforts to tilt the balance from private toward public responsibility, just as it would be a disservice to resist, out of self interest, programs needed by society. Thus, wise industrial leadership, supported by an informed work force, is a necessity to meet the challenges of the 1980s.

20-7 CONCLUSION

These are but a few of the major challenges facing industrial management in the immediate future. Each single enterprise has an obligation to do what it can toward their solution. The method of approaching each challenge is relatively simple. Find out the precise nature of the problem. Get the facts. Break down the larger problem into its elements or parts. List the conflicting interests. Set up the desirable objectives and note the difficulties standing in the way of their achievement. Explore the means of overcoming each difficulty as far as that can be done within each enterprise. In weighing the sacrifices demanded against the advantages sought, take the long view. Put the public interest and the general welfare above the private one. Do everything possible to solve problems within the enterprise itself because that is where management exercises its most effective power. Where the problem is too large for the single management, turn to the industry's trade associations, to general business and commercial organizations, and to community bodies, private and public. Do not wait for others to attack problems or to make improvements; open the new trail yourself.

We live in a day of great opportunities. They call for a new, inspired, and crusading spirit upon the part of industrial, business, and labor leaders. Instead of remaining on the defensive, these leaders must be willing to go forth and meet the great human problems of the times. That is what all this industrial organization and rationalization is for: to release management and to give it the freedom to pioneer. There is a great demand for the imagination that will take industrial management beyond the stage of self-interested corporate combination to the wider group action needed to solve problems too big for the single enterprise. There is a demand that the same zeal be devoted to public interests as has been displayed in securing private advantages. There must be a willingness to reason and to sacrifice—the ability to take the broader view, to suppress the heat over a problem, and to work on it with opposing groups. *The imperative challenge of our times is to find the way by which owners, managers, financiers, labor, government, and the general consuming public can work in harmony toward full and efficient use of our resources, factories, and distribution system with the goal of greater productivity and higher living standards for all.*

20-8 REVIEW QUESTIONS

1. What is the importance of coordination in the functioning of an enterprise? What must management do to achieve better coordination?

2. What are two types of coordination? Are they independent of each other?

3. Why are intermanagement communications important? What are some of the methods of achieving effective communications?

4. How is the problem of external coordination different from that of internal coordination? What is its importance?

5. Describe the four worlds external to an enterprise and indicate their importance to the enterprise.

6. How are the problems of management different in overseas operations?

7. Why should an enterprise adapt itself to changing conditions?

8. What is the objective of studying the practices of industrial organization and management?

20-9 TOPICS FOR DISCUSSION

1. It has been said that the establishment of American plants overseas amounts to a transfer of American jobs to manufacture overseas. Is this true, and if so how does a nation compensate for the loss of these jobs?

2. In complaints about the rising influx of imports into the United States from foreign countries, the charge is made that "American producers are pricing themselves out of world markets." If you believe the charge to be true, develop (orally or in writing) a substantiation of the charge; if you believe the opposite, develop a refutation of the charge.

3. A wag has claimed that we will have solar power as soon as the public utilities find a way to put a meter on it. Comment.

4. Attempt to answer the questions posed in the titles of the Perspectives included in this chapter.

   - Can Rising Costs of Paper Work be Controlled?
   - Can Anyone Grasp the Big Picture?
   - What is the Cost of Pollution and the Price for Control?
   - Will We Run out of Resources?
   - Can We and Should We Cut Energy Consumption?
   - What Problems Do Multinational Corporations Face?

5. Case 20A: *The Need Not to Know*
"What we need is a data implosion to counteract the information explosion. In a way it is unfortunate that the big advances in data processing and storage arrived in concert with the big burst in new knowledge. I am reminded of a saying I learned in grade school: 'The more you study, the more you know. The more you know, the more you forget. The more you forget, the less you know. So why study at all?' A similar saying for information might go 'The more you store, the more you have. The more you have, the more trouble it is to find what you want. So why store at all?'

   The obvious answer to information problems is to start a program to teach everyone about throwing things away, erasing taped memories, and getting off distribution lists."

   Questions

1. What arguments can be made to support both sides of the issue?

6. Case 20B: *One, Two, Three, Change!*

"We are a large corporation and we know large corporations are prone to be slow reacting. We also know that we have to keep on top of fast-changing trends if we hope to remain competitive. Therefore, we try to force change. We feel change is important even if we can't see its immediate profit; just being alert and ready to move is vital. Sometimes we do it by planting a seed: experimenting with an idea or starting a pilot study. Our transfer policy of purposely trading managerial assignments not only provides training, it also encourages change as a new manager picks out what worked in the last assignment and installs it in the new one. We intentionally construct emergencies: surprise visits by management auditors and annual reviews by a blue-ribbon panel. These visiting teams want to see the changes since their last visit. Our conferences and training sessions stress the dangers of complacency and stagnation.

We believe you have to change to grow, and we want to keep growing."

Questions

1. Do you believe that a business environment can be designed to make people feel changes are expected, natural, and desirable?

7. Case 20C: *A Louder Voice for Consumers?*

It is an old saw that every issue has at least two sides. Even the celebrated cause of consumerism can be faulted. The worthiness of Federal action to protect consumers was discussed in Perspective 18A. The other side of consumer-oriented activities emphasizes inequities that may result from precipitous rulings to calm emotional fears originating from isolated incidents, the eventual cost to consumers of broadside attacks on a whole class of products, and spreading economic disruptions that seem to follow intervention of new federal agencies committed to correcting a problem.

Assume you have been asked by a "Great Decisions" study group to represent the negative side of a proposal to create a tax-funded Office of Consumer Protection to operate at the federal level. Opposing you are representatives from the Consumer Federation of America and Common Cause.

Proponents can cite examples of the need for a national watchdog agency to assure children's sleepwear is flameproof and borrowers know exactly the terms of their loans. Supporters feel too that a superagency is needed to act as a countervailing force to other regulatory agencies, they contend, are captives of business and unresponsive to the consumer.

Wariness about creating a powerful consumer-advocate body was expressed by Special Prosecutor Leon Jaworski in April, 1977, when he stated that a consumer agency "would be vested with authority so broad it could easily be turned to political advantage of those who control it." Examples can also be cited of less than successful consumer-oriented regulations established by federal agencies, such as the ill-fated ignition interlock that did not allow cars to start unless the driver was fastened into a harness of seat- and shoulder-belts. A flurry of protests caused the law to be rescinded, but not before it had cost consumers $2.4 billion extra for their new cars. The total cost of consumer protection by government regulations was estimated at $65.5 billion during 1976 by Washington University's Center for the Study of American Business, that is, $300 per citizen per year.

Questions

1. To prepare for the Great Decisions debate, list examples and arguments against the creation of a superagency in Washington to handle consumer protection.

2. What arguments in favor of a Federal consumer protection agency should you be prepared to rebut?

SELECTED REFERENCES

Chapter 1: INTRODUCTION: AMERICAN INDUSTRY

Cochran, Thomas C.: *Business in American Life: A History,* New York: McGraw-Hill, 1972.

Krooss, Herman E., and **Charles Gilbert:** *American Business History,* Englewood Cliffs, N.J.: Prentice-Hall, 1972.

Michael, Stephen R., and **Halsey R. Jones:** *Organizational Management: Concepts and Practice,* New York: Intext, 1973.

Owens, Richard N.: *Management of Industrial Enterprises,* 6th ed., Homewood, Ill.: Irwin, 1969.

Riggs, James L.: *Production Systems: Planning, Analysis, and Control,* 2nd ed., New York: Wiley/ Hamilton, 1976.

Thirlwall, A. P.: *Growth and Development,* New York: Wiley, 1977.

Weimer, Arthur M.: *Introduction to Business: A Management Approach,* 4th ed., Homewood, Ill.: Irwin, 1970.

Whyte, William F.: *Organizational Behavior: Theory and Practice,* Homewood, Ill.: Irwin, 1969.

Chapter 2: MANAGEMENT STRUCTURES

Gibson, James L., John M. Ivancevich, and **James H. Donnelly, Jr.:** *Organizations: Structure, Processes, Behavior,* Dallas, Tex.: Business Publications, 1973.

Katz, D., and **R. L. Kahn:** *The Social Psychology of Organizations,* New York: Wiley, 1966.

Lorsch, Jay W., and **Paul R. Lawrence:** *Studies in Organizational Design,* Homewood, Ill.: Irwin, 1970.

O'Shaughnessy, John: *Patterns of Business Organization,* New York: Wiley, 1976.

Shrode, William A., and **Dan Voich, Jr.:** *Organization and Management: Basic Systems Concepts,* Homewood, Ill.: Irwin, 1974.

Wieland, George F.: *Organizations: Behavior, Design, and Change,* Homewood, Ill.: Irwin, 1976.

Chapter 3: OPERATIONS ANALYSIS

Cook, Thomas M., and **Robert A. Russel:** *Introduction to Management Science,* Englewood Cliffs, N.J.: Prentice-Hall, 1977.

Eck, R. D.: *Operations Research for Business,* Belmont, Calif.: Wadsworth, 1976.

Hillier, F. S., and **Gerald J. Lieberman:** *Introduction to Operations Research,* San Francisco, Calif.: Holden-Day, 1974.

Levin, Richard I., and **Charles A. Kirkpatrick,** *Quantitative Approaches to Management,* 3rd ed., New York: McGraw-Hill, 1975.

Miller, David W., and **Martin K. Starr:** *Executive Decisions and Operations Research,* 2nd ed., Englewood Cliffs, N.J.: Prentice-Hall, 1969.

Riggs, James L., and **Michael S. Inoue:** *Introduction to Operations Research and Management Science,* New York: McGraw-Hill, 1975.

Chapter 4: RISK AND FORECASTING

Box, G. E. P., and **G. M. Jenkins:** *Time-Series Analysis, Forecasting, and Control,* San Francisco, Calif.: Holden-Day, 1970.

Bright, James R.: *Technological Forecasting for Industry and Government,* Englewood Cliffs, N.J.: Prentice-Hall, 1968.

Brown, R. G.: *Smoothing, Forecasting, and Prediction of Discrete Time Series,* Englewood Cliffs, N.J.: Prentice-Hall, 1966.

Montgomery, Douglas C., and **Lynwood A. Johnson:** *Forecasting and Time Series Analysis,* New York: McGraw-Hill, 1976.

Nelson, C. R.: *Applied Time-Series Analysis for Managerial Forecasting,* San Francisco, Calif.: Holden-Day, 1973.

Ostwald, Phillip F.: *Cost Estimating for Engineering and Management,* Englewood Cliffs, N.J.: Prentice-Hall, 1974.

Wheelwright, Steven C., and **Spyros Makridakis:** *Forecasting Methods for Management,* 2nd ed., New York: Wiley, 1977.

Chapter 5: FINANCING AND BUDGETING

Fabrycky, W. J., and **G. J. Thuesen:** *Economic Decision Analysis,* Englewood Cliffs, N.J.: Prentice-Hall, 1974.

Mayer, Raymond R.: *Capital Expenditure Analysis,* Prospect Heights, Ill.: Waveland Press, 1978.

Pyhrr, Peter A.: *Zero-Base Budgeting,* New York: Wiley, 1973.

Riggs, James L.: *Engineering Economics,* New York: McGraw-Hill, 1977.

Taylor, George A.: *Managerial and Engineering Economy: Economic Decision-Making,* 2nd ed., Princeton, N.J.: Van Nostrand, 1975.

Weston, Fred J., and **Eugene F. Brigham:** *Essentials of Managerial Finance,* Hinsdale, Ill.: Dryden Press, 1974.

Chapter 6: RESEARCH AND DEVELOPMENT

Burman, P. J.: *Precedence Networks for Project Planning and Control,* New York: McGraw-Hill, 1972.

Gordon, William J.: *Synectics, The Development of Creative Capacity,* New York: Harper, 1968.

Niebel, Benjamin W., and **Alan B. Draper:** *Product Design and Process Engineering,* New York: McGraw-Hill, 1974.

Ostrofsky, Benjamin: *Design, Planning, and Development Methodology,* Englewood Cliffs, N.J.: Prentice-Hall, 1977.

U.S. Department of Commerce Patent Office: *General Information Concerning Patents,* Washington, D.C., 1971.

Weist, Jerome D., and **Ferdinand K. Levy:** *A Management Guide to PERT/CPM: With GERT/PDM/DCPM and Other Networks,* Englewood Cliffs, N.J.: Prentice-Hall, 1977.

Chapter 7: PHYSICAL FACILITIES

Apple, J. M.: *Material Handling Systems Design,* New York: Ronald Press, 1972.

Chapanis, A.: *Man-Machine Engineering,* Belmont, Calif.: Wadsworth, 1965.

Francis, Richard L., and **John A. White:** *Facility Layout and Location: An Analytic Approach,* Englewood Cliffs, N.J.: Prentice-Hall, 1974.

Reed, Ruddell: *Plant Location, Layout and Maintenance,* Homewood, Ill.: Irwin, 1967.

Woodson, W. E.: *Human Engineering Guide for Equipment Designers,* Berkeley, Calif.: Univ. of California Press, 1964.

Chapter 8: PRODUCTION PLANNING

Bierman, Harold, Jr., Charles P. Bonini, and **Warren H. Hausman:** *Quantitative Analysis for Business Decisions,* 4th ed., Homewood, Ill.: Irwin, 1973.

Blanchard, Benjamin S.: *Engineering Organization and Management,* Englewood Cliffs, N.J.: Prentice-Hall, 1976.

Buffa, Elwood S.: *Operations Management: The Management of Productive Systems,* New York: Wiley/Hamilton, 1976.

Schmidt, J. W., and **R. E. Taymor:** *Simulation and Analysis of Industrial Systems,* Homewood, Ill.: Irwin, 1970.

Shannon, Robert E.: *Systems Simulation: The Art and Science,* Englewood Cliffs, N.J.: Prentice-Hall, 1975.

Shore, Barry: *Operations Management,* New York: McGraw-Hill, 1973.

Wagner, Harvey M.: *Principles of Operations Research,* 2nd ed., Englewood Cliffs, N.J.: Prentice-Hall, 1975.

Chapter 9: PRODUCTIVITY IMPROVEMENT

Box, G. E. P., and **N. R. Draper:** *Evolutionary Operation: A Method for Increasing Industrial Productivity,* New York: Wiley, 1969.

Mali, Paul: *Improving Total Productivity,* New York: Wiley, 1978.

McGreath, G.: *Productivity Through People,* New York: Wiley, 1974.

Norman, R. G., and **S. Bahiri:** *Productivity Measurement and Incentives,* London: Butterworth, 1972.

Riggs, James L.: *Production Systems: Planning, Analysis, and Control,* 2nd ed. New York: Wiley, 1976.

"Work in America," Report of a special task force to the Secretary of Health, Education and Welfare, Washington, D.C., December, 1972.

Chapter 10: PRODUCT FLOW

Blanchard, Benjamin S.: *Logistics Engineering and Management,* Englewood Cliffs, N.J.: Prentice-Hall, 1974.

Chase, Richard B., and **Nicholos J. Aquilano:** *Production and Operations Management: A Life Cycle Approach,* Homewood, Ill.: Irwin, 1973.

Elmaghraby, S. E.: *The Design of Production Systems,* New York: Reinhold, 1966.

Moore, Franklin G.: *Production Management,* 6th ed., Homewood, Ill.: Irwin, 1973.

Moore, Harry D., and **Donald R. Kibbey:** *Manufacturing: Materials and Processes,* rev. ed., New York: Grid, 1975.

Muth, J. F., and **G. L. Thompson** (eds.): *Industrial Scheduling,* Englewood Cliffs, N.J.: Prentice-Hall, 1963.

Chapter 11: MATERIAL FLOW

Ammer, Dean S.: *Materials Management,* 3rd ed., Homewood, Ill.: Irwin, 1972.

Buffa, E. S., and **W. H. Taubert:** *Production-Inventory Systems: Planning and Control,* rev. ed., Homewood, Ill.: Irwin, 1972.

Hesket, James L., Nicholas A. Glaskowsky, Jr., and **Robert M. Ivie:** *Business Logistics —Physical Distribution and Materials Management,* 2nd ed., New York: Ronald, 1973.

Naddor, Eliezer: *Inventory Systems,* New York: Wiley, 1966.

Niland, P.: *Production Planning, Scheduling, and Inventory Control,* New York: Macmillan, 1970.

Orlicky, Joseph: *Material Requirements Planning,* New York: McGraw-Hill, 1975.

Chapter 12: QUANTITY FLOW

Barnes, R. M.: *Motion and Time Study,* 6th ed., New York: Wiley, 1968.

Grimaldi, John V.: *Safety Management,* 3rd ed., Homewood, Ill.: Irwin, 1975.

Hammer, Willie: *Occupational Safety Management and Engineering,* Englewood Cliffs, N.J.: Prentice-Hall, 1976.

Niebel, Benjamin W.: *Motion and Time Study,* 6th ed., Homewood, Ill.: Irwin, 1976.

Riggs, James L.: *Engineering Economics,* New York: McGraw-Hill, 1977.

Smith, George L., Jr.: *Work Measurement: A Systems Approach,* New York: Grid, 1978.

Chapter 13: QUALITY CONTROL

Duncan, Acheson J.: *Quality Control and Industrial Statistics,* 3rd ed., Homewood, Ill.: Irwin, 1965.

Grant, E. L., and **R. S. Leavenworth:** *Statistical Quality Control* 4th ed., New York: McGraw-Hill, 1972.

Juran, J. M., and **Frank M. Gryna, Jr.:** *Quality Planning and Analysis,* New York: McGraw-Hill, 1970.

Kirkpatrick, E. G.: *Quality Control for Managers and Engineers,* New York: Wiley, 1970.

Ott, Ellis R.: *Process Quality Control,* New York: McGraw-Hill, 1975.

Smith, C. S.: *Quality and Reliability: An Integrated Approach,* New York: Pittman, 1969.

Chapter 14: HIRING AND TRAINING

Ginzberg, Eli: *The Development of Human Resources,* New York: McGraw-Hill, 1966.

Glueck, William F.: *Personnel: A Diagnostic Approach,* Dallas, Tex.: Business Publications, 1974.

Jucius, Michael J.: *Personnel Management,* 8th ed., Homewood, Ill.: Irwin, 1975.

Lyton, Ralph P., and **Uda Pareeq:** *Training for Development,* Homewood, Ill.: Irwin, 1967.

Terry, George R.: *Supervisory Management,* Homewood, Ill.: Irwin, 1974.

Chapter 15: LABOR-MANAGEMENT RELATIONS

Beal, Edwin F., Edward D. Wiskersham, and **Philip Kienast:** *The Practice of Collective Bargaining,* 5th ed., Homewood, Ill.: Irwin, 1976.

Cohen, Sanford: *Labor in the United States,* 4th ed., Columbus, Ohio: Merril, 1975.

Jenkins, David: *Job Power: Blue and White Collar Democracy,* Garden City, N.J.: Doubleday, 1973.

Mabry, Bevars D.: *Labor Relations and Collective Bargaining,* New York: Ronald Press, 1966.

Serrin, William: *The Company and the Union,* New York: Alfred A. Knopf, 1973.

Simon, Raymond: *Public Relations: Concepts and Practice,* New York: Grid, 1976.

Chapter 16: JOBS AND WAGES

Anthony, William P., and **Edward A. Nickolson, Jr.:** *Management of Human Resources: A Systems Approach to Personnel Management,* New York: Grid, 1977.

Best, Fred: *The Future of Work,* Englewood Cliffs, N.J.: Prentice-Hall, 1973.

Lawler, E. E., III: *Pay and Organizational Effectiveness: A Psychological View,* New York: McGraw-Hill, 1971.

Lundgren, Earl F., and **William J. Engle, Jr.:** *Supervision,* New York: Grid, 1978.

Meyer, Mitchell, and **Harland Fox:** *Profile of Employee Benefits,* New York: The Conference Board, Inc., 1974.

Chapter 17: MOTIVATION

Bolles, R. C.: *Theory of Motivation,* New York: Harper and Row, 1967.

Chung, Kae H.: *Motivational Theories and Practices,* New York: Grid, 1977.

Dalton, G. W., and **P. Lawrence:** *Motivation and Control in Organizations,* Homewood, Ill.: Irwin, 1970.

Herzberg, Frederick: *Work and the Nature of Man,* New York: World Publishing, 1966.

Maslow, A. H.: *Eupsychian Management,* Homewood, Ill.: Irwin, 1965.

Siegel, Laurence, and **Irving M. Lane:** *Psychology in Industrial Organizations,* 3rd ed., Homewood, Ill.: Irwin, 1974.

Chapter 18: MARKETING

Asker, David A., and **George S. Day:** *Consumerism: Search for the Consumer Interest,* New York: The Free Press, 1974.

Bartels, Robert: *The History of Marketing Thought,* 2nd ed., New York: Grid, 1976.

Burton, Phillip Ward, and **J. Robert Miller:** *Advertising Fundamentals,* 2nd ed., New York: Grid, 1976.

Kelley, William T.: *New Consumerism: Selected Readings,* New York: Grid, 1973.

Lazer, William, and **Eugene J. Kelley:** *Social Marketing: Perspectives and Viewpoints,* Homewood, Ill.: Irwin, 1973.

Sanford, David: *Who Put the Con in Consumer?,* New York: Liveright, 1972.

Schwartz, George: *Science in Marketing,* New York: Wiley, 1965.

Chapter 19: INTERNAL CONTROLS

Drucker, Peter F.: *The Effective Executive,* New York: Harper and Row, 1967.

Llewellyn, Robert W.: *Information Systems,* Englewood Cliffs, N.J.: Prentice-Hall, 1976.

Malone, Robert L., and **Donald J. Peterson:** *Effective Manager's Desk Book: Improving Results Through People,* Englewood Cliffs, N.J.: Prentice-Hall, 1974.

Riggs, James L., and **A. James Kalbaugh:** *The Art of Management,* New York: McGraw-Hill, 1974.

Solomons, David: *Divisional Performance: Measurement and Control,* Homewood, Ill.: Irwin, 1968.

Tricker, R. I.: *Management Information and Control Systems,* New York: Wiley, 1976.

Chapter 20: CHALLENGES TO INDUSTRIAL ORGANIZATION AND MANAGEMENT

Ball, George W. (ed.): *Global Companies: The Political Economy of World Business,* Englewood Cliffs, N.J.: Prentice-Hall, 1975.

Barnet, Richard J., and **Ronald E. Muller:** *Global Reach: The Power of the Multinational Corporation,* New York: Simon and Schuster, 1974.

Bauer, Raymond A., and **Dan H. Fenn:** *The Corporate Social Audit,* New York: Russell Sage Foundation, 1972.

Blumberg, Phillip I.: *The Megacorporation in American Society,* Englewood Cliffs, N.J.: Prentice-Hall, 1975.

Chamberlain, Neil: *The Limits of Corporate Responsibility,* New York: Basic Books, 1973.

Hill, David A., *et al.* (eds.): *The Quality of Life in America,* New York: Holt, Rinehart and Winston, 1973.

Steiner, George A.: *Business and Society,* 2nd ed., New York: Random House, 1975.

Sturdivant, Frederick D.: *Business and Society: A Managerial Approach,* Homewood, Ill.: Irwin, 1977.

Tugendhat, Christopher: *The Multinationals,* New York: Random House, 1972.

Walton, Clarence C.: *Ethos and the Executive: Values in Managerial Decision Making,* Englewood Cliffs, N.J.: Prentice-Hall, 1969.

INDEX